The CORRESPONDENCE *of* JEREMY BENTHAM

Volume 3
January 1781 to October 1788

edited by
IAN R. CHRISTIE

This edition published in 2017 by
UCL Press
University College London
Gower Street
London WC1E 6BT

First published in 1971 by The Athlone Press,
University of London

A CIP catalogue record for this book is available
from The British Library.

PREFACE TO THE NEW EDITION OF VOLUME 3

The third volume of Jeremy Bentham's *Correspondence* was originally published in 1971, under the editorship of the late Ian R. Christie and the General Editorship of the late J.H. Burns. The *Correspondence* volumes represent the 'backbone', so to speak, of the authoritative edition of *The Collected Works of Jeremy Bentham*, giving scholars the orientation that enables them to begin to make sense of Bentham's published works and the vast collection of his unpublished papers, consisting of around 60,000 folios in UCL Library and 12,500 folios in the British Library.

The present volume has been attractively re-keyed in a typeface that is sympathetic to the original design, and crucially the exact pagination of the original volume has been retained, so that referencing remains stable. The opportunity has been taken to incorporate the corrigenda printed at the conclusion of Volume V of the *Correspondence* and further corrections identified by the Bentham Project. Professor Anne Brunon-Ernst (University of Paris II) has kindly checked the accuracy of the reproduction of the French material according to the conventions currently adopted in the edition as a whole.

The current volume opens as the American War of Independence was coming to a conclusion and closes on the brink of the French Revolution. In early 1781 Bentham, who was living in Lincoln's Inn, received a visit from the Earl of Shelburne (raised in the peerage to Marquis of Lansdowne in 1785). Shelburne, who was known for his intellectual interests, was also a major politician, becoming leader of the administration from July 1782 to March 1783, with responsibility for negotiating the peace with America. Bentham could not but have been flattered by Shelburne's attention, and he accepted Shelburne's invitation to visit his country home Bowood House in Wiltshire, where he stayed for several weeks in the autumn of 1781. Bentham's detailed letters from Bowood to his friend George Wilson give a fascinating insight into life in one of the country's major aristocratic houses.

Bentham's correspondence is, however, dominated by Russia. In March 1780 his younger brother Samuel had arrived at St Petersburg, where he had begun to establish his reputation as an engineer. Having undertaken an expedition to Siberia, Samuel was taken into service by

Prince Potëmkin, a powerful aristocrat with a large estate at Krichëv in the south of Russia, where Samuel took charge of Potëmkin's industrial and military concerns. In August 1785 Bentham left London, travelled through the Mediterranean to Constantinople and then overland via Bucharest, and arrived at Krichëv in February 1786. He stayed for nearly two years, living with his brother in a farmhouse provided by Potëmkin, and spending most of his time writing, but also dealing with various aspects of Samuel's affairs. In late 1787 Bentham set off back to England, travelled overland via Warsaw and Berlin, and arrived home in February 1788.

Bentham had hopes of presenting his penal code to Catherine the Great, Empress of Russia, but, remaining in his farmhouse, he failed to seize the opportunity to meet her when she visited Krichëv early in 1787. As was often the case, Bentham had not brought his work to completion, despite composing a large mass of manuscripts (in French, for the benefit of the Empress) under the headings of 'Projet Forme' and 'Projet Matière'. While in Krichëv, Bentham wrote *Defence of Usury*, which George Wilson, his friend in London, saw through the press, and which was published in late 1787. Bentham's essay was highly influential over a course of years in presenting the case for the abolition of legal limits on rates of interest. It has appeared in the *Collected Works*, along with other related material from these years, in *Writings on Political Economy: Volume I*, edited by Michael Quinn, published in 2016.

A further work to emerge from Bentham's visit to Russia was his scheme for a panopticon prison, which was eventually printed in 1791 as 'Panopticon: or, The Inspection-House'. Samuel had proposed to build a manufactory, arranged around a central point, from where he could continuously inspect the activities of his workforce. Bentham realized that the central-inspection principle might be applied to a whole variety of institutions, including factories, schools, and hospitals. The pressing need in England at the time was for a penitentiary, and so Bentham focused his attention on prison design. He imagined a circular or polygonal building, with the cells on the outside, and an inspection tower in the centre. The attempt to build a panopticon prison in London would come to dominate his life for over a decade following his return to England.

As Christie explains in the 'Introduction' below, up to 80 letters sent by Bentham to Samuel between 1781 and 1785 are missing. Christie wondered whether the letters might surface in a Russian archive, but they have not yet done so. He also explains that, while all Samuel's letters to Bentham appear to have survived, he excluded from the present volume those letters and parts of letters that dealt exclusively with Samuel's affairs. Christie went on to produce a detailed account of Samuel's activities, including his involvement in the Russian defeat of the Turks at Ochakov in 1788, and of Bentham's hazardous and eventful journeys to and from Krichëv in his *The Benthams in Russia, 1780–1791* (Oxford and Providence, RI: Berg, 1993), which may now be supplemented with Roger Morriss's *Science, Utility and Maritime Power: Samuel Bentham in Russia, 1779–91* (London: Routledge, 2015).

Philip Schofield
General Editor of *The Collected Works of Jeremy Bentham*
UCL, March 2017

PREFACE

The thanks of the Bentham Committee are due to the following for access to and permission to print Mss. in their possession as well as for assistance afforded to the General Editor and to the editor of this volume: The Trustees of the British Museum; The Deputy Keeper of the Public Records, the Public Record Office; The Librarian, University College London; The Librarian, the William L. Clements Library; The Most Hon. the Marquess of Lansdowne; Col. Sir John G. Carew Pole, Bt., D.S.O., T.D., of Antony House, Torpoint, Cornwall; Mr D. R. Bentham. The Committee also thanks the National Maritime Museum, Greenwich Hospital Collection, for permission to reproduce the picture which forms the frontispiece. The grateful acknowledgements of the Committee are also due to the following bodies for financial assistance towards the cost of the editorial work on this volume: The Rockefeller Foundation; The Pilgrim Trust; The British Academy.

My labours as editor of this volume have been helped in the highest degree by Mrs Sandra Hole, who bore the brunt of the work of copying from manuscripts, checking typed transcripts, and collecting information for footnotes; and by Miss Judith Stafford, who gave valuable assistance in checking the proofs and compiling the index. I am most grateful to them both, and to Miss Helen Nowell, and also to Mrs Hilary P. Evans and Mrs Audrey Munro who between them produced the typescript. It has been a pleasure and relief to know that the great knowledge of Bentham possessed by the General Editor, Professor J. H. Burns, has been available in case of need, and I much appreciate the help he has given on many points. I owe debts of gratitude to various colleagues in University College, Professor R. A. Humphreys, Dr J. Kells, Dr W. A. Smeaton, and Dr M. Winterbottom, who came to my aid on particular matters; and special thanks are due to Dr C. L. Drage of the School of Slavonic and East European Studies of the University of London for his help in transcribing Russian documents, providing typed transcripts of them complete with idiosyncrasies of spelling, and correcting my attempts at translation. Dr A. G. Cross of the School of European Studies, University of East Anglia, kindly provided identifications of a number of more obscure Russian personalities not to be found in the Soviet Encyclopaedia or the

Russian Biographical Dictionary; I regret that the late stage of preparation at which his help was obtained has precluded full use of the information he furnished.

University College London I. R. C.

CONTENTS

LIST OF LETTERS IN VOLUME 3

INTRODUCTION

1. The Letters

About three-quarters of the letters included in this volume have not been published before. The place of first publication of all but a few of the remainder was Sir John Bowring's Memoirs of Bentham, in volume x of his edition of *The Works of Jeremy Bentham*. Wherever possible the present text has been taken from original manuscripts, and at times the inadequacy of Bowring's editing stands clearly revealed—a fact which renders the more unhappy the circumstance that the originals of a few of the letters he printed have disappeared, leaving his text as the only source.

The main manuscript sources for the letters in this volume are the two great collections of Bentham's papers, in the library of University College London, and in the manuscript department of the British Museum. Since the relationship between their contents is not altogether clear, some recapitulation is given here of explanations made in the Introduction to volume i. The first of these collections came into the hands of Bowring as Bentham's literary executor, and was deposited by him at the College in 1849. Although the main bulk of this collection is made up of Bentham's works, it contains a substantial number of letters written to Bentham during the period covered by this volume, and also some of his drafts—in a few cases it has been proved, by the discovery of the originals elsewhere or of replies to them, that these represent letters actually sent.

The second collection, now in the British Museum, was not known to Bowring when he edited Bentham's papers. This collection contains the main mass of the family correspondence—for this period Bentham's letters to his father and those received by him from his brother which he regularly forwarded on to his father. Bentham himself believed this correspondence had been destroyed by his stepmother before her death in 1809. However, at some time presumably after his death it passed into the hands of his nephew George or sister-in-law Mary Bentham—possibly after lying forgotten in a lawyer's vault—and Mary Bentham, when writing her sketch of her husband's life, probably incorporated with it a mass of Samuel Bentham's correspondence which it now contains. After the death of her son George Bentham, the collection passed to Joseph Dalton

Hooker, and from Hooker by purchase to the British Museum.

There are problems relating to the contents of this collection, to Bowring's possible indirect connection with it, and to its connection through him with the papers now in University College. There are two apparent intrusions. One consists of a number of Bentham's letters to George Wilson, to the Davieses, to James Anderson and to one or two other addressees. The other is made up of letters to him from such correspondents as Lord Lansdowne, Baron von Raigersfeld, Reginald Pole Carew, François Xavier Schwediauer and Jacques Pierre Brissot de Warville.

How did these letters reach their present location? It seems certain that at some point Bowring was involved. The letters written by Bentham must have been assembled by him as an artificial collection to assist him with the Memoirs; and in some cases where only his printed text is now known, presumably he either returned the manuscripts to the addressees or their heirs, or else disposed of them in some other way. The letters to Bentham, of which he printed only a selection, can only have been extracted from the papers which passed into his keeping in 1832 and which still contain other letters from some of these correspondents. There is later evidence, referred to below, that a private Bowring collection was formed out of these papers; but there is no information as to how this group of letters, or most of it, came to be amalgamated with the papers now in the British Museum.

A small proportion of the letters in this volume are printed from originals in private collections: among these are to be noted especially the Lansdowne Mss. at Bowood and the Pole Carew Mss. at Antony, Cornwall. Bowring's handling of the correspondence between Bentham and Lansdowne merits comment. It is evident that he did not obtain access to the Lansdowne archives, for in cases where a manuscript is known to exist, his texts of Bentham's letters to Lansdowne are derived from drafts or copies in what is now the University College collection. There is also evidence that he abstracted a personal collection of the more interesting of Lansdowne's letters to Bentham from the papers under his control: his grandson Wilfred Joseph Bowring sent one of these to the 5th Marquess in 1910 and mentioned his possession of many others.

All known letters of Bentham's belonging to the period covered by this volume have been printed in full; so have practically all letters to him, save for those from his brother.

In one respect this volume contrasts markedly with its predecessor. Bentham's side of the voluminous correspondence which was being carried on with Samuel Bentham in Russia has disappeared—clearly through some artificial division of the papers, since the break comes at the beginning of the calendar year 1781. In Samuel's replies, and occasionally in Bentham's letters to his father, and elsewhere, there are specific references to some thirty-eight of Bentham's letters to Samuel, but there is sufficient indication that the number missing is far greater than this. In the year 1780, the last for which the archive seems complete, Bentham wrote nineteen letters to his brother. Fourteen are known by reference for the first ten months of 1781. One he wrote in September 1783 was numbered 'XXV' in a sequence relating to that year (only this one and five of its predecessors of that year are known by specific reference). He sent at least thirteen in the first seven months of 1784. To judge by these figures an average of twenty letters a year seems a conservative estimate. On this basis at least ninety letters are missing for the period from January 1781 till Bentham's departure from England for Russia in August 1785, plus two sent to Samuel from Constantinople at the end of 1785 and at least another two written towards the end of 1787. The possibility that these exist in some portion of Samuel Bentham's papers left behind him in Russia cannot be excluded, although the Institute of History of the Soviet Academy of Sciences, which has kindly provided information on surviving letters of Bentham in Russia, has not found trace of them. Of this great series there survive only three incomplete drafts and also one long letter which may have been preserved in special circumstances because of its particularly intimate personal character.

Something of the contents of Bentham's missing letters to his brother can occasionally be deduced from Samuel's replies. Judging by their number Samuel's letters to Bentham have survived almost completely and their bulk has presented a considerable problem of selection. In order not to destroy the balance and proper emphasis of this volume it has seemed advisable rigorously to exclude material dealing with Samuel's own activities in Russia, and to print only those letters or parts of letters which yield information about Bentham by reference to what he himself had written or to activities in which he was involved on Samuel's behalf.

Bentham's surviving correspondence with his father during this period is irregular but not unsubstantial. In the main it falls into three periods; 1783, when the chief topics were Samuel Bentham's love affair with the Countess Sof'ya Dmitriyevna Matyushkina and the momentary prospect that Samuel might become temporary

British *chargé d'affaires* at St Petersburg; 1786–7, when Bentham was writing to his father from Russia; and 1788, when they were both avidly following the naval war news from the Black Sea. As might be expected from the relations between father and son, there is little evidence in this run about Bentham's intellectual pursuits. But a rich vein of description and narrative characterizes the second group, and this is also a notable feature of the long journal-letters which Bentham wrote about his stay at Bowood in 1781 and again, between August 1785 and February 1786, about his journey to Russia. Throughout this period it was George Wilson who, more than anyone save his brother, shared his confidence and his intellectual interests. This stands out both in the striking run of the letters to Wilson from Bowood in 1781 and in those exchanged between them while Bentham was in Russia.

The remainder of the letters printed in this volume reflect the growing range of Bentham's contacts. For the most part these are letters to Bentham. Practically all such known letters have been included, as they yield information about his activities and his intellectual interests not otherwise available, and sometimes, as in the case of Brissot de Warville, provide the only evidence for the widening of his circle which was taking place at this time. Some of them have a biographical interest, not least one or two which show him at work as the business assistant of his brother at Krichëv. Two long and difficult drafts to Lord Ashburton in 1782 provide the fullest information available on the development of his writings on jurisprudence at this time. Every item relating to Bentham's contact with Lord Lansdowne has been included, however slight, on the ground that for both men it has a cumulatively important biographical significance. Unfortunately Bentham's own letters to a number of these correspondents remain undiscovered (if they still survive) notably those to Prince Grigoriy Aleksandrovich Potëmkin, Count Sergey Ivanovich Pleshcheyev, François Xavier Schwediauer, James Trail and Brissot de Warville.

For notes on details of editorial practice, see the Introduction to volume i at pages xxi–xxii. In transliterating Russian names the Russian modified 'e' (= 'yo', or 'o' after 'ch' and 'sh') has been rendered as 'ë' in preference to the also frequently-used 'yo' or 'o'.

2. Outline of Bentham's life, January 1781 to October 1788

1781 The beginning of this year was marked by the break-down, for reasons not disclosed in the correspondence, of Bentham's plans for a German translation of the *Introduction* of his *Plan of a Penal Code* (later published as *An Introduction to the Principles of Morals and Legislation*). The English text had now been set in type, but he proceeded no further with this, being hard at work on part of what he regarded as the main body of his future publication, his *Plan of a Penal Code* itself, which is referred to for short as 'Code' in the Correspondence of this and the following years. In February some light relief was afforded by his cousin Gregory Bentham's discovery of a graft being carried on over the sale of admiralty appointments, which Bentham took upon himself to report to the First Lord of the Admiralty. There is some indication of continued contact with Shelburne House, for about the end of April a correspondence with the earl's librarian seems to show that Bentham had agreed to look out for copies of Prynne's tracts and in exchange he was offered duplicates from Shelburne's collection. It was possibly this matter that gave Shelburne the opening at the beginning of July for his descent upon Bentham's chambers at Lincoln's Inn. Shelburne seems there to have enjoyed a lively and critical discussion of Bentham's work. He was sufficiently impressed to borrow a copy of the *Fragment on Government* for perusal at leisure, and to follow up his visit with a pressing invitation to Bentham to spend part of the summer at Bowood and bring his work so that it might be submitted to the judgment of Shelburne's legal friends, Lord Camden and John Dunning.

Though Bentham showed some hesitation, it was impossible to refuse. At the beginning of August he stayed for a fortnight with the Davieses at Chatham, where he went sea-bathing on his doctor's instructions. He then travelled down to Bowood where he remained until the middle of October. It was a memorable experience of gracious living in an intellectual household which was also a focus of national politics. During this period, apart from much stimulating conversation he had the diverse pleasures of romping with Shelburne's infant son, performing violin and harpsichord duets with Lady Shelburne, playing chess with the future prime minister, William Pitt, and indulging just a little (but not too much) *tendresse* towards one of Lady Shelburne's kinswomen. Long afterwards he wrote: 'Those days with the exception of a few months passed in the same company about eight years afterwards, were the happiest of my life'; and his zestful descriptions of the people he met and the gossip he heard in a long series of letters to George Wilson form the major part of his correspondence during this year. During his stay at Bowood, Lord Camden looked through the

Fragment and made little of it; but John Dunning was not able to do so, his wife's pregnancy obliging him to leave Bowood almost immediately after he arrived. At parting Shelburne urged Bentham not to let his brother stay too long abroad, and gave advice that he should take in the naval yards of the Scandinavian countries on his way back to England. If he were ever in a position to do so he would bring Samuel forward in public employment; meanwhile he held out the offer to him of a house at Wycombe, where he had an estate, and a retainer of £1000. Puzzled and not wholly convinced of the sincerity of these offers, Bentham duly relayed them to his brother, but with a caution not to take them too seriously. Leaving Bowood in mid-October Bentham travelled via Oxford and Slough to Thorpe, where he stopped briefly—for the last time, for Wilson was abandoning the cottage he had shared with him there—and by the end of the month he was back at Lincoln's Inn.

1782 The scanty information available suggests that during most of this year Bentham presumably remained at Lincoln's Inn at work on his writings. He spent the autumn at Brompton near Chatham, staying with the Davieses, whose home was now to some extent to take the place for him of Wilson's cottage at Thorpe as a retreat from London.

Shelburne kept in touch with him, and in June, on Shelburne's insistence, he sent to Lord Ashburton (as Dunning had now become) the printed sheets of the *Introduction* and a plan, now some months out of date, of the way he intended to develop his study. According to a later memorandum these were never returned to him. Later on Shelburne seems also to have pressed him to tell his brother to return, holding out the prospect of a commissionership of the Navy Board. Bentham reported this proposal to his brother with strong warnings to treat it with caution; he was anxious that Samuel should not on this ground throw up promising prospects in Russia. In fact, for various reasons, Samuel stayed at St Petersburg after his return (in October) from the long tour of exploration in Siberia which had occupied him since February 1781.

Towards the end of the year Bentham had evidently gone some way towards producing a French version of the general treatise on jurisprudence which, in one form or another, had occupied him since about 1770. In a letter to his brother he referred to this as a 'projet d'un corps de droit' and as being near completion—the latter statement, however, being characteristically over-optimistic. About this time, too, he made a new friend in the person of the

French journalist, Jacques Pierre Brissot de Warville, who in November came over to London in connection with various literary ventures.

1783 This year saw the development of an intimate friendship between Bentham and Brissot, marked by several exchanges of letters, of which only Brissot's side appears to survive. Bentham's relationship with Shelburne remained cordial: in February he sought his favour to help in securing French publications on law questions. In the spring of 1783 he found a new friend in the young Cornish member of parliament, Reginald Pole Carew of Antony. Pole Carew had travelled in Russia and had become friendly with Samuel Bentham. After he returned to London it is not clear which sought out the other—possibly the first approach to Carew was taken by Jeremiah Bentham—but a common interest in Samuel's romance with the Countess Sof'ya Dmitriyevna Matyushkina drew them together. Bentham obtained information about the Countess, owing to Carew's friendship with Prince A. V. Vyazemskiy, who was then on a visit to England and who, as a relative of the Countess, was making enquiries about Samuel's family on her behalf.

Bentham's intellectual interests are reflected in correspondence with an old acquaintance, Baron von Raigersfeld, the secretary of the Austrian legation, who tried to get information for him about German law, and also with a new one, David Steuart, recently provost of Edinburgh, who promised to help him on the subject of Scottish criminal law. His old friend, James Anderson, consulted him about the draft of his pamphlet concerning the development of the Scottish fisheries. Out of the blue an obscure Russian army surgeon, whom his brother had met in southern Siberia, sent him a consignment of seeds which had to be acknowledged; and when a proposal came up for Samuel to act as temporary *chargé d'affaires* at St Petersburg on the retirement of Sir James Harris, he was drawn into a flurry of correspondence and personal consultation with the new ambassador's brother, his old friend, William Fitzherbert.

At the end of July Bentham once again left London to join the Davieses at Brompton, and in the autumn he removed with them to their new home at Linstead near Sittingbourne. There is some indication that at this time Bentham was continuing to eke out his slender allowance by hack-work for London booksellers, including the translation of works into English. Meanwhile Samuel Bentham, finally settled in the imperial service in the civilian rank of *conseiller de la cour* at St Petersburg, began to press his brother to pay a visit to him in Russia, an idea which seems already to have crossed Bentham's mind. Bentham returned to Lincoln's Inn about the middle of November. Towards the end of this year he received the first of a string of letters from his brother about his want of skilled craftsmen of various kinds who might be recruited to help him with the mechanical inventions he was trying to develop.

1784 The correspondence of the early part of the year reveals little about Bentham's activities, save that he was in London. A growing interest in things Russian is evident from his brother's replies to his enquiries and from his draft of a letter to Samuel discussing the qualities of a possible recruit for service in Russia. In April the reopening of a brief correspondence with his old friend, Francis Villion, who for some years had been dropped from his acquaintance, about the return of books which each had lent to the other, may indicate a desire to tidy up his affairs before going to visit Samuel. There was. discussion of plans for employment in Russia for James Anderson and indications multiply that Samuel, who in March was transferred to the army as lieutenant-colonel under the immediate patronage of Potëmkin, was beginning to use his brother as a private recruiting agent for technical experts.

About the end of April, however, the normal tenor of Bentham's life and whatever plans he had in view were disrupted by the death of his uncle George Woodward Grove. This event brought Bentham a small legacy, which, together with his father's allowance, was just sufficient to save him from some of the shifts to which hitherto he had occasionally been driven to make ends meet. But the duties of executor involved him in several months of wearying toil at Grove's country house at Whitchurch in Hampshire—he was back in London for a week or so at the end of May to deal with probate, but did not finally leave Whitchurch till some time in early November. For some weeks his eyes suffered severely from overstrain: in July he wrote that for two months he had been unable to make any progress with his work. Apart from a stream of letters from Samuel Bentham about workmen wanted in Russia his correspondence during this period included letters to his father about the disposal of Grove's estate, a long letter to Anderson discussing Russian prospects, two from F. X. Schwediauer about the supply of a set of the new *Encyclopaedia Britannica* for Samuel and containing chit-chat about intellectual life in Edinburgh; and London gossip from his Lincoln's Inn friends, George Wilson and James Trail.

1785 During the winter and spring Bentham, now back at

Lincoln's Inn, was actively preparing for his forthcoming trip to Russia. He was again in fairly frequent contact with the Marquis of Lansdowne (as Shelburne had now become); in April, perhaps in view of favours to come, he offered a gift of drawings to Lady Lansdowne; and before his departure Lansdowne provided him with some letters of introduction. He now had specific commissions from Samuel on Potëmkin's behalf. These related to taking out a botanist to serve in the Crimea and arranging the movement of other craftsmen to help develop Potëmkin's White Russian estate of Krichëv. Somewhat to his brother's dismay, he wrote at least four letters direct to Potëmkin on these matters. Lansdowne's friend, John Symonds, the professor of modern history at Cambridge, furnished information about Italy which Bentham planned to visit briefly on the way.

At the end of June Bentham's baggage was sent off on board the *Mary Frances*, commanded by Captain Richard Brine, which he planned to join about the end of August at Nice after travelling overland across France. In the following weeks his last preparations were completed. These included a visit to the Foreign Office to pick up letters of recommendation, when he took occasion to draw the secretary of state's attention to his brother's interest in commercial development in eastern Siberia and the North Pacific. Early in August he set out from London, reached Brighton on the 6th, and on the night of the 7th–8th crossed to Dieppe. This time there was no dallying as there had been in 1770 along the pleasant country of the looping Seine between Rouen and Paris: leaving Dieppe on the 11th by Saturday, 13 August, he reached the French capital. Here he stayed barely a week, entertained by friends of his father's, paying a courtesy call on Lansdowne's friend, the secretary of the French department of foreign affairs, Gérard de Rayneval, who provided him with further letters of introduction, and gathering up the rest of his party which was to accompany him to Russia—the Scottish adventurer, Logan Henderson, whom he had recruited as a botanist and the two Miss Kirtlands, whom he understood to be Henderson's nieces, who were to run a dairy in the Crimea.

In the small hours of Saturday, 20 August, the party left Paris. They travelled partly by coach and partly by river, via Châlons, Lyons and Montpellier to Marseilles and then to Nice, which they reached on 9 September. They rested there for the weekend, and set out again on the 12th travelling by felucca to Genoa, where, on the 14th, they caught up with the *Mary Frances*. Here they embarked on the 17th for the voyage to Smyrna. However, the ship's captain passed ten days or so (20 September–1 October) doing business at Leghorn. This enabled Bentham to spend three days at Florence, where he lived 'lodging excepted', at the house of the British resident, Sir Horace Mann, to whom Lansdowne had given him an introduction. Finding, when he returned to Leghorn, that Brine was not sailing so early as he had at first intended, he made a further expedition to Pisa.

About 1 October the *Mary Frances* left Leghorn on the last stage of her voyage to Smyrna with no further planned port of call *en route*. Prone to sea-sickness, Bentham seems to have been ill for the next ten days, but after the passage of the Straits of Messina the weather was good and he found energy to write an ample letter-journal. After encountering a severe storm off the Asian coast, the *Mary Frances* anchored at Smyrna on 24 October.

On 3 November Bentham and his party, together with a Russian merchant named Schneyder, a surgeon named Griffiths escaping from his creditors, and a slave dealer with a group of African girls bound for the slave market embarked on a heavily overladen Turkish caique for Constantinople. Uncertain weather and the caution of the Turkish captain held up their arrival at the Dardanelles until the 13th and they might have been delayed still longer but for the appearance of an English vessel which took them on board at Kvemed on the 15th and brought them to Pera on the 21st.

By this time the season was too advanced for Bentham to follow his original plan of taking ship from Constantinople to the Crimea; and on reaching Pera letters from Samuel Bentham advised him that his brother was at Krichëv and not in the Russian south. An initial scheme proposed by the Russian ambassador, that Bentham's group should travel in the company of a Moldavian royal party as far as Jassy, on the first leg of the circuitous land journey to Russia, came to nothing owing to the bad state of the roads west of Constantinople. To a coach (necessary for the women-folk) these were impossible. Accordingly Henderson and the Miss Kirtlands waited at Constantinople till the Black Sea should be open again to navigation; and on 10 December Bentham set off by this route on horse-back. To serve him he borrowed Schneyder's Polish-born servant Ludwig (who was to stay with him for the duration of his Russian visit). A janissary conducted the party, as Turkish law required, either till it caught up the Moldavian party or else passed out of Turkish territory. With him went a servant. The party was completed by a guide who was responsible for bringing back from Bucharest the horses ridden by Bentham and Ludwig and the two pack-animals, which carried their baggage. In all the expedition consisted of five men and seven horses. He reached Bucharest on 26 December.

1786 Bentham continued his journey to Russia, leaving Bucharest on or about 2 January after about a week's stay. Three days later he was at Jassy. After delays caused by the Greek Orthodox Christmas festivals, he got away from here on the 9th, crossed the Dniester into Polish territory near Soroka, and by 5/16 January had reached the Polish side of the Russian frontier at Bohopol, at the confluence of the Sinyuka and the Bug. Here he was held up first by the crossing of the Sinyuka and then by quarantine regulations at the Russian frontier town of Olviopol; but in a few days he was on his way, taking a roundabout route by Kremenchug to Krichëv, where he arrived on 10/21 February.

Bentham's letters from Krichëv during the rest of 1786 give only a general impression of his life there. Early in the year Potëmkin gave his brother tenancy of a farm in the village of Zadobrast in a bend of the river Sozh about three miles from the township, and here Bentham spent much of his time busy writing in seclusion. Early in the spring a hint that their peace might be disturbed by a visit from their father was met by a superbly tactful intimation that circumstances might not then make this advisable. By the end of the year Bentham was well advanced with the drafts of what he described as 'Essai sur les Recompenses' (the basis of the *Rationale of Reward*) and had completed his work on the nature of civil law. At the same time he found energy to write his Panopticon Letters, describing his brother's invention of a new form of industrial building described by him as an 'inspection house', which Bentham was quick to see also had other possibilities. At the end of December two copies of this work were dispatched to London, one to Jeremiah Bentham, the other, under cover of his agent, Richard King, to George Wilson, who was asked to see the work through the press.

Occasionally this existence was varied by a visit from one of Samuel's Russian friends or still more rarely by a call on one of their neighbours. In August the brothers entertained the English member of parliament, Sir Richard Worsley, now on the last lap of an extended foreign tour, whom Bentham had already encountered at Smyrna and at Constantinople during his journey the previous autumn; and Bentham accompanied Worsley on a trial voyage some sixty miles down the Sozh on the prototype of his brother's newly-invented articulated barge-train, which the brothers had christened the 'vermicular'. Reports Worsley brought with him to the effect that the British government intended to impose new legislative restrictions on rates of interest set Bentham's mind at work on the composition of the *Defence of Usury.* Now and again Bentham wrote business letters for Samuel, and at the end of the year a crisis in his brother's affairs at a time when Potëmkin demanded Samuel's attendance in the south occasioned for him a veritable flurry of correspondence.

1787 Although the Empress Catherine II passed through Krichëv early in February on the start of her great tour of south Russia and the recently annexed Crimean territory, Bentham remained secluded at Zadobrast. By this time he had carried his 'Essai sur les Recompenses' to such a state of completion as to send a copy to Wilson for his comments. He also wrote a long description of 'vermicular' to Wilson, in case there should be any way in which a provisional claim to a patent might be lodged. About the same time he was writing the *Defence of Usury*, which he sent off to Wilson for publication at the beginning of May. This was dispatched via St Petersburg, through the hands of Sergey Ivanovich Pleshcheyev, who, in accordance with Bentham's request, made some minor corrections to references to rates of interest in Russia. Despite a refusal to undertake any more such editorial work, which had crossed this in the post, Wilson did in fact see this pamphlet through the press and it was published towards the end of the year. However, further action on the Panopticon Letters was postponed on Bentham's instructions, chiefly, it seems, because of a temporary misunderstanding between him and his father due to interruption of mails. They were not to be published till 1791.

With the spring the settled life of the Bentham brothers at Zadobrast and Krichëv came to an end. At the beginning of May Samuel was called away to dance attendance on Potëmkin in the south, at least for so long as the Empress's tour lasted. Three weeks later Bentham learned that Potëmkin had sold Krichëv in connection with his purchase of a new estate further to the south-east at Smolian lower down the Dnieper. This was soon seen to imply the transfer there of various undertakings with which Samuel had been concerned. During the early summer Bentham was conducting a slightly embarrassed correspondence with his father about the repayment of money which had been advanced by the elder Bentham in connection with some of Samuel's projects. He was now anxious to set out for home, but his brother's desire to see him once more before he left obliged him to give up the idea of taking ship from Riga and to plan an overland journey home in the autumn as soon as ice and snow had hardened the winter roads. However, a Turkish declaration of war on Russia on 5/16 August made a meeting between the brothers out of the question. Bentham had no wish to travel hundreds of miles further away from his homeward direction. Samuel was fully employed in the arming of a flotilla of light vessels in the Dnieper estuary. In Samuel's absence Bentham found himself inevitably drawn into the task of settling up Samuel's concerns and in particular seeing to the paying off of some of the British workmen for whom Samuel had no further employment. In consequence on the eve of his departure he became the victim of legal proceedings for the recovery of money claimed (unjustifiably Bentham thought) by one of his brother's Russian creditors. Though the details are not available, he appears to have extricated himself successfully, and he left Krichëv on his way home on 19/30 November. He reached Warsaw on 16 December, after a gruelling journey, of which he left a detailed account; stayed there only forty-eight hours; and by 27 December was at Berlin.

1788 Bentham passed about a fortnight at Berlin, leaving on or soon after 9 January. He spent the next two weeks 'crawling post from Berlin to Holland through vile roads' and reached home early in February. For some time he idled, feeling 'like a fish out of water', and renewing old acquaintanceships. Lansdowne was affable, consulted him on legal points connected with the trial of Warren Hastings, and asked him what sort of office he would like if he, Lansdowne, got back into power. By early May he was ready to move into a new country lodging—a farm-house at Hendon—where he could have absolute peace to get on with his writings and amuse himself with a 'superb' harpsichord on which he decided to squander sixty guineas. Here he spent most of his time henceforth with occasional visits to his parents and his step-brother Farr, at Farr's country house at Putney Heath. Save for one reference to affairs in France in a letter from Lansdowne, his correspondence up till the end of October reveals little but his absorbing interest in the Russian naval operations in the Liman of Ochakov, in which his brother (though he did not yet know this) was for a short time actively engaged.

MISSING LETTERS OF JEREMY BENTHAM REFERRED TO IN THE CORRESPONDENCE

January 1781 to October 1788

	1780	*Letter*
To S. I. Pleshcheyev	December	384 and n. 7
	1781	
To Samuel Bentham	January	389 and n. 2
	30 January	392 and n. 1
	23 February	(do.)
	26 February	(do.)
	13/31 (*sic*) February	393, n. 1
To James Matthews	end of April	391 (indicated)
To Samuel Bentham	22 May	408 and n. 5
	early July	409 and n. 2 and 424 and n. 4
	1 August	427 and n. 2
	13 August	(do.)
	15 August	435 and n. 4
	11 September	427 and n. 2
	15 September	(do.)
	21 October	(do.)
	[?] 24 October	433 and n. 4
To Shelburne	late October	423 and n. 1
To Captain Blankett	late October	(do.)
	1782	
To Charles Hanbury	30 April	428
To Samuel Bentham	November	436 and n. 3
	21 November	436 and n. 8
	late December	438 and n. 5
	1783	
	28 January	440, n. 2
	[?] late April	444, at end
To Brissot de Warville	10 July	453 and n. 8
To Samuel Bentham	10 July	(do.)
Three unknown addressees	10 July	(do.)
To Samuel Bentham	mid-July	459 and n. 5
To Baron von Raigersfeld	August	463 (indicated)
To Samuel Bentham	August	469 and n. 3

	1783	*Letter*
To Thomas Payne (bookseller)	September	468
To Samuel Bentham	about September (numbered xxv)	516
To F. X. Schwediauer	October	480
	1784	
To Samuel Bentham	2 January	516
	15 January	(do.)
	9 March	495 and 516
	26 March	516
	5 April	(do.)
	8 April	(do.)
	11 or 12 April	(do.)
	14 April	497
	28 April	516
To James Trail	May	499
To Samuel Bentham	13 May	516
To I. M. Simolin	6 June	501
To James Trail or George Wilson	June	502 and n. 2
[?] To William Browne	June	502 and n. 3
Two letters to Samuel Bentham	June	502 and n. 5
[?] To Brissot de Warville	June	502 and n. 4
To James Trail or George Wilson	4 July	506
To Samuel Bentham	7–12 July	516
To James Trail	early August	511 and 512
To John Mulford	August	511
To F. X. Schwediauer	September	514
To Robert Hynam	23 September	518
To Brissot de Warville	mid-November	521
To John Howard	26 November	520, n. 1
To Samuel Bentham	24 December	526 and n. 1
	1785	
	7 February, and an unspecified number between this and the previous date	526
To Ribeaupierre	[?] February	526
To Prince Potëmkin	[?] February	526
Two letters to Prince Potëmkin	[?] March	529
To John Symonds	March	523 and 527
To Samuel Bentham	early April	528
To Prince Potëmkin	April	529
To Lansdowne	mid-June	533 (indicated)
To James Lee	*c.* 1 November	558

	1783	*Letter*
To Samuel Bentham	26 November	554, n. 6
To Samuel Bentham (2)	early December	562
	1786	
To James Lee	March [?]	568, n. 2
To George Wilson	29 May/9 June	576, n. 2
To James Trail	early summer	576, n. 4
To Christian Trompovsky ('general letter')	18/29 December	577 (memo)
To Walter Shairp, Petersburg	(do.)	(do.)
To James Anderson	(do.)	(do.)
To M. Malartie [?] of Paris	(do.)	(do.)
	1787	
To George Wilson	early March	589 and n. 2
To Jeremiah Bentham	early March	589, n. 4
To S. I. Pleshcheyev	*c.*11/22 May	595 and n. 1
To Jeremiah Bentham	31 May/11 June	594 and n. 7
To S. I. Pleshcheyev	29 June/10 July	595, n. 1
To Prince A. V. Vyazemskiy	August	601 and n. 2
To Jeremiah Bentham	*c.*16/27 August	603 at n. 9 and n. 12
To Mrs Bentham	*c.*12/23 September	602, 619
To Samuel Bentham	late October	614 and n. 6
	17 December	615, n. 28 (journal)
	1788	
To S. I. Pleshcheyev	early April	620 and n. 14
To Lord Wycombe [?]	June	622 and n. 5

KEY TO SYMBOLS AND ABBREVIATIONS

SYMBOLS

/ In /	Interlineations. Sometimes these are insertions, sometimes alternative versions. Interlineations are not indicated in all cases.
| |	Space left in Ms.
~~Oxford~~	Word crossed out in Ms.
[to]	No such word in Ms.; it has been supplied by the editor according to sense.
< so >	Conjectural restoration of mutilated word.
< . . . >	Word torn away or hidden in binding of Mss.
[?]	Reading doubtful.
[. . .?]	Word proved illegible.
	Editorial comments are printed in italics within square brackets.

ABBREVIATIONS

Apart from standard abbreviations, the following should be noted:

B.M. I, II, . . . etc.: refers to the main series of Bentham papers in the British Museum, Additional Mss. 33537–64, the volumes of which are numbered from I to XXVIII. Thus B.M. I = Add. Ms. 33537 and so on.

U.C.: refers to the Bentham papers in the Library of University College London. Roman numerals refer to the boxes in which the papers are placed, Arabic to the leaves in each box.

Bowring: refers to *The Works of Jeremy Bentham*, published under the superintendence of . . . John Bowring (11 vols.), Edinburgh, 1838–43. Volumes x and xi contain Bowring's Memoirs of Bentham.

NOTE

Apart from sources cited in the notes, the following standard works of reference have been in frequent use and have not usually been cited:

Dictionary of National Biography

Joseph Foster, ed., *Alumni Oxonienses . . . 1715–1886*, 4 v., 1887–8

John & John Archibald Venn, comps., *Alumni Cantabrigienses*. Pt. I (to 1751), 4 v., 1922–7. Pt. II (1752–1900), 6 v., 1940–54

G. F. R. Barker & A. H. Stenning, eds., *The record of old Westminsters*, 2 v., 1928

Sir Lewis Namier & John Brooke, *The History of Parliament. The House of Commons, 1754–90*, 3 v., 1964

J. F. Michaud, ed., *Biographie universelle, ancienne et moderne*, 52 v., 1811–28

J. C. F. Hoefer, *Nouvelle biographie générale*, 46 v., 1853–66

Russkiy Biograficheskiy Slovar', 21 v., 1897–1916

N. Ikonnikov, *Noblesse de Russie*, 2nd edn., 20 v., 1957–1963; supplements, 1963, in progress

Bol'shaya Sovetskaya Entsiklopediya, 2nd edn. 51 v., 1949–57

Dizionario Enciclopedico Italiano, 12 v., 1955–61

Correspondence

January 1781 to

October 1778

383

From Samuel Bentham[1]

12/23–13/24 January 1781

Jany. 12th 1781

It is too much to be sure for me to expect that you should go to work blindfold upon the presumption of my infallibility without any data to judge from: but I really cannot at least at present give you those data.[2] As to the letter I am rather inclined to advise that there should be none at all and am pretty well persuaded that a Compliment or two dispersed in the different parts of the book itself like the one which you mean to be inserted in that part of the introduction which I have already received will answer much better than any letter.[3] Though there is scarcely a possible chance of her reading the work yet it may be contrived that these particular parts should be pointed out to her. Consult Burkitt[4] about the binding and let it be as elegant as possible. If there are some silk strings to it they will serve to point out the places where she is alluded to. Your idea of having thin as well as fine paper is certainly a very good one. Take care that the sheets are not pressed before they are dry and that all the proper precautions are used to prevent the printing on one leave blackening the other. Let the leaves be all turned over after they are gilt to prevent their sticking. Let the other copies be cut but not bound on account of cheapness and neatness. If you should have such an opinion of her discernment as

383. [1] B.M. III: 127. Autograph. Docketed: '1781 Jan. 13 O.S. 24 N.S. / S.B. Petersburgh / to / I.B. Linc. Inn / Code [. . .].'

[2] See letter 380. In several letters Samuel had been making discouraging comments about the probable reception of 'Code' in Russia.

[3] I.e. a letter to the Empress introducing 'Code'. Bentham had sent Samuel a draft of such a letter for consideration and amendment on 10 April 1780 (letter 351). Samuel here refers perhaps to what became part of a footnote to Ch. ii, § 16 of the *Introduction to the Principles of Morals and Legislation*, pointing to the need for governmental detachment in handling civil disputes: 'The ministers of Catherine II are better *instructed* than to take any other part in such disputes, than that of preventing the parties concerned from doing one another a mischief.'

[4] Burket, from the scanty information about him, seems to have been a mechanical inventor and model-maker. Samuel Bentham had known him at least since 1773 (*Correspondence*, i, 158 n., 166, 170, 171–3; ii, 399, 405).

to imagine the appearance of the outside would give no merit to the contents you will [*three or four words crossed out*] I believe be mistaken and most certainly /many of/ those about her who should see a book better bound than any other will be very much inclined to give the greatest merit to the work itself. An old Aunt of my freind Pleschijeff[5] gave a bible to a Convent the binding of which cost about 10,000 £ sterling. Happy is the man who can get a kiss at this transcendent binding: the precious stones as they glisten in it make many a chop to water. The expence of 2 or 3 guineas may distinguish the merit of your work above others in as great a degree as this said bible is exalted. If you could think of a short but most flattering motto to put on the outside that would certainly succede best of all. Some few however I am in hopes there are who we may get to read it who may be sensible to its real merits and who if it does not appear to oppose their interest may puffe it, and gain it that reputation which a book of inferiour merit however handsome the binding could not acquire. It is not even the 10,000 £ binding that would warm the hearts of the devout if it was said to be /the covering of/ any other book than the bible although the inside is perhaps never seen. In short what all this fair reasoning comes to is that a /outside ornaments/ handsome binding would distinguish it in the first instance and if the inside be ~~found to have~~ approved of would make it more universally liked. [*Several words obliterated*] I now give you according to your desire the first 2 or 3 words of each paragraph of your proposed letter.[6]

1. Voici un livre...2 Il y a dix ans...3 A peine j'avois commencé...4 Que je vous voyes 5 Le livre qui doit accompagner... The last Paragraph has no number but begins Pardonnez moi. I have sent you a copy of verses made by a polish Abbé and presented to her but do not know what reward she bestowed, however as they were spoken highly of to me and given me by the Bishop of Wilna in my last excursion I thought you might finding some hint of a good flattering expression. The worst of it is that the new laws and

[5] Sergey Ivanovich Pleshcheyev (1752–1802), at this time captain of the second rank in the Russian navy. For Samuel Bentham's first meeting with him, see *Correspondence*, ii, 422 n. Destined from an early age for the Russian naval service, he spent some of the most impressionable years of his life (1765–71) as a midshipman serving on ships of the British fleet on the North America station, and ever afterwards he was more at home with English than with his native tongue. From 1780, though still on the active list, his main avocation was service in the court of Catherine II's son and heir, the Grand Duke Paul, later Paul I. Highly gifted as a linguist, he had wide cultural interests and was the author of several works of travel and topography. By this date he and Samuel had become close friends (*Russkiy Biograficheskiy Slovar'*).

[6] See letter 380. The references are to passages in letter 351.

form of Government is already established in most of the Governments in that of Peterbourg for example though not yet in Moscow this however it will be very soon.[7] I do not think she may be much inclined to change anything now as there has already and still continues to be a great deal of plague about it and besides the purpose of ostentation is already answered and I believe that is the only purpose designed. The Heir to the bigotted old woman deceased from the disposition and penetration which he showed on his late visit here as well as by general report promises to be more likely to give that attention to it which may make it of real use.[8]

I congratulate you on your translation's appearing to be in such good hands.[9]

I am sorry that Peake and Mosberry are not inclined to seek fortune,[10] I am in hopes however to be able to prevail on the latter if I should have occasion for him.

I have sent also the arms which might serve as ornament on the outside of the book. Although I think all that can be done may be done without a letter yet at the same time with attention to the critisisms which I sent you I am persuaded you would write the best of all possible letters. Will you when you read it allow me [*two words crossed out*] in case of my observing any parts which I and Pleschijeff ~~think~~ do not approve, and if they be such as can be left out without breaking the thread, to write it over myself leaving those parts out. You will perceive I mention this on the supposition that there will

[7] A considerable reorganization of local government had been in progress in Russia since the autumn of 1775, involving the creation of provincial and district elected chambers. See Sir Bernard Pares, *A History of Russia*, new revised edn., 1947, pp. 283–90, which requires correction regarding the role of locally elected representatives and officials by reference to Mark Raeff, *Origins of the Russian Intelligentsia: The eighteenth-century nobility*, New York, 1966, pp. 96–101.

[8] In June 1780 the Emperor Joseph II, seeking a diplomatic understanding, had travelled to Russia *incognito*, had met the empress, Catherine II, at Mogilëv, and was subsequently entertained by her at Tsarskoye Selo. The death in the following November of his mother, Maria Theresa of Austria, gave him at last full control over the Habsburg inheritance and his desire to apply the lessons of the Enlightenment to the rule of his dominions was well known.

[9] In August 1780 Jeremy Bentham had begun to arrange with Johann Friedrich Schiller, a native of Württemberg, for a German translation of the *Introduction to the Principles of Morals and Legislation*; and on 26 December he reported the excellent progress made with the translation and Schiller's plans for arranging publication at Stuttgart (*Correspondence*, ii, 478 and n., 482–3, 518–19). Nothing further is known of this project. Owing to circumstances not disclosed in the surviving correspondence it seems to have been stopped early in 1781 (letter 393 n.).

[10] Henry Peake was Master Shipwright Assistant at Chatham dockyard, 1774–79, and Master Shipwright at Sheerness, 1779–84. Mosberry, who remains unidentified, was probably a craftsman unconnected with the government yards: for previous reference to him see letter 343 n. 7.

not be time for it to come here return and come again before the work itself may come.

Do not think that the *Police* is good in this country or that there is more justice or more impartiality in the decisions of the law Courts than in other despotic countries. There is however more mildness in the present reign than there used to be. How much I wish that you could see and hear what I do.

I am very much rejoiced at the account you give me of the happiness of the D's[11] but you tell me nothing about the light I am considered in. I wish you could send me out by a messenger a tollerable good waistcoat or even two for these things are very dear here. Any which you have worn yourself will do better. I told you that a Messenger will bring to the size of 2 4to volumes. If you have a mind to give the Verses to Charles[12] do with the cover.

384

From Samuel Bentham[1]

12/23–13/24 January 1781

Jany. 12th 1781. Conveyance of Packets.

Remember for the future that messengers either Russian or English are very frequently passing between Petersbourg and London and that you may certainly hear of their going from London at the Secretary of State's Office. Remember also that packets as large as two quarto volumes may be sent by this mode of con-

[11] Joseph and Elizabeth Davies of Brompton, near Rochester, and their daughter Elizabeth. Samuel Bentham, from 1775 onwards, during the latter years of his apprenticeship, had lodged at Davies's house and been placed under his tuition, and a close friendship developed between the two families. After being a clerk in the office of the Navy Commissioner at Chatham, Davies, in 1776, secured appointment as chief secretary to Admiral Lord Howe, who was then British naval commander-in-chief at New York. He returned from two years' service in North America with sufficient capital to provide an income of £300 a year and an appointment to a pursership. The latter was worth a further £400 or more, clear of the payments which he made to the deputy who performed the sea-going part of his duties on board the *St Albans*, a ship-of-the-line in the Channel fleet based at Portsmouth (letters 131, 282, 317).

[12] Their step-brother, Charles Abbot (1757–1829), the future Speaker.

384. [1] B.M. III: 128. Autograph. Docketed: 'S.B. / Lr datd Petersburg / Jany 13 1781.' Annotated by Jeremiah Bentham: 'recd 26 Febry 1781.' Copy of parts of this by Jeremiah Bentham, B.M. XXII: 17v–18.

veyance directed to Sir James.[2] Pallas[3] conveys and receives parcels of seeds and minerals of even greater bulk by these means. This letter is to go by a /Russian/ messenger whose going is kept as secret as possible.

I recieved yours of the 26 Dec.[4] by the last post and above all things am rejoiced to learn that I may expect 'Div' and 'Experimenting' by the next post or (allowing you to be as unpunctual as myself in such kind of promises) in 2 or 3 posts for certain.

I thank for your Naval news. I long to hear of poor Lohmann after the storm his ship was exposed to.[5] The more storms the more actions and the more difficulties of all kinds he gets into the better if he do but escape safe and sound.

You have sent me a packet sealed and entitled 'Champaigne's papers.'[6] I have not as yet received any account of what you wish me to do with them or why you have sent them. If it was with a view of my assisting in the execution of the plan he proposes it is possible I might be of use in it if I had my directions. I suppose you said something of it in the letter which was sent to Constantinople and which is not yet come to hand: but the papers themselves are imperfect, There are pages marked 5 and 6 but none of any of the preceding numbers nor any which leads to what is written on page 5, it even begins with half a word -chant which I suppose had mer— on another page. The observation of the Monopoly in the hands of the English factory is certainly very just. As to the mutual interchange of goods that cannot well take place with respect to the proprietors of iron mines as they do not deal in any other merchandise. Money is what they require in exchange for their iron.

This goes by a Courier who is said to be setting off in an hour. I have not time to send by this opportunity the Certificate which my father desires of me but will do it by my next letter.

[2] James Harris (1746–1820), K.B. 1779, created Baron Malmesbury, 1788, and Earl of Malmesbury, 1800, M.P. Christchurch 1770–4, 1780–8, was British ambassador at St Petersburg, 1776–83. He proved a good friend to Samuel Bentham.

[3] Peter Simon Pallas (1741–1811), the famous German naturalist, who settled in Russia. On him see letter 366, n. 3.

[4] Letter 380.

[5] Samuel Bentham had become friendly with the Russian, J. Lohmen, early in 1779, when both men were studying at the Royal Naval Academy, Portsmouth (letter 301). In 1780 Lohmen sailed on the *Thunderer*, one of a British squadron detached to the West Indies. This ship disappeared with all hands in a hurricane during October 1780 and was eventually presumed lost.

[6] Champaign, a member of the firm of Champaign, Booth and Tull, 143 Upper Thames Street, and a friend of Alderman Richard Clark (see letter 62, n. 1), was interested in the iron trade with Russia (letter 325). Nothing more is known of these papers. Presumably they had something to do with this subject.

We have not as yet had a degree of cold here more than 20 degrees of Reumur's Thermometer. This is to be sure a vast deal colder than in England. The rooms are hotter than one would wish them and even in walking or driving in open sledges the face and ears only feel the cold. I expect to set out shortly for Arcangel and had intended to have gone from thence through a part of Siberia, but now I rather believe I shall return straight in which case I shall not be absent from Petersbourg above a month. This depends however [*crossing out*] many circumstances which I cannot enter into a detail of. Be satisfied in the assurance that it is not the pleasure of the present moment that I pursue. My friend Ples[chijeff] is very ill of a disorder which though not immediately very dangerous yet plagues him a good deal every now and then. It is the Asthma. What are the remedies and regimen usually employed in England? He frequently reads over your letter[7] to him with the strongest sensation at the pleasure of having received such a letter from you but of shame at the same time for not having answered it. It is his constant occupation and the habit he has been now for some time in of neglecting by necessity his own affairs that seems to have prevented him.

Mr. Carew[8] is still here and will stay I believe the winter at least. He is a man certainly of great abilities a vast stock of knowledge from all opportunities I have had of judging, of a most excellent heart. He is as much attatched to his country as possible and Sir James cannot but find a great satisfaction in his political assistance.

I am affraid you wont read all this.

Jan. 13th 1781 O.S.

We have no news to tell you. It is from you in England that we are anxiously expecting news. What a havock you must make among the dutch ships.[9]

[7] Missing.

[8] Reginald Pole Carew (1753–1835) of Antony, Cornwall. On him see letter 375 and n. 6, and letter 379, n. 2.

[9] Great Britain declared war on the United Provinces in December 1780 in order to preclude the Dutch from obtaining protection under Catherine II's league of armed neutrality (to which they were on the point of acceding) for the important trade in Baltic naval stores which the French were pressing them to continue (Ian R. Christie, *The End of North's Ministry, 1780–1782*, London, 1958, pp. 243–50).

385

To Samuel Bentham[1]

13 February 1781 (Aet 32)

Tuesday Feb. 13. 1 o'clock 1781.

Now for a very odd sort of a story which our travelling cousin G.B.[2] has just now been and told me. As I told you before Banks[3] had promised him his interest with Ld. S.[4] for a Pursership: /that was I believe about 6 weeks or 2 months ago/. Being dunned from time to time, Banks had put him off from time to time telling him that he must wait a little, that his L'dship as he might imagine was much pester'd with Sollicitations, and hamper'd with former promises. In the mean time Allen (Master Painter at Woolwich) had talked to him about the state of his expectations, and told him he could put him into a much surer channel. Thereupon he gave him a letter to a Mrs. Steele at a shop where they sell Essence of Spruce for beer, and which is opposite to the Admiralty. I dare say you remember it; a very *spruce* shop indeed; where they sold nothing else: (now indeed they *do* sell a few other things). The *firm* of the shop is Steele and Townson. The history of them is as follows. There are two sisters, Mrs. Steele, and a Mrs. with a german name, (he could not recollect it precisely) something like Switch: we will call her Mrs. Switch. They have a brother whose name is Hughes, and who is a slater (I think it is) by trade: they have also a cousin

385. [1] B.M. III: 144. Autograph. Docketed by Jeremy Bentham: '1779? or 1780 / J.B. Linc. Inn to S.B. Russia / Greg. B.'s story about the Admiralty Place Sellers. Not sent.'

A large amount of space left unfilled suggests that the letter was not completed, or Bentham may have decided not to send it owing to its libellous nature. A letter begun on this date and finished later was received by Samuel in May, but his acknowledgement makes no reference to this matter (letter 393, n. 1). Bentham's opinion of Gregory's story appears in the next letter, which was presumably drafted about the same time. The ladies mentioned have not been identified.

[2] Jeremy Bentham's second cousin, Gregory Bentham, had recently returned to England after serving as captain's clerk and purser under Captain Charles Clerke on the *Discovery*, the ship which accompanied the *Resolution* on the circumnavigation of 1776–80 during which Captain Cook lost his life in Hawaii. Clerke took over the command but he himself, a victim of consumption, died a few months later, in August 1779. The expedition arrived back in the Thames during October 1780 (See letter 378 and J. A. Williamson, *Cook and the opening of the Pacific*, London, 1946, pp. 191–217).

[3] Sir Joseph Banks (1743–1820), President of the Royal Society from 1778 till his death. Bentham's previous reference to this matter was in letter 378.

[4] John Montagu, 4th Earl of Sandwich (1718–92), First Lord of the Admiralty, 1771–82.

a Mrs. Townson who is the other partner. Mrs. Steele Mrs. Switch and Mrs. Townson are all married. Mr. and Mrs. Steele and Mr. and Mrs. Townson live together in this house: and I believe Mr. and Mrs. Hughes likewise. Mrs. Switch and Mrs. Steele are both visited by Ld. North.[5] Mrs. Switch does not live in that house, but in another in Queen Street, which has a door into the park. She lives very retired, but had a Coach called for her at 3 o'clock /one/ day that G.B. was at Mrs. Steeles. I observed that there was a report of his having kept a woman in one of the Courts near Charing Cross (Johnson's or Craig's) and asked whether it was the same: he answer'd he believed it was: he had heard of her having lived thereabouts. This Mrs. Steele has several daughters: the eldest 17, and very beautiful: the next 13 and very pretty for her age: she has fair hair. They are supposed to be Ld. N's: the eldest is just going into keeping with Ld. S. She said to Miss Allen a few days ago, 'in less than a month I shall be at Black-heath: then I shall come and fetch you in my coach, and we shall see one another often.' The connection between Allen and them comes in this way. Allen's father and their father lived next door to each other in or near Parliament Street: there Allen and these girls used to be play-fellows. When G.B. carried this letter he was received upon terms of familiarity and confidence. The first idea was, that he shou'd have one of the new forty-gun frigates: and Mrs. Steele was to have so much a year for three years. She began that topic by throwing out a distant hint, to which he replied a compliment must be given of course: then there was no farther difficulty, and matters were treated of in plain terms. This was | | days ago: he has been there several different times: he is going there now he has left me. A day or two ago, upon his calling there, Mrs. Steele said to him. 'Well, now you have got your frigate, and the warrant is made out: but suppose a larger ship could be had, you would have no objection to it.—No certainly.—Well then; there is a new 74 which you may have if you please: but as the warrant for the frigate is already in your name, it will not be so proper that another warrant for another ship should be made out in the same name immediately after. Ld. S. and Ld. Dudley[6] (Qu. what can the latter have to do in the business?) are to lay papers before the house next Thursday, and such a change might appear odd. Some other person's name must therefore be put into the warrant /for the 74/ of which mention is

[5] Frederick North, Lord North (1732–92), First Lord of the Treasury, 1770–82.

[6] John Ward, 2nd Visc. Dudley and Ward (1725–88). He was a supporter of North's ministry, but he had no particular connection with the affairs of the Admiralty.

to be made in those papers Mr. Hughes's for example: but as soon as ever the accounts are deliver'd in then that to Mr. Hughes may be cancelled, and another made out for you.' What the consideration was to be for the frigate, he either did not tell me, or I do not remember: that for the 74 was to be £100 a year for three years; but he proposes to pay a sum down at once—But how, /said I,/ do you settle about the time of payment? I hope you /do not/ pay any thing first—Oh no, said he, never fear me; not a penny till I have the warrant in my pocket: on Thursday or the next day, I hope to have it: and when I have it I will bring it you.

Miscellaneous particulars—Mrs. Steele asked him whether he should not like to have a boy of his brought in to the Charter-house. (Ld. N. and Ld. S. are both Governors of that charity.) This he declined for the present, fearing to disoblige a friend who had undertaken to get the boy into the Blue-coat School.

Mrs. Switch's husband is a German: he is abroad in the service in some capacity or other of some minister of our's at some foreign court. Berlin was mentioned for one. I suppose the place is one of the highest that a man can have and yet be in service: that of maitre d'hotel for example. You don't remember any such person at Berlin do you?

One day that B. was there, he saw a gentleman there who he understood was Sr. John Dick,[7] who is or has been Consul at Leghorn.

Admiral Rodney took out with him /to the W. Indies/ (from this house I believe) 2000 lb. weight of essence of spruce and would have taken more, had there been time: Admiral R. and Sr. Hugh Palliser[8] used often to call in there and chat. I forget whether B. did not say it was for the sake of seeing Mrs. Townson.

Spruce beer seemed to answer extremely well in G.B.'s long voyage, and the men liked it very well. Notwithstanding they had nothing but salt provisions from the Cape of G.H. till they had reached Scotland which was 17 weeks, (and that very bad and stale) there was no scurvy till they had been sometime in harbour in Scotland and had drunk quantities of Whiskey: and then only two men had, who were presently cured by coming on shore.

G.B. mentioned it as an idea either of his, or that is likely to be

[7] Sir John Dick (1720–1804), holder of a supposed baronetcy of Charles I's creation, was British consul at Leghorn, 1754–76. For his services to the Russian fleet in the Mediterranean during the Russo-Turkish war of 1768–74 Catherine II made him a Knight of the Order of St. Alexander Nevski.

[8] Sir Hugh Palliser, 1st bart. (1723–96), captain R.N. and M.P., had been Sandwich's right-hand man at the Admiralty during the years 1775–9.

adopted, the giving spruce beer to the men throughout the navy, every third day. Why, said I, not oftener? because it is so much dearer than common beer

	pr. Tun £ s d
Common beer has cost Government in an ordinary year	1 – 10 –
This or the last year on account of the extraordinary cheapness of malt	1 – 2 or 1 – 3
Spruce beer – – – – –	1 – 10 – 0

Several of the sailors who had had rheumatic pains, lost them upon drinking of this beer.

386

To the Earl of Sandwich[1]

c. 13 February 1781 (Aet 32)

Asand

If the information I have received is true, there exists at present close /under your Ldship's eye/ to the Admiralty a nest of /Sharpers from/ whose practises if not put a stop to, /the reputation of/ that branch of his Majesty's service which is in /within/ your Lordships department may receive a very essential prejudice. The principals are two women of the names of Townson and Steele,[2] who keep a /grocer's/ shop directly opposite the Admiralty. These people pretend to sell places in ~~in your Lordship's gift~~ the gift of the board, and in order to give colour to their pretences, they point out a girl the daughter of one of them who, they have the impudence to insinuate, is on the point of occupying such a station about your Lordship's person, as according to the notions commonly entertained of female influence might naturally enough be expected to

386. [1] U.C. CLXIX: 49. Autograph draft, much corrected.

The folder containing this letter is marked: 'Legislaturientes epistolae, Brouillons Unsent, 1774? to 1784?' Probably it was not sent. Mr A. W. H. Pearsall of the National Maritime Museum kindly confirmed that the letter is not to be found among the Navy Record Society's transcripts of Lord Sandwich's naval papers and the present editor did not come across it when he inspected some years ago the non-naval papers which form part of the collection owned by Mr Victor Montagu. Although undated it would appear to have been drafted about the same time as letter 385. Round brackets indicate marginal additions to the initial draft.

[2] On Mrs Townson and Mrs Steele see letter 385.

give more than a due weight to any applications she might choose to make. I have heard of two attempts of theirs, ~~which they have made~~ one of them by the immediate relation of the party concerned and whose testimony if the story he told me was true would in both cases be legal evidence. ([3]/In the instances I allude to/ A person /man/ of judgement who had the honour of a personal ~~acquaintance~~ /intimacy/ ~~knowledge~~ with your Lordship or who had been thoroughly acquainted with the forms of office might, without hesitation, /I suppose,/ have pronounced it a fraud from the beginning: but as the bulk of ~~intendants~~ expectants are in neither of these predicaments, I should ~~apprehend~~ not wonder if there were many who suffer'd themselves to be imposed upon: /especially as/ for the business /imposition/ seems to be conducted with a considerable share of artifice, and they set out with pretending not to take money till the places are actually in possession). I have been told that some intimation is given of them in a recent publication on the subject of swindling ~~which I have not seen~~ in which Mrs. Steele is characterized by the initial letter of her name. I understand that it is in 2 vols. 8vo. and written by one Parker I think the name is, but I have never seen it.[4]

The distress that may be brought upon individuals by this species of sharping is I apprehend but a small concern in comparison of the national mischief it /occasions/ tends to produce, by the false imputations it gives birth to, and the discredit it tends to bring upon so important a branch of //the national /King's/ service// administration. Many people hear of the first beginnings of a transaction, who hear nothing of the conclusion; and thereby imbibe prejudices which they have no opportunity to get cured of, and propagate false /erroneous/ notions which they have no opportunity even /supposing them to have/ if they had the inclination to correct. (so that setting aside the force of party prejudice, and the propensity of ~~which~~ the multitude ~~have~~ to give credit to ~~every~~ any thing that tells to the disadvantage of their superiors, I should not wonder if) In /the very instance in question/ my own case it was my fortune to hear of the beginning of the machination /to which I allude/ a considerable time before I heard of any of those /the/ circumstances which render'd the /fraudulency of it/ falsehood

[3] This passage between brackets has been substituted for a crossed-out passage of similar length.

[4] This probably refers to *A View of Society and Manners in High and Low Life*, 2 vols., 1781, by George Parker, an itinerant actor. Parker gives an account (ii, 10–19) of 'Place-Sellers' among other swindlers; but neither here nor elsewhere in his book is there a reference of the kind Bentham describes.

of the story incontestible; and if I had not had the good fortune to /have seen the impropriety of saying any thing of the matter in that stage/ set /put/ a bridle on my tongue in the mean while even so obscure an individual as myself might have been the ~~undesigning~~ innocent or at least excusable cause of /stirring up/ raising /some degree /share// of national discontent ([5]against a minister altogether undeserving of it, (and of doing more mischief than I would choose to have to reproach myself with.)[6]

(They sell not only places of profit, /stations/ but offices of high trust the command of ships: in short any kind of moonshine that a man will buy.)

If this information should happen to be thought worth attending to, a sheet of paper or thereabouts would contain as much more as I know about the matter. The misfortune is that as no money has been taken, /in either of the instances to which I allude/ there could be no means I doubt of[7] (punishing them in an adequate degree upon the statute which makes it /an offence punishable by hard labour/ to obtain money upon false pretences. They might[8] be punished /perhaps even/ for what is past by a civil action, or /by/ an ordinary indictment; but) The only means I can think of /for punishing them is the method first mentioned/ would be for your Ldship to employ a confidential person who should appear to fall into their snares, and /should/ suffer himself to be cheated of such a sum as it should be thought proper to lay out for that purpose. No very capital sum /I imagine/ would be necessary: for they catch at small sums as well as great, pretending disbursements and the like.

387

From Samuel Bentham[1]

6/17 February 1781

At last then my journey is absolutely determined on and will most probably be a long one. I have everything ready and set off

[5] This parenthesis is in pencil.

[6] The draft continues in pencil: 'which I should be very sorry to have to reproach myself with having started without cause'; and another variant passage is pencilled in the margin: 'more mischief than I would choose to have to answer for'.

[7] Crossed out: 'inflicting a punishment adequate to the mischief'.

[8] In pencil: 'be called to account'.

387. [1] B.M. III: 146–7. Autograph. Docketed by Jeremy Bentham: '1781 Feb. 6 O.S. / Feb 17 / S.B. Petersburgh / to / I.B. Linc. Inn / Setting out for Archangel.'

early tomorrow morning. Where to? What for? When shall I be back? are questions which you will expect me to give a good account of, but which I could wish to put off the answering of. My dislike to setting about giving you these answers does not I do most sincerely assure you procede from any suspicion that you would not be satisfied with them; but merely from the impossibility of letting you know all my reasons. Will you be satisfied in knowing that ~~nobody ever set out to~~ I am pursuing the plan which cannot fail of succeding either here or at home. It is my own fault if my connections in both are not very firmly established by my return. My very good freind Sir James has [*several words crossed out*] given himself a good [deal] of trouble to serve me Mr. Carey[2] also in whose power it may probably be to do me very essential service is disposed to spare no pains in exerting himself for me. Whether I shall begin here or at home is as yet uncertain. I have just now written a letter to Ld. Sandwich which Sir James incloses in one from himself about me by the first Courier which he dispatches. My letter is about my Copper Sheathing plan.[3]

I hope my father will forgive my having taken up so much money just now. I have not spent 20 pounds since my return from the last journey except for things for my present journey and which I hope will well pay me. Besides I shall certainly not want any more for a year.

After visiting some saw mills and some copper mines which are almost in the streight road I shall I suppose in less than a fortnight be at Archangel. From thence you will hear from me and there I may be able to give some better account of the route I take. I promise to be a much better correspondent than I have been yet, and shall be much more particular in my journal as I may probably make some use of the /general/ observations I make.

Our correspondence will henceforth seldom cost either of us any-

Copy in a clerk's hand, B.M. III: 150. Part-copy by Jeremiah Bentham, B.M. XXII: 18v–19.

Addressed: 'Jere^{y} Bentham Esqr., Lincoln's Inn, London.'

This letter reports the beginning of a long tour for the purpose of surveying possibilities of industrial enterprise in the interior of Russia, which occupied Samuel Bentham for the next twenty months and took him as far as points on the Chinese frontier south and east of Lake Baykal. He arrived back in St Petersburg in October 1782. His absence interrupted almost completely the delivery to him of Jeremy Bentham's letters and for most of this period his own give little information about their contents.

[2] Probably Pole Carew. See letter 384, n. 8.

[3] Samuel Bentham's copper sheathing plan was rejected—Navy Board to the Secretary of the Admiralty, 28 April 1781, copy, B.M. III: 173, and Lord Sandwich to Samuel Bentham, 3 May 1781, autograph, ibid. 174–5.

thing. I have since I have been here paid a monstruous deal of money for postage. You will always direct your letters or packets to Sir James. I have received a few days ago your packet of 'Div.' 'Experimenting' which I wanted most you promise me in a month I think; however if you send it me in 3 or 4 it will be time enough.

When your Code is finished send 3 or 4 copies in English and ½ a dozen in German directed to Sir James. One he will take care the Empress shall have. One in English direct yourself to Mr. Petroff[4] from the Author. Inclose it also in a cover apart directed to Mr. Petroff St Petersburg. The other copies leave Sir James to dispose of as he pleases.

When Mr. Sambouski[5] goes to England cultivate his acquaintance. Of late we have been more together than we were before. What would I give for an hour or two's chat with you just now. A dinner at Q.S.P. and a dish of tea at Lincoln's Inn before I set out on this journey would be more relished than ever they have been yet.

I set off directly. Feby. 6th O.S. I am in the best spirits owing to things which I cant write about.

public things go on very well here.

Pleschijeff promises to write to you.[6]

388

From Sergey Ivanovich Pleshcheyev[1]

14/25 February 1781

St. Petersbourg Feb. 14th 1781

I have no more time than just to forward to you your brother's letter which he left with me at his setting out, and to tell you, Sir,

[4] Vasiliy Petrovich Petrov (1736–99), Catherine II's librarian. See *Corr.*, ii, 115.

[5] Andrey Afanas'yevich Samborskiy (1732–1815). The Benthams always mis-spelt the name. Their acquaintance with him began in 1779 (letter 294, n. 3).

[6] See letter 388. On 14/25 March Samuel Bentham wrote to Pleshcheyev from Velikiy Ustyug forwarding two scraps of letters for onward transmission to his brother. He urged: 'I wish you would take a copy of all my letters which you get a sight of and send to my brother otherwise notwithstanding my promise to him I am affraid he will hear but little from me. If you get a sight of [...?] letters to Sir James copy them also.... Yes I do pray you, write to my brother. Your writing will be at least next to my writing myself.' Pleshcheyev forwarded these, adding a scribbled note in which he apologised for the fact that his attendance on the Grand Duke precluded his writing at length (B.M. III: 168).

388. [1] B.M. III: 148–9. Autograph. Docketed by Jeremy Bentham: '1781 Feb. 14 O.S. Mar 23 / Pleschejeff Petersburg / to I.B. Linc. Inn / S.B. set out for Archangel.' Copy in a clerk's hand, B.M. III: 152.

that his business goes on very well, he has two excellent strings to his bow, in short I know not how he could be better off, but you must not be in a hurry, that is the worst in our country; It will be a twelve-month, or let us say, for the most 18 months, before his affair can be determined on. I must tell you that I am not a stranger to his pressing circumstances in other respects. He has been very uneasy, I could see, at his /having/ drawn on his father for so much, I could have prevented him, taking away the necessity; this however he would not allow. But although my allowance is but scanty for the expences I am necessarily, from my situation drawn into, yet you may make his father, if you please, easy as to apprehensions of more demands, I will save my friend from that and I shall have a bad opinion of him if he does not permit me to satisfy his further wants: I shall one day or other have a sufficiency, and indeed as my wants are not very extensive, an affluency, and then I am sure my friend cannot want my assistance, it is merely that I may have an opportunity of tasting of that pleasure, and one would imagine he grudges it me.

I have had lately so little leasure, that I was always hinderd to write to you, and particularly to answer the several questions in the letter you did me the honour and the pleasure to write to me, which however I shall not fail to do in my next. I am with the truest attachment and esteem

Your very faithful humble

servt.

Sergius Pleschejeff

389

FROM SAMUEL BENTHAM[1]

26 February/9 March 1781

Archangel Feby. 26 O.S. 1781

Poor Lind![2]

I can't help thinking of the man He was alltogether a very extraordinary character. For my part I was under great obligations

Addressed: 'To Jere^{y} Bentham Esqr / Lincoln's Inn / London.'
Postmark: 'ST PETERSBOURG' and 'MR / 26'.

389. [1] B.M. III: 154. Autograph. Docketed by Jeremy Bentham: '1781 Feb. 26 O.S. / Mar. 9 / S.B. Archangel / to / I.B. Linc. Inn.'

[2] John Lind died on 12 January 1781. Jeremy Bentham's letter, to which this is a reply, is missing.

to him. I received your letter containing the news of his death the day after I arrived here when I was at dinner at the house of a Merchant whose acquaintance I made by his means at Mr. Raikes's[3] in London. I could not help starting at seeing the words 'Lind's death' just at top.

The papers which you tell me of your having dispatched I hope to receive by my next packet from Petersbourg.

I got yours of Dec. 29th[4] containing the first parcel of 'experi.' by the last post, and 'Div.' came to hand before I set out. As to the matter between Peake and Harrison I know no more of it than the man in the Moon.

Sir Charles Douglas's method of splicing the yards certainly a good one: but I cant say so much of your description of it. If it were not for the bright genius of thy younger brother, thy scribbling would have been to little purpose.

390

From James Matthews[1]

25 April 1781

Sir

I humbly conceive it would be troubling you with too long a List to give the particulars of such of Prynne's Tracts as Lord Shelburne has already got; and equally so of such as he has not. I would therefore rather beg the favour of you to oblige me with a note of such as you have by you of no use, imagining them to be not many; or give me leave to wait on you at your Chambers at some leisure hour to look at them; hoping you will excuse this freedom; and being

Sir

Your most obt. humble Servt.

Ja: Matthews

Shelburne House 25: Apr: 1781
Jeremy Bentham Esqr.

[3] Either William or Thomas Raikes, who were leading Russia merchants with offices at 3 Bishopsgate within. Both brothers were extremely prominent in the Russia Company in London.

[4] Letter 381.

390. [1] B.M. III: 171. Autograph. Docketed by Jeremy Bentham: '1781 Apr. 25 / Matthews Shelburne House / to / I.B. Linc. Inn.'

Addressed: 'Jeremy Bentham Esqr. / Lincoln's Inn.'

The writer was the Earl of Shelburne's librarian. See also the next letter.

391

From James Matthews[1]

7 May 1781

Sir

Inclosed is a List of Prynne's Tracts not in Ld. Shelburne's Collection,[2] the length of which I hope will excuse my taking time to answer your Favour of a Week ago.[3] His Lordship to whom, in writing, I have been attentive to mention your kind Offer, orders me to return you his Thanks. It is understood that you are not to have any trouble, and only favour him with such as may happen to fall in your way. He has already all the several pieces you send a note of, except the Seventh, which not being mentd. in any of the printed Lists is doubtful whether by the same Author or not. My Lord has already near 60 pieces of Prynne's writings besides many duplicates which would be much at your Service or any of your Friends, were you disposed to make a similar Collection. Many of the single Sheets and half Sheets are probably not to be met with anywhere but in Lincolns Inn Library and the late Judge Blackstone's, (which last is said to have rather a compleater collection /(of Prynnes)/ than the first)—and therefore are not expected to be procured. I have omitted noting many of the mere puritannical Tracts which deserve certainly to be no Object of collects, in comparison with the many others that are esteem'd on account of the Authors uncommon depth of Reading in the Records, Laws, Politics and History of England and am

Sir

Your obed. humble Serv.
James Matthews

7th May 1781

391. [1] B.M. III: 179–80. Autograph. Docketed by Jeremy Bentham: '1781 May 7 / Matthews Shelburne House / to / I.B. Linc. Inn.'

[2] B.M. III: 181–2. Matthews's list contains 91 titles. All but seven of these correspond, though not always accurately, with those given in William Prynne's own list published in 1660, *An Exact Catalogue of all Printed Books and Papers written by William Prynne of Lincoln's Inn Esq.; before, during, since his imprisonment.* The fullest account of Prynne's writings is by Mary Isabel Fry and Godfrey Davies—'William Prynne in the Huntington Library', *The Huntington Library Quarterly.* (1956–57), 53–93, listing 289 works either attributed to or known to be by him.

[3] Missing.

392

From Samuel Bentham[1]

3/14 May 1781

To IB

Just as I was sealing up the whole sheet to send to Petersbourg to be forwarded from thence to you came a man sent to me by the Governor of Catherinberg with a large packet of letters containing yours of the 30th of Jany. another of 26th Feby. 'Experimenting.' Anderson's agriculture paper. 'Div'. 'Destruc.' and scraps of Reviews. Your reproaches to me for writing so seldom affect me at present to such a degree that they can not fail of producing a greater degree of /punctuality/ in that respect. Can you believe that every day and often in the day I regret this negligence of mine and yet that I cannot sit down to write and draw my attention from other things to that but now and then just as the post is going out? Thus it is that I am always in a hurry and that my letters are filled as it were with excuses for not writing.

I have relied on Pleschejeffs sending you copies of whatever I write to Petersbourg as it will most of it come into his hands.

Was there a Bell man to ring every night I should certainly [*words obliterated*] better correspondant. How unlucky that even at this mo[ment] when a man is waiting to set off /for Catherinberg/ the instant I give him this and that I could yet keep him an hour to give you another sheet, that at this moment there is a couple waiting at the church to be married and the preists even I see at the church door looking out for me. The fact is I had desired the

392. [1] B.M. III: 183. Autograph. Docketed by Jeremy Bentham: 'S.B. Nigni Taghil / 140 versts from / Catherinburgh in Siberia / to I.B. Lincoln's Inn / Reced July 17.' Copy by Jeremiah Bentham, B.M. XXII: 23v.

Addressed: 'Jere. Bentham Esqr. / Lincoln's Inn / London.'

Making fullest possible use of the winter sleigh roads Samuel Bentham had arrived before the spring thaws set in at Nizhniy Tagil, about eighty miles north of Yekaterinburg (now Sverdlovsk). Founded in 1725 on the upper reaches of the river Tagil on the eastern slopes of the central Urals, 58° N., 59° 58′ E., Nizhniy Tagil was one of the oldest centres of the iron industry in this region. Having sent no news to his brother since the brief note printed as letter 389, Samuel, on 14/25 April, began a lengthy account of his activities, which included the construction of a special amphibious vehicle in which to continue his journey. On 3/14 May he added a final portion to this letter, acknowledging the receipt a week previously of Jeremy Bentham's letter of 23 February (missing), (B.M. III: 169–70). This was the sheet which he was about to seal up, when he received the packets including Jeremy's letters of 30 January and 26 February (also missing) to which this note refers.

principal preist to let me know when there was to be a marriage that I might see that ceremony performed according to the true uncorrupted Russian custom. He sent me word this morning and now lets me know that they wait only for me. Surely this excuse is admissible.

May I never hear a single word from you again if I sleep before I have filled one sheet of paper for you. [*Whole line crossed out*] Some good public news from England I have just learnt by a letter from Mr. Carew at Petersbourg of whom you have written to me and I I dare to say several times spoke of to you. Poor Lohmenn little hopes of the Thunderer!

393

From Samuel Bentham[1]

12/23 May 1781

Patent

I thank you for your information about Patents as to what you are pleased to say to the disfavour of my invention which you know

393. [1] B.M. III: 184. Autograph. Docketed by Jeremy Bentham: '[1781] May 12 (23) / S.B. [Nigni Taghil] / to / I.B. Linc's Inn / Sheet 3 / Planing Machine / first hinted.' Note by Jeremiah Bentham: 'S.B. / Le. dat. Nigni Taghil, Siberia /12/23 May 1781 / Recd in a 1r from J[y] B. dated / 13th Aug. 1781 / Inclosing a copy of a letter / from S.B. to Sir Ja[s] Harris / at Petersbourg / Dat. Nigni Taghil / 13 May 1781'. A briefer version appears in Jeremiah Bentham's letter book, B.M. XXII: 24v–25.

The opening sentence presumably refers to one or other of Jeremy Bentham's letters of 30 January and 26 February which Samuel had received nine days previously (letter 392 n.). Samuel mentions his preoccupation with an invention in a sheet filled up between 28 November/9 December and 20/31 December 1780, sent presumably just after the latter date (B.M. III: 115). It was probably the planing machine, reference to which is found later in his correspondence. A second note of 12/23 May 1781, not printed here (B.M. III: 185) contained an inquiry about entering a caveat at the Patent Office, so that action might be taken to prevent Samuel's being forestalled by another inventor. In a third note of the same date (B.M. III: 186) Samuel acknowledged the receipt that day of a further letter from Jeremy (now missing) 'dated in the former part Feby 13 and at the latter *Jan* intended for Feby 31st [*sic*]'. See letter 385, n. 1. Yet another undated and partly indecipherable sheet which, from internal evidence, can be assigned to this packet of Samuel's, indicates that Jeremy, in whichever letter Samuel was acknowledging, was still concerned about the presentation of 'Code' in Russia. Samuel wrote: 'I have got into a much better channel for pushing Code or anything else forward, so don't give up this but sending us copies is all you have to do. Leave the rest to us wise ones.' Possibly in one of these missing letters Jeremy explained the lapse of the German edition of the *Introduction* which had been in progress, for Samuel wrote: 'Don't attach yourself to Germans. There is something in their general character' [*remainder illeg.*] (B.M. III: 192).

nothing of, I care not one farthing for it notwithstanding you enforce it by 'Mind I told you so.' A Model of it I hope to find made and in good order at my return to Petersbourg. The reason of my /not/ telling you what it is for even was only least the letter should be seen, and my over-great circumspection makes me fear that it would be in anybody's power to invent it if they even know the object of it. A further reason indeed was that one person I thought necessary to trust with it and ~~therefore did not choose that there should be a possibility of its being known by other means~~ if I trusted no one else with it should it become known I might conclude it was from him. What I can tell you is that it is for working in wood and that from calculations made as ample as possible with respect to the expences of the work done by it; it cannot fail of being profitable under the most disadvantageous circumstances. In the part of the country where I am and indeed in this whole country, it would be exceedingly usefull. I /have great/ hopes of getting it set on foot so as for me to have the profits without any advance for the expence of it. I may say I am sure of having it tried whenever I please that is of having the machine erected and worked without any expence to me whatever, /but then it will belong to another/. This would serve with respect to profiting by it afterwards in England, but what I want is an exclusive privilege for it here. I have been advised (by a person whose judgement you would have a very good opinion of if you knew him) to get a Patent by some means or other in Holland at the /same/ time as in England. He has spent a long time in that country and is well able to judge how well it would answer there. Indeed there is no country in which it would not, but I want to introduce it here first.

394

FROM SAMUEL BENTHAM[1]

16/27 May 1781

Nigno Taghil le 16 de Mai 1781

I dispatched 2 or 3 scraps of letters to you from hence a few days ago:[2] but I shall not let pass an opportunity which just offers of giving you another scrap.

394. [1] B.M. III: 187–8. Autograph. Docketed by Jeremy Bentham: '1781 May 16 O.S. 27 N.S. / S.B. Nighi Taghil / 120 versts from Catherinburgh / in Siberia / to I.B. Lincoln's Inn / Mills.'

Addressed: 'Jere^{y} Bentham Esq / Lincoln's Inn / London.'

[2] Letter 393 and n.

The commissions which I gave you for *wearables* I drop entirely: but I must give you another of a different kind. I do not sufficiently understand the mechanism of wind mills, or rather I am not acquainted with the dimensions to which they may be extended. The Principles on which they act can need no illustration to anyone who has sailed in a boat. What I want then is the dimensions of the Vanes as well as of the axis and the means of presenting them so as to suit all directions of the wind, and of increasing and diminishing the quantity of sail. All this I can easily enough invent, but I wish to know how it is /actually/ practised in the most approved mills, and at the same time whether any new mode of applying the force of wind to produce a circular motion has made its appearance lately. Remember that those parts of a Windmill which are to adapt it to the grinding of corn I am not in want of. Now how are you to get this information. I dont know of your having any mechanical freinds who could give it you directly.

You might go to Nairne[3] and inventing some story or other to account for your curiosity desire him to inform himself if he does not know of the length of the Vanes of a windmill. This is the principal Quere.

There are 2 or 3 remarkably large windmills on the River Thames below Wapping at Limehouse or the Isle of Dogs, which I have been used to see in passing. They had a contrivance which I much admired of staying or supporting the extremities of the Vanes by /a/ rope to each which were fastened at their other ends all to the *axis produced. I give you leave* and desire you to employ two *afternoons* to procure me this information but no more. Do it however immediately and send also by the first Courier directed to Sir James Harris any good book there may be on the subject of both wind and water mills. The bulk must not be greater than 2 small quartos.

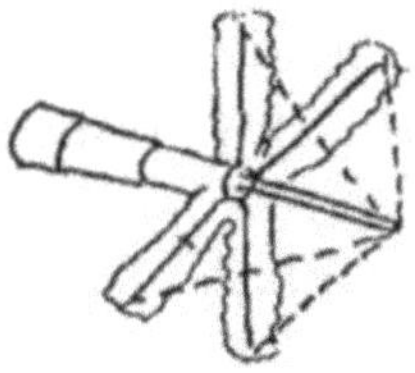
the axis produced

There is a change in my plan since I wrote my last /which/ though contrary to my usual *prudence* I will e'en tell you of. Finding some clever workmen and being likely to be detained a month longer by the making this new invented travelling carriage, I have determined to try /here/ my machines of which I wrote to you in my last. I mean that the work which requires 10 hours for a man to do in the present method he shall do in 10 minutes by my machine /and much better in quality/. That the general idea of the machine can

[3] Edward Nairne (1726–1806), instrument maker. On him see letter 149, n. 4.

be made to succede is what I have not the least doubt of. How far my abilities with respect to invention and my patience in the pursuing the ~~experiments~~ alterations which may be necessary after trial will /carry me/ I shall see in time. I have however set a man to work on a model and shall in a day or two set half a dozen more to begin the machine itself and the dread of shame if nothing else will carry me through it. Keep however, I beg of you, your former ideas of its coming to nothing, and recollect that it will not be the first project which I pursued at first with vigour and dropt again without fruit.

If I succede in this to my wishes I shall most likely return immediately to Petersbourg to take such steps as may turn it most to my advantage. I reckon upon 2 months as necessary to make any trial. You who may imagine my calculation is very *bare* may set down 3 4 or 5 before you will expect that I shall give you any account of the result. Give me only in the mean time your *prayers* that I may be endowed with perseverance. Amen. Dont find fault with the coarseness of my paper, I am just going to write a few lines on some of the same to a Governor who has some hundreds of thousands /of/ people under his Government.

Adieu.

The making the master of the fabrick where I am some return for the obligation I shall be under to him for the work which has been done for me first put me in the head of erecting such a machine for him. Otherwise there are other places where I could have made my trials of it.

I hear that the best house in Tobolsk has been got ready for me for this month past. I have at present possession of the best house in Catherinberg where I left all my books and other things, with a soldier to take care of them. I shall however desire my books to be sent to me.

395

To Joseph Davies[1]

June 1781 (Aet 33)

Saturday June 1781

A friend of mine Dr. Schwediauer[2] has some notion I understand of putting people in his country to export hither the fossile Alkali from thence where it can be had cheap, now at a time that /the price of/ that from Spain which is what we used to have is enhanced greatly by the war. In this view he is endeavouring to come at the prices that are given here by the manufacturers who make use of it. The soap-boilers I understand are the principal: it being better for their purpose than the vegetable: it makes the soap harder it is said. But he knows no soap-boilers in town; nor I neither. Now I happen to recollect that there is a person of that business who lives either at Chatham or at Rochester: I believe at Chatham. I forget his name; but I remember well that by Mr. Guy's[3] means I hired a horse of him to wait upon Mrs. D. Miss Guy and poor Mrs. Wise[4] the summer before she died to Coxheath: Mrs. D. I am sure remembers it very well. I remember seeing some of his vats when I called there with Mr. Guy to talk about the horse. Now who is it that will go for me and examine and Xexamine this honest man, and ask him what he gives for his fossile alkali (upon the supposition that he uses any) or what it is that people in general (for nobody wants to pry into the secrets of his particular dealings) give for it these hard times. It will do him no harm to tell: for peradventure means may be found of letting him have it at a cheaper price than he pays now.

As to the scientifical name of fossil alkali some of the glassmakers

395. [1] B.M. III: 195. Docketed: '1781 J.B. / to / Davies Brompton / To enquire prices of / Fossile Alkali for / Swediar.'

[2] Dr François Xavier Schwediauer (1748–1824), an Austrian doctor of medicine. Bentham had become acquainted with him in October 1778 (letter 279 and n. 5), and their friendship had ripened on the basis of common scientific interests. There are many references to him in the correspondence of 1778 to 1780.

[3] Presumably the G. Guy with whom Bentham had some dealings over the affairs of the Wise family in the winter of 1776–7. See letters 196, nn. 10 and 11, 199, 203, and 212.

[4] Mrs Wise was the sister of the Benthams' friend, Mrs Elizabeth Davies. For her death, some time in March or April 1779, see letter 313 and n. 2. Bentham and the Wise family were all at Brompton during the latter part of September 1778 and this would appear to be the occasion of the visit to Coxheath, which is not mentioned in the correspondence (letters 274 at n. 5, and 277).

here know it by that name: but that I suppose is hardly the case with soap boilers. Exclusive of that there are three names by which it is known in trade: *Kelp*, Barilla, and Soda. It is called Kelp when it is in its ⟨im⟩purest state; Barilla is purer, and Soda is purer still: but still this last wants much of that purity to which it may be brought, and to which it is brought in the state in which it is sold by the Chemists. Therefore what I wish to know is

1. Which of all these if any he buys?
2. At what prices and whether by the ton, hundred, or what other measure?
3. What is the least quantity he ever buys, or would choose to buy?
4. Whether he does anything to refine it after he has got it, or whether he would wish to have it purer than it is when it comes to him?

I should like to know likewise what the difference is between what he pays for the vegetable alkali if he uses any, and this.

396

To the Earl of Shelburne[1]

18 July 1781 (Aet 33)

Lincolns Inn July 18 1781

My Lord

In the course of the conversation[2] I was last honoured with (no part of which will very speedily be forgotten by me) your Lordship, I think, was pleased to drop a hint or two concerning a plan you had in contemplation for the improvement of the Poor Laws. Since then I have received a letter which if your Lordship should happen not to be particularly apprised already of the footing on which that matter stands in Scotland, I thought it might perhaps be a satisfaction to you to peruse. A copy of so much as relates to this subject I therefore take the liberty to enclose. I do not mean to put your Lordship to the trouble of returning it, having got a

396. [1] Lansdowne Mss. Autograph. Docketed: '18 July 1781 / Mr Bentham / about Poor Tax / Improvidence.'

Addressed: 'Earl of Shelburne.'

[2] This conversation had taken place perhaps as much as a fortnight earlier at Shelburne House (see the beginning of the fourth paragraph). Up till that time, Bentham, though corresponding with Shelburne, mainly on Samuel's behalf (letters 327, 338, 362, 364, 367, 369), had avoided meeting him, chiefly on the ground that he ought first to establish his reputation by bringing out the *Introduction to the Principles of Morals and Legislation* (*Correspondence* ii, 480, 504 and n. 3). Early in July Shel-

similar copy for my own use. The writer is a *Mr. James Anderson,*[3] a very observing intelligent man, who has added the experience of a farmer to the studies of a man of science. He is advantageously known in the world of letters by several publications on the subjects of Agriculture, Chemistry and Political Œconomy; particularly by a book entitled Essays on Agriculture in 2 vols. 8vo, and by another entitled Observations on national industry, 1 vol. 4to: both of which contain very liberal and extensive views.

As to the paper in question, when I consider it with a view to any application that can be made of it to what I understand to be your Lordship's purpose, it is fit I should acknowledge, that I look upon it more as a matter of curiosity than of use: since the view it presents to *us*, is rather that of a state of things to be envied and of a system of manners to be admired than that of a plan of policy to be pursued. If one may give credit to it (which from the knowledge I have of the author's accuracy and talents for observation I am much disposed to do) the three great hinges upon which the perfection of the Scottish management of this business turns, are the virtues of humanity, frugality and honest pride: the first on the part of the contributors, the second on the part of the managers, that and the last together on the part of the receivers. As to the first of these qualities, I make no doubt of our possessing it to at least as high a degree as they: it is to this that we owe, such as they are, the present system of the Poor Laws. But in both the other points we have been hitherto, and perhaps ever shall be, far behind

burne at last decided to seek the acquaintance of his elusive correspondent and descended upon him at his chambers in Lincoln's Inn, and Bentham's visit to Shelburne House appears to have been an immediate sequel to this (B.M. XVII: 26). Bentham then gave Shelburne some explanation of the work on which he was engaged. When he came to write this letter, he was in great doubt how far he should enlarge upon the subject and he eventually decided to discard lengthy passages of explanation. Four drafts of this letter exist: U.C. CLXIX: 113, 114, 115, and 116. The first of these is a fair draft of the letter as sent, practically identical in wording, but with one or two pencil emendations, and with a final paragraph referring to Samuel Bentham, which is given in note 8. The second is apparently the first draft of the opening portion of the letter, which Bentham abandoned, and in view of its interest this has been printed as an appendix. The third and fourth drafts represent different stages in the evolution of the final letter, during which Bentham decided to omit still other passages of explanation, and two material extracts from these appear in notes 4 and 5.

[3] James Anderson (1739–1808), farmer, journalist, and author of works dealing with agricultural and economic questions: on him see Charles F. Mullett, 'A Village Aristotle and the harmony of interests: James Anderson (1739–1808) of Monks Hill', *Journal of British Studies*, viii (1968–9), 94–118. Bentham's dressed-up copy of his letter to him became dissociated from this covering letter and is now in the collection of the Shelburne papers at the William L. Clements Library, Ann Arbor, Michigan. It is printed below as an enclosure.

them. Accordingly, with *them* the business is done by *manners* only, and as far as taxes are concerned for nothing: with us, by a most complicated system of laws and an immense expence.[4]

The arrangement of the paper your Lordship will see is not very methodical: which is the less to be wondered at as it was a mere letter of friendship, written without being so much as asked for and without the least idea of any such honour as is now done to it: not that I can say much, indeed, for either his method or his stile at any time. It stands word for word as I received it, except that I have broken it down into paragraphs, equipped it with a set of marginal contents, and at the conclusion given the heads of it in another order. The marginal-contenting (that your Lordship may not be startled at it) is a sort of hobby-horse exercise of mine, which the weakness of my frame forces me to be practising upon all occasions: upon mole hills as well as upon mountains; upon sheets as well as upon volumes: so that without it I can never fancy myself master of any thing I either write or read. The result of it when performed, cannot I think but be a matter of some convenience even to minds of stronger grasp finding it necessary to my own.

Since I was at Shelburne-house, the nature of my design has led me to bestow upon the constitutional branch of law a share of attention which certainly has not been the less sollicitous for a hint which fell from your Lordship on that subject. My way is (in the order of *tractation* I mean which in many respects is a very different thing from the order of *investigation*) first to consider what is

[4] The following paragraph follows in draft U.C. clxix: 115 at this point, but was later discarded: 'The affairs of nations are conducted /led influenced/ by two sorts of institutions laws and manners. Ask your Gardener my Lord, and he will tell you that there are some plants /so tractable/ ~~which will bear transplanting and which are of so tractable nature that wherever he wants to [...] them~~ he has but to stick them ~~in the ground~~ /any where/, and they will be sure to /take root and/ grow; but /while/ that there are others ~~of~~ so untractable and fastidious that they come up only /no/ where ~~they are self sown, nor will they have any other soil than what they choose themselves~~ /but where they have sown themselves in a soil of their own choosing/. Laws /are ended/ (I believe it will be found are) many of them in the former /case/ : but manners, I believe are mostly in the latter. ~~I do not pretend to~~ /Far be it from me to/ say that ~~the~~ in (the formation of) /forming/ manners the sovereign /legislator/ has no influence /can do nothing/ : but that the /chief of the/ influence he ~~has~~ /can/ ~~belongs,~~ exercise /exert/ will be that which he exercises in the capacity rather of a leader than of a governor) but that it is only in ~~an~~ a very indirect way and by a roundabout and tardy process that he can exercise any effectual influence over them in ~~the~~ his particular character of a legislator, and that in an immediate way ~~the only influence it is only in the capac~~ if he acts with any effect it must be in the capacity of a leader—In making manners he can do little more than the first fiddle +[*pencil note in margin:*+ or the director] of a band in making music: if the others follow, well and good: but if not, there is no help for it,' [*A further short continuation in pencil is not fully legible*].

possible, next what is *eligible* and lastly what is *established*. The first object I have got pretty well within my grasp, having drawn a circle, as I think, round the possible modifications which the powers of government admitt of: and this is all that is necessary or indeed pertinent to the purpose of the volume I am upon. These are things which are not done in a day, my Lord: and yet in point of extent this affair has been but a parenthesis, as in point of difficulty it has been but an amusement in comparison of the other contents of a provoking chapter which still sticks with me.[5]

This packet I have ventured to trouble your Lordship with as the lawyers say, *de bene esse*: taking the chance of your having any leisure to bestow a thought upon it. If the report which has been in circulation within this week or a fortnight have any truth in it,[6] the care of the poor must give way to those more extensive cares which embrace the interests of poor and rich together. But we have the gloomy English notion of the incompatibility between good news and true to prevent our giving that credit to it which it might receive otherwise.

The visit your Lordship was to make to Cheltenham is, I suppose by this time at an end.[7] Wherever this meets you, I sincerely [hope] it will find you in possession of the share of health which you proposed going in quest of to that place.[8]

I have the honour to be with great respect

My Lord

Your Lordships most obedient humble servant

Jeremy Bentham.

[5] In draft U.C. CLXIX: 116 there is a colon at this point, and then the following passage which was later discarded: 'and of which the object is to ~~give~~ an analysis /exhibit the possible varieties in/ the texture of a /compleat/ body of laws quelconque, to settle the individuation of a law what it is that makes one entire ~~bu~~ yet single law, and what parts of the total mass of the laws belong to the ~~several~~ three great branches into which that body is not uncommonly divided: all which ~~though~~ announced separately are points which / however separate in appearance are in reality so connected that they / must come [...] together / [...] [...] / (upon the analysis of the matter of a body of laws) or not at all. What sort of work I shall /poor Davus will/ make of it after all, God knows: but I believe in my conscience if ~~Eurystheus~~ /the Sphynx/ I think ~~her~~ /the lady's/ name is had, happened to have thought of it these [*three words crossed out*] /are the problems she would have put/ given / ~~Hercules~~ /Oedipus/ to /solve/ instead of the questions she took it into her head to puzzle him with.' The 'provoking chapter' is Ch. XVII of the *Introduction to the Principles*, the continuation of which eventually became the separate work published in this edition as *Of Laws in General*. See also letter 426.

[6] The allusion is obscure.

[7] This was not the case. A week later Shelburne dated his reply from Cheltenham (letter 398).

[8] In the letter as sent Bentham omitted this final paragraph which appears in his

Appendix[9]

Asel

My Lord

In the last conversation I had with /was honoured with/ your Lordship, (no part of which will very speedily be forgotten by me): ~~Your Lordship was pleased to put the~~ I well remember /one/ question/put/to me/ by your Lordship was/ how it happen'd that I had not made the constitutional branch of the law the first object of my enquiry [*marginal note*: tho' the first in dignity not first in the order of demonstration]. The question is one of those which convey /bestow/ instruction while /as/ they seem to demand /ask for/ it: had it been my good fortune to have been earlier in the way of receiving such lessons, my book would have been better (than it is) and sooner written than it has been: (however) but let that pass—it becomes me rather to be thankful for /to make the most of/ the advantage which my good fortune has put /thrown/ into my hands than to repine at the thoughts of its not having befallen me any sooner [*marginal note*: had I possessed sooner the advantages of which a prospect has /is/ now open'd to me]. /But to return to/ To this question time did not then allow me /so much/ to attempt giving an answer that could in any degree be satisfactory—conscious of which I remember well, the answer /all the answer/ I gave was that the opposite course to that which the question suggested was that which the order of my ideas had prescribed to me. The answer which /for the reason already assigned/ I could not then give for myself my book will be found I hope to have already given for me. The passage I allude to is in ch. 16 paragraph | | beginning with these words, | | [*marginal note*: see also Indirect Legislation].[10] The general /[...?]/ end of government in all its

final draft, U.C. clxix: 113: 'With relation to my Brother, I obey'd your Lordship's commands within a few days after they were delivered /given/: but it may be a long time before I (can) hear of his having received them. The last letter I have of his was written so long ago as the 25th of March at a town, /called Ustjago/ on the road between Archangel and Catherineburgh in Siberia, called Ustjago: it is a place of some note, and is inserted in the maps. He was setting out from thence in great diligence, loaded with the benedictions and more substantial favours of the good Archbishop; who seems to have had more hospitality than religion, having broken the fast in that season of mortification in a very conspicious manner, for the accommodation of his young guest. The kind part your Lordship has been pleased to take in what relates to him will, I hope render it pardonable in me to have made this mention of a young man who otherwise has so little title to your notice.'

[9] U.C. clxix: 114.

[10] Bentham did not complete the reference to *An Introduction to the Principles* and it is impossible to locate with any certainty in the very long sixteenth chapter the

branches is the happiness of the community: the happiness of the community is made up of the several happinesses (if one may so) of the several individuals /members/ of which that body is composed —these happinesses are all reducible into such and such pains or evils averted—and such or such pleasures and advantages procured or secured.

If I have profited any thing /reaped any profit/ by a course of twelve years study it will shew itself in the /my/ capacity (I shall manifest) of receiving instruction from such /further/ questions as your Lordship may think fit /be pleased/ to put to me. [*Marginal note*: my ideas will receive a polish from]

The general end of government taken in all its branches being the happiness of the people that is etc. the laws which belong to the constitutional branch are those which /of all others [*Marginal insertion*: as I hope your Lordship will perceive]/ stand the farthest from that mark in the chain of causes and effects.

If what is there said should not be found sufficiently explicit, any farther elucidations would be most commodiously given by means of such occasional /viva voce/ /extemporaneous/ illustrations as the turn of the conversation may demand /seem to call for on the spot/.

I remember also ~~that~~ to have confessed to your Lordship that the constitutional branch was that which of /above/ all others had /hitherto/ occupied the smallest share of my attention. But that it either has or could have been altogether unattended /unnoticed/ to by me—that it has not may be seen by several /various/ passages in my book (refer to them) that it could not have been will be sufficiently plain to anyone who considers how inextricably all the several branches (into which the principles of government may be divided) are interwoven. The *loom* being set, I can at pleasure take up the thread and carry /spin/ it on wherever it is broken.

If in return for the /rich harvest of/ instruction I shall be sure to reap (it should be my good fortune to afford any) I should be able to flatter myself with the notion of having afforded any, it will be

passage intended: perhaps the discussion in para. 65 of the 'Characters...of PUBLIC offences, or offences against the *state* in general' (in *CW*, pp. 278–9).

The marginal reference to 'Indirect Legislation' likewise cannot be precisely located. It relates to what was originally conceived of as a further chapter of *An Introduction to the Principles*, and subsequently as a separate essay (see letter 426). The Mss. for this essay were used by Dumont for the section on *Moyens indirects de prévenir les délits* in *Traités de législation civile et pénale* (Paris, 1802: t. iii, 1–199; cf. Bowring, i, 533–80).

one of the most honourable as well as the most flattering circumstances of my life.

Enclosure[11]

Anderson on the maintenance of the Poor in Scotland.
Account of the manner in which the
Poor
are maintained in Scotland.

In a Letter from Mr. James Anderson of Monkshill near Aberdeen, to Jeremy Bentham Esq. of Lincoln's Inn,—Dated March 1781.

1.

Occasion of the ensuing Paper.

...I have hardly forgot any of the Conversation I had with You while I was in London, and in particular I just now recollect one of a very interesting nature concerning the Poor Law in England, and the mode of providing for the Poor in Scotland—as I consider the Poor Laws in England as the most destructive system of Laws that ever were invented, which must at last prove the ruin of that Nation, I cannot help thinking that it is a Subject which claims your particular attention in the important work you are engaged in; and altho' it is possible that a more œconomical or more judicious mode of providing for the Poor may be discovered than that which is followed in Scotland, yet it is so much preferable to the mode adopted in England as to deserve to be particularly explained to You; which I shall do by giving You an Extract from a Letter published some years ago in a Scots Magazine on that subject with such remarks as will tend to make it intelligible to You.

2.

Form of Parochial-Government in Scotland.

You are acquainted with the general form of Church Government in Scotland. The Affairs that relate to the Poor are left to the management of the *Parson* of the Parish (who always resides

[11] Shelburne Mss. William L. Clements Library. The copy Bentham preserved for himself is at U.C. CLI: 35–8.

upon the spot) and a set of Men who are called *Elders.*+ These Elders consist of grave well behaved Persons, selected by the Parson from among the Parishioners, without whose concurrence he can do nothing regularly in this and many other lesser Matters. Their function is pretty much like that of the Privy Council; *Si parva licet componere magnis.* Their number is not limited, only they must consist of three at least: usually there are ten or twelve in a Parish. In choosing these Elders regard is had in some respect To their local situation in the Parish; and they have it in charge to enquire into the circumstances and behaviour of the Poor in their Neighbourhood, and to make a report to the Parson in Session (for this is the Name of the Court when assembled) of the situation and circumstances of any necessitous Persons. If these necessities proceed from idleness, extravagance or misbehaviour, they Cite the necessitous Person before them and accompany the Charity with a monitory reprimand. If any necessitous Person has Relations who are in affluent Circumstances, particularly the Children or near Relations, a Deputation of the Elders sometimes waits upon these Persons, and represents to them the calls upon them to relieve their poor Relations; but they have no compulsory Power whatever. To the Honour of their Country, however, it must be said, that this is seldom necessary. I never knew it done but in One instance, where a Brother was inattentive to the wants of a Sister, and it produced the desired effect.

+ V. Postea 17.

3.

Funds for relief of the Poor.

The Funds for relief of the Poor are entirely gratuitous Donations, unless in a few Cases that shall be afterwards mentioned.

1. Bequests.

It often happens that Charitable Persons at their Death Bequeath some Money to the Poor of the Parish where they were born or resided.

4.

2. First Fruits of Livings.

The Patron of every Parish likewise has it in his Power to keep the Church vacant so long at every change as to obtain the disposal of Half a Years Stipend. This Money may be applied by him for any work of public utility within the Parish, or may be given to the Poor. Custom has made it a pretty general Rule, that the widow or Children of the deceased Parson (who are seldom left in affluent Circumstances) get this Half Years Stipend; and on some Occasions it is applied for the behoof of the Poor.

5.

[The Funds /are/ managed by the Kirk Session.

This, together with the Charitable Donations, becomes a Fund under the management of the Parson and Session, who lend it out to interest, and apply the Interest for the behoof of the Poor, if Necessary, or allow it to accumulate if they find it can be done, or encroach upon the Stock, if any extraordinary Exigency require it.

6.

/Whose/ proceedings /are/ registered.]

The proceedings of this Court are regularly entered, in a Book kept for that purpose, by the Clerk of Session, which any *Heritor* has a right to Examine when he sees fit: who can also Cite them before a civil Magistrate in case he sees any appearance of malversation.

7.

3. Ordinary Contributions at Kirk.

The Ordinary Fund for the Current Expences, is the voluntary Contribution given by the Parishioners at each time of public Church Service. In most cases there is placed at the Door of the Church a Bason or two, into which any One as he passes may drop just what he pleases. One of the Elder's has the charge of this Offering, which is carried directly to the Session House, and as soon as Church Service is over, is there told over and the amount of it entered into the Session Book. It is at this time also that the

Court give out to the Poor such proportion of the Money as they see proper for each, which is then entered also in the Book. Such of the Poor as are able to attend, come in Person and receive it themselves: and the proportion that is assigned to such as cannot attend is given to the Elder in whose district the poor Person lives, who gets it Conveyed to them.

8.

In Country parishes the Sacrament of the Supper is usually Administered once a year, at which time there are frequent Preachments, and as most of the Parishioners then attend the Church, and it being a Season of extraordinary Sanctity, the Contributions for the Poor are at that time more abundant than at any other Season. 4. Extraordinary, at Sacrament time.

9.

Besides these Funds, they have fallen upon a mode of raising another kind of Contribution upon the People. Custom has made it necessary for all Persons, unless it be those in extream indigent circumstances to have a *Mort Cloth* over the Coffin, when the Corpse is carried to interment. Every Kirk Session therefore has provided itself, out of the Poor's Money with at least One Mort Cloth of Black velvet with Silk fringes; for the use of which is paid at each time a stipulated Sum. As these Mort Cloths become Old, new Ones are bought and the Old Ones still kept, which are let out at an inferior Price, Some Parishes have three of these, by which means the Rich and the Poor are equally accommodated; as every one may chose that kind, the price of which is best adapted to his circumstances. 5. Profit upon lending out Mort Cloths.

10.

Since Roads became good in Scotland, another improvement of this Nature has taken Place. The Session buy a kind of two wheeled Herse which 6. and Herses.

they let out at so much each time to such as choose it, with or without Plumes and Trappings as the Persons Circumstances require. They keep no Horses, but these are usually borrowed from any Farmer in the Neighbourhood.

11.

7. Fines for Fornication.

Another Fund for the Poor arises from Fines imposed for Fornication, formerly it was the Custom to Cite Fornicators to appear before the Parish, to be seated in a public Seat erected for that purpose (called the *Stool of Repentance*) for three several Sundays; there to be as often rebuked by the Parson. This they were Obliged to submit to under the Penalty of being excommunicated: which was then deemed a very severe punishment. But as the Opinions of mankind in these matters are much altered of late, the repentance Stool has been gradually allowed to fall almost into total desuetude, and instead of that, the Guilty Persons are Cited privately before the Session, where they receive a private rebuke and admonition from the Parson, and upon paying a moderate Fine proportioned to the Circumstances of the Person, they are then absolved. These Fines are for Servants and Labourers, usually from ten to twenty Shillings for each of the Parties.

12.

8. Seat Rents at Kirk.

+See also 20, 21.

All these (together with Seat Rents in Church in some parishes) are the Funds out of which the Poor are supported.+ The Seat Rents however in Country Parishes are seldom any thing. In what manner these are distributed, you will in part learn from the following Letter upon this Subject, which You will now be able fully to comprehend.

13.

Proportional number of Poor, what.

This Letter is introduced by a Quotation from Bishop Burnet which I Omit. The writer then proceeds thus. 'The design of this quotation which I have taken from Harriss's Collection is to introduce a few Observations relating to the Poor of our own Country. What the proportion was between the numbers of Poor and the rest of the Inhabitants of England or of any other Country through which the Doctor had Occasion to travel at that time, I don't know' (his Calculation supposes that the Thirtieth or Fortieth part of the Inhabitants of every Country are Poor and require to get Alms) 'but in the several Country Parishes around where I live, I understand, from good authority, that the real Poor are in the proportion of one only to an Hundred. By real Poor, I mean such as stand in need of dayly supply: there are others indeed who need some small thing once in the year or oftener for Cloaths, Fuel or for the support of their Families, when by distress they are rendered unfit for Labour.'

14.

Contribution for the helpless Poor, what and how raised.

'What Sum may be necessary for the annual maintenance of the last class of Poor, cannot, as their need depends upon a variety of circumstances, be easily ascertained. I shall however endeavour to shew how the Poor of both these Classes are supplied in some Parishes, and may be supported in every Parish in Scotland, so as to prevent all Occasions of begging.

'Few Kirk Sessions give more, and many less, than the Price of a peck of Oatmeal to any One of the Poor in a week. If we suppose a Family to consist of Five, of an Hundred Persons there will be twenty Families; If each of these Families gives, one with another, an half Penny every Sabbath Day, the Amount will be Ten pence; the weekly Pension of a Person really necessitous when the Oatmeal is at ten pence the peck. (The average Price of Oatmeal is about Eight pence the Peck consisting of Ten pounds Amsterdam weight.) If it is higher as at this Season, 1772, they can easily afford the necessary additions; or supposing that of these Twenty Families there are three Farmer's Families,

	s	d
The Farmer and his wife each Sunday may give	.0:	1.
His Son and Daughter	.0:	1.
His two men Servants and two maid Servants	.0:	1.
Three Families	.0:	9
So the remaining Sixteen, the 17th. being supposed to be the Poor Family, will have only to give	.0:	3.
	1:	0

Being the weekly supply to a Poor Person when the price of Provisions is high. Whatever be in this Calculation, I know that a Parish consisting of three Hundred Persons, ten years of age and upwards (who you know can never all attend the Church in One day) contribute every Sunday at an average through the Year, three Shillings Sterling and upwards to the Poor, and a Parish of a Thousand twelve Shillings'. (Upon enquiry I find this is a higher Sum than is usually collected; it usually runs on an average between 8d. and 10d. p. Hundred Persons.)

15.

For those who require only a partial Relief.

'Having shewn how the real Poor in some Parishes are supplied, I shall in the next Place endeavour to point out, how the Other Class of Poor may be provided for. From the above Calculation it appears that of Ten hundred Persons, ten are really Poor, and that these Ten hundred contribute weekly Twelve Shillings for the ten Poor, that is two Shillings /more/ than is required.

	l s d
The two Shillings overplus weekly amounts in a year to . .	5. . 4 . . 0
(This Article should be thrown out, as being above the average Collections, even his own Parish of three hundred contribute only three Shillings) 'Every Parish almost has besides the weekly Collection, a small Fund for the support of the Poor: many 100, some two, some three hundred pounds. The One I have in my Eye has £100, which at 5£ p Cent. is 5£. But supposing it to be only 50£, the Interest yearly will be—	2. . 10. . 0
If two in an hundred die in a Year, and if a mort Cloth is made use of upon such Occasions, the hire of it for 20 dead of 1000d. at 4s. 6d. each, would be 4£. . 10s. . 0d. but supposing it 2s. at an average	2. . 0. . 0
	9. . 14. . 0'
(I find upon enquiry that in a parish of 1000d. Persons, where two Mort Cloths are employed at 12s. and 4s. the Average Revenue that accrews from hence is abt. 2£. . 12s.)	
'The Parish which contributes weekly 10 or 12s. will at the Sacrament give twelve times that Sum—hence	6. . 0. . 0
Total	£15. . 14. . 0

'Thus the managers of the Poors Funds, in a parish consisting of such Numbers, will have £15. . 14. . 0 Sterling to answer all incidental Charges. I might have mentioned SeatRents and Fines for Fornication which in many places add greatly to the Sum' (At an average my information would lead me to conclude, that in a parish of the Size mentioned, twenty Shillings p.ann. is about the average Sum drawn from the first, and about 15s. from the last Article).

16.

Conclusion, that the Provision made for the Poor is sufficient.

'Many of the above Calculations are too low; but the design is to shew, that all parishes, however mean in their Circumstances, may if they will, easily maintain their own Poor. In my Calculation I have laid no Stress upon the contributions of the Heritors or their Families for one Reason among others, because few of them attend their parish Churches. It may appear surprising, but upon enquiry it will be found true, that generally through Scotland, the Poor are supported by the Poor, I mean by Tradesmen, Mechanic's, Labourers, Servants Etc.'

I think it unnecessary to quote farther, a very few Observations on the above, will give You a pretty just Idea of the management of the Poor in Scotland.

17.

Poor's Money by whom distributed.

+Supra 2.

Since writing the first part of this Letter,+ I have been more particular in my enquiries than I had been before, and I find that every Proprietor in the Parish is entitled to a Vote in the Session with respect to the distribution of the Poors Funds, if he pleases to attend; on which Account the Parson gives public intimation from the Pulpit, before each distribution of Money to the Poor, when it is to take place.

18.

Accounts when and how made up and audited.

The Accounts of the Poors Money of each Parish must be regularly made up Once a year, and laid before the whole of the Ministers who constitute the Presbytry in which that Parish is included; who Examine the Accounts, and Check such abuses as they see necessary. The custom is to appoint some individual to Examine the Accounts and to report at a subsequent Meeting.

19.

The Poor, you will easily Perceive, are in general allowed to live in their own Houses, or with their Friends. What they can Earn for themselves goes in part for their maintenances: and the deficiency that may arise from their inability to provide for themselves is made up by the public Money. If any One is in a condition to earn his own Bread, he can expect no sort of supply.

Poor suffered to live at Home.

20.

Besides the public Charities collected at Church,// well-disposed Persons have an Eye over such Poor as thro' accidental Sickness or other misfortunes may be in distress in their Neighbourhood, and contribute by private Alms what they can easily spare, or represent their Case to the Parson, who gives such relief as can be Afforded. The chief burthen of this kind of Charity, falls upon the middle Ranks of People; chiefly Farmers in the Country. Those of higher Rank are in general above the knowledge of these lower Scenes of distress; unless it be when a Charitably disposed Matron fixes her Residence in the Country; which is but seldom the Case.

9. Source of maintenance occasional Donations of Opulent Neighbours.

// Supra 7, 8.

21.

Well disposed Persons of Rank, sometimes mortify a small Annuity to the Poor of the Parish in which they reside. This was formerly more common than at present.

10. Source—regular Annuities.

22.

By these means the Poor are in general out of all danger of being in want of the common necessaries of Life. But when they are reduced to get public Charity, they never can hope for any

Disgracefulness of an Eleemosynary support, the cause of the fewness of the Poor.

Superfluities; and as it is esteemed a disgraceful thing to receive Charity, every One thro' the whole of Life, does as much as is in his Power to prevent himself From being reduced to that humiliating Situation: And as it reflects a kind of disgrace upon his Relations also, these contribute what they can, whether by temporary assistance or occasional Remonstrances, to prevent any of their Kindred from being in that situation. This tends to inspire a kind of industry and frugality into the Minds of the poorer Classes, which is productive of much good to the Community. To these circumstances we must attribute the very small proportion that the necessitous Poor in Scotland, bear to those of Other Countries; from all that I can learn, the proportion of One in a Hundred is very near the truth.

23.

—And of the good behaviour of the lower Classes.

I apprehend that it is chiefly owing to the difference in the Idea that a Scotsman and an English Man in the lower Ranks of Life, entertain in regard to the acceptance of Charity from the Public, that we are to ascribe the superiority that the former enjoy above the latter, as Servants in England. The lower People in England work hard, but spend their Earnings with an improvident Prodigality, which in any slight reverse of Fortune tends to throw them upon the Parish. The Habit of Drinking on Sundays, which too much prevails among them must be in a great measure ascribed to that Cause; and nothing so entirely unfits a Man for an Office of Trust as a habit of Drunkenness. A Scotsman when he comes to England, knows that he must depend upon Himself alone for his Subsistence, even in cases of Distress: He is therefore obliged to be Sober and diligent, which renders him much fitter for an Office of Trust than another Person who has not the same motives for attention and uninterrupted watchfulness.

24.

But altho' the mode of providing for the Poor here is at present and ever has been sufficient for the purposes required (except in some great Communities, where the management of the Funds is more liable to abuses than in other Cases) yet there are Abuses even here, and there are circumstances which tend to make these Funds defective in certain Cases: which will probably one day or other destroy the System that has so long prevailed. Misapplications of the Poors Funds.

25.

There is one radical defect of the institution, which is indeed but of a venial Nature. At every Parish Church in Scotland is settled a public Schoolmaster, who has a small Salary appointed to him by Law, in the same manner as the Parson, but these Salaries are in general so very Small as hardly to be an Object of desire to Men who have got an Education to fit them for the Office; usually from five to ten pounds pr. Ann., To render their Situation somewhat better, the Schoolmaster is usually made Session Clerk with a small Salary annexed which is paid out of the Poors Funds, because no Other Provision has been made for that purpose. These Salaries tho' small tend to diminish the pittance that the Hand of Charity means to apply to the relief of the Poor. 1. Allowance to parish Schoolmasters.

The Salary of the Sexton which for the same reason is paid in the same manner is liable to the same Objection. These two Salarys amount together from three to six pounds pr. Ann. in different parishes. Each of these has certain Fees besides; the Clerk for registering marriages and Baptisms, and the Sexton for Burials. It is a pity that these Fees are not so high as to prevent the necessity of giving any Salary at all; but this is only a small abuse. 2. Do. to the Sexton.

26.

3. Do. to Students in Divinity.

Every parish likewise gives a certain Sum annually from the Poors Money towards Educating a poor Student in Divinity. This tho' a trifle (being from 6s. and 6s. . 8d. to 13s. and 4d. p. ann. on a parish) is a very unnecessary Alienation, which ought to be corrected.

27.

4. Do. to the Dissenting Clergy.

But what cuts deeper than any of these is, that Sectarists of all denominations, having no legal Funds for paying the Salaries of their Parsons, appropriate among themselves all those Contributions, which in the Established Church go to the Poor, to the payment of their Parsons Salaries; and are besides Obliged to tax themselves very heavily in other ways. Hence it happens that the Poor of all these Sectarists become a heavy burthen upon those Parishes where they abound: and as the lower Classes among these Sectarists feel these Taxes very heavy, there is always a greater proportion of Poor among them than in the Established Church. The Funds for support of the Poor by these means in some Parishes are much more deficient than in Others, and as those of the Established Church who contribute their proportion to the support of the Poor, See that Money in many Cases applied to the relief of those Sectarists who do not contribute at all, it is to be feared that they may sometime or Other adopt the Idea of compelling them to contribute to the support of their own Poor. This has never yet been done, and I hope if ever it should be necessary, they will be cautious what Plan they adopt: but I have no Hesitation in affirming that if the Poors Funds are deficient in any part of Scotland for the purposes wanted it arises from that Cause. When a Foundling is at any time thrown on a Parish, it also becomes a very heavy load upon the Poors Funds. But that is not now so often the Case as it has been; the Crime of Fornication not being now accounted a damnable Sin, People are less ashamed at contributing to the support of their illegitimate Offspring.

Table of Contents.
in another order.

1 Proportionable number of the Poor. 13.	6. None taken from their own Houses. 19.
2. Allowance requisite for each Person. 14.	7. Distribution of the allowance, by whom performed. 17.
3. Funds out of which the allowance is supplied. 3, 4, 7, 8, 9, 10, 11, 12, 20, 21.	18. [*sic*] Accounts of the Poors Money, how made up and audited. 18.
4. Calculation of the manner on which the burthen of the voluntary Contributions is distributed. 14.	19. Improper defalcations made out of the Poor's Funds. 24, 25, 26, 27.
5. Distinction between the Poor who require to be maintained *in toto*, And those who need only /to/ be maintained ex parte 13, 15.	20. Fewness of the Poor, owing to what Cause. 22. 21. Good behaviour of the lower Classes owing to the same Cause. 23.

397

FROM SAMUEL BENTHAM[1]

10/21 July 1781

It would be better that the Copies of Code should be *bound*, neatly though not richly. Suppose 4 Copies in English and at least

397. [1] B.M. III: 198. Docketed by Bentham: '1781 July 21 N.S. 10 O.S. / S.B. Nigni Taghill / to / I.B. Lincs Inn / Sheet 2 / Reced at Bowood / Oct 5th.'

6 better 10 in German. I was misinformed when I understood that the making of a Code in this country was dropt. It is here that the happy efforts of a reformation in jurisprudence are to be seen daily. Parts of this /new/ Code which make their appearance (which are promulgated) occasionally from time to time prove the attention which is still given to this subject. How earnestly I wish this work of yours was ready! If it is not now too late do not leave out the note on *asectism* unless you have any particular views which that would be adverse to: at least let my advice get the better of your German freind's. In this country at any rate anything said indirectly against Religion will not hurt the credit of a book in the eyes of those whose judgement will be attended to. The Religion, here tis true consists of a vast number of ceremonies: but the preists have no influence in the jurisprudence nor in the Education. They have no respect shown to them but what they show to each other. Indeed they have their hands kiss'd as a salutation from the devout and as a ceremony in the church upon certain festivals; but they are never seen in /fashionable/ company. A Governor or Commander may on a particular holliday invite the principal of the preists, but he has only to eat and drink, he is taken little or no notice of, and when dinner is over he makes his bow and marches off.

What think you of a Governor who rules over 110,000 people whose sole object is to avail himself of the power that is given him only to produce as much happiness as he can. Such a man it is my good fortune to have formed a freindship with. [*long crossing out*] What I tore off and have scratched out was what I had ⟨by⟩ mistake written on this piece of paper instead of in a letter to this

This is a separate sheet forming part of a packet including B.M. III: 196–7, which is addressed: 'Jere[y] Bentham Esq / Lincoln's Inn / London', and which bears a similar docket. Both sheets were copied, with some omissions, as a single letter by Jeremiah Bentham in his letter book, B.M. XXII: 28–29v. The omitted portion contains Samuel's description of an excursion to Yekaterinburg (now Sverdlovsk) and the surrounding district. In the concluding passage of it he wrote: 'You certainly would give one of your ears to have such an opportunity as I at present have of informing yourself of the Jurisprudence of this country. Some of the more recent regulations respecting criminal matters I have beg'd the Governor to have written out for me and they shall then be translated. As my head is full of other things of more importance to *me* I do not wish to bestow a great deal of thought on this subject neither perhaps should I do it to your contentment. If however you will send me immediately some Queries more especially if you write them in french, I shall most likely have a very good if not quite so good an opportunity of answering them. You have no occasion to menager to me any caution in your *questions*, all information of that kind is allowed and even encouraged to be given in this country, as witness the sources I have laid open to me for acquiring information by the express desire of the Empress.'

said Governor. His name is Lambe.[2] He says that he is of English or rather Scotch extraction. An ancestor of his was taken into the service by a Czar before Peter the Great. but in short this is a matter which is so little interesting compared to his good qualities that I have forgotten it.

The machine I wrote to you last about is tried in the model to the perfect satisfaction of every body.[3] It would be almost ready in the great but 6 weeks hollidays at this season of the year for the men to make their hay etc. puts a stop to it. You shall hear more of it as soon as it can be finished. I beg'd you in my last[4] to give me information about windmills. All mechanical information would be highly acceptable.

398

From the Earl of Shelburne[1]

26 July 1781

Cheltenham 26 July 1781

Dear Sir

I am very much oblig'd by your Letter of the 18th.[2] I consider your Attention as a Mark of your Friendship, of which I am ambitious. I remember reading some of Mr. Anderson's papers, and that they contain'd more usefull matter, tho' not such fine Language as is commonly to be met with among Scotch Writers. I entirely agree with him about the Poor Laws—They not only appear to me productive of all the Inconvenience commonly apprehended and Felt, but likewise are daily destroying all natural Subordination and affection—The Master Manufacturer uninterested in the Fate of the hands whom he employs becomes a mere Negro Driver—while the man of Property loses that political Influence, which it has been a Fundamental Principle of all constitutions to suppose attendant on Property, by the Poor being taught upon all occasions to look up to the King's Justices for Relief and I shall not be surpriz'd to see the Poor make as seperate an Interest in the State as the Clergy do.

[2] Not identified.
[3] His planing machine (see letter 393).
[4] Letter 394.

398. [1] B.M. III: 199–200. Autograph. Docketed by Jeremy Bentham: '1781 July 26 / E. of Shelburne Cheltenham / to / I.B. Linc. Inn / Poor Laws / Invitn to Bowood.' Printed, Bowring, x, 88–9, and Everett, 123–4.
[2] Letter 396.

I brought the *Fragment*[3] here meaning to read it again, which has been the means of discovering to me that I am here in company with a Friend of yours—Captain Blankett.[4] He returns with me to Bowood at the end of next Week, from whence he accompanied me here, and I should be very happy if it might prove an Inducement to you to meet us there.

You say nothing of your Brother I hope he has not embark'd himself in a Service, which among others he has given me the worst opinion of.

It is ridiculous to say in this Idle Place, that I am oblig'd to conclude my Letter for want of time, but I was impatient to acknowledge yours, and an early Dinner does not leave me more time than is necessary to add the Truth and Regard, with which I have the Honour to be Dr. Sr.

Your Faithfull
Humble Sert.
Shelburne

[3] Bentham's *A Fragment on Government*.

[4] John Blankett (d. 1801), a second lieutenant on Admiral Keppel's ship, *Victory*, in 1778, when his path first crossed that of the Benthams (letter 286 and n. 2). In 1779, on being promoted commander and appointed to command the *Nymph* (14) detailed for the East Indies with an expedition under the command of Rear Admiral Sir Edward Hughes, he made a proposal, which was declined, that Samuel should accompany him (letter 302). He received rank as captain in 1780. Long afterwards, reminiscing about this period of his life, Bentham told Bowring: 'Blankett was a retainer of lord Shelburne, one of the numerous hangers-on who were tale-bearers to my lord, and was familiar with the Whigs [i.e. the followers of the Marquis of Rockingham and of Charles James Fox]. He was an ignorant, confident, amusing fellow, an object of great aversion to the Bowood ladies from his coarse manners. But he was employed by Lord Shelburne to repeat to him what passed among the Whigs, and especially to report the conversations at the Admiralty. I was once playing a duet with Lord Shelburne's upper servant, when this Captain Blankett pushed against me. I lounged at him with my bow, and broke my bow... though ill-read and assuming, and addicted to falsehood, rather from temerity than mendacity, he was a necessary instrument to Lord Shelburne' (Bowring, x, 116).

399

To the Earl of Shelburne[1]

29 July 1781 (Aet 33)

Lincolns Inn July 29 1781

My Lord

Late last night I received the honour of your Lordship's letter.[2] In answer to the obliging invitation it contains, I will take the liberty of telling your Lordship how I am circumstanced. My health not being altogether as I could wish, my Physician has for some time past been wishing me to take the benefit of sea-bathing. Business however has confined me to town hitherto, and will confine me till next thursday: on which day I am under a promise to pay a visit to a friend of mine who lives in the neighbourhood of Chatham,[3] where the water, I am told, is salt enough for my purpose. There, it was my intention, before I received your Lordship's letter, to have staid a considerable part of the summer: but my physician says a fortnight's bathing there will answer my purpose, he thinks, pretty sufficiently, if it be succeeded by bathing in fresh water, the means of which I take for granted I should find at Bowood. For this reason, if it were entirely equal to your Lordship, I could rather wish to defer paying my respects at that place till *Friday fortnight*: but if on any account whatever an earlier day should be more agreable, any intimation to that effect should be obey'd as soon as it was received. I hope I should not then be too late for the pleasure of Captain Blanket's company, to whom I beg my compliments. It would be an indulgence to me to be permitted to talk over with him the travels and adventures of his old acquaintance, whom he was kind enough to wish to have for his guest, but would not accept of for his carpenter.

This same would-be carpenter (for it is he whom your Lordship condescended to reproach me for not mentioning) has *not* embarked himself in the Russian service. His last letter dated May 14th was written at a place called Nigni Taghill a house of the famous Dimidof's[4] whom I dare say your Lordship has heard of,

399. [1] B.M. III: 201–2. Autograph, draft or copy. Headed: 'I.B. to the E. of Shelburne then at Cheltenham in answer to his of July 26th.' Docketed by Bentham: '1781 July 29 / I.B. Linc. Inn / to / E. of Shelburne / Cheltenham.'

[2] Letter 398.

[3] Joseph Davies, of Brompton, near Rochester. See letter 383, n. 11.

[4] Samuel Bentham's references to 'the famous Dimidof' are in a portion of his

not a hundred miles (to use a newspaper phrase) or at least not much more than a hundred miles from the nearest post-town, which is Catherineburgh in Siberia. He was going in high spirits /in pursuit of I know not what/ I know not whither: but he tells me that if I make haste and answer him immediately, my letter will probably find him at Astracan. More than this I need not say of him at present. I am—etc.

400

From the Earl of Shelburne[1]

15 August 1781

Bowood Park 15 August 1781

Dear Sir

I should have written to you some days since to acquaint you of my return home, but I was in doubt whether you expected an answer, or how it might find it's way; In this doubt therefore I only write to be of the sure side to acquaint you, that Captain Blankett and I will be[2] in such an addition to our Society and that I have no engagement whatever except to pass Monday with Ld. Pembroke,[3] whose House etc. I shall be proud to shew you if you continue your last Resolution of coming here on Fryday next.[4]

I am with great Regard
Very Truly Yours
Shelburne

letter to his brother of 14/25 April–3/14 May 1781 not printed in this volume (letter 392, n. 1). This was Prokopiy Akinfiyevich Demidov (1710–88), at this time the senior member of a numerous family which for several generations had played a distinguished part in developing metallurgical industries in the central Urals. He had inherited an enormous fortune and was a munificent patron of education. He owned a large iron works at Nizhniy Tagil and had made Samuel free of his house there while he was in the district.

400. [1] B.M. III: 203. Autograph. No address or docket.

[2] Shelburne here omitted 'delighted' or some such expression.

[3] Henry Herbert, 10th Earl of Pembroke (1734–94). His family seat was at Wilton.

[4] 17 August 1781.

401

To George Wilson[1]

19 August 1781 (Aet 33)

Sunday 12 o'clock

Where shall I begin? let me see—the first place belongs of common right to the ladies—The ideas I brought with me respecting the female part of this family are turned quite topsy turvy: and unfortunately they are not yet cleared up. I had expected to find in Lady Shelburne a Lady Louisa Fitzpatrick sister of an Earl of Ossory whom I remember at school instead of her I find a lady who /has/ for her sister a Miss Caroline Vernon.[2] Is not this the maid of honour, the sister to Lady Grosvenor, the lady who was fond of Ld. Caermarthen of whom he was fond, and whom he quitted for an heiress, and a pair of horns?[3] Be they who they may, the one is loveliest of matrons, the other of virgins: they have both of them

401. [1] B.M. III: 204–5, 206–8. Autograph. Undated, but clearly written on the first Sunday after Bentham arrived at Bowood, 19 August 1781.

First sheet addressed: 'George Wilson Esqr. / Lincoln's Inn / London', and redirected: 'Thorpe near / Staines.' Postmark: '21 / AV.'

First sheet partly printed under incorrect date, Everett, p. 128, and without dating, Bowring, x, 90–2; second sheet printed without dating and in incorrect order, Bowring, x, 89–90. The last few lines of this letter, being on a separate sheet, were inadvertently left out when Bentham made up his packet and were inclosed with his next letter: see n. 16.

Bentham's friends were avid for news about this first plunge into high society and the possibilities for advancement which it might bring, and he pledged himself to write long detailed accounts of his experiences to George Wilson, who was to post them on afterwards to Joseph Davies (letters 402, 414).

[2] Bentham soon unravelled these relationships: see p. 51 below. Shelburne's second wife, whom he married in 1779, was Louisa, da. of John Fitzpatrick, 1st Earl of Upper Ossory, and sister of the second earl who had been an almost exact contemporary with Bentham at Westminster. Lady Shelburne's mother had married as her second husband Richard, fifth son of Henry Vernon of Hilton, Staffs, and in due course presented her with three Vernon half-sisters: Henrietta (1760–1838), who married (1776) George Greville, 2nd Earl Brooke of Warwick Castle and Earl of Warwick; Caroline Maria Vernon (1761–1833), who married (1797) Robert Percy Smith, ancestor of the Barons Lyveden—she is the Miss Vernon of this correspondence; and Elizabeth (1762–1830), who died unmarried. At this time Bentham was confused over Caroline Vernon (1751–1829), at one time a maid of honour to Queen Charlotte. She was the daughter of Richard Vernon's eldest brother, Henry, and so a first cousin to the Countess of Warwick but with no blood relationship to Lady Shelburne.

[3] Francis Godolphin Osborne, Marquis of Carmarthen (1751–99), who succeeded his father as 5th Duke of Leeds in 1789, married in 1773 Amelia Darcy, da. of the 4th Earl of Holderness. She eloped in 1778 and was divorced from him by Act of Parliament in 1779.

more than I would wish, of reserve: but it is a reserve of modesty rather than pride. The quadrupeds whom you know I love next consist of a child of a year old,[4] a tyger, a spaniel formerly attached to Lady Shelburne, at present to my Lord, besides poor plebian cats who are taken /no/ notice of, horses etc. and a wild boar who is sent off on a matrimonial expedition to the farm. The four first I have commenced a friendship with; especially the first of all, to whom I am body Coachman extraordinary en titre d'office—Henry, (for that is his name) for such an animal has the most thinking countenance I ever saw: being very clean I can kiss him without disgust—and even with pleasure, especially after having been rewarded as I have just now, for my attention to him by a pair of the sweetest smiles imaginable from his Mama and Aunt. As providence hath order'd it they both play upon the Harpsichord, and at Chess. I am flattered with the hopes of engaging with before long either in war or harmony. Not to day, because whether you know it or no it is Sunday. I know it, having been paying my devotions, our church, the hall; our minister a sleek young parson the curate of the parish: our saints, a naked Mercury an Apollo in the same dress, and a Venus of Medicis; our congregation the two ladies Capt. Blankett and your humble servant upon the carpet, by the minister, below the domesticks superioris and inferioris ordinis: among the former I was concerned to see poor Matthews the librarian, who I could not help thinking had as good a title to be upon the carpet as myself.

Of Ld. Fitzmaurice[5] I know nothing but from his bust and letters: the first bespeaks him a handsome youth, the latter an ingenious one. He is not sixteen and already he writes better than his father. He is ⟨in⟩ the care of a Mr. Jervis[6] a dissenting minister ⟨who⟩ has had charge of him since he was 6 year old. ⟨He has⟩ never been at any public place of education—he has now for a considerable time been travelling about the kingdom, that he may

[4] Henry Petty-Fitzmaurice (1780–1863), who succeeded his elder half-brother in 1809 as 3rd Marquis of Lansdowne.

[5] Shelburne's eldest son, John Henry Petty (1765–1809), styled Lord Fitzmaurice. He succeeded his father as 2nd Marquis of Lansdowne in 1805. According to Bentham's later recollection, much at variance with the passage which follows, he appeared in youth to be somewhat retarded in intellect (Bowring, x, 118), but this is probably to be discounted as prejudice or lapse of memory. The Rev W. B. Stevens, meeting Fitzmaurice in 1794, thought him 'an eloquent, sensible, young man' (*The Journal of the Rev. William Bagshaw Stevens*, ed. Georgina Galbraith, Oxford, 1965, p. 147).

[6] Perhaps the Rev W. Jervis whose obituary is printed, *Gentleman's Magazine*, 1792, i, p. 385. A relationship with Shelburne's friend, Captain John Jervis, R.N., later Earl of St Vincent, seems probable but has not been traced.

know something of his own country before he goes to others, and be out of the way of adulation—

I am interrupted—adieu—le reste l'ordinaire prochain.

(Circular) Sunday 8 o'clock

It is true—Lady S. is a sister of Ld. Ossory's: my Lord was mentioning it just now in a parenthesis—then Miss Vernon must have been a half-sister by another father: and so /part at least of/ the mystery is cleared up—The Countess of Warwick is also a sister of Lady S's: whether half or whole I can't pretend to say—What is it now you want of me?—Tabletalk? get Selden's[7]—there you have a whole volume of it—Politics? I know nothing about the matter. Does he come in? that I know nothing about no more than you—He went some little time ago to town for a couple of days only—that came out accidentally in conversation yesterday when there was company—'people fancied that I was gone upon politicks'—I have been told at different times in the /way of/ parenthesis that I should see Ld. Camden[8] here, and Col. Barré[9]—at present there is not a soul but Blanket. Tomorrow my Lord and I and Blanket (I beg his pardon Blanket and I) go to Ld. Pembrokes to see Wilton: we are to stay there all night: it is about 30 miles off. On what account we go I can't pretend to say: it was proposed as if it were only on mine. On Thursday we go to Calne[10] to a corporation dinner. Hamilton of Bath[11] has been mentioned as another person whom I shall see /and that/ in a few days: It is he who was the creator of Payne's-Hill: he is the oracle for the gardening works that are carrying on here: and has been employ'd in undoing what Capability-Brown[12] had done. To day we had no company at

[7] Bentham was referring to John Selden, *Table-Talk: being the Discourses of John Selden Esq.; or his sence of various matters of weight and high consequence relating especially to Religion and State*, London, 1689.

[8] Charles Pratt (1714–94), cr. Baron Camden, 1765, Lord Chancellor, 1766–70. A former protégé of the Earl of Chatham, he was somewhat loosely associated in politics with Shelburne at this period.

[9] Isaac Barré, M.P. (1726–1802). For over twenty years he was Shelburne's closest friend and spokesman in the House of Commons, where he sat for one or the other of Shelburne's boroughs.

[10] Calne, a 'pocket borough', where the franchise was confined to the twenty or so members of the corporation, was under the controlling influence of Shelburne, who owned most of the property in the town.

[11] Charles Hamilton (c. 1704–87), 9th son of the 6th Earl of Abercorn, formerly a member in both the British and the Irish parliaments, was noted in his later years for the fine garden he created at his seat at Painshill, near Cobham, Surrey.

[12] Lancelot Brown (1715–83), the famous landscaper, head gardener to George III at Hampton Court, who made a sufficient fortune to establish his son as a country gentleman and M.P.

dinner: yesterday we had a Mr. Bayntun, (son of a Sir Edw. Bayntun an old courtier whose name you will find in your Bible) and his wife:[13] and who should this wife be but a Lady Maria a daughter of Ld. Coventry's by Miss Gunning, and who notwithstanding her ancestry is as dowdy as a country girl, and as ugly as a horse: and yet they say she had on her best looks. Her husband is a plain young country Squire in dress with something of Croft's[14] manner in his address, yet better spoken and without his affectation: he is cultivated *par cause de vicinage*: being the nearest neighbour there is, and yet three miles off, neighbours being *eloigned* by the extensiveness of the demesnes.

All this while I have said nothing of the manner of my coming here. I began in the middle like an epic poem. I travelled very snug in my Coach as far as Marlborough, with a set of people not worth recounting. At Marlborough where we dined our Coach joined issue with another: the company Alexander Popham[15] and a certain female: he appeared to know who I was, and we made a sort of *bande a part*. I determined to pursue your plan with regard to the quitting the hackney vehicle at Marlborough—but alas! what availeth human, nay Scottish, even Wilsonian prudence? Heaven's great amusement is to make mock at it. Necessity obliged /me/ to make enquiries before these people which led them to conclude I was going to Ld. Shelburne's—'*ed io anchio*—and I too, said the chambermaid' (for some such personage was she) 'am going to Ld. Shelburne's.' Thank your stars you were not in my shoes—if you had been not all the hartshorn in Godfrey's shop would have recover'd you. *Je tins bon*, but the chambermaid's back being turned, I unbosomed myself /Gallicé/ in pathetic strains to Alexander Popham—'Qu'y faire? cette femme-ci quoique ce soit une femme, il n'y a pas moyen de la mener avec moi: cependant c'est precisement a cette maison la que je vais: voila ce qui s'appelle un rencontre.' It was some consolation however to me that the turpitude of my situation was shared with Alexander: who upon first meeting took care to enlarge upon the pre-eminence of post- /stage-/ coaches to postchaises, of the former's being the more

[13] Andrew Bayntun Rolt, M.P. (c. 1740–1816), eldest son of Sir Edward Bayntun Rolt, 1st bart., M.P. (1710–1800). His wife's mother had been a famous beauty. The Bayntuns were ministerialist in their politics.

[14] Probably the barrister Herbert Croft (c. 1752–1816). See letter 201, n. 6.

[15] Alexander Popham, M.P. (?1729–1810), a barrister of the Middle Temple, represented Taunton on his own interest there for many years but failed to secure re-election in 1780. Contemporaries sometimes reckoned him a member of Shelburne's political group.

expeditious vehicle, of his being urged to have recourse to it by a disinterested Innkeeper at Newbury and of his being determined by so pure a motive as the hope of company: had it not been for this, I should rather have attributed it to the expences of a lost election: at parting, 'to let you into a secret', says he, 'I ought not by-rights to go so near without paying my respects at the house you are going to: and I would not wish you to mention your having seen me—But how long do you think of staying?'—'Indeed I can't tell.'—'A month or thereabouts?'—'it is not impossible'—'Oh then,' says he, 'I hope we shall meet.'—'Well but why not now? Come get into the postchaise with me'—the fact was I should not have been sorry to have had him (supposing him upon such a footing, as a sort of instrument to break the ice with). However he would[16]

End of letter 1—omitted in my last

not go. When I arrived here the family were not at home—They were gone, at least the gentlemen were, to dine with Sr. James Long, the /nephew and/ hæres designatus of Ld. Tilney.[17] When my Lord came in, he ran up to me and touched one of my cheeks with his, and then the other. I was well satisfied with it since he meant it kindly, and since such, I suppose, is the fashion: but I should have been still better satisfied, if he had made either of the ladies his proxy.

402

To Joseph Davies[1]

24–25 August 1781 (Aet 33)

Bowood Saty. Aug. 26 1781

I wrote a letter to Wilson t'other day,[2] and am now writing another[3]—these he will have my direction to transmit to you, with a frank to do it in. I wrote to him first, having commissions for

[16] The sheet ends here. Bentham's heading to the next sheet, which follows on the next line, was omitted by Bowring (x, 90).

[17] Sir James Long, M.P. (? 1737–94), of Draycot Cerne, Wilts, was a supporter of the North ministry. In 1784 he succeeded to the estates of his uncle, John Child, 2nd Earl Tylney (I) and took the name of Tylney before Long.

402. [1] B.M. III: 219. Autograph
Addressed: 'Joseph Davies Esqr.' No postmark or docket. Friday was 24 August.

[2] Letter 401.

[3] Letter 403.

him to execute—You won't have the unconscionableness to expect that I should write separate letters about the same things only that you may have the contents a day or two the sooner.

Ld. S. has a project for making a grotto; and for collecting fossils to ornament it with: of course the most shewy would be the most suitable. You were speaking I remember of fossils that are found in the Isle of Sheppy—Could you manage any how for me to get a parcel of them here. Are there any people upon the island who make it their business to hunt for them and keep little collections by them? If any thing that will make any sort of figure can be got for the value of half-a-guinea or so, I wish you would get it and send it forthwith to Shelburne House Berkeley Square /I shall in that case be generous and make him a present of it/—Carriage and Porterage let him pay for: if it should exceed that, then only write me word about it, mentioning the particulars and the price—All this supposes that either you would have no objection to take a trip over thither yourself, or that you have access to somebody else who has occasion to go thither. In short if you could manage the matter for me in some way or other you would oblige me. Whether the things are scarce or no, signifies not a straw; for we dont pretend to understand any thing about the matter: brilliancy, singularity or magnitude of appearance are the qualities most desirable. Take the Dr.[4] into counsel: his friend Schnebbelie[5] could probably furnish us with some lights. The Dr. is bound in conscience to do all he can to help us; for we are as great Croakers as himself.

The Ld. Howe with whom I told you mine was intimate is your's indeed[6]—For the history of this family vide other letters—We are still very good pax, only the women beat me cruelly at chess.
Bowood Friday Aug. 25th I believe it is.

Saturday.

The inclosed is /a copy of/ the 3d of three sheets I have just sent to Wilson. I fear it will hardly be legible all over—it was taken by Bolton's copying machine.

[4] Probably Dr John Simmons. On him see letter 123, n. 1.

[5] Jacob Schnebbelie (1760–92), a noted artist, who was for some years draughtsman to the Society of Antiquaries. His father, a native of Zurich, had come to England many years previously and established a confectioner's business in Rochester which was afterwards carried on by one of his sons (*Gentleman's Magazine*, 1792, i, 189–90).

[6] Admiral Lord Howe, whom Davies had served as chief secretary for nearly two years at New York (letter 383, n. 11).

403

To George Wilson[1]

24 August 1781 (Aet 33)

Friday evening Aug. 25th or thereabouts

On Monday we went to Wilton, as proposed—Ld. S. Blanket and I in my Lord's Coach with hacks—It was not as I had at first apprehended—My Lord was /almost/ as much a stranger at Wilton as myself—He had been there but once before, and then without acquaintance. Ld. Pembroke's defection from the court had begun an intercourse /in London/, and this visit was the first fruit of it in the country. We sat out at 6: got there to breakfast (it is about 26 or 27 miles off) and staid to breakfast the next morning. It was seeing the place to some advantage—having the master and the mistress of the house for Cicerones: a very pretty part of the gardens planned and just finished by Lady P. is not shewn to strangers. At dinner the only company beside ourselves were an officer who is quarter'd at Salisbury (a Major Nooth of the 4th Dragoons) and young Beckford of Font-hill,[2] who on the 28th of this month comes of age and gives a grand fête to all the world—the family consist only of Ld. and Lady P. Ld. Herbert[3] who is with his regiment, and Lady Charlotte[4] a little girl of 9 or 10 year old, who is at home. It is odd enough that though he and she are by no means on good terms, they should neither of them have a creature

403. [1] B.M. III: 209–12. Autograph. No address or docket.

Misdated by Bentham, Friday being the 24th. Printed, Bowring, x, 91–3. Partly printed, Everett, 129–31.

According to the last paragraph of no. 401, this letter would appear to have been despatched on the evening of Saturday, 25 August and to have then consisted of three sheets. Only two sheets, each folded into four pages, now exist, and their contents seem to be in complete continuity with nos. 400 and 404. The missing sheet apparently contained separate subject matter and may have also borne the now missing address. Its absence is accounted for in a letter from Wilson to Davies of 21 September (B.M. III: 239): 'I inclose some more letters and scraps of letters from Bentham. For want of room I have been obliged to cut off the least material parts of many of them, and by that means have sometimes sent you imperfect sentences, but I believe you dont want anything of consequence.'

[2] William Beckford (1760–1844), of Fonthill, Wilts, the novelist, youngest but only legitimate child of the elder Pitt's political associate, Alderman William Beckford (1709–70). On him see Boyd Alexander, *England's Wealthiest Son. A Study of William Beckford*, London, 1962.

[3] George Augustus Herbert, M.P. (1759–1827), who succeeded his father as 11th Earl of Pembroke in 1794. He was a captain in the first regiment of dragoons.

[4] Charlotte Herbert (?–1784).

with them. Ld. P. is one of the best bred most intelligent pleasantest fellows I ever /met with/ in my life—they say he is mad, but if his madness never shews /itself/ in any other shapes than it did then, I wish to God I could be mad too. He talked with infinite vivacity and legeretè, saying many good things and no foolish ones. I got a most exquisite lesson on the art of small-talk from the breakfast conversation of Ld. S. and Lady P. (Ld. P. being absent for near an hour) They had been old cronies 20 or 25 year ago and had never come across one another since—you may imagine what stories they had to cap, and notes to compare. In those days Lord S. used to frequent Marlborough-house—You know the genealogy—Lady P. and Lady Di—Beauclerk sisters to the present D. of Marlborough.[5] It was pleasing enough to contemplate at leisure the remains of a beauty which was one of the first that I remember to have heard celebrated *au sortir de l'enfance.* Lady P. and Lady Egremont[6] whom /also/ I shall probably have the opportunity of being acquainted with were the two heroines of a copy of verses, /which/ I remember made some noise at Tunbridge when I was there with my Father about 20 year ago.[7] She is grown fat, and by that means a little out of shape: but she has still a fine face and very fine light brown hair which she wears neatly done up without powder to serve as evidence of youth. To apologize for the attention with which I survey'd her, and to make up for the little I could have to say upon such topics I threw into my looks as well as I could an air of respect mixed up with a small dash of tenderness. She is at that time of life at which a woman thinks herself obliged to any man who will give to understand that he thinks her still desirable. It was by this manoeuvre I suppose that I escaped contempt: for it did not appear to me that I was worse looked upon than others who had so much more to say for themselves. They (I mean, Ld. and Lady P.) are to be here in the course of the summer: but separately, it being so contrived, thinking it would be the more agreable to them. The Dutchess of Bedford is also to be here: she is you know related (I dont know yet precisely in what manner) to Lady

[5] Elizabeth, Countess of Pembroke (1737–1831) was the 2nd daughter of Charles Spencer, 2nd Duke of Marlborough. Her elder sister, Diana (1734–1808) married firstly Frederick, 2nd Viscount Bolingbroke, and secondly, after this marriage had been dissolved by Act of Parliament, Topham Beauclerk, only son of Lord Sidney Beauclerk.

[6] Alicia Maria (d. 1794), daughter of George Carpenter, 2nd Baron Carpenter of Killaghy (I), was the widow of Charles Wyndham, 2nd Earl of Egremont (d. 1763). She married secondly Hans Moritz, Count Von Bruhl, of Saxony.

[7] This visit to Tunbridge took place in August 1760. See letter 7.

Shelburne:[8] so also I believe is a personage of a nature very disparate to the former I mean Dunning.[9] /I mean that he is expected here./ You have in the newspapers of a day or two ago a mighty pretty paragraph about the Dutchess's being all summer long in town: the fact is she is at Wooburn. Yesterday we had at breakfast old Sr. Edw. Bayntun: tomorrow we have at dinner Sr. James Long nephew and hæres designatus to Ld. Tilney. This morning went away honest Jo. Townsend, a parson, brother to the Alderman:[10] we found him here on our return from Wilton on tuesday. He seems a very worthy creature, has been a good deal abroad, and has a great [deal] of knowledge: his studies have lain a good deal in the same track with mine. He is a utilitarian,[11] a naturalist, a chemist, /a physician,/ was once what I had like to have been a methodist: and what I should have been still had I not been what I am, as Alexander if he had not been Alexander (I am wrong in the story but never mind) would have been Parmenio.[12] In short we are become great friends, and he has given me the *carte du pays*. There is a mixture of simplicity candor, and a composed earnestness temper'd with good breeding that has won upon me mightily: and upon the terms of my indulging him in his patriotism and antipathy to your countrymen (some of whom however he has a great respect for) I am apt to think we shall be fast friends. He is to come here again ere long that I may cast an eye over a work of his part of which is printed; and he in return is to assist me in the revisal of mine, which he enters into the spirit of most perfectly. He has made me promise to go over and see him at his living, which is about 14 miles from hence. Ld. S. and Barré when he comes are to go and dine there: I shall then go with them and stay behind them for a few days. Blanket is to go on Monday. I am glad of it: he seems to be an honest /sort of a/ man enough, but has one of the most confused heads I ever met with: he embroils every topic that is started.

The master of the house to judge from every thing I have seen

[8] Gertrude, dowager Duchess of Bedford (1715–94), widow of the 4th duke, was the elder sister of Lady Shelburne's mother.

[9] John Dunning, M.P. (1731–83), one of the most brilliant barristers of his age. Next to Isaac Barré he was at this time one of Shelburne's closest friends and political spokesmen in the House of Commons. Shelburne secured his elevation to the peerage in 1782.

[10] Joseph Townsend (1739–1816), a well-travelled man interested in science, with a good knowledge of mineralogy and geology, was rector of Pewsey, Wilts., a few miles from Bowood. His brother, Alderman James Townsend, M.P. (1737–87), of Bruce Castle, Tottenham, was a political associate of Shelburne and his chief representative in the political world of the City of London.

[11] This appears to be the first known use of the term 'utilitarian'.

[12] Over this word is a later insertion, 'Diogenes', probably in Bentham's hand.

yet is one of the pleasantest men to live with that ever God put breath into: his whole study seems to be to make every body about him happy:[13] and in their countenances one may read the effects of his endeavours: in his presence they are as cheerful as they are respectful and attentive; and when they think they are alone you may see them merry; but at all times as quiet as so many mice. I have no need to rue the rencontre mentioned in a former sheet: for to such a poor devil as I they are as respectful and attentive as if I were a Lord. The mistress has more reserve and less conversation: but as much mildness as the master. The only instances of fire I have seen him exhibit have been when he has been declaiming about politics: yet though I frequently oppose him and scarce ever join with him he takes it all in the best part imaginable.

I'll tell you how the matter stands between the Pr. of W. and *Perdita.*[14] The common story is that she has got letters of his in which he speaks disrespectfully of the King: and that she is making use of them to extort money from him. This is not the case: but the fact is that she has a direct promissory letter for £20,000 /written, I think it was, before possession/: This is what Ld. P. told us on Monday: before he left town he called on Ld. Southampton to pump him about it. Ld. S. could not immediately see him: meantime came in Ld. Malden, who was come /as plenipo. for the lady/ for the express purpose of negotiating the matter with Ld. S. Ld. P. devined his errand as he says, and by pretending to know more than he did, picked the story out of him.

As to myself I have hitherto been compleatly idle; and that partly from inclination, partly upon principle. Strangers are lodged in a part of the house quite separate from that which is inhabited by the family. Adjoining to my bedchamber I have a dressing room and should have a servants room if I had one to put into it. They are plain: but neat, spatious and convenient: the dressing room I make my study. People here do just what they please—eat their

[13] Inserted in pencil, perhaps in another hand: 'servants not excepted.'

[14] In 1780 the Prince of Wales conceived a violent passion for the actress Mary Robinson, who had made her mark as Perdita in *The Winter's Tale*. Not only did he give her the promissory note for £20,000, here referred to, for the surrender of which she subsequently obtained an annuity from him; but he wrote a 'multitude' of indiscreet letters which, when his passion cooled, she threatened to publish, and for the return of which his father, George III, found himself obliged to pay the sum of £5000. She had previously been the mistress of the Earl of Exeter's heir, George Capel, Viscount Malden, through whom the prince had made her acquaintance, who was apparently therefore considered a suitable go-between. Charles Fitzroy (1737–1810), created 1st Baron Southampton in 1780, was groom of the stole and head of household to the prince.

meals either with the family or in their own apartments. The only gêne I feel is that which conscience imposes of dressing twice a day: that you know eats time.

We learnt at Wilton that Ld. Porchester comes off with little loss: the witnesses against him discredited themselves.[15]

Saturday afternoon

Ld. Bristol is here—a most excellent companion—pleasant intelligent, well bred and well read—liberal-minded to the last degree—He has been every where and knows every thing. Sr. J. Long is a little stiff-rumped fellow and knows nothing—except persons and so forth in the Q. S. Pian stile. Ld. B. has with him one of his sons a fine boy of 12 year-old who is just going to sea.[16]

404

To George Wilson[1]

25–28 August 1781 (Aet 33)

Bowood Saturday Aug. 26 1781

The revenue of the Bishoprick of Derry is at present £7200: and in a few years will be £9000: the patronage 14,300£ none of the livings less than £250: some 8, 10, 12, up to 1500. / Of all the advowsons in his diocese he has 40, some Lay Lord five; and another (I forgot who) two or three./ This from the honest Bishop,[2] who at the same time declares it to be a wonder and a shame that the Clergy should be suffer'd to remain in possession of so much wealth. Of the /above/ parsons scarce one resides: they pay a curate £50 a year: which he observes according to their own estimation is what the service that is done is worth.

Ld. B. says he is well assured and persuaded that Neckar[3]

[15] Henry Herbert (1741–1811), of High Clere, Hants, created Baron Porchester in 1780 and Earl of Caernarvon in 1793, a distant kinsman of the Earl of Pembroke. The lawsuit has not been traced.

[16] Frederick Augustus Hervey, 4th Earl of Bristol (1730–1803) was bishop of Derry and at this time a strong supporter of the movement for constitutional reform in Ireland. For an account of Bentham's conversation with him see letter 404. The boy accompanying him was his second son, Frederick William (1769–1859), who succeeded his father as 5th earl.

404. [1] B.M. III: 214–18. Autograph. Docketed: '1781 / 27 Aug. / Bentham / Bowood'.

Printed, Bowring, x, 93–6. Saturday was the 25th. This letter, although despatched later, was clearly written in immediate continuation of letter 403.

[2] I.e. Lord Bristol, referred to subsequently as 'Ld. B.'

[3] Jacques Necker (1732–1804), a Genevese banker who established himself in

acted corruptly: that as Minister he borrow'd of his own house at 7 pr. Cent, when the Farmers would have lent at 5. Neckar and Turgot[4] (who you know died about 8 months ago) were bitter enemies: this makes it the more generous for N. to speak of T. in the handsome manner he has done in his pamphlet. What turned out Turgot was a jealousy of Maurepas.[5] When the Prince of Conti[6] who found himself affected by some of Turgot's arrangements raised the insurrection at Paris, Turgot went to the King and got an order upon the Marechal de Biron[7] Governor of Paris for as many men as he chose to have: purposely or through inadvertence he failed to communicate this to Maurepas. M.'s jeaulousy took fire: and in two days Turgot was dismissed, Madame Blondel[8] who was closely liée with Turgot took upon herself the blame: but all would not save him. Neckar ow'd his dismission to the Parliaments: whose assumed negative in legislation his project of Provincial assemblies went to supersede. The K. of F. who is timidity itself was apprehensive of a quarrel with the men of the long robe. Caron de Beaumarchais,[9] one of the busiest and most succesful of intriguants has amassed /realized/ (Ld. S. says) to the tune of $S 30 or 40,000 a year. He was sent over to get I know

business in Paris and in 1777 became director-general of finances and principal minister of state under Louis XVI. He resigned in 1781, in consequence of a combination of pressures and intrigues, among which the personal rivalry of Maurepas (see n. 5 below) may have counted for as much as the Parlement's dislike of his scheme for provincial assemblies. In 1781, in his *Compte Rendu au Roi de l'Etat des Finances*, published by the king's order, he presented an unduly favourable picture of the country's financial situation, which he had in fact seriously damaged by reckless borrowing at high rates of interest in order to finance French participation in the American War of Independence.

[4] Anne Robert Jacques Turgot (1727–81), Baron de l'Aulne, controller-general of finance under Louis XVI, 1774–6. He had connections with the Physiocrats. Maurepas distrusted his desire for vigorous financial reforms and was jealous of his popularity. Some of his policies were violently attacked by Necker. For this episode, and for the riots instigated by the Prince de Conti, see D. Dakin, *Turgot and the* Ancien Régime *in France*, 1939, pp. 177–94.

[5] Jean Frédéric Phélypeaux, Comte de Maurepas (1701–81) became principal adviser to Louis XVI on his accession in 1774 and presided over the council of state though not himself holding any executive office. Strongly conservative by instinct, he blocked the efforts at reform of both Turgot and Necker.

[6] Louis François de Bourbon (1717–76), Prince de Conti, was the instigator of bread riots which spread to Paris in 1775. His aim was to embarrass Turgot, whose reforms he opposed.

[7] Louis Antoine de Gontaut (1700–88), Due de Biron, for many years commander of the *gardes françaises* in Paris.

[8] Mme Blondel, daughter of Bataille de Francès-Daville, receiver-general of finances at Soissons, and sister to the diplomat Francès who was sometime French ambassador in England, was the wife of the diplomat Jean Blondel. Turgot acted as a patron to both her husband and her son.

[9] Pierre Augustin Caron de Beaumarchais (1732–99).

not /forget/ what papers /of consequence/ from De Morande:[10] but /that story/ you remember: he was even employ'd once in making up a quarrel between the K. and Q. of France; which had gone to such a length that the Empress Queen was impliquèe in it: at present his credit /interest/ is equal to almost any thing.

He is at the head of the project[11] for publishing 3 magnificent editions of Voltaire's works at 15 (25 I think it is) and 40 guineas with Baskerville's types. He has sent Ld. S. a number of proposals. By the bye he has written to Ld. S. a letter which I suppose I may see: whether it has been answer'd or no I can not say.

Monday 27th Aug. 8 in the evening

Last night came in Elliot of Port Elliot,[12] St. Paul's friend. This morning Ld. Bristol and Blanket went away: Ld. Bristol I believe to Oxford: Blanket to London, taking Hackwood (the D. of Bolton's) in his way. One of the most wrongheaded blockheads I think I ever met with: putting in his oar upon every occasion, taking a tort and a travers and spoiling every discussion that is started. Yet he is connected with many of the first people in opposition, and in particular has the ear of the maitre de la maison to a degree I am sorry to observe. His great merit is the having been a Lieut, to Keppel,[13] whose ame damnée he is and has written paragraphs and pamphlets on his side. Before he went he took me into confidence and consulted me about a nonsensical project of his for discovering polished and commercial nations where Cook has been and found none: the most absurd idea supported by the most /absurd/ arguments in the most confused methods, and in the most slovenly and awkward stile. He it is who brought home the Rippon from the E. Indies. He is personally acquainted with Rumbold,[14] and defends him without argument and without shame. Sed de hoc plus satis.

[10] Probably Charles Theveneau de Morande (1748–92) who, after a period in restraint under *lettres-de-cachet* for his irregularities, about 1770 settled in London and wrote scurrilous pamphlets against French public men. On this episode see Eloise Ellery, *Brissot de Warvlle*, Boston and New York, 1915.

[11] This project resulted in the great 70-volume edition of Voltaire's works issued during the years 1785–9, in which Beaumarchais collaborated with Condorcet and J. J. M. Decroix. Condorcet supplied a biographical sketch.

[12] Edward Eliot, M.P. (1727–1804), of Port Eliot, Cornwall, was at this time supporting the opposition and at the last general election had accepted a nominee of Shelburne for one of the six parliamentary seats under his control.

[13] Admiral Augustus Keppel (1725–86). For Bentham's earlier interest in him, see *Correspondence*, ii, as index.

[14] Sir Thomas Rumbold, M.P. (1736–91), governor of Madras, 1777–80. His conduct during office was the target of severe condemnation and the subject of investigation

Talking with Ld. B. yesterday (nobody else in the room) about the riots he took notice that in the Scotch assembly /(national ecclesiastical assembly what d'ye call it)/ there were but 2 voices against the toleration: O yes says I, I understand it was not with the Clergy that it originated, but with a parcel of low-lived fellows /of laymen/ in the neighbourhood of Glasgow—No, no, says he—not with them—With whom then?—with people here—These last words were pronounced with an air of mystery and with a hush of the voice—Who he meant I can not pretend to say: it could not be the ministry: for besides that nothing could be more against their interest, if he had meant them he would have spoken out: it could not, I think be the Rockinghamites: it could not have been Ld. G.G.:[15] for nobody could have thought of making a mystery of his name. I leave you to form your own conclusion.

Ld. S. says that when he was in town (about 3 weeks ago) a Mr. Oswald[16] who is a strong Royalist and much connected with Ld. Mansfield[17] told him that it was a certain fact that the French had at last seen the necessity of supplying the Americans with money that they had accordingly sent 600,000£St: and that if it reached them, there must be an end of all our hopes.

Ld. B. said he had met with French officers and seen letters from others (Fayette[18] was one who was mentioned on the occasion) who all joined in giving the Americans the worst of characters: 'they had all the vices of the Athenians', said somebody, 'without any of their virtues'. Franklin,[19] it was agreed by both their Lordships, found /finds/ his situation to the last degree uncomfortable: despised and neglected by the French Ministry, thwarted and persecuted by Arthur Lee's[20] party of whom he has been heard to

by two parliamentary committees; but by the end of 1783 the charges against him had been dropped.

[15] Lord George Gordon (1751–93), instigator of the anti-Catholic riots in London at the beginning of June 1780.

[16] Richard Oswald (1705–84), a merchant engaged in the American trade. He was employed by Shelburne in the peace negotiations with the Americans during 1782.

[17] William Murray (1705–93), 1st Earl of Mansfield, Lord Chief Justice, Court of King's Bench, 1756–88. At this time his nephew and heir, Lord Stormont, was Secretary of State for the Northern Department and one of the most energetic of the cabinet ministers.

[18] Marie Joseph P.Y.R.G. du Motier, Marquis de la Fayette (1757–1834) served as a volunteer in the American army, 1777–8, and returned with a French military force sent to assist the Americans in 1780.

[19] Benjamin Franklin (1706–90) was at this time principal American representative at Paris.

[20] Arthur Lee (1740–92) nursed seeds of suspicion against his two colleagues as American ministers at Paris, Franklin and Silas Deane, secured Deane's dismissal, and continued his intrigues against Franklin after his return to America in 1780.

say 'he could not have thought there had been so much venom in human nature'.

Elliot has brought down a /strange/ story of the Chancellor[21]—that he had promised a man a living—that afterwards he came to learn that the man who is a Yorkshire man had concurred in some of the opposition measures of that county, and that thereupon he had revoked his promise: by way of contrast the care was mentioned that Ld. Northington[22] took to make an equal distribution of church preferments to all parties: a strange circumstance in the story is that Ld. Loughborough[23] went to the Chancellor and forced him into it: the reality of the promise is mentioned as being so clear, that it was /as to have been/ confirmed by I know not what overt acts.

Ld. S. pretends to have heard from very high authority at N. York, that Ld. Cornwallis being sick of his situation had begged of Clinton to come in person and gather the laurels that were ready for him: but that Cl. had begged to be excused.[24]

Repartee of Ld. Mulgrave[25] when in opposition—Being introduced to the Queen of Sardinia—On dit said her majesty que Milord n'est pas bien a la cour.—Madame, c'est la cour qui n'est pas bien chez moi.—This was by Ld. Bristol, who is Uncle to Ld. M.

Ld. B. assumed to me (unless I much mistook him) a principal share in the merit of carrying the toleration act through the Irish House of Lords—He was /in his own mind at least/ for going further, and admitting them to all offices, that of Member of Parlt. not excepted. Of a little more than 3 millions of which the people /population/ of Ireland he says consists upwards of 2 millions are Catholics, about 600,000 Presbyterians, and only about 400,000 Church-of-England men. He has made an exact numeration of all

[21] Edward Thurlow (1731–1806), created Baron Thurlow in 1778 on his appointment as Lord Chancellor, an office which he held till April 1783 and again from December 1783 until 1792.

[22] Robert Henley (c. 1708–72), 1st Earl of Northington, was Lord Keeper, 1757–61 and Lord Chancellor, 1761–6.

[23] Alexander Wedderburn (1733–1805), created Baron Loughborough in 1780 on his appointment as Lord Chief Justice in the Court of Common Pleas. For previous reference to him see *Correspondence*, ii, 18 n.

[24] This passage probably refers to rumour about the patently absurd proposal made in April 1781 by General Cornwallis, then in North Carolina, that New York should be abandoned and the whole British army there under the commander-in-chief, Sir Henry Clinton should be thrown against Virginia in conjunction with his own forces moving up from the south (William B. Willcox, *Portrait of a General. Sir Henry Clinton in the War of Independence*, New York, 1964, pp. 347–91, esp. 382–5).

[25] Constantine John Phipps (1744–92), 2nd Baron Mulgrave (I), R.N., began his political career in opposition, but in 1775 went over to the administration. From 1777 to 1782 he was one of Lord Sandwich's colleagues on the Board of Admiralty.

the people in his diocese distinguishing them according to their religions, occupations, sex ages and the like.

Elliot says that Adm. Parker[26] is loud in his complaints against Ld. Sandwich for not giving him force enough: that the Royal visit was a contrivance of Ld. S.'s to stop his mouth: but that it won't do.

Elliot and Ld. S. agreed that Ld. Chesterfield[27] is quite broke up and gone to live altogether in the country: he says of himself that he is much obliged to the P. of W: that he had not thought of his owing above £30, or 40,000: but that in consequence of that affair, he had the advantage of knowing that it amounted to £90,000: that the notice of his being a short life had brought all his creditors about him; that now he knew how his affairs stood, and 7 or 8 years spent in the country would set them right again. Otherwise, going on in the notion of owing but 30, or 40,000, he should have ruined himself past redemption. Ld. S. says that upon the breaking out of that affair, the K. was exasperated /to the highest degree/ with Ld. Chd.: that he had appointed a day for visiting him: but that upon that he broke the appointment, without sending any word.

Ld. Br. told me that Ld. Shannon[28] used to send 22 or 23 members to the Irish Parliament: but that since the octennial act that influence was diminished.

I write you every thing higgledy piggledy just as it happens to come in my head. There is no end of the anecdotes of all kinds I hear about the politics as well of France as of this country: about one in fifty I shall remember; the others will be lost to me. I wish to

[26] Admiral Hyde Parker (1714–82) commanded a small fleet covering commercial shipping in the North Sea and Baltic during the summer of 1781. On 5 August he fought a hot engagement against an equal Dutch squadron, whose accompanying convoy went back to port. In the circumstances his complaints about the Admiralty's failure to give him more ships were unjustified, but, 'hostile in the highest degree to the Ministry', despite a state visit to his flagship by the king, who tried to soothe his feelings, 'he refused a knighthood, resigned his command, and would serve no more' (P. Mackesy, *The War for America, 1775–1783*, London, 1964, pp. 394–5).

[27] Philip Stanhope (1755–1815), 5th Earl of Chesterfield. In May he had suffered some accident in which broken bones were suspected (H.M.C., *Carlisle Mss.*, p. 480). Possibly this had caused the anxiety among his creditors which led to the enumeration of his debts.

[28] Richard Boyle (1727–1807), 2nd Earl of Shannon. The Irish Octennial Act of 1768 reduced to eight years the maximum duration of Irish parliaments, which had hitherto usually endured for the length of each sovereign's reign. More frequent general elections stimulated competition for seats and rendered the maintenance of a controlling interest more expensive. After 1768, while Shannon's connections in the Irish House of Commons numbered about eighteen to twenty, only nine seats were under his direct control (Edith M. Johnston, *Great Britain and Ireland 1760–1800*, Edinburgh, 1963, p. 261).

God I could get your great carcase and squeeze it through a key-hole like a fairy's, that you might get by heart the things I hear and give them me back as I wanted them.

Ld. S. says that Ld. Chatham who governed every body else with so high a hand was /himself/ governed in a manner by the K. of Prussia, who gave him information and suggested ideas to him even for his maritime operations. This appears from a suite of letters from the K. to Ld. C. of which Ld. S. has either the originals or copies, and which I, I believe, may see.[29]

I mistook—Ld. Porchester upon Ld. Pembroke's account loses about £3500—Supposing that he should be ruined, he had sent over an agent to the continent to look out for a retreat.

Tuesday Aug. 28 8 in the evening

'A Historical account of the settlement and possession of Bombay and of the rise and progress of the war with the Mahratta nation. Printed for Robson New Bond Street 1781.' It is not yet published: Ld. S. says it is by Master Pechel:[30] it contains information which there is no other means of coming at: in that respect it is valuable: but for composition it is I think the vilest stuff I ever met with. I have just read it. This is one of the pleasant incidents attendant upon great houses: meeting with inedited books, or books of the day before they are to be had elsewhere.

This morning came a packet to Ld. S. from France. It contained 2 /ms/ papers: the one a journal of the operations of de Grasse[31] from his sailing from France to the day of the /troops/ abandoning St. Lucia: the other a letter of Count Dillons[32] from that period to

[29] Shelburne built up a considerable collection of copies of diplomatic papers but no correspondence of this kind, referring to Pitt's conduct of the Seven Years' War, is listed in the guides to the Lansdowne Mss. (H.M.C., *Third Report, Appendix*, pp. 126–32, and Howard H. Peckham, *Guide to the Manuscripts in the William L. Clements Library*, Ann Arbor, 1942).

[30] *A Historical Account of the Settlement and Possession of Bombay* was published in 1781. The British Museum catalogue attributes authorship to S. Pechel.

[31] François Joseph Paul, Comte de Grasse (1723–88), one of the most capable and enterprising of the French naval commanders during the American War of Independence. On 22 March 1781 he sailed from Brest with about twenty ships-of-the-line and supporting vessels. Towards the end of April he was indecisively engaged off Port Royal, Martinique, by the British West India squadron under Rear-Admiral Samuel Hood, but this did not prevent him from assisting in the French capture of Tobago early in June. In answer to appeals from America de Grasse sailed north from the West Indies early in August, and a day or two after Bentham completed this letter his arrival in the Chesapeake closed the trap upon the British forces under Cornwallis at Yorktown, a move which spelt final defeat for the British in the War of American Independence (H. Doniol, *Histoire de la participation de la France à l'établissement des Etats-Unis d'Amérique*, 5 vols., Paris, 1886–92, ii, 558–666).

[32] Edouard, Comte de Dillon (1750–1839), who became colonel of the regiment of

the taking of Tobago. The first man says the port in St. Lucia is so strong, (What do they call it? Morne Fortuneè?) that it might bid defiance to an army of 20,000 men: that it has cisterns and I dont know how many other things bomb-proof; and that part of it is undermined. But then he adds some other circumstances that are plain lies: viz: that there were 2500 regulars in it and as many sailors. It appears plainly that the attack upon St. Lucia was designed principally if not wholly as a feint to draw our attention from Tobago. At this latter place it looks as if we had made but a scurvy figure: the island was surrender'd without so much as firing a gun; though we had one post Dillon says extremely strong, and a defence of 24 hours might as they had reason to expect, have given time for the fleet to come to their relief. On the other hand their fleet appears from the first paper to have cut as scurvy a figure in the engagement with Adm. Hood: it talks of a *'fatalité'*, and then again of another fatalité, and so I believe to the tune of 3 fatalités that prevented them from gaining the advantages they might have done: and yet this was written by an apologist of de Grasse's.

I believe I shall pack this off to night: tomorrow Elliot leaves this place: a modest civil good kind of man: sensible enough, but without those pretensions which one would expect to find in a man whose station in his county is so commanding and political influence so great. He is moderate enough in his conversation about politics, but desponding: he says he scarce ever looks into a newspaper; nor dares he for fear of ill news.

I have just been playing at billiards with Lady S. Miss V. looked on, but would not play, saying she never had play'd before. There is an event for you: by and by I shall come to telling you every time I buckle my shoe. I almost despair of getting them to the harpsichord: tomorrow however the house I hope will be clear; and then perhaps I may have some chance: the chess and the billiards were her own proposal: the harpsichord I must beg and pray for.

The sheet is not filled, and you'll grumble if I leave any of it blank. There seems no want of money here: grounds laying out and plantations making /upon/ a large scale. A gate going to be made with a pyramid of each side of it for an approach to the house at

Provence and eventually rose to be a general in the French service. His father migrated from Lancashire to France when he was a child, and from 1773 he was on the staff of the Comte d'Artois. In 1779 Dillon took part in the French expedition against Grenada and was wounded and invalided home, but he went out again to the West Indies with de Grasse in 1781. In 1778 and again in 1784 he was employed on diplomatic missions to the court of Catherine II of Russia.

six miles distance: the pyramids to be at least a hundred foot high. At this place a road which is to be made from the house is to join the /road from/ London to the Devizes: the new road will leave Calne /(through which the present road runs)/ on the right hand and save a mile or two. I call it Egypt: in the way you have deep vallies with meadows and a watermill at the bottom of them; and on the sides craggy rocks with water gushing out of them, just for all the world as if Moses had been there. Ld. S. in a téte a téte we had the other day talked to[33]

405

To Jeremiah Bentham[1]

31 August–2 September 1781 (Aet 33)

Bowood, Friday, August 31, 1781.

Honoured Sir,

A day or two ago, I received your letter, dated Brackley, August 25. I write this in expectation of its meeting you at Bath: as soon as I hear of your arrival there, I will see about fixing a day for paying my duty to you in person: as that will, I hope, be a speedy one, there will be the less occasion for my entering into any epistolary details; characters, therefore, and descriptions, and conversations, you will not now expect from me; I shall content myself with giving you a very short account of my motions, and the company we either have seen or expect to see. Yesterday se'ennight, (Thursday, August 16,)[2] at four o'clock in the morning, I got into one of the Bath post-coaches: diligences there are none. At Marlborough, where we dined, I quitted the coach, took a post-chaise, and got here about light. The family consists at present only of Lord and Lady Shelburne; a little boy of theirs, who is no more than a year old; and Miss Caroline V., a half-sister of Lady Shelburne's by the mother's side. Lord Fitzmaurice,—the only child Lord S. has left by his first lady,-–a youth not quite sixteen,

[33] For explanation of the break in the text see letter 403, n. 1.

405. [1] One sheet containing the last two hundred or so words of this letter is preserved as B.M. III: 221. The original of the remainder has not been located, and the text is reproduced from Bowring, x, 96–7. For most of the persons mentioned see annotations to letters 402–4.

[2] The date in the parenthesis should be the 23rd. The mistake here and at the word 'se'ennight' may be either Bentham's or Bowring's.

is travelling over England, with a Mr. Jervis, a dissenting minister, who has had the care of him ever since he was six years old. He is not to come to Bowood before the family leave it for the summer. Visiters there were none, except Captain Blankett, whom you know of: he left us on Monday last, but is expected again in October. On the Saturday, there dined here a Mr. Bayntun, and Lady Mary his wife, daughter of Lord Coventry by the celebrated Lady Coventry, whom we used to hear so much of. She has nothing of her mother's beauty. Mr. Bayntun is the youngest son, but heir-apparent, of Sir Edward Bayntun, an old courtier, who has an estate in this neighbourhood. On Sunday, there was nobody. On the Monday, Lord Shelburne, Captain Blankett, and I, went in my lord's coach to Lord Pembroke's at Wilton. We got there to breakfast, and staid to breakfast the next morning: Wilton is about twenty-seven miles from Bowood. At breakfast, there was not a creature but Lord and Lady Pembroke; but at dinner came a Colonel Nooth,[3] who happened to be quartered at Salisbury, and young Beckford of Fonthill, who was to give a grand fête upon his coming of age, the 28th. This was the first visit Lord S. had ever paid at Wilton upon the footing of an acquaintance. Sunday, September 2d. On Tuesday, (August 21st,) on our return from Wilton, we found a Mr Townsend, a clergyman, a brother of the alderman's. He has a living about fourteen miles off, and is upon a familiar footing here. He staid till the Thursday or Friday after. What I have seen of him, I like much; his thoughts have run pretty much in the channels that mine have run in. He was to go for three weeks into Northamptonshire; but he made me promise, that, on his return, I would go over and spend a few days with him. On Wednesday the 22d, or Thursday the 23d, I forget which, Sir Edward Bayntun breakfasted here. On Saturday, to dinner, came a singular sort of personage, who, not in Falstaff's sense, but in another sense, may be termed a *double* man: I mean the Earl of Bristol, *alias* Bishop of Derry. He brought with him a fine boy of his, about twelve years old, whom he is just going to enter in the navy. On Sunday evening came Elliot of Port-Elliot; he who is knight of the shire, and puts in seven borough members for Cornwall. Lord Bristol went away on Monday, (the 27th,) as likewise did Blankett. Elliot staid till Tuesday after breakfast. On the Sunday, (the 26th,) Sir James Long, the nephew and *hœres designatus* to Lord Tilney, dined here. Since the Tuesday, I think we have had nobody, except yesterday, when we had to

[3] Read as 'North' by Bowring; but this must be the Major Henry Nooth mentioned in letter 403 (p. 55 above). He became Lieut. Colonel in November 1781.

dinner a Mr. Bull,[4] who lives at Calne, and a Captain Onslow,[5] late of the Blues, who is upon a visit to him. Oh, yes: on Friday we had a Mr. Dickinson,[6] a rich old Quaker in the neighbourhood, who called here and drank tea. Several whom I hear spoken of as being expected here, are Lord Dartry, Lord Camden, Dunning, Colonel Barré, Hamilton, late of Payne's Hill, William Pitt the orator, Lady Warwick—Lady Shelburne's sister, and the Duchess of Bedford. It was not till t'other day that I understood from Lord S., as we were sitting tête-à-tête after dinner, that there was a probability of her bringing the duke with her, which, he said, he hoped might be the case, 'That the duke might have the advantage of making my acquaintance.' Lord Dartry[7] has been expected for this day or two. He is an Irish lord made out of a banker,—his name was Dawson: Lord S. speaks of him as one 'with whom he is much connected.'[8] As to the other people, I have been successively told at different times when they have happened to be mentioned, that I should see them here; Lord Camden in particular, with a view to his looking over my book. This throws my departure to an indefinite distance. Indeed, I have no need to wish to be in a hurry to go away, as I am as much at my ease as I ever was in any house in my life; one point excepted, the being obliged by *bienséance* to dress twice a-day. I do what I please, and have what I please. I ride and read with my lord, walk with the dog, stroke the leopard, draw little Henry out in his coach, and play at chess and billiards with the ladies. My lord's custom is to read to them after tea, when they are at work; and now nothing will serve him but, in spite of everything I can say, he will make them hear my driest of all dry metaphysics.

He takes the advantage of my being here to read it in my presence, that I may explain things. This has gone on for several evenings. I must cut short; for while I am writing this in my dressing-room

[4] Daniel Bull (c. 1727–91). His father, who died in 1768, had long been steward in charge of the Bowood estate, with management of parliamentary elections at Calne, and Bull himself continued to act as election manager for Shelburne. His own interest in the borough was by no means negligible: in 1789 his lands in the parish were valued at nearly £9000.

[5] Not identified.

[6] Not identified.

[7] Thomas Dawson (1725–1813), of Dawson Grove, co. Monaghan, son of Richard Dawson, an alderman and banker of Dublin, represented co. Monaghan in the Irish parliament, 1749–68, and was created Baron Dartrey of Dawson's Grove (I) in 1770. In 1785 he was elevated as Viscount Cremorne. In later life Bentham asserted that Dartrey had lent considerable sums to Shelburne (Bowring, x, 116).

[8] B.M. III: 221 commences here. This sheet is docketed, by Jeremiah Bentham: 'Fils J^{y} / Lr. datd. Bowood / Sep. 2d. 1781.'

above stairs, they are waiting for me half-a-mile off in the library below stairs. You will, I dare say, excuse me; succinct as my letter has necessarily been, it is already not a short one. My best respects wait upon my mother. How fares it with our friends at Oxford?

I am, Hon. Sir, your dutiful and affectionate Son,

Jeremy Bentham.

I forgot to mention that Lord and Lady Pembroke are also expected here. It is contrived that they shall come separate.
Sunday, Sept. 2d, 1781.

406

To George Wilson[1]

5 September 1781 (Aet 33)

Septr. 5th 1781

The Ladies being retired Ld. S. and I are left alone in the dining-room. He is writing to his son, and I, having no son to write to, to keep my hands from mischief, will write to you.

This morning he had a letter from Blanket, telling me that there was certainly foundation for the report of the insurrections in Peru,[2] and asking him if he had not, or rather taking for granted that he had, received a Copy of the manifesto of the insurgents from Sr. John Hort at Lisbon is it or Oporto?[3] Blanket appears to have had it from Pinto the Portuguese Minister[4] with whom he is well

406. [1] B.M. III: 224–5. Autograph.

Addressed: 'To George Wilson Esqr. / Thorpe / near Staines.' In bottom left corner: 'Wycombe.' Stamped: 'FREE'.

Printed, Bowring, x, 98.

[2] These reports were well-founded. Resentment at increasing imperial taxation produced anti-tax riots among the creoles in various Peruvian towns during 1780. Late in that year these events were overshadowed by the formidable Indian rising led by Tupac Amaru in protest against taxation, forced labour, and the tyranny of local officials. Tupac Amaru was captured in April 1781, but order was not fully restored in Peru till the end of the year. During 1781 New Granada was the scene of a creole rebellion with similar objects (R. A. Humphreys and John Lynch, *The Origins of the Latin American Revolution, 1808–1826*, New York, 1965, pp. 16–18. A full account of the rising of the Peruvian Indians is given in Boleslao Lewin, *La Rebelión de Túpac Amaru y los orígines de la emancipación americana*, Buenos Aires, 1957).

[3] Sir John Hort, 1st bart. (1735–1807), was British consul-general at Lisbon, 1767–96.

[4] Luiz Pinto de Sousa Coutinho, 1st Viscount of Balsemão (1735–1804). He was leader of the pro-English party in Portugal and was minister resident in London from 1775 till 1788.

acquainted—Pinto was at one time expected here but I believe is not now.

A day or two ago I received a letter from you your second I think it is, from Thorpe[5]—One of mine there was which you did not acknowledge—I believe there was hardly time for it to have reached you—it contained inter alia a frank for Davies.

Q.S.P.'s are got at last to Bath—Q.S.P. I see is hankering to come here—but he will be disappointed—Nothing but plague to my noble hosts as he calls them and shame to me could come from such a visit. As to your fears about my conversion, they are altogether vain. This is all I can say about the matter at present faute de tems —for when my Lord has done I have done as the Packet is then closed.

Yesterday was it? or the day before I forget which we had a Turtle and therefore company to eat it. A Mr. Methuen, and his son and his son's wife[6]—The father was Member for some place, but has given up to his son—you will see him in the Bible. The Son is married to a sister of your friend Gooch's that had the whore of a wife. With them came also young Bouverie, youngest son of Ld. Radner[7]—Methuen the father has £16,000 a year—Bouverie when he comes of age which will be in a few months has £20,000 all told: among them all they have not the tenth part of an idea. Young Methuen is the very moral of Mylord What-then in the Princesse de Babylone,[8] except that instead of my Lord's crustiness he seems to have good nature.

No Ld. Dartry yet, and Hamilton does not come this month.

What think you of L.G.G. opposing Clark?[9] Ld. S. knows nothing of the latter thinks it will be the best thing ⟨for⟩ him that could happen, dividing the Opposition party.

[5] Both of Wilson's letters are missing.

[6] Paul Cobb Methuen (1752–1816), of Corsham, Wilts., heir of Paul Methuen (1723–95), succeeded his father as M.P. for Great Bedwyn in March 1781. He married, 1776, Matilda, daughter of Sir Thomas Gooch, 3rd bart., of Benacre, Suffolk. Her second brother, William Thomas Gooch (1749–1833) secured in 1781 the dissolution by Act of Parliament of his marriage (1775) to Elizabeth Sarah, daughter of William Villa Real of Edwinstow.

[7] Edward Bouverie (1760—1824), born 20 September, 5th son of William Pleydell-Bouverie (1725–76), 1st Earl of Radnor, and youngest brother of Jacob (1750–1828), the 2nd earl.

[8] Voltaire, in his novel, *La Princesse de Babylone*, introduced, as part of a satire on life in England, a character, 'milord Qu'importe', as representative of the boorish type of Englishman.

[9] At a by-election for the City of London, which ended on 2 October, Richard Clark was the candidate favoured by the government. He was defeated by the Lord Mayor, Sir Watkin Lewes. Lord George Gordon did not stand.

Send me any election news you pick up—as likewise any thing you can get from St. Paul's[10]—Ministerial news he may be more in the way of picking up than we. It will be shortest to direct to Shelburne house. Ld. S. has just written to Dunning to ask him here.

407

To George Wilson[1]

10 September 1781 (Aet 33)

Bowood Sept. 10th 1781 Monday morning 9 o'clock

I have just received your's of Friday the 7th[2]—this is expeditious. I tremble at the threaten'd acquaintance with the Bennets: even Parson Bridger's I would have gladly spared:[3] if things go on thus the post at Thorpe will be no longer tenable.

I am distracted at the thoughts of losing Miss Vernon. She leaves us in a day or two: I fear on thursday. I had taken for granted her home was here: but Ld. S. says it is at the Dutchess's. She is gone to Lady Warwick: 'because' Lady W. is some time or other to lay in /*lay* in, is it, or *lie* in?/ However one of these days it will come to our turn to lay in: and then we shall have Miss Vernon back again. She is not very conversible indeed, as I have already told you ten times over: but then she is very sensible, has great good nature in her, and is altogether one of the sweetest pictures to look at you ever saw: we shall muzzy enough I doubt when she is gone. I can't help pitying poor Lady S. who will not have a creature of her own sex to speak to: this will not however last long. There is another Miss Vernon, younger than this, whose name is Elizabeth.[4] She is not so beautiful, I understand as this: but a little upon the squat, as I learnt from her similitude to a tree that I was commending. Lady Holland[5] was another sister of Lady Shelburne's: she I

[10] Horace St Paul. On him see letter 325, n. 16.

407. [1] B.M. III: 226–7. Autograph. No address or docket.

Printed, Bowring, x, 98–9. This letter was sent at the same time as letter 412 (see p. 86, below).

[2] Missing.

[3] Not identified; presumably new acquaintances made by Wilson at Thorpe. 'The Bennet's' were perhaps the Rev Wolley Leigh-Bennett (1733–90), lord of the manor of Thorpe since 1768, and his family.

[4] See letter 401, n. 2.

[5] Mary (d. 1778), daughter of John Fitzpatrick, 1st Earl of Upper Ossory, who married (1766) Stephen Fox (1745–74), 2nd Baron Holland.

believe was by the same father, the E. of Ossory: she I understand is dead to the great grief of Lady Shelburne. So far so good: but then if my memory does not much deceive me, Ld. S. told me yesterday that the Dutchess of Marlborough again is another sister.[6] Yes, he certainly did: but with the Marlborough family I see not the least sign of any communication. Perhaps /however/ the Dutchess of M. is only a cousin; being the niece of the Dutchess of B. by another sister: as the Dutchess of Grafton and Baroness Kutzleben are.[7] Be this as it may, sure I am that the Dutchess of M. was spoken of by Ld. S. as one of the ladies of whom the Dutchess of B. had the breeding up. Lady Shelburne was with old Gertrude for 9 years. What an exquisite brood that old hen has sat upon!

Compliments to Trail and Douglas: with my best thanks to the former for this trouble he has been kind enough to give himself about the books.

Ld. Dartry I believe is not now expected here: at least not yet a while: Lady Dartry I understand is much in favour with the Queen. Ld. Camden is expected here the 15th: Dunning on the 25th. Mrs. Dunning comes a week before, to be here while her husband is at Bristol. I am kept here for the professed purpose of Ld. Camden and Dunning's looking over my book: hence it appears that I shall not at any rate leave this place till the month is out. As soon however as there is no particular reason assigned for my staying here I intend to go: so that by the first week in next month it is probable we shall meet: this however can not be, if Douglas and Trail /are/ both with you at that time: since the house would not hold us all: tell me how that matter stands.

When the Dutchess of B. comes seems not to be yet fixed: there is some expectation that she will bring the Duke[8] with her. Ld. S. said to me t'other day as we were sitting after dinner tête a tête, that he hoped she would, 'that the Duke might have the advantage

[6] Caroline (née Russell), Duchess of Marlborough (1743–1811), was the sole daughter of the 4th Duke of Bedford and through her mother, Gertrude, first cousin to Lady Shelburne.

[7] Elizabeth (1745–1822), Duchess of Grafton, and Dorothy (d. 1822), who in 1780 married Baron von Kutzleben, minister to the Landgrave of Hesse Cassel, were daughters of the Rev Sir Richard Wrottesley, 7th bart., by his wife Mary (née Leveson-Gower), sister of Gertrude, dowager Duchess of Bedford.

[8] I.e. her grandson, Francis, the 5th Duke (1765–1802). His father had died *vita parentis* from a riding accident in 1767.

of making my acquaintance'. This, I have a great notion, I told you in my last: if I did you must excuse me.

So Lady Warwick, you see, is not to be here, as I once thought she was: it was not here that Miss Vernon and she were to meet, but at Warwick castle. Did you ever hear of this same Warwick castle as a place worth looking at? Ld. S. has mentioned it to me as one of the most beautiful spots in England. I may possibly one day or other be able to tell you more about the matter: he has told me two or three times that he should be glad to shew it me. This I should like well enough, I must confess; if it were only for the sake of seeing the fair owner. Ld. W. he says is a pleasant good natured little man, and that I shall like him very well: upon my asking about his political bias, he spoke of him with some little mark of regret as being a courtier: and of Greville who is in the Admiralty (I think, is it not?) as a 'rank one.'[9] Is not all this very handsome? It would please you to see how attentive he is upon all these occasions to keep out of sight every idea of protection: every thing that could give me to understand he looked upon it as a favour done me to introduce me to these great people. His plan, indeed, seems to be at[10]

408

FROM SAMUEL BENTHAM[1]

30 August/10 September 1781

Nigno Taghilsky Fabrick August 30th O.S. 1781

In my last[2] I told you that the season being /come/ for hay-making and collecting /laying up/ the different kinds of provision for winter, there was a stop to all work in the fabricks here about. I had slackened the working at my vehicle to give time for the perfection of the machine I told you of and at the same time to

[9] George Greville (1746–1816), 2nd Earl of Warwick. He had two brothers: Charles Francis Greville, M.P. (1749–1809) was at this period a lord of the Admiralty, and Robert Fulke Greville (1751–1824) had recently (June) been appointed an equerry to the king. His wife, Henrietta, was the eldest of Lady Shelburne's Vernon half-sisters.

[10] The remainder is missing.

408. [1] B.M. III: 228–9. Autograph. Docketed: '1781 Aug. 30–Sept. 10 / S.B. Nigni Taghil. / to / I.B. Linc. Inn / Amphibious finished / Planing dropt / Copper sheath rejected / Magnets.' Letter-book copy with minor omissions by Jeremiah Bentham B.M. XXII: 30v–32.

[2] Letter 397.

have an answer from Petersbourg about the propriety of erecting it. [*Word crossed out*] In the meantime I have been taking a tour above a thousand versts on horseback to the mines and works belonging to a Mr. Pogodashin[3] and some others belonging to a Mr. Sabakin.[4] Pogodashin's Copper mines are the richest in the country. They produce sometimes upwards of 50,000 poud of copper in a year each poud is 40 pounds. I deprived him of several pounds sterling worth of copper in the rich and curious specimens which he gave me. I dare to say I collected in the course of this journey 8 or 10 hundred weight of different kinds of minerals which will all make their way next summer by water to Petersbourg. I think I shall have enough 2 or 3 decent collections of the mineral productions of this country. In my way I visited one of the highest of the Ural mountains where at present the best magnets are found. The Commander of the fabrick belonging to the crown nearest it conducted me there and took half a dozen men to work in search for some better pieces of magnet than were to be picked up of those lying loose on the ground. I collected about a hundred weight of different sizes from 10 pounds to ¼ ounce. I have had at different times to the number of 4 or 5 given me mounted: the largest of these weighs 5 pounds and lifts up 27 or 30 but among those not mounted will be some stronger. One I found and work't out myself weighs about ½ ounce and lifts ½ a pound badly mounted probably a pound when in order. I dont know whether magnets are scarce in England or not but of such curiosities I shall be well stockt.

At my return here I found yours of the 22nd May[5] directed to Pleschejeff I found also one from S.J.[6] or rather from my friend Carew containing both their advices (the answer to my letter about my machine) to '*look forward to old England for the first recompence of my ingenuity.*' [*two words crossed out*] This however does not prevent my trying some experiments relating to it although it sets me a wavering with respect to part of my intentions.

My Amphibious vehicle is just now finished and I shall set off in it shortly for Perme[7] a town that is or rather will be situated (for

[3] Maksim Mikhaylovich Pokhodyashin (d. 1781).

[4] Perhaps Lev Fëdorovich Sabakin (1746–1813), a Russian engineer who twice paid visits to England, where he met James Watt, and who produced the first account written in Russian of Watt's universal steam engine.

[5] Missing.

[6] I.e. Sir James Harris.

[7] Perm, situated on the left bank of the Kama in the western foothills of the Central Urals, 58° N., 56° 15′ E., was soon to be an important centre of the Urals copper industry. It became the government centre for the administrative district of the same

it is scarcely begun) between Catherinberg and Cazan it is to be the Capital of the Government which is henceforth to be called by the same name and which will take in a great part of that which hitherto has been called Siberia.

The /establishment of the/ new mode of Jurisdiction or the opening this new Government is to take place the beginning of October with great ceremony which I it is *to be understood* have been staying in this part of the country to be eye witness of. I shall send you an account of this when it takes place and shall at the same time be able to tell you which way I turn from thence.

I recived a letter at the same time from Pleschejef telling me that he was in expectation of setting out in September with the Grand Duke on his travels for a year or more. No more letters therefore must be directed to him. Let them be all directed to Sir James Harris. I am sorry on my own account at Ples travelling but on his part he may establish his health. I received also a letter from Ld. Sandwich[8] enclosing that from the Navy board it was written in his own hand, but *hang* him for not taking notice of the hint I gave him of having other proposals to offer. I suppose it is the varnishing the Copper which is the method superiour. I send you a copy of both letters for your amusement.

What the deuce is come to you that makes you so inquisitive about affairs between man and wife. You are told that Sir Gilbert Elliot goes to fetch Lady Harris to England[9] to see her freinds and the knowing ones in such matters conclude there must be a misunderstanding between them. Let the prattlers settle the matter among themselves or *put on petticoats.*

You tell me Howard[10] is set out for Petersbourg. He must be there then long before now. I wonder my letters from thence dont mention his arrival as they are of $\frac{20}{31}$ July. I may probably write a letter to him at least I have such a idea in my head just this minute.

To Hanbury[11] I will write but not these month or 6 weeks when

name later in this year, and Samuel was present at the inauguration ceremonies (letter 424, n. 1).

[8] Lord Sandwich's brief letter and the copy of the report from the Navy Board are at B.M. III: 173–5.

[9] Sir Gilbert Elliot, 4th bart. (1751–1814), of Minto. His wife and Lady Harris were sisters, and owing to a deterioration in Lady Harris's health he had travelled to Russia to escort her home.

[10] John Howard, the prison reformer, had set off in May 1781 on a tour of continental prisons. He arrived in Russia about the end of July and left again on his way to Poland early in September.

[11] Presumably Charles Hanbury, or his father John, with whom Samuel had stayed at Hamburg in 1779 on his way to Russia.

I shall have something more amusing to tell him of. I mean after the opening the new Government.

At Mr Pogodashin's where I have told you of my having just now been I was delighted to find the Encyclopadia. I spent almost 2 days in reading several different articles in it. The /moulin à vent/ article [*two words crossed out*] furnished me with almost all the information I asked for on that head.

The appearance of the country I have been passing through in this excursion is in general very beautifull: a great part of the way I appeared to be riding through an English park. The Weather was very fine. The hay perfumed the air, and one can seldom go 10 or a dozen miles without meeting a river or a rivulet. Birch trees and the several different kinds of fir form the principal parts of the woods. The larch tree is in great abundance and grows to a great size but is a very unprofitable production in this part of the country, though so very valuable near Arcangel. It is the best of the fir tribe for building ships and little inferiour to the oak of this country but as the woods are used here only to make Charcoal for the mines, and this makes the worst of Charcoal it is almost entirely useless. Corn grows; but seldom thoroughly ripens on the ground: so that the Cultivation of it is not much followed. It is a good crop that produces 10 fold what was sown, whereas in the Government of New Russia it is said to produce 100 fold.

The Puddles were covered with ice for some nights running near 3 weeks ago and the appearances of winter come on apace.

With my loadstones and other such curiosities I have put up 2 or 3 small bundles of ravens' quills enough to supply your harpsichord for your life time, I think they are very dear and scarce in London.

409

FROM SAMUEL BENTHAM[1]

1/12 September 1781

Sept. 1st O.S. 1781

I.B.

Code (I must call it so for shortness). How much I have wished it were possible to have received it at Perme at the opening the new Government. Whenever it does come it will find however as good a channel as possible. How comes it that nothing is said of it in your

409. [1] B.M. III: 230. Autograph. Docketed: '1781 Sept. 1–12 / S.B. Nigni Taghil / to / I.B. Linc. Inn / [...?] / Code—Ld. S. etc.'

last?[2] I expected it according to your former letters to be at Petersbourg in July.

As to Ld. Shel's views and plot upon you. Is not his desire to have your advice on the plans of Legislation he has to shew you, sufficient to account for his importunity? I should be hoping that at this instant you were laying your heads together were it not for the other prospects which you delight me so much by the kind of confidence with which you tell me they promise much better.

Honey costs here from 10 to 20 copecks the pound and sugar 70. Might not one make sugar from honey so as to take away entirely the peculiar flavour of the latter and give it the colour and texture of the former?

Is there no drawing published or could you not secure me a description last improved Steam Engine. Bolton[3] of Birmingham I think is the improver. Nairne[4] certainly could give it. You may best judge whether you would choose to ask him. The improvement I think consists in condensing the steam in an apart reservoir and not cooling the piston or the principal Cylinder. Also in one or more little air pumps which extract that part of the vapour which is not condensible, the permanent air discharged from the water by boiling.

You never tell me anything about the Davieses.

Call at Nairne's or anywhere else you can see some Magnets, and enquire the weight of each stone, how much it will lift up alone without being mounted, how much when mounted, what it is worth without and with the mounting. I may from knowing these particulars of 4 or 5 magnets be able to judge what pains it is worth my while to take to procure more than I have. If they /those which you see/ are of different sizes I should judge also what size is most prized. Would it /one be/ very rare and valuable which should weigh 50 pounds and lift up 150, or weigh 100 lift up 200. I mean when mounted, for it is scarcely possible to find one that shall lift up 10 pounds without being mounted though it should weigh 200. In

[2] Taken together with the reference to Shelburne at the beginning of the next paragraph, this would appear to indicate that Samuel had just received a further letter (now missing) from Bentham, written not earlier than the beginning of July when Shelburne forced his acquaintance on him (letter 396, n. 3). There can have been no such reference to Shelburne in the letter of 22 May acknowledged by Samuel in letter 408.

[3] Matthew Boulton (1728–1809), founder of the Soho engineering works at Birmingham, was at this time engaged with his partner, James Watt, in developing the steam engine into an effective power unit, primarily for pumping water out of mines.

[4] Edward Nairne (1726–1806), instrument maker. On him see letter 149, n. 4.

the Encyclopedia I find Knight[5] (the compass maker I suppose) was possessed of the secret of being able not only greatly to augment the force of all magnets but also to change the direction of the poles at pleasure. If that secret is known at present by other mathemat. instrum. makers I could procure some large stones which by the change of the situation of the poles might from being very indifferent become very excellent.

You mentioned to me a publication on Cements if you send any parcel to me send me this also if it is to be had.

410

From Samuel Bentham[1]

c. 1/12 September 1781

Everything that may be usefull for /in/ the erecting wind water or horse mills and particularly for flower mills saw mills and coining business. Go to the mint observe all the machines at present in use but chiefly those for half pence. Send me ½ a dozen new coined halfpence. Have you no acquaintance who has a mechanical genius enough to draw the engines exact enough for me to form an idea of the proportions. If not do what you can yourself. Make Wilson or somebody go with you to correct you or assist your memory. Do they make use of aqua fortis to brighten them when finished or before stampt or by what other means do they brighten them after they have been the last time heated red hot to soften them.

A plane fowling piece for Gov. L. Send me at the same time all manner of Queries that you please they shall all be answered especially if they be written in french. Give me Instructions with respect to Code. You may be sure it will be made some use of.

[5] Gowin Knight (1713–72), sometime physician, and from 1756 the first principal librarian of the British Museum, conducted important research into magnetism and the construction of compasses. A number of his reports were published in the *Philosophical Transactions* of the Royal Society.

410. [1] B.M. X: 604. Autograph. No date, address, or docket.

The general contents and especially the reference to Governor Lamb indicate that this letter belongs to the sequence written by Samuel to Bentham from Nizhniy Tagil about the beginning of September, and from the references to steam engines and cement it appears likely that it was closely associated with the previous letter. Windmills had also been a subject of recent enquiry in Samuel's letters (see letters 394 and 397, at the end). On the back of the sheet are some pencil drawings of what look like candelabra and the faint pencil notes: 'saw mill worked by wind either from the Encyclopaedia or some other work / To have drawings of the coing. machine directly to be sent by the post.'

It must be a great expence at the Tower to move (produce the primum mobile of) the coining machines without wind or water. I suppose they do it by horses.

I should like much to know how the copper is purified at the mines for it is somehow or other made much finer than the copper here.

How long do the stamps last. If long enough to stamp 2 or 3,000 you might get me a few made or at any rate a stamp for making the stamps. These /first/ stamps should have made ½ a dozen stamp to try them which ½ dozen should be sent.

How may the power of a windmill be treasured up so as to act at the intermissions. This would be of most importance for moving bellows to Iron furnaces. If by a calm the furnaces must be let to cool the loss would be very great. It might perhaps be better to have a steam engine which possibly might be worked by the heat of the furnace itself without diminishing from it so as to require more fuel.

The heat at the upper part of an iron casting furnace is not confined at all instead then of escaping into the air it may be applied to the working the machine. Endeavour to inform yourself if there be any such machine also how a furnace may be erected for the melting iron and copper ores without the help of bellows.

The Publication you mentioned to me about Cements

A Description of the process and mill for making oil from Linseed. Might not the oil be extracted by compression from the bark of the birch tree or is it in some measure the *creature* of the fire

Drawings and descriptions of the improved Steam Engine

A Steam Engine distills the fluid employed this fluid might be turned to some account. If water only it should be said but perhaps some more valuable fluid might be thus distilled. It is to be considered that the degree of heat to which it will be exposed will by the compressure be far greater than the boiling heat of that fluid. Some substances might be made to act on each other in the state of vapour which could not meet together in that state but under such a pressure. Portable soup might be made either open in the still or enclosed in a vessel to which the compressed over-heated fluid in the still serves as a bath.

Get also what information you can about the making of Steel. There are mines here that produce the best of Iron but the steel they make is very coarse grained and indifferent. There is a good deal about this in the chemical dictionary

Potash from the ashes of great [...?]. Oil mills. Sugar honey and soup[?] Pot

411

To George Wilson[1]

13 September 1781 (Aet 33)

Sept. 13th Thursday

Yesterday came here in the evening a Mr. Ernest,[2] a heavy-looking good humoured sort of a German, intimately connected somehow or other (I can't yet tell how) with Count Bruhl,[3] through whose means he came known to Ld. S. /In the chaise/ With him came his servant also a German who before bedtime got drunk, and deposited his carcase in the housekeeper's room, instead of his ⟨own. Go⟩[4]ing downstairs to a certain place after I had been up to ⟨bed I me⟩t the housekeeper upon the staircase, who being a neighbour, open'd her hard case to me. Finding remonstrances ineffectual, we got a couple of the men who hawled him away and left Mrs. Housekeeper to her repose.

Yesterday also came Parson Townsend. I have not yet had any private communication with him. Illness in his family prevented his intended journey into Northamptonshire. The same illness may perhaps prevent my visit to him.

Today came a letter announcing an intended visit from a certain Ld. /and Lady/ Tracton.[5] This Ld. Tracton is Ld. Ch. Baron in Ireland. His father was an attorney and did Ld. S's. business there.

411. [1] B.M. III: 231. Autograph. Written on pages 3 and 4 of a double sheet of notepaper (page 4 bearing the address), from which the other half bearing pages 1 and 2 has been detached and is now missing.

Addressed: 'George Wilson Esqr. / Thorpe / near / Staines.' Postmark: '15 / SE.' Printed, Bowring, x, 99–100.

[2] Not identified. Bentham understood him to be the Saxon minister in London (letter 412).

[3] Presumably Hans Moritz, Count von Bruhl, of Saxony, on whom see also letter 403, n. 6.

[4] Here, and also a few words further on, the writing has been obliterated by the seal.

[5] James Dennis (1721–82), who held the office of Chief Baron of the Exchequer in Ireland with the title of Lord Tracton. In 1769 he married Elizabeth Pigott.

412

To George Wilson[1]

15–17 September 1781 (Aet 33)

Saturday night Septr. 15½ after 10. 1781

Arrived here a little before dinner Ld. Chatham,[2] /his brother/ Will Pitt,[3] and Prat,[4] Ld. Camdens son, member for Bath. /I find they had none of them been ever here before./ Do you know Ld. Chatham? In his appearance upon the whole he puts me in mind of Danl. Parker Coke:[5] but he has his father's Roman nose, and if events should concur to make him have ⟨a goo⟩d opinion of himself, will soon I dare say acquire his commanding manner: at present one sees little more than a kind of reserve, temper'd with mildness, but clouded with a little dash of bashfulness. Will Pitt, you know for certain: in his conversation there is nothing of the orator: nothing of that hauteur and suffisance one would expect: on the contrary he seems very good natured and a little raw. I was

412. [1] Bowring, x, 100–3. The first part printed from B.M. III: 234 (autograph).

This letter presents considerable editorial problems, but the case for regarding the whole as a single letter is clearly indicated. Towards the end of the letter Bentham wrote: 'Send to Davies everything except what is mentioned as secret between us two, or marked with the initials of your name.' B.M. III: 234 is a single foolscap sheet, filled up on both sides. It matches other double foolscap paper, on two sheets of which Bentham wrote the next letter but one (B.M. III: 235–8, letter 414). It contains about 750 words, much the same as the printed passages for which there is no manuscript appearing as Bowring, x, 101a–102a. Its content is personal chit-chat, very different from the political information in the second part which Wilson is instructed to keep to himself. The probable explanation for its survival in the Bentham collection is that Bowring, when preparing his edition, obtained letters from the descendants of both Davies and Wilson. The former did not press for their return; but the latter probably did, for the Bentham collection now lacks the manuscripts of a number of Wilson's letters printed in Bowring. On this supposition, when Wilson received this letter he tore off the first part, which is now B.M. III: 234, and forwarded it to Davies, retaining the second part and also another sheet on which Bentham wrote the 'Relation', which forms a kind of postscript to the rest, and which now appears as Bowring, x, 102a–103b.

A word count indicates that this other sheet could also have borne the address.

[2] John Pitt (1756–1835), 2nd Earl, heir of the famous William Pitt, 1st Earl of Chatham.

[3] William Pitt (1759–1806), the future prime minister, second son of the 1st Earl. Entering parliament in January 1781 he had immediately engaged in active opposition to the North ministry.

[4] John Jeffreys Pratt, M.P. (1759–1840), who succeeded his father as 2nd Earl Camden in 1794. He became one of William Pitt's close political associates.

[5] Daniel Parker Coke, M.P. (1745–1825), a barrister attached to the Midland circuit.

monstrously frighten'd at him: but when I came to talk with him he seemed frighten'd at me: so that if anything should happen to jumble us together, we may perhaps be good pax which however is not very likely; for I don't know very well what ideas we are likely to have in common. After beating Miss Vernon I have just been beating him at Chess: an inglorious conquest, as he is scarce so much in my hands as I am in yours. Ernest and the rest of the people have been playing at Crown Whisk. Supper being announced I stole up here. Ernest it seems is the Saxon Minister: an honest good-humoured kind of man. I find it necessary to rise before 6, and for that purpose to go to bed by 11. I lie on straw. Prat has more distance and more suffisance than either of the others: yet there is a sort of giggishness about him too: he puts me in mind of a young Jew broker in the city. About an hour after /dinner/ passes now quite happily: as I have established a habit of accompanying Lady S. on the harpsichord: and she is pleased with it. She has nothing at present /here/ but a shabby little spinnet, that I should be ashamed to use myself: but I have set her agog after a variety of new-fashioned harpsichords and she vows to have some of them. There being nothing here in the fiddle way that is tolerable she has made me send for mine to town.

Sunday morning.

I mistook about the time of Dunning's visit: his wife does not come till the 24th and he not till a week afterwards. He therefore will not be here till the 1st of October allowing a week for his stay, I shall not leave this place till the 27th: then I am to pay a visit to Parson Townsend, from whom I shall hardly get away under a week. I shall then come to you en droiture without going to town provided always that your spare room is not preoccupied. On se dechaine ici most violently against Governor Cunningham:[6] indeed his conduct at Barbadoes seems to warrant it. A brother of his also in the army and to be looked on as a ~~ward~~ mignon of Ld. G. G's in Germany, when Ld. S. was serving there: Cunny was very nice about his hair which used to make Ld. S. take a pleasure in discomposing it. Besides his connection with Ld. G. G. he is a toad-eater at Marlborough house where he had his entrees at any time notwithstanding the reserve so remarkable in that family: the first

[6] Major General James Cuninghame (c. 1731–88) was appointed governor of Barbados in February 1780 by the favour of the secretary of state for the colonies, Lord George Germain. On him and his brother, Lieutenant General Robert Cuninghame (c. 1728–1801), see Sir Lewis Namier and John Brooke, *The History of Parliament. The House of Commons, 1754–1790*, 3 vols., London, 1964, ii, 283–5.

time of his being there he was invited for a week: he staid six, in spite of continual hints of his having staid long enough.

A story of Ld. Bristol—some time ago coming from Paris directly to London he carried a verbal message as he pretended from Franklin to who would you think of all men in the world but Ld. Spencer,[7] telling him that if he would come to Paris immediately, they two would be able to settle a peace. Ld. Spencer was very much distressed: could scarce credit the information: but willing to do what he thought right, thought he could not justify to himself the taking no notice of it. He accordingly set out and /actually/ got as far as Calais but the wind proving contrary, or some other obstruction arising, he found it impracticable to get to Paris time enough, and so went back again. This Ld. S. says he has from an authority which he is not at liberty to mention but which he can absolutely depend upon. He has told it twice in my hearing the last time yesterday to Ld. Chatham. He accounts for it to the flightiness of Ld. B. who he says is equally known for his spirit of intrigue and his habit of drawing the long-bow. Indeed there does seem to be something of that in him: besides that they say that there is something of a crack in the brain runs throughout the family.[8]

Sunday Morning, September 16.

The hints thrown out by Lord S. in one of our tête-à-têtes in London, about offers made to entrap him, and which I was then disposed to look upon as a way of speaking, have, in some of our country tête-à-têtes, been particularized. To break the connexion between him and Lord Chatham, propositions were first made to the latter to come in with Lord S., afterwards to Lord S. to come in without Lord C. One day, when Lord S. was dining at Lord Beauchamp's, Eden having been to Shelburne House, and not finding him at home, he followed him thither; calling him out, he said he came by order of the king; and made him three propositions: the first, to come in and act with Lord North and Lord Suffolk; another, to act with either of them without the other; and a third, to come in without either of them. This latter he would have

[7] John Spencer (1734–83), 1st Earl Spencer. He was the principal beneficiary under the will of his great-grandmother, Sarah, Duchess of Marlborough, but subject to the proviso that should he accept 'from any King or Queen of these realms any pension, or any office or employment civil or military' (other than the rangership of Windsor Great or Little Park) then the estates were to pass to the next heir, as if he 'were actually dead'. He thus played virtually no part in public life, a circumstance which explains the piquancy of this particular frolic of Lord Bristol.

[8] B.M. III: 234v ends here.

accepted, had not his friends, some or all of them, been excluded. I know not whether Lord Chatham was living at that time, but I believe he was.[9] Barré, he says, has been repeatedly and constantly refusing £3,000 a-year, which would have been given to him if he would have deserted Lord S. He values himself much on his friends, and on their mutual fidelity. With Alderman Townsend, he says, he has been connected twenty-two years; with Lord Camden, about twenty-one; with Dunning, eighteen; and with Elliot, I think, he added sixteen. Elliot brought in seven Members, he says, the last time. Gibbon he brought in for private friendship; though, as it turned out, much to his regret.[10] Elliot offered, he says, to take his recommendation for some of them; but, at that time, he neglected the offer through despondency. At his outset, I myself, he says, could scarcely be barer of connexions than he was: his father had scarcely any others than with Lord Holland. At a former time, when he was laughing with Blankett and me about his being called Jesuit, I asked him who was his godfather on that occasion. This would be an occasion, if he thought proper to lay hold of it, for telling his own story about the rupture between him and Lord Holland, and so it proved. He said that Lord Holland, previous to his resignation, (the history of the day will show when that was,) of his own accord, for some reason or other, not specified, I think, by Lord S., mentioned his tedium of public business, and his wishes to resign; that, for some reason or other, it was convenient he should resign; and so Lord S. took him at his word. Having thus over-reached himself, he was enraged, and inveighed against Lord S., as if it were he that overreached him. Lord S., I think, mentioned somebody as having been a witness, and as justifying him, but I forget whom.[11]

[9] There is no complete narrative of this attempt by Lord North to escape his responsibilities or else strengthen his administration, but the main moves can be followed through the king's correspondence. In mid-February 1778 a tentative approach was made to Chatham through the Duke of Northumberland. In March a more direct approach, authorized by the king, was made to Shelburne, William Eden being employed as an intermediary; but Eden's memorandum on the subject gives no indication of an attempt to separate Shelburne from Chatham (*The Correspondence of George III*, edited by Sir John Fortescue, 6 vols., London, 1927–28, iv, nos. 2184, 2193, 2219, 2220, 2221, 2223–6, 2228–9, 2232, 2235, 2237, 2239–40, 2255–7. See also *Memorials and Correspondence of Charles James Fox*, edited by Lord John Russell, 4 vols., London, 1853–57, i, 180–7).

[10] Edward Gibbon, M.P. (1737–94), the historian, was a cousin of Eliot's wife. Eliot brought him into parliament for Liskeard at the general election of 1774 but refused to sponsor him again in 1780, when the two men were on opposing sides in politics.

[11] This explanation was too self-exculpatory. Holland accused Shelburne of lack of frankness. The explanation Shelburne recorded at the time indicates that although he may not have been blameable in that respect, at any rate he was too inexperienced

Yesterday morning, Lord S. spoke of a letter which he had received from an officer high in rank in the West Indies. He said that De Grasse, with twenty-four or twenty-five ships of the line, (he had had a reinforcement of six or seven,) sailed, on the 31st July, for New York. That Hood, with seven or eight, was only then on the point of setting sail. This looks bad, and was mentioned with great triumph. If you mention it, you must not say how you came by it; for the officer, whoever he be, would get a d—— rap of the knuckles if he was known to correspond with us.[12]

Monday Morning, September 17.

Now, from other advices, we have altered Hood's number from seven or eight to fifteen. At eight o'clock this morning, I received yours of Friday the 15th.[13] You are a good fellow enough for the news you send me; but an ungrateful bear for pretending to complain of the shortness of my letters; while I, to the utter neglect of my whole business, spend whole mornings in cramming your insatiable maw with politics. It takes me, indeed, a monstrous long while to write a letter to you; for I have so many things I might write, that more time is spent in determining which of them I shall write than in writing. I have a hundred and fifty subjects at this moment which are ready to pull me to pieces for the preference. My notions of the characters of the people here; conversations about Sam and about myself; what sort of connexion I hope or wish to form or to preserve; these are topics I find myself continually solicited to touch upon, yet I think it better not to do it at all than to do it imperfectly. They will keep; and political stories that I chance to hear, if they were not set down instantly, would be forgotten. Your queries about my visit at Thorpe I have answered by anticipation, in a letter which will go with this.[14] Send to Davies everything except what is mentioned as secret between us two, or marked with the initials of your name: but wait for franks from me unless you can get others.

or insufficiently alert to see the necessity of keeping everyone accurately informed of the reports he made (Lord Fitzmaurice, *Life of William, Earl of Shelburne*, 2 vols., London, 1912, i, 160). For a discussion of the whole episode from Shelburne's point of view, see ibid., pp. 149–65, and from that of Holland, Lord Ilchester, *Henry Fox, First Lord Holland*, 2 vols., London, 1920, ii, 241–60.

[12] This bold move by de Grasse led to French control of the waters of the Chesapeake and made impossible any attempt to relieve the British army under Cornwallis cornered at Yorktown by Washington and La Fayette.

[13] Missing.

[14] Letter 407.

Bowood, Monday,
17th September, 1781.

Relation of an overture made by Lord North to the Rockingham party for a coalition, in the summer of 1780, as given by Lord Shelburne to Mr. W. Pitt, on Sunday, September 16th, 1781, after dinner—present, Lord Chatham, Mr. Pratt, and J.B.[15]

It was introduced with some little preparation, as if in compliance with a request made on some former occasion. Lord North, meeting his cousin Montague upon the steps of the House of Commons, went up to him and said, he was glad to understand there was a disposition among his friends to *coalesce*; that, if that disposition were real, he would authorize him to propose such terms as the Court meant on their part to insist upon. That, however indelicate it might sound in his mouth, yet it was necessary he should say, that, at all events, he must be continued where he was: that the case was the same with respect to Lord Sandwich. Or, if it should happen that the king could be prevailed with to give up Lord S., which he could not vouch for, he was sure it could not be done upon any other terms than that of a very honourable provision being made for him. That, in this case, whoever should come into the Admiralty, it must not be Admiral Keppel: that Charles Fox could not be received, at least immediately, into any of the high and confidential offices, such as that of Secretary of State; but that, as to any lucrative office out of the great line of business, such as that of Treasurer of the Navy, there would perhaps be no objection; that after the length he had gone, and the offences he had given, it could not be expected that his majesty should be immediately reconciled to the idea of a confidential communication with him; but that such a place as was suggested might serve him as a place of probation, and that it would give him opportunities of smoothing the way to a more perfect reconcilement.

Thus far I am perfectly clear, not only as to the facts, but as to the colouring. This being reported to Lord Rockingham, he returned an answer of himself, without consulting with the party; my recollection is not clear as to the stipulations contained in it, but I think he stood out for Keppel, and insisted that the Duke of Richmond and Charles Fox should be secretaries of state. In all this,

[15] Shelburne did not know all the details of this political negotiation, but his account was in general correct (see Ian R. Christie, 'The Marquis of Rockingham and Lord North's offer of a coalition, June–July 1780', *English Historical Review*, lxix (1954), 388–407). He had however overlooked grounds he had given Rockingham for thinking that it would be useless to notify him of the pourparlers.

it does not appear that anything was said about Lord Shelburne. Upon Lord Rockingham's communicating the offer and the answer to the Duke of Richmond, the duke blamed him for including him in such a proposition; whether as meaning that he would not serve the king on any terms, or not on those terms, I did not understand. The duke intimated, at the same time, that there 'were other persons' (meaning, as I understood, Lord Shelburne himself) with whom, considering such and such things, it would have been but decent to consult. It seemed to me that the information of this negotiation had come to Lord S., first from the Duke of Richmond; though it seems as if the matter had afterwards been the subject of discussion between the former and Lord Rockingham. The interpretation put upon Lord R.'s answer, whatever it was, is a matter of contestation between him and Lord S. Lord R. calls it an absolute rejection of the offer, and a virtual refusal to treat: Lord S. considers it as an acceptance of the treaty, and thereby as a sort of treachery, or, according to the footing they were then upon together, at least a violation of amity towards himself. Pitt or Pratt asking Lord S. what it was that in all this business Lord R. was expecting for himself, the answer was, Nothing that he ever heard of; clearly nothing, unless, perhaps, it might be that he had Ireland in view, on account of the advantage it might give him in thwarting the Absentee Tax; but this was not pretended to be anything but surmise. Was not this very creditable to Lord R.? From what I have heard of him, since I have been here, I am disposed to entertain a good opinion of him: I have heard a good deal against him in the way of general disapprobation; but as to any grounds for it, I have heard of none, but what appeared to me to be either inconsistent, nugatory, or unintelligible. Being asked what was to have been done for Burke, he answered that he was not clear; that certainly he was not to have been neglected, but that there was something of an inferior negotiation, in which he was more particularly concerned. The terms were so ambiguous, that I could not distinguish who were the parties, with whom he was meant to be represented as having been negotiating; whether the ministry, or the people of his own party; or even so much as whether he was himself a party to this under or interior negotiation, in which, in point of interest, he was represented as being concerned. There is a prodigious deal of ambiguity in the general tenor of Lord S.'s language on party subjects; whether genuine or affected I cannot be certain: I rather believe it genuine; because I find it the same on subjects in which party has nothing to do. As to the negotiation above-mentioned, it is scarcely necessary to add that the demands on Lord Rockingham's side being such, no reply was given.

In Burke's pamphlet on the affairs of Ireland, at least in one of his late pamphlets, if I do not mistake, he tells us that Lord Rockingham had not apprized anybody of his determination to apply for the audience he had about Ireland with the king. Lord S.'s account of that matter is, that about one o'clock on that day, Lord R. came to him, to take his advice about it, mentioned his determination to demand the audience, but that he wished for Lord S.'s advice about what he should say; and to know, in general, whether he approved or disapproved of it. Lord S. observed to him, that it was too short a warning by much, for taking a step of so much importance; for, considering what it was then o'clock, they should not have more than half-an-hour to deliberate upon it. I am not certain whether it was not that Lord R. wished Lord Shelburne to go with him: whichever was the case, he confessed to us that, from reasons regarding his own reputation, he declined taking a part either way, on a sudden. Considering the importance that it might appear to be of to the nation, that the king should hear what information Lord R. had to give him, he, Lord S., did not care to have it said that he had put his negative upon it; and, on the other hand, there might, for aught he could satisfy himself about on a sudden, be other reasons, which he did not state, especially why it might not be advisable to him to be known to have concurred in it.[16]

[16] On Rockingham's interview with the king on 5 May 1779 concerning the need to make commercial concessions in order to bolster up the Irish economy, which had been hard hit by the American War of Independence, see *The Correspondence of Edmund Burke*, vol. iv, *July 1778–June 1782*, edited by John A. Woods, Cambridge, 1963, p. 67. Burke referred to this interview in his pamphlet on Irish affairs, 'A Letter to Thomas Burgh Esq.', dated 'New Year's Day, 1780', *The Works of Edmund Burke*, Bohn edition, 8 vols., London, 1894–1900, v, 502. See also Sir John Fortescue, op. cit. iv, 335, and T. H. D. Mahoney, *Edmund Burke and Ireland*, London, 1960, pp. 75–92.

413

To George Wilson[1]

25 August–17 September 1781 (Aet 33)

Aug. 25th 1781
Saturday morning 9 o'clock

Yesterday when I gave my Lord some directions to copy there was one to Jeremiah Bentham Esqr. Bath—'What is that your father Mr. B? Is there any attention we could shew him? is there any thing we could do for him? would it be agreable to him to come over here and see us?' The answer was—'Your Ldship is very good —but he is full as well where he is.' Was not this obliging? What a pretty scene would have been exhibited had I suffer'd my Lord to send for them? What a mixture of hectoring and pressing, and self-complacency and cringing and self-ostentation and forced civility?

Sept. 17th

Since writing the above, Q.S.P. in one of his letters[2] spelt for me to get him here—would I come over to him? or ⟨sh⟩ould he come to me? I went over to him without taking any notice of the other branch of the alternative. T'other day however upon my Lord's making the offer of sending them some game I accepted it, and the game was sent.[3]

For some time I could not make the copying press do: but now I am got into the way of it; so that you will probably not have any more packets to send to Davies. This however there was no taking an impression of, owing to the antiquity of the first paragraph.

This day just as we were sitting down to dinner came Ld. and Lady Tracton—They are a curious couple: but I have no time at present to give you any account of them—tomorrow Pratt and the Pitts leave us, and go to Banks's of Corfe-Castle. I am sorry they go so soon. Ld. Camden we expect the day after tomorrow.

413. [1] B.M. III: 213. Autograph.
This single quarto sheet bears no address and was probably slipped in with letter 412.

[2] Missing.

[3] The present of game was acknowledged in a letter from Bentham senior to his son, dated Bath, 13 September 1781 (B.M. III: 233).

414

To George Wilson[1]

17–24 September 1781 (Aet 33)

Bowood Monday evening ½ after 10 Sept. 17 1781

The Whist table is just broke up: supper is announced, the game at chess between Ld. Chatham and Miss Vernon is drawing near to a conclusion, and while the rest of the people are hovering round them waiting for the event, I have taken french leave of them all, and stolen up here, that I may be a good boy tomorrow and rise betimes. This Ld. and Lady Tracton are the queerest gigs you ever saw: my Lord wears his bob wig black coat and /coloured/ worsted stockings and looks like a plain stout thick set country parson. My lady is a little shrivelled figure of about sixty, with a hook nose and ferret eyes, a long white beard and a parchment mahogony-coloured skin, in a /gray/ riding habit with a black hat and feather. Nobody speaks to her nor she to anybody: she has been sticking close to her husband's side, while he has been playing at whist but would not play herself.

Tuesday evening 10 o'clock Sept. 18.

We have just now a monstrous heap of people. Departed before breakfast Pratt and the Pitts. Remain Ld. and Lady Trackton: Arrived before dinner Ld. Dartry and Col. Barré seemingly in company. Arrived before tea, Ld. Camden, Miss Pratt his daughter,[2] and a Mr. Smith, now or formerly a Captain in the E. India service.[3] The carriages came in together: but whether Smith belongs to Ld. Camden and his daughter I can't tell; no signs of converse between them have I seen. Ld. Dartry is a chatty sort of man, and seems to know everybody: does not seem to trouble his head about party, but mixes with ~~opposition~~ government as well as ~~government~~ /with opposition/ men. His wife is a good deal in favour with the Queen,

414. [1] B.M. III: 235–8. Autograph. No address or docket.

Printed, Bowring, x, 103b–107b. The manuscript consists of two sheets of double foolscap, each folded to form four pages, and Bowring's arrangement completely obscures the fact that the whole was written in sequence as a kind of journal. The final lines indicate that these sheets were despatched as a separate letter.

[2] Of Lord Camden's four daughters only the second, Elizabeth (d. 1826), remained unmarried at this time.

[3] Nathaniel Smith, M.P. (1730–94), an East India Company director, was for several years Shelburne's spokesman at East India House.

and often with her. She is of the family of the *Penns.*[4] Miss Pratt is very fat, not handsome nor very young: but well-bred, conversible, sensible and as far as one can judge, good-natured. Ld. and Lady S., Ld. Tracton, Ld. Dartry, and Col. Barré have been at the Whist table: the rest of us round the book ⟨table⟩ à l'ordinaire: except that for the last half hour Ld. Camden has been walking in a passage room with Barré. With Ld. Camden I have had as yet scarce any communication: but while the women have been at their work, and I with my book before me, I have been joining in conversation occasionally with his daughter: and Ld. C. and S. I observed were in close conversation for some time with looks that seemed to indicate they were talking about me.

Wednesday afternoon 8 o'clock.

This morning before breakfast Ld. and Lady Tracton took themselves away: Joy go with them; they were a pair of cursed sangliers: the latter more particularly to my dear Lady Shelburne whose footsteps I adore. Miss Vernon alas! leaves us the day after tomorrow without redemption. I forgot to tell you of a dinner visitor we had the day before yesterday, a Mr. Talbot,[5] a name he has taken for an estate instead of that of Davenport. He is a young man but lately come of age, he has been to Christ Church in Oxford, and has now thoughts of going into the army. His family house is in the neighbourhood at or near Causham /Cosham/ where Methuen lives: it is an old monastery, one of the most perfect they say in England. It is a vast place and the estate though a nominal £2,000 a year is so reduced by incumbrances as to bring him in, it is said, scarce £500: so that a profession is absolutely necessary to him. The man whom he has his estate from was obliged to fly the country for Italian eccentricities. In the young man himself there is nothing that seems remarkable.

Barré loves to sit over his claret, pushes it about pretty briskly, and abounds in stories which are well told and very entertaining. He really seems to have a great command of language: he states clearly and forcibly; and upon all points his words are fluent and well-chosen. Ld. Dartry is also intelligent and entertaining. They were talking over Irish affairs this afternoon. Their conversation

[4] Lord Dartrey had married in 1770, as his second wife, Philadelphia Hannah, only daughter of Thomas Freame by Margaretta, daughter of William Penn.

[5] William Davenport Talbot (c. 1760–1800), son of Dr William Davenport, rector of Bredon. He took the name of Talbot in 1778 on inheriting the estate of Laycock Abbey. In 1796 he married the eldest daughter of the second earl of Ilchester, at whose town house he died (*Gentleman's Magazine*, 1800, ii, 801).

was instructive: when they differed, as they did now and then, about matters of fact as well as opinion, it was with great frankness and urbanity. I put in a word now and then to keep the ball up and to avoid appearing a perfect ninny: but it was pain and grief to me. My health some how or other is in cursed order: I scarce know how to get up early enough: even six o'clock is too late.

Hyde Parker it is said (this is Barré's story) is not to have anything after all. Being offer'd the command of the fleet against the Dutch, he demanded a reinforcement; but was denied. Afterwards a reinforcement was order'd; then he declared himself willing to serve; but then they would not let him. This Col. Barré said he had from an officer who is intimate with Parker. 'Ah Johnny,' said the old man to his friend, ''twas a rare bout, twould ha' done thy heart good to have seen it: there was not a shot that did not take place on either side.'[6]

Sept. 24. Monday evening ½ after 10 o'clock.

This morning at 8 received yours of the 20th:[7] but let pass. I will go on at present with my journal.

Thursday nothing happend that I can recollect worth mentioning no fresh visitors.

On Friday the prediction given of Miss Vernon's departure in the last page was but too well verified. There was a little incident—no I won't go on with that sentence—A little piece of attention she show'd me the night before, while it flatter'd my vanity, made me feel the loss of her the more sensibly. On the Sunday before she and I had been playing at Chess. Pitt who did not play at the whist table, and Ld. Chatham who cut in and out had been occasionally looking on. After she had lost two games to me, which was as many as she had ever been used to play, she gave it up; whereupon Pitt proposed we should play, which we did, and I beat him. Finding he had no chance with me, he complained of it's hurting his head, and gave it up immediately. Towards the close of the evening Ld. Chatham gave me a challenge—I accepted it. From something that Pitt had said I expected to have found him an easy conquest; especially as there was something /seemingly/ irregular in the opening of his game; but it was a confounded bite, for I soon found his hand as heavy over me as I ever have felt your's; in short he beat me shamefully: and the outcries I made on that occasion were such as would naturally convey to other people a formidable

[6] See letter 404, n. 26.

[7] Missing.

idea of his prowess. Now what is all this to Miss Vernon? Why the next evening, Tuesday, Pitt first proposed a game to her: they plaid, and I don't know which beat: but after playing one game, she declined playing any more, the words were scarce out of her mouth, when Ld. Shelburne from the Whist table, by way of saying something, called to me as if pitying me for not being able to get a game: upon that each of them proposed I should play with the other. After some *pourparlers*, as Miss V. had before declined playing any more /with Pitt/, I thought it wou'd be civiler to both of them for me not to make any proposal to her: so I asked Pitt, but he declined it, saying as he had done before that his head would not bear more than a game at a sitting: accordingly the chess board laid aside and we took to our books à l'ordinaire—About an hour or an hour and a half afterwards, Ld. Chatham, having cut out at the Whist table, came to the library table and proposed to Miss Vernon to play a game with him. She consented, and they had just time to play a game before supper: he beat her of course, though not with so high a hand as one would have expected. Tuesday morning, as I told you, Ld. Chatham etc. went away and on Tuesday and Wednesday evenings, as Miss Pratt was there, /and not playing at Whist/ I thought it not proper to say anything about Chess to Miss Vernon. Well now comes the mighty favour. On Thursday, towards the close of the evening, she called me to her, and asked me (which was what she had never done before) whether I would play a game at chess with her: observing that she had used me excessively ill in refusing me and then playing with Ld. Chatham. Mighty thankful I was as you may imagine: we sat down immediately and we were mighty sociable and merry; more so than I had ever observed her on any occasion before; insomuch that Ld. Shelburne from the Whist table took notice of it, adding that, whatever was the reason, he never saw her laugh so much with any body as with me. When I talked to her about her going, and asked her what time it was to be in the morning, she said that I should not see her, for that it would be before I was up. 'Well, and what of all this?' you may say; 'a fine long-winded story this is à la mode de Bentham to cook up about nothing at all. 'Why to be sure it is: and if this had happened with some women I should never have made any reflections on it even in my own mind, much less have thought of boring you with it. But were you but acquainted with the girl, and *à portée* (as Clinton would say) to observe the extreme dignity and coldness and silence and reserve (as much as is consistent with great good nature which it would be injustice to deny to her,) you would then and not otherwise be able to estimate the value of any such *little* expression of complacency as what I have been mentioning. Oh, and I have not told you neither that it was by her means that I got upon the footing that I am upon of playing upon the harpsichord (I mean upon the fiddle with the harpsichord) every afternoon with Lady Shelburne: but that story I shall spare you; nor of the air of cordiality and attention with which she received the whisper in which I took my leave of her at night: in short she actually took the sort of notice which no well bred woman could have avoided taking of any man who was paying her a compliment of that sort: In the morning you will have concluded I made a point of being in the way to hand her to her carriage: but I did not, thinking it might be deemed an act of impertinence, and might give occasion to her maid, or to people who did not know the great gulphs of 150 kinds that are fixed between us, to prate. You can't imagine what a reserve there is in the manners of this house, nor how little there has been of gallantry towards her in the behaviour of all the men that have been here, young and old, as far as I have had occasion to observe.

Ld. Shelburnes carriage took her but one stage: there it waited (it was at Malmsbury) for Miss Fox, who is sent here from Warwick castle (you will excuse me but it really is the Earl of Warwicks castle, at Warwick and not Capt. Donnellan's) in exchange. Miss Fox is a little girl between 13 and 14: a sister and the only one of the present Ld. Holland who is about 9: consequently niece to Ch. Fox, and to Lady Shelburne, and great niece to the Dutchess of Bedford.[8] The D. of Bedford is now at this same Warwick castle: we shall hardly see him here, at least I shan't. She is very prettily made, and has already a very womanly sort of bosom I assure you; as much so as a certain friend of our's at Brompton[9] notwithstanding the difference of age. By the bye I have a letter from that same friend at Brompton, who is a saucy slut, and tells me of her being just going to write to you, and that she likes you as well, aye better than she does me. Ld. Shelburne introduced me to Miss Fox in a more particular manner than he did any body else, as 'a favourite of Miss Vernon's.['] We are very good friends; she too plays at chess: she is very fond of it, we play'd yesterday, and I suppose shall be

[8] This was Caroline Fox, born 3 November 1767, only surviving daughter of Stephen, 2nd Baron Holland and Mary, daughter of John, 1st Earl of Upper Ossory. Her brother, Henry Richard Fox, had succeeded to the barony in December 1774 when only just one year old. Lady Shelburne was her mother's sister; Charles Fox her father's brother.

[9] Miss Elizabeth Davies.

playing every evening. She seems a good natured pleasant kind of girl, but has not much to say for herself as yet, as you may imagine. Her face, I had like to have forgot her face, is far from an unpleasing one: but the form of it which is rather too long, a mouth which is the Fox mouth, and a set of teeth which though white are rather too large, save her from being a beauty.

On Friday at dinner we had again Mr. Bull and Capt. Onslow and now for the first time a Mr. Brooke[10] who was upon a visit to Mr. Bull. Brooke is or has been something in the law: probably at the Bar. I have a notion of having seen him taking notes in the K[ing]'s Bench: a little man dapper made with a sharp face. Capt. Onslow told me that Brooke had lately met the Q.S.P.'s at Bath drinking tea at Mr. Poole's, a man who is a son of Sergt. Poole's has a good fortune, but was once at the Crown Office with Abbot.[11] Brooke has a house some where in this country.

On Saturday there dined with us a Mrs. Johns.[12] Mrs. Johns was a sort of dependent of Lord S.'s first wife: lives gratis in a little house of my Lord's close by; is a methodist, comes a begging to great people for money to give ⟨to⟩ charity, is a conversible woman who has seen the world and has court connections. She has distributed money for the Queen: and though she has the dress and appearance of an upper servant has had correspondences with all manner of great people, and could be made use of /occasionally/ to find news about. This is the account Ld. S. was giving me of her.

On Sunday nothing happend that I recollect.

On Monday Ld. Dartry left us. It was he that pushed the bottle about and not Col. Barré: I beg the Colonel's pardon. He is a valetudinarian: finds it necessary to have a bottle a day in his guts is fond of religion, and of cards; does not know very well what to do with himself, hunts out oddities and knick-knacks, and frequents auctions.

On Tuesday in the morning Capt. Smith took his departure. He was once an E. India Director: has a house in Bloomsbury Square and another at Ashsted near Epsom. He found out that I was profoundly conversant in E. India affairs (you know how profoundly) offer'd me access to inedited Maps and Ms. of various kinds, and gave me pressing and repeated invitations to both /his/ houses, mentioning connections he had with people who were

[10] Not identified.

[11] Josiah Poole, son of David Poole, serjeant-at-law, who died in 1762. Josiah went up to Queen's College Oxford a little after Bentham, matriculating, aged 17, on 11 February 1763.

[12] Not identified.

philosophical men and would be glad to be acquainted with me. Shall I go? I can't tell. We'll talk about it. He wrote a pamphlet once on India affairs which Ld. S. had taken notice of as one he approved of mightily and never knew Smith to be the author till Monday night. It is entitled Observations on the present posture of affairs in India. 8vo. 17| |pp. | |[13]

The same morning Ld. Camden and Miss Pratt went off to Beckford's at Font-hill; but they return tomorrow or next day. Beckford I told you before was to have a grand fete the 27th or 28th upon his coming of age. Ld. Camden went yesterday in order to be before the fete I suppose on account of Miss Pratt's not being prepared for it in the articles of cloaths. Ld. Shelburne goes on Friday and returns the next day. Ld. Camden likes all these bustles: Ld. S. not: nor would he go, I believe, but in view of fixing or drawing young Beckford into his party. Between him and old Beckford the Alderman you know I suppose that there was an intimate connection.

This was the day Ld. S. was to give the second and last treat to his Corporation people: the first had been given since I have been here. Having missed that opportunity I was very glad of this occasion of being witness to such a scene. I accordingly went and dined at Calne with my Lord and Col. Barré. We drank tea at Mr Bull's and coming home found Mrs Dunning. She had left her husband at Bristol, and he is expected on Friday or Saturday. She plays the harpsichord most divinely. I have just been accom-⟨panying her⟩ [*some words obliterated.*] Well, but I must go down—Miss Fox is waiting for me. Parson Townsend came today to dinner; and now we shall probably settle a day for Ld. S. and Barré to go and dine with them: and that will probably fix the date of my departure from this place.

What do you think I heard from Barré yesterday in the Coach? That Mrs. Armested[14] had taken or bought Lady Tankerville's on

[13] Nathaniel Smith's *Observations on the present state of the East India Company and on the measures to be pursued for insuring the permanency and augmenting the commerce of the company further considered*, was published in 1771 and was followed by two more pamphlets on the same subject during the next two years.

[14] Elizabeth Bridget Cane (1751–1842), commonly known as Mrs Armistead, was one of the great courtesans of the decade from about 1770. Previously in the protection of the 3rd Duke of Dorset, by 1779 she had become the mistress of the 12th Earl of Derby, and for a short time in 1781–2, she was intimate with the Prince of Wales. Towards the end of 1783 she became the mistress of Charles James Fox, whom she eventually married in 1795. The house with thirty acres of ground which she bought at St Anne's Hill near Chertsey had belonged not to Lady Tankerville but to the Duke of Marlborough, who had acquired it from Lady Trevor and Lord Charles

St. Anne's hill: so that you will have her for a neighbour: who pays for it, whether Ld. Derby or the Prince I have not learnt. Send these two sheets to Davies as soon as you get a frank together with all the others which are not exclusively to yourself. The copying machine does [not do]

415

FROM MISS ELIZABETH PRATT[1]

29 September 1781

Sir,

Your ungentlemanlike behaviour, the last time I din'd at His Lordships did not pass unnotic'd, I am sir a Man of *honor* tho' I believe *you* did not think so, *Sir* behind the Lodge is a convenient place, where I shall expect you to give me Satisfaction for Winks, and Nods,—and in short sir behaviour that I don't understand and won't take tamely.—Swords, or Pistols, /chuse/ your weapon as they are equal to your humble and offended Servant

J. Brookes.

Calne Septr. the 29th.

By Seven oclock to morrow I shall be at the Place appointed.—No *seconds*.

416

TO JEREMIAH BENTHAM[1]

30 September–2 October 1781 (Aet 33)

Bowood Sept. 30th 1781 ½ after 10 at night
Sunday.

Hond. Sir

Today at dinner I had the favour of your's of the 29th,[2] which according to my calculation was yesterday. As to my not seconding

Spencer in 1778 (E. W. Brayley, *History of Surrey*, edited and revised by E. Walford, 4 vols., London, 1878–81, ii, 30).

415. [1] B.M. III: 240–1. Autograph. Docketed: '1781, September 29. Miss Pratt Bowood / to / I.B. ibid / Challenge given in / drollery under the / name of Brookes'.

416. [1] B.M. III: 244–5. Autograph. No address or docket. 'Alas! poor Clark!' is written upside down above the greeting.

Printed, Bowring, x, 110–12.

[2] Missing.

my last letter sooner, my own reproaches anticipated your's: but the fact is, it is with the utmost difficulty I have been able to find time for even this short tribute of duty whatever it may prove. All the time I can get in the morning before breakfast I find it absolutely necessary for my health to devote to exercise: nor is even that always enough: for between breakfast and dinner, even although there should be no party made for anything, I sometimes find it necessary to get on horseback and shake myself. It is but now and then that I have been able to get a morning ~~for~~ to bestow upon my book or on a few letters which for one purpose or other I have had occasion to write. After dinner, while the gentlemen are still at their bottle, I steal away to the library where I meet Lady Shelburne and wait on her to her dressingroom: there we have music of some kind or other, unless there happen to be ladies in the house who are not musically disposed; when the Gentlemen leave the dining room, or if the weather admitts of it have done walking, we meet them again in the library to drink coffee: after which, unless Lady Shelburne wants me to make one at whist, it is absolutely necessary I should be in readiness to play at chess with Miss Fox, whose cavaliere serviente I have been ever since she came here from Warwick castle in exchange for Miss Vernon. Our company consists at this present writing of the persons following: Ld. Camden, Miss Pratt and Mr. Pratt: Mr. Will. Pitt (Ld. Chatham's brother there are such a heap of Pitts it is necessary to distinguish.) Mr. Banks—(your Banks) ~~Mr. and Mrs. Dunning:~~ Col. Barré. Mr. and Mrs. Dunning. Mr. and Mrs. and 2 Miss Sturts (Sturt member for Dorsetshire): Miss Fox I have already mentioned. All these (Miss Fox excepted) are actually at supper. Mrs. Dunning came on Tuesday; she is just ready to fall to pieces: Mr Dunning today after dinner, very much fatigued with the hard work which you have seen and heard of. Mrs. Dunning is a perfect mistress of the harpsichord; and a very agreeable woman though not very young nor handsome: but that's Mr. D's concern not mine. Miss Pratt sings extremely well and plays on various instruments. She is lively, sensible, goodnatured, and has every accomplishment but beauty, in which however she is not remarkably deficient. Miss Fox is a sprightly goodnatured little girl not 14, but forward of her age: she too plays on the harpsichord.

Monday ½ after 10 at night

By tomorrow a whole posse of people will be gone: some of them to my very great regret: among these Mrs. Dunning and

Miss Pratt. Mr. and Mrs. Dunning went off in a violent hurry this morning under the apprehension of Mrs. D's being brought to bed: if it had not been for this accident, they would have staid some time. I had not an opportunity of exchanging ten words with him: so that I had not time to make an acquaintance with him, which was what for Mrs. D's sake much more than for his, I greatly coveted: Miss Pratt while she was here drew Miss Fox's picture, and has just been making me a present of it. Before Coffee was over they made me leave the company and come with them into Lady S.'s dressing room, where we very frankly avowed to one another our regrets at parting. There we had been about an hour, when Lady S. stole away from the company and staid /with us/ almost another hour, leaving the Sturts to take care of themselves. She took the precaution however to cut them out employment some at Cards some at chess, that they might not come and interrupt us. They are but odd sort of people: Miss Sturt has been suffered to fancy she plays in a superior manner on the harpsichord, without having the least notion of it. Would you have thought of my being in such favour with the ladies? yet so it is; and to crown all, it was under favour of a good word which was put in for me by Miss Vernon, notwithstanding all her reserve, that I first got the *entrées* of this same dressing room which I am so fond of.

Tuesday morning

This morning departed Ld. Camden and Miss Pratt, the Sturts, Will Pitt and Banks: it was the first time of Banks's being here. Mr. Pratt staid after the rest: but goes away tomorrow. Mr. Hamilton is expected in a day or two. It was at Font-hill t'other day, I believe, that Ld. Shelburne first met with Banks; and it was from seeing him with Pratt and Pitt who were come with him from Kingston Hall that he took occasion to invite him here. There he likewise saw Count Czernichef[3] and had some conversation with him; but did not invite him hither, though as he says he ought to have done it. It was rather odd he did not, considering the notice he takes of foreigners in general: the reason he mentioned was the awkwardness of having his Polish tutor with him. Some little time ago I had the pleasure of hearing of you from a Mr. Brookes[4]—oh, but you know that already. You know, I suppose, that I must be

[3] The reference to a tutor suggests that this was Count Grigoriy Ivanovich Chernyshëv (1762–1825), son of Count Ivan Grigor'yevich Chernyshëv, who had been Russian ambassador in England in the years 1768–70.

[4] He is mentioned above as Brooke, letter 414, p. 96.

at Oxford before the 17th,[5] and on what account. I have written to Poore[6] as he desired me. How I shall be disposed of in the mean-time I do not as yet exactly know: but my paper is at end. Pray send me back Wilson's letter.[7]

417

To George Wilson[1]

2–3 October 1781 (Aet 33)

Bowood Oct. 2nd 1781

It was a cursed foolish thing in me to set myself such a task as that of sending you a diary of every thing that passes here: and now I do not recollect where I left off. Oh, I think it was on Saturday that I dispatched my letter[2]; and I believe I told you of Banks's[3] coming in from Font-Hill with Pratt and Will Pitt.

Sunday Sept. 30th came in to dinner a whole heap of Sturts, like-wise from Font-hill: Mr. and Mrs. Sturt, Miss Sturt a girl about 17 or 18 and Miss Eliza Sturt about 11.[4] Banks, it appeared, is intimate in that family. After dinner came in Dunning, piping hot from Bristol.

Monday (yesterday) Oct. 1st. A party of us went to Methuen's at Cosham about 5 miles from this place to see his pictures: it is a famous collection made by Sr. Paul Methuen[5]: the family were not at home. They are at Ld. Boston's, who married a daughter of

[5] To support Charles Abbot's candidature for the Vinerian Scholarship. See letter 420.

[6] Edward Poore, a friend of Bentham of Oxford days—he matriculated from Queen's College, aged 16, in 1761—had been called to the bar at Lincoln's Inn in 1772 and subsequently practised on the western circuit. On him see letter 57, n. 2.

[7] Missing.

417. [1] B.M. III: 247–8. Autograph.
Addressed: 'George Wilson Esq. / Thorpe / near / Staines.' Postmark: '5 OC.'
Printed, Bowring, x, 112–13. For the enclosure, see n. 12.

[2] Missing.

[3] Henry Bankes, M.P. (1756–1834), of Kingston Lacey, Dorset, part-owner of the pocket borough of Corfe Castle; one of the young men who were beginning to group themselves under the political leadership of William Pitt. This passage may indicate that a portion of letter 414 is missing.

[4] Humphrey Sturt, M.P. (?1725–86), of Crichel More, Dorset, his wife, Mary, da. of Charles Pitfield, and his two eldest daughters, Mary and Eliza-Bizarre.

[5] The owner of Corsham at this time was Paul Methuen, M.P. (1723–95), who had inherited the estate from his cousin, the diplomat Sir Paul Methuen (1672–1757). His only daughter, Christian, was the wife of Frederick Irby, 2nd Lord Boston (1749–1825).

Methuen's: I should have said Methuen's daughter, as he has but one. The party consisted of Lady Shelburne, Ld. Camden Miss Pratt and Miss Fox in Ld. S's Coach: Pratt, Pitt, Banks and your humble servant on horseback. On our return, to my great mortification we found Mr. and Mrs. Dunning were set off for London. It was absolutely necessary: Mrs. Dunning and her maid were expecting every hour to fall to pieces.

Tuesday Oct. 2. In the morning before breakfast Ld. Camden and Miss Pratt went off for Hereford-shire: Banks and Pitt for Kingston-hall, Banks' house in Dorsetshire: the Sturts to their house which is 4 miles from Kingston-hall.

Wednesday Oct. 3. This morning before breakfast Pratt went off for Bath, where he is gone to cultivate his corporation:[6] so that there is nobody left but Barré and I. Sir E. Bayntun has been breakfasting here. One would think he came here as a spy of the court: for he always comes at breakfast, the time that people are collected together. This is at least the sixth time of his breakfasting with us since I have been here.

I see by the Dutch papers that are come today that the Dutch depair of saving their Prince William. That will be a great loss to them: as she is one of the most capital ships they have or can have, a 74.

Affairs seem to wear but a very unfavourable aspect in Minorca. Barré's character of Murray is that he is obstinate and wrong-headed, but brave to desperation.[7] He has seen a letter from Draper[8] to a person here who is a Government man. Draper says that the effective men in garrison are but 1800 regulars: /consisting upon Barrés computation of/ 2 battalions English, 3 of Hanoverians: upon paper 2400. The Spanish account speaks of 400 of the latter deserting: God forbid it should be true. Draper writes that with infinite perseverance he has succeeded in putting and keeping himself upon good terms with the general: but that he is the only man /in the island/ who is so: reckoning as well the army as the inhabitants. Barré who has been in the island speaks of Fort St. Philips as being excessively strong: the garrison cover'd every

[6] John Jeffreys Pratt had been returned for Bath at the general election of 1780. The franchise was confined to the members of the corporation.

[7] Lieutenant General James Murray (?1719–94), governor of Minorca. In August 1781 a combined French and Spanish force of 14,000 men, with naval support, besieged the British garrison at Port Mahon. By February 1782 Murray's forces had been so reduced by sickness that he was obliged to capitulate.

[8] Lieutenant General Sir William Draper, K.B. (1721–87) was lieutenant-governor of Minorca. He was at odds with Murray and was later reprimanded by a general court-martial for preferring unfounded charges of misconduct against him.

where in a surprizing manner: that the fault of it if it has any is that of its being over-worked: the souterreins so intricate, that a man must have a better head than the Governor to understand them.

This morning (Wednesday) I reced. your's of Saturday Sept. 29.

As to all that concerns my adventures in the family, and the footing I am upon, I must be as concise as possible: there would be no end in giving the details, and as these are things there is no danger of my forgetting, there is no occasion for it. What I fill my letters with in preference are anecdotes concerning persons, places, number, weight and measure, which relating to persons I have no personal acquaintance with and therefore making but a faint impression, might be lost if they were not quickly consigned to paper:[9] temporary ones more especially, as for example the foregoing. The greater part however are inevitably lost, either on account of their being but imperfectly heard (for my hearing is in reality very dull) or but imperfectly related, the relators having their reasons for not being perfectly explicit, or in short but imperfectly remembered. A disadvantage I labour under is the want of power to cross-examine. A thousand considerations intervene to limit the exercise of this power, which however I do exercise at least as much as is agreeable to the deponents: the fear of being troublesome: the fear of galling them, by obliging them either to give an answer apparently evasive, or to betray something which would subject them either to disrepute, or some other inconvenience.

Suffice it that I tell you in very general terms that with Dunning I could have no communication: there was no time for it; except a joke or two which the Devil tempted me to crack upon him immediately upon his coming in: with Ld. Camden, /I had/ but little, for reasons I will tell you at large: with Miss Pratt, who is a charming girl in every respect but beauty, pretty much: she has given me a sketch of Miss Fox in crayons, which she was two days about: it is not ill done considering, and has some resemblance: with Mrs. Sturt [*two words crossed out*] who is a good fine woman at the age of 42 after bearing 18 children 14 of whom are alive, I had a little ⟨flirtation⟩ but left her after seeing a little more of the ton of the family, which I did not like. With Sturt I had some general conversation, but saw nothing about him that made him very interesting to me. With Barré /although we have few ideas in common/ I am upon terms of some familiarity; owing to the good nature and companionable-

[9] See the enclosure to this letter and n. 12.

ness of the man Dunning's health seemed not so much amiss, notwithstanding the fatigue he underwent at Bristol. He had got up a good deal, before that happened to throw him back; and the morning he went away, he told me he had /already/ recover'd himself to a considerable degree. All these are heads for you to examine me upon: as such I set them down without farther particularity.

As to my health it is still but so so: but I promise myself something from the comfort and ease of Thorpe, and something more from the winter which seems to agree best with me. For a long time I had no notion of riding out, because my lord did not ask me: but at last I found out /that/ his reason for not asking people to ride out with him, was that all he rides out for is to superintend his workmen which takes up his whole attention for the time and is rather sitting on horseback than riding: since that I have taken heart of grace and rid out almost every day before breakfast, independently of casual excursions in company.

As to the D. of Bedford's being an opposition man, I understood as much from Ld. Shelburne.

I desire no reflections upon Miss Mercer[10]: it is the greatest satisfaction to me imaginable to hear of handsome girls falling in love with ugly fellows.

Alas poor Clark![11] Commend me to them and the St. Paul's; with whom I please myself with the thoughts of spending a comfortable day or two ere the month is out.

Enclosure[12]

Bowood, 28th September, 1781.

One of Lord Shelburne's channels of American intelligence, is through General Grey,[13] with whom he appears to be on a footing of some intimacy. Grey is, at present, at Plymouth, and from

[10] Perhaps the relation of an old friend of George Wilson (see letter 179).

[11] Alderman Richard Clark had been defeated in the recent by-election for a member of parliament for the City of London. See letter 406, n. 9.

[12] The following text is not known in manuscript and exists only in Bowring, x, 107b–110a. The style of this material differs from the personal chattiness characteristic of the letters to Wilson, and the content corresponds with Bentham's description in the letter above (at n. 9). Presumably Bentham wrote down these informative notes under the successive dates as the various points were gathered in conversation.

[13] General Charles Grey (1729–1807), cr. in 1801 Baron Grey de Howick, and advanced in 1806 as Viscount Howick and Earl Grey (the father of the prime minister). He had served in the British army in North America since 1776. His fairly regular correspondence with Shelburne is noted in H.M.C., *Sixth Report, appendix*, p. 239.

thence sends him letters which he (Grey) has received from America. Lord Camden was giving instances that have come very lately within his knowledge of the freedom used at the Post-office with letters that come from thence. In one letter, which he seemed to have seen, a part was actually cut out; but it was managed so clumsily, that what remained announced the contents of what was taken away. Lord S. was telling me, upon a former occasion, that there was a whole department in the office on purpose for that business.[14]

The same accounts still continue that we have heard before, of Clinton's eccentricities: that he shuts himself up for three or four days together, and is seen by nobody. It seems to be true that he has recalled Lord Cornwallis, either through jealousy or necessity. A paper received by Lord S. makes Washington upwards of 11,000 strong, including 4000, and, I think, *two* hundred French, but exclusive of militia: pieces of cannon, eighty-six. I saw the particulars in his hand; but I must not think of copying. There was a talk of 7000 or 8000 militia. Clinton was said to have about 9000 men that he could spare from posts and garrisons. Washington's vicinity straitened him, it is said, for provisions; and that was mentioned as the chief reason for his recalling Cornwallis.

When Lord Bristol came here, it was, as he said, to thank Lord Shelburne for favours; I mean the share he had in getting him the bishoprick. When the late Lord Bristol was Lord-lieutenant, the bishoprick being vacant, he got a promise of it from the king. Meantime, Lord Townsend succeeded; and he, regardless of his predecessor's promise, made interest for somebody else.[15] Lord Shelburne, when Secretary of State, reminded the king of his promise, and obtained the necessary document, which he sent over without delay. After this, Lord S. thought himself well entitled, upon the present occasion, to ask Lord B. for an Irish living, which he wants just now to satisfy the cravings of a man of Calne, who has a son a parson, and whose political chastity is assailed by Robinson of the Treasury.[16] Lord Bristol changed the discourse, and would not hear him. This is exact: having heard Lord S. repeat it two or

[14] On interceptions by the post office, see K. Ellis, *The Post Office in the eighteenth century*, 1958, pp. 60–77—in this context especially pp. 63–5.

[15] George William Hervey, 2nd Earl of Bristol (1721–75) was Lord Lieutenant of Ireland during 1766–7, but never visited the kingdom during his lieutenancy. He was the eldest brother of the 4th earl (see letter 403, n. 16 and 404). He was succeeded in Ireland by George Townshend, 4th Viscount Townshend (1724–1807), who held that office for five years.

[16] John Robinson, M.P. (1727–1802), one of the secretaries to the Treasury under Lord North, 1770–82, and in charge of political patronage.

three times, Barré says, and says it seriously, that now he has some chance; but that, had Lord B. promised, he would have none. Everybody seems to be agreed about two things: that he is touched in his noddle, and that he draws a long bow.

Lord Dartry says, the Irish exports, by the last accounts, were four millions a-year. Barré doubts, but Lord Dartry insists. Barré says he will write over to know.

Some time after Lord Hertford had been Lord-lieutenant of Ireland, umbrage had been taken by the House of Lords there at something relative to one of their clerks. Being closely interrogated, he confessed at length, with much agitation, that the profits of his place were not what they might seem to be; for that, on being appointed to it, he had been forced to undertake for paying so much to Lord Beauchamp, whether a gross sum or an annuity, I forget. The House, therefore, transmitted a state of the case, with a complaint, to be laid before his majesty. It came, as in course, to Lord Shelburne; he being then Secretary of State. Lord S., from a notion of decency, thought proper, before he presented it, to give notice to Lord Hertford. He, accordingly, wrote a note to Lord H., saying that he had some particular business which he wished to talk to him about, and that he would be glad either to wait on him or to receive his visit. Lord H., little thinking how nearly it concerned him, gave rather a cavalier answer, appointing Lord S. to wait on *him*. What passed afterwards was slurred over in an obscure way, as usual; but so it was, that the complaint was stifled (as Lord S. says he must acknowledge to his shame,) and never reached the king. This is odd enough; for how came the Lords, when they saw it stick, not to follow it up? This was told after dinner to-day, in presence of all the company, except the ladies. Lord Beauchamp, it was also said, rides an Irish bishop. This the bishop bolted out one day, out of patience with hearing himself accused of stinginess for not living up to the apparent value of his income.[17]

[17] Francis Seymour-Conway, 1st Earl of Hertford (1718–94), Lord Lieutenant of Ireland August 1765 to September 1766, was described by his successor, Lord Bristol, as 'an excellent solicitor', who 'has a constant appetite for all preferments for himself and family, with the quickest digestion and the shortest memory of past favours of any of the present noblemen of this moderate and reasonable age' (cited, Sir Lewis Namier and John Brooke, *The History of Parliament. The House of Commons, 1754–1790*, 3 vols., 1964, iii, 424). His heir, Francis (1743–1822), styled Lord Beauchamp, was for some years a member of both the Irish and the British Houses of Commons. On 12 March 1768 Lord Townshend reported to Shelburne, then a secretary of state, the odd case of the parliamentary clerk, Dr Gayer, who had confessed 'that he was under a point of honour to Lord Viscount Beauchamp' to pay any emolument he received in excess of £200 a year or session 'to a person unknown'. (*Calendar of Home Office Papers, 1766–69*, pp. 314–15, 553–4, and *Journal of the House*

Lord Dartry says, Penn,[18] the proprietor, is living in Philadelphia in a state of the utmost indigence. After paying rent-charges created in favour of younger children, etc., or what encumbrances there are, he does not receive so much as £200 a-year. This is what Lord Dartry is in a way to know; Lady Dartry being a great-grand-daughter of the first Penn's.

Saturday, September 29.

On Thursday, (27th,) pretty early in the morning, came from Bath a Mr. Hodgson:[19] he was kept to dinner; and Lord Shelburne, not to be bored with him, consigned him to my hands. He is going on a secret expedition, the destination of which appears clearly, from circumstances, to be some place in the narrow part of the Spanish main. He is to have the conduct of it, together with the command of a regiment, and is to embark in about a week from Falmouth. His business at Bath was to settle some matters relative to it with Knox, Lord G. G.'s secretary. Dealing in generals, he says it will be but a small affair at first, but he hopes it will swell to something greater: doubtless by the accession of Indian, or other malcontents, as you will see. From circumstances which it would take up too much time to enumerate, he was led to place a confidence in me; and even, however odd it may seem, to look up to me as a sort of protector; and, in consequence, he gave me, for me

of Lords (Ireland), iv (1753–70), pp. 461–3. In 1769 the Irish House of Lords approved a resolution that the moneys given up by Gayer had been applied to charitable purposes but resolved also that he was henceforth quit of any such engagement.

[18] The reference appears to be to Richard Penn (1735–1811), who, in 1775, had brought over the Continental Congress's 'Olive Branch' petition, and who by this time had returned to Philadelphia.

[19] Robert Hodgson (fl. 1748–90), formerly superintendent of the British settlements on the Mosquito Shore, 1749–76 (for his appointment see R. Pares, *War and Trade in the West Indies, 1739–1763*, 1936, p. 540, where he is, however, confused with his father). For the affair which ended his superintendency and involved him in a quarrel with his successor, James Lawrie, see his pamphlet, *The Defence of R. Hodgson*…, 1779, and R. White, *The Reply… of the principal inhabitants of the Mosquito Shore* …, 1780. The Board of Trade was plagued with this business for several years but refused to reinstate him (see *Journal of the Commissioners for Trade and Plantations from January 1776 to May 1782*, as index references). In 1780 Hodgson went to Jamaica to concert plans for raising the Mosquito Indians against the Spaniards as part of a British bid to secure control of the region of Nicaragua (H.M.C., *Stopford Sackville Mss.*, ii, 274–90, esp. 287–90). In 1781 he returned to England to make further arrangements and was given local military rank as a commander of the projected expedition; he had already been in touch with Shelburne about this earlier in the year (letter of 6 June 1781, noted H.M.C., *Fifth Report, appendix*, p. 246). Early in 1783 he was intercepted off the coast and taken captive by the Spaniards, together with a large file of military plans (J. T. Revello, 'Escritos hallados en poder del espía inglés Roberto Hodgson', *Boletin del Instituto de Investigaciones Hist.*, v (1926), 76–100).

to give to Lord S., two papers open, of which the following are extracts.

One is a copy of a letter to Lord Hillsborough, dated September 10, 1781, in which he speaks of his having been informed that he is again to be sent on service, and therefore desires Lord H. would witness for him to Mr. Knox of the truth of the following particulars:—

'1*st*, That the first matter which brought him to his lordship's notice was a survey he took,' (when employed as an engineer,) 'of all the Spanish coast, from Honduras to Puerto Bello, together with a geographical account of it; which,' says he, 'were put into your lordship's hands, and I never made any other use of them.

'The next was the manner in which I ventured, against every local opposition, to execute the 17th article of the peace, by which I gained the time for your lordship's interposition in favour of the Mosquito shore to have its effect—that of saving it to the crown.'

He then speaks of 'the manner in which he afterwards undertook the *superintendency* of that country; that he was asked to go; that some time after, when he had again come into his lordship's hands, he made no hesitation, at his lordship's instance, at leaving his military commission behind him, and going out in a manner which his lordship thought better for the public service.' The case was, I suppose, that the treaty did not allow his going out in a military character, and so he was to *hug* the Indians underhand. He talked to me about the open house he used to keep for the Indians.

That after his accepting his 'letter of instructions,' his lordship presented his memorial to the king, for military rank.

Lastly, that he was turned out of his superintendency in the manner stated in a letter to Mr. Knox, which he encloses. I should have said, he began with observing, that what Knox himself could know of him was little more than that, as far as his conduct had relation to the late sad Nicaragua expedition, it had been satisfactory. (In talking, after dinner, he computed the loss in men to be 4000, including what were lost with Walsingham; and in money £500,000.)

In the other letters to Knox, dated July 28, 1781, he refuses having any concern in the expedition in question, with one Lawrie, who appears to be the present superintendent. He says, that Lawrie is ignorant and incapable; that he has been labouring under a proclamation, under the great seal of Jamaica, for forgetting his allegiance, and erecting a new government; and was also officially accused by 'him (Hodgson) to the Secretary of State, of rebellion.'

That Lawrie got Hodgson turned out of that place, and himself put into his room, by alleging that he was absent from his duty, and so the country left without a superintendent; when, in truth, not only was he there all the time alleged, both before and after, but another person was sent by the king to be his '*locum tenens*,' in case of his 'coming home to give informations;' and that Lawrie had imposed upon the Board of Trade, (on that or some other occasion,) 'as an answer from Hodgson to his memorial, a paper written a year before that memorial.'

H. is to write Lord S. an 'account of his expedition,' and there is a chance of his letters being addressed (enclosed at least) to me.

Hodgson told me he was first of all taken up by Lord Shelburne, but what appointment he got from him at first does not appear. Afterwards, he says, he was to have been the man with whom, in connexion with Macleane, the business was to have been managed with the Marquis d'Aubarede; but, upon examination it was found that d'Aubarede had undertaken far too much, and that he had not the credit with the people he pretended to have.

October 3d.

Upon mentioning this to Lord S., a day or two ago, as what Hodgson had told me, he did not directly confirm it; but he denied it in such a manner as made me rather conclude it to be true. Speaking of him in company, Lord S. said, he had given him a little place, but did not mention what. He must have meant, I think, the superintendency Hodgson mentioned in his letters. Lord S. says, he is a little maddish; it may be so, but I see nothing but what appears to me full as sober and consistent as anything about his lordship. His writing, indeed, is bad, but his discourse is better. His knowledge seems to be pretty extensive, and his observations just —his constitution is of iron; which is a capital point in the service he is to go upon. He went once to Omoa with a flag of truce: thirteen men whom he had with him all died. Another time, of three who went out hither, not one came back. I asked Lord S. whether there was anything against him; he said no. Yet, although he has constantly corresponded, which is all that a man in that situation could do, he seems not to be in favour.

418

To Jeremiah Bentham[1]

6 October 1781 (Aet 33)

Honoured Sir

A word or two just to acknowledge the receipt of your kind letter a day or two ago.[2] I have been in daily expectation of doing it in person: but I have been waiting for Mr. Townsend who has been expected here ever since Tuesday, in order to settle with him the time of my going over to his house. I write now, ~~because~~ foreseeing that I shall not be able to wait on you tomorrow (indeed being Sunday it would not answer one of my purposes) nor probably on Monday. Will you be kind enough to lend me that letter I wrote to you last?[3] I mean the whole sheet; in which there is nothing I think that I need have any scruple about shewing to my friends, Wilson or Davies. I have thoughts of getting it copied at Mr Davies's to send to Sam, to whom any thing of that sort would be a treasure.

We are as quiet here as mice—Nobody left but Miss Fox and Col. Barré—Mr. and Mrs. Hamilton of your city have been here for 4 or 5 days—They left us but this morning.

Yesterday came a letter from Sam[4]—which I believe I shall enclose.

My hearty congratulations to my Mother on Charles' honourable success—[5]

Yours dutifully and affectionately
Jeremy Bentham

Bowood
Oct. 6. 1781.

418. [1] B.M. III: 249–50. Autograph. Docketed by Jeremiah Bentham: 'Fils Jy Jy B. L. Datd. Bowood / Oct. 6 1781.'

[2] Missing.

[3] Letter 416.

[4] Samuel's packet dated 10/21 July 1781, received at Bowood on 5 October, B.M. III: 196–8, part of which is printed as letter 397.

[5] His unopposed election to the Vinerian Scholarship.

419

To George Wilson[1]

7 October 1781 (Aet 33)

Bowood Oct. 7. 1781

Your's of the 29th of Septr.[2] I think I acknowledged in my last, which I believe was dated Wedn. 3d instant:[3] since then nothing very particular has occurred in this place. That same day I think it was, came Hamilton (of Payne's-hill) and his wife from Bath:[4] Ld. Shelburne sent his carriage for them; and sent them back yesterday. Hamilton has been giving his assistance in laying out the grounds here. He is an old man of 75 or 76, and is besides very much afflicted at times with the stone: but this time he was very cheerful and alert. There came at the same time a Mr. Tonge or Tongue,[5] who has no connection with them; but as it happen'd came and went on the same day with them. An insipid insignificant man, who lives at Bristol: I could perceive no other bond of connection than the circumstance of his having once rented a house about a mile from Ld. Shelburne's which his Lordship has just pulled down.

On Thursday came General Johnson, a neighbour of Ld. Shelburne's: he is Equerry to The King, and had been in waiting.[6] He is an old man, is deaf at times, and has got the nick-name (so I learnt by accident) of Old Sulky. He travels in a leathern conveniency of the same name. The account he gives of Governor Murray quadrates very exactly with that which Barré was giving; and being a government man may the better be depended upon. He has a son there, to whom he acknowledges that Murray has been very kind, and that there does not appear to be anything of passion to corrupt his judgement.

419. [1] B.M. III: 251. Autograph. No docket or address, but from internal evidence clearly to George Wilson, and so printed by Bowring (x, 113–14).

[2] Missing.

[3] Letter 417.

[4] See letter 401, n. 11.

[5] Not identified.

[6] Probably lieutenant general James Johnston, colonel of the 11th regiment of dragoons (d. 1795). He appears to have been an equerry continuously since 1761. As this office required periodic attendance at court, identification of its holder with his namesake, lieutenant general James Johnston (c. 1721–97), colonel of the 6th regiment of dragoons, seems less likely, since this man was lieutenant-governor of Minorca from 1763 to 1774 (*The Yale Edition of Horace Walpole's Correspondence*, ed. W. S. Lewis, ix, 245, n. 1 and 28 n.).

Since my last I have reced. a letter from Q.S.P. at Bath,[7] in which (blessed be God therefore) he tells me there will be no occasion for me to go to Oxford, for that C. Abbot has no competitor, and looks upon himself as sure. I had asked him about the price of ratteen cloth, which I had heard from Barré was as cheap there as Broad-cloth in London, viz 18s.: Q.S.P. upon inquiry confirmed that idea, and in the overflowings of his affection offer'd me a coat of it as a Bath present: so away go I on cock-horse to Bath tomorrow morning to be measured for it. I shall return in the afternoon.

A day or two ago I received a letter from Sam, dated Catherineburgh and Nigni-Taghill.[8] The bad news it contains is that he has lost a portable Barometer and gold to the value of £13 or 14 by the breaking of a phial of quicksilver by the overturning of a trunk: the good news that the model of his plane-engine is finished, and 'succeeds to the satisfaction of every body.['] The Engine itself would have been finished but for a vacation of 6 weeks which the workmen have on account of the harvest; the time for which in that country being short requires as many hands as can be muster'd.

I wait only for Parson Townsend to quit this place. I can not think what is become of the man—he leaves me in an ⟨awkw⟩ard predicament—he was to have been here on Wednesday ⟨There⟩ is now nobody but Miss Fox and Col. Barré. Adieu—I send you a frank for Davies.

420

From Charles Abbot[1]

9 October 1781

Dear Jerry,

Having of no Opposition I am very glad that I can spare all my out-lying friends the trouble of coming hither to vote.

With many thanks for your good wishes believe me ever

Sincerely and faithfully
Yours
Chas Abbot.

Ch. Ch. Oxon
Octr. 9th 1781.

[7] Missing.

[8] B.M. III: 196–8, partly printed as letter 397.

420. [1] B.M. III: 252. Autograph. Docketed by Bentham: '1781 Oct 9 / C. Abbot Oxford / to / I. B. Bowood [written over Thorpe] / Election sure / Reced at Thorpe'

421

To Miss Elizabeth Davies[1]

12–17 October 1781 (Aet 33)

Oct. 12. 1781 10 o'clock.

Here am I at a place called Beckington[2] in the road from Bath to London, as also in the road from Bath to Oxford, and having nothing else to do, it comes into my head that I may as well write to you. This morning I left Bowood to seek my fortune: found two Bath Coaches full (I mean Coaches from Bath to London) took a Post chaise at Calne and came to this place which is 6 or 7 miles from it. I am bound for Thorpe. All the Coaches that go to London before night being full, I am just stepping into a Coach that goes from Bath to Oxford, which latter place it reaches by 7 in the evening. Providence has therefore order'd it that I shall spend this evening with my friend Abbot of Christchurch college, who little expects me.[3] I have parted very good freinds with the people at Bowood, a thing which I cannot but wonder at, considering that it was politics that first brought us acquainted, at the same time that according to the discoveries we have reciprocally made nothing can be more opposite than [*two or three words faded*] as to every thing that concerns present measures—This is incorrect, and will not convey the meaning I wish it should, but I have not time to set it right. But as a proof that we are well together, one of the last things my Lord said to me was, 'you will leave nobody here who does not love and admire you.'[4] He has given me a letter to Ld. Fitzmaurice /at London/ that I may be acquainted with him before the family come from Bowood, and charged me to come and dine with them as soon as ever they come to town. I have hurt my finger: therefore don't be surprized if my writing is not quite so elegant as usual.

421. [1] B.M. III: 253–4. Autograph.
Addressed: 'Miss Davies.'

[2] Although Bentham's rendering of this name reads clearly enough, the place he meant is Beckhampton, where the Bath–London road is crossed by the road from Devizes to Swindon.

[3] I.e., his step-brother, Charles Abbot.

[4] Bentham long afterwards, in 1828, in a memorandum concerning his 'intercourse with the Lansdowne family', wrote of the visit to Bowood which had just ended: 'Those days with the exception of a few months passed in the same company about eight years afterwards, were the happiest of my life.' (B.M. XVII: 26).

Thorpe Monday Oct. 15th.

I got here on Saturday evening about 7. It was quite dark before I reached Oxford on Friday: the town pretends to be lighted and paved upon the plan of London: but the lighting is very indifferently performed: however there was just light enough to enable me to patch up some sort of recollection of the old place, where so much of my youth was idled away. I had learnt by that time that the only Coaches that would suit me in point of time for the purpose of reaching this place before night set out at 8 the next morning: so that I could not have much time for looking about me; unless I made a day of it, which I was determined not to do, since in that case there would be no avoiding a multitude of sanglierical visits. In the remainder of the evening added to what little I could make up by good husbandry out of the morning I got time enough to see whatever there was new in the appearance of the town without breaking my incognito: the public observatory, a new bridge or two, and the principal of the new houses. I got to Slough about ½ after 4: after dining on the road. Slough is about 20 miles from London, the nearest place of any upon that road to Egham. I had no other baggage with me than my fiddle case and a hat box with a little linen in them. I thought to have taken a post chaise at Slough: but to my surprize I found there were none kept in the place. So I left my baggage at an Inn there, and /had the plea of/ necessity for following my own original inclination, which was to march on foot. The main body of my luggage I had left in the great trunk which you saw under the care of Monsieur Fombel my Lord's Valet de chambre to be sent after me to Slough by the Bath Waggon which is to reach Slough this evening Wednesday 17th: and by way of disposing the people at Slough to take the more care of it, it was my intention to have taken a post-chaise from thence: but Providence order'd it otherwise. God send it safe to me tomorrow: I spoke to a man at Slough to dispatch it to me here; provided it came into his hands: it is directed to be left at an Inn which as I found had been shut up these two years.

Did you ever see a prettier letter about nothing at all written by a man with a lame hand? You won't be able to make out one word of it out of ten: you must get the mother of you to decypher it.

You must absolutely learn chess: it is all the *ton*, for persons of all ages and both sexes: yes, you must; were it only to play at it with my handsome young Lord with a hard name, who, they say, is very fond of it. The plan is at present, if it does not change, for him to spend some little time at Chatham, in lodgings which must be found out for him: if so you may see him often. This your father and mother will like much; for his gentleman, I understand, is a shentleman of Wales and plays upon the Welsh Harp most notably: as to you, who are a poor tasteless creature that does not love music, he may strum his fingers off, and you not care any thing about the matter.

Hark ye, young woman, now I think of it, I have a job for you: what shall I give you now to copy out all the letters that have been sent you since I went to Bowood, this included, that I may send a copy to Siberia? I have told Sam I would get it done for him if I could. As to the originals I can not send them; for Wilson claims them as his property. /You must write small, and get the thinnest paper that is to be had./ Well, but I have written enough to you with my lame hand and so, good b'w'ye to you. My finger, (the third finger of my right hand) is crooked, and I am under some apprehension it will remain so: it was at first /very black and/ very much swelled; but the swelling as well as the blackness is /now/ almost gone off. How did it come? Why, my horse got his foot entangled in the curb-rein: and when I went to lay hold of it in order to disengage him, he gave a violent jerk with his head which wrenched my finger on one side.

Don't wonder at the rumpled state in which you will find this paper: I have been carrying it about in my pocket for this week.

Thorpe Wednesday evening: Oct. 17th.

Wilson desires his Compliments. I stay here till Novr. 4th.

422

To the Earl of Shelburne[1]

18 October 1781 (Aet 33)

October 18, 1781.

Since my arrival at my 'villa,' (a subject on which the public prints have been scandalously silent,) I have been honoured with

422. [1] Bowring, x, 114–15. The original is not at Bowood and has not been traced. The care which Bentham devoted to his correspondence with Shelburne at this time is attested by the existence of a draft of this letter, not corresponding exactly with the text as printed, but not departing materially from it in context (B.M. III: 255). A copy by Bowring is at U.C. ix: 93.

two testimonies of your lordship's kind attention.[2] In the first I am told that 'all Bowood desire to be remembered by me:' as if any part of Bowood could ever cease to be remembered by me, while gratitude, or any quality I could ever value myself on, remained in me. In the latter, I am informed that my 'Bowood friends are impatient to know how my hand does.' These reproaches, as they might seem if literally taken, for not writing, may, I think, upon the fairest and least flattering interpretation, be construed into a permission to write. In this light I avail myself of them: for without some especial warrant, my lord, I should hardly have ventured to have given you any trouble with my pen, in addition to the unconscionable bond which particular circumstances, and the kind injunctions on your lordship's part, which they gave birth to, were the means of my laying on 'all Bowood' by my company. I had indeed, as I have still, a pretence for writing in store, which I treasure up accordingly: I mean the commission I was honoured with to Colonel Skene;[3] but it may be some time yet before I may have anything to say to your lordship on that subject. The time of doing it, I take for granted, is not very material, so as it be in the course of three weeks or a month; that is, till your lordship comes to town at the meeting of parliament. I shall, therefore, look upon myself as being at liberty, as things stand at present, to defer going thither myself for a week or ten days, by which time I hope to have put off the guise of an invalid. At present, though I make with some difficulty such use of my hand as your lordship sees, it is still so tender that I am obliged to attend to every motion I make. If, however, any reason should occur to your lordship, for wishing me to see the colonel sooner, any intimation to that effect shall be obeyed the instant I am apprized of it. In the meantime, I have written to Mr. Hodgson to inquire where Colonel Skene is to be met with. Having no answer, I suppose he had left London before my letter got there. I am concerned for the poor captain:[4] henceforward, should he ever feel bold enough to mount again, your lordship, in order to act the more completely the part of the good Samaritan, would do well, I think, to 'set him upon your own

[2] Missing.

[3] Philip Skene (d. 1788), colonel 69th foot, perhaps associated with Robert Hodgson (see letter 417, n. 19) in his Caribbean schemes. He distinguished himself while on active service in the West Indies in the following year and received promotion to major-general in 1783. The business to which the following passage relates concerned Shelburne's brother (see letter 423).

[4] Captain Blankett was seriously indisposed, apparently as a result of a riding accident (see also letter 423). It appears that this piece of news was contained in one of Shelburne's two missing letters.

beast,' meaning either Lord Abingdon's or Mr. Miller's: upon either of these he would be comparatively safe; for, granting that he might stand a chance of stumbling every other step, yet I have too good an opinion of their prudence to suppose that either of them could ever be prevailed upon to rise to a pace sufficient to make a tumble serious.

As to the fiery courser which stands at present dignified by his name, I would humbly propose that he be new christened; and that some man of skill and spirit—myself, for example—be pitched upon for his godfather; in which case, I would further move, that an act of oblivion be passed at Bowood, forbidding, under the severest penalties, everything that could tend to revive the memory of the Corsham expedition.

I beg my most respectful compliments to Lady S. and Miss F.; it would be a most flattering circumstance to me, if I could persuade myself that they, or either of them, were actually, as well as virtually, included under 'all Bowood;' and that they or either of them—I speak as a lawyer—took any distinct and individual part in the kind remembrances that were sent me. I am particularly anxious to know whether Miss F. has found anybody to give check to since the only man she could depend upon in that way has had the misfortune to quit her service; whether, for example, the gallant colonel, after the rebuff I was witness to, has ever mustered up courage to face her during any of the truces of the cribbage table. If I have entertained anything like a wish on the affirmative side, it must be acknowledged to be an effort of the highest generosity, the colonel being too formidable a rival not to destroy any chance I might otherwise have of procuring an odd corner in her memory. Missing the chess-board, it is possible that, for a week or so, she might be led to bestow a straggling thought upon the once happy man who used to sit on the other side of it.

423

From the Earl of Shelburne[1]

1 November 1781

B.P. Thursday Octr. 31 1781

Dear Mr. Bentham

I have only a moments time to obey your commands and send you the Inclos'd by Col. Barré—If you chuse it, you may give it to be printed, provided you can answer for its being return'd to me within a fortnight.

I have many thanks to return to you about my Brother's business[2]—I never meant to give you the trouble of seeing Col. Skeene—your writing what I dictated to Mr. Hodgeson is fully sufficient—I return you his Letter.

Blankett intends answering your Letter,[3] as soon as he thinks himself well enough. When that will be does not seem certain—I can answer for every body else without their writing that they would be very ready and very happy to prove the regard and good Wishes with which We all are

Your Faithfull
Servants
Shelburne

423. [1] B.M. III: 258–9. Autograph. Docketed by Bentham: '1781 Nov. 1 / Ld. Shelburne Bowood / to / I.B. Linc. Inn / Sends Necker's pamphlet.' Shelburne headed the letter, 'B.P. Thursday', and the dating was added later, perhaps by Bentham. 1 November fell on Thursday.

This letter discusses the business mentioned in Bentham's letter to Shelburne of 18 October (letter 422) but is not a direct answer to it—rather, it suggests the existence of an intervening exchange of letters now missing, the last of which had just been received by Shelburne. Necker's pamphlet was presumably a copy of the *Compte Rendu.*

[2] Thomas Fitzmaurice (1742–93), of Llewenny Hall, Denb. He was in business on a considerable scale at Llewenny as a linen merchant and linen bleacher.

[3] Missing.

424

FROM SAMUEL BENTHAM[1]

16/27 February–15/26 April 1782

Kiachta[2] 16 Feby. 1782.

I send from this place to Petersbourg by 2 different Couriers 3 parcels each sewed up in rawhide. One of them consists /only/ of a box of tea containing I suppose about 12 pounds. This I have beg'd the favour of Sir James Harris to send by a Courier or the first other opportunity to Ld. Shelburne. The other two parcels I have desired to be sent to Queen's Square Place. One of these 2 parcels consists of 1st /a box of/ About 10 pounds of green tea, 2d a box of about 7 pounds bohee tea, 31y, a box of Rhubarb the very best that could be picked out of the whole stock in the magazines here. 4th a small cannister of tea of about a pound. 5, 2 small boxes of indian Ink and larger sticks without a box. These two large boxes of tea I would wish to be divided equally between my mother and you. My mother I would at the same time desire to give Farr

424. [1] B.M. III: 285–6. Autograph. Bentham docketed this letter twice; first, '1782 / April 15/26 / April 12/13 / Feb. / S.B. Kiachta / and Irkutsk / to / I.B. Linc. Inn. / Collections sent', and, second, '1782 / April 15/26 / S.B. Nerchink / and Irkutsk / to / I.B. Linc. Inn / Priv. Code.'

Addressed: 'Jere[y] Bentham Esqr. / Lincoln's Inn / London', and redirected, 'At Mrs. Davies's / Brompton / Near Chatham.' Postmark: '16 / OC.'

Samuel filled up the pages of this double sheet of notepaper at different dates, but not in order on the pages. Between mid-February and mid-April his journeyings had taken him as far east as Nerchinsk, in what is now Chitinskaya Oblast of the U.S.S.R., a silver mining settlement on the Shilka river, a tributary of the Amur.

Since September 1781, when Samuel had dispatched letters 408 and 409 he had written further letters to Bentham on 20/31 October 1781, 2/13 December 1781 and 2/13 January 1782 (B.M. III: 257, 268–9, and 278–80). Throughout this period Bentham's letters to him were miscarrying, and his own therefore contain little reference to Bentham's activities. He stayed at Perm during October to witness the institution of the new mode of provincial government: 'On the 12th these Ceremonies began, on the 18th they finished,' he wrote. 'I keep as exact a journal as possible of what passes from which I shall be able to give you shortly some account of the good effects of the introduction of this new mode of Jurisdiction and some observations on different branches of the laws themselves.' This promised account does not seem to have been sent. On 2 January, about to depart from Yekaterinburg (Sverdlovsk) for Tobolsk on the start of his journey into Central Siberia, and having heard nothing from Bentham since a letter written the previous July, he inquired: 'Can you as yet determine when *your work* according to its enlarged plan will be compleat? Is it possible some copies may find their way to Petersbourg by this time twelve month?'

[2] Kiachta, otherwise Kyakhta, is located at 51° N., 106° 50′ E., south of Lake Baykal, north of the present boundary between the U.S.S.R. and Outer Mongolia. It had been established as a Russian frontier fortress in 1728.

and Charles some of her share, and you give my Uncle or Cousin and my other freinds with whom you have more intercourse parts of your share. The small cannister may be better sent either to my Cousin or to any other of my freinds who live at the greatest distance from town as it is already securely packed up. The Rhubarb to my father at his disposal only that I beg him to be *bountifull* to Farr. I have packed it up as securely as I thought might preserve it from all injuries during its journey, and I trust apothecary's hall can but very rarely if ever furnish such choice pieces. The indian ink to be given where it will be most acceptable.

The other parcel consisting only of one box I wish you to take into your possession, as some part at least of the contents is more likely to be to the taste of your acquaintance than of my father's. Not however that I mean that you should give away the contents of this box as I have nothing more of the sort.

The 2 sorts of black silk you may make breeches waistcoats etc. of, one sort may serve for winter, the other for summer, I have cut off a part from each for that use. You will find also in this box a small wooden box of tea of a sort not to be purchased here, but made me a present of by a lady as a great rarety. This you may take in your pocket when you go to drink tea with any of our freinds and give them a taste of it, provided always that it proves better than ordinary tea ...[3]

I have full employment here in acquiring information about the Kamtschatka trade which is under the direction of this Government, and compleating my information about Nerchinsk and the connection with the Chinese.

Do above all things let me know immediately when for certain I can receive at Petersbourg some copies of a translation of your 'Principles of Jurisprudence' I think that is the title or tell me if you have any other work in hand which may be acceptable here. I have not received a letter from you since October last. The last was dated July 1781.[4] If you write about nothing else tell me how your works go on. Be *ye but as happy as I hope to be*!

Irkutsk April 15th

I send by the same Courier who takes this letter to Petersbourg two more parcels which I shall desire some of my freinds there to send by sea to you...[5]

[3] A passage of about 150 words relating to a sample of 'fossile alkali' is omitted.

[4] Missing.

[5] A passage of about 350 words relating to the contents of these packages—mineral specimens from the region of Nerchinsk—is omitted. Samuel informed his brother

I think of reaching Petersbourg not before the winter.

If it should so happen that you have acquaintance by whose means you could procure some English minerals in consideration of a promise of furnishing them with some from this country they would be wonderfully acceptable at Petersbourg.

425

TO LORD ASHBURTON[1]

3 June 1782 (Aet 34)

My Lord

The book /printed sheets/ herewith inclosed waits upon your Lordship at the desire of Ld. Shelburne. (He) /who/ had the patience to read them over with me last summer at Bowood: ~~where I was one of a crowd whom your Lordship's and Lady Ashburton's precipitated departure consigned to disappointment.~~ /Since then he has/ He had frequently intimated to me his wishes that it might (have the honour of coming) /come/ under your Lordship's eye: /and/ Last Tuesday ~~he repeated them in a manner too peremptory to be resisted~~ in particular he desired I would /myself send ◫/ furnish

◫Take upon me to

that a further twelve sets of his collections would be dispatched by water. Meanwhile, of the three sent he was to keep one, Pole Carew should have a second, and he might dispose of the third as he pleased.

425. [1] U.C. CLXIX: 124. Autograph. Draft, much corrected.

On Dunning (now Lord Ashburton) see letter 403, n. 9. Bentham had met him briefly at Bowood the previous summer but had had no opportunity for extended conversation—and if Shelburne had then hoped to have Dunning read and assess the incomplete printed proofs of the *Introduction* he was disappointed—because Mrs Dunning's advanced state of pregnancy caused them both to leave Bowood within forty-eight hours of Dunning's arrival (letters 416 and 417). Since that time Dunning had become Chancellor of the Duchy of Lancaster with a peerage, and he had been brought into the cabinet as Shelburne's chief legal adviser in the unharmonious ministry formed by Rockingham in March 1782. No collection of Ashburton's papers is known to survive and there is no acknowledgement from him in Bentham's papers, but this letter, the next, and the printed sheets of the *Introduction* were presumably sent, since Bowring (x, 124) records seeing a memorandum made by Bentham to the effect that the proof sheets were neither acknowledged nor returned.

This draft proves that Bentham's memory was at fault when, many years later, in the historical preface to the *Fragment on Government*, he stated that Shelburne had (according to his own admission) put the *Introduction* into the hands of both Camden and Dunning during the autumn of 1781 and had visited him in London not long after his return from Bowood to tell him that neither had found it very comprehensible. Shelburne may have made this comment, but not earlier than the summer of

your Lordship with a copy without delay.[2] Thus much, /my Lord,/ I thought necessary to apologize /account/ for the liberty I take in sending your /putting into/ ~~Lordships~~ hands a book /which is not only/ without beginning or end:⊞[2] circumstances which I reminded him of but without effect /which he was/ pleased to overrule. The approbation of (so discerning /enlightened/ a judge as) Ld. Ashburton would /indeed of course/ naturally have been one of the first objects of, my ambition: but /if left to myself ⊞/ ~~I should not of myself have chosen so premature a period for becoming a candidate for that honour~~ /I inclose in another paper[3]/ A short account of the views with which it was written /as well as/ ~~and~~ of the undertaking of which it makes a part.⊞ I take the liberty /also/ of inclosing a pamphlet ~~which made its appearance~~ written three or four years ago upon the spur of the occasion (relative to) on the ~~occasion~~ /subject/ of a measure of detail which happened to come /then/ upon the carpet (three or four years ago.)[4] This and an anonymous ~~pamphlet called~~ book entitled a Fragment on Government /of which I have no copies left/ is all I have yet ventured to /make/ (lay before the) public.

P.S.

~~Of the sheet which contains from p.p. 313 to 320 inclusive there exists no other copy and /than the loose proof sheet herewith inclosed: and/ the press has been manuscript has been long ago destroy'd and the press broke up.~~ Of the loose /proof/ sheets herewith inclosed there exists no other copy either in print or manuscript than this, which your Lordship will therefore have the goodness to preserve.[5]

⊞~~and~~ /but/ which must undergo several alterations before it sees ~~presented to the public~~ /faces/ the light /the public eye/.

⊞[2] I should certainly not have /thought it advisable/ ~~proper prudent declared myself a candidate for it at so premature a period~~ produced my titles to that honour is so imperfect a condition

⊞To contrast /in some measure/ with that dry cargo of /speculative/ general metaphysics.

1782. Although this document bears no date, its form and content leave little doubt of its being a covering letter to the more detailed statement which constitutes letter 426.

[2] This is interesting evidence of continued contact between Shelburne and Bentham during the first half of 1782.

[3] Letter 426.

[4] I.e. his *View of the Hard Labour Bill.*

[5] If the page numbers in the crossed-out version of the postscript are relevant, this passage refers to the second last proof sheet of the *Introduction* as set up in print by

426

To Lord Ashburton[1]

3 June 1782 (Aet 34)

My Lord

The ~~other~~ sheet which is in a (hand) different /hand/ ~~from my~~ own contains a prospectus of my plan as it stood ~~as little~~ about a year ago; since which ~~[...?] it has /unavoidably/ undergone /a variety of/ considerable~~ /a number of/ alterations have unavoidably taken place in it.[2]

As the distinction between the penal branch of the law and the civil is so familiar, I had all along taken for granted that the line of separation between those objects might be traced within the compass of a page or two. When I came to make the experiment, I found that this /such/ separation could scarcely be said as yet to exist: and that to set up one of my own in such manner as to answer as nearly as possible the purposes for which the /verbal/ distinction /in words/ is made, would involve a multitude of problems of the most intricate kind which nobody /seem'd/ ~~had~~ hitherto ~~seems~~ to have thought of solving. I found in short that the substance /matter body/ of the penal law was /almost/ inextricably interwoven with the civil on one hand and the constitutional on the other: and it became necessary to carry /pervade/ my eye through the whole mass of /the/ law in every direction in order /ere

November 1780. The corrected version of the postscript suggests that Bentham decided to cut the proof sheet into separate pages before sending his packet. Although there is no other evidence to support the conclusion, it would appear as if the last pages of the *Introduction* written up to that date were never printed off, and therefore, if (as stated in n. 1) these pages were never returned to Bentham, the passages they contained must have been re-written and reset later.

426. [1] U.C. CLXIX: 125–8. Autograph. Draft, much corrected. Sheet 125 crossed through with a pencil line.

Pages one and four of the double foolscap sheet forming document 126 both bear at the top what appears to be Bentham's own ascription: 'I.B. to Ld. Ashburton', with the date: '1782 June 3.' The subject matter indicates that this letter is close in date to letter 425, and its general character and the unprefatory nature of the opening paragraph suggest that it was the 'another paper' to which reference is there made. It is of exceptional interest as an indication of the way in which, about 1782, Bentham envisaged the development of his study of jurisprudence; on this see the introduction to *Of Laws in General*, edited by H. L. A. Hart in *CW.*

[2] Missing. This was evidently a prospectus for Bentham's 'Plan of a Penal Code', similar to that sent to Russia in the autumn of 1780 (*Correspondence*, ii, pp. 488–9, n. 18).

I could/ to disentangle /from the rest/ the part to which I had at first originally intended to confine myself. By this means what I had originally designed for sections to the chapter which your Lordship will find unfinished, grew to such a bulk as to be /some of them/ almost too big for chapters. I had however the satisfaction of finding that ⊞ ~~the introduct~~ (which I had ~~would~~ /thus/ written) would ~~serve~~ as far as it went serve for an introduction to the principles of legislation in general as well as to the penal branch in particular: and that the branch which I had happen'd to take up first was the very branch (which in a natural arrangement would take the lead of the other two and serve best to exhibit the lineaments of the whole) /For this being the branch/ in which those characters of imperation /which ⊠ are essential to everything that bears the name of law/ were most distinct: /marked;/ (by visible) /it would/ form a natural center of aggregation for the disjointed /heterogeneous/ parts of the civil branch on the one hand, and either a center of aggregation or a standard of comparison for the equally heterogeneous parts of the constitutional branch on the other.

The chapters[3] then which contain the remaining part of the matter designed for the introduction stand at present as follows

Chap. 18. (dismembered from Chap. 17) Jurisprudence its branches.

Ch. 19. A law defined and distinguished. See Ch. | | Here the difficulties are stated which occur in common speech from the want of [*In margin*: any settled] distinction between acts of legislation, acts of administration and acts of judicial authority, and acts of

Ch. 20. *Source* of a law or of the persons of whose will ~~the law~~ it may be the expression. (Here it is shewn) in what manner covenants, conveyances, /judicial/ orders, /orders/ of executive magistrates, by-laws, /treaties entered into by the executive magistrate with foreign states/ etc. connect with those permanent laws which emane /directly/ from the sovereign legislature: and how /in the current language/ covenants and conveyances are confounded together under the name of *contracts*.

Ch. 21. *Ends* /or purposes/ to which a law may be directed

Ch. 22. Of the *things* and *persons* which a law may take for its *subjects*.

⊞the additional matter I had thus been forced to introduce
⊠how much soever they may be obscured

[3] Document 126, a double foolscap sheet, written on all four pages, begins here

Ch. 23. Of the *acts* which a law may take for its *objects*

Ch. 24. Of the parties on whom a law may operate. (Here it is shown) by what means the chief /executives/ magistrates and even the entire sovereignty may stand in the capacity of parties bound.

Ch. 25. Of the ~~local extent of a law~~ modifications a law is susceptible of in point of local extent.

Ch. 26. Of the /modifications/ ~~extent of~~ a law in /is susceptible of/ point of *time*

Ch. 27. Of the modifications ~~which~~ a law may admitt of in point of generality. Here the⊞ indeterminateness and instability of the distinction between public and private acts (is laid open /exposed/) brought to view. ~~In~~ the course of this and the 24th chapter I found it necessary to give an analytical view of the several simple modifications, of which the powers of /government or dominion/ public as well as private are susceptible: for the modifications expressed by the common distinction /division/ into legislative and executive⊞$_2$

Ch. 28. Of the *aspects* of a law. Here are exhibited the several *aspects* which laws /and parts of laws/ may bear to one another as well as to the acts to which they /bear a common/ relation, ~~and of~~ as also the several changes and combinations of which they are susceptible: such as command, prohibition permission, repeal, alternation confirmation, continuation etc.: likewise when it is that there is a repugnancy /takes place/ between the ~~laws of a province or colony and the mother country~~ acts of a superior and the subordinate legislature.

Ch. 29. Of the (*force* of a law: of the) ways in which a law exerts its force. Herein is given an ~~notion~~ /idea/ of the connection of the laws of procedure with the ~~main body~~ /rest/.

Ch. 30. Of the /certain remedial/ *appendages* /with which/ laws of a certain class may be provided. ~~This relates to the provisions that may~~ These are of less extensive application than the penal. Herein of procedure in *praeveniendum*, in *compescendum*, and *in compensandum.*

Ch. 31. Of the words or other *signs* by which a law may stand *expressed.*

Ch. 32. What is it that constitutes a *compleat* law. ~~The general~~

⊞[*In margin*]: nature of the several sorts of privilegia is placed in a new light, and the

⊞$_2$ [*In margin*]: or legislative executive and judicial I found to be very complex in themselves, and very ill distinguished from one another.

~~laws of liberty form a sort of expanse in which the several coercive laws have a /their respective locality/ place as islands in the ocean, or stars in the immensity of space~~

Ch. 33. Of the /common and/ customary law: that no such thing as *a* compleat law is to be found in it. [*In margin*: From these may be ~~They seem to give~~ collected the plan of a compleat body of laws.]

Ch. 34. Of the *separation* of the *civil* branch of the law from the penal—That the former is only a development of certain parts which belong in common to the latter.

[*Long marginal note, beginning beside point* 34] From where it puts /enables/ the legislator /is put in a way/ to know /how far/ ~~when~~ /any given/ ~~his~~ body of laws he has before him is compleat if compleat /to see at once [?]/ ~~gives room~~ the whole effect and influence ~~forsaking~~ of any amendments ~~within~~ as well in point of amplitude as discrimination.

Hence any impropriety in point of substance may be the easier discover'd—Tendency which such a method has to check the license of interpretation—to facilitate the ~~drawing comparisons between~~ /confrontation/ of the laws of different nations—and the communication of the science of legislation to beginners.

Ch. 35. The division of the laws into civil and criminal—That this division /as it stands at present/ is arbitrary and unsteady ~~[and till some positive line of separation shall be drawn can tend only to mislead]~~ /fallacious and productive of confusion./

Ch. 36. Of the distinction between penal and civil *procedure.*

Ch. 37. Uses of the eighteen preceding chapters

Ch. 38. Idea of a compleat *Corpus Juris*, and of the different ways in which it may be divided for different purposes, into the ~~penal~~ /internal and the international; and the former into the penal/ civil, and constitutional branches—into the general code and the system of particular codes as determined by the particular ~~denominations~~ /classes/ of persons interested: into the law of procedure or adjective law as it may be called, and the substantive, or that to which the adjective is subsidiary: into the main body of the law, and the /appendix or/ book of *formularies*, including precedents of conveyances, /pacts/ covenants, judicial orders etc. all which as far as circumstances permitt /admitt/ should be settled by the legislator.⊞

⊞[These 19 chapters taken together form a sort of /universal/ anatomy of ~~the~~ any /entire/ body of the law whatsoever considerd nakedly as a collection of expressions of will, abstraction being made of the propriety of the volitions so expressed. In this part of my course as well as in that which your Lordship has before you I found there was no trusting for a single step to the beaten tracks. I was travelling a new road, and had every step of the road to make. This /would/ of course render the /progress/ business the more toilsome: both to myself ~~who have written~~ /in writing/ and to the few if any who /may ~~will~~/ have patience to read.]

Ch. 39. Of Indirect or preventive Legislation: or of the several ways of preventing misdeeds otherwise than by (force of) punishment /immediately/ ~~directly~~ applied to the very act which is obnoxious. Indirect Legislation may be levelled 1. against *delinquency*: or 2. against *misrule*.

Ch. 40. Influence of *time* and *place* on the expediency of a law. Some parts of a perfect body of law ~~will~~ /would/ be equally adapted to all times and places: others not.

The plan being thus enlarged, so as to take in the whole body of the law as well as the penal branch, ~~I saw~~ /it occurred/ that the subject of reward would now require the same development as that of punishment had received before: the one being as much a spring of action and instrument of government as the other.⊞[2] The /most/ proper place for /it which/ would have been immediately after the chapters relative to punishment (Ch. 13, 14, and 15). ~~But~~ was pre-occupied. 2. ~~Although~~ As the influence of this spring of action in government lies comparatively within a narrow compass, the whole of what I should find to say about it (~~would /might~~/ I thought) ~~being brought into the compass of one volume which would /might~~/ /I thought/ form a work /volume/ of itself which from the nature of the subject might be rather /more readable/ less unpopular than the rest. /other./ /In/ This volume might even /be/ comprised what relates to the application that may be made of the instrument in question towards the production of particular services: whereas the whole of the penal and civil branches of law is included /comprized/ in what concerns the application of punishment.

Of[4] all the matter /above spoken of/ no more is printed off than what ~~I send accompanies this letter /I have taken the liberty to send~~/ accompanies this address. However Book the first containing

⊞[2] [*In margin*]: But several considerations concurred in determining me to allott to this subject a separate work. 1.

[4] Documents 127 and 128, two single foolscap sheets constituting a single series of paragraphs concluding the letter, commence here.

the whole of the penal code except what relates to procedure was at one time thought to be finished in readiness for the press: but the /analytical/ (exhaustive) view I took afterwards of the system of offences in the introduction suggested the necessity of /a multitude of/ ~~several~~ additions /~~insertions~~ and corrections/ which have not /all of them as yet/ been made. There are however titles enough ~~to serve all~~ in a legible state to /serve as specimens of/ the manner in which the general principles contained in the introduction are applied, and of a method by which I have attempted /endeavoured/ to reconcile amplitude /plenitude/ with discrimination and brevity, with /perspicuity and/ precision. Indeed any one in which the law is proposed in *terminis* may be considered as an integrant part⊞ of the whole. Book 2 relating to procedure is not in equal forwardness: however the ~~general~~ /leading/ principles are settled, the outlines marked out, /most of the matter determined in idea,/ and some of the titles /set down *in terminis*./ The case is nearly the same with the several titles destined for the appendix.

My present design is to publish what is printed of the Introduction by itself: making only a few /inconsiderable/ alterations in the last chapter in consequence of the ~~new lights which~~ /enlargement which the whole plan/ have come /has undergone/ since this /part/ was printed off. I ~~shall~~ /propose mean to/ wait however for the completion of the book on Indirect legislation. These I propose to publish ~~at the same time~~ together, in order to take at the same time the sense of two different sets of readers: the Introduction ~~being~~ /is/ destined for the few (who have ~~patience and capacity~~ strength of mind to ~~comprehend general~~ /embrace a set of fundamental/ principles /in all their extent, and patience/ to follow up a long thread of metaphysical discussions) ~~who are capable of digesting metaphysics~~ The Essay on Indirect legislation being /like that on Reward/ full of /propositions/ of detail, and illustrations drawn from the actual laws of different nations, will I hope /like that/ be somewhat ~~more popular~~ /less unpopular/ and better suited /less ill suited/ to the relish and the powers of the bulk of readers. /What I shall finish next/ Whether ~~when these are off I shall apply proceed in the next place to finish print~~ the Essay on Reward, or that on the influence of place and time which I think likewise of throwing into a small but separate work, the ~~matter of Legislation,~~ or Book the 1st of the penal code, or whether before I publish the latter I shall wait till I have settled the terms as well as the plan of the civil code, in

⊞[*In margin*]: and ~~sufficient~~ /characteristic/ specimen

order that ~~the connection with~~ /the boundary line between that and/ the penal code may be /distinctly and/ specifically marked out in every part, I have not yet determined.

Your Lordship will easily perceive that a book of law upon this plan is virtually a project of reformation,⊞[1] and that every title of it ~~is virtually contains~~ may be considered as /construed into a/ proposal for the alteration of the laws at present in force in as far as they differ from the model of supposed perfection which /it is the design of/ such title ~~is calculated~~ to exhibit:⊞[2] But the most signal and perhaps impracticable reformation of ~~the whole~~ /all/ is that which would be effected were the present indefinable extent /indeterminable prospect/ and immeasurable /~~indefinable~~/ bulk of the whole reduced to the ~~comparatively slender~~ /moderate/ dimensions /within/ which upon this new plan ~~it would be~~ it would be confined ~~/included/ an improvement~~ /a proposal/ an improvement the proposal of/ which cannot be exhibited /stand expressed represented considered as [...?]/ in any of the titles taken separately but which must be /looked upon /~~considered as standing exhibited in~~ resulting in/ from the (connection which is established between the titles) /as the general result/ method and expression /which will have been/ given to the whole. It is evident that the plan as far as it went could in a certain sense be the destruction of the *customary* or as it is so uncharacteristically termed by us, the *common* law: since whatever goes at present under that name would either be abrogated or *homologated* as the Flemish writers call it, that is expressed in assignable /authoritative terms/ and /thereby/ converted into the form of statute law.

I shall trouble your Lordship at present I shall give your Lordship no further trouble: but in the course of a day or two I shall take the liberty of sending one sheet more containing the /titles of the/ chapters of the three essays on indirect legislation or reward,

⊞[1] [*In margin*]: addressed to /any and every/ ~~the~~ nation to the circumstances of which it is meant to be applied:

⊞[2] [*In margin*]: In the /a model/ /construction/ of this model the law of England was of course the principal but /by no means/ the only established body of law (whose excellencies I studied to avail myself of, ~~which~~ in trying to remedy its defects) of which I /studied/ tried to avail myself of the excellencies as well as to provide /exhibit/ a remedy for the defects: abstraction being made of all local prejudices which whatever /tenderness/ respect they may claim from the hand of the legislator ought never to stop the eye of the individual inquirier.

and on the influence of time and place, in the state they are in at present, exhibited at one view.

I have the honour to be etc.

If the form be what I have endeavoured to make it, the *substance* of the law would ~~lose much of~~ /by being thrown into any other form lose/ a great part of any utility it ~~might have if not thrown into that form~~ /otherwise possess/. But the *form* might be given to any body of laws ~~how inexpedient soever~~ /whatsoever were its imperfections in/ point of substance /those excepted that/ except the ~~what~~ depends upon the want of amplitude and discrimination the indeterminateness, contradiction, /tautology/ ambiguity, and obscurity /and unwieldiness/ which it is the special purpose of the form in question to remove. As a ~~plan~~ model of a digest it might be made use of /have its use/ (were the matter/included under contained in it/ by it ever so much disapproved) looked upon as ever so expedient or impracticable although as a system of legislation /code of new law/ it should be deemed useless or impracticable.

427

From Samuel Bentham[1]

16/27 June 1782

Irkutsk June 16th O.S. 1782.

Not a Scrap of a letter had I received from England or scarcely from Petersbourg since October last while I was at Perme till today when the post brought me at once 7 from my father and you. My father's are dated one Septr. 14th, the other Octr. 18th. Yours are of the 1st and 13th of August, 11th, and 15th of Septr. and the 21st of October.[2] I have also received some interesting news from Petersbourg, and I would wish to take the opportunity of the post which sets out in 2 days to answer yours at least. Some of your letters

427. [1] B.M. III: 289–94. Autograph. Docketed on each sheet, the last reading: '1782 June 16/27 / S.B. Irkutsk / to / I.B. Linc. Inn / Sheet III.'

Addressed: 'Jere^{y} Bentham Esq. / Lincolns Inn / London', readdressed: 'Brompton / near Rochester'. Notes: 'No such person to be found at Brompton near Chatham'; and: 'Returned to Lincolns Inn for the reasons assigned. I.H.' Three postmarks: '22 SE', '26 SE', and one illegible.

Bentham considered that Samuel intended this letter for Shelburne's eye (letter 434). See also letter 436, n. 9.

[2] All missing.

and more particularly your representation of the advice which Ld. Shelburne is so kind as to give me quite disconcerts all my plans: but I believe I must begin by giving you some account of them as they hitherto stood which is what I have not attempted to do since I left Catherinberg. In a letter from that place dated the beginning of January last I mentioned to you the terms which I thought the best to make engagements on with private people relating to improvements in fabricks, manufactaries etc. The saltworks near Solikamskaja[3] served me as an example and I told you how much one of the proprietors seemed disposed to enter into such terms. I about the same time wrote to Petersbourg to my freind Hynam that he might sound a person who had before wished to have some such engagements with me how far such terms would be agreable to him. By this post I have in answer to that enquiry an assurance that he most perfectly approves of the terms and further assurances of the liberal sentiments of this said person together with pressing advice to enter into such a kind of association with him immediately. . . .[4]

Now after reading your letters I would fain hasten my journey homewards, but on account of a determination and promise not to excede the bounds of expences set me by my father I have marked out the plan of my journey in such manner as to make use of water carriage in the summer half year when post horses are dearer and to profit by the cheapness to travel by land the winter half. by this means without *migardness* I shall be able to squeeze my absolute expences as required, having alotted the overplus money which I have taken up to the making small purchases. The only part then of my general plan which this requisite œconomy will permit me change in consequence of the sentiments his Lordship seems to entertain in my favour and the advice he is so kind as to give me is that dropping the idea of asking for any employment for the purpose of acquiring honour to myself in this country, that I should confine myself to the sources of profit, and whether the mine should or should not be given me to make what haste I can to come to terms with my freind at the black sea and perhaps the proprietor

[3] Sol'kamskaya, now Solikamsk, situated on the left bank of the Kama river on the western slopes of the Urals at 59° 40′ N., 56° 45′ E., was at this time the most important centre for salt-mining in Russia. It was also a trade centre on the route to Siberia, though in this respect then in decline. Samuel was here referring to his letter of 2 January 1782 O.S. (B.M. III: 278–80); see also letter 431, n. 5.

[4] A passage of about a thousand words omitted. Samuel detailed the activities of this 'person' who, though not named, was clearly Potëmkin. He also wrote at length about the possibilities and the difficulties of taking on the management of an iron mine belonging to the crown in the vicinity of Yekaterinburg.

of the saltworks, and when I may thus have put things in a *thriving* way and get a thousand or two pounds in my pocket leave affairs to take their chance under the best agents I can pick out and pursue my travels as his Lordship proposes. In the meantime if you have in England patriotism enough left to refuse any longer to be ruled by those whose administration have been cursed by so many [*word underlined and crossed out*] misfortunes at least, misfortunes which /to judge/ by their number alone seem scarcely possible but to have arisen from /any thing but/ misconduct. and if at that happy period his Lordship should take a part in a new administration I may hope that from the favourable disposition he seems to have towards me I may be put in a way of exerting my tallents such as they are in the service that of all I should most wish for. You seem indeed by your letters to insure this. The great attention however which has been paid me here, the manner of life I have now been used to, and to confess the truth a sense of pretensions I have on the score of qualifications will not permit me to accept such places as I should before my travels have been eager for. You mention indeed Commissioner of the Navy or something equivalent in power I suppose as well as in emolument, such a place tis true is the greatest I could think of at first; but what expectation of procuring such a place under the present Ministry?

Do I consider my profit only or marks of favour and distinction of the Sovereign without regard to the country it is here I seem to be in the best track for acquiring them. If however at any rate you continue to give me expectation of the continuation of the freindship which through your means his lordship seems to have acquired for me I will abandon my plans of serving for honour in this country and pursue these only which will be the most immediate sources of profit a profit however in itself cannot but be honorable in some degree as it will be the entire fruit of improvements at the expense of no one and to the advantage of many individuals as well as the country in general.

I set off from hence the 23d and in less than a month I shall reach Barnaoul.[5] There I intended spending more than a month I will however not excede a fortnight there and will make scarcely any stop in another place till I get to the environs of the black sea, to

[5] Barnaul, a town in south-west Siberia, situated at 53° 21′ N., 83° 48′ E. on the left bank of the Ob by the confluence with its tributary, the Barnaulka. It had been founded in 1738 as a centre for a silver industry by the great Siberian entrepreneur, Akinfiy Nikitovich Demidov (1678–1745), with whose son, Prokopiy Akinfiyevich Demidov, Samuel was acquainted.

do this however I must be obliged to take up some more money I am affraid, and what will my father say to this?

At dinner today at the Governors the Russian Gazettes which this post brought were read. From the English news I had the supreme satisfaction of learning that the long-wished for total change of the Ministry is at last effected.[6] And now why I dont know very well what to say now, the best thing is to go and take a walk to compose my spirits a little, and when I have considered the matter a little cooler and thought of what further alterations it may be proper to make in my plans, I will set me down again to take advantage of this post. This news as if on purpose to revivify a poor forlorn Englishman has found its way to this part of the world in 2 months and a half.

This change of affairs cannot but make me very anxious to be at home, and on the assurances in your letters (when this matter was only as possible) I shall not let the trifling expence attending the different seasons or the manner of my travelling be any cause of delay. But there also other objects of consideration. 1er. whether my connections in and knowledge of this country may not be turned to some account while I am yet in it. 2nd. If I may not be able to leave open at the same time a channel for my turning to profit the observations I have during my stay made on the improvements applicable to this country. I have no time to giving any order to my thought on these subjects but as they come will clap them down as I now have but an hour or two before the post goes out. . . .[7]

You will then let me know how far such ideas of mine are thought worthy of notice, or what other plan you would have me pursue. I will be hastening towards Petersbourg so as to get there or rather about the black sea at the time when I can have an answer to this. It is to Chremenchuk[8] that you should beg Sir James Harris to

[6] I.e. the replacement of North's ministry by that headed by Rockingham at the end of March 1782. Shelburne held office as a secretary of state.

[7] A passage of about a thousand words omitted. Samuel mentioned the possibilities of ship-building at Archangel and on the Black Sea, and discussed timber resources in south Russia and southern Poland. He speculated as to whether he might be employed in Russia or elsewhere abroad on behalf of the British government to get ships built for the British navy.

[8] Kremenchug, an important town on the left bank of the Dnieper, situated at 49° 03′ N., 33° 25′ E. At this time it was the temporary capital of the southern province

forward my letters unless in consequence of any letters of later date from you I may see cause to change my plan and should of course write to Sir James other directions about the disposal of my letters. If you were to beg Sir James to send an express with my letters it would cost but 5 pounds English....[9]

428

From Charles Hanbury[1]

19 July 1782

Hamburgh 19 July 1782.

Sir.

I have received Your Letter of 30th April,[2] which I must beg leave to defer answering fully 'till my Return from a Journey which I am about to make tomorrow for about a Month.—I should not have deferred writing You so long if the Books You ordered had been compleatly ready sooner. I now have the pleasure to tell You they are to go on board of Captn. Man, who will be ready to sail in abot. a Week or ten days—Inclosed You will find a Rect. for them, which will entitle You to recieve them from the Ship—The Account of their Cost will follow in my next. I am much obliged to You for the Account of Your Brother, who is become a great Traveller — We may probably soon hear of his having been Physician and Prime Minister to the Prince of Abyssinia, and having stepped over the Source of the Nile, like Mr. Bruce[3]—but to do him Justice I believe him more inclined to be original, than an Imitator even of Mr. Bruce. His Shoes and Stockings etc. have

known as New Russia, of which Potëmkin was governor; and it was a transit point through which had to pass practically all supplies connected with the colonization of the south which Potëmkin was pressing forward with great vigour (E. I. Druzhinina, *Severnoye Prichernomor'e, v 1775–1800 gg*, Moscow, 1959).

[9] A final passage of about 250 words is omitted.

428. [1] B.M. III: 295–6 Autograph. Docketed: '1782 July 19 / Hanbury Hamburgh / to / I.B. Linc. Inn. / Brought to Chambers / July 27. Reced by / mistake not till Aug. 3d.'

Addressed: 'Jeremy Bentham Esqr. / Lincoln's Inn / London.' Two postmarks, the first indecypherable, the second, 'IV/30.'

For Samuel Bentham's meeting with Hanbury during the course of his journey to Russia, see letter 333, n. 1.

[2] Missing.

[3] James Bruce (1730–94), carried out a number of explorations in North Africa, the Levant, and Abyssinia between the time of his resignation from his post as British consul in Algiers in 1765 and his final return to Scotland in 1775. He claimed to have discovered the source of the Nile.

been in the mean time travelling to Russia and are returned safe to Hamburgh—I shall cause them to be redelivered to you by some Opportunity—I hope to have the Satisfaction of enjoying Your Friendship on my Return to England, and in the meantime I beg You will be assured that I am very ready to do You any Service—being with Esteem

Sir,

Your sincere hble. Sert.

C. Hanbury.

Jeremy Bentham Esqr.
Lincolns Inn, London.

429

From Samuel Bentham[1]

2/13 August 1782

Barnaôul, August 2d O.S. 1782.

At my arrival here I was most vexatiously disappointed at not finding a letter from you. Yet I am certain that upon the change of the Ministry you must have had something to say to me. The packet containing the last news I had from England I answered from Irkutsk by a long letter which on account of the time I sent it should reach you before this: but on account of the different manner of its going probably this will follow close after. My last news then from England except what I learn by the Russian Gazettes is of the 21st Octr. 1781 nearly 10 months ago. This delay in sending me letters I attribute to the impossibility that my freinds at Petersbourg think there is to send letters to any person in Siberia. The truth is the post goes every week and there is no more difficulty with respect to the examination of letters or any other account whatever in sending letters to Siberia than to any other part of the Russian or for what I know any other Empire. One letter and one only I have reason to believe is lost in its way to me, but that probably was [*several words crossed out*] not sent by the post.

The Gazettes tell us that the Duke of Richmond[2] has reduced

429. [1] B.M. III: 297–8. Autograph. Docketed by Bentham: 'S.B. to J.B. 2 Aug. O.S. 1782 / Barnaoul.'

[2] In March 1782 Charles Lennox (1735–1806), 3rd Duke of Richmond, took the post of Master General of the Ordnance in the second Rockingham administration. He immediately mounted a crusade for economy within his department (Alison Gilbert Olson, *The Radical Duke*, 1961, p. 74).

the yearly expences of his department 400,000£. God grant it may be true! God grant also that the same spirit of Œconomy and patriotism may inspire those who preside in other departments! and that particularly with respect to the Marine that it may be perceived that everything is not as it were to be wished it should be and as it may be made to be. Inspired by the hopes that what I might have to say on the subject might now meet with some attention I wrote 2 or 3 Sheets on the Œconomy of the Dockyards while I was descending the Angora river to Jeneseisk[3] which with what I had before written at different times during my journey and while at Petersbourg will make a very considerable addition to what you know of my having on the subject. /On the other hand/ my judgement being become more comprehensive than it was when I left you I see the frivolousness of some few of my former ideas. /and on that account/ [*two words crossed out*] Upon reflection the errors of my own and of your judgement also seem to have had one general and frequent source namely that passionate desire of making *every* thing perfect, without sufficient attention to the relative importance of the different subjects which present themselves. Hence it has frequently happened that we have laboured long to effect a purpose very little worthy our attention. The consequence of this is not only a waste of time but an injury to one's reputation. The public seems much rather to support /admit of/ a man's doing nothing, than of his being occupied about what appears trifling. So in writing I [*words crossed out*] cant help being affraid of an appearance of an overgreat accuracy and of your pursuing your examinations and observations to too minute details. A reader will not readily pardon your leaving nothing for his invention to supply; the little confidence you put thereby in his understanding perhaps even touches his vanity; besides when the ideas are very consequent they rise in his mind before he can have time to read the words by which you impart them thus he is under the tiresome necessity of entertaining the same trifling idea twice. The motive I believe of this over accuracy is more often that of appropriating to yourself the whole of the merit by shewing you had those ideas than out of any apprehension that the reader might not have them, /at least I think I have caught myself acted upon by such a motive./ I do not precisely recollect from what particular

[3] The river Angara in central Siberia rises out of Lake Baykal and follows a course over a thousand miles, first northward, then westward, eventually joining the upper waters of the Yenisey. Yeniseysk lies some distance downstream (north-west) from this confluence, at 58° 27′ N., 92° 13′ E., and at this period was an important commercial and administrative centre.

examples in your writings that I entertain these fears. I think however they may be seen in the View of the hard labour bill, perhaps respecting the devise for ornaments to the building, perhaps in your examination of instruments of punishment, or /perhaps in the consideration of/ means of marking the Convicts.[4]

430

From Samuel Bentham[1]

28 August/8 September 1782

Tobolsk August 28th 1782 O.S.

At Omsk fortress[2] on the frontiers of the Empire towards the Kirgisian territories, I learnt by the Russian Gazettes of Rodney's success in the West Indias.[3] At my arrival here yesterday I learnt the death of the Marquis of Rockingham, of his being succeded by Ld. Shelburne and the further changes in the Ministry.[4] The post arrived today brings the disagreable news of the critical situation of Ld. Howe who with only 22 sail seems liable to be exposed to and even determined to engage with the combined fleet of the enemy amounting to 40 sail. Some little hopes the same papers give us /indeed/ that our fleet may be reinforced to 35 sail if so (as according to my calculation ~~Ld. Howe's abilities =⅛ in addition to the force in a clearer expressed~~ 35 + Ld. Howe's abilities = 40) we shall be a match for them.[5] Such very interesting public news together with

[4] For the respective passages in *A View of the Hard Labour Bill*, see Bowring, iv, 32–3, 10, 20–2.

430. [1] B.M. III: 299–300. Autograph. No address or docket.

[2] Founded in 1716 at the confluence of the Om and Irtysh rivers, 55° N., 73° 20′ E., Omsk, during most of the eighteenth century, was one of a line of forts forming the defences of south-western Siberia.

[3] This was Rodney's victory over de Grasse at the Battle of the Saints, 12 April 1782, which checked any aggressive move by the French in the West Indies for that year. De Grasse was taken prisoner and five French warships captured (P. Mackesy, *The War for America, 1775–1783*, 1964, pp. 457–9).

[4] Rockingham died on 1 July 1782. Shelburne succeeded him as First Lord of the Treasury and chief minister. Thereupon Charles James Fox and the members of the Cavendish connection, who had aspired to dominate the administration, resigned their offices.

[5] Early in July, while cruising off the Scillies to cover the arrival of the Jamaica convoy, Howe encountered the joint Franco-Spanish fleet in much superior strength. In hopes of getting a windward position to compensate for his inferior numbers he boldly sailed his squadron northward through the treacherous strait between the Scillies and Land's End. A storm dispersed the Bourbon fleet to the southward and the convoy, arriving a little later, had a safe passage into the Channel. Rumours

the circumstance of my not having received a single letter from England of a date later than October last makes me anxious to an extreme degree to reach Petersbourg and therefore almost in'cable of supporting the least delay in my journey.

The opening the new mode of Jurisdiction in this Government takes place here the day after tomorrow and though this is what I wished much to be present at and had promised to stay for, yet upon the receipt of this last news I lost all patience I went directly to the Governor General for the purpose of taking my leave. Nothing however would he hear about taking leave, he vowed ~~to me that~~ he would not let me have horses /till/ the day after tomorrow and in short will not permit me to set off before that time. In the mean time 'tis true I shall rest myself ~~after my~~ a little which upon the whole may not be time lost. . . .[6]

How Vexatious it is that I cannot know a syllable of what you write. ~~My anxiety to know what you are about (which increases at every place I come to where I had expected to find letters) is now got to such a degree that I know not scarcely what I do~~ At such a time as this certainly you must be otherwise employed than in the pursuing your former works. For my part /when I reflect on the probability of my being employed now in founding the dockyard works were I at home and at the same time read of the reinforcement for Ld. Howe not being ready I am as it were ready to [. . .?]/ the hopes I have that what I have to say may now meet with some attention my Zeal is without bounds. Was I in authority I should I believe never sleep but in my way from one dockyard to another. Messrs. The Commissioners of the navy and dockyard officers should have no more rest than I have /now/ on my journey. The fear of such a whip before their eyes as one of my Grenadiers puts life into the postillions with when they are lazy, would make these Gentlemen a little more alert. A little Russian discipline would now work wonderfull changes in such *lukewarm* dispositions. The master Shipwright himself when he has nothing better to do should blister his hands in setting an example to the workmen. Not one bit of ornament or accomodation for an officer should be a moment's delay. Is it possible that Carved work and mouldings, planing and polishings make at such a time as this a part of the employment of these workmen whose labour is of such great ~~value~~ /moment/? Is an hour in the day that is ½ day in the week *still* spent in cutting up and

about the reinforcements available to Howe were greatly exaggerated—no doubt deliberately (P. Mackesey, op. cit., pp. 478–9).

[6] A passage about his plans for returning speedily to St Petersburg is omitted.

secreting of *chips*? Is it by such lying reports that the Lords of Admlty as well as Navy board or whosoever else it may concern still judge of the progress of the works in the dockyard? They would get better information from the newspapers.

431

To Jeremiah Bentham[1]

3 October 1782 (Aet 34)

Brompton Oct. 3. 1782.
near Chatham

Hond. Sir

I have been looking out I don't know how long for the pleasure of a letter from you: your plan being of the itinerant kind, and mine stationary, I took it for granted you would let me know as soon as you were fixed. Possibly you may already have sent me a letter which owing to a misapprehension of my *homme d'affaires* in town, may have failed hitherto of coming to hand. As a letter I received from him last night contains some public intelligence to which you might not otherwise have access, I do not know but I may send it you with this.[2]

An enclosure which will be rather more interesting to you is a pretty long letter of Sam's dated Irkutsk June 16th that is the 27 1782.[3] I received it last night, but not till after the post was gone: what part of it I shall send you by this post, or whether any part I can not yet determine, as I must keep it by me till I have had time to send him the answer he requires.[4] You will regret with me that the account I gave him through Lord Shelburne's repeated importunities of the conversations I had with his Lordship relative to him, that this I say added to the accounts which had since reached him of the change of the ministry should have produced the effect which it appears to have produced upon him. At the same time you will doubtless rejoice with me at the prospect he has of /any one of/ three different establishments /which/ all of them promise to be lucrative to a very extraordinary degree, and two of which probably,

431. [1] B.M. III: 301–2. Autograph. No address or postmark. Docketed: 'fils Jeremy / Lr. datd. Brompton / Octr. 3 1782.'

[2] Missing.

[3] Letter 427. This letter had arrived before letter 424, which did not reach Bentham till the end of October (see letter 434).

[4] This 'answer' is missing.

certainly one of them, wait only for his acceptance. One is the undertaking the management of Baron Strogonoff's salt-works:[5] another is the undertaking the management of works of various kinds belonging to a person whose name he has thought it prudent not to mention, but who I think must be Mr. Dimidoff.[6] The third is the farming an iron mine of the Crown.[7] The second you will find he is actually pressed to undertake: the first you will see reason to think from the enclosed would be at his option: the third he /himself/ thinks he should obtain were he to apply for it. As the terms Mr. Dimidoff has declared his willingness to accede to are precisely the same as those you will see were approved of by Baron Strogonoff, you will be perfectly able to judge of the nature of them, though in the instance of the former he has given us no *data* from which we can judge of the precise nature of the undertaking, or of the profits to be reaped from it. The sheets I now send you, to confess the truth came with his last letter. I forbore shewing them to you, first, because as you will see he desired it,[8] and secondly because I did not like you should be harrassed with projects which might prove abortive. As he has it now absolutely in his power to engage in a plan which he seems to prefer even to that very advantageous one, this latter objection as well as the former is now at an end. Till I knew of this of Dimidoff's, I was a little vexed at his not closing immediately with the other; though at the same time I imagined several other good reasons as possible at least which to you I feared might not prove so satisfactory as to me. Within a day

[5] In two long letters, one dated 2/13 December 1781 but completed on the Russian New Year's Day 1782, and the other of 2/13 January 1782 (B.M. III: 268–9 and 278–80), Samuel Bentham gave a full narrative of his encounter with the wealthy Count Aleksandr Sergeyvich Stroganov (1733–1811), a member of a notable family of Siberian entrepreneurs, a favoured councillor of Catherine II, a count of the Holy Roman Empire, and a patron of the arts and sciences. At Stroganov's request Samuel made an examination of the count's salt-works at Solikamsk, put forward a number of suggestions for improvement, and outlined terms on which it might be worth while to a western expert to engage to make improvements. He was tempted himself by the prospects: 'A man I dare to say may be found, but why not undertake it myself? to clear by the salt works only about 50 or 60 thousand pounds in 10 years without any capital and without the necessity of above one or two years residence on the spot is no such contemptible object. I have already pretty well invented all the machines necessary for the improvement /of/ these works.' And after a further consideration on paper of various technical improvements he reached the conclusion that the profit might even reach the figure of £100,000.

[6] Bentham's guess was incorrect. The person concerned was Potëmkin. See letter 427, n. 4.

[7] Ibid.

[8] In his letter of 2/13 January 1782 (B.M. III: 278), Samuel had written, without explanation: 'I would rather you should not show my father this nor the other small sheet.'

or two after I received the sheets herewith inclosed, I wrote to him a long letter /turning/ chiefly upon the philosophy of the Salt-works, and the manner of negotiating with the Baron: this latter part in French, that being the language in which the treaty would be carried on. The warmth with which I enter'd into that project, with /some/ other circumstances which I cannot particularly recollect will I am sure be sufficient to stop the alteration which you will see he had thoughts of making in his plans in consequence of what I had written to him by the direction of Lord Shelburne.[9] That letter he must have had a chance of receiving very soon, after the time of his writing that which I have just recieved; and if that should not have been sufficient, I wrote him another a month after. He will therefore have received /some sort of/ satisfaction as to that point long before the period which you will see he says he should look out for, viz: that of a letter's reaching him /from me/ in answer to this last of his, which letter *ex majore* cautilâ I am now writing. He acknowledges the receipt of your two letters: the last he had received from us was one of mine written from Thorpe the 21 Octr.

The Bell-man is ringing, and I must put a speedy period to this letter—Sam's you may look for in a post or two.

The /real/ profits of the mine, which he says he thinks he could get the farming of he estimates at £12,000 a year after the two first years, which two first years would not be altogether without their profit. Bolton and Watt from whom he says he had the idea of the terms, are getting I have been told at the rate of 60,000£ a year by Watt's improvement on the Steam-Engine. What I now send is all that remains of Sam's last letter but one.[10]

My best respects wait upon my mother—What news from Scotland.

I may possibly make use of the frank to 'Patrick Barclay Esqr. Bath' in my next.—

Your's dutifully and affectionately
Jeremy Bentham.

Wolsey[11] is very well and goes about with a stick by himself: I have seen him several times. He has let the house built in the room of that you were in; and lives in another hard by.

[9] That is, written at the end of Bentham's stay at Bowood.

[10] The letter of 2/13 December 1781, B.M. III: 268–9.

[11] Not identified.

432

To Jeremiah Bentham[1]

5 October 1782 (Aet 34)

Brompton near Chatham Oct. 5 1782.

Hond. Sir

I wrote to you the day before yesterday by a frank of Mr. Gascoyne's.[2] I now enclose Sam's promised letter:[3] you have every scrap of paper that belongs either to that or the former one. You, /who/ have the convenience of books and maps, I wish you would be kind enough to tell me whether you can meet with any thing about *Chremenchuk* and *Barnaoul*, and what /longitudes and/ latitudes they are respectively in: *Irkutsk*, the place the letter is dated from, we both know. I remember visiting it with you not only upon Voltaire's map,[4] but upon the globe. If you have a mind to astonish the politicians at Bakers (is it not?) with the extent of your political intelligence, you may tell them as a great secret, that Franklin has had a fit of the apoplexy from a (see the other leaf)[5] retrograde gout, as I am informed by a friend of mine, /a physician/ who ⟨...⟩ to see him: but that on the 16th of last month (the day when my friend's letter was dated) which was three weeks after the fit, he was pretty nearly recover'd: on such a text, at this critical period, with a little management, a sermon of decent length, might I humbly conceive, be preached.

The ground I tread on here is classic ground. 'Give us our rights' lives next door but one:[6] and Capt. Douglas /the engineer/ author of the anonymous imitation of Sterne entitled Travelling Anecdotes,

432. [1] B.M. III: 303–4. Autograph. Docketed by Jeremiah Bentham: 'Fils Jere[y] Bentham / Two letters dated at / Brompton near Chatham / Kent the 3rd and 5th Octr. / 1782.' He added another docket: 'Barnaoul / Chremenchick.'

Addressed: 'Jeremiah Bentham Esqr. / Bath.'

[2] Probably Bamber Gascoyne (1725–91), of Bifrons, Barking, Essex, M.P. for Truro (see letter 342, n. 9). However his son of the same name was also sitting in parliament at this time, for Liverpool.

[3] Letter 427.

[4] The first edition of Voltaire's *Histoire de l'Empire de Russie sous Pierre le Grand*, 2 vols., Paris, 1759, included two maps of Russia between the preface and p. 1. Bentham and his father may have been consulting this, or one of the later editions (1760 and 1775).

[5] These four words were added by Bentham at the foot of the page.

[6] Major John Cartwright (1740–1824), the radical reformer. *Give us our Rights! or, A letter to the Present Electors of Middlesex and the Metropolis*, one of his best-known pamphlets, was published in 1782.

a stock book I warrant you at Bakers's, is somewhere in the camp.[7] The Duke of Richmond at the review here was observed to take a good deal of notice of Major Cartwright, a bird of his own feather.[8]

The length of my last will account for, and, I hope, excuse, the shortness of this. Once more therefore adieu, and believe me ever your's dutifully and affectionately

Jeremy Bentham.

I hope it will not be long before I hear of the gouts you would have had, had it not been for the waters: and of the stock of health you have laid in against the winter.

433

From Samuel Bentham[1]

11/22 October 1782

Petersbourg October 11th 1782.

I arrived here the day before yesterday this was 10 days later than I had intended and should have done had I not stopt at Wolidimer a town 150 versts on the other side of Moscow[2] while I sent here to have my letters forwarded to meet me at Moscow. The reason of my wishing to receive my letters before I came here was the assurance I was in to receive a letter from you in answer to the last I sent from Irkutsk[3] in which I desired your advice respecting various matters and which it would have been infinitely better that I should receive before my return here. Finding however no letter from you or any body in England I came on here full of hopes of having some news from you from some body here. But how great is my vexation at not being able to learn one syllable of

[7] Captain James Douglas (1753–1819) published in 1782 his *Travelling Anecdotes*, a description of a journey through Europe told rather in the manner of Sterne's *Sentimental Journey*.

[8] At this time the Duke of Richmond, like Cartwright, favoured constitutional reforms of an extreme kind, including universal male suffrage.

433. [1] B.M. III: 305–6. Autograph. Docketed by Bentham: '1782 Oct. 11 / S.B. Petersburgh / to / I.B. Lincs. Inn / Shairpe.'

Addressed: 'Jere[y] Bentham Esq. / Lincolns Inn / London'; readdressed: 'At Mrs Davies's / Brompton / near Chatham.' Postmark: '...NO.' Stamp: 'STPETERSBOURG.' Note: 'Opened by G.W and J.T.'

[2] Vladimir, about 120 miles east of Moscow, situated at 56° 8′ N., 40° 20′ E. A small town of little commercial importance—it was a centre mainly for local trade—it had recently (1778) been made the administrative centre of a generality.

[3] Letter 427, which had only reached Bentham on 2 October (letter 431).

news from you. As you must have /been surprised/ that you had not received more regularly news from me, I should have thought you would [have] addressed yourself to Sir James Harris or at any rate to Hynam to make some enquiries about me. Besides if you meant that I should come home and that by the way of Sweden and Denmark I could not but expect ~~that you~~ to be furnished with further credit at some of the merchants' houses for that purpose. Tis true I know of 2 parcels of letters which have missed me and are sent to distant parts of the country from whence they cannot return [*words crossed out*] for some weeks, now am I to stay here an indefinite time to wait for these letters the contents of which most probably are to advise me to be as expeditious as possible on my return, or am I trusting to that probability to resolve on setting off as soon as possible and contrary to all my former resolutions about money matters, take advantage of the credit I have from freindship and run a risk of rendering myself unpardonable in my father's /eyes/ and unhappy to desperation. The last letters I have from you namely of the 24th of October[4] now a year ago I read over and over again and when I attend only to their contents I cannot but resolve to [*two words crossed out*] set off for Stockholm directly. But to do this I must be indepted here at least 400 pounds. 200 I have already drawn upon Mr. Shairpe[5] for while I was on my journey, and for expences I must now be at here, together with those on the way home, I cannot take less than 200 more. He 'tis true without my asking has offered to supply me with that or more. My determination is after a most tormenting consideration to accept of Shairpe's offer and set off as soon as I have taken leave of tho⟨se⟩ in this country to whom I am under so great obligations.[6] This will be perhaps a week or a little more. I believe I shall pass by Abo. I cannot hear from you in answer to this until I reach Copenhagen. By the next post I will give you further instructions about places where I may find letters from you. If those letters encourage me in my return I may see you before the year is out. But if by this step I have displeased my freinds God knows when I shall see you. Adieu.

[4] Probably a mistake for 21st of October [1781], referred to in letters 427 and 431—but if not, this is yet one more missing letter of Bentham's.

[5] Walter Shairp, British consul at St Petersburg from 1776 till his death in 1787.

[6] Samuel did not adhere to this intention. A scrap of paper in his hand dated 22 October 1782 O.S. (B.M. III: 311) states: 'Here am I still and I cannot as yet fix the day of my departure. When I was at Court on Sunday the Empress did me the honour to express a wish of talking with me and therefore till she gives me an opportunity of doing so I cannot think of setting off. After that I must spend a day at Cronstadt and 2 or 3 more in taking leave.' In fact he was kept dangling round the court for many weeks and by the time he could have gone he had decided to stay.

434

To Jeremiah Bentham[1]

1 November 1782 (Aet 34)

Brompton Novr. 1: 1782.

Hond. Sir

Many thanks to you for your account[2] of that 'immensely distant place *Kiachta*': whereupon, be pleased to take notice that I have now lying before me a letter dated half of it from that same Kiachta, and the other half from Irkutsk: the former Feb. 16/27, the latter April 15/26.[3] I have had it by a week or more, but on account of its staleness scarcely thought it worth writing about on purpose. It is short, and was written only for the purpose of announcing some good things he had been sending for us from that same Russo-Chinese town, from which or at least from the government in which it is situated, the Kamchatka trade is also carried on. Teas of various sorts, silks, indian inks, minerals, and above all some delicious rhubarb for you, enough to make one's mouth water but to think of. All sew'd up in raw hides: but God knows when, if ever, we shall set eyes on it. As to the letter I shall not I [think] send it by this conveyance, partly because I have ne'er a frank to Q.S.P. partly because I don't care to let it run any unnecessary risks, and partly because it will not be long before I shall hope for the pleasure of delivering it to you in person. I imagine in about a fortnight: if I outstay that term any time to signify I will contrive to let you have a copy.

The observation made in your second letter[4] with relation to Sam's throwing out to me the idea of engaging *Mosberry*[5] admitts of a very satisfactory answer: the letter though addressed to me,

434. [1] B.M. III: 312–3. Autograph. Docketed by Jeremiah Bentham: 'Fils Jere^y^ Bentham / Lr. datd. Brompton near / Chatham Kent Novr. 1st 1782.'

Addressed: 'Jeremiah Bentham Esqr. / Queen's Square Place / Westminster.' Postmark: '⟨. . .⟩ NO.'

[2] Missing.

[3] Letter 424.

[4] Missing.

[5] The final passage omitted from the printed text of letter 427 which alluded to the idea of building ships in Russia for the British navy begins: 'For any schemes of Shipbuilding here it might be proper to send such a man as Mosberry.' On Mosberry see letter 383, n. 10. Samuel had thought of recruiting him on a number of previous occasions, but he had then shown reluctance (see *Correspondence*, ii, 350 and n., 387, 397, 430, 437, 507 n., 516, and 519).

was written for Lord Shelburne: nor was there to be any question about Mosberry's going, but upon the condition of his being sent on the account and in the pay of government; which might very well have taken place /if necessary, as Sam proposed/, without his knowing who the money came from. This consideration of the letters being an ostensible one, it will be necessary to bear in mind throughout, in order to put a right construction on several passages in ~~his letter~~ it: but all these are matters that will very well wait for our discussion till we meet.

As to the question concerning the personality of his great friend whom he has it in his choice to close with, my inference concerning Dimidoff was drawn /principally/ from the very passage from which you drew the contrary one. I could not very well imagine to whom the epithet of the greatest proprietor in the whole Empire could well belong to unless it were to a man who in his life could afford to spend £150,000 upon one single charity, which is what Cox in his account of the Russian prisons (a pamphlet which I shewed you once) says Dimidoff laid out upon an hospital at Moscow.[6] As to his /Sam's/ mentioning Dimidoff as a third person, I thought that might perhaps only be a blind as I have known him I forget on what occasions lay great stress upon the necessity he said there was of being a good deal upon the reserve with regard to names. Upon farther consideration however it has appeared to me not improbable but that the person might be Count *Resamousky*[7] whom he mentions in a letter written not a great while after his first arrival at Petersburgh as having about 70,000 £ a year. It was at this man's house I believe that Sam dined in company with the Empress, which squares very well with what he ⟨said a⟩bout the persons interest /at court/ being so strong.

The circumstance that Sam alludes to in the conversations that passed between Ld. Shelburne and me relative to him was one which I suppose did not occurr to me at the time of my giving you an account of those conversations. It was, that of his Lordship's advising that on his return home he should not omitt visiting the dockyard in Sweden and Denmark. In reply to that, I talked of the expense such a measure would require, and of the opportunities he had of staying where he was and trying some experiments from the success of which he had expectations, without any such expence.

[6] Archdeacon William Coxe, the historian, published in 1781, *An Account of Prisons and Hospitals in Russia, Sweden, and Denmark.* Demidov is mentioned at p. 14.

[7] Probably the extremely wealthy Count Kirill Grigor'yevich Razumovskiy (1728–1803), until 1764 last Hetman of the Ukraine.

Then came the offer about the house at Wycomb, and the thousand pound, and so forth as I told you, and as I told him not omitting at the same time to express my wonder at so extraordinary a proposal, and my doubts about the sincerity of it; which doubts however it would have been very improper for him to have ecchoed back in a letter intended for his Ldships. eye.

I am sorry I omitted answering your second letter before you left Bath, which from that letter I had no idea of your quitting so soon. I wish you may happen to have brought with you the Chart you mentioned: it may go very well by a messenger.

435

From Samuel Bentham[1]

8/19 November 1782

St. Petersbourg Novr. 8th O.S. 1782.

Here I am and this is all I can tell you as yet. As the Empress has done me the honour to tell me that she would wish to talk to me, it certainly depends upon her fixing a time. I have received at last a letter from you of a late date, but what alteration that may make in my determinations I cannot as yet let you know. In either case be of good cheer. I dispatched by the Kingston a vessel belonging to the duchess of Kingston[2] formerly her yatcht now a merchantship under russian colours, 10 boxes and parcels directed for Lord Shelburne. I took the liberty of directing them to his Lordship partly because a part of the contents are destined for him and partly that the people at the custom house might be more civil. I must write to his lordship to explain the matter.[3]

The box of books and a parcel including a letter of the 15th of August 1781[4] is come to hand but no Phosporus have /I/ as yet found. Adieu for the present.

You know all letters are opened, but that is nothing.

435. [1] B.M. III: 314–15. Autograph. Docketed by Bentham: '1782 Nov. 8/19 / S.B. Petersburgh / to / J.B. Linc. Inn. / Cathn. visenda.'

Addressed: 'Jerey Bentham Esqr. / Lincolns Inn / London.'

[2] The notorious Elizabeth Chudleigh (1720–88). See letter 248, n. 1.

[3] This, an entirely non-committal letter, was written on 25 November 1782 O.S. (B.M. III: 316–17).

[4] Missing.

I am very happy in the freindship of the young Prince Dashkoff:[5] did you know him?

Cannot you get me copied out the Contents of your Code ~~either~~ in English if it is not as yet in any other language upon the chance of my being still here.

436

From Samuel Bentham[1]

13/24 December 1782

Petersburg 13th Decr. 1782.

Here I am still and the Lord only knows how long I shall be here. By one of the last ships which sailed from this port I sent so much of my minerals other natural productions etc. as have reached this place. There were 10 separate parcels the boxes marked G. H. I. and K. you should open because they contain a mixture of things, the rest contain minerals only, except the large basket which contains *stuffed birds*. The box I is rather smaller than the rest and covered with green oiled cloth, it contains 5 bottles of Astrackan wine....[2]

I received yours of the | | of November[3] and have written to Mr. Eden[4] at Copenhagen to beg him to forward to me the letters you tell me you sent there. I directed all these parcels to Ld. Shelburne in hopes that the contents would be less rummaged and damaged in the custom house. I wrote to his Lordship apologising for that liberty and offering him one of the collections when

[5] Prince Pavel Mikhaylovich Dashkov (1763–1807), son of Catherine II's favourite, Princess Yekaterina Romanovna Dashkova (née Vorontsova). He was brought up to have command of a number of foreign languages, including English (which the letters in the Bentham papers show that he wrote with idiomatic fluency), and he spent a period at the university of Edinburgh which awarded him its degree of M.A. In 1782 he was attached to Potëmkin as an adjutant, and from 1783, when he was made a colonel (at the age of 20), he engaged seriously in a military career. He and his mother were on bad terms, and later on Samuel, on at least one occasion, tried to pour oil on the troubled waters of their relationship.

436. [1] B.M. III: 318–20. Autograph. Docketed by Bentham: '1782 Dec. 13/24 / S.B. Petersbourg / to / I.B. Linc. Inn / Inclosing Sambouski's. Reced Jan. 24.'

Addressed: 'Jere^{y} Bentham Esqr. / Lincoln's Inn / London', and, 'Via Ostende'. Postmark illegible. Stamped 'ST PETERSBOURG'.

Copy in Jeremiah Bentham's hand, B.M. III: 321.

[2] A passage of about 150 words detailing the contents of various parcels is omitted.

[3] Missing. The date was omitted by Samuel.

[4] Morton Eden (1752–1830), later 1st Baron Henley, British envoy extraordinary at Copenhagen from 1779 to 1782.

put in order.[5] In the meantime you will take possession of the whole....[6]

You have however magnets enough I hope. On espère que si vous n'avez pas d'autres qualités, vous deviendrez au moins *attraiant* par là et moi comme un imbecile, je vous ai envoyé toute ma portion d'attraits. Je m'en apperçois helas trop tard! This is feminine dictation.[7]

Comme je ne vous reverrai pas bientôt encore, mon cher frère, je veux que vous ayez une idée de ce que je suis apropros[?]. Me voici, il me semble que je suis un *demi* degré moins gauche que lorsque je suis parti de l'angleterre. J'ai pris un peu de coquetterie, ce qui fait que j'ai soin que mes habits soient mieux faits, que j'ai des manchettes propres à l'habit que je porte. Il me paroit aussi que je marche moins mal, et que je salue avec un peu plus de grâce, et quand je me tiens tranquile je ne me jette pas si fort en arrière. Voici ce que concerne ma figure. Quant à ce que je peux avoir acquis en fait de connaissances, sciences, etc. etc. etc. je n'en parlerai point. Je veux vous donner le plaisir de les decouvrir petit à petit, pour ce qui concerne la langue françoise, vous voyez comme je l'écris; mais je n'ose me flatter de parler aussi bien; car je trouve des gens assez francs pour rire à gorge déployée de quelques unes de mes expressions. Pour ce qui s'agit de ma conduite, je ne puis cesser de m'étonner, mon cher frère, que vous ayez pû me laisser aller sans guide clair-voyant; car il y a des occasions ou je suis aussi *helpless* qu'un enfant de quatre ans; et si je n'avois trouvé des âmes charitables qui voulussent bien me servir de (нянка) /(a kind of russian nurse)/ et qui me disent, ne faites pas çeci, faites ça, n'allez pas là, allez ici, je ne puis pas répondre de tout ce que ma maladresse, mon peu de prévoyance auroit pu me faire faire. Ç'aurait été à vous à repondre de tous les accidens, désagréments, malheurs, catastrophes, dans lesquels je me serois precipité. Mais j'ai eu le talent de me faire des amis, voilà mon bonheur. Vous sçavez que la *faiblesse* et l'*ignorance* sont quelquefois *intéressantes*.—Sachez, mon cher frère, que je suis intéressant dans plus d'un genre, car on m'assure que j'ai fait quelques conquettes dans ce pays, la première par où je débutoit à mon premier sejour ici étoit brillante, mais j'étois une bête alors. Je fis le dédaigneux et l'on me planta là; et l'on dit tout haut que j'étois un imbecile. Depuis je suis devenu plus

[5] B.M. III: 316–17.

[6] About six lines relating to his mineral collections omitted.

[7] These four words were added afterwards at the foot of the page.

prudent et plus coquet. Je ne traite pas ces choses avec autant de rusticité

All this French you will perceive to be dictated par un esprit feminin. I am chiefly indebted to the dictatrice for what little improvement I have made in the french language, but as to any further consequence of such a liason you have neither to hope or to fear.

I am busy at present in writing a paper of my observations on *cases meet for improvement* in the economy of the works which constitute the greatest part of the riches of the country I have been visiting. In a day or two it will be finished and soon afterwards presented. I shall then be able to give you some news that will be interesting.

I have received yours of which the last date is Novr. 21st.[8]

The thoughts of abandoning such brilliant prospects were the effect of an excess of sincere patriotism and a greater excess of what might be stiled pretended.[9] Neither were the grounds on which they were to be abandoned so slender as they appear to you. But the business of Justification as it cant be done on many accounts fully, may as well be deferred.

My good freind Mr. Sambouski[10] begs me to intreat you to send the inclosed by some safe hand. There are few men whom I esteem more than this same Sambouski, and the degree of respect he meets with here is exceedingly great. Pleschejeff and he were both with the grand Duke on his travels and of course are come back. I certainly have as many and as firm freinds as come to the share of one man. A propos of freinds. You or my father have heard something to the prejudice of my Mechanical freind. It proceded partly from some money concerns in which some people here were the sole causes of what appeared a want of probity in h⟨im⟩ ⟨a⟩nd partly from his professing, and associating with those who profess'd no great respect for religious concerns. Notwithstanding these circumstances his probity and moral character is more interesting than his mechanical abilities.

---

[8] Missing.

[9] The degree of Samuel Bentham's subtlety (he is referring to letter 427) is not fully revealed, but it is probable that not only was he playing off Russian prospects against Shelburne's promises but, in the knowledge that his letters home were opened as a matter of course, also trying to create an impression of interest, but not eagerness, for Russian consumption.

[10] The Benthams had first come to know Samborskiy when he was chaplain to the

'Projet d'un corps de droit'.[11] How I rejoice that it is nearly finished! but cant the word Projet be changed for one less obnoxious. I who am more *prudent* have entirely blotted out that word from my dictionary.

You will pay double I suppose for this letter but I cant help it.

437

FROM JACQUES PIERRE BRISSOT DE WARVILLE[1]

26 January 1783

Ce Samedi Matin

Monsieur

Me pardonerés vous de n'avoir pas tenu ma parole la dernière fois. J'ai été lié enchaîné par un devoir, et j'ai bien regretté de ne pouvoir voler au rendézvous. Je sens plus que jamais le désavantage

Russian embassy in London. He returned to Russia early in 1780 to become director of an agricultural institute at St Petersburg (*Correspondence*, ii, 202 n. 3 and 392–3).

[11] This probably indicates that Bentham had at least made substantial progress in the major enterprise of producing a French version of the elaborate treatise on legislation on which he had by now been at work, in one form or another, for a dozen years (the abbreviated title 'Projet' appears on many of the Mss. in French dating from this period). If so, there had evidently been a substantial modification in Bentham's plans since letter 426 to Ashburton was drafted in early June. The claim that the new project was 'nearly finished' was characteristically over-optimistic: in fact Bentham never did finish the work in this or any other form. The materials for the *Projet d'un corps de droit* were among those used by Dumont for *Traités de législation civile et pénale*, Paris, 1802.

437. [1] B.M. III: 324–5. Autograph. Docketed: '1783 Jan. 25 / Warville Brompton Row / to I.B. Linc. Inn.' Saturday was the 26th.

Addressed: 'Jeremy Bentham Esqr. / Lincoln's Inn Old Buildings / No. 6.' Above the address 'Not Chief' is added in another hand.

Printed, *J.-P. Brissot, Correspondance et Papiers*, ed. C. Perroud, Paris, 1912, p. 59, where it is incorrectly attributed to June 1783; and, omitting the compliments, in English translation, in Bowring, x, 191.

Jacques Pierre Brissot (1754–93) trained for the law but decided to pursue a literary career. In 1778 he was engaged to undertake the French edition of the *Courrier de l'Europe*, a journal published in London. In November 1782 he came to London to engage in various literary ventures. From that December until November in the following year he was producing the *Correspondance Universelle, ou ce qui intéresse le bonheur de l'homme et de la société*, under a Neufchâtel imprint, though the printing was probably done in London by Cox, the printer of the *Courrier de l'Europe*. Late in 1783 he managed to launch his *Licée de Londres*, a periodical aimed at French readers, and in part printed at Paris, dealing generally with literature, politics and

de vivre si éloigné de vous, de tous les secours littéraires que je pouvois me procurer à Londres; et cela va me forcer de prendre dans un mois un autre logement. Mais pour le Changement, j'atens la fin d'un ouvrage que j'ai entrepris, et qui sera terminé dans 8 jours. Agréez mes excuses et faites les agréer je vous prie à votre ami Monsieur Swediar, que je suis honteux et désolé de n'avoir pas encore vu—. Le tems est afreux—Il est impossible de sortir—Je suis avec respect

Monsieur

Votre très humble et obt. Serviteur

Brissot de Warville

438

FROM SAMUEL BENTHAM[1]

31 January/11 February 1783

Petersburg Jany. 31st 1783 O.S.

I have written by this Post to Sir Joseph Banks[2] President of the Royal Society to inform him of the late director of the Academy of Sciences being turned out of his place and Princess Dashkaw

society in England. He also published various other productions. But his undertakings did not prosper, he ran into debt, and he returned to Paris in May 1784. This letter is one of a number which passed between him and Bentham during his stay in London, and the beginnings of the French Revolution later occasioned a renewal of their correspondence. Their acquaintanceship seems to have commenced almost immediately after Brissot's arrival in London: in the first issue of the *Correspondance Universelle* he gave notice of forthcoming publication by Bentham under the title, 'Principes de Législation sur les lois pénales' (*Correspondance et Papiers*, ed. Perroud, xxiv–xxvii, 58). Brissot's own account of his sojourn in London, including a pen-portrait of Jeremy Bentham, is in his *Mémoires*, ed. C. Perroud, 2 vols., Paris, n.d., i, 302–97.

438. [1] B.M. III: 326–7. Autograph. Docketed by Bentham: '1782 Jan. 31/Feb. 10 / S.B. Petersburgh / to / I.B. Linc. Inn / Princess Dashcoff Directrice. Reced Mar. 12.'

Addressed: 'Jere[y] Bentham Esq. / Lincoln's Inn / London. Via Ostend.' Postmark: 'MR 12.' Stamped: 'ST PETERSBOURG'.

In a previous rather terse and uninformative letter dated 30 December 1782 O.S. (B.M. III: 322–3), Samuel had told his brother that a paper of his on the economy of mines and saltworks had been received with pleasure by the Empress, but that the holidays were holding up further approaches to the court. Potëmkin had been taking an interest in his information about Siberian industry. For his father's and brother's concern at the lack of real news about his prospects see letter 440.

[2] Sir Joseph Banks (1743–1820), the naturalist. A manœuvre to get Samuel Bentham introduced to him before his departure on his continental tour is mentioned in letter 309. Samuel's letter to Banks is in the Dawson Turner Copies of Banks Correspondence at the British Museum (Natural History), South Kensington (vol. iii, pp. 15–16). It establishes that a meeting between them had taken place.

appointed directrice in his stead. I at the same time offered to satisfy any curiosity he might have respecting the interiour parts of this country. I enclosed him a copy of the speech the Princess made at the first meeting. Now you must bestir yourself to afford all scientific information, and as any proposals for the improvement of Science will at present stand an excellent chance of being forwarded you may rummage up all you have of that kind. My great intimacy with the Princess and more particularly with the son ensure me a great deal of attention. Tomorrow the Princess will present to the Empress a plan of mine of a chart for exhibiting a view of the absolute and comparative state of Population of the whole or any parts of the Empire. It is a little thing too simple to have much merit but may probably take very much. Mechanical digest If I have time I should like to put in order and propose. I have also some new ideas on the motion of water in rivers at different depths.

I wrote to you by a Mr. Capper[3] who set off from here about a /fortnight/ week ago by him I sent you copies of papers I gave in on the Empress's desire on the mines and saltworks in Siberia.[4] I have but just received your letter [*long unreadable crossing out*] to which Wilson had put a Postscript.[5] I cant answer it by this post. When I can tell you more about my Chart I will write again.

Would you give some of the seeds I sent you by Mr. Capper to Sir Jos. Banks. The flower seeds some of them I hope will be propagated in Queen's Square Place.[6] You never tell me what Charles is about.

439

To the Earl of Shelburne[1]

5 February 1783 (Aet 34)

Lincoln's Inn, February, 5, 1783.

My Lord,

Upon my happening at Streatham to mention the Code lately promulgated by the French king for the government of Corsica,

[3] Capper seems to have been in business at St Petersburg. Samuel later contemplated going into partnership with him to run an oil-pressing plant and did join with him in a venture to import English cloth into Russia.

[4] Missing.

[5] Missing.

[6] This was a 'collection of the seeds of plants peculiar to Siberia' (B.M. III: 322–3). It may have been the occasion of the acknowledgement which forms letter 445.

439. [1] Bowring, x, 126.

your lordship had the goodness to offer to procure me a copy of it. If no measures should yet have been taken for that purpose, I would not wish to take up any portion, however small, of a time so precious as your lordship's, about a matter that might be effected by ordinary means.[2]

But, my Lord, there is a work which less than your lordship's influence could hardly be sufficient to obtain, and which your lordship, if not already apprized of it, will, I hope, not be displeased to hear of. The title of it is, 'Mémoires concernant les Droits et Impositions en Europe.' It is said in Smith's Wealth of Nations, b. v. ch. 1, to have been compiled by order of the French Court 'for the use of a Commission employed for some years then past in considering the proper means for reforming the Finances of France.'[3]

I have been told that there were but 100 copies printed of it, and that it has been never sold. Mr. Anstruther, lately elected Member for ———, happening to be at Paris just as it was printed, obtained a copy.[4] I have asked him for a sight of it by means of a common friend; but he had given it to Lord Loughborough, whom nobody, that I am acquainted with, cares to ask.[5] The case is the same with regard to Lord Stormont, who I thought might possibly have another.[6]

M. de Rayneval, I should think, must know of it, if he thinks proper to acknowledge.[7] Should there be one copy of it procurable, and but one, I would humbly beg the use of it for a few weeks: should there be two, I should even hope your lordship might think proper, as a matter of grace, to grant me the informer's share.

[2] This was, *Code Corse; ou Recueil des édits, declarations, lettres patentes, arrêts et reglemens, publiés dans l'isle de Corse depuis la soumission à l'obeissance du roi*, 3 vols., Paris, 1778.

[3] Adam Smith, *An Inquiry into the Nature and Causes of the Wealth of Nations*, 2 vols., 1776, makes reference to these *Mémoires* at Book v, ch. ii, p. 413.

[4] John Anstruther (1753–1811), 2nd son of Sir John Anstruther, 2nd bart., was M.P. for Anstruther East Burghs from 21 January 1783 till 1790.

[5] Alexander Wedderburn (1733–1805), 1st Baron Loughborough, Chief Justice of the Court of Common Pleas.

[6] David Murray (1727–96), 7th Viscount Stormont, nephew and heir to William Murray, 1st Earl of Mansfield, Lord Chief Justice of the Court of King's Bench. Stormont, a professional diplomat, had been British ambassador at Paris, 1772–8. He was now associated with Lord North and Charles James Fox in opposition to Shelburne's ministry, which was on the point of collapse after defeats in parliament, and was shortly to become Lord President of the Council in the Fox-North Coalition.

[7] Joseph Mathias Gerard de Rayneval (1746–1812), French diplomat. During the last three or four months he, as French special envoy, had been conducting with Shelburne the negotiations which led up to the Peace Treaties of 1783.

To save your lordship the trouble of getting the title transcribed, I have repeated it on the other leaf.

I have the honour to be, with all possible respect.

Your Lordship's much obliged, and
Most obedient humble Servant,
J. B.

Mémoires, etc., en plusieurs volumes en 4to., composés et imprimés il y a quelques ans par ordre de la Cour de France, mais jamais publiés.

440

FROM SAMUEL BENTHAM[1]

9/20 March 1783

Petersbourg March 9th 1783.

It is now above a fortnight that I have your letter of the 28th Jany.[2] in my pocket reading it every day and have not as yet sent any answer to it. The indeterminateness of my situation, your vehement reproaches and a consciousness of my deserving them for the trouble and uneasiness I have given to my father and you and in short all my freinds in England render me hitherto incapable of writing any kind of letter to him. And I must own to you that I feel that nothing less than your threat of writing to Sir J.H.[3] at the expiration of the 3 months could force me to get the better of this reluctancy. You need not doubt however but that that threat will operate the desired effect, of such importance I conceive it to be to me in every respect to stand well with him.

The papers which I sent to you by a Mr. Kapper[4] I trust to for giving you some little satisfaction, by proving to you that I have not been quite idle. Every day since my having given in those papers, I have been expecting to have a private audience with the Empress and I trusted to the courage that that event would give

440. [1] B.M. III: 330–1. Autograph. Docketed by Bentham: '1783 Mar. 9/20 / S.B. Petersburgh / to / I.B. Linc. Inn. / Catha. visa.'

Addressed: 'Jere[y] Bentham Esqr. / No. 6 Lincoln's Inn / London.' Postmark illegible. Stamped: 'ST PETERSBOURG'.

[2] Missing. The reference to Shelburne at the end of this letter seems to indicate that Bentham's had contained reports of the first moves by the parties of Charles Fox and Lord North to combine against him.

[3] I.e. Sir James Harris.

[4] See letter 438.

me to write to my father. I have now had that honour. Her majesty expressed herself much pleased with my observations and very sensible of the Utility of them. Since that ~~she has let me know~~ I have through Princess Dashkoff asked leave to communicate to her in future such ideas as appear /to/ me usefull towards the improvement of the parts of the country I have been in /for/ which offer she expressed herself much obliged to me, and gives me leave to address anything to her through the Princess's hands. She also ordered a Chart of one of the provinces to be done according to a plan of mine for exhibiting an absolute and comparative view of the state of population, which Chart I am in hopes may be ready to present to her in a fortnight. An English Courier which Sir James will dispatch shortly, shall bring you a full account of all this, together with the letter which you require. [*two lines crossed out*] I expected from what you said to have heard something from you about Davies's freind. Ld. Sh. reign will not be long I suppose.

The Courier perhaps may set off in 3 or 4 days perhaps not this fortnight or more. I have begun my letters for him.

441

To Samuel Bentham[1]

23 April 1783 (Aet 35)

Epithalamica.

Permitt me, my dear Sir, to express my grateful acknowledgements of the honour done me in condescending to consult me on your proposed marriage. The observations which I took the liberty of submitting to you in consequence have reached Petersburgh I imagine, about ten days; before which time I take it for granted the question they relate to has one way or other been decided. But from

441. [1] B.M. IV: 46–9. Autograph.

Addressed: 'I.B. to S.B. / Epithalamica / Don't open this if the match fails. / It will only plague you. / It is *badinage* Castle-building etc.'

Although filed among papers of the year 1784 the contents of this letter exclude it from that sequence. The only explicit indication of date is a heading of a paragraph near the end: 'Wednesday April 23rd at night.' In 1783 April 23 was a Wednesday. Moreover, in no other year could Bentham have written: 'Alas, poor E. Florida! Jack Spaniard /you know/ is to have it again' (p. 158 below)—a reference to the preliminaries of the peace of Versailles which had been made public about three months before. This letter appears to be a reply to the missing letter mentioned in letter 438 at n. 3.

a gentleman in your situation much consistency is not to be expected: love seeming to have been as generally admitted as charity, to the privilege of covering a multitude of sins. As my good star would have it I did not take a very peremptory part on the one side or the other: and as you were pleased to ask me whether I had anything to say for or against I accordingly made the compleatest use of the liberty thereby given me, by offering such arguments as occurred to me on both sides. ~~With regard to one argument~~ /On one topic/ I must confess I was altogether silent; viz: the degree of your affection for the fair object: not as holding it to be the least material of the number, but that some how or other I could not help looking upon it as more than probable that some time or other it might present itself to your consideration of its own accord. The event has proved that presumption not to have been ill grounded: insomuch that the stone, which the builder thought it unnecessary to lay, has accordingly danced into its place with as much alacrity as if /Apollo/ Neptune or Amphion had piped a country dance to it, and is become /after all/ the head-stone of the corner. To these observations you, Sir, who after having been long enough the pupil of a court are now arrived to the dignity of prescribing to it its topics for conversation, have doubtless the answer ready: You knew /me/ too well ~~not to be assured that~~ to imagine it possible that any advice of mine on such an occasion could be of any other than the moderate and impartial stamp of which it proved to be. And now, I think, it may be time the account of compliments should close on both sides.

This is the first reference in the correspondence to the love affair between Samuel Bentham and the Countess Matyushkina, which dragged on until finally broken off under pressure from her parents about the end of 1783. Sof'ya Dmitriyevna Matyushkina (1755–96) belonged to the highest circles of Russian society. Her father, Count Dmitriy Mikhaylovich Matyushkin (1725–1800), was a privy councillor and chamberlain. Her mother, Anna (1716–1804), belonged to the proud family of the Gagarins, being the daughter of Prince Aleksey Matveyevich Gagarin. She was Grand Mistress and Lady in Waiting at the empress's court, and at one time had been a favourite with Catherine II though, to judge by the reported critical comments of the empress on her opposition to a match between her daughter and Samuel, this was the case no longer. Anna's younger sister, Dar'ya, was to show, out of family pride, the most determined opposition to any such match. She was married to Prince Aleksandr Mikhaylovich Golitsyn (1718–83), a distinguished soldier now holding rank as field-marshal, who, until his death in October, seems to have occupied some sort of *locus parentis* in the affairs of his wife's niece during the absence of her father in Moscow. Countess Matyushkina herself was about twenty-eight years of age at this time. The French diplomat Bourrée had known her a few years earlier and described her as pretty, lively, and pleasant, 'la tête fort romanesque', but summed her up as a heartless flirt. However, her feelings for Samuel seem to have been quite genuine. For a less critical description of her see letter 464.

Ever since I have decypherd the *arcana*[2] I have been as full of cogitabundities as ever Mambrès was.[3] That Miss or Countess or Princess or whatever she is should have her nose burst out a bleeding, upon Mama's speaking to her, that this bleeding should produce a recal of the fatal prohibition, and that notwithstanding such recal and Miss's being at her own disposal into the bargain and having made so many and such explicit tenders of her sweet self there should be any 'fear' of her resolution to bring the matter to a conclusion. *Encore* if there had been a father: but I don't find there is any such personage in the case. Certainly if you have stated the matter accurately and fairly, the knot must have been tied and the zone bound long enough before this. So say I, and so says Wilson, who is the only person to whom I have yet communicated it. My hypothesis is, that whatever want there may be of resolution is on the side of the gentleman: who has always been a shilly-shally sort of a gentleman, more so even than his brother, ever since I have had the honour of his acquaintance.

And to think of my Sam's getting a wife, and being by and by a father! and of my having a sister, and by and bye being an Uncle, by God's blessing, and having a parcel of mongrel animals half children and half bears for nephews and nieces! I shall expect a full and exact description of her whether she is hairy all over, how long her claws are, and whether she has got a tail—One thing appears, that whatever may be her excellencies in other respects, she wants the property the E. Florida bears have (you remember) of 'never attacking a man'. Alas poor E. Florida! Jack Spaniard /you know/ is to have it again. Lucky enough we did not go there.[4]

I hope by the Courier we shall hear the name, and something about the assets. I wish it may prove a Princess (not that a Princess is anything with you) or at least a Countess or a Baroness, /only/ for Jezebel's[5] dear sake. The passage in which you spoke of your intimacy with Princess Dashcoff was a dagger to her.[6] Not long after /our receiving/ that letter, Far asked me at table to give you that commission which I suppose you have received before now,

[2] This may be an indication that part of Samuel's missing letter was written in sympathetic ink.

[3] The sorcerer in Voltaire's *Le taureau blanc*, which Bentham had translated in 1774 (see *Correspondence*, i, 185 and n. 4).

[4] Some references to East Florida in earlier correspondence suggest that Bentham had then toyed with the idea of emigrating there (*Correspondence*, i, 170 n., 174 and n., 179, 235).

[5] Their step-mother, Mrs Bentham.

[6] This passage is in letter 438.

about Brompton the Painter;[7] adding that he understood he was intimate with Sr. J. Harris. Hardly intimate said I: he was not the sort of man for Sir J. to be intimate with: though he used, as I understood to take some notice of him. 'Oh' says Madam, /with one of her angelic looks,/ 'but at that distance, very slight acquaintances are always magnified into great intimacies.' The malice was so apparent that even her first-born and best-beloved reprimanded her for it before my face. If it should be a Princess, to be sure poor dear Jezebel will break her heart: there will be no occasion for a Jehu to throw her out of the window.

Then as to assets I wonder whether her expectations are equal to poor Miss Pleschijeff's? What will she and her brother, your bosom friend say to this abandonment? Were all thoughts of that affair perfectly given over by all parties?[8] She has got some little matter, you say, of her own. This I suppose we shall one of these days know the quantum of: as also who the two rich people are to whom she is heiress, and what she may expect from each. Her mother, I suppose, is one of them. But pray, Mr. Sir, what do you mean by *'heiress'*? Do you mean that their assets *must* come to her at all events, or only that they will come to her, if they do nothing to prevent it? Tell me in either case where their estates, if on land, are situated, that I may find them in the maps, and send me a map in which they may be found, if there be such an one, /colouring/ marking the spot distinctly. I suppose if they bring in a hundred a year they will be as large as an English county. And tell me the ages of the Mother and the other friend.

If these friends, or either of them, should come to at last, you and she will of course be presented at Court on the occasion of the marriage. If so, it will probably find its way into the Petersburgh Gazette. Would it not be a great treat to Mrs. Q.S.P. if from thence /or otherwise/ it could be made to find its way into our Gazette? Could not Sir James, by writing word of it in a particular manner, ensure it a place there? If I do not mistake, Frazer who when Under Secry. of State wrote you your recommendations, is writer of the Gazette. All that is woman against woman; but independant of all that, which is not worth crossing the threshold for, there may be a real advantage in becoming the topic of conversation here on a ground rather creditable than otherwise. It might contribute to

[7] Richard Brompton, who died in 1782, spent the last few years of his life at St Petersburg holding an appointment as portrait painter to Catherine II.

[8] For Miss Pleshcheyeva and Bentham's earlier jesting on that subject, see *Correspondence*, ii, 429 n., 445 and n.

smooth the road for example to a Commissionership should that be eligible.

You /who/ know what a Castle-builder I am, may imagine what a number of Castles I am building upon this ground.—/Behold a specimen./ You, who want to revisit England, and to have the pleasure of shewing it to the Princess Beareoff or Oursoff whatever her name is, as likewise of shewing her to your friends, pretend to yourself and make yourself believe (though it is no such thing) that a visit hither is necessary to your carrying on whatever projects of improvement you may have upon the anvil. The Princess, her own revenue not being able to keep her in cloaths, much less to pay the expence of such a ramble, profers an humble petition to the Princess Dowager. A grant of 3 or 400 pounds passes the seal: whereupon the Princess attended by Sammy Sneak, and the favourite lady of the bed chamber, visit this once happy isle /like the Princess of Babylon./ Coming in summer, they find nobody in London: they stay therefore no longer than just to take up Jerry Sneak. That makes just a Coach-full, or in short, as no Coach but the Q.S.P.-ian ever travelled with less than 4 horses, two Postchaises, which would cost no more. They then take a ramble over England, to look at Saltworks, Mines and Mechanism.

They go first to Cornwall, taking Bath in their way, and Bowood in their way to Bath. In Cornwall they visit Basset with whom Carey is intimately connected:[9] and from Bowood they get a heap of other recommendations. From Cornwall instead of returning to London, they visit the copper-mines in Gloucestershire, then the Salt works which I have seen at Northwich in Chester. Not far from Chester is Manchester, where liveth a very capital Manufacturer whom Capper knows, and who dined at Q.S.P. the day Capper dined there. In the Manufactories in the neighbourhood of Manchester is to be seen a variety of mechanism. *Farr* was telling me t'other day of a man with an odd name who had in a short time made a matter of 50,000£ /in that neighbourhood/ by the invention of machines for abridging labour. The mines in Derbyshire, and the manufactories at Birmingham, would then be on the way to London.

Q.S.P.s when they went to Scotland paid for Postchaises for 1100 miles, which came to I don't know whether it was £50 or 70£. This would not be quite so many miles but as there has been a tax since

[9] Sir Francis Basset, 1st bart., M.P. (1757–1835), of Tehidy, later Lord de Dunstanville, a great mine-owner in Cornwall, and a friend of Jeremiah Bentham (cf. letter 354 at n. 3. 'Carey' is probably an error for [Reginald Pole] Carew.

of I think it is 1½ or 2d. a mile, we will say it would come to 60£. This for two Post-chaises would be £120. I am afraid there must be something of a Swiss servant to dress hair, who would ride in one of the chaises as the ton is, except when one came to a great house, then he must ride post thither and from thence. This say would make it £130. Two guineas a day for travelling expences for two months 60 guineas allowing 7 pound for extra expences that would make it £200. If /it could be/ ten weeks so much the better. While the Sneaks were examining mines and manufactures the Princess would be reposing her sweet person. If she could be prevailed upon to trust the said person to the sea the whole expence might be brought within £300: and in coming at least that way they would probably save time. If an additional £100 could be obtained they might return by land in the winter, which they should do by way of Sweden. There there would be a great deal in the chemical and mine- way to be seen. This way Capper says is rather cheaper than the other. An English carriage bought secondhand at Tattersals /for £40 or £50/ would make a great figure during the journey, and even at Petersburgh on the return.

The Princess would doubtless be wild for all this, and £200 a piece supplied by her two rich friends would do the business.

I take for granted the ordinary revenue would suffice for a fortnights stay in town, to see the Opera house, the Play-houses, the Pantheon, the Waxworks, and the Lions.

Neither Basingstoke (the Drs. abode) nor Whitchurch, humble as the appearance of things /is, then/ should be passed by unvisited: the expectations will reconcile her Highness to the humiliation. A pilgrimage should also be made to Browning-hill, to visit the dead Ancestors: more especially as I understand that estate is intended to be your's.

Was there ever a prettier scheme cut out upon paper? As a lawyer I cannot avoid turning my thoughts to the legal consequences of this hybridous conjunction. It won't be the first time of my reckoning my chickens, or what comes to the same thing, your chickens, before they are hatched. One good thing is, that as to all English privileges, you being an Englishman, mauvais sujet as you are, it is all the same where *Ursa minor* litters. They may inherit Q.S.P. and Browning-hill, trade without paying alien's duty, and sit in Parliament if they can bribe anybody to choose them. With regard to Russian privileges and disadvantages, it will be well worth your while to inform yourself, whether it would be for their advantage or otherwise to be whelped in Russia. Is there not for example, a foolish sort of law forbidding Russian subjects [*several words totally obliterated*] without leave? Can children born out of Russia, of a father not a Russian, inherit lands in Russia: and in particular lands in the province in which Ursina's lands, if she has any, are situated?

Then as to yourself, do not /let/ the sound of the word tempt you to accept, much less to sollicit '*naturalisation*' without obtaining a distinct conception of the advantages or disadvantages that may attend it. You would not for example forfeit any of your English rights exercisible in England: but I am apt to think you would forfeit your claim to any protection from the Ambassador of England.

Nor is the plan of marriage perhaps a matter of intire indifference. You are not so bewitched, I hope, as to be incapable of acknowledging, that marry what you will, ~~there may be~~ occasions may hereafter happen, which may render it eligible to a man to have the possibility of recovering his freedom: and that even upon easier terms than that of having been previously made a notorious cuckold. In England a man who has been married in England may for adultery get a divorce by act of Parliament after a deal of trouble and at a most enormous expence. In Scotland he may be divorced for the same cause at much less trouble and expence. In Sweden and Denmark he may get a divorce for mere incompatibility of tempers /In a Catholic country no divorce at all./ Learn /if not too late/ how that matter stands in Russia: and if it be possible, marry in the place which is best for marrying in. Take notice that the foolish nincompoops called Legislators have not made provision for a tenth part of the varieties that may take place with relation to such an affair. The parties, natural born subjects the one of one country, the other of another: the marriage contracted for in a third; celebrated in a fourth: a cause of dissolution takes place in a 5th. dissolution applied for in a sixth: they have children born and estates in all: and they want to marry again in each. A pretty number of instances to ring changes upon!

Understand all this while, that I know perfectly well as I was telling Wilson, that this is a great Jack Whore you have got, and that all my nephews and nieces instead of going now and then upright with only a little of the Bentham stoop, will be all -offs and -wisky's and go constantly upon all fours: for Capper tells me no Russian female ever could remember the time of her having her maidenhead. I have accordingly promised Wilson a parcel of the tickets which I am going to get engraved with her picture taken from the best dancer I can find in London, and under it 'Admitt the bearer and his friends.' And when you send over to [*words obliterated*] portion of the shift according to the Russian etiquette ⟨...?⟩ for to offer to palm off upon us and particularly upon such a Chemist as myself, a parcel of hog's blood or blood made a la mode de St. Januarias, but hold a bottle for the blood that comes from the next nose-bleeding produced by the next 'prohibition'.

Now you talk of whores /Jones is dead and/ Miss Ousnam is come back and lives with her father and mother.[10] La Folle[11] and they however do not visit. What could you do about La Folle? Unless Orsina were in good earnest what I have been telling you she is out of compliment, I never could bear any wife of your's should be two minutes alone with that cursed woman or her equally impudent daughter. One single pissing-bout with either of them would be sufficient to wash away all her delicacy. The young one met me once on the staircase in her shift without a blush: discussed with me the choice of the parts it was properest to cover; and the mother who was within hearing though not within sight, thought it a good joke. Poor thing! (I mean your Orsina) I cannot help thinking of her by the hour together, as I can conceive a man to think of a girl that his wife has just been brought to bed of.

Your rogue you, what a deal of life of one sort or another, good and bad together, have you seen at your age, while I have been but vegetating!

Oh, I'll tell you how I will manage La Folle: I will tell her you are afraid of seeing her, for fear of etc. again, after which you would never be able to endure your wife. She told me once, you yourself said to her that would be the case: and whether you ever said so or no, and whether you thought so or no when you said /it/, she will make no difficulty of believing it as true as the gospel to the world's end. Queen Elizabeth used to /sit and/ hear tag rag and bobtail talk in strains of rapture of her beauty when turned of seventy.

Wednesday April 23rd at night

I have been trying to get some lights out of Smirnof[12] about Orsina: but he is as dark as pitch. I asked him whether he knew of any lady of one of the first families (Remember, Mr. Two shoes you said one of the first families) who had no husband living and only

[10] In 1778 Miss Ousnam had eloped with a second lieutenant of marines (presumably Jones), who had evidently not married her (letter 234, n. 4).

[11] I.e. Bentham's hostess at Brompton, Mrs Elizabeth Davies.

[12] The Rev. Yakov Ivanovich Smirnov (1759–1840), chaplain to the Russian church in London from 1780 till his death and also to the Russian embassy. (See letter 501.)

one daughter who was just of age. He knew of no such person. I asked him when a girl was of age to dispose of herself in marriage? I could not get any distinct answer to that neither. He seemed however to think that no girl who had a mother living could dispose of herself at any age without her mother's consent, unless impower'd to do so by the father's will. And as to the marriage of a girl of the Greek religion with a man of another religion [*many words obliterated*] I a⟨lso⟩ thought of asking him ⟨…?⟩ He ⟨…?⟩ Russian Statutes at large, and is to ⟨…?⟩ what he finds in a day or two. I did not tell him you were ⟨the⟩ party concerned: but neither had I any apprehension of what might be his suspicions. As you say the whole Court is up in arms about it, every thing of a secret is out of the question. You ninniest of all ninny-hammers! as if after describing her to the knowledge of any body that could have open'd the letter at Petersburgh you could not as well have told her name. It would be a great treat for example to M⟨rs⟩ Q.S.P. if her name were Yssoupof: Princess Yssoupof: attendu that one of the Dutchess's of Courland the last before Madlle. Medern was a Princess Yssoupof; whom poor Lohmen upon my mentioning her, called an old whore.

Smyrnof was as busy as a bee packing up fine things in abundance for Count Soltakoff,[13] the man that whilom commanded a Russian army.

442

From Reginald Pole Carew[1]

25 May 1783

Dear Sir,

If I were not in Expectation at this Moment of seeing Prince Wiasemskoy[2] here, to go with me into the Country this day, I

[13] Nikolay Ivanovich Saltykov (1736–1816). A distinguished soldier, who saw active service during the Seven Years War and the Russo-Turkish war of 1768–74, he later succeeded Potëmkin as president of the college for military affairs.

442. [1] B.M. III: 338. Autograph. Docketed by Bentham: '1783 May 25. Pole Carew—Lower Gros/venor Street / to / I.B. Linc. Inn. / Matushkina's expectations.'

On 2 March 1783 Jeremiah Bentham wrote to Carew, seeking an interview in order to obtain first-hand accounts of Samuel. This move opened up a new friendship to Bentham. Samuel sent further news, both about the favourable progress of his approaches to Catherine II and about his love affair, in a letter to his father dated 23 April/4 May 1783 (B.M. III: 334–7). Possibly it was the arrival of this letter which set off the inquiry about Sof'ya to which this letter refers.

[2] Available information about the prolific stock of the Vyazemskiys (Prince Pëtr

would have desired to have the Pleasure of seeing You at the present Moment. If Nine be a convenient Hour Tomorrow I shall be happy to see You.—I have sounded him a little on the subject.—I cannot learn that there is any Thing in the Absolute Disposal of the Lady, tho' much in Expectancy, dependant however as far as I can learn on the Will of others—

Yours etc.
in haste,
R. Pole Carew.

443

To James Anderson[1]

28 May 1783 (Aet 35)

Wednesday, May 28th, 1783.

Dear Sir,

I am sincerely sorry you do not seem to acquiesce in Mr. Wilson's opinion, which is entirely mine. I will own myself anxious that this pamphlet may never see the light, and that much more on account of your reputation than your purse. There is really a combination among your friends—who are indeed very much your friends, or they would never undertake so invidious a task—to strangle this unhappy bantling in its cradle. Without pretending to assign all *their* reasons, to which I might not be able to do justice, I will take the liberty of giving you a few of *mine*. I say a few, for you will not expect that I should write a pamphlet, in order to prove that you ought not to publish another pamphlet. Why it is you should be so much attached to it, I cannot conceive; for I really do not see a syllable in it that is new. Whether the observations relative to the difficulty of collecting a revenue in thinly-peopled countries,

V. Dolgorukov, *Rossiyskaya Rodoslovnaya Kniga*, 4 parts, St Petersburg, 1854–7), does not permit positive identification of this member of the family nor the establishment of his relationship to Countess Matyushkina. It seems probable that he was also the writer of letter 601 and that the perpetration in that letter of a confusion of cyrillic and roman lettering in the signature conceals the identity of a Prince Aleksandr Vasil'yevich Vyazemskiy, one of two men of this name, uncle and nephew, known to be living about this time.

443. [1] Bowring, x, 127–8.

The subject of this letter was a pamphlet which Anderson printed privately later that year, entitled: *The True Interest of Great Britain Considered: or, a Proposal for establishing the Northern British Fisheries.*

are originally yours or not, I will not pretend to say, though I confess I suspect the negative; but sure I am they are yours already: witness your last pamphlet. Those relative to the inefficacy of bounties, and the injudicious, or supposed injudicious, conditions annexed to them, I thought ingenious when I read them, and well worth more attention than it suited me to bestow; but they, too, are yours already: witness your Observations on National Industry, in which this very subject is treated more satisfactorily, as far as I can speak upon recollection, than in the very pamphlet which professes to treat of nothing else. What you say of the difficulties attending infant manufactures, is there also anticipated. What is there in all this that you should be so anxious to 'discover' and to 'preserve?' Look back to your own works, and you will find it discovered and preserved already, as far as printing and publishing can discover and preserve it. Is it the idea of getting towns built on the spot in question? This has been suggested, and, you will excuse me for saying, suggested, I think, in a more instructive manner, almost these twenty years, by Sir J. Stewart, in the concluding passage of book ii. chap. 30, which I have before me;[2] and, I am told, over and over again, in Campbell's Political Survey, which I have not seen.[3] Is it the idea of engaging people at large to build, by grants of land? America, a country in much better repute, justly or unjustly, than the Scottish Isles, gives land without stint, without such conditions; and with timber on it that cries, 'come cut me,' as plain as ever a herring cried 'come catch me.' Is it the idea of giving the son of Abraham, of Isaac, and of Jacob, a place to rest his head on? America is large enough for him, and as open to him as to any disciple of Christ. I question whether you are aware that Jews, native Jews, are already, and have been for hundreds of years, upon just as good a footing, as to the acquiring of land, as native Christians; and that the object of the act (are you aware of that act?) which was so soon repealed, in consequence of a temporary and party clamour, was only to hold out naturalisation to foreign Jews.[4] I speak from Blackstone, and from the act itself. Is it the

[2] Sir James Steuart, *An Inquiry into the Principles of Political Economy; being an Essay on the Science of Domestic Policy in Free Nations*, 2 vols., London, 1767.

[3] John Campbell, *A Political Survey of Britain; being a Series of Reflections on the situation, lands, inhabitants, revenues, colonies and commerce of this island: intended to show that we have not as yet approached the summit of improvement*, 2 vols., London, 1774.

[4] The Jewish Naturalisation Act (26 Geo. II, c. 26) was passed in 1753 and repealed the following year in response to fierce public agitation. For the whole episode see Thomas W. Perry, *Public Opinion, Propaganda, and Politics in eighteenth-century England. A Study of the Jew Bill of 1753*, Camb. Mass., 1962.

idea of getting Parliament to venture the sum required, because that sum would not exceed, as you suppose without any calculation, the amount of *one month's* expense of the war, as you have written it in huge letters? My dear sir, do you consider that one month's expense of the war *is about a million of money, more or less*?—that a work not of supererogation, but of pressing necessity, long ago begun, and far advanced in the building,—I mean a penitentiary house for the home circuit,—stands still for the want of a tenth or a twentieth of that sum?—that a house somewhat upon that plan is wanted for Edinburgh, that £6000 would do the business, and that this trifle, as it may seem to you, is more than Mr. Stewart,[5] late Provost of Edinburgh, the patron of the scheme, a most intelligent and public-spirited man, has any hopes of getting?—so he told me himself within these three weeks.

Catching fish in the Western Isles might be made a very beneficial business,—a business much more beneficial than it is,—a business more beneficial than any other that could be carried on with an equal capital; but not unless conducted by people, and they in considerable numbers, having fixed habitations in those isles. All this may be true; but what reason have you offered further than your own averment (repeated, and enforced in abundance of declamatory language) for thinking it so? What *data* have these twenty years' reflection and experience of yours (experience of what?) furnished, upon which any, even a most superficial judgment of the matter, can be grounded? What are the trades and manufactures, the association of which would be necessary for carrying on this branch of industry? Net-makers, hook-makers, and so forth. This might be known by surveying and analyzing the furniture of a fishing ship, etc., and considering whence it came. What would be the capital necessary for the stocking of those trades and manufactures? How is that capital to be supplied? If too great for one private undertaker, would it be too great for a partnership? If too great for a partnership, would it for an incorporated company? If too great for an incorporated company, who would be working for their own profit, is there any chance of its being carried

[5] David Steuart (d. 1824), 5th son of John Steuart (1689–1776) 7th laird of Dalguise, Perthshire. He was Lord Provost of Edinburgh, 1780–2. For many years a banker and merchant in Edinburgh and Leith, as a young man he had spent some years abroad, had a wide-ranging mind, and included bibliophily and penal reform among his interests. John Howard received the freedom of the city in 1782 during his provostship, and in that same year Steuart published at Edinburgh, in collaboration with Archibald Cockburn of Cockpen (1738–1820), *General heads of a plan for erecting a new Prison and Bridewell in the City of Edinburgh* (William Anderson, *The Scottish Nation*, iii (1868), p. 511; *The Book of the Old Edinburgh Club*, xii (1923), p. 223).

on by agents appointed by the crown, working for the benefit of I don't know who? What do the Dutch lose by the disadvantages of distance? Is that disadvantage more than equal to the habitual and inveterate difference between British and Dutch economy? Supposing a greater profit might be made by a given capital employed in this way, than by the same capital employed in any other, (a point necessary to be made out, with at least some general show of probability,) why am I, who am carrying on a flourishing manufacture at Manchester, to be taxed, to have money taken out of my pocket, to be given to you to catch fish with in the isles of Scotland? Certainly I ought not, unless with that money you could bring to market a great many more pounds' worth of fish than I could of cloth. When you have given something of an answer to these questions, I may perhaps be able to supply you with as many more; and when you have answered those, then perhaps your pamphlet may have some claim to the title it assumes: supposing all the while that I, who am a mere novice in political economy, can, in the course of a most hasty and superficial glance, have gone any part of the way towards exhausting the considerations necessary for founding a judgment upon this complicated question. When you have collected the matter above alluded to, you may then the better afford to leave out all general disquisitions about human nature, especially if they should have nothing either very new in the matter, or pointed in the manner: all histories of the European transactions in the East Indies: all controversies founded on loose expressions of Mr. Howlett,[6] or Mr. anybody else, relative to abstract propositions on the subject of population: all caveats against Dr. Tucker,[7] or Dr. anybody else, about the property of supposed new ideas: all invectives against ministers, in or out of place, on the score of measures which have no other connexion with that in question, than in so far as they relate to money: all declamations founded on the supposition that the ruin of a country, which is to be starved this summer, is no otherwise to be prevented than by raising piles of brick and mortar, which may come to be lived in two or three years hence; but of all things, all passages tending to insinuate, in terms more or less explicit, that all political men, if not all men whatever, are equally blind and profligate, and that the whole stock of intelligence, as well as probity in the world, happens, by

[6] John Howlett (1731–1804), vicar of Great Dunmow, Essex, wrote several works on population, including *An Examination of Dr. Price's Essay on the Population of England and Wales; and the Doctrine of an Increased Population in this Kingdom Established by Facts*, Maidstone, 1781.

[7] Josiah Tucker (1711–99), Dean of Gloucester, writer on economic subjects.

some odd accident, to centre in a single person, whose censure, without the weight of proof, is to stamp indelible infamy on every head it lights on. It is now past one—I began at past eleven; and these representations, I see but too plainly, are coloured by the impatience which late hours, and multiplied avocations, give to a sensible temperament and feeble constitution: but if you make the requisite abatements, you may profit: and as you know the motive, (for what motive but one could have induced me to give us both this plaguing-bout,) you will forgive.

In the other sheet[8] you have my opinion on your pamphlet; if, notwithstanding, you persist in printing it, all I have to say to you further is, that your orders will be obeyed. And yet, why in London? —in Edinburgh, printing is not only cheaper, but better done. But that you must doubtless have made up your mind about.

444

From Samuel Bentham[1]

30 May/10 June 1783

Petersbourg May 30th 1783 O.S.

I have just been writing to my father to give him some little account of my love matter and telling him at the same time of my being in all probability left *Chargé d'affaires* here for 2 or 3 months at Sir James's departure.[2] It is today only that Sir James proposed it to me and writes to Mr. Fox[3] to acquaint him with his intentions of leaving the business in my hands. I believe you have had very little expectation of my ever being engaged in political business and I believe not much inclined to imagine me fit for it. If I am not, I shall endeavour to make myself so while Sir James is yet here, and

[8] Bowring states that this last paragraph was written on a 'second sheet'.

444. [1] B.M. III: 345–6. Autograph. Docketed by Bentham: '1783 May 30/June 10 / S.B. Petersburgh / to / I.B. Linc. Inn.'

Addressed: 'Jere^y Bentham Esqr. / Lincoln's Inn / London. [...?]' Postmarks: 'IV.5,' and one illegible. Stamped: 'ST PETERSBOURG'.

Copy by Jeremiah Bentham, B.M. III: 347.

[2] Samuel Bentham's letter to his father is at B.M. III: 343–4. Harris's plan to hand over the care of the British mission at St Petersburg to Samuel in order to expedite his own return to England did not take place, because Catherine II decided that Samuel could not be admitted into the Russian service if he were also holding an official position under the British crown.

[3] Charles James Fox had recently returned to office as Foreign Secretary in the Fox-North Coalition ministry headed by the Duke of Portland.

for that purpose I will /begin to/ go to school to him tomorrow. Besides the opportunity this may afford me of making freinds at home, it cannot but assist my views here of which I shall give you some account in a packet I send by sea.

Your poor brother is become very bare in several necessary articles, but in none so intollerably as in linnen. A reinforcement of a dozen of shirts is absolutely unavoidable. They would be much cheaper and better if you could continue to send them from England washed and marked.

With respect to my love affair, from the *first* to the last approve of my conduct. Whatever blame there is falls only on her for not acting now more resolutely in my favour. So that I shall have at any rate the consolation of having distinguished myself much to my advantage. The highest compliments imaginable I have received on the occasion. This to one of *our* disposition cannot but have alleviated much the vexation from the disappointment hitherto.
Sir James's freindship and confidence is very flattering to me and I doubt /not/ will be on all accounts advantageous.

As thou art so good and provident a brother I dare to say thou wilt endeavour to furnish me with such kind of knowledge as may be subservient to the employment I am going to engage in and in which I am most wanting. I dare to say Sir James has all kind of works which can afford any assistance, therefore dont plague yourself till I can give you some better account of what I think you could procure me.

Anderson. Yes it is probable that something very advantageous for us both may be brought about. Of this I will tell you more by the packet I send by sea.

On Monday last I gave in a letter for the Empress to her principal Secretary[4] which I dare to say he presented yesterday. In a few days I may be able to guess of the event of it. It was an offer on my part to put into execution the improvements I proposed in my paper of which you have a copy. If She accepts the offer and grants me such terms as /to/ make such an employment desirable it may take place as soon as a new Minister is come here to take the political business out of my hands. In the meantime I shall be able to settle the conditions probably more advantageously than if I had not been in such an employment.

[4] Aleksandr Andreyevich Bezborodko (1747–99). He became secretary to Catherine II in 1775 and after the dismissal of Count Panin towards the end of 1781 he was virtually Russian minister for foreign affairs. A draft of Samuel's letter to the empress offering his services is at B.M. III: 339–40.

I wonder I hear nothing about 'Principles of Penal Jurisprudence.'[5] My present situation viewed on all sides is interesting enough. Be of good spirits. I ought to be notwithstanding my despondancy in my love affair. The coals may be blown up again now.

Letter of attorney you shall also have by shipping.

Although I have received your packet of letters I have not as yet got the box of books. I suppose the Custom house delays them.

445

To Mr Klangen[1]

June 1783 (Aet 35)

Jeremias Bentham Londinensis Domino Klangen Chirurgo Imperiali pro fodinis apud Barnaoul in Siberia salutem.

Misit mihi aliquot abhinc mensibus frater meus junior Samuilis ~~quindecim~~ sexdecim plus minus summum specimina, quae tuae humanitati accepta rettulit. Acceptissima sane evaserunt nostris Botanophilis, utpote quorum ~~nonnulla~~ alia heic culta sed rara, alia specimine sicco, alia icone tantum, alia ne nomine quidem (specifico ingenuo) nota. Sic mihi pronuntiavit Josephus Bankes baronettus, Societatis nostrae Regalis Praeses, Solomon noster quod ad plantas attinet. Plantas ille non asservat nisi siccas: ejus autem /consilio/ communicavi semina ~~a te missa~~ supradicta variis cultoribus, inter quos Dominus Eaton, Hortulanus Regius apud Kew (juxta Londinium) magnopere laetatus est. Idem dixerim de Dno. Hope, Med. Doct. horti publici custode apud Edingburgenses, in Scotiâ. Chartas curavi tuo nomine inscribi ~~ut ne~~ donati cui debent, nesciant. O /Tu qui/ Botanicam amas, ~~valde~~ /ut/ delectareris si sentire posses quanto sit ea scientia apud nostrates in honore! Ut

[5] Cf. letter 437, n. 1 (near the end). It would appear as if earlier in the year Bentham had given his brother good reason to think that he was about to publish the work on criminal jurisprudence which Brissot had announced.

445. [1] B.M. III: 363–4. Autograph. Draft with many corrections. Docketed by Bentham: '1783 June / J.B. Lincoln's Inn / to / Klangen Barnaoul.'

See letter 438, n. 6. Samuel Bentham had passed through Barnaul on his way back from Irkutsk to St Petersburg about the beginning of August 1782. Evidently Klangen had been extremely helpful; for, in a long letter of 20 June/1 July 1784 (B.M. IV: 70–80), about Russian plans and prospects, Samuel wrote to his brother: 'Microscope I wanted to give to Klangen at Barnaoul in consideration of what he has given and what in future he may give me in the way of Nat. Hist.'

taceam optimates et generosos, duodena aliquot imo et centena puto numerari posse /in hac vicinia/ eorum qui negotium faciant plantas alendi [*two words crossed out*] delectamenti causâ emendas inter quos non desunt qui ~~opibus~~ doctrinâ opibus, moribus etiam generosos aemulantur. Ut /conjicias/ in quantum divitiae /opes/ nostrae in hoc genere crescunt, ostendit mihi unus ex his 400 novarum ~~seminum~~ plantarum species, ab ipso solo hoc viro satas, quibus et aliae multae postea accessêre: alter, mesembryanthemae /specierum/ ~~dupl~~ numerum duplo /fere/ majorem /quam/ eorum quae Linnaeo innotuêre. [*Seven words crossed out*] /Ratus tibi non molestum fore symbolum tuum/ denuo ~~addire~~ /conferre/, quod ex liberalitate tuâ jam experta ~~nullus~~ /non est/ quod dubitem, catalogum adjeci plantarum Sibericarum /aliquot/ quae heic adhuc desiderantur.

1. Salicornia Arabica.
2. Cornûs variae species.
3. Cortusa Mathiolia
4. Cortusa *gemele* (non sum certus de scripturâ
5. Phlox Siberica
6. Campanula Siberica.
7. Robiniae variae species.

Surrexerunt jam ex tuis jam missis plurimae, /inter quas Dryae geoidis, Robinia Halodendri, et Berberidis Sibericae memini./

Tune plantas colis, sicut et amas? Si ita est, fac sciam, /seminum quae viam ~~tam longam~~ patiuntur tam longam/ non indigebis. Si rescissem, misissem jamdudum, sicut aliis misi petente fratre ex catalogo: ~~perpauca~~ /species/ equidem perpaucas, quoniam aestas praeterita omnium quas novimus /colligendis seminibus/ maxime inopportuna. Egomet ~~studiis~~ urbanus merus et studiis politicis deditus non sum botanicus, sed /attamen/ botanices a pueritiâ amator. Quod ad experitus /portationes/ attinet, ~~egomet~~ mihi curae ~~esset~~ /feret/ eas tibi ad Petroburgam usque non molestas fieri: sed de reliquâ viâ opus fuerit me docueris, quo aliquid tibi et certius /et nullo aut saltem/ et minimo ~~aut nullo~~ pretio perveniat, praesertim postquam frater meus, qui id negotium potuerit curare, ~~Russiam~~ Petroburgam liquerit. ~~Scripsi~~ /Scribo/ tibi Latinâ, /compertus/ ea te usum linguâ: eadem licet rescribas, aut si magis tibi conveniat Gallicâ. Vale vir erudite, meque inter tuos numera.

Maximum est hie plantarum Pincusicum desiderium; ex borealibus partibus inquam quae tuo imperio conterminae, nostrum climata ~~convenirent~~ potuerint sine cura tolerare: exempli gratiâ

Pelinensis. Si arbor fructifera nobis nova /posset hie mitti/, aut etiam legumen aut etiam flos ~~adeo speciosus~~ ejus speciositatis ut posset /[...?] (favente eventu)/ per vulgum ~~multipl~~ venundari (~~de seminibus semper loquor) ita ut his succederet,~~ nullus dubito, adeo liberales generosorum imo et hortulanorum /nonnullorum/ animi, quin collatione facta, munus pecuniarum conflare vellent quod dignum feret ut mittatur /ad regiones etiam adeo dissitas/. Tu istis regionibus nimis sane es remotus: sed [*three words crossed out*] /nostri/ forsan aliquem botanicum qui eas ~~regiones~~ est aditurus.

Translation

Jeremy Bentham of London to Mr Klangen, Imperial surgeon at the mines at Barnaoul in Siberia, greetings.

My younger brother Samuel sent me some months ago about sixteen specimens which he said he owed to your kindness. They have certainly proved most welcome to our Botanophiles, for some are cultivated here but are rare, others are known by dried specimen, others only by picture, and others not even by the name in its native form. Such was the information given me by Joseph Banks, baronet, president of our Royal Society, our Solomon when it comes to plants. He only keeps dried plants; but on his advice I sent some of the aforesaid seeds to various growers, among whom Mr Eaton,[2] Royal gardener at Kew (near London) was exceedingly pleased. I could say the same of Mr Hope, keeper of the public garden at Edinburgh in Scotland. I had the documents inscribed with your name so that those who received this gift might not be unaware to whom they are indebted. O you who love botany, how delighted you would be if you could feel how great honour that science is held in among our people! To omit the aristocrats and men of breeding, I think about 112 could be named in this area who make a business of raising plants to be bought for pleasure: among them some who rival even the well-born in learning, wealth and character. So that you may guess to what heights our riches in this department are growing, one of these people showed me 400 species of new plants sown by this one man alone, and afterwards many other species have accrued to these; another showed me species of mesembryanthemum to about twice the number of those known to Linnaeus. Thinking that it would not be troublesome to you to contribute your portion anew—this I can hardly doubt in view of the liberality we have already experienced from you—I have added

[2] William Aiton (1731–93).

a catalogue of some Siberian plants still lacking here:

1. Salicornia Arabica
2. Various species of cherry
3. Cortusa Matthiolii
4. Cortusa Gemele (I'm not sure about the spelling[3]
5. Phlox Siberica
6. Campanula Siberica
7. Various species of Robinia

Many plants have already come up from the seeds you sent, among which I recall Dryas Geoides, Robinia Halodendron, and Berberis Siberica.

Do you cultivate plants as well as loving them? If so, let me know, and you shall not lack for seeds that can stand so long a journey. If I had found out, I should long ago have sent them, just as I have sent to other people when my brother made requests from the catalogue: but a few kinds only, for the past summer has been the most unsuitable we have known for collecting seeds. I am a townsman pure and simple, devoted to politics and I am no botanist, though I have loved botany since I was a boy. As to safe transport, I could take care that they give you no trouble as far as Petersburg; but as to the rest of the journey, I must be given information as to how something may come to you both safely and at little or no expense, especially since my brother, who could have seen to the matter, has left Petersburg. I write to you in Latin, having heard that you are conversant with the language: you may write back in the same, or, if it is more convenient to you, in French. Farewell, learned man, and count me one of your friends.

There is a great want here of [...?] plants: I mean from the northern districts bordering on your empire—[such plants] will be able to withstand our climate without trouble: e.g. the *Pelinensis*. If a fruitful tree that is new to us could be sent here, or even a vegetable, or even a flower so beautiful that it could be (with luck) sold publicly, I have no doubt—so generous are the hearts of the aristocracy (and even some of the gardeners)—that they would be willing to make a collection and get up a gift of money worth sending even to regions so far removed from us. You are certainly very remote from those parts; but perhaps you know of some botanist who is going to visit them.

[3] Bentham meant 'gmelinii'.

446

From Jacques Pierre Brissot de Warville[1]

11 June 1783

Londres 11 Juin

La quantité de Lettres, Monsieur, que j'ai eu à expédier m'a empeché de répondre plutôt à la vôtre. Je me rapelle très bien avoir vu dans le Courier[2] quelques pièces relatives à la Neutralité armée,[3] et je vais les Chercher.

La critique que vous faites de M. Pr. de R.[4] doit être fondée; car je vous crois bien versé dans les lois de votre pais. Mais si vous connaissiés aussi bien le Nôtre, vous verriés qu'il n'est pas mal d'y equilloner [*aiguilloner*] les esprits par des Comparaisons avec les Constitutions étrangeres. Vraies ou non, elles font un certain effet et le bien se fait toujours.

Je n'ose pas vous répéter que j'espère bientôt avoir le plaisir de me rapprocher de vous, et de vous voir plus souvent.[5] Je ne veux pas vous fixer le tems, car je vous ai appris à ne me plus croire sur cet article et les circonstances m'y ont forcé. Cela viendra plutôt que vous ne comptés, croiés moi tout à vous sans cérémonie

De Warville.

446. [1] B.M. III: 348–9. Autograph. Docketed by Bentham: '1783 June 11 / Warville Brompton Row / to / I.B. Lincoln's Inn.'

Addressed: 'Jeremy Bentham Esqr. / Lincoln's Inn Old Buildings No. 6.' Postmark '13/IV.' Stamped: 'PENNY POST NOT PAID. T'.

Printed, *J.-P. Brissot, Correspondance et Papiers*, ed. C. Perroud, Paris, 1912, pp. 58–9.

[2] I.e. the *Courrier de l'Europe.*

[3] In 1780 Catherine II of Russia had taken the lead in forming an alliance of northern neutral states for the mutual protection of their merchant shipping against interference by the western Powers which were engaged in the American war of independence (Isabel de Madariaga, *Britain, Russia and the Armed Neutrality of 1780*, 1962).

[4] Antoine Francois Prost de Royer (1729–84), of Lyons, a writer on jurisprudence, had begun in 1781 the publication of a new edition of Baillon's *Dictionnaire de Jurisprudence* (*J.-P. Brissot, Mémoires*, ed. C. Perroud, 2 vols., Paris, n.d., i, 258–64).

[5] In July Brissot was still at Brompton Row, but he later found accommodation at 26 Newman Street.

447

FROM SAMUEL BENTHAM[1]

2/13 June 1783

Petersbourg June 2nd O.S. 1783.

I told you by last post[2] of my having given in a letter for the Empress offering my services to inspect the execution of the improvements I had proposed in my paper of observations. I cannot as yet tell the answer which she gave immediately on reading it, verbatim, but the tenour of it was a desire of having me, and the liberty of choosing the place with a kind of intimation that I should propose the terms and mode of engagement. In short the whole of the manner in which the letter was presented and the answer given was very flattering. I shall know much more about it tomorrow morning, but in the mean time I cannot but let you know thus much: besides something came into my head yesterday which though I have not sufficiently considered yet the sooner I give you /time/ to think about /it/ the better. First there is no reason to doubt her Majesty's being already disposed to engage me. Secondly when she comes to know that I am to be entrusted with the ministerial business from the time of Sir James's departure to the coming of the next minister, my being thought in my own country capable of executing that business cannot but raise me in her opinion. The alarm that several persons in power must be in from the idea of a person being employed in an economical department with the probability of his having permission to address himself directly to the Sovereign, has already begun to shew itself; and there is reason to imagine that alarm may be increased. My situation then in this respect joined to my chargé d'affaires business must render my situation for these 6 months to come particularly interesting. I do not say anything here about my love concern because that I think must now be determined one way or the other in a fortnight.

It occurred to me yesterday that you would receive infinite

447. [1] B.M. III: 350–1. Autograph. Docketed by Bentham: '1783 June 2/13 / S.B. Petersburgh / to / I.B. Linc. Inn / Cath. accepting offers.'

Addressed: 'Jeremy Bentham Esqr. / Lincoln's Inn / London', and redirected, 'Brompton / near Chatham, Kent', and endorsed: 'Missent to Maidstone'. Three postmarks: '12/IV'; '7 o'clock.'; 'KENT POST PAID' [*date illegible*].

[2] Letter 444.

satisfaction and some advantage in being witness to what I shall be doing for these 6 months to come. In some /respects/ you could help me /very/ much; but then in other respects I fear you would govern me too much. Have you anything to prevent your spending 3 or 4 months here. You might come out and even return also by sea: but it must be unknown to all but your most intimate freinds, or to all if possible. It must be under another name and without going with public company. Could you not pretend to go into the country. You would be at the same time my Mentor and my Pupil. You would be witness to my outset /at/ the most important period of my life, and be assured you would receive instruction.

I have a sheet or two ready to go by shipping. I shall add another today and dispatch it by the first opportunity. I shall by that opportunity answer your last letters.

448

To Jeremiah Bentham[1]

13 June 1783

Lincolns Inn June 13. 1783.

Hon:$_d$ Sir

I am just now returned from Barking, where I went on foot, and came back by the same conveyance. Tyser[2] told me he happen'd to be at Waters's[3] at the time the Bailiffs came with the Appraiser: but since then he knows nothing of Waters, nor of the key, nor of the house nor any thing that belongs to it. He took a walk with me thither: but the windows were shut up, the door fast, and no getting in. I thought it would answer no purpose breaking in: it might have two bad effects; the discharging the Sheriff, upon the supposition of his remaining hitherto responsible: and the making a breach which might afterwards be made use of [by] idle boys and thieves.

Your old dwelling-house is in better luck. The gentleman you heard of who made use of it to entertain ladies in, continued in it but a fortnight. For some time past young Tyser has been tenant

448. [1] B.M. III: 352. Autograph. Docketed by Jeremiah Bentham: 'Son Jeremy's letter about The Houses at Barking in Essex / dat'd June 13 1783.'

Addressed: 'Jeremiah Bentham Esqr. / at the Black Boy Inn / Chelmsford.' Postmark: '13/IV.'

[2] Not identified.

[3] Not identified.

to it; not much, as it should seem to the old man's liking. After laying out about thirty pound upon it he has let it *again* to a Major *Cameron*,[4] who is related to Cameron[5] who is in partnership with Sir Charles Raymond,[6] and who (I mean the Major) is married to a sister of Lady Raymond. They are expected in it to day. Tyser and I went thither together; and I explored every nook and cranny of the premises: house, garden, fields, out-houses, and every thing. Young Tyser I did not see: he being at work at Sir Charles Raymond's: but I saw old M^rs^. Tyser, and young M^rs^. Tyser, and five ⟨...⟩ children, out of, I think, nine they have in all. Further particulars, being rather tired I hope you will excuse my deferring, till we meet. Indeed the above is every thing that is material: except that I should have told you, Major Cameron has taken the house for a year and no longer. I beg my best respects to my Mother, and am

Hon:$_{d}$ Sir
Your's dutifully and affectionately
Jeremy Bentham.

449

From Samuel Bentham[1]

? 12/23 June 1783

Code

Certainly they would not bear to have any imperfections pointed out. Where what you have to say agrees with their plan

[4] Not identified. [5] Not identified.

[6] Sir Charles Raymond, 1st bart. (1713–88), of Valentine House, Essex, was a prosperous London banker. His wife was Sarah, da. of Thomas Webster of Bromley, Kent.

449. [1] B.M. III: 466. Autograph. Docketed by Bentham: '1783 / S.B. Petersburgh / to / J.B. Linc. Inn / Code advice / xviii.'

The dating of this letter presents difficulties. This attribution is suggested by the fact that this letter is now located next to a draft of a letter written by Samuel to his father dated 12/23 June 1783, recounting the crisis when his love affair became known to Countess Matyushkina's family (B.M. III: 468–9, copy sent ibid., 353–6). However, it may not have been dispatched until a few days later, with other letters dated 26 June/7 July (B.M. III: 365, 366). The most indicative piece of internal evidence is the passage: 'Made in the manner above mentioned suitable to this country it might be published here free of all expence by Princess Dashkoff's im-

say so and give them as much of the merit as you can spare where what you have to say contradicts their plan go on and take no notice of their's. There seem to be two ways in which a work of this kind can meet with credit here. One is from being the production of an author who either on account of this very work or some former one has acquired great reputation in Europe. The other is from ~~taking all the example~~ appearing to found the whole of it from an amplification of the principles which may be discovered or which a devout admirer may think he discovers in the Instructions which the Empress has given for that purpose or from the laws themselves which She has hitherto made. On this latter plan what the author has to say is, I have been employing myself for these 10 or 15 years in pursuing your principles to all the cases imaginable so as to produce an exhaustive code. The immediate exigencies of improving particular branches of legislation must be supposed to be the reasons which have prevented her having completed herself a work of this kind, not but what the 'Instruction pour le Code' alone was sufficient for the Sovereign. /In/ this said 'Instruction' then or in some of the laws themselves *hints* at least totidem litteris must be found for every reform and expedient proposed. In this manner if the work be published in french it will be certain of success. Would the success be purchased in this way at too dear a rate? All this which you may conceive exceptionable might be brought in in the form of an Appendix of notes and preface. The work itself might appear pure in English and even in the french edition as published in other countries.

Made in the manner above mentioned suitable to this country it might be published here free of all expence by Princess Dashkoff's immediate power. Besides I could appear myself as the Editor of the french edition published here, which would gain me credit and save you that independency of Character in England which I hope you will never deviate from. If you can make the Americans adopt in some degree your ideas you will then shine most nobly, but could you have the most flattering offers here, I should oppose your accepting them with all my might. I may sell my independance in a great degree and in more ways than one, and that I hope may serve for us both.

To be sure were you here just now we might cook up several things which would advance my interest exceedingly. Without

mediate power.' About a month later, on 16/27 July, Samuel wrote to his brother: 'I told you in my last packet that your work might be printed here, but I am affraid I was mistaken' (letter 457).

you, Love, indecision, and if you will have it indolence render me very little able to profit of the favorable opportunities which present themselves. The freinds I have now may shortly be unable or unwilling to serve me. This certainly is the crisis of my good or bad fortune in this country.

450

To David Steuart[1]

27 June 1783 (Aet 35)

June 27th, 1783.

Sir,

I take advantage of your very obliging permission, to trouble you with a memorandum of the documents I wish for, relative to the criminal law of your part of the island.

By way of a clue, give me leave to mention the purpose. Upon the supposition that the influence of religious instruction is beneficial, upon the whole, to the temporal interests of society, and that the labours of the clergy do a certain degree of service by what they contribute towards turning this influence to account; I know of no observable standard more exact for estimating the value of that service, than the comparative paucity of such mischievous acts, as the law has stigmatized under the denomination of crimes. England, which, containing such a number of people, and such a quantity of wealth, pays to its clergy such a sum, (which is distributed among them in such a manner,) has, in a given period, such a number of criminals: Scotland, which, containing such a number of people, and such a quantity of wealth, pays to its clergy, so much less in proportion, and that distributed in a different manner—has, in the same period, such or such another number of criminals. I am apt to think it would turn out that this latter number, instead of being greater than that in England, in proportion as the pay of the clergy

450. [1] Bowring, x, 129–31.

Bowring identified the recipient as Dugald Stewart (1753–1828), one of the notable scholars at the university of Edinburgh about this period, who became professor of moral philosophy in 1785. However, internal evidence makes it certain that this letter was addressed to David Steuart, recently Lord Provost of Edinburgh (about whom see letter 443, n. 5). He, but not Dugald Stewart, was interested in prison reform and in the work of John Howard (hence Bentham's 'claiming kin to you and Mr. Howard as a kind of brother in the trade', with a reference to his pamphlet on the Hard Labour Bill). The phrase 'that I may pay the amount of it to your house in London' also indicates that the letter was sent to a man who was in business.

in Scotland is less, is in fact less; and that therefore, in Scotland, the clerical work is not only done for less money than in England, but better done. This is the inference I am disposed to draw from the Table of Convictions in Scotland, already published by our excellent friend Mr. Howard.[2] But, as that table extends to no other than capital crimes, the information it affords can be, as you must perceive, but very unsatisfactory with a view to my purpose. It is the more so, inasmuch as the same crimes which are capital in England, are not so, in every instance, in Scotland, and *vice versâ*. To be sure, in both countries the denominations of crimes, etc., are, in but too many instances, determined not so much by the real nature of the mischief, as by extraneous and accidental circumstances, such as the punishment or mode of prosecution—but this is an imperfection I cannot help. I must take the information, and be glad to get it too, as it stands. What I wish for is, therefore, a table of the crimes, that within a certain period (suppose from the beginning of the century) have been *known to be* committed in Scotland,—the more extensive as to the sorts of crimes, and the more minute the distinctions, so much the better. As to the distinctions, those given in Mr. Howard's table are, as far as that goes, sufficiently particular: the head of murder excepted, inasmuch as it makes no distinction between homicide in prosecution of robbery, and the murder of a defenceless person through particular enmity, fair duelling, and I don't know how many other species I could point out, but which are as different from one another as guilt from innocence.

I say, have been *known to be* committed; and, therefore, a table of the *trials* would be much more satisfactory than a table of the bare *convictions*,—and still more so, an account, which I suppose it is impossible to obtain, of *informations* lodged before a magistrate. You have a method, I have heard, of transporting suspected persons, with their consent, without a trial; of these, some, I presume, would, were it not for such provision, have gone into the class of those informed against, but discharged for want of sufficient evidence—others into the class of convicts.

I dare say it is but a small part of all this information that is attainable; but any part that it should be in your way to obtain for me, without too much trouble, I should think myself infinitely obliged to you for.

[2] See J. Howard, *The State of Prisons in England and Wales*, 2nd edn., Warrington, 1780, p. 445: 'Table X. An Account of the Number of Prisoners convicted of Capital Crimes in Scotland from 1st January 1768 to 1st July 1779.'

To a man of Mr. Stewart's turn of mind, the various public uses which at any rate such a sort of document might be put to, and the credit which (if my conjecture be well-grounded) the result would reflect upon his friend, must, if fame says true, hold out inducements infinitely more favourable than any that could be presented by the acknowledgments of so insignificant an individual as myself. And that the information may receive a much greater degree of circulation than I could expect to give it, we will make Howard insert it in his next publication. He will, I dare say, be very glad of it, for he seemed to acquiesce in my remarks on the incompleteness of that printed in his own appendix. Be there more or less of it, the copying of it must necessarily be attended with some expense. —You will be kind enough to direct the copyist to make a memorandum of it, that I may pay the amount of it to your house in London.

I took the liberty, as you may perhaps remember, of claiming kin to you and Mr. Howard as a kind of brother of the trade, which I certainly am, as far as endeavours go at least, however inferior in point of means. The only proof I can as yet produce to you, in support of such a pretension, is contained in a little pamphlet,[3] a copy of which herewith sent, I hope you will do me the honour to accept.—I am, with great truth and regard, Sir, your most obedient humble servant,

J.B.

The expense and trouble it cost me, were not wholly thrown away, as the Bill, which was the subject of it, underwent a number of alterations, several of which, I understood by a note from Sir W. Blackstone, were the consequences of my remarks.

[3] *A View of the Hard Labour Bill.*

451

To Jeremiah Bentham[1]

8 July 1783 (Aet 35)

Brompton near Chatham
July 8th 1783

Hond. Sir

I write now, only that, upon your weekly visit to town you may find a letter to thank you for your favour of the 3rd. instant.[2] It gives me the highest satisfaction to see you so well reconciled to the miscarriage. When I see you uneasy, I never can be easy myself: and when I see you satisfied, I never can be much otherwise. As to the rest I have two recipes for content: one is to look always forward and never backward: the other is to look to the bright side of things, and never to the dark. By the facility I have acquired of practising these two lessons, I think I have made myself a tolerable good practical philosopher: but on this occasion, I must confess, you have got the start of me. The disappointment does not now sit, /nor even/ did it from the first *fall* heavy on me, because I never suffer'd myself to entertain any thing more than a very faint expectation of success, and because no disappointment ever could for these many years, or ~~heavy~~ ever can sit heavy on me: but you are not even so much as disappointed. To be sure /in/ what light soever we ought to look upon the news, good or bad, nothing can be more flattering than the manner in which it has been convey'd to us. I have sent your letter, as it is, to town, to be forwarded to my Uncle and to Mr. Mulford.[3] It is the more agreable to me inasmuch as I look upon it as affording no inconsiderable presumption that the air of the Terras agrees with you.

For my part I am here very much at my ease, in a situation very favourable to the only occupation and the only amusement I am capable of. Owing to a variety of causes I get forward here much better than at London.

451. [1] B.M. III: 367–8. Autograph. Docketed by Jeremiah Bentham: 'Fils Jeremy / Lr. datd. Brompton / July 8 1783.'

Addressed: 'Jeremiah Bentham Esqr. / Queen's Square Place / Westminster.' Postmark obliterated.

The matter to which this letter relates has not been ascertained.

[2] Missing.

[3] I.e. his mother's brother, George Woodward Grove (d. 1784), and Grove's cousin, John Mulford (1721–1814).

The Mr. and Mrs. Bentham you missed of were the very persons you conjectured:[4] you were in better luck than I. What grounds they could have for the surprise they expressed at finding you out of town, I know not, If they had asked me about it, they would have heard: as they did not, I said nothing to them on the subject. I received them civilly while they staid, but it was no object of mine to protract their visit. I hear the Bellman, and must therefore conclude rather precipitately with assuring you with what respect and affection I am

Ever Your's
J.B.

452

From Jacques Pierre Brissot de Warville[1]

8 July 1783

Londres 8 Juillet.

L'occasion qui devoit, mon Cher Confrère, me faire passer par Chatham, n'aura pas lieu; ainsi je ne Compte plus sur le plaisir que je m'étois promis d'aller y passer deux Jours avec vous. Je ne vous cacherai pas, quel était l'objet de mon voiage à Douvres. Je suis marié, mais jusqu'à ce jour mon mariage a été secret pour plusieurs raisons. Mon amie vient me rejoindre à Londres, et je devois aller au devant d'elle à Douvres. Mais d'autres motifs font que je fattens à Londres à Chaque Jour, à Chaque Instant.

J'espere bien cet hiver en étant plus près de vous avoir les moiens de m'instruire sur mille points qui sont loin d'être éclaircis. En attendant je vous souhaite toutes le plaisir que vous ne pouvez

[4] Perhaps Edward William Bentham (d. 1785) and his wife. See the genealogical table, *Correspondence*, i, p. xxxviii.

452. [1] B.M. III: 369–70. Autograph. Docketed by Bentham: '1783 July 8 / Warville Brompton Row / to / I.B. Brompton / 5.'

Addressed: 'Jeremy Bentham Esqr. / at Mrs. Davies Wood Street / Brompton / Near Chatham.' Postmark: '8/IY'.

Printed, *J.-P. Brissot, Correspondance et Papiers*, ed. C. Perroud, Paris, 1912, p. 64; and incomplete in English translation in Bowring, x, 191.

Brissot married Felicité Dupont in September 1782, but the marriage was kept secret for several months so that his wife might retain a post as governess which she had obtained under the auspices of Mme de Genlis (*Correspondance*, xxiii–xxiv).

manquer de goûter à la Campagne, et vous prie de me croire sincèrement tout à vous, et sans ceremonie

Brissot de Warville

P.S. Je n'ai pas encore entendue parler de la Caisse de Virchaux —J'ai quelqu'un qui veille sur l'arrivée du Vaisseau.

453

To Jeremiah Bentham[1]

10 July 1783 (Aet 35)

Hond. Sir

I sent you a day or two ago through Wilson[2] a copy of a letter from Sam,[3] to which I now refer. I wonder whether he will get any thing from people here for doing that sort of journey-work for them, besides the credit of it, and the collateral advantages he may make of it? I think they can't sweat him for two or three months /together/ without giving him what the French call a *pot de vin*, and what in vulgar English may be rendered 'something to drink,' after he has done—I wonder when Fitzherbert sets off[4]—I wonder how long he will be upon his journey? I wonder whether it would be within the sphere of possibility to make him take the latest rather than the earliest of two days that might be indifferent to him, by enchantment or any other means less supernatural, supposing it would be of any use? I should not mind writing to his brother[5] in that view,

453. [1] B.M. III: 371–2. Autograph. Docketed by Jeremiah Bentham: 'Fils Jeremy / Lr. datd. Brompton / 10 July 1783.'

Addressed: 'Jeremiah Bentham Esqr. / Queen's Square Place / Westminster.'

Samuel Bentham had written on 30 May O.S. about Harris's plan to leave him in temporary charge of the British mission at St Petersburg (letter 444). Unaware as yet that this proposal had been ruled out by Catherine II as incompatible with Samuel's entry into the Russian service (Samuel to his brother, 16/27 July 1783, B.M. III: 378), Bentham and his father were anxious to pull any strings they could in Samuel's favour.

[2] George Wilson.

[3] Presumably letter 444.

[4] The man designated as Harris's successor at St Petersburg was the able professional diplomat, Alleyne Fitzherbert (1753–1839), who was later created (1794) Baron St Helens (I). During the winter of 1782–3 he had been the British representative at Paris in the negotiations leading up to the Peace of Versailles, now reaching their final stages. On him see also letter 189, n. 2, where the periods of his service in France and Russia are mis-stated.

[5] William Fitzherbert (1748–91), of Tissington, elder brother of Alleyne, had become acquainted with Jeremy Bentham about 1773, when he was studying for the

if it wou'd answer any purpose. Concerning all these matters you might get some light from Sneyd.[6]

I have written to Far, to beg the favour of him to order the shirts on my account from Barker, and cause them to be dispatched according to directions I have given.[7]

I can write no more. I have before me half a dozen letters going on at the same time—[8]

Yours' dutifully and affectionately
J.B.

Brompton near Chatham
July 10 1783.

454

From Jacques Pierre Brissot de Warville[1]

14 July 1783

14th July, 1783

There is, my dear colleague, in your letter, a tone of dryness and drollery which grieves me. I have been separated from *mon amie* for fifteen months, and you do not forgive me for setting aside, for a few moments, books and commissions. You have, then, never loved me,—me whose sensibilities mingle with legislation itself. I am less severe.

bar at Lincoln's Inn. He was sometime recorder of Derby, a gentleman-usher to George III, and was created baronet in 1784. See letter 138, n. 30.

[6] Jeremiah Sneyd, member of a Staffordshire family, but born in Ireland, had for some years held clerical posts in the old southern department which had recently been converted into the Foreign Office, and he was now chief clerk.

[7] Samuel's request for the shirts is in letter 444.

[8] None of these letters has been found. One was probably to Brissot de Warville, to which letter 454 is an answer. Another, to Samuel, was acknowledged by him on 1/12 August (letter 459).

454. [1] Bowring, x, 191.

Bowring's rendering in English. Probably incomplete. This letter is evidently in reply to Bentham's answer to letter 452. If it was couched in the sort of jocular style displayed in letter 441, Brissot's comment is understandable.

455

To Jeremiah Bentham[1]

23 July 1783 (Aet 35)

Brompton near Chatham
Wedy 26th July 1783.

Hond. Sir

Yesterday came here a letter from Sam, shorter indeed but much sweeter than that to you which my Mother was so good as to copy for me. You have it on the other leaf. His offers to the Empress you will find are now actually accepted: and he has nothing left now but to choose the scene of action and negotiate about the terms. This is better than presenting a begging petition and getting kicked out of Court with a few hundred roubles in his pocket. It is better also in his judgement even than engaging with the Strogonoffs,[2] which he has all along considered only as a *pis-aller* and which Sir James mentioned to you only as being then the only thing actually in his power. (With regard to the Debt it is certainly no pleasing news:[3] but let us give the devil his due and not condemn him beyond his demerits. We are not told the times of his contracting it: but if you recollect, from the distant period of his last draught /upon Grill/[4] during his Siberian excursion you inferred,

455. [1] B.M. III: 374–5. Autograph. No address or docket.

The year to which this letter belongs is not in doubt, and in 1783 Wednesday fell on 23 July. The address and date at the top of the letter were added by Jeremiah Bentham. Copy by Jeremiah Bentham, B.M. XXII: 120–1. Another copy, B.M. XXI: 259–60.

Samuel wrote a long letter to Jeremy, partly before, partly on or after 1 June O.S. (B.M. III: 357–60), explaining how he had submitted a letter to the Empress offering his services, and that he understood that in principle his offer was accepted, although the question where he should serve still lay open. Some weeks were still to pass before these arrangements were completed. Meanwhile Bentham and his father were still not aware that the idea of Samuel's being chargé d'affaires had now been dropped.

[2] Samuel had outlined at the beginning of the letter referred to above (n. 1.) the terms on which he might enter into an agreement with the Stroganovs. He described them as 'the most honest to be found' but he was disheartened by their indifference to business. 'There indolence is as great an obstacle as dishonesty', he wrote. 'I have spent 3 or 4 afternoons with the Baron playing at Billiards with him to get ½ an hour to talk on a business he is so much interested in: yet he is one of the good economists.'

[3] Samuel, in a letter to his father of 30 May O.S. (B.M. III: 343–4), presumably received in England at the same time as the one just received by Jeremy, had confessed that he had been obliged during recent months to borrow nearly £100 to meet expenses.

[4] A firm of shippers in the Russian trade.

and very justly, the probability and indeed almost /a/ certainty of some other charge that had not been brought to account. We must not therefore impute to him the crime of incorrigibility on that account. A great part, /certainly/ perhaps, the greatest, was ~~certainly~~ contracted within that interval in order to bring him back. None of it has been contracted with Grill. It must therefore all of it have been contracted upon his mere personal credit at Petersburgh. This circumstance though it does not diminish the burthen affords some consolation by the proof it gives of the warm friends he has acquired, and the estimation he is held in there. If by the money already laid out he has purchased an honourable and lucrative establishment in any degree approaching to the amount of his calculations you certainly can not grudge it or look upon it as mis-spent. (The appointments of his /ministerial employment/ will be some little temporary relief to him while it lasts.) Several of my friends from whom I have lately received letters concur in looking upon it as the most honourable and desirable thing for him in every point of view that could have been imagined. Far from thwarting or superseding his more lucrative enterprizes, it cannot but contribute in the highest degree to forward them, as he himself observes, and as is manifest enough from the nature of the thing. A stronger certificate of abilities and integrity no young man in his situation could ever have received. The state of our negotiations with that country appears to be particularly critical, both on account of the approaching war with the Turks on which the French and we must be keeping an attentive eye, and on account of the commercial concerns that come to be discussed between Russia and us in consequence of the Revolution in America.[5] If Sir James had not been fully persuaded of his sufficiency he would never have staked

[5] At this time a war between Russia and Turkey over the Crimea seemed most probable. By the peace of Kutchuk-Kainardji of 1774 Turkey had agreed that the Crimea, formerly part of the Ottoman Empire, should become an independent khanate, subordinate to the Sultan in religious matters only. In April 1783, after the khanate had been for nearly ten years rent by the quarrels of pro- and anti-Russian factions, Catherine II issued a decree annexing it to Russia. Despite this breach of the treaty the Turks dared not retaliate with a declaration of war at this time, and hostilities between the two Powers did not break out until 1787 (see letter 603). France was deeply concerned, both as the traditional ally of Turkey and as the patron of Sweden, which was likely to be drawn into any anti-Russian combination. Because of British hostility towards France, Russian activity round the Black Sea was in general regarded with complacency in London. Not for another five or six years did the British attitude begin to be influenced by fears of Russian expansion southwards. Meanwhile the loss of the American colonies was causing the government to be concerned about the supply of various naval stores otherwise mainly obtainable from the Baltic region, a major potential source being western Russia.

his own character /upon it/ to the degree in which he must do it by his recommendation to our Ministry; and that recommendation can not be a cold one to justify his taking so extraordinary a step. As to Sam this is a prize which /nothing less than/ very extraordinary fortune, added to what in Sir James's opinion at least is very extraordinary merit could have thrown into his lap: nor does it appear that this has been purchased by any expence. This at least is so much clear gain: and I hope and trust the expence that has been incurred has not been ill laid out in the purchase of that /other/ situation /to the attaining of/ which it was directed. I must own I can not help looking upon that as a thing that may be depended upon: the Empress and Sam have both of them gone too far, I think to retreat. It would be a thousand pities were any disgrace to befall him, in consequence of any pecuniary difficulties, that should tumble him down just as he is arrived at the summit of his wishes: nor would you ever be able to forgive yourself should such a thing happen for want of any exertions that are not absolutely out of your power: it would be like leaving a rich harvest to rot in order to save the expence of gathering it in. /It is for you and not me to determine what may be in your power./ But whatever else may be or may not be in your power at the long run, I hope and trust it will not be long out of your power to let him have his regular allowance of which three quarters became *due* if you will allow me to use the word, last midsummer. This besides supplying immediate demands which may come upon him before his ministerial pay becomes due, and preventing his being under the necessity (if it should be in his power) of adding to his debts, may perhaps enable him to do some small matter towards satisfying his creditors whoever they may be, of his disposition to do them justice. I must however beg you to reserve £12 all but about 8s. in order to pay Barker for the dozen shirts I have bespoken of him. You may well imagine that what I have will not bear any such deduction.

You desired, my dear Father, to have my thoughts upon this subject. You have them just as they occurred to me, as far as the paper would hold them. If you see the matter in the light I do you will look upon the news we have received from him since Sir James's letter as good news, and very good news upon the whole, even after allowance made for the unwelcome drawback that has accompanied it. I have room for no more than that I am Yours ever dutifully and affectionately

J.B.

456

To Jeremiah Bentham[1]

26 July 1783 (Aet 35)

Lincolns Inn Sat. July 27. 1783

Hond. Sir

Sir James's departure is certainly fixed for the 12th of August. Fitzherbert's is fixt *apparently* for the 20th. He told Pole Carew who called on me yesterday evening that he should take Brussels in his way: and whether Sam's continuances in his office be desirable or otherwise, which is what it is not worth thinking about, I have heard enough to satisfy me that he can hardly get out of it in much less than three months if so soon. ⟨But⟩ this you must be careful to know nothing about; even ⟨such⟩ an idea were it to get round to the office might be very prejudicial to Fitzherbert. Willm. Ft. who is a most friendly creature, took a good deal of pains to get his brother (Allan) to meet me yesterday. Allan called at W's on Thursday, and regretted much to Mrs. F. (W. himself being out) that he could not, but said he was engaged to dine that day with the Provost of Eton[2] (whom I believe you know) in his way to Bath where he stays till the 12th.

W. had told me he thought it would be proper to make an early application to Sneyd about Sam's appointments the payment of which might depend /as he thought/ in point of time, as well as the allowance of charges under the head of extraordinaries upon favour: and he had proposed various expedients to me for that purpose, such as his going with me that afternoon or at any future day; he being in the habit of talking to Sneyd and I believe sometimes to Frazer about his brother's affairs. It seems that in the meantime he had written about it to Allan to ask his advice. I very luckily declined every thing of that sort for the ⟨purpose of⟩ telling him of the acquaintance you had with Sneyd. This morning came a note from W. inclosing a letter from A.[3] in which he says that I should

456. [1] B.M. III: 376–7. Autograph. No docket.
Addressed: 'Jeremiah Bentham Esqr. / Queen's Square Place / Westminster.'
Saturday was 26 July. This letter follows up business first discussed in letter 453.

[2] William Hayward Roberts (1733–91), Provost of Eton, 1781–91.

[3] A copy of Alleyne Fitzherbert's note to his brother, dated 'Windsor, July 26th', in Bentham's hand, is preserved in Bentham's papers (B.M. III: 373). Except for the transference into *oratio obliqua* it reads virtually as reported by Bentham. The note from William Fitzherbert is missing.

do very well to get myself introduced to Mr. Frazer[4] upon the occasion of my brother's remaining in that station, but that there would be the greatest impropriety in my talking to Frazer either about credentials or appointments, as persons in that situation never have credentials, and that as to appointments though the office commonly allows 2£ a day, yet it is given as a matter of favour /rather/ than of right: my sollicitations therefore he continues would wear particularly at so early a period a most ungracious appearance, and do Mr. B. of Petersburgh the greatest disservice.—W. however repeats to me what he had said before, that whenever the affair of the appointments came upon the carpet, it would be highly advisable to employ Sneyd as *Agent* in the business. Sneyd is a sort of Banker to the office; he keeps all the money in his hands: and the time of payment depends in good measure upon him. Sneyd has been always employ'd as Agent by F.; some agent there must be: and what other person (if it be not Hopson's choice) so proper as Sneyd? But pray remember that neither you nor I are to say any thing at the office upon that subject, unless it should be mentioned to us there, or we should be desired so to do by Sam. As to the securing to him whatever ⟨...⟩ will make it his business we may be sure ⟨Pole Carew⟩ wanted nothing more than to know whether ⟨our⟩ wishes were to forward the match or to throw cold ⟨water⟩ upon it, that he might act accordingly.[5] I told him I believed your wishes upon the subject were not very decided, but that for my own part, as I should not think of throwing cold water upon

[4] William Fraser (c. 1727–1802), a career official, served as Under-Secretary in the Northern Department, save for brief intervals, from 1765 to 1782, and continued to hold the same-ranking position in the new Foreign Office from 1782 till 1789. For fuller details of his career see Leslie Scott, 'Under-Secretaries of State, 1755–1775', unpublished M.A. thesis, University of Manchester, 1950. He also held the sinecure post of Gazette Writer from 1771 till 1802. His second son, Charles Henry Fraser, began his diplomatic career at Vienna, and then served under Alleyne Fitzherbert at St Petersburg from 1783 to 1787.

[5] Pole Carew's visit was in connection with the affairs of Countess Matyushkina. On 15 July 1783 he had written to Bentham, then at Brompton: 'I saw a Letter from the Fair one in question, a few days since; in which She complains to her Friend of the hardship of not being able to marry the Person her heart approved etc.; in such a stile that I have no doubt She is in earnest. She complains likewise that her Friend here had not given her any account of a certain Family about which She had desired to be informed. This explains the mystery: two or three of her Letters have miscarried: possibly they have been stopped by her Friends.... He is gone into Scotland. It is possible that some future Letter may lead him to converse with me on the subject: I should be glad, in that case, to know what language you would wish me to hold. If you could resolve to take your breakfast here any day of this week, you will find me at home' (copies, B.M. XXI: 235 and B.M. XXII: 118, the second in the hand of Jeremiah Bentham). The 'friend' referred to in his letter was the young Prince Vyazemskiy, who was on a visit to England (see letter 442, n. 2).

any match of his, were it with a Tinker's daughter, if I thought his affections were set upon it, any otherwise than by endeavouring to dissuade him from it, of course I could have no other wish than what concurred with his with regard to a match that promised to be so advantageous. I hope to God Sam's new station will bring credit with it sufficient for the necessary expences, such as postage of letters etc. which must be considerable: otherwise his situation will be a rueful one indeed.

It will be very comfortable by and by my being upon such a footing with W. F. the intercourse between us and Petersburgh will be so much the more easy: and the friendship between the brothers here will contribute to cement that between the brothers there.[6]

457

From Samuel Bentham[1]

16/27 July 1783

I told you in my last packet[2] that your work might be printed here in french cost free; but I am affraid I was mistaken. At least it would be contrary I find to the Princess's notions of economy to undertake it merely on my proposing it to her. Indirectly however I still think it might be brought about. I have not propos'd it to her as yet nor shall I till I have some further account of it from you. The heads you sent me on half a sheet of paper does not give sufficiently an idea of the work to be shown with that intention, unless it were for want of a more ample account of it in case of the starting up of a rival work, and of that there is scarcely the least apprehension. I wish you had accompanied these heads by a kind

[6] I.e. the friendship between Jeremy Bentham and William Fitzherbert in England would assist the establishment of one between Samuel Bentham and Alleyne Fitzherbert at St Petersburg.

457. [1] B.M. III: 380. Part autograph, part copy by Bentham. Docketed: '1783 July 16/27 / cont. Aug. 13/24. / S.B. Petersburgh / to / I.B. Lincolns Inn / Projet insitens. / from Sh. III.' And: '⟨S⟩B Zarsko Selo / ⟨J⟩B Linc. Inn / Reced at Brompton.'

This extract is on a separate sheet but part of a packet (B.M. III: 378–9) in which Samuel discussed possible future Russian projects and also explained that, in view of the Empress's objections, the plan for him to act as temporary chargé d'affaires had been abandoned. It appears as if this is the bottom half of a sheet from which the top has been separated by cutting: and that, having cut a line too low by mistake, Bentham then copied in the first fourteen words here printed and also the latter part of the passage, from the words 'was added'.

[2] Letter 449.

of Prospectus on the same plan as that which you sent me once before at the time your work was beginning to be translated into German.[3] If to this was added one of the chapters the most striking to serve by way of specimen such as Procedure which I think you proposed, or that in which other expedients are proposed instead of imprisonment for debt it might then be shewn to the Empress, and by that means it seems more probable that she wou'd get an idea of the work than if the work were in the first instance presented to her. As you profess it to be a Corps de Droit detaillé and complet ensemble, 700 or 750 pages 8vo. however closely printed appear to be very little to contain so much matter.

458

To Jeremiah Bentham[1]

28 July 1783 (Aet 35)

July 29. 1783.

Monday morning—just setting off for Brompton. The answer within mentioned as given by Alleyne F. was given to a note of Willm. simply enquiring whether any thing and what was to be done.—I saw W. again on Saturday.

W.F. still persists in recommending strongly that one of us should get introduced by Sneyd to Fraser, only to recommend Sam to Fraser's countenance and attention. In the mean time he will get Sam mentioned to Frazer by an intimate friend of his (W.F's) who is intimate with Frazer.

[*Beneath this note, upside down, is written*:
Jeremiah Bentham Esq.]

[3] See letter 372, n. 18.

458. [1] B.M. III: 381. Autograph. Docketed: 'Fils Jeremy / Lr. datd. Brompton July 27th and 29th, 1783.'

Addressed: 'Jeremiah Bentham Esqr. / Queen's Square Place / Westminster.'

This letter appears to have been written as a final accompaniment to and explanation of Bentham's previous letter of Saturday 26 July (letter 456). Monday was 28 July.

459

From Samuel Bentham[1]

1/12 August 1783

You are very good to have got me the Shirts. I have in the mean time got a supply of half a dozen only of a coarser sort the cloth of the fabrick of this country. The silk stockings and divine Marinerian shoes[2] by all means send I am not a bit less in want of these articles than of the former. Every thing should be washed and if possible marked to avoid the duty.

I have now been tormented these four years for want of tollerable razors. You knew I never recieved those which were sent after me to Hambourg.

Sikes[3] is out of humour and vows he wont write to me nor will he have me write to him, because he hears all letters are opened particularly at this time. I believe he may be in the right, but he is a strange fellow. He is terribly affraid anybody should see what he writes.

Here am I still uncertain with respect to the time and conditions on which I am to be taken into the Empress's service. I have in the mean time very flattering promises to feed on. I have given up the being chargé d'affaires here understanding that though it were to be for ever so short a time the taking upon me that charge would not be approved of by her Majesty.

Sir James has no certain news as yet when Mr. Fitzherbert is to come out, therefore as he has fixed his departure he must find some of our countrymen here to whom he can entrust his correspondence.

This last letter of yours dated Brompton July 10th is not numbered as usual.[4]

My good friend Prince Dashkoff is just arrived from the Crimea. He was sent by P. Potemkin as Courier to bring the detailed account of the taking possession of the Crimea, and he is made a Colonel, though he is not yet 21.

459. [1] B.M. III: 386–7. Autograph. Docketed by Bentham: '1783 Aug. 1/12 / S.B. Petersburgh / to / I.B. Linc. Inn / Reced at Brompton / Chargéship given up.'

Addressed: 'Jere^{y} Bentham Esqr. / No. 6 Lincoln's Inn / London', with an addition: 'At Mr. Clarke's Stationer, Portugal Street Lincoln's Inn Fields.' Two postmarks: one, 'SE/6', the other illegible. Stamped: 'ST PETERSBURG'.

[2] I.e. made by Mariner, the Rochester shoemaker mentioned in earlier letters (cf. *Correspondence*, ii, 62, 255).

[3] Not identified. [4] Missing.

Augt. 1st O.S.

I have received yours in which you speak of [*heavy crossing out*][5] I doubt whether he will like to come out now that I am not to be chargé d'affaires. I write by shipping in 2 or 3 days.

460

To Jeremiah Bentham[1]

16[?] August 1783 (Aet 35)

Brompton near Chatham Aug. 16[?]—1783

Hond. Sir

I have two letters[2] to thank you for since my return hither, the last copying that of Mr. Fraser. Of this copy I sent a copy to W. Fitzherbert, under the idea of thanking him for it as the fruit of his good offices. To those good offices (which as I told you he had offerd me) it may naturally be supposed to have been owing, at least in part; and at any rate, you will easily concieve my having more than one motive for ascribing it to that cause. His answer you will find on the other leaf. As to my seeing A. Fitzherbert, or your seeing him, I can't see any use it would be likely to be of adequate to the trouble it would give to either of us, and the expence, as well as loss of time it would necessarily be productive of to me. Indeed to speak the truth, I do not see any /real/ use it could be of /at/ all, /even/ were those considerations out of the question. Nothing can be more favourably disposed to us than there is all the reason to be assured the Fitzherberts are already: and when no more good remains to be done, the effect, if any, of any nearer intercourse could only be to do harm. If there were any such use concievable, it could only be that from being witness to your stile of living he might be led to entertain a higher idea of the situation of the family than possibly he may have imbibed from what his brother W. has been used to see of mine. But this could not take place without your getting him to your house: and that you could not do without offering him a dinner; which possibly though not probably, by a stretch of civility, he might enable himself to accept. This you might

[5] Missing.

460. [1] B.M. III: 388–9. Autograph. Docketed by Jeremiah Bentham: 'Fils Jeremy / Lr. datd. Brompton / Augt. 18. 1783.'

Addressed: 'Jeremiah Bentham Esqr. / Queen's Square Place / Westminster.' Postmark: '20/AV.'

[2] Missing.

think it necessary (though I should not) to be at some expence about; and at any rate it must occasion a good deal of trouble and inconvenience to my Mother; especially as at this season the house is not in order. After all it could not signify a farthing, unless it were with a view to any ideas he might be able and disposed to get convey'd to the Countess's friends. But as to that matter, it is not very improbable he may be disposed of himself to convey such ideas as he may imagine you would wish to have convey'd: and be that as it may, I think it quite as well for us to follow Sam's example, and let things speak for themselves, and represent themselves as they are.

In answer to your questions about Pole Carew; it was not in his way to /have/ heard any thing more from the Prince her cousin, and still less was it in his way to write on that subject to the Prince. The Prince was then gone to Scotland, from whence, if I recollect right, he was not to return for this month or more /to come/. The Countess in that letter which the Prince received, did not mention my Brother's name: and Carew, as I thought the letter which you saw of his to me mentioned, took care not to give him that information.

It has occurred to me that Mr. Fraser's letter to you,[3] might possibly be of the greatest use to Sam at Petersburgh: the fact of his appointment if they know there how the matter stands, will prove nothing more to them than the opinion entertained of him by Sir James. It is from Frazer's letter only they could learn that somehow or other a similar opinion is entertained of him here. If you concur with me, I wish you would send it directed to my Brother under cover to Mr. Wilson of Lincolns Inn whom I shall have apprised of it, and who will forward it to Petersburgh by the next packet he sends for me. You will observe it must be the original; a copy would be nothing.

The things for my Brother were deliver'd without loss of time on board the Dolphin Captn. Robinson whose receipt was sent him by the Post.

[3] A copy is preserved (B.M. III: 385). In acknowledgement of Jeremiah Bentham's letter of thanks for his advice, dated 3 August, William Fraser replied the following day with flattering references to Samuel which must, it is to be presumed, have been partly based upon a recommendation of him from Harris: 'The very distinguished Character which your Son has so very deservedly acquired will make me very desirous to recommend it to my Son to cultivate his Acquaintance and intimate Friendship, and there are so few young Men who endeavour to acquire useful knowledge that Those who do have a just right to every possible encouragement, and I shall be happy if I can in any Shape be of the least use to Mr Bentham.'

Copy of a letter from W. Fitzherbert Gr. Russel Street to J. B. Brompton.

Aug. 13th 1783.

'Dear Sir,

Your Brother's character stands so high, that it is difficult to ascertain from what source any commendation or recommendation arises. I endeavoured to serve him through two channels to two persons the most able to be of any use to him, and lately had an opportunity of speaking myself to Mr. Frazer. I now write to say my Brother goes about the 20th; and that if you have any letters he will carry them. As he goes by land, I can not venture to say he will charge himself with anything heavier. I mention this as an opportunity on⟨ly of⟩ writing confidentially, as I apprehend he will make so⟨me⟩ short stay on the road, and you will write much more expeditiously by the Post.

I am etc.

If your father should happen to be in town, and should wish it, I would willingly introduce him to my Brother.'

I have written to W.F. to tell him that I do not see any occasion for wishing to put his Brother to the trouble: but that if he sees the matter in a different light, you would certainly be very happy to receive either of their commands—that you are in town commonly of a Wednesday, but seldom stay beyond Thursday morning on account of Mrs. B's health (this to account for your not offering them dinner etc.)—that your house is so and so—that I direct you at other times to Datchet where you have a house for the summer.

461

To Jeremiah Bentham[1]

27 August 1783 (Aet 35)

Hond. Sir

A few days ago I received from Sam the packet herewith inclosed:[2] it came by Sea. As soon as you can spare it, I wish you

461. [1] B.M. III: 398–9. Autograph. Docketed by Jeremiah Bentham: 'Fils Jeremy / Lr. datd. Brompton / Augt. 27 1783.'

Addressed: 'Jeremiah Bentham Esqr. / Queen's Square Place / Westminster', and redirected, 'Datchet / near Windsor / Berks.' Postmark: '28 AU.'

[2] B.M. III: 378–80, dated 16/27 July 1783, the last part of which is printed as letter 457.

would send it to Mr. Carew; I have just been writing to him to tell him you will do so. I have desired him as soon as he has done with the letters to send them to Mr. Mulford /instead of returning them to me/. As I have written, it will not be necessary that you should, and perhaps it might be rather better you should not, unless you have any thing particular to say to him, as your writing would put him to the trouble of an answer, by which means his politeness in which he seems to abound, would be laying a tax upon his indolence, in which he seems to abound also.

I have just received your favour of the 25th.[3] I congratulate [you] on the fortuitous concourse of atoms which jumbled you among our diplomatic friends: but infinitely more upon your having let the house upon terms which with deference to your better judgement, I think excellent. I am, ever your's

Dutifully and affectionately
Jeremy Bentham

Brompton near
Chatham Augt. 27 1783.

After I had directed this letter /and sealed that to Mr. Carew/ it occurred to me that the packet unless you had notice of it might lie at Q.S.P. a considerable time. I therefore thought it best to dispatch this by the Post, to apprise you of the packet, that you might give what order about it you please. It will reach Q.S.P. before this letter reaches you. I should be rather loath to trust it to any of the stages that go farther on and may carry it to Wales or the Land's end. For the like reasons as above I inclose with the packet my letter to Carew for you to send him instead of me.

/As to Frazer's letter/[4] It is more probable than not that Sam would have *no* opportunity of shewing it: but as the contrary is not impossible, it would be a pity /I think/ he should lose the chance. Suppose for example he should be brought into discussions with the Countess's friends, and they were to say to him who are you? who knows anything of you in your own country? True it is, that the good opinion /entertained/ of Sam here at the office probably came from Sir James Harris: (though this is not certain: it might possibly have arisen in part in a way more or less roundabout from Ld. Shelburne, Ld. Sidney,[5] or Pole Carew) But this is more than people

[3] Missing. [4] Letter 460, n. 3.

[5] Thomas Townshend (1733–1800) had been Secretary of State for the Home Department in Shelburne's short ministry of 1782–3 and early in 1783 received a peerage with the title of Baron Sydney.

would know in Russia: they might think Sir Js. Harris's good opinion of him was grounded originally on the character he bore here, even among people of that class.

If it were a matter of intire indifference, it is a letter you would naturally be glad to keep: but if you think with me that there is a faint chance of its being of service to Sam you will as naturally prefer sending it to him—I have sent him mine from Fitzherbert.[6]

462

To Reginald Pole Carew[1]

29 August 1783 (Aet 35)

Brompton near Chatham Aug. 29th 1783

Dear Sir

After the proofs I have received of your friendship for my Brother, I shall never henceforward look upon any apology as necessary for the liberty I may take of communicating /to you/ any intelligence I may obtain of him. A day or two ago I received a packet from him by sea, which I have desired my father as soon as he can open it to forward to you. In one of the sheets you will observe a paragraph or two in answer to some questions I put to him immediately in consequence of the enquiries made by Mr. Rashleigh.[2]

By a letter from Mr. Frazer to my father,[3] as well as through other channels I have the satisfaction of finding that my Brother is well thought of in that department, an advantage of which I make no doubt your friendly partiality has been principally the cause. I have the honour to be, with the sincerest regard

Dear Sir
Your most obedient humble Servant
Jeremy Bentham
Turn over

[6] See the concluding portion of letter 460.

462. [1] Pole Carew Mss. Autograph. Docketed: 'r 6 Septr. / a 10 –.'

[2] See letter 461 and n. 2. No passages relating to enquiries made by a Mr Rashleigh can be identified in the surviving letters of this period. He was Philip Rashleigh (1729–1811) of Menabilly, Cornwall, M.P. for Fowey, 1765–1802, a noted mineralogist, and it was probably Samuel Bentham's mineralogical reports on places in Siberia which had excited his attention.

[3] Letter 460, n. 3.

Your candour will find no difficulty in making the requisite allowances for some passages which if addressed to any other persons than those which they were in fact addressed to, might appear justly chargeable with indelicacy. I mean those in which he speaks of his conduct being 'admired' and so forth.[4] If such a way of speaking of one's self can ever be pardonable, it must be, I should think, in the mouth of a young man who is giving the best account of himself he can to a father or an elder brother or to both.

When you have done with the letters, instead of returning them to me, I will beg the favour of you to address them by the post to an old relation of my brother's with whom it concerns him to be on good terms. The direction is—John Mulford Esqr. Basingstoke.

463

From Baron von Raigersfeld[1]

1 September 1783

Dear Sir

I was in hopes of giving you the information you desired, sooner than I find I shall be able, for knowing Mr. Vigneules, the Prussian Secretary,[2] to be a man of letters and born at Berlin, I thought he could inform me, but tho' he is of opinion that the translation of the Code Frederik having been made by authority and for the use of the many french Subjects of the king's, there is nothing more in German but what has been translated, and that the same Code is still in force, yet he would not be quite positive, and has therefore promised me to send your queries with the next post

[4] These words seem to refer to passages in Samuel Bentham's letter to his brother of 30 May/10 June (letter 444), in which he had written: 'With respect to my love affair, from the *first* to the last approve of my conduct. Whatever blame there is falls only on her... The highest compliments imaginable I have received on the occasion'; and to similar expressions in another of the same date to his father (B.M. III: 343–4).

463. [1] B.M. III: 402. Autograph. Docketed by Bentham: '1783 Sept. 1 / Bar. Raigersfeld Tinterden Street / to / I.B. Brompton / Code Frederic.'

Addressed: 'Jeremy Bentham Esqr. / Brompton near Chatham / Kent.' Postmark: 'I/SE'.

Johann Lukas, Baron von Raigersfeld, came to London as secretary to the Austrian legation about 1767 and held the post till about 1807, acting on a number of occasions as chargé d'affaires in the absence of an Austrian minister. Bentham had been introduced to him in the summer of 1780 and found him friendly and helpful (*Correspondence*, ii, 479, 482–3).

[2] Not identified; presumably a member of the staff of the Austrian embassy.

to Berlin, from whence they will be answered in about a month, with more certainty, than he could do; and you shall have 'em as soon as they arrive. I can say nothing about the regular intercourse betwixt Vienna and Petersburg nor whether the present situation of affairs with Turkey is likely to give your brother much to do. The russian Manifesto which you have in the Gazette, is I believe, the first communication that has been made to this court relative to the Empress's views in that part of the world, and I know not what has since been done.[3]

I have the honour to be with the most perfect regard and esteem

Dear Sir
Your most obedient hble. Servant
Barn. Raigersfeld

London Septr. 1st 1783

464

From Jeremiah Bentham[1]

1 September 1783

Datchet near Windsor
Monday 1st Septr. 1783.

Dear Jere,

In consequence of the Intelligence, yours of the 27th ult.[2] gave me, I was in hopes, Sam's packet wo'd have been forwarded to me before now. Your's reach'd me on fryday, and that day /as/ I was inform'd by a Letter recd. by your Mother from Farr, that he called at Q.S.P. but no Letter was there, i.e. at that time of the day arrived thither of any kind. So that the means you took to expedite the Packet did not keep pace with your intelligence. However, I have still hopes of its reaching me tomorrow afternoon by means of

[3] *The London Gazette* of 26–30 August 1783 gave nearly three columns to an English text of Catherine II's manifesto justifying the annexation of the Khanate of the Crimea to the Russian Empire. The attempts to maintain a friendly puppet regime in the Khanate had been resisted by constant intrigue fomented by the Turks. In any case, however, expansion into the Crimea was a logical extension of the gains made in 1774 under the treaty of Kutchuk Kainardji.

464. [1] B.M. III: 404. Autograph. Incomplete, and without address. Docketed: '1783 Sept. 1 / Q.S.P. Datchet / to / I.B. Brompton / Sophia known by / Mrs. Winder.'

[2] Letter 461.

Mr. and Mrs. W. Browne[3] who are to come to us then on a Visit till Thursday morning, and I have desired him to send to Q.S.P. for what Letters may be come to me there by that time and to bring them with him. So that possibly I may be able to satisfy you of my having the Packet, before I close up this.

I think with you that upon a possibility that Sam may have an occasion, some way or other, of making use of his being possessed of the original of Fraser's Letter to me it may not be amiss to get it convey'd to him, but your friend Wilson, I could not but think was upon the Circuit he go's, therefore sending it to him yet awhile co'd not be the means of forwarding it to Sam. I therefore thought it best to transmit the original to you herewith for you to send it when and how you see best, and imagining you wo'd not dislike to see a Copy of the Letter from me to Fraser which produc'd that answer, and upon a conjecture, that you might be willing Sam sho'd see that too, I have herewith sent you /a Copy of/ that of mine together with the original of Fraser's answer.[4] It will at least serve to satisfy Sam of my attention to whatever is in my power to promote his Views—My Letter to Fraser was written in a hurry but nothing co'd shew more how welcome it was, than the immediate answer given to it—and I don't know anything I co'd have written more to the purpose if I intended or wish'd that, even, Mr. Fox[5] sho'd see it from Fraser, but if you send the answer to Sam, caution him not to let Chas Fraser, the son, know that Sam is in the Possession of the original tho' it may not be amiss for Sam, to let him know the purport of my Letter to his Father, as it might answer the purpose of a Letter, which Fraser intimated in his, I wou'd write to his son; and which I have not done, as nothing more of that kind was said at the time, I told you, I saw both Father and Son, and it may be proper for you when you write to Sam again to let him know, I have not only seen Fraser the father and son but also A. Fitzherbert, and what I told you passed between us at that time, as otherwise it may appear a little strange to the Latter that Sam sho'd not be /made/ acquainted therewith before his, A. Fitzherbert's, arrival.

As soon after my Receipt of Sam's Packet as possible, I will take care to transmit it to P. Carew together with your Letter to him and think with you, it will be better for me not to appear in it since I

[3] William Browne and his wife Jane (see letter 45, n. 3). He acted as business agent for Jeremiah Bentham (see letter 346 at *Correspondence*, ii, 383), and the two families were on friendly terms.

[4] B.M. III: 384–5. The relevant portion of William Fraser's letter is quoted above (letter 460, n. 3).

[5] The Foreign Secretary.

am not unaware that both of us interfering with the same Person may lessen the Weight of Each of us.

Since my last I have been in company with a Lady a few miles from hence, that was several years with the Court at Petersburg, was acquainted with every Lady belonging to it and particularly the *Countess*, as you call her. This Lady told me, She was handsome, genteel, in her Person, and very aimable and agreable in her behaviour and deportment and esteem'd by every body, and in a manner adored by her own Family, that She is one that cou'd not but please here in England; that whenever she went out, it was in a Carriage with a Set of Six Horses to attend her, and She gave me much the same account of her Family, as Sam's to me. Speaking of the Father she said he was look'd upon to be rather a weak man, and was made a dupe of by some designing Persons, who, to answer some views of their own put him upon behaving in a manner slighting or offensive to the Grand Duke and Dutchess, on which account it was /that/ he was ordered out of the way, to Moscow, but that his wife the Countess's mother was not thought the worse of on his account. You will probably want to know by this time, who this same Lady is, that cou'd give me so partial an account. It is a Mrs. Winder,[6] who is daughter of Lady Knowles by Admiral Sir Chas Knowles, who, you know, was some time at Petersburg. His daughter is married to a young gentleman, /an officer/ of the Guards, but he and she live chiefly with Lady Knowles her Mother, at Thorpe. Mrs. Winder is a very pretty agreable young Lady, plays admirably well on the Harpsichord, and, when /she was Miss Knowles at Petersburg /She/ was, it seems, a great Favorite of the Empress, in so much, as to be a kind of maid of honour, and I once saw her dressed in Town, when she appear'd to have some Jewels in some form, on one side, wch. if I understood aright were a Present from the Empress, expressive of some order or other, but as to that circumstance, perhaps, I may be mistaken, however she appear'd to be perfectly well acquainted with the Names, Persons and Characters of everybody abt. the Court at Petersburg—you may imagine, I co'd not but be pleas'd that a young Lady of such a description and character as the Countess, had avow'd such a Passion for Sam, tho' nothing may come of it, as it never the less

[6] Anna Charlotte Christiana Knowles (1752–1839), daughter of Admiral Sir Charles Knowles (d. 1777), married in 1781 Captain John Winder of the King's Dragoon Guards. Her father had entered the Russian service in 1770, and she became for a time a maid of honour to Catherine II.

465

TO JEREMIAH BENTHAM[1]

5 September 1783 (Aet 35)

Brompton
Friday Septr. 5 1783

Hond. Sir

It is but this day that I have reced. your favour of the 1st.[2] It is necessary on more accounts than one that Mr. Carew should see the whole of Sam's Packet, that part relative to Mr. Capper excepted.—That part that concerns the Countess, that he may be the better prepared to say what he thinks proper to say to her Cousin[3]—That part that concerns the Mine-negotiations that he may see the grounds of Sam's proceedings with regard to the Baron, and that Sam may have better reasons than he (Carew) might otherwise have imagined for not closing with the Baron at all events and in the first instance[4]—I could add other reasons had I nothing else to do with my pen and paper: but what supersedes them all is that Sam's papers are announced in the letter of mine to Carew,[5] which since it has not passed through your hands as I intended must have been sent to him *en droiture* by Mr. Wilson through whose hands the packet passed.[6] The letter which you received of mine was written or at least finished in town: I came thither on the Thursday (I think it was) and returned hither the next day. Thursday evening I supped with my Uncle left Sam's packet with him /open/, with directions to him to send it to Wilson when he had done with

465. [1] B.M. III: 407–8. Autograph. Docketed by Jeremiah Bentham: 'Fils Jeremy / Letter datd. Brompton / Septr. 5 1783.'

Addressed: 'Jeremiah Bentham Esqr. / Datchet near / Windsor / Berks.' Postmark: '6 SE'.

[2] Letter 464.

[3] Prince Vyazemskiy; see letter 442, n. 2.

[4] The order of arrival of Samuel Bentham's letters is difficult to unravel as it did not always correspond with the order in which they were written and Bentham's acknowledgements are missing. This passage suggests that Bentham had included in his missing packet both Samuel's letter of 16/27 July 1783 (see letter 461, n. 2) and also his earlier letter of June 1783 (B.M. III: 357–60), in which he had given details about his proposals for a business agreement with the Stroganovs and his belief in the need to secure the legal protection which would be his as a servant of the Russian imperial crown before he entered into any private engagement.

[5] Letter 462.

[6] Bentham later discovered that this packet of Samuel's letters had been left by Wilson at Pole Carew's town house in Grosvenor Street (letter 470).

it. The letter to Carew being sealed /and directed/, Wilson I conclude must have sent it according to the direction. As to Mr. Mulford, the packet will afford him amusement, he will I know expect to see it, and there is nothing in it that can give him any alarm more than he has received already. I think that by the details Sam has now given us his ground appears more solid than it did by the /short/ letter received by the post, as it appears more plainly that the Empress was in earnest, and has gone too far to retreat with decency.

I wish you most sincerely every benefit you may expect from Bath, though I flatter myself it is only *ex majori cautela* that you think of performing that pilgrimage at present—I have a cover for you, directed thither, which I reserve to forward any packet from Sam, if any such should come while you are there.

I am, Dear Sir
Yours most dutifully and affectionately
Jeremy Bentham

I had like to have forgot to tell you that in about a fortnight or three weeks this family[7] is going to remove to a place called Linstead, 4 miles from Sittingbourn, 1 mile from Green-Street in the road from Sittingbourne to Canterbury: and I believe I shall go with them—If I do, or wherever I go in consequence I shall give you timely notice.

466

To Jeremiah Bentham[1]

10 September 1783 (Aet 35)

Hond. Sir

I obey your commands in the instant of receiving them[2]—By all means send the originals—Mulford as you well know is suspicious —Carew can not be at a loss to know how much a frank can carry— Paper never can be an object with people of that class: and the

[7] The Davies's.

466. [1] B.M. III: 409–10. Autograph. Docketed: 'Fils Jeremy B.m. / Letter datd. Brompton Kent / 10th Sept. 1783 / Directed to me at Bath.'

Addressed: 'Jeremiah Bentham Esqr. / Queen's Square Place / Westminster'. Postmark: '12 SE'.

[2] Missing.

difference between folding one or two covers or even three which as I know by trial is the utmost that can be requisite, can not be an object with people of any class—(The endorsements ~~which I have~~ made in red ink will shew the order in which the sheets should be read) You may mention that if you think proper in the cover in which you inclose them—The weight which a Frank will carry I know is not less than 2 ounces—I forget whether it be more—I have sent three printed sheets in a cover which by trial I found came within the weight. /A sheet of printing paper is I dont know how many times as heavy as one of such writing paper./ Carew will certainly not communicate to the Prince[3] either originals or copies —I send them him merely as instructions for himself.

It makes me very happy to find they have given you satisfaction —I was in hopes they would as they did me; I said nothing, however, wishing you to form your own opinion.

Adieu—this I hope will be sufficient—It is as impossible for me as for you to comprise a letter in a 'line' or even in a page—

Yours dutifully and affectionately,
Jeremy Bentham.

Brompton
Wedsy. 10 Septr. 1783.

I wrote you a few days ago a letter which I find you had not as yet received.[4]

467

From Reginald Pole Carew[1]

10 September 1783

Antony House Sept. 10th 1783.
near Plymouth.

Dear Sir

Your Favor of the 29th Ult.[2] did not reach me at this Place till the last Post; I shall ever esteem it an Honor to be reckoned among the Friends of Your Brother, and shall be ever very thankful to you

[3] I.e. Vyazemskiy.

[4] Presumably letter 465.

467. [1] B.M. III: 411. Autograph. Docketed by Jeremiah Bentham: 'Mr. Pole Carew's letter / dated Sept. 10, 1783.' Copy by Jeremiah Bentham, B.M. III: 412.

[2] Letter 462.

for the Communication of any Facts which tend either to his Satisfaction or advantage. I fear that I may have given to Mr. Bentham a Fruitless Walk into Grosvenor St: it shall be my Business when I return to Town (which will be very shortly) to wait upon him. And I will be careful to forward as You desire, the Letters you have received.—Mr Rashleigh whom I saw yesterday thinks himself much obliged by Your kind attention to his Enquiries—I have just now sent him Your Translation of Bergman's Essay on the Usefulness of Chemistry,[3] the Method and Purport of which pleased me much; but as I am unfortunately no Chemist, Parts of it were too Chemical to be read by me with Ease. They have however served to confirm a strong Desire I have ever had, tho' without a proper Opportunity of gratifying it, to make myself Master of the Elements of Chemistry—

I have this very Day received very great Satisfaction from the Perusal of Your Observations upon the Draught of the Hard-Labour Bill.[4] As I am almost a Stranger to the Modern Parts of Our Legislation, I may venture to ask if any Advantage was taken of the many Useful Hints you have furnished?

I am perfectly Innocent of having contributed to the good Impression which has been made of Your Brother on the Secretary of State's Office. He is guilty of the whole himself. He has ever had as far as I can find an unlucky Knack of producing similar Sensations upon all those that know him.

Prince Wiasemskoy has just now left me, he has. had pressing requests to enquire into the Family and Situation of your Hero; I endeavoured to satisfy him on that Head—I find from questioning in my Turn that She really has received from her Parents to the Amount of 9000 Roubles Yearly as a Donation; a Donation made with a View to her marrying Advantageously but of which She does not enjoy above 1500 for her own Expences, the rest going to defray those of the Family. How far She could command the

[3] Torbern Olof Bergman (1735–84) had been appointed professor of chemistry and pharmacology at Uppsala in 1767 and was one of the foremost scientists of the age. His *Anledning till föreläsningar öfver chemiens beskaffenhet och nytta samt naturliga kroppars almännaste skiljaktigheter* (Stockholm, Uppsala and Åbo, 1779) appeared in an English version in 1783 under the title *An Essay on the Usefulness of Chemistry and its application to various occasions of life*. The translation seems to have been a joint production by Bentham and Schwediauer from the German edition, and yet each man spoke in correspondence of it as his own (Bentham to his brother, *Correspondence*, ii, 433; but see also p. 405; Schwediauer to Bergman, *Torbern Bergman's Foreign Correspondence*, edited Johan Nordström, Uppsala, 1963, pp. 331, 346). See Bertel Linder and W. A. Smeaton, 'Schwediauer, Bentham and Beddoes: Translators of Bergman and Scheele', *Annals of Science*, xxiv (1968), 259–73.

[4] *A View of the Hard Labour Bill*, which Bentham had published in 1778.

Remainder during the Life Time of her Parents if she marryed against their Consent I could not learn—It seems that the Mother who was born a Princess Gagarin,[5] and Who is the first Dame D'Honneur de l'Imperatrice, Dame de Portrait etc. and long her first Favourite, has ever had the most ambitious Views in the Mariage of her Daughter, and Prince Wiasemskoy tells me that the Marechal Galitzin would rejoice in seeing her Pride a little Hurt, for hurt it would be that her Daughter should marry an untitled Gentleman, tho' he had the Merits of an Angel to recommend him. —Prince Wiasemskoy was to embark on Sunday last for Lisbon, whether he did nor not I have not yet learnt.—I have the Honor to be with the Highest Respect and Esteem Dr. Sir

Yr. most Obedt. Hle. Servt.
R. Pole Carew

468

From Thomas Payne (bookseller)[1]

23 September 1783

London Sept. 23. 1783

Dear Sr.

I recd. the favour of yours[2] and as the game you offer is of so high a nature, think I cannot refuse to accept if not too high seasoned. I think were I to give two Guineas for every sheet of translation, making 16 pages in 8vo., it would be a handsome offer. Translation is generally but one Guinea a sheet.

As to title, that might easily be Settled, and a knowledge to the publick easily insinuated, without any Appearance from whence it came or who is Concerned in the writing.

I shall be very Secret in the business, you shall not appear without your own Consent.

The last ship that goes for Petersburgh, is the Hannah Capt. Battington and sails on Saturday, she is at present at King Stairs.

[5] See letter 441, n. 1.

468. [1] B.M. III: 413. Autograph. Docketed by Bentham: '1783 Sept. 23 / Payne Mews-Gate / to / I.B. Brompton / Offer accepted.'

Addressed: 'To / Jer. Bentham Esqr. / at Mrs. Davies's / at Brompton near / Chatham.' Postmark: '23/SE'.

Thomas Payne and son were booksellers at the Mews Gate, Castle Street, Leicester Fields. It is not known what Bentham proposed to translate for them.

[2] Missing.

Brownrigg on Salt[3] is very Scarce, I will endeavour to pick up one for you.

I am Sr.
Yr. humb. Servt.
Tho. Payne

Written with the Solution trebl[?] de Sutill[?][4]

469

FROM SAMUEL BENTHAM[1]

13/24 September 1783

Petersbourg Septr. 13th O.S. 1783.

I am at length taken into the service of this country. The rank given me is that of Conseiller de la Cour, which is only equal to that of Lieutenant Colonel in the army. Considering that I had had no Military rank in any other country to found my pretentions on, I ought to be perfectly satisfied with such a beginning: but the flattering treatment I had received and the promises made me, gave some reason to expect something better. The salary I have is /as great if not/ greater I am told than is given to any other person of the same rank; yet it is but a thousand roubles which according to the present ordinary course of exchange falls considerably short of 200£ a year.

As to what I am to be employed in, I know nothing as yet, except that it will be in some department where Mechanical Knowledge is more particularly necessary. The Priviledges I acquire by being in her Majesty's service enable me to pursue private concerns with much greater advantage, and these are what will occupy me now as much as my situation in other respects will admit of.

[3] W. Brownrigg, *The Art of making Common Salt, as now practised in most parts of the world*, London, 1748. This was wanted for dispatch to Samuel Bentham.

[4] This is an almost indecipherable jotting in Bentham's hand.

469. [1] B.M. III: 414–5. Autograph. Docketed by Bentham: '1783 Sept. 13/24 / S.B. Petersburgh / to / I.B. Lincs. Inn / Appointment fixed / Oil-mills with Capper.'

Addressed: 'Jere[y] Bentham Esq[r] / Lincoln's Inn / London', and re-addressed to 'Linsted near Sittingbourn / Kent / To be left at the Post Office till called for.' Two postmarks: '18 OC'.

Samuel Bentham had now gained what he had come to realise was essential for any successful enterprise in Russia—rank as a government servant and its accompanying prestige and privileges.

What *interests* me most of all is still undecided; I have very little hopes of success, yet she[2] is not at all disposed to give it up.

I have received your packet[3] by Capt. Keddy,[4] and I will send you what you wish for by a Ship that is nearly ready to sail.

You intended sending me a paper of Anderson's on the application of falling water to millwheels;[5] but I have not found it yet in any of the parcels you have sent me. 'tis true I have not yet got the one containing the cloaths from the customs-house; for I have had much plague about it. So far from not paying duty every article will pay at least 40 p. ct. and the silk cloaths are according to law confiscated and a fine of the amount of their value to be paid likewise. No assurances of their being exported back again immediately can save them: yet I have some hopes of getting out of the reach of the rigour of this ⟨law⟩. In future never send any parcel but by means of a freind who can secure it with his own baggage.

When you see Anderson or anybody else likely to be acquainted with the subject ask him if he has ever known Wheels of cast iron used instead of rolling *stones* to bruise the seed in oil mills, and what objections he sees to such a substitute. In many places I imagine the rollers of stone may be cheaper; but that would not be the case here.

Capper is returned and his having seen you all has attatched me to him. It is probable we may be concerned together in the erection of an oil mill which gave rise to the above question. In a model he has brought with him from England there is an apparatus for bruising the seed by making it pass between two iron rolers of small diameter which the seed is to be subjected to before it is exposed to the pressure of the great stone rolers: this he says is a late invention; but as it requires more workmanship than is easy to be had here I think cast iron rollers to act in the manner the stone ones do at present may be made to do the whole business.

[2] The Countess Matyushkina.
[3] Missing.
[4] Not identified.
[5] This publication has not been traced.

470

To Reginald Pole Carew[1]

3 October 1783 (Aet 35)

Linstead near Sittingbourn Oct. 3d. 1783

Dear Sir

I am infinitely obliged to you for your very interesting intelligence: to say nothing of the kind offices which may be seen through it without a microscope.[2] It is the [*word crossed out*] interesting, inasmuch as by a packet later than that which I hope has reached you before now, I find the lady's flame, which for some time seemed to have been in a smother, /has/ broken out afresh: the vows of constancy have been renew'd: and even an appointment made, which however did not come to hand time enough to be kept.[3]

You desire to know whether any and what effect was produced by my 'View of the Hard-Labour Bill'. Understanding the 12 Judges had a hand in the Bill, and particularly Blackstone, I sent each of them a copy. Sometime after Blackstone wrote me a civil note telling me that several of my observations had occurred to the friends of the Bill (since the printing of the rough *draught* which was the subject of my comment.) and that 'many more were well deserving of their attention.' When the Bill itself was printed, as such, for the use of the members, somebody sent me a copy: no note or letter accompanied it, but the direction seemed to be in Blackstone's hand.[4] Upon glancing over that copy, I remember it seemed to me that, upon a loose computation, about the half of my suggestions seemed to have been adopted: but I would give you a good while to guess which they were. I could easily enough have furnished fresh animadversions upon the intermediate alterations: but as my assistance was not asked even by those who acknowledged they had profited by it when spontaneously given, I thought it would not be the more likely to be made use of for

470. [1] Pole Carew Mss. Autograph. Docketed: 'r — 6 / a — 7 —.'
Addressed: 'R. Pole Carew Esqr.'

[2] Letter 467.

[3] This episode is mentioned in Samuel Bentham's letter to his brother of 13/24 August 1783 (B.M. III: 394–7). It appears probable from the endorsement on B.M. III: 390–1, another letter of about the same date, that it reached Bentham about 19 September.

[4] See *Correspondence*, ii, 103, 122 and n.

being flung at their head. If after all the delays the measure has met with and all the cold water that has been thrown upon it, it should at last be carried into effect, I shall not grudge the £20 or £30 which it cost me to give it a helping hand: but it is a /sort of/ satisfaction which a man cou'd not afford to give himself every day at the same price.

I wonder whether in all this time my Brother's letters have reached you: they were left at your house in Grosvenor Street a month ago. If they had been disposed of in the manner I had desired they might, they would have been distributed into parcels small enough to have travelled after you by the post: as it happen'd, I doubt that part of my instructions was not observed.

Since then two successive Couriers have brought me a continuation of the romance: but as anticipating it would spoil it, I will leave it in due time to speak for itself.

I am glad to hear of your pious dispositions in behalf of Chemistry: I wish they may prove something more than mere velleities: had I the gift of tongues, I should be as devout a preacher of that science as Dr. Tucker has been said to be of trade: and nothing could be more flattering to me than to reckon you in the number of my proselytes. I will beg my best Compliments to Mr. Rashleigh,[5] should he chance to be at your elbow. Believe me to be, my dear Sir, with the most perfect respect

Your much obliged
and most obedient humble Servant
Jeremy Bentham.

471

To Jeremiah Bentham[1]

6 October 1783 (Aet 35)

Linstead near Sittingbourne Oct. 6th 1783.

Hond. Sir

On Wednesday the | | I received your short letter in which you desired I wou'd not fail to give you a line by the return of post

[5] See letter 462, n. 2.

471. [1] B.M. III: 416–7. Autograph. No address or postmark. Docketed by Jeremiah Bentham: 'Fils Jeremy B—m / Letter datd. Linstead near Sittingbourne Kent / October 6 1783 / directed to me at Bath.'

to tell you whether you shou'd send P. Carew the originals or the copies. On that same day I sent an answer in due time and by the ordinary conveyance, desiring for the reasons which I there gave that it might be the originals.[2] I was pleasing myself with the thoughts of the proof you wou'd recieve of my punctuality and my attention to your commands when I learnt first by your note to my Uncle which Wilson inclosed to me in a packet,[3] and afterwards by your letter of the 17th last[4] to me, that that letter of mine had never come to hand. I must leave you to judge how much I /was/ mortified at this intelligence: how to account for the fact I know not. I now write for little other purpose than to enclose two packets of Sam's on which as before I shall make no comments: only begging you to read /the sheets/ ~~in the order in which they lie~~ /the order of the dates/ without which you might lose a good part of whatever pleasure they may afford. /The dates you will find by the endorsements I have made to them./[5] I inclose also a letter of P. Carew's[6] to me written at a time when being at Plymouth he had not received the originals of Sam's letters which Wilson sent to his house in town by my desire.

When you have done with these letters of Sam's pray send them to Mr. Mulford. You will do as you please about sending them or copies of them first to Mr. Carew.

Chit-chat for Bath.

Extract of a letter from Baron Raigersfeld Septr. 30.[7]

'I dare say you know by reputation M. de Kempelen,[8] Conseiller au Gouvernment in Hungaria, or rather the famous Automaton Chess-player: he is arrived in London, where he will stay several months: He has also brought with him a figure that speaks, or to say better the figure is not made yet, but it speaks. The Chess-player is not to be seen yet, he not having got yet a house where to

[2] The missing date is 10 September. See letter 466.

[3] Both Wilson's covering letter and the note from Jeremiah Bentham are missing.

[4] Missing.

[5] The reference is probably to some or all of Samuel Bentham's letters dated 1/12 August (letter 459); 13/24 August (B.M. III: 394–7), which refers to a letter of his to Sir James Harris (see n. 9 below); and letters of 21 August/1 September and 22 August/2 September (B.M. III: 400–1, 405–6—see ibid.). The order in which these letters reached Bentham is not recorded.

[6] Letter 467

[7] Raigerfeld's letter is missing.

[8] Baron Wolfgang von Kempelen (1734–1804), Referendary to the Hungarian chancellory in Vienna, Director of saltmines in Hungary, and inventor, in 1769, of a mechanical chess player which he exhibited in Paris and London.

unpack him: but I have heard the speaking automaton, of whose contrivance he makes no secret in so far that you can see that it is play'd like an organ, uttering articulations instead of simple sounds. I think nobody ever brought it so far, and I can assure you that M. de Kempelen is a gentleman of very great ingenuity and worth your knowing him.'

This packet will have been an outrageous long while a reaching you. It has been retarded /by the want/ first of Carew's letter which had hid itself among some other papers in the hurry of moving; next of a frank: for some how or other that which I thought I had is gone; and how or when these presents will reach you I can not very well tell. I am

Hond. Sir Ever your's dutifully and affectionately
J.B.

It will depend upon the weight whether I inclose a letter of Sam's by the post, completely superseded by those others, and the copy he refers to of one of his to Sir James.[9] There never was such thick heavy paper as this of Sam's. It is as much as two franks will do to convey these few sheets: and the weight comes so near that I have been obliged to clip the paper and use other contrivances to avoid the overcharge.

[9] The copy of Samuel's letter to Harris apologising for his misbehaviour at Harris's farewell party, dated 13/24 August 1783, is at B.M. III: 390–1. It is docketed by Bentham as received at Brompton on 19 September. The first of Samuel's letters referred to is presumably one of that same date (B.M. III: 394–7), referring partly to his negotiations with the Russian court, partly to the renewal of his love affair. The reference to 'those others' is not clear, but may be to letters dated 21 August/1 September and 22 August/2 September (B.M. III: 400–1, 405–6). In the second of these Samuel related the gist of a conversation with Bezborodko about the rank which he hoped to be given in the Russian service. It seems unlikely that Samuel's letter of 13/24 September announcing the completion of his negotiations (letter 469) could have reached Bentham by 6 October.

472

From Samuel Bentham[1]

28 September/9 October–12/23 October 1783

St. Petersbourg Sept 28th O.S. 1783.

I sent to my father by last post a letter[2] which I fear will give him much vexation. I could not avoid settling my money concerns here with Mr. Shairp without hurting myself very materially and irreparably, and as it is the last time I shall ever make any demand on my father for money I hope he will forgive it. Great as the sum may appear it does not amount to so much as he must have deprived himself of ~~to have made me~~ in giving me into my hands at my coming of age something analogous to what he gave you, and which I remember there were thoughts of his doing.

In my letter to him I promised to send a packet by Sea; but the departure of an English Courier I thought a better opportunity. For the purpose of assuring my father that he need not be under the least apprehensions of my drawing upon him for any more money, I have desired him to write to Mr. Shairpe here to tell him that he will not be responsible for me in future. I myself give people here to understand that I expect no further assistance from my father while I am in this country during his lifetime. That his displeasure at my declining the flattering offers made me by Ld. Shelburne, and after that my refusing to be Chargé d'affaires here, together with my determination of staying from home, have made him resolve that I shall shift for myself. I have given a sketch of the letter I wish you would persuade my father to write in which the expressions should be as strong as possible.

Octr. 12th

Yesterday died the Field Marshal Prince Gallitzin.[3] He had been ill for more than two months and given over for a fortnight. He has left I hear all his property to his widow at her disposal. The sister and niece will most likely now live with her. Some people are

472. [1] B.M. III: 427–8. Autograph. Docketed by Bentham: '1783 Oct. 12/23 / S.B. Petersburgh / to / J.B. Lines. Inn / (No. 1).'

[2] B.M. III: 418–9, dated 26 September 1783.

[3] Countess Matyushkina's uncle by marriage. See letter 441, n. 1.

disposed to flatter me now with hopes that the Widow's pride will be let down so as for her to oppose with less vehemence her niece's inclinations: but I for my part have scarcely any the least hopes of the neice's taking any decisive step. More than once have I been upon the point of renouncing the matter altogether when some new intimation of her disposition towards me brings me back to my former state of indecision.

Mr Fitzherbert has been arrived here these 10 days. From him but more from Mr. Frazer[4] I was happy to hear how well my father looks. Frazer says he appears as well in every respect as he remembers to have seen him. Frazer seems to be a very openhearted and promising young man, and this news he brought me could not but make me the more wish to contract a freindship with him. Mr. Fitzherbert and I are as good freinds as possible, and I am happy in being of some little use to him in giving him a carte du pays as far my knowledge extends. He on his part by the confidence he puts in me assures me of his freindship. He tells me that Ld. Shelburne and his lady whom he saw at Spa spoke much of me. I mean to write to his Lordship as soon as I can find time.

I send you a letter for Miss Harris enclosing one for Miss Gomme.[5] You will hear when Sir James is in town and thereby find out how to get this letter to his Sister. You will seal them both. I send you likewise a table of the comparisons of the scales of Thermometers. Also a famous law of the King of Prussia, which most likely you have already.

I have not as yet got my box out of the Custom house. The Cloaths are certainly confiscated though I am promised that they shall be sold very cheap if I choose to buy them. Every article will pay duty, none less than ⅓ of their value.

Since I have got into my lodgings I have kept an exact journal in a book destined for that purpose. I have not as yet brought myself to write every day what belongs to that day but I have seldom let pass more than one day. I have hopes therefore that in a little time you will find me more regular in my information. I have so many objects of attention that method is to be sure of the highest importance, but the case is that there are so many things happen to me of the affecting kind that they break through the firmest resolutions I can make about method. If the answer to my letter to my Father about settling my money concerns should set my mind

[4] Charles Henry Fraser. See letter 456, n. 4.

[5] Not identified. She belonged to the Harris family circle and was possibly a companion to Lady Harris. Letter book copies of these letters are at B.M. XXI: 274–6.

at ease in that subject, I think a little time will suffice to put me in good order.

Continue to direct your letters to me at Petersburg without any regard to my title here.

473

To Reginald Pole Carew[1]

10 October 1783 (Aet 35)

Dear Sir

I cannot reconcile myself to this idea of confirming by my silence an error to which, however unimportant and however easily rectified by other means, I have myself given occasion. It was not you that had been misinformed, but I that was inexplicit. The Bill has indeed existed in the shape of an Act for years: but were the business to stop where it stands at present, and where it seems not very unlikely to stop, that Act will have been worse than ineffectual. Supervisors have /been/ appointed for the future receptacle: first, Sr. T. C. Bunbury,[2] Dr. Fothergill[3] and Mr. Howard:[4] then, upon the death of Dr. F. and resignation of Mr. H., Sir Gilbert Elliot[5] and a Dr. Bowdler.[6] A plan has been made choice of by the present Supervisors upon the most liberal principle: premiums offer'd to the public at large, and which produced between 60 and 70 candidates. Ground has even been bought (near Wandsworth) at a vast expence: but, without any blame upon the Supervisors,

473. [1] Pole Carew Mss. Autograph. Docketed: 'r — 11 October 1783 / a — 23—.' Addressed: 'R. Pole Carew Esqr.'

Carew misunderstood Bentham's letter of 3 October (letter 470), and in his reply, dated 7 October (B.M. XXI: 257–8, copy), wrote: 'I...had conceived that the Bill did really pass...but you speak of it as a thing yet in uncertainty.' The Bill had been enacted as 19 Geo. III, c. 74, 'An Act to explain and amend the laws relating to the Transportation, Imprisonment, and other Punishment, of certain offenders.' Since convicts could no longer be sent to the American colonies, by then in revolt and on the way to independence, the Act provided, among other things, for the appointment of three supervisors, who were to buy land—the value, if necessary, being ascertained by a jury as a preliminary to compulsory purchase—and there build one penitentiary for men and another for women (see letter 238, n. 1).

[2] Sir Thomas Charles Bunbury, 6th bart. (1740–1821), M.P. for Suffolk, 1761–84, 1790–1812, had concerned himself with reforms of the criminal law at least from 1771. This preoccupation was to bring him later into direct relationship with Bentham.

[3] John Fothergill (1712–80), a physician and botanist, and also a philanthropist.

[4] I.e., John Howard, the prison reformer.

[5] Sir Gilbert Elliot (1751–1814), M.P., later first Earl of Minto.

[6] Thomas Bowdler (1754–1825), physician, philanthropist, and literary editor.

that ground, I believe, remains as yet unbroken. You may observe that I speak only of *one* building instead of the *eight* that were at first designed: for when the 'Draught of a Bill' ripen'd into a Bill, the *noble* was not improperly, I think, reduced to *nine* pence. It would be to little purpose for me to trouble you with a detail of particulars which are public and which could be much better stated to you by hundreds of your friends: but if it were worth your looking at, I could shew you when I have the pleasure of seeing you in town, a correspondence I had with Mr. (now I believe Sir W.) Eden, upon the occasion of a part of my Preface which in compliment to him I left out: at least I could shew you Mr. Eden's notes, for I don't recollect whether I kept copies of my own.[7]

If my child, whom I am certainly not the less disposed to be proud of by the regard you are kind enough to express for him, should be settled at *Olonitz*, which at present seems highly probable, I shall certainly contrive if possible, to pay him a visit in the spring. Olonitz you know is but a stone's throw from Petersburgh; not above 350 versts. Were you ever there? and if you were can you tell me whether the salt-works or the iron mines in the neighbourhood afford any thing of a house for him to live in? In short any thing you could tell me about the place I should be much obliged to you for: not meaning that if you can tell me nothing you should be at the trouble of writing to me to say so.[8]

I am, My Dear Sir, with the sincerest respect
Your most obedient humble
Servant
Jeremy Bentham

Linstead near Sittingbourn
Oct. 10. 1783.

[7] For these exchanges between Bentham and William Eden, see letters 238–41 and notes. Eden had not become 'sir'.

[8] When Samuel Bentham, on making application to enter the service of Catherine II, had expressed interest in imperial manufactories in Siberia, the empress's comment had been that he might prefer to be at Olonetz (a place just to the east of Lake Ladoga), because, he suspected, she thought this conveniently near to St Petersburg so that he could pursue his love affair with Countess Matyushkina. 'I have been informing myself about Olonitz', he wrote to his brother, 'and find that the mines there are so indifferent that although they furnish cast iron pretty good for Cannon and Shot yet of this cast iron none but very bad wrought iron can be made. From any cast iron whatever there seems to be no doubt but what wrought iron (forged iron) may be made: but to know without a number of previous experiments by what process this may be done with respect to the particular cast iron in question, and at the same time how far the expence of such process can be born according to the usual price of Siberian iron, is not to be expected. The Siberian mines seem to be the only ones where I could be certain of making very striking improvements. As to Saltworks

474

From Reginald Pole Carew[1]

23 October 1783

Exeter Octr. 23—1783

Dear Sir

In[2] *the letter which this answers I had asked him whether he knew anything of Olonitz, where Sam seemed then likely to be settled, throwing out in general terms the idea of my paying him a visit there one of these days.*

Your obliging Letter of the 10th Inst. reached me as I was just setting out a second Time for this Country, and tho I shall not write to tell You the Nothing I know of Olonitz yet you will suffer me to do it for the Purpose of thanking You for the kind Information which You have been pleased to give me of the State of the Hard Labour Bill and of the Effects it has produced.—This I can say to You of Olonitz, or of Russia in General, that as Houses grow /there/ like Mushrooms, if You will give Your Brother a Month's Notice of Your Intention of making him a Visit, I will answer for it, that he will build you a Palace at Olonitz, that shall be ready for Your Reception at Your Arrival.—I have been writing to him by this Post a Letter[3] that may be read at the Four Quarters of the Empire, and therefore such an one as I should rather they copied at the Post, than otherwise. My first Object in writing was to desire

there are some near Novgorod, but they are very trifling compared to the Siberian ones.' As with all Samuel's letters from Russia, this may have been written in the knowledge that it would be intercepted, to create a misleading impression about his views. In fact he was kept at St Petersburg. On 6/17 October 1783 he wrote to Bentham: 'I expect every hour to receive my orders which are already written, by which I am destined for the present at least to a part in the direction of the principal canal that is making here in the town. It is called the Fontanka canal. I believe I have already made it known to you that the instant the Empress had put her hand to the order for me to be in her service, I became *omniscient*...I have...some reason to believe it was done with a view to finding me any kind of employment whatever here at Petersburg and that because it was thought I would wish to be here for the present at least to finish in one way or other my matrimonial connection' (B.M. III: 357–60 and 425).

474. [1] B.M. III: 429. Autograph. Docketed by Bentham: '1783 Oct. 23 / Pole Carew Exter / to / I.B. Linstead / Writes to S.B. about Rashleigh and Pallas / Russian houses / mushrooms.'

[2] The italicized passage was inserted in red ink by Bentham below Carew's greeting but above the body of the letter. It refers to letter 473.

[3] Missing.

him to explain Matters between Mr. Rashleigh /*a Cornish Member*[4]/ and Mr. Pallas[5] /*a German Professor of Nat. Histy.*[6] *at Petersburgh*/ and I thought this a good Opportunity of introducing what might be of use on other Topics.

I look forward with Pleasure to the hopes of meeting You frequently in the Winter and am with great Veneration and Regard

Most unfeignedly Yours
R. Pole Carew

P.S.
I shall probably leave this Place soon.

475

To Jeremiah Bentham[1]

24 October 1783 (Aet 35)

Linstead near Sittingbourn
Friday Oct. 24. 1783.

Hond. Sir

I am to thank you for two letters, one of the 12th inst: the other of the 19.[2] The reflections they contain would have been in great measure superseded could I have convey'd along with the packets to which they allude the letter I now inclose to you:[3] hopes and fears have now given place to certainty: but whether you will think that a *certain* Lieutenant-Colonelcy is equal to a *possible* Colonelcy, or a certain 1000 roubles to an expected nay promised 1200 or 1500, is more than I can venture to assure myself. One thing I can inform you from the best authority, that this 1000 roubles, shabby as it is, is more by 150 roubles than is given to the

[4] An insertion in red ink by Bentham.

[5] Peter Simon Pallas (1741–1811). Born and educated at Berlin, he later studied medicine at Leyden, and became professor of natural history at St Petersburg in 1763. In 1764 he was elected to the Royal Society of London. He spent many years in Russia, travelling and writing. Samuel Bentham had met him on a number of occasions at a scientific coterie during the autumn of 1780 (*Correspondence*, ii, 501, 511 n.), and at the beginning of 1781 he had given Samuel material assistance at the start of his Siberian journey, both with advice and letters of recommendation.

[6] An insertion in red ink by Bentham.

475. [1] B.M. III: 430–1. Autograph. Incomplete. Docketed on the edge of the fourth page: '1783 Oct. I.B.—Q. S. P.—Commissioner / of the navy.'

Beginning with the third paragraph the underlinings are in red ink, a frequent practice on Bentham's part at this time.

[2] Missing.

[3] Letter 469.

chief Judge of the principal court of justice in a Province of the first magnitude: and four times as much as is given to a Captain in a Regiment. This I speak from the Empress's Constitutional Code which is lying before me on the table. The rank, such as it is, will at any rate, I hope, answer his main purposes, as he seems to think it will.

You will be vext no doubt at perceiving the scrape which you have been the innocent cause of drawing him into: though you have proved an Eutrapelus to him it certainly was not with Eutrapelus's intentions. [*Inserted at the foot of the page*: Eutrapelus cuicumque /nocere volebat/ Vestimenta dabat pretiosa, says Horace who knew him.][4] If it had not been for an accident this little misfortune might not have happen'd. I had no reason to suspect that in Russia French silks were contraband: but partly for certainty /security/ and partly to save expence, I had been accustomed to send every thing for Sam through Mr. Shairpe the Russia merchant of Broad Street,[5] whom I have never seen. Some little time before the cloaths were sent I had had occasion to write to him and had received no answer: from thence I became apprehensive that I had *worn him out*; and the things not being all ready at the time of my leaving town, I saw no better means of managing the matter than by leaving it in the hands of my Lincoln's Inn friends, who sent the things in the ordinary way through some master of a vessel whom they did not know. About a month or six weeks afterwards I received a very civil letter from Mr. Shairp, apologizing for not having answer'd mine sooner, and mentioning as the reason of his silence his having been absent on a /long/ journey, /from which he was but just arrived and/ at the end of which and not before my letter had come into his hands.

All together we have very little reason to be pleased with Custom-houses: for this is not the only misfortune /of the kind/ that has befallen us: we shall on both sides of the water have bought experience at a pretty dear rate. *You remember* the old story of *the minerals which came directed to Ld. Shelburne*: and among which the box of Rhubarb, by passing as it would seem for a box of minerals /as it was inclosed in a larger box which contained

[4] Horace, *Epistles*, I, xviii, 31–2. Eutrapelus, a political figure in Rome in the first century B.C., was an associate of Mark Antony.

[5] Mr Shairp of Shairp, Maude, and Co., Russia merchants, 8 Broad Street Buildings. In fact the garments concerned were not contraband. The Russian customs officials had been under a misapprehension about their nature, and Samuel eventually rescued the whole consignment from their hands after paying duty amounting to twenty-six rubles (B.M. III: 462, 14/25 November 1783).

nothing else but minerals/ happend to escape duty.[6] *I told you* at the time or soon afterwards of what passed on that subject between Ld. Shelburne and myself; and *of his taking the matter upon himself in the most explicit manner.* As he told me at the same time of having franked *Linguet's* goods among which was a very large cargo of French wines, with /the/ public money, *I concluded of course that whatever charge, if any, there might be upon the very trifling articles that were consigned to me, would be paid for* in the same manner. It would have been a very improper application of the public money, doubtless: but that was his concern. I certainly should not have asked him to do any thing for me in any such way; *but when he offer'd it, it would have been ridiculous* /and very offensive to him/ *to have stopped his hand. After a number of delays, at last,* /as/ you know I *got the minerals*: *but of the silks and tea as I told you, nothing positive could as yet be said. In the mean time came one day to my chambers Monsr.* Fombel, *my Lord's Valet de Chambre, with a bill for the charges attending these things, and a receipt to it given by a man of the name of* Marshall, *to the amount of £19 within a few shillings*; *which bill upon my asking him, he said he had just been paying. Having by good or ill luck*, but at any rate by rather extraordinary luck, *a £20 note by me at that time, I gave it him in discharge of the receipt, which I took together with the difference.* Now are you, and will be for some minutes or some hours (for the experience of 35 years has taught me what to look for on occasions of this sort) full of indignation and contempt at the thought of my suffering myself to be gulled, as you will call it, out of this money. The fact was that I was nearly as unwilling to part with the money as you could have been: but a day or two hence you will be sensible of the force of what I have to observe to you. *It was then the beginning of March*: *at that time I could not be certain* notwithstanding the cautions I had subjoined *but that my brother might be coming post-haste from Petersburgh in consequence of what Ld. Shelburne had in a manner forced me to write to him about the Commissionership of the Navy*:[7] nor had I any demonstrative proof but that his Lordship might have intentions of some sort or other in *my* favour. *Had I even been disposed to wave* both *those prospects and contest the matter it seemed very problematical to me whether* that *letter of Sams to Ld. Shelburne* which you have seen *would not have furnished legal evidence to fix some of us with the responsibility for*

[6] Concerning the consignments of mineral samples from Russia, see letters 424 and 436.

[7] See letter 433.

476

FROM SAMUEL BENTHAM[1]

14/25 October 1783

I.B.'s Visit

I am now in a situation to turn to the best account any ideas of improvement applicable to this country. Anything of the Scientific kind which the Empress would be likely to approve of, Princess Dashkoff would be happy to present to her. Anything which relating to any particular department the Princess would not think proper to meddle in, the *Favorite*[2] who is very powerfull and seemingly much disposed to be my freind would I am persuaded be ready to promote. Now then how happy I should be to have you with me. How many things we might dress up together that would make a figure, and the making a figure seems all that is sought after here. Usefull things are certainly adopted sometimes, when they could not be spendid without being usefull.

I for my part can neither fix upon anything nor execute it to my satisfaction where it is a litterary production: the models necessary to give an idea of 2 or 3 of my inventions is as much as I can be able to manage by myself. I could certainly furnish ideas for ½ a dozen people to work on independent of my mechanical inventions.

I have now got comfortable lodgings where you would not be exposed to shiver with cold and blister your legs as in your chambers and where you would be delivered from the agonies of rising in a morning from a warm bed to a cold room.

With respect to comforts you should have many. Besides what

476. [1] B.M. III: 433–4. Autograph.

This letter, together with letters 477 and 478, and B.M. III: 435, 446–50, and 441–3, not all of them fully dated, clearly forms part of a large packet which Samuel Bentham wrote to his brother on 14/25 and 15/26 October 1783. All these letters reflect the release and effervescence of his energies in the weeks after his appointment in the Russian service was finally confirmed, and his renewed concern with Bentham's fortunes now that his own seemed settled. In the forefront of his mind was the desirability of his brother's visiting Russia—an idea which Bentham now had seriously in contemplation (letter 473). Secondly came the question of some sort of publication in Russia of a summary of Bentham's ideas on legal codes, in the pages of the new periodical, *Sobesednik* (See letter 478). Samuel was on good terms with its conductress, Princess Dashkova, who edited it in close collaboration with the empress herself. Samuel's own concerns are reflected in his inquiries about craftsmen who might be sent out to assist him, and also in a long description (B.M. III: 441–3) of his observations about the behaviour of objects floating in rivers.

[2] Potëmkin.

I hope we should enjoy from each other's company, there are 2 or 3 of my freinds from whom you would receive the greatest satisfaction and now and then for a treat we would go and drink tea with my female friend /Made. Scherbinin/[3] in her own apartments. She is certainly far superiour to any of her sex among our acquaintance in England. You need not appear in propriâ personâ, she, the prince her brother, Pleschijeff, Hynam and Capper /and if you please Fitzherbert/ must be in the secret, all the world besides need know nothing of the family connections of Mr. John Clark, unless to account for the likeness such as there is between us, you might be a distant relation. You might be a James Bentham why not? and then you might go to one or two of the English houses and as many of the Russian ones where I am most intimate, particularly one a few doors from me where Pleschijeff spends every evening and where there is a harpsichord, fiddle, and harp playing every day. And this would require no expence worth speaking of, you might wear the same coat always while it held together and yet be as much at your ease as if your cloaths were ever so costly. If however it would be losing too much time to go out to dinner very good eatables might be dressed at home at a very trifling expence. Were you to determine on coming now, and could bear the disagreeableness of the voyage the season is not too far advanced for you to come by sea as far as Dantzic or even Memel. From the latter place you would find carriers who would bring you to Riga, from thence others who would bring you here; so that the whole of this land carriage would not amount to more than 5 or 6 pounds and yet you would have a sledge to yourself in which you might put a large cloak bag a small flat trunk and other smaller packages.

Supposing Anderson,[4] Burkit or the clever weaver[5] would come

[3] Princess Dashkova's daughter, Nastas'ya Mikhaylovna. Her husband was a Brigadier Sherbinin.

[4] The idea of James Anderson going out to Russia to join Samuel in some enterprise or other was aired on a number of occasions during this period and eventually gave rise to letter 508. Nothing came of it.

[5] On Burket, the mechanical inventor and model-maker, see letter 383, n. 4. The 'clever weaver' is not identified. In another sheet belonging to this packet (B.M. III: 445), docketed by Bentham, '1783 Oct. / S.B. Petersburgh / to / I.B. Linc. Inn / Workmen accersendi', Samuel wrote: 'Have you heard anything more of your ingenious fellow of a weaver, of whom you told me such great things on the faith I suppose of a freind of yours of the name of Townsend. Such men as Burkitt and he would be treasures indeed to me, and I could be sure of putting them in a way of making money though I should not be able to find employment for them myself.

'There are no exclusive priviledges in favour of particular bodies of men exercising a trade any more than there are in favour of any particular invention. Any body exercises what trade he pleases, so that Burkitt might make fiddles, harpsichords, and guittars, set in artificial teeth, make milk punch, shine in high varnishing, and

with you at so short a notice the disagreeableness of the journey would be lessened and the expenses not doubled, at so short a notice however there is scarcely a possibility of the two latter being ready; possibly Anderson may agree to it. Were you to come in this economical way I could bear the whole of your expences in coming out, living here till the middle of next summer, and returning by sea. Your coming out I suppose not to cost more than 30£. I have not as yet bought me the new carriage for which I have taken up money of Shairpe and for which 350 roubles (the price I was going to give for one) were not in the account I sent my father. The real advantages which would arise to me from your assistance independent of the pleasure which [we] should both feel and the use I imagine I should be of to you, outweigh the portion of *infamy* arising from the shifts I must make for want of a carriage: besides I am in hopes of getting an old one that would serve my purpose at a very low price.[6] Besides at any rate at this important crisis of my life I would rather borrow a small sum of a freind here than that anything but your own concerns in England should be an obstacle to our meeting. Do not however think of coming unless you can stay at least till the spring or even if we see occasion to the latter end of the Summer. The general purposes of your coming would be. The Cooking up my most striking projects in a way to make a figure at least here and most probably to get some profit from some of them. The consulting on means of turning my ideas of improvement in the Marine at home to some account so as to be preparing the way before me there. The reading over your works together and gutting them to make them pallateable to this country. The drawing up 2 or 3 philosophical papers which would be of use both at home and here.

If however you are persuaded that I can be of little or no use to you in my examination of your work before you publish it, if you have already began to print it; then postpone your visit till the spring. I can jog on in the mean time making my models; and that I may apply myself the closer to them I think of shamming ill in 2 or 3 weeks time, and then not going out till they are done.

But if your work is not as yet printed and you think my criticisms might be of use, if at the same time you could conceal the place of your residence from people in general at home under the pretence

cut paper without the least molestation in selling his handyworks, and without paying a farthing of taxes.

'His handicraft abilities independent of his inventive tallent might be turned to his and our common advantage in various ways.'

[6] Bentham added here in red ink: 'N.B. in his letter of Feb. 2d 1784 he says "Coach is bought".'

of going into the country a good way off, Why not try to come. By trying I mean enquiring if there are Vessels sailing for Dantzic or Memel and if the passage be not dangerous at this season. Coming by land all the way would be too expensive. There are no such post waggons as you speak of which come from Vienna here.

No it will be exposing yourself too much to make such a voyage by sea at this time of the year. I must first get some money to send you to pay for coming by land, and in the mean time I shall know more of my destiny, and shall have had news from you about your work.

Princess Dashkoff could now be made usefull in any thing that would please the Empress and She is well capable of judging what will do that. There is some fear that when Potemkin returns she may lose her favor; but I do not fear the finding other channels of coming at the Empress.

Octr. 14th O.S.[7]

477

From Samuel Bentham[1]

14/25 October 1783

The price as well as every thing relating to the means of getting by land from Ostende Hamburg Helvoetsluys, etc. you can learn much better from Germans. People here either travel expensively by land or else come by sea.

From Memel to Riga. I am told the Russians whom you will find there will bring you for 5 ducats from Riga to Petersburg 5 more. 20 or 25 pounds is the most that the whole of the journey would cost in this way, but then in the post waggons I believe you can carry but 14 pound weight.

You would want no books but a german grammar in your pocket. If there should be a Courier coming to Mr. Fitzherbert he might

[7] A further passage is omitted in which Samuel proposed that, instead of money, his brother should bring some firearms and razors. These could be sold at a profit, having been commissioned by men whom he was anxious to oblige, the firearms by Count Vorontsov (possibly Count S.R. Vorontsov, who became Russian ambassador in London in 1784), the razors by Baron Stroganov (possibly Baron Aleksandr Nicolayevich Stroganov (d. 1789)).

477. [1] B.M. III: 444. Autograph. Docketed by Bentham: '1783 Oct. / S.B. Petersburgh / to / I.B. Linc. Inn / Route to Petersburgh.'

take your papers. A pair of boots large enough for me you might wear on the road with 2 pair of warm stockings under them.

Ostende Bruge gent Brussel	By Canals
Mastricht Dusseldorff Munster Osnabruck Hanover Braunschweig Berlin Custrin Konigsberg	In post waggons
Memel Mittau Riga St. Petersbourg	At Memel or even at Konigsberg there are always Russian Yemschik[2] who have brought merchandize or people from Riga or even from Petersburg with their own horses and sledges and are returning back so as to be contented with a very moderate price. They go about 70 or 80 versts a day.

478

From Samuel Bentham[1]

14/25 October 1783

Code

I cannot help wishing that *Projet* should not be printed till we meet. Considering your engagement here in the light you now seem to consider it, were you to have advantageous offers made you, I should be far from opposing your accepting them. Such an employment might certainly by distinguishing you promote the execution of your ideas of reform at home, and therefore if it were for a short time not exceeding 2 or 3 years I should rejoice exceedingly at such

[2] *Yamshchik*, carter, or postilion.

478. [1] B.M. III: 455. Autograph. Docketed 'S.B. Petersburgh / to / I.B. Linc. Inn / Code [...?] and Sobecednick.'

an event. I have however very little expectations of any such offers being made you, and I cannot bear your offering your services. The Empress herself will never read your work, nor any one of her Ministers beyond the title page. It is therefore only from your reputation elsewhere that She would think of making you offers and that reputation once gained and you would not want her assistance.

An idea just now strikes, of a possible means by which the Empress might be made acquainted with the principles on which your work is founded, and by which the most striking ideas might be exhibited so as to make her interest herself in the work itself.

I told you of a periodical work that is published here at the Academy under the immediate management of the Princess Dashkoff, it is in this work that the Empress herself is giving the history of this country.[2] She also writes some other things in which the aim is wit and humour more than scientific knowledge. The rest consists of Poetry, Satire and some moral tales. 2 or 3 months ago there was published in this work a paper containing about 20 questions relating to the government which would astonish you by their freedom. One of them was 'why are not trials in courts of justice printed?' another was 'why do men of merit quit the service?[']

Princess Dashkoff shewed this paper to the Empress before she dared permit it to be printed. Leave however was obtained. Now in this same work one might In the way of dialogue cooked up into a tale introduce all your striking observations on jurisprudence. And in short through this channel we might exhibit all our remarks and criticisms whenever they do not attack the Empress herself more than that question of 'Why do men of merit quit the service?'

We certainly could shew off in this work and at present while it is yet new the Empress sees everything that is in it. Anything on the subject of Education would be well received.[3]

[2] *Sobesednik Lyubiteley rossiyskago slova soderzhashchiy raznyya sochineniya v stikhakh i v prose nekotorekh rossiyskikh pisateley*, 12 parts, St Petersburg, 1783–4.

[3] A final brief paragraph is omitted. This relates to B.M. III: 435, 446–50. These documents are an explanatory letter and a copy of the questions and answers to which reference is made above, which had recently appeared in *Sobesednik*. They are printed in full and critically discussed in K. A. Papmehl, 'Samuel Bentham and the Sobesednik, 1783', *Slavonic and East European Review*, xlvi (1968), 210–19.

479

FROM GEORGE WILSON[1]

3 November 1783

Wallace[2] is gone down to Tinmouth in Devonshire; they say it is the place where Dunning died, and in all probability Wallace goes on the same errand. Everybody says that Erskine[3] will be Solicitor-general—and if he is, or indeed whether he is or not, he will have had the most rapid rise that has been known at the bar; it is four years and a half since he was called, and in that time he has cleared £8,000 or £9,000, besides paying his debts, got a silk gown, and business of at least £3,000 a-year—a seat in parliament,—and over and above, has made his brother[4] Lord Advocate. For my part, I have great doubts whether his coming into parliament was a wise thing; he sacrificed his House of Commons' business, which was very profitable; and besides, his success seems to me very doubtful. He has several of Burke's defects, and is not unlikely to have his fate; and the expectation from him will be too great to be satisfied. We expect a match between him and Pitt, and another between Fox and Flood.[5]

The apprehensions about Ireland are not quite so great since the Leinster meeting, where there was not the same appearance of unanimity as at Dungannon. We have not yet heard of any meeting of the other two provinces;[6] and their parliament has been

479. [1] Bowring, x, 131. Incomplete.

[2] James Wallace (1729–83), of Carleton Hall, Cumberland, a distinguished barrister. He held the offices of Solicitor-General 1778–80 and Attorney-General 1780–82, and took office as Attorney-General in the Coalition ministry as one of North's followers. He died on 16 November.

[3] Thomas Erskine (1750–1823), 3rd son of Henry David Erskine, 10th Earl of Buchan, a brilliant barrister who had attached himself to the circle of Charles Fox and the Prince of Wales, to whom he became Attorney-General. The Fox-North ministry fell a few weeks later and he did not at this time obtain public office.

[4] Henry Erskine (1746–1817), 2nd son of the 10th Earl of Buchan, was appointed Lord Advocate for Scotland, in place of Henry Dundas, in August 1783, but lost his place in December on the dismissal of the Fox-North Coalition. On him see G. W. T. Omond, *The Lord Advocates of Scotland*, 2 vols., Edinburgh, 1883, ii, 163–74.

[5] Henry Flood (1732–91), formerly a member of the Irish parliament, had just entered the House of Commons as M.P. for Winchester. He opposed Fox's East India Bill during the following weeks.

[6] The meeting at Dungannon on 8 September 1783 had been attended by delegates from about 270 corps of volunteers of the province of Ulster and there had been substantial agreement upon a programme of radical parliamentary reform. At the meeting of volunteers of Leinster province on 9 October, dissensions due to conservative elements were much more in evidence. Meetings of volunteers in the provinces of

adjourned for some time.[7] The Bishop of Derry goes to the House of Peers, attended by a troop of horse, who remain on duty during his stay there.[8] He quite eclipses the Lord Lieutenant.[9] What a pity he is not captain of a man of war, and his son a bishop!

480

From François Xavier Schwediauer[1]

4 November 1783

Dear Bentham!

It would be very much out of your way to go to Petersburg by the way of Vienna. If you intend to go by land there, your nearest way is by Berlin, but from Vienna as well as from Berlin you may go with the diligence, which goes regularly twice or three times a week, tho' I am not informed and it would be indeed difficult to get information whether the diligences from Berlin to Petersburg (because this is always even by the way of Vienna the *route* to Petersburg) are so ~~good~~ /convenient/ as those from Vienna to Berlin. These latter go day and night and are covered like those in france: but in some parts of his prussian majesty's /dominions/ the diligences are nothing but open carts. The best what you could do would be to go either from Vienna or Berlin with a Russian *Courier* which pass and repass very frequently between these three courts; you go thus as Cheap as with the diligence (about 10 or 12 guineas from Vienna to Petersburg) but must at any rate always provide for your nourriture. But as I think upon the whole, that you are not able to put up with the inconveniences of Such a journey (the

Connaught (6 October) and Munster (1 November) had in fact adopted programmes substantially in line with that adopted by the Ulstermen at Dungannon (R. B. McDowell, *Irish Public Opinion, 1750–1800*, 1944, pp. 99–100).

[7] The Irish Parliament had been in recess from 27 July 1782 until 14 October 1783, when its next session began. Wilson had evidently not seen any report of its activities. It had stood adjourned from 16 to 27 October.

[8] On the Bishop of Derry, see letter 403, n. 16.

[9] Robert Henley (1747–86), 2nd Earl of Northington, had been appointed Lord Lieutenant of Ireland after the formation of the Fox-North ministry and resigned early in 1784 after its dismissal. He was generally considered to be very unequal to the position.

480. [1] B.M. III: 458. Autograph. Docketed by Bentham: '1783 Nov. 4 / Swediar Edinburgh / to / I.B. Linc. Inn. / Route to Petersburgh.'

This letter appears to reply to a letter from Bentham which is now missing. It affords further clear indication that Bentham, now that it was known that his brother was settled in the Russian service, was himself seriously thinking about visiting him.

couriers as well as the diligences go on day and night) I would rather advise you to go from London to Gothenburg or Copenhagen by sea and from thence by land /to Petersburg or Stockholm/ which is a very quick journey in winter (*in Sledges*).—I have received a letter from Bergman[2] last week, and likewise the 3d volume /of which/ you shall have a copy. Bergman gives to my knowledge two courses of chemistry, of which that of the winter season is the compleatest and best, but I do not recollect now when it begins, tho' I have it written down somewhere in my Notes. I am yours, and am happy to hear of your brother's establishment

Schwediauer

Edinbr. 4th Nov. 1783.

481

From Samuel Bentham[1]

10/21 November 1783

Novr. 10th

Wax Candles. Yes you certainly shall have them here. They may be bought I think for 13 pence lb. As to your general relaxation I make no doubt you would find great benefit from your journey. With respect to conversation, you will meet with such here as will certainly be infinitely more interesting to you than that of your /present/ acquaintance; but nevertheless the result of it will be your enjoying afterwards your pursuits in England far beyond what you can do without such a companion or rather without the advantages which you will derive from what you will learn here.

Power of Atty. I did not execute on account of my not having as yet made any such engagements as I considered to have been the reason for executing it. I now send it you.

There are no *Dilligences* in the country but Russian carriers go as far as Memel Dantzic or even Vienna and Berlin. No dependence however can be put on finding them at either of these places, and they are very tedious as they never change horses.

[2] On Bergman see letter 467, n. 3.

481. [1] B.M. III: 459. Autograph. Docketed: '1783 Nov. 10/21, Reced 1784 Mar. 6 / S.B. Petersburgh / to / I.B. Linc. Inn.' This docket in Bentham's hand obscures the beginning of another which appears to be in the hand of Samuel Bentham and to read: 'Sent[?] Jan. 22/Feb. 2nd.'

You tell me of a wonderful decypherer of whom you seem to have spoken in a former letter, if so that letter never came to hand.[2]

La Mechanique appliquée aux Arts aux Manufactures à l'Agriculture et à la Guerre, par M. Barthelot à Paris 1782 2 Vol. 4to. I have had only a glimpse at this book but it seemed to contain a vast number of mechanical inventions, some of them new to me, and the stile of the descriptions seemed to be particularly simple.

Steam Engine the simple one you speak of and the distilling apparatus by the same inventor would be great acquisitions.

If you were to bring with you a good fowling piece and a brace of small pocket pistols also another brace of larger proper for a travelling carriage they would serve you in the road and might be sold here to advantage. A freind of mine has beg'd me very much to procure him the above articles from England.[3]

482

From the Earl of Shelburne[1]

22 November 1783

Dear Sir

Lady Shelburne and I think it a great while since we had the pleasure of seeing you, and wish to tempt you to spend your Holydays here. If You are not better engag'd you'll find us from the 15th of next month to the end of it, and I shall be happy to assure you of the constant Truth and Regard with which I am

Dr. Sr.
Your Faithfull
and Obedt. Serv.
Shelburne.

Bowood Park
22d Novr. 1783.

[2] See letter 493. The 'decypherer' is there identified as a Captain William Skinner of the marines. In a letter dated 'Novr. 14th O.S. 1783' (B.M. IV: 462–3), Samuel added an interlineation in sympathetic ink: 'Novr. 29th O.S. I also received a fortnight ago a small parcel containing seeds two razors and some letters chiefly about Skinner. I have [not] yet an opportunity of doing any thing for him nor of informing myself of what can be done. I think however I shall write to you about him in the course of next week.'

[3] See letter 476, n. 7.

482. [1] B.M. III: 460–1. Autograph. Docketed by Bentham: '1783 Nov. 22. / Ld. Shelburne Bowood / to / I.B. Linc. Inn. / Invit. to spend Xmas.'

Addressed: 'To J. Bentham Esqr. / Lincoln's Inn / London.' Franked: 'Wycombe' Postmark illegible. Stamped: 'CALNE' 'FREE'.

483

To Reginald Pole Carew[1]

24 December 1783 (Aet 35)

Dear Sir

I have at length muster'd up exertion enough to tell you, what I might and should have endeavoured to tell you in another manner six weeks ago, that I am in town. I can give you no good reasons for the omission, nor any reason at all, but my apprehension of interfering with your better engagements, and the time it would have cost me to take the chance of doing so. Of your having been in my thoughts you will perhaps in a few days receive a proof which instead of affording an apology requires one. A few days ago an opportunity happen'd to present itself on the sudden of getting over from Ireland a pamphlet I had a curiosity to see: of the few friends I have in the house you happen'd at that moment to stand uppermost in my thoughts. I accordingly desired that it might be directed to you by the post. If you have a mind to take toll of it in its passage to Lincoln's Inn, you may have an opportunity of making yourself a perfect master of the art of legislation in all its branches, at a cheap rate: for in the compass of 88 pp. 12mo. loosely printed Mr. Dobbs Barrister at Law, will there present you with a Corpus Juris for Ireland *in terminis* if I am informed aright and compleat in all its branches.[2]

As to Monsr. le Conseiller de Cour de sa Maj. I. de T. 1. Russies,[3] some general idea of his destiny you have probably collected from Sir James. I have at present by me some of his scrawl posterior to any that you may have seen.[4] Is it worth sending or bringing to you? Shall I send this very scrawl of my own or bring it and leave it for you myself in the event of your not being at home? These are

483. [1] Pole Carew Mss. Autograph. Docketed: 'r—29 Decr. 1783 / a — 31.'
Addressed: 'R. Pole Carew Esqr.'

[2] Francis Dobbs (1750–1811), an Irish barrister, author of *A History of Irish affairs from the 12th of October 1779 to the 15th of September 1782*, Dublin, 1782, one of several pamphlets which he wrote at this time in support of a reformed Irish representative system with greater independence from British control. Between 1779 and 1784 he was an active supporter of the political agitation carried on by the Volunteer Movement in Ireland. No publication by him of the description here given has been traced.

[3] Samuel Bentham.

[4] Carew's reply (letter 484) identifies this as Samuel Bentham's letter to his brother of 6/17 October 1783. See letter 473, n. 8.

questions, which being of such importance it is great odds whether I decide upon before I fold up this paper: in the mean time, I hope you will do me more justice than to impute it to any want of respect if I tell you that I am in my garret every morning after 9, (till 3½) and most evenings after 7: and that it would be very flattering to me if at this bustling crisis you could find time to honour it with a visit. In said garret there is a manufactory of tea at work at all hours after the one last-mentioned. I am, My dear Sir, most entirely your's

J. Bentham

When you have done with the papers herewith enclosed, I will trouble you, instead of returning them to send them to Mr. Mulford Basingstoke, as before.

Lincoln's Inn
Decr. 24 at night.

484

From Reginald Pole Carew[1]

31 December 1783

Exeter Decr. 31st–1783.

Dear Sir

And I say unto my Servant, do this and he doth it: where does that happen but in Russia? does not this give You as great an Idea of the *Omnipotence* of a Russian Monarch as of the *Omniscience* of the Conseiller de Cour.—You see likewise by this Example, that the forming Men to the Various Arts, Sciences, Professions and Trades â *Coups de Baton* which has been so much talked of, is not confined in this extraordinary Country to the lower Ranks of the People, nor to the Natives alone, but that it is extended to all Ranks, and to /the Individuals of/ all Nations who breath the Russian Air.—They have found out that Your Brother has great Knowledge and Skill, in Mechanics, Chemistry, Physics, etc., and they make a Stone Mason of Him, a Hewer of Stone and Drawer of Water.—I am very much obliged to You for the Perusal of these

484. [1] B.M. III: 464–5. Autograph. Docketed: '1783 Dec. 31 / P. Carew Exeter / to / I.B. Linc. Inn.'
This is a reply to letter 483.

Letters, as I take a very sincere Interest in what Regards the Writer of them; there is no Man whom I more wish to see well rewarded for his Ingenuity, but I cannot help harping upon the same String, I wish it were upon an English Ground, and in doing His Mother Country Service, instead of Prejudice. The Country he is in is really unworthy the Pains he will take to serve it, and not in the same Want of the Helps of Ingenuity that our Taxridden Land is.—Would to God he had made his Fortune, and got the *Heimweh*; if I knew how to make him hear I would play up the *Ban des Vaches* quickly to him, which has the powerful Effect of sending every good Swiss home to his Mountains.

By the Date of my Letter, You will see I have been playing Truant, it has been much against my Inclination; and is become doubly so since the Temptations which You hold out to me between 9 and 3 and between 7 and Midnight.—I beg You not to think that Tea is one of those Temptations; for tho' I am very well disposed to cultivate its Acquaintance, I have ever met with so bad a Return, that I have been obliged to give it up.—The Attraction is centred in the Manufacturer, for whom I have a sincere Predilection, and from whom I have met with so obliging Receptions as to encourage very much the Renewal of my Visits.—

Mr. Dobb's *Code of Laws* followed Your Letter, and as he says he employed some Months in Composing it, I spent some Minutes in cursorily reading it; I like his Compendious Way of exposing his System of Legislation; but as we do not start well together, and tho there may be some Good Ideas, and a great Part of what Relates to the Courts of Justice and to Property may have its Advantages, yet I differ from Him in several of the most important Parts of His Political or Publick Law.—The Objections which strike me would extend beyond the Limits of a Letter, but I could not help marking what appears to me an Inconsistency in Our Author; in Page 23, he tells You that all Barristers and Attornies will be rendered useless by the Simplicity of this Code, in Page 32, he says (in the Chapter on Real Property) that all Parties may attend and plead their own Cause or *authorise others* to plead for them, giving them what Reward they choose.—What is this in Fact but restoring things to their Present Footing.—No Man would trust to his own Pleading, when he could get a Professional Man learned in the Laws to do it for him—

I think we never have had a Digest of the Laws of England made tho' a Work proposed by Chancellor Bacon, and which I conceive would be of considerable Use. It is to be lamented that he did not execute it as he had intended in his own Time, he would have laid an excellent Corner Stone for future Workmen to build upon.—

You will receive Mr. Dobbs in Company with this Letter and with it the Assurances of the great Respect and attachment of Dear Sir

Your most devoted Hble. Ser.
R. Pole Carew.

P.S.
I have forwarded your Brother's Letters as You desired—

485

To an Unknown Attorney[1]

8 January 1784 (Aet 35)

Jan. 8th 1784.

Dear Sir

On the other leaf you will see what I have undertaken for you. The Revd. Mr. Wilder, as I have heard is Mrs. Best's Brother and one of two Trustees to her marriage settlement—I have nothing to add but to beg you would do yourself justice as far as the occasion allows, which is what I should not know how to do.

I am Dear Sir, most sincerely

Yours
Jeremy Bentham

485. [1] Ms. in the possession of Mr D. R. Bentham of Loughborough. Autograph. Wrapper torn and the addressee's name missing.

Addressed: '⟨...⟩ Esqr. Atty. at Law / ⟨...⟩l's Inn / Holborn / London'. The only location which seems to fit is Furnival's Inn, where a number of attorneys had their offices. Postmark: 'BASINGSTOKE' (no date preserved).

The business to which this note relates is unknown, and so are the identities of the persons concerned. There was a Rev Henry Wilder, LL.D. (1744–1814), of Purley Hall, Berks, who was rector of Sulham, a place near the border of Hampshire with Berkshire. The will of his father, John Wilder of Nunhide, Berks (d. 1772) makes no mention of a sister, but if he was the person involved, the reference might be to a sister-in-law—his wife was Joan, née Thoyts.

486

To Samuel Bentham[1]

12 January 1784 (Aet 35)

Monday Jan. 12th.

Come give me a halfpenny, and I'll tell you a spick and span new *primum mobile* that you may make your fortune by. I have discovered it within these two hours. You remember the old /tea-table/ experiment of the tea-cup, which having a piece of lighted paper put into it, and being inverted, sucks up the saucerful of water. By means of a large tea-cup as many foot in diameter as you please I get a running stream out of a still pond. The tea-cup /being turned down/ rests on posts with the rim plunged a few inches under water. About half way up it in the middle is /the

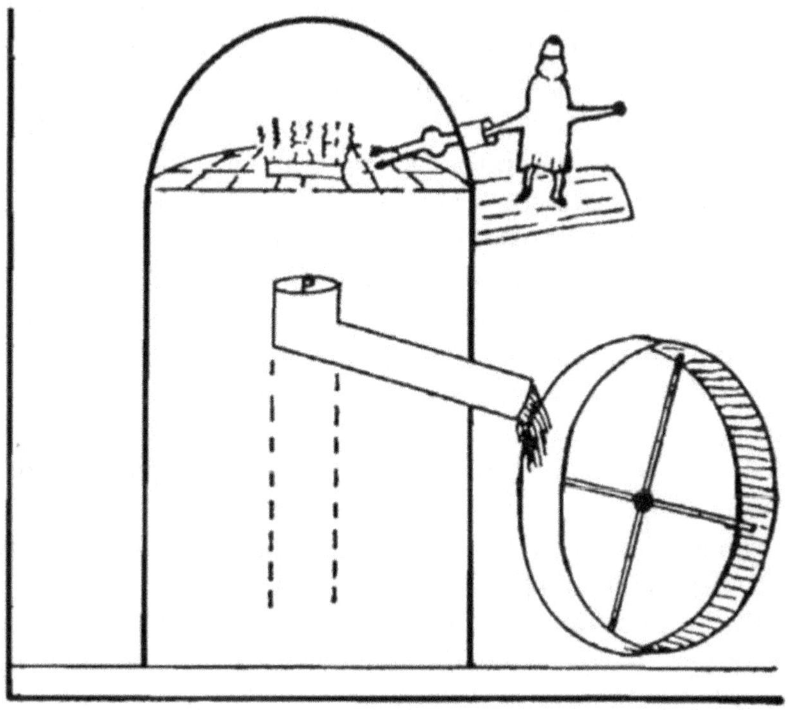

486. [1] B.M. X: 605. Autograph. Docketed: 'J.B. to S.B. Petersburgh.'

Address (crossed out): 'Samuel Bentham Esq., Petersburg.'

The dating, 'Monday, Jan. 12th' identifies the year as 1784 and this is also confirmed by internal evidence. The last paragraph refers to the first manned flight in a balloon organized by the brothers Montgolfier and undertaken by Francis Pilatre de Rozier and the Marquis d'Arlandes, which took place on 21 November 1783. D'Arlandes's account is quoted in full in L. C. T. Rolt, *The Aeronauts. A History of Ballooning, 1783–1903*, London, 1966, pp. 46–8. Newspaper accounts of the flight

upper end of/ a pipe (P) like what you see in cisterns to carry off the superfluous water and to prevent their overflowing at the edges. The lower end of the pipe hangs over a ~~water~~ wheel, which the water, by running upon it out of the pipe, is to turn. About ⅔ way up the tea-cup just above the upper mouth of the pipe, is a *stage* where I make a fire to rarify the air. If /by this rarefaction/ I can drive out half ⟨...⟩ atmosphere, 32 /Foot/ ÷ 2 = 16 Foot, ⟨...⟩ /get a/ fall of 16 foot of a column of water which might be of any diameter greater than half that of the tea-cup. Yes but then the fall can continue but a moment, unless the cause of the rarefaction, the ~~burning~~ fire-making be continued. Qu— what communication the fire-room at the top of the tea-cup have with the external air? There must be a hole to let out the air driven out by the rarefaction. There must be also a hole to let in the air for the combustion. This should [be] by a pipe fitting exactly into the fire-place so that no more air should get in than was necessary to keep up the fire, which necessary position would of course be heated by that means. To keep the fire supplied with fewel, I have two holes in the fire-room, closed with gloves long enough for an operator on the outside to thrust his arms through: and an Athanor[2] closing another room might be contrived for letting in the fewel from the outside.

The upper-part of the tea-cup is well great-coated /on the outside/ as you may imagine with the worst conductors that are to be had for love or money. The heat need not be so great as to prevent a man's thrusting his arms /into/ ~~through~~ the gloves. We shall see perfectly ⟨...⟩ /well/ what we are about /in the fire-room/ as there ⟨is⟩ no law against having as many little glass windows as we please. Shou'd the burnt air be let out at once, or should it be fogged round the room through an iron funnel /flue/ in order to force it to deposit its heat?

Would it be possible to produce the same effect by an air pump? the upper end of the pipe (P) being closed by a valve ~~opening outward~~ which should not go down untill the water rising above it should press it down? The Fire Pump to Bolton's Steam engine is worked not through leathers but only by tow wrapped round the piston, squirt-like.

appeared in *The Morning Chronicle*, 25 November 1783 (p. 3) and *The London Chronicle*, 25–27 November 1783 (p. 515). Reports also appeared in *The Gentleman's Magazine* for December 1783 (vol. 53, p. 1059) and in *The European Magazine* for January 1784 (vol. 5, pp. 25–7).

[2] A type of furnace constructed so as to maintain an equal heat and to burn for a long time without the addition of fresh fuel.

Tell me whether out of this rough hint you think any thing can be made. I could write ten times as much about it, if I had the time.

In order for the air in the fire-room to be kept in a rarified state it is by no means necessary that the fire-room should be air-tight. Mongolfier's Aerostatic Machine rose upon every fresh combustion, after the top was burst full of holes.[3]

487

From William Fitzherbert[1]

16 January 1784

Dear Sir,

Captn. Gotsched, an acquaintance of mine, a very Deserving young Man, wishes to ask you Some Questions relative to Russia, where He Has some Ideas of Going; If you will Give him time He will wait upon you, and I shou'd be oblig'd to you for any information you will give him.

Dr. Sir
Yours sincerely,
W. Fitzherbert.

Do not trouble yourself to answer this.

488

From Samuel Bentham[1]

20/31 January–22 January/2 February 1784

Petersburgh Jany. 20th 1784 O.S.

No time was as yet fixed for the departure of the English Courier who has been here some months and by whom I have given

[3] Bentham's device was impracticable. It rested upon both a misunderstanding and also the confusion of two distinct phenomena: the buoyancy of a bubble of hot air in relation to a colder surrounding atmosphere, and the contraction in a given volume of air when the oxygen is consumed within a bell-jar upturned in water.

487. [1] B.M. IV: 2–3. Autograph. Docketed by Bentham: '1784 Jan. 16 / Fitzherbert Gr. Russel Street / to / I.B. Linc. Inn / To introduce Cap. Gotsched.'

Addressed: 'Jer. Bentham Esqr.'

488. [1] B.M. IV: 7–12. Autograph. Docketed by Bentham: '1784 Jan. 22/Feb. 2 / S.B. Petersburgh / to / I.B. Linc. Inn.'

Some other notes of the same date (B.M. IV: 19–21) are omitted. Copy by Jeremiah Bentham, ibid., 13–16.

you to expect news from me, but as another is just arrived with the news of the change in the ministry Mr. Fitzherbert dispatches one of them as soon as possible. A small part only of what I had written in readiness for the opportunity will be to be sent now as my circumstances of late are entirely changed.

First I have to tell you that my love affair is entirely put an end to. Gen. Landskoy[2] ~~had~~ immediately on the death of the Uncle without any application on my part to him had interested himself so much in the affair as to let the aunt and mother know that the Empress thought they did wrong to oppose the young Countess's inclinations and promised that her Majesty would premote me and do anything to give them satisfaction. This only irritated the Aunt the more. When the Uncle and father came the girl was watched more closely than ever: yet she found means to write to me frequently and everybody seemed to be in our interests. She was ill, kept her room, and her bed, and allarmed her freinds, but could not soften them. She offered to make her escape with me, or take any steps which I would point out, could She but escape the vigilance of her keepers. She offered money and diamonds to one of her chambermaids, but could not gain her assistance. When things were in this situation the parents summoned all their force against her, and at length after having her Mother at her feet foaming at the mouth through despair, She, after half an hour's reflection sat down and wrote me a *renounce.* telling me that all had been tried and that a sense of the unhappiness She caused in her family forced her to give up all hopes....[3]

One consequence however is that my plans in this neighbourhood must be abandoned, at least for the present. I must certainly quit Petersburgh till the affair is blown over out of delicacy to her, so that it is lucky that an offer of Prince Potemkin's affords me a good opportunity. He wishes me to go to Cherson. He makes me lieutenant Colonel in the army, with a promise of promoting me as soon as possible to Colonel, perhaps within a year, to give me 12,00 Rubles salary, and as much more for table money. As for employment I am to do anything I think myself fit for and choose to do. He tells me he means to transport the Dockyard below the bar, and I may have the directing the new one, and for this purpose he

[2] '(The Empress's favourite)' is added above the line in another hand. Aleksandr Dmitriyevich Lanskoy (1758–84), a carefully-chosen client of Potëmkin's unlikely to undermine his political favour, had been for several years the latest of the handsome men with whom Catherine II took her sexual pleasures.

[3] About 600 words concerning the break with Countess Matyushkina are omitted.

preposed my being in the Navy, but as I should then be in some measure under Czernicheev's orders,[4] and depend in some degree on him for premotion, and as a freind of mine told him of Czernichev's being not well disposed to me; he then said he would take me in the army, by which means I should depend on himself alone. He means I should erect planing machine and my other machines usefull under his command which are no less than almost all machines possible, for his immediate command is all the southern part of the country and his indirect command is the whole Empire: but he is so indolent as not to have given yet the orders necessary to take me under his command....[5]

Consider then my inventive disposition and the imperfect state of every department here and you will have no doubt but I must have a multitude of proposals for improvement which have arisen from what I have seen in this country, over and above those which /we/ have talked over together and which are applicable to most countries....[6]

My difficulty in writing, in drawing up any paper, and more particularly in finishing it to my mind, has I fear rather increased upon me, and this partly from want of habit and partly because the number of objects of attention being increased each separate /one/ becomes of less importance. It will be to no purpose to fill sheets of paper in discussing the causes of this inability of mine; the effect of it I fear will be that unless you *do* pay me a visit and unless I can get some such man or men as Anderson whose Character would allow me to place the confidence necessary to derive assistance from his abilities I may live here with ease and repute, but shall never make a fortune. I can enjoy a great share of esteem and perhaps respect here, but shall have nothing to procure it me whenever I return home. Could you resolve to come and spend six months with me, you would make a new man of me, you would enable me to turn to account any ideas /of improvement/ which at present lay perfectly useless. You who so well spun out and displayed a few improvements in the details of the practice of constructing Ships would now have much richer materials to work on.

[4] Count Ivan Grigor'yevich Chernyshëv (1726–97), head of the Russian admiralty. For Samuel Bentham's dealings with him in 1780 see *Correspondence*, ii, as index. In the spring of 1780 Samuel had in some unspecified way given him offence, probably by using other channels to urge his pretensions to an office with privileges higher in rank than Chernyshëv thought it right to concede (B.M. III: 46, 52–3).

[5] About 800 words about his acceptance of Potëmkin's offer and his future prospects are omitted.

[6] About 100 words on the same subject omitted.

But how could you, who can scarcely bear the motion of a coach, make such a Voyage by Sea? once landed at Petersburgh I would endeavour to make you comfortable in the journey you would most likely have to make in the Country. Whether I shall reside at Cherson or, whether I shall have to shift about wherever there may be anything going forward in Potemkin's Governments ~~which~~ where he may see or I may see that I can be of use, I cannot tell as yet, he certainly will get me to his estate on the borders of Poland to give directions for the erecting some machines /there/, though he has not /yet/ told me so. But be it where it will, tell me the time you will be at Riga or Petersburg and I will meet you there to conduct you wherever my fate destines me. As soon as you are in the country all expence of living and travelling is mine, and I think you wont find it troublesome. I have just this instant learnt that it is probable I shall have the directing of the building some Corn mills in the Crimea /as one of my first commissions/ they must some of them at least be worked by wind or possibly by oxen as their fodder will be very cheap. . . .[7]

I sent you a letter about 3 weeks ago to which you can well imagine I am very anxious for an answer.

You have desired me to send you Guldenstaedt's account of the productions and commerce of this country.[8] I have got it ready to send you; but upon looking into and turning over page after page without finding any article of it true I determine not to send it at all unless I can go over it and correct it.

A Russian Grammar I send you.

A Catalogue of Books published in the Russian langage I asked Princess Dashkoff for yesterday; but she refused to give me one and insisted on my not thinking of sending one till the middle of next month when there will be a new one ready with all the prices as She has changed them and an addition of a great many important works. Among others there will be a history of the The Manjures and Mongols translated from the Manjure language and which has been translating and printing for these 24 years past. It is in 16

[7] About 500 words repeating his proposals about Bentham's visit to Russia omitted.

[8] Johann Anton Güldenstädt (1745–80), a native of Riga, educated in Germany, a doctor and naturalist, who travelled widely in Russia and became professor of natural history at St Petersburg and president of the economic society there. In 1776, at a public meeting of the imperial academy of sciences, he delivered an address which was afterwards published: *Discours académique sur les produits de Russie propres pour soutenir la balance du commerce exterieur toujours favorable*, St Petersburg, n.d.

volumes 8vo. There will be likewise a collection of all Plato's works in the russian language in 3 volume 4vo.

You ask some account of the Sobecednick.[9] The 10th volume is just now printed it is in small 8vo. It began in May last. Each volume contains about 12 sheets.

As to a book of the Custom house duties in this Country you may by enquiry among the Russian Merchants in London learn where it is to be procured in English. I think it is published by Spilsbury.

Czarawitch Clore the Empress's tales of which you asked are not to be had in French.[10]

The answers to those questions of which I sent you what you call a very bad translation were written by the Empress I thought I told you so. The stile was so indifferent in Russ that it would have been difficult to make the translation tollerable.

I think I write worse and worse. I dont mean the hand alone but the stile also. I am really affraid you will scarcely understand some parts of this letter.

I send you the Eloge of the famous Euler,[11] and a Peterburgh Court Calendar.

~~I send you a copy of a letter written by Sir Robert Walpole to the late king. I had it from Pleschijeff who got it when he was in England~~

[9] See letter 478.

[10] *Skazka o Tsareviche Khlore*, i.e. 'Story of the Tsarevich Khlor'. An English translation appeared in 1793 in James Anderson's journal, *The Bee*, and was then published separately, with authorship attributed to Catherine II, under the title, *Ivan Czarowitz, or The Rose without Prickles that Stings Not.* The prefatory note to it states: 'The original of this little tale in the Russian language was given to Dr. James Anderson, editor of a periodical paper called THE BEE, published at Edinburgh, by a gentleman of literary eminence, who had been some time ago in Russia, with an assurance that, upon the most undoubted authority, he could say it was actually the performance of the august personage whose name it bears in the English title.' Possibly the conveyor of the original was Jeremy Bentham, who returned to England early in 1788 after his sojourn in Russia. See A. G. Cross, 'Arcticus and *The Bee* (1790–4): An Episode in Anglo-Russian Cultural Relations', *Oxford Slavonic Papers*, new series, II (1969), 62–76.

[11] Leonard Euler (1707–83), a distinguished Swiss mathematician. At the age of nineteen he was second in a contest for a prize given by the Paris academy for the best treatise on masting of ships. While still in his twenties he became professor of physics and then of mathematics at St Petersburg. After 1741 he spent a period at Berlin, but he later returned to St Petersburg, where he died. His various important mathematical treatises established his reputation as one of the founders of modern mathematical analysis. Possibly the 'Eloge' was that by the Marquis de Condorcet, which was later published at the beginning of the first volume of *Lettres de M. Euler à une Princesse d'Allemagne*, 3 vols., Paris, 1787.

(I send you likewise a magnificent Chart of Moldavia Walachia etc.[12])

I send you also a Chart of the Empire[12] in which the acquisitions made to it in each reign since Peter the great inclusive are distinguished by different colourd inks. It takes in the late discoveries by Kamschatka I must write a few lines to Miss Harris which you will forward[13] although it is 1 o'clock in the morning and the Courier's horses are ready.
22nd at night.

489

To Jeremiah Bentham[1]

3 February 1784 (Aet 35)

Linc. Inn Tuesday eveng.

Hond. Sir

Tomorrow after Mr. Mulford comes to town to dispatch the business of advancing the £600.—You will therefore look out the writings of what you propose to offer him in the way of Mortgage, and be prepared for whatever else may be proper on the occasion—After waiting on you at dinner time I shall call immediately on him at his lodgings in King Street Golden Square

Yours dutifully
J.B.

Some difficulties had occurred, and I was obliged to call forth all my rhetoric: but now I hope everything is clear.

[12] Missing.
[13] A copy of this letter by Jeremy Bentham is at B.M. IV: 23–4.

489. [1] B.M. IV: 25–6. Autograph. Docketed by Jeremiah Bentham: 'Fils Jeremy B / Lr. Datd. Lincoln's Inn / Dated Tuesday Eveng. / 3d. Feby. 1784.'

Addressed: 'Jeremiah Bentham Esqr. / Queens Square Place / Westminster.' Postmark: 'KENT POST PAID', date illegible.

The transaction here mentioned is not explained, but it probably related to the clearing up of Samuel Bentham's final outstanding debts at St Petersburg (see letters 472 and 491).

490

TO JEREMIAH BENTHAM[1]

11 and 12 March 1784 (Aet 36)

Linc. Inn. March 11(th) 1784.

Honoured Sir

I /write this merely to/ beg you would make my apology to my Mother for the abrupt manner in which I left the room yesterday afternoon, without taking my leave of her any more than of you. ~~Nothing could be further from my thoughts than~~ Conceiving that after the turn the conversation had taken, that room was by no means a proper place for me to be in, as indeed it had not been for some time, I took myself away accordingly: (~~a little sooner perhaps than I should have done otherwise, but not so soon as I wish I had done~~) but the idea of the cause that made my intention no longer tenable affected me in such a manner as to deprive me of all power of utterance. The reason therefore why I did not speak to her ~~at parting~~ a circumstance that ~~must~~ might naturally appear ~~disrespectful on my part if not explained~~ /to shew a want of respect if not explained/ was a very simple one: viz that it was as much out of my power as if my tongue had been cut out to speak at all. ~~As to~~ That nothing ~~disrespectful to her~~ of that sort could have been meant by me will I hope ~~appear the more manifest~~ /the more easily find credit/ when it is recollected that /~~of/ whatever unkindness I had been the object of in the [...?...?] you may have given me to complain of an unkindness, she who had been a silent auditor the whole time~~ [*further correction obscure*] Whether the ground I concieved I had to complain of unkindness be just or otherwise, she had not the smallest share in it. I am with all respect

Honoured Sir
Your dutiful son
J.B.

Letter 2d in reply to the answer to the above

490. [1] B.M. IV: 27–8. Drafts, with corrections. Autograph. Docketed by Bentham: '1784 March 11 and 12 / I.B. Linc. Inn / to Q.S.P. Q.S.P. / Brouillons / Post Phillippi [...?] / coram [...?] / and / Reply to answer.'

No information has been found throwing light upon the nature of the dispute between Bentham and his father referred to in these letters.

Hond. Sir

It gives me great satisfaction to find my Mother had the kindness not to put that construction upon my behaviour to which I own it was so liable: ~~but the~~ /As to my waiting upon you today, the/ same considerations which in my conception rendered it improper for me to stay on in the room in question, render it equally improper for me to return to it, untill some points have been cleared up, which can /not/~~with propriety be opened up discussed (between persons so related as you and I are) according to my notions~~ (be discussed with propriety before any) third persons whatsoever. Such at least are my notions ~~on the matter~~ /in/ which from ~~what~~ /incidents/ I have so often been witness to in that same room, I have the satisfaction of knowing that I am by no means singular. ~~If I am~~ Singular ~~in them~~ /or not/ I am at least so consistent that /as often as/ my Brother has happened to have ~~any of those~~ /certain/ points to discuss with you which ~~from my experience /my experience/ the disposition of the parties I have judged~~ /have appeared to me/ to be of a delicate nature I have been as anxious to leave him alone with you as now I am to be alone with you myself. Some day or other your business will call you my way; whenever it happens to suit your convenience I shall be happy the opportunity of assuring you /in person/ of the affectionate respect with which I am Hon Sir Your dutiful Son J.B.

491

From Samuel Bentham[1]

6/17–9/20 March 1784

Petersburgh March 6th O.S. 1784.

I can at length tell you something more certain relating to my destination although it is but very little. Prince Potemkin sets off from hence in less than a week to visit Cherson and his new Government of *Chersonesus Taurica* (the name given to the Crimea since its being annexed to the Russian dominions). I am to go with him in the quality of Lieutenant Colonel in the army: but /as to/ what employment I am to have either at Cherson or elsewhere

491. [1] B.M. IV: 30. Autograph. Docketed by Bentham: '1784 March 6–9/17–20 / S.B. Petersbourg / to I.B. Linc. Inn / Going to Cherson with Potemkin / Reced Apr. 13.'

Addressed: 'Jere^{y} Bentham Esqr. / Lincoln's Inn / London.' Postmark: 'ST PETERBOURG', dated '3' otherwise illegible.

under his command I can tell you nothing [*a line and a half almost entirely obliterated*] When we are on the spot I shall ⟨be⟩ able to ⟨judge better⟩ of what I should be most capable as ⟨well⟩ as what will be most desirable. While I enjoy the share of a Prince's good opinion and confidence which I flatter myself I possess at present, my situation cannot be disagreeable: and there ⟨...⟩ little doubt of my having some advantageous opportunities ⟨of⟩ distinguishing myself.

March 9th I send you enclosed a draft on Sutherland's house for 100£ which you will give to Burkitt.[2] I have but just received it but will not delay a post to send him the news of it and to let you know that I set off today or tomorrow. You shall have further particulars by next post. I am all anxiety to hear from you about your Visit. About the beginning of June P. Potemkin will be back here and probably I may come with him although my stay in that case would be short here as my business will lie at Cherson or in the Crimea. I could however though it should be impossible for me to come to meet you make provisions for your having every accomodations. and John Clarke[3] might ~~move~~ /travel/ with Burkit from Petersburgh free of all expenses. Letters will be forwarded to me.

[*Added upside down at foot of page*]

I have not written to my father yet in answer to his. The Packets you left with Frazer are not come. Mr. Thorpe tells me my Father has paid the money. I am therefore as easy /as/ I can be: but the effect of payment being once refused must remain.[4]

[2] As well as inclosing the draft for Burket, Samuel Bentham also sent, on the other page of this sheet of paper (fo. 29) a letter for Burket, dated 9/20 March, informing him that the draft was sent to provide money for clothing and other things he should bring with him to Russia. He would receive 600 rubles a year (about £100) while in Samuel's employment. An 'English' journeyman watchmaker (he was a Scotsman, James Love) had already been engaged to work under him. Samuel defined Burket's employment as 'the assisting me in any machines I may erect, any mechanical construction I may introduce, the directing the making of models, and the executing such parts yourself as others under you can not do'. Burket was to come by sea, arriving in June, and in case of Samuel's absence he was to report to Hynam, the empress's watchmaker, through whom any necessary arrangements for him would have been made. Samuel's next letter (letter 492) included a list of things Burket should bring with him. However, Burket decided not to go to Russia.

[3] I.e. Jeremy Bentham.

[4] The final clearance by Jeremiah Bentham of the debts Samuel had incurred at St Petersburg prior to receiving his commission in the Russian service may have been effected with the money borrowed on mortgage from Mulford (see letter 489). Samuel's letter to his father, dated 5/16 April 1784, acknowledging this help is at B.M. IV: 33–4.

492

From Samuel Bentham[1]

13/24 March 1784

Petersburg Wednesday March 1784

I am just this instant setting out for Moscow where I shall find Prince Potemkin. Different things detained me here 3 or 4 days after him. By the last post but one I sent you a letter half of which was intended for Burkit as I suppose you saw by the contents although I forgot to tell you so explicitly.[2] It enclosed a draught on a Banker for 600 rubles of which I now send you the duplicate in case of any accident with the first, according to custom. I hope Burkit will be preparing for his journey and that he will get here by the end of May. As to John Clarke I am affraid he would be troublesome and still more that it would not suit himself to come out: but surely you might pay me a visit yourself. Could I but know it in time I make little doubt but I might come and see you here and then if you liked it you could go with me to my *station*. Even without such a motive it is probable that I may return here with the Prince at the end of May or beginning of June to receive more fully his orders about what I am to have to do. The idea of a journey of two thousand versts may appear a little formidable to you: but in this country it is nothing. You cant concieve how lightly I think of my /future/ journie now that the expence is out of the question. Should you be here a little time without me: you would meet with the most hospitable and freindly reception possible from Fitzherbert. Pleschijeff would be overjoyed to see you: and you would find some others here in whose company you could be happy. There would be no need of your going into public company for there you would find no satisfaction. You would profess the having come out on purpose to see me and that you would wait till you heard from me if that were practicable. As to Anderson I have not had an opportunity to do anything in the way of providing

492. [1] B.M. IV: 31–2. Autograph. Docketed by Bentham: '1784 March / S.B. Petersburgh / to / I.B. Linc. Inn.'

Addressed: 'Jere[y] Bentham Esqr. / Lincoln's Inn / London.' Postmark: 'AP/20'.

This letter can be exactly dated to 13/24 March 1784, by Samuel's reference to the departure from St Petersburg of Potëmkin, which took place on Saturday, 9/20 March (Bezborodko to S.R. Vorontsov, 15/26 March 1784, *Arkhiv Knyazya Vorontsova*, 40 vols., Moscow, 1870–95, xiii, 48).

[2] Letter 491.

for his expences in a manner that would be agreable to him but as a visitor he would have every conveniency I could procure him. I am in too great agitation in leaving my freinds here at this moment to be able to depend on what I write now so that I shall only add a few things that I think Burkit should bring.

1. Portable furnace[3] such as you once mentioned in a letter.
2. My tools which I left behind as well as of course /his/ your own.
3. A Microscope of some kind or other.
4. Book of drawings of Machines sold at Sharpe's the Iron-mongers with their prices.
5. Models[3] if to be procured of the best constructed wind mills for grinding corn.
6. For me. Cook's last voyage to the South seas.
7. Smith on the Wealth of Nations.

493

TO SAMUEL BENTHAM[1]

25 March 1784 [?] (Aet 36)

J'ai entendu souvent attribuer à l'Imperatrice ou pour vrai dire, au Prince P. deux grands objets: l'acquisition de la Crimée c'est à dire la navigation de la mer noire, et l'ouverture d'une communication avec celle du Japan par le fleuve Amour ~~C'est surtout~~ /Voilà surtout le rapport ~~ce qui a fait~~ /de Pole Carew que ~~j'appris celle particularitè je tiens suis redevable de cette idée~~/ qui me parle sans cesse de M. le Prince et jamais sans éloge. Or de ces deux objets le premier est heureusement accompli: /reste done le second pour lequel actuellement/ on doit donc se

[3] Over this is written in pencil: 'To Anderson'.

493. [1] B.M. X: 618–19. Autograph. Draft with corrections. No date, address, or docket.

The reference to Skinner (n. 2 below) is in answer to a query in Samuel Bentham's letter of 10/21 November 1783 (letter 481), which was received in London on 6 March 1784. Bentham's next letter to Samuel was dated 9 March and acknowledged by Samuel from Orsha on 7 April (B.M. IV: 35–7). However, this draft would appear to be of a later letter, because Bentham's query about the Amur river route only received an answer in Samuel's letter of 20 June/1 July 1784 dated from Kremenchug (B.M. IV: 70–80, extracts of which were sent or handed by Bentham to Lord Carmarthen at the Foreign Office in July 1785–see letter 536). Samuel moved south from Orsha soon after 7 April, and his own letters indicate that those from England were taking two or three months to reach south Russia. His next acknowledgement of letters from Bentham lists those dated 25 March, and 5, 8, 11 (or 12), and 28 April, and 13 May (B.M. IV: 98–9). The first of these dates seems the most likely for this draft, though an early date in April cannot be excluded.

trouver en /toute/ liberté ~~de poursuivre.~~ Mandez-moi, je vous prie, s'il paroit qu'on y songe, et où l'on en est à cet égard? entreprise commencée et quand? preparatifs /faits ou commencés?/ projet arrêté ou simplement conçu? Vous savez comme j'ai pris l'Empire Russe sous mon auguste protection: et je vous avoue que toutes les fois que j'ouvre la carte, je ne puis regarder sans un mouvement de regret ce beau fleuve qui pourroit être si utile et qui ne l'est guère, ce beau fleuve qui ne coule que pour des barbares. Les fourrures de Sibérie /n'y/ pourroient-elles pas trouver un meilleur chemin à la Chine qu'elles n'en trouvent à travers cet affreux desert de Gobi? Le plomb de Nerchink qu'on n'exploite dit-on que pour la petite portion /d'argent/ qu'il renferme, et qui /faute de debit/ pourriroit, si le plomb pouvoit pourrir sur les bords de la mine, ne pourroit-il pas s'échanger contre l'or et l'argent du Pérou? Une poignée d'hommes ne suffiroit-il pas pour aider les Coréens /les/ Hilites comme l'on dit des Chinois, à secouer le joug de leurs tirans. Ne seroit-il pas là un moyen d'acquérer dans ces mers des alliés utiles, ou plutôt des dépendans dévoués, et de jouer ~~avec un~~ à meilleur titre et avec ~~plus~~ meilleur /~~fruit~~/ le rôle qu'ont joué les François dans l'Amerique? Dites-moi là dessus si vous en avez le tems ce que vous savez et ce que vous pensez. ~~C'est~~ Ce sont ces idées qui m'ont fait penser derechef à Skinner: au Capitaine William Skinner:[2] c'est ainsi que cet homme⊞ dont vous avez demandé des nouvelles [sous] le nom du wonder-working decypherer.[3] J'ai d'abord jetté les yeux sur lui à l'occasion des démêlés avec les Turcs:[4] il s'est prêt à l'idée que je lui ai suggeré de faire offre de ses services: mais il l'a abandonné avant même que

⊞ [*Marginal addition*] le jeune ~~officer~~ /Capitaine/ de Gardes-Marines dont je vous ai parlé dans une lettre que vous dites avoir manqué, et de qui

[2] William Skinner appears to have been an illegitimate son of Lieutenant General William Skinner (1700–80) by his housekeeper, Elizabeth Prior. He does not appear in the contemporary army lists, but Bentham's description of him as a captain of marines is categorical and repeated, and presumably correct. The references to Admiral Arbuthnot, naval commander at New York from August 1779 to September 1781, and to Howe's relief of Gibraltar in October 1782, fit well with the description of Skinner as a young officer, aged scarcely twenty-five.

[3] This phrase occurs in letter 481.

[4] After the Russians annexed the Crimea in the summer of 1783, some little time elapsed before it became clear that the Turks would not make this a *casus belli*. In these circumstances, with the American war of independence over, Russia was one place where officers thrown on half-pay looked for possible active employment. However, Skinner does not seem to have pursued any opening in Russia through the Benthams. On 23 December 1784 Samuel complained to his brother: 'You tell me nothing more of Skinner.' (B.M. IV: 129–30.)

l'attente de la guerre [se soit] rallentie, à cause de la resolution où ont eté nos puissances de ne pas donner permission aux officiers /reformés/ de ce corps là /le corps des gardes-marines/ à moins qu'ils ne résignassent leur demi-paye.

En effet depuis l'intérêt que vous m'avez fait prendre à la prosperité de /votre pays adoptif/ je ne vois dans aucun genre un homme de talent sans dire à moi-même, mais cet homme-ci n'y auroit-il pas moyen de ~~le faire~~ /s'en servir/ utile à la Russie? Quand à celui-ci je vous ai marqué dans le tems ses principaux titres: plusieurs années de service auprès de Gibraltar avec le Lord Howe, en Amerique, dans les Indes occidentales: commission importante reçue, confiance insigne /distinguée/ reposée en lui par l'Admiral Arbuthnot qui ne le connaissait que de reputation, à une occasion où sans l'imbecillité de Clinton c'en étoit fait de la flotte Françoise: courage et san[g] froid deploiés à l'occasion* de ces émeutes à Chatham où tant d'autres trembloient et ne savoient que faire: sa douceur, sa modestie et sa sagesse: le bon sens qu'il a /fait voir/ temoigné dans /des/ quelques lettres que j'ai tenu de lui, et ce /qu'on recontre si rarement/ ~~qui est si rare~~ dans un militaire surtout dans un militaire si jeune car à peine a t'il vingt cinq ans) l'élegance de son stile: enfin ce talent singulier qu'il possède parfaitement comme j'en ai fait la preuve, et qui semble faire fin d'un esprit robuste et exercé qui pourroit s'appliquer a tout.

*[*Marginal addition*] Zèle avec lequel Skinner a executé cette commission et qui s'est /lui fit subir volontairement/ manifester par des fatigues lesquelles pendant deux mois faisoient désespérer de sa vie.

494

FROM FRANCIS VILLION[1]

13 April 1784

Dear Sir

Upon my returning to town today on account of the election of E. India Directors,[2] I have been,—shall I say, agreably, or,

494. [1] U.C. IX: 1. Autograph. Docketed by Bentham: '1784 Apr. 13 / Villion / Lothbury / to / I.B. Linc. Inn.'

Partly printed, Bowring, x, 132.

Villion, a Genoese merchant in business in London, had been thick with Bentham in the early 1770's; but he displayed a streak of meanness which Bentham found distasteful and seems to have dropped out of his intimate circle by about 1775. See *Correspondence*, i, 144 n., 174, 262, 270, and Bowring, x, 131.

[2] The election of East India Company directors took place on 14 April, and the

disagreably?—surprised, at finding at home your obliging letter of the 8th instant.[3] It hath recalled to my mind a friendly connection, which, as long as it lasted, was at once the pride and the delight of my life. But this connection not being supported equally on both sides, it necessarily grew by slow degrees, weaker and weaker, till it broke at last.

This event, although long-foreseen, and according to the common course of Nature, which seldom, very seldom indeed, admits the continuation of an intimacy between *unequals*, hath however affected me so much, that I do assure you, Time hath hardly afforded me any relief; even Time itself, whose ever-working hand, hath almost obliterated out the very deep impressions, made upon me by the heavy strokes of repeated misfortunes: misfortunes which the generality of people would agree, in looking upon as the most severe ones. I have endeavoured to reconcile myself to that event, by the consideration, that, when we leave nothing at all behind us to regret, we are prepared to meet Death with fortitude and indifference.

But I beg your pardon Dear Sir, for wandering so far out of the way, and making these moral reflections, which, I own, are quite foreign to the subject of your letter, and must be indifferent to you. I have been naturally enough, tho' unawares, led into them.

I do not find that besides the history of Opticks by Dr. Priestley[4] in a large Qto., I have any other book of yours, excepting his answer to Beattie, Oswald and Reid. As to Hasselquist's voyage,[5] I do not remember to have ever borrowed it of you; on the contrary, I am /pretty/ certain I have not, because it was lent to me, soon after its publication, by my friend Mr. Hinde of Hampstead.

I see by a memorandum of mine, that you have along with the 3 Voles, of Livy,[6] Sheridan upon elocution in Qto. covered with blue

friends of Pitt's administration succeeded in excluding all six candidates put up by Fox's party (C. H. Philips, *The East India Company, 1784–1834*, Manchester, 1940, pp. 28–9).

[3] Missing.

[4] Joseph Priestley (1733–1804) was the author, among other works, of *The History and Present State of Discoveries relating to Vision, Light and Colours*, 2 vols., London, 1772, and *An Examination of Dr Reid's Inquiry into the Human Mind on the Principles of Common Sense, Dr Beattie's Essay on the Nature and Immutability of Truth, and Dr Oswald's Appeal to Common Sense in Behalf of Religion*, London, 1774.

[5] Fredrik Hesselquist (1722–52), *Voyages and Travels in the Levant, in the years 1749–52, containing observations in Natural History... written originally in the Swedish Language... published... by Charles Linnaeus*, London, 1766.

[6] *T. Livii... historiarum libri qui supersunt omnes ex recensione A. Drakenborchii ...Cum indice rerum locupletiss. Accessit praeter varietatum lectt Gronovianae et Crevenanae glossarium Livium, curante A. G. Ernesti*, 3 vols., Leipzig, 1769.

paper.[7] I shall be obliged to you, to look for the last, and if you will be so kind as to send the whole to my lodgings by your servant, he will carry back your own books. I shall give orders that they be delivered to him, should I happen not to be at home, when he calls for them.

I am with very sincere regard, and always shall be,

Dear Sir
Your most obedient
humble servant
Francis Villion

No 26 Lothbury
Tuesday evening 13 April 1784
Jeremy Bentham Esqr. Lincoln's Inn
Old Buildings No 6.

495

From Samuel Bentham[1]

7/18 April 1784

April 7th 1784 O.S.

I have just now received your letter III of which the last date is March 9th.[2] I have not as yet received any letter from Burkit, but your letter seems to give me assurances that I shall see Anderson as well as him. Before I left Petersbourg I sent at 2 different times duplicates of a draught on Sutherland's house in London for 600 rubles for Burkit. With respect to Anderson I have not been

[7] Thomas Sheridan (1719–88), *A Discourse... by T. Sheridan, being introductory to his course of Lectures on Elocution and the English Language*, London, 1759.

495. [1] B.M. IV: 37. Autograph. Docketed by Bentham: '1784 Apr. 9/18 / S.B. Orska on the Dnieper / to / I.B. Linc. Inn / Sheet / Received at Whitchurch.' The letter reached Bentham on 4 July (see letter 506).

In other portions of this letter, of the same date (fos. 35–6), Samuel explained how, in the course of his travels with Potëmkin, he had fallen into intimacy with the prince's first aide-de-camp, Lieutenant Colonel Jean François Ribeaupierre (1754–90), a Swiss who had settled in Russia. Ribeaupierre owned an estate in the vicinity of Orsha, and Samuel discussed at length ways in which it was farmed and might be developed, a task which he thought Anderson might take on under his auspices. A further long discussion of this subject, still on the asumption that Anderson would come to Russia, is contained in another letter, dated 9/20 April, possibly dispatched in the same packet (B.M. IV: 38–42). Bentham relayed the suggestion to Anderson: see letter 508.

[2] Missing.

able to do the like for him chiefly from the reasons which I before gave why almost any kind of previous engagement would be unsuitable to him. I hope however to be able to inform him by this same packet of a plan that presents itself from which he may derive some advantage. In the mean time I sit down to answer this last letter of yours.

As to Messengers it is very improbable that you will receive any more letters from me through that channel. It is an opportunity that happens so seldom that when I send my letters to Petersburgh to be forwarded to you, I should not think of lying them so long in waiting. Mr. Fitzherbert is so exceedingly freindly to me on all occasions that I believe I shall charge him with the forwarding my letters from me. As to those I receive from England it will be sometimes one person sometimes another as circumstances require. No matter to you you may direct to me always the same. But if ever you should have occasion to direct to me straight to any other part of the Country then you will call me Lieut: Col: au service de S.M. L'Imp. de toutes les Russies. I will however not fail to use the precautions you require.

Henderson[3] and Dinwidee[4] are new names to me but from the manner in which you mention them I should have been glad you had made acquaintance with half a dozen more such. I long for this packet of which you have more than once given me tidings.

Dont think anything about the expence of such guests, be assured we shall all find where withall to eat and drink. As to travelling expences to come to me I can also engage for that some way or other, either at public or even at my own expence. My Salary I understand is 1200 rubles to which I am to have 100 rubles pr month equal to 1200 more for table money, besides four men servants who are fed without my expence. I told you I was to be made Lieutenant Colonel in the Army. I am so, and wear the uniform accordingly as you will see by my portrait which I have sent my father and which he will receive by shipping.[5] I rejoice that *Projet* is so near finished but I had wished so much to see it before it had been printed, besides that I shall lament so much the impediment to your visit. If however the gods will that you should be thus detained I will console myself with the hopes that

[3] See letter 543, n. 5.

[4] Not identified. There is no indication in the correspondence that a man of this name went to Russia under any arrangements with the Benthams.

[5] This portrait is now in the National Maritime Museum, and is that used for the frontispiece of this volume.

in the course of these 6 or 8 months I may contrive your visit to be more comfortable to you. Happy we will be when we are together....[6]

496

From Francis Villion[1]

18 April 1784

Mr. Villion came to town last night at 11 o'clock on account of an engagement to dine with some friends at Mr. Chalie's in Bedford Square. He is exceedingly sorry not to have had the pleasure of meeting Mr. Bentham at his chambers, so much the more as he is obliged to postpone it for two or three days, very much against his inclination—

Sunday 2½ o'clock
J[y] Bentham
Esqr.—

497

From Francis Villion[1]

19 April 1784

Lothbury No. 26 Monday morning
19 April 1784

My Dear Sir

An ingagement for yesterday, brought me to town very late on Saturday evening. I had been pressed in an obliging manner to stay till the next morning, but I congratulated myself for having luckily withstood the civil importunities of my friends, as I antici-

[6] A final passage is omitted. Samuel hoped for a full description of a steam engine about which he had been inquiring. Anderson and Burket were to bring some seed potatoes. The chart of the empire he had sent was in Russian characters as one in roman lettering was not available.

496. [1] U.C. IX: 2. Autograph. Docketed by Bentham: '1784 Apr. 18 / Villion Lothbury / to / I.B. Linc. Inn.'

This note, written on a scrap apparently detached from a larger sheet, was left at Bentham's chambers—see letter 497.

497. [1] U.C. IX: 3. Autograph. Docketed by Bentham: '1784 Apr. 19 / Villion Lothbury / to I.B. Linc. Inn.'

Addressed: 'Jeremy Bentham Esqr. / No. 6 Old Buildings / Lincoln's Inn.'

Printed, Bowring, x, 132–3.

pated by some hours the inexprimable satisfaction and comfort which your letter of the 14 Inst.[2] gave me. So kind, so friendly, so moving,—so artless a letter, dictated by the heart, coming from you to me, makes more than ample amends for full ten years trouble and uneasiness of mind. I am sure in the course of a very long life, I should never forget a single word of it.

I look upon it as a pledge that promises to me the continuation of what will soften the unavoidable misfortunes of this world, will increase greatly the enjoyments it may afford, and what I value more, will add dignity to me, not only in my own estimation, but in that of others.

Had it been a more early hour, had I not been affraid to disturb you, had I been sure you could give me a bed, I should have flyed directly to your Chambers. I called there yesterday. To my very great disappointment I did not find you at home, and I left a Note[3] which I scribbled at the Coffee House in a hurry and under the first impression of my chagrin at seeing my hopes frustrated.

It is very unlucky for me, that I cannot absolutely see you nor to day, nor to morrow. If you be disingaged next wednesday evening I shall call upon you. Should not that day suit you? chuse any other you please, and be assured that I shall make you a sacrifice of any engagement of mine, let it be of duty, business or pleasure, for I can have none greater than that of assuring you in person how affectionately and truly

I am My dear Bentham
your humble servant and sincere friend
Francis Villion

498

To Jeremiah Bentham[1]

16 May 1784 (Aet 36)

Whitchurch Sunday May 16th 1784
½ after 4.

Hond. Sir

Your letter is this instant received

The post sets off before 5. As far as the catching tame fish can

[2] Missing. [3] Letter 496.

498. [1] B.M. IV: 56–7. Autograph. Docketed by Jeremiah Bentham: 'Son Jeremy Bentham / Lr. datd. Whitchurch / 16 May 1784.'

be depended upon, you may depend upon having at least the quantity you wish for by the Salisbury two-horse Coach which gets in by 7 on Friday morning. They will be directed to be left till called for at the Three Kings Piccadilly. They will be put onto the Coach at 8 in the evening leaping alive. This is all that is material at present, and all that I have time to say to you, unless it be that I am ever Yours dutifully and affectionately

Jeremy Bentham

You must send the fish to the painters, for our's are unfortunately very white; but the learned say not the worse tasted.

Affairs will I hope turn out somewhat better than we expected. I am happy in the thoughts of being able to accommodate you on the present occasion, and still more in the hopes of being able to accommodate you not unfrequently in the like manner in future.

499

From James Trail[1]

22 May 1784

Dear Bentham

I received your short letter last night.[2] I am much obliged to you for thinking of my wants—I should feel them more if you had

Addressed: 'Jeremiah Bentham Esqr. / Queen's Square Place / Westminster.' Postmark: '17 MA'. Stamped: 'WHITCHURCH'.

Bentham spent most of the rest of 1784 at Whitchurch, discharging his duties as executor of the will of his uncle, George Woodward Grove. The exact date of Grove's death has not been ascertained: the signature to the last codicil of his will (B.M. Add. Ch. 44535) is dated 20 April 1784. By this will a number of his properties in Hampshire were to be sold to raise a sum of £6000 bequeathed to his natural daughters, Ann and Susannah. Bentham and his brother were left property in Essex, formerly belonging to Thomas Woodward, their mother's uncle, and also a house in Half Moon Street.

499. [1] U.C. IX: 5. Autograph. Docketed by Bentham: '1784 May 22 / Trail Linc. Inn / to / J.B. Linc. Inn.'

Addressed: 'To / Jeremy Bentham Esqr. / Whitchurch / Hants.'

Printed, with short omissions at the beginning and end, Bowring, x, 135, but there misdated 22 January.

This is the first of a number of letters addressed to Bentham by the able but unsuccessful young barrister, James Trail. He came into Bentham's circle through a close friendship with George Wilson, formed when the two men were together on the Midland circuit, which Trail gave up in the course of this year. See Bowring, x, 134–5 and 135 n. The third son of the Rev William Trail, of Fife, he had been admitted to the Middle Temple in February 1772, but he was not called to the bar till February 1782. His name appears in the list of matriculations at the University of St Andrews dated 16 February 1773.

[2] Missing.

not already indulged me with the use of your edition of the Statutes —I do not wish to relinquish my claim to keep it till you want it yourself but notwithstanding that, if you really have no way of disposing of the copy you mention, I cannot refuse to receive what you so readily offer.

[*Several words crossed out*] I have no news to send you. How can you expect any before the Session of Parliament is fairly begun—on Monday we expect a motion from Fox or some of his friends relative to the conduct of the High bailiff of Westminster.[3] Most people agree that his conduct is irregular in not making a return of the two candidates who were highest on the poll—but the great difficulty is what the House of Commons ought to do to remedy this irregularity—whether they call the High bailiff to the bar and order /him/ to make a return—or if they ought to refer it [to] a committee under Grenville's act to determine what he ought to have done and what he ought now to do. Some think that as his power expired on the day the writ was returnable and no return being then made the House can only declare the election void and order a new writ to be issued. Whatever turn it may take it is expected to be a popular topic for opposition and I suppose we shall hear of it as often as they possibly can introduce it.

It is reported that Pitt means to repeal Mr. Burke's act, or at least some part of it in order to restore the board of Trade[4]—Sr. James Lowther has been exceedingly offended that Lord Abergavenny was made an Earl before him, because the Daughter of John Robinson formerly his steward may eventually take rank before his wife—It is said that he is now pacified but on what terms I have not heard—according to some, he remains a commoner and will notwithstanding continue to support the administration—others say he takes his six titles and has obtained besides the promise of a blue Ribband.[5]

[3] For the dispute over the Westminster election of 1784 see Sir Lewis Namier and John Brooke, *The History of Parliament. The House of Commons, 1754–1790*, i, 337.

[4] This rumour was incorrect. Pitt acted in accordance with provisions made in Burke's Establishment Act (22 Geo. III, c. 82) by setting up by order in council a committee of the privy council on trade to exercise the functions of the former Board of Trade.

[5] On 3 October 1781 Mary, the only child of John Robinson (1727–1802), Lord North's secretary to the Treasury, had married Henry Nevill (1755–1843), heir to the 17th Baron Abergavenny. As a reward for the material assistance given by Robinson over the general election of 1784, Pitt secured an earldom for Mrs Nevill's father-in-law, which took effect on 17 May 1784. Sir James Lowther, 5th bart. (1736–1802), whose dominant position in Cumberland and Westmorland gave him control of eight or nine seats in the Commons, swallowed his pride and accepted his

We hear that Pitt has prepared an India bill nearly the same with that [of] Fox's—The Trade to be left in the hands of the directors the government to be vested in Comnrs. for a term of years but named by the Crown—Probably his plan establishing the succession to offices in rotation will make a part of this bill and in that case it will be nearly the same with what Fox proposed after his first bill was rejected by the House of Lords.[6]

The only changes talked of are Lord Carmarthern to be Privy Seal—Lord Sidney to be Secretary of State for foreign affairs and Dundas to be secretary for the home department.[7]

Wilson desires his compliments and is very happy to hear that affairs turn out better than the time you mention.

I am Dear Bentham yours etc.
James Trail

London
22nd May 1784

500

To Jeremiah Bentham[1]

25 May 1784 (Aet 36)

Hond. Sir

It gave me great pleasure to find the trout and chickens were so acceptable—I had blamed myself for not thinking of the latter in time to announce them along with the former: but I thought you would hardly provide yourself till you had inspected the cargo from the Three Kings.

I am much obliged to you for your kind offer about taking the house /here/ off my hands and setting up your own standard here that

election reward from Pitt: on 24 May he became Earl of Lonsdale. During the 1760's Robinson had been Lowther's steward and principal law agent and political manager.

[6] Pitt's East India Bill differed from Fox's (*inter alia*) in establishing a board of commissioners to control East India affairs, who held office at the pleasure of the Crown and not, as here suggested, for a term of years. There was no provision for a system of rotation.

[7] These ministerial changes did not take place.

500. [1] B.M. IV: 58–9. Autograph. Docketed by Jeremiah Bentham: 'Fils Jeremy / Lr. datd. Whitchurch 25 May 1784.'

Addressed: 'Jeremiah Bentham Esqr. / Queen's Square Place / Westminster.' Postmark: '26 MA'. Stamped: 'BA ⟨SING⟩STOKE'.

I may make it my head quarters in the excursions you suppose I should have to make to Baghurst: unfortunately Miss Grove[2] had taken measures for disposing as soon as possible of the furniture, and Mr. R. Skeat[3] if he gets the management of Lord Sydney's affairs[4] which he has been made to expect proposes to take up his residence in this house.

It is not improbable but I may follow up this letter pretty closely, in order to prove the Will.[5] ~~I could wish you could~~ but I stand engaged to be back here by Monday in order to meet a gentleman who comes on business. It would save time if you would be kind enough to send to my chambers as soon as you receive this to give me a direction to your Proctor and tell me any thing you may happen to know about the times of doing business—I hope to reach town tomorrow afternoon, and on Thursday I think to go to the Commons.[6] I am Dear and Hond. Sir

Your's ever
Jy. Bentham

Whitchurch May 25.
1784

[2] Anne Grove, born 1761, elder daughter of George Woodward Grove by his housekeeper, Elizabeth Ragg (or Riley).

[3] Richard Skeat was appointed an executor, vice Samuel Bentham, in the second codicil to Grove's will, drawn up in November 1782 but not signed till April 1784.

[4] Thomas Townshend (1733–1800), created Baron Sydney in 1783, and at this time secretary of state for home affairs. His mother's family, the Selwyns, had a controlling electoral interest in the borough of Whitchurch, and he received a bequest of some properties in the borough under the terms of Grove's will.

[5] Bentham, as executor, was present on 3 June 1784 to prove his uncle's will before Dr Ducarel, surrogate of the commissary of the prerogative court of Canterbury (P.C.C. 322 Rockingham).

[6] I.e., Doctors' Commons.

501

From Ivan Matveyevich Simolin[1]

8 June 1784

Londres le 8 Juin 1784.

Monsieur,

Hier j'eus le plaisir de recevoir votre lettre du 6 de ce mois,[2] et je m'empresse de vous répondre, que l'aumônier de la Chapelle russe Mr. Smirnoff m'a communiqué une lettre de la part de Mr. votre Frère, où il s'agissoit d'une proposition à faire à un certain Mears[3] demeurant actuellement dans les Chantiers de Portsmouth. Il a fallu beaucoup de précaution à l'égard des actes du Parlement,[4] pour faire parvenir au dit Mears l'invitation dont il s'agissoit. Ce n'est que depuis samedi que la lettre m'a été rendue avec une réponse verbale que le Sr. Mears inclinoit assés à accepter la proposition, si l'on obtenoit pour lui le consentement et la permission du Lord Howe.[5] Or cette condition étant impraiticable, il faut necessairement y renoncer. Il y a deux mois que j'ai proposé un autre sujet et j'attends d'un jour à l'autre la réponse et la résolution qu'on aura prise à cet égard. Si votre ami sait d'autres sujets capables de se charger de la besogne qu'on destine à Mears, il ne seroit pas mal d'en avoir connaissance et d'y revenir, en cas que les conditions de celui qui a été proposé ne fussent pas agréées.

501. [1] B.M. IV: 62–3. Autograph. Docketed by Bentham: '1784 June 10 / Simolin Londres / a / I.B. Whitchurch.'

Addressed: 'To / Jeremy Bentham Esqr. / Whitchurch / Hampshire.' Postmark: 'IV', otherwise illegible.

Ivan Matveyevich Simolin (fl. 1743–96) was a successful professional Russian diplomat of Swedish extraction, who entered the service in 1743, acted as secretary at various legations during the next thirty years, obtained his first ministerial appointment at Stockholm in 1774, and was sent as Russian minister to the court of St James in 1779. His services during the period of international strain after the formation of the Armed Neutrality (see Isabel de Madariaga, *Britain, Russia, and the Armed Neutrality of 1780*, London, 1962) gained him honours and promotion. Later in 1784 he was succeeded in London by Count S. R. Vorontsov and early in 1785 he was transferred to Paris with the rank of ambassador.

[2] Missing.

[3] For Samuel Bentham's interest in the shipwright Mears, see letter 505. Samuel had met him when he was at the Royal Academy at Portsmouth in 1779 (*Correspondence*, ii, 247 n.).

[4] Under the statutes 5 Geo. I, c. 27 and c. 28, and 23 Geo. III, c. 13, it was an offence to entice a skilled craftsman to go abroad.

[5] Richard, Viscount Howe (1726–99), at this time First Lord of the Admiralty.

J'ai l'honneur d'être avec la plus parfaite estime,
Monsieur

Votre très humble et très
obéissant serviteur
Simolin

502

From George Wilson[1]

19 June 1784

Saturday Night
June 19th 1784

Dear Bentham

Trail and I having divided tho not very equally the labour of your commissions,[2] he has sent Browne's letter[3] and put that to the Frenchman in the Penny post,[4] and I have sent one letter to your brother to Mr. Shairp's and put the other marked No. 1 in the Post Office paying with it 2s[5] and have also ordered your wax candles from Thorley's in Lombard Street which come, including the box they go in, to 18s.—Your Proctor's bill was £14.18.6. so that I have remaining of yours £4: 1: 6—

I saw in one paper about 10 days ago an account of the Arrival of the Gibraltar, Burford and Hound at Spithead, but as I have not seen it repeated nor heard any thing of Macneill or Davies I conclude the account is premature—[6]

The Westminster scrutiny goes on rapidly[7]—In this first week 2 votes of Mr. Fox's have been decided upon and both confirmed—A third has been heard and the decision adjourned till Monday. The mode agreed on is that Sr. Cecil shall first go thro' all his

502. [1] U.C. IX: 6. Autograph. Docketed by Bentham: '1784 June 19 / G.W. Linc. Inn / to / I.B. Whitchurch. / Probate paid for.'

Addressed: 'Jeremy Bentham Esqr. / Whitchurch / Hants.' Postmark: '19 / IU'. Partly printed, Bowring, x, 136.

[2] A letter from Bentham to Wilson or Trail is missing.

[3] Presumably a letter to William Browne, missing.

[4] A Frenchman to be reached by the penny post was possibly Brissot de Warville, though it is not certain that he was in London at this time. Bentham's letter is missing.

[5] These two letters to Samuel Bentham are missing. In letter 517 Samuel acknowledged receipt of the news of Grove's death, but without specifying the date of Bentham's letter which conveyed it.

[6] The press carried news dated 10 June 1784 of the arrival of these ships—*General Advertiser*, 12 June 1784, 3, iii.

[7] For the Westminster scrutiny see letter 499 and n. 3.

objections in the parish of Soho and then Fox go through his, after which they go to another parish—But many people think they will never get out of Soho—

We understand Sr. R. Hotham is to come in for the Borough[8] —Lord North made a great speech and Pitt a miserable one on the reform[9]—on that subject and the receipt tax people may now judge of the Minister's sentiments[10]—Adam has got another son and what is better he is getting a deal of money by Scotch appeals.[11]—

Trail is drawing like a waggon horse from morning to night and from Monday to Saturday—I am as usual attending the King's bench and idling away the afternoon. Douglas[12] has had a relapse of his ague but is no[w] pretty well again and his inside thoroughly tanned—Lord Mansfield[13] looks tolerably well but it is understood he is not to sit after term nor go any circuit—In short his resignation cannot be far distant—Some people talk of the following arrangement Which as it stops so many mouths may not be improbable—Kenyon Ch. Justice. P. Arden M. of the Rolls. Macdonald Ch.J. of Chester. Parry a Welsh Judge. Bearcroft Atty and Scott Sollr Genl. Pepper is to be ⟨marr⟩ied after his circuit to Miss Bootle.[14] I can think of nothing more—so good Night

G.W.

[8] Sir Richard Hotham (1722?–1799), M.P. for Southwark, 1780–4, was narrowly defeated in the by-election at which the result was declared on 25 June.

[9] In a debate on 16 June 1784, the Opposition tried to cast doubt upon Pitt's zeal for the cause of parliamentary reform (Ian R. Christie, *Wilkes, Wyvill and Reform*, London, 1962, p. 205).

[10] The previous day, 18 June, an opposition M.P., Nathaniel Newnham (*c.* 1741–1809) had moved in committee of supply for the repeal of the tax on receipts, a move which would be popular to his constituents in the City of London and politically embarrassing to William Pitt as head of the Treasury. Pitt declared his firm opposition to this proposal, which was thrown out by a large majority (J. Debrett, *The Parliamentary Register*, xv (1784), pp. 216–24).

[11] William Adam (1751–1839), M.P., a member of the Foxite party and a successful barrister.

[12] Sylvester Douglas (1743–1823), a barrister of Lincoln's Inn, who through Wilson had become an intimate friend of Bentham. See *Correspondence* ii, 123–4, 329–30.

[13] Chief Justice of the King's Bench.

[14] None of these legal promotions, all dependent on Mansfield's expected resignation, took place at this time; most of them took place when he did resign in 1788. Richard Pepper Arden (1744–1804), M.P., Attorney-General, and Chief Justice of Chester, married, 9 September 1784, Anne Dorothea, daughter of Richard Wilbraham Bootle, M.P.

503

From Samuel Bentham[1]

18/29 June 1784

Kremenchuk June 18th O.S. 1784.

May I be not disappointed in the hopes I have that you will not fail to come and see me this year and if possible this summer. I hope I shall be able to make you comfortable and you would make me happy beyond measure.

Consider also that I am for the first time engaged in a real business on which my reputation will depend. Consider the favourable circumstances I am in to turn to account my different speculations. Consider that my mind has been unbent from business. That I have long been out of the habit of application. Consider the weakness of my memory and judge yourself of the assistance you would be of to set me once more in the right path.[2]

Take notice that besides Ships building I have an unlimited field to employ such tallents as I either have or may acquire. The Empress ~~will~~ is expected to embark at this estate of the Prince's to descend from thence down the Dnieper. If my rowing Yatcht is found preferable to those built by the Admiralty for her, the Prince will certainly give it for her use. This will be a flattering way of renewing the notice She has before honoured me with. I think therefore if you can conveniently that you should stay with me till that time.

This Estate of the Prince's is called Kreetchoff it is /in the

503. [1] B.M. IV: 66. Autograph. Docketed by Bentham: '1784 June 18 / S.B. Krementchuk and Kreetchoff / to I.B. Linc. Inn / I.B. visit.'

Potëmkin's estate of Krichëv lay in the eastern part of the gubernia of Mogilëv in White Russia, a province seized from Poland at the first partition in 1772. Catherine II granted the estate to the prince in 1776 and he immediately began to develop it as a supply centre for the Russian colonization of the south and the military and naval preparations against the Turks in the area of the Crimea. At this place, eight hundred miles from the Black Sea, but from which vessels of up to two hundred tons burthen could be floated down on the spring floods by way of the rivers Sozh and Dnieper, Samuel Bentham was set to train soldiers to act as seamen and to build ships of various kinds as transports, auxiliaries and fighting units for the Russian Black Sea Fleet. Soon, as the correspondence shows, he also took on other responsibilities and enterprises. On this subject see E. P. Zakalinskaya, *Votchinnye Khozyaystva Mogilevskoy Gubernii vo vtoroy polovine XVIII veka*, Moghilev, 1958, and Ian R. Christie, 'Samuel Bentham and the western colony at Krichev, 1784–1787', *Slavonic and East European Review*, xlviii (1969–70), 232–47.

[2] Parts of the next two paragraphs are lightly scored through in pencil.

province of White Russia/ about 100 versts from Mohilew near the borders of Poland from which it was restored in the last division of that Country. Riga is the nearest port in the Baltic. Could I know but /near about/ the time you could come there, I would meet you there at least I think I could, and if not I would at any rate send somebody to conduct you. It is less than 600 versts from Riga to Kreetchoff therefore about 3 days journey at the rate people travel here. Vitepsk[3] I believe is about 200 versts from Kreetchoff and heavy luggage may be transported so far by water up the Dwina.

Books.

By all means without binding were it only for the better stowage. I cannot tell you anything certain about the price of binding here. The materials are much cheaper.

Cook's Voyage. I had some reasons for wishing to have it but as you tell me it is so dear let it alone.

Smith on the Wealth of Nations.

Certainly the new edition would be better.

Yes by all means Encyclopaedia Britannica.

504

From Samuel Bentham[1]

19/30 June 1784

June 19, 1784.
Credit for Commissions

Kremenchuk June 19th

I asked the Prince this morning if I should write by the Courier that is now going to Mr. Sutherland to order him to give credit in London for the Commission I had to execute relating to the Botanist etc., etc. He said by all means but though I wished him to fix some bounds to the credit 'What is necessary' was the

[3] Vitebsk, situated on the upper Western Dvina, at 55° 10′ N., 30° 11′ E., was a commercial centre on the river route from Riga to the centre of European Russia via Smolensk.

504. [1] B.M. IV: 68. Autograph. Docketed by Bentham: '1784 June 19 / S.B. Krementchuk / to / I.B. Linc. Inn / Received at Whitchurch / Sept. 11 / Credit for Commissions—Journey-expences.'

As a result of the opening up of Samuel Bentham's new activities in Potëmkin's employment, Jeremy Bentham was becoming an unofficial agent for recruiting technical experts for service in Russia.

only answer I could get. I therefore wrote the following letter to Sutherland the Court Banker at Petersbourg.

Kremenchuk June 19th O.S. 1784

'Sir,

Prince Potemkin wishes me to execute some Commissions for him in England, and has ordered me to write to you, to desire you would furnish money in London for the expences of them. You will therefore be so kind, Sir, as to order your Correspondent in London to pay to the order of Jeremy Bentham Esqr. of Lincoln's Inn as much as may ⟨be⟩ demanded. I cannot judge at present what the sum may amount to; but at any rate you may limit it to three thousand Rubles.

'You will be so kind at the same time to write a few lines to the above-mentioned address to inform my brother on whom he is to draw for the money in question.

I am, Sir, your most obedient Servant

S.B.

'Mr. Sutherland St. Petersbourg'

The 3,000 Rubles will make 500£ a little more or less /the one you have makes 600/ and this I think will fully suffice to execute all the Commissions I have given in case it is convenient to you and you are able to execute them. With respect to the Botanist I conceive there can not be the least difficulty /in finding a man of Science who would be glad of that employment./ besides the expences of his Voyage he should have ~~30 ducats or even 40 if you please~~ 40 or 50 ducats for expences or casualties from Riga to Kreetchoff. You might give as much to the *Dairy Lady.*[2] As to their Assistants and in general the other persons mentioned half that sum would suffice.

If you should collect a number of persons, you must be as Economical as possible for the travelling expences because the idea of the advantage arising from having a number of persons will not encrease as as to keep pace with the idea which a great sum expended on that account might produce. I am however at a loss how to restrain you in this respect I think however that the money furnished to people for their expences in coming out should not

[2] The demand for a botanist and a dairy lady led to Bentham's becoming entangled with the egregious Mr Henderson and his entourage: on Henderson see letter 543 and n. 5.

exceed 2,000 Rubles. /however many/ there be. If there are but few you may be more generous in proportion. Money must be furnished for what seeds the Botanist may think proper to bring with him.

As the Prince leaves these things so much at my discretion so must I leave them entirely at yours. If therefore you have any reason to think the credit is not sufficient let me know immediately and you will certainly have more. As all the Commissions I have given you (excepting articles of dress) are literally speaking *for the good of the Service* you need not think of employing any other money for them; and you may add a few more books such as you may judge usefull.

[*Added in pencil*]: I must leave this to be sealed by a friend ⟨in⟩ case ⟨the⟩ Courier goes before I come back.

505

From Samuel Bentham[1]

c. 10/21 June–20 June/1 July 1784

Shipwright wanted

I know not how to go about to get a good practical Shipwright to *ballast* me in the execution of my idea of improvement in Ship-building. A man whom from having been to sea knows well the use and necessity of all the parts as well as how to make them. I would [pay] the expences of bringing such a man from England and sending him home again the next year if he pleased or continue him probably on an encreased Salary. I could not well engage to give him more than a guinea a week /and should hope to get him for less/ but then he should have lodging and boarding. ~~Were it not for the plague and fuss it would make I can't see why permission might not be given for a few workmen.~~ I ought not to be grudged a good workman or two and I think you might with safe conscience in-

505. [1] B.M. IV: 70–1, 72, 73, 74–5, 76–7, 78–9, 80. Autograph.

These sheets, all self-contained as to contents, are identified as part of one packet only by Bentham's endorsements, which begin: '1784 June 20 / S.B. Kremenchuk / to / I.B. Linc. Inn', and then continue with appropriate phrases to indicate the general nature of the contents of each sheet. The date 'June 11th' occurs at the head of a paragraph on folio 71v, indicating that the letter may have been begun earlier than this date. Folio 76 begins with the date 'June 20th'. As letters 503 and 504 were written between these dates, Bentham's different docketing may indicate that they were sent separately by another route.

fringe that foolish law which stands in the way of engaging artizans to go to foreign countries when they are to be employed in experiments which if usefull at all may be /so/ to all who choose to profit by them.[2]

Timber-Measurer

I want also very much a man well conversant in the quality and comparative value of Timber. It would be better that he should be a Shipwright too that he might understand the conversion of it. I mean Timber while standing in the woods. Possibly Mr. Mulford might find such a man. The one for example who gave me lessons on that subject though he be not a Shipwright might serve. What I should want of him is to accompany me or go without me to pick out Timber of such and such description. Such a man I think might come for less wages if he has lodging and board as the other.

Mill-wright.

The man next in utility whom I could wish to have is a millwright capable of erecting by himself, that is with men unacquainted with the business, windmills for flower as well as for sawing. Such men I fear it will not be in your way to meet with.

Remember that the 3 persons above mentioned are not to be attached in any way to the service of the /crown/ unless they afterwards wish it, where they might make their own terms.

It is with me only they would be engaged.

As to Steam Engines I have no immediate use for them although it is certain they would have their use, as for the raising of water for the working machines: But I should have no hopes of getting a man capable of erecting them for any Salary I could at present offer.

Any clever people capable of introducing improvements in the Prince's Government might meet with good encouragement but I should be very sorry to recommend any who in the end should fail in their proposals.

But the sort of person whom above all I have the most occasion for and whom you and such of my freinds as find pleasure in hearing from me are most interested in the procuring me is a somebody who could assist me in my correspondence. Any Englishman who could be attached to me and whom I could depend on. Who when I had given him and that at different times the ideas I wish to communicate would put them into a Stile adapted to the mode of

[2] See letter 501, n. 4.

communication required. If he understood French enough to translate from it that would be an extraordinary merit. There certainly do exist poor Curates for example who with all the qualifications desirable cant get more than 30 pounds a year to live on. I certainly could give that besides living and expences of coming out into the bargain. One of that profession would be more suitable on every account except one he but free of Pedantry. A few prejudices might be put up with and if they are not firmly rooted they would soon die away here of themselves. Your finding me such a person seems the only chance of my becoming a tollerable correspondant. This Salary it is plain must be at my own expence.

I am in hopes that among the different people I may get from England they may be one understands brewing so that I may get good beer an article much prized here and which might also be advantageous in point of profit at least to the brewer. The Prince wants much to introduce the use of Beer in his Governments and permits the sale of it without any excise. He would give a Salary to a man who was a professed brewer: but as that art is universally understood in England I think there would be no occasion for a man on purpose.

I much doubt whether I shall be able to send you any more money on credit by this opportunity. In the mean time employ the 600 rubles intended for Burkit at your discretion.[3] It would bear the expences of 8 or 10 people's coming out by way of Riga. Those who have the Captain's table pay certainly not more than 8 guineas.

The Prince will have a Botanical garden in the Crimea in which if possible all the vegetable productions of the world are to be collected. For the direction of this garden he wishes to have an English Botanist. I have told him that I would give you the commission to search for one. This Botanist I proposed should have an assistant —Agreed to.—He means also to have an elegant Dairy in which the best of Butter and as many different kinds of cheese as possible should be made. For the direction of this dairy none but an Englishwoman will serve.

This Lady must have her Assistante. agreed to.—The salary of these 4 persons he leaves to my discretion, and tells me that he will order Sutherland the Court Banker to give credit in London for the purchase of Seeds etc. Expences of the voyage it is understood are to be defrayed besides.

[3] See letter 491 and n. 2.

I suppose there would be no doubt but what Mr. Anderson's Botanical abilities would be equal to such an undertaking, especially if One particularly skilled in such branches as he may not have so much attended to, be chosen out for his Assistant. Were he to accept of this offer, I /think I may/ venture as far as twelve hundred rubles a year Salary. He would also have a piece of land to cultivate for himself, house, servants, and I suppose fireing. Add to this opportunities of travelling all about the Prince's Governments, ~~and~~ the being treated by the Prince in a manner which cannot but be agreable to him, leizure to pursue other studies and occupations, liberty to quit his employment and the country when he thinks proper, and even I dare to say he might take a trip hereafter to see his friends.

The Salary of the Assistant must not exceed 600 rubles.

The Salary of the Directrice of the dairy might be 5 or 600 rubles and of her assistante 200. The directrice of the dairy might be wife of the director of the Botanical Garden, in like manner the Assistante of the former might be wife to the Assistant of the latter. This arrangement however must depend on the qualifications of the ladies. I have so much bragg'd of the neatness and excellency of the English dairies that I shall lose all credit if that business is not in perfection.

I cannot judge how far Mrs. Anderson would like such an undertaking: Why not if she has been used to the employment? If such employments do not suit A: then be as sparing as possible in the account you give of the Salaries: since it would be much better if I could surprize them with more advantageous terms than they bargained for.

A: if he came might bring out his whole family. The expences of coming out would be defrayed, but I suppose he would rather come alone first. Yet the directrice of the dairy should come as soon as possible because the Prince would wish to have all in readiness for the Empress who perhaps will be in the Crim next May. You will conceive that it must be a woman of good deal of spirit to bear the difficulties of bad lodgings uncleanly servants etc. which must be encountered with till she has herself put it in rather better order and a house is fitted up. The Prince wishes also to have a whole colony of English. They might have their Church and all manner of priviledges not ~~hurtful~~ /injurious/ to other settlers. They would have each family quantity of land for nothing. How much I know not as nothing of that kind is as yet settled.

On every occasion there appears a partiality in favour of our country that is very flattering. In speaking of Anderson you make a comparison between Tuscany and this country so much to the disadvantage of the latter that I can not pass it by 'certes il fait mieux se promener dans un jardin que dans des deserts.' Moi je viens de parcourir des deserts qui valent bien votre jardin. They are at least happy deserts that produce vines, figs, Pomegranetes, Mulberries and laurel trees etc., etc. without culture. Better wine than half what you drink is to be bought for twopence a bottle and sometimes much cheaper. The Ukraine has long been reputed among the finest countries in Europe, the Crimea is much superior to the Ukraine. The Prince has promised me an Estate there, but none are as yet given.[4]

June 11th

I have just received news from Petersbourg of the arrival of Men women and children to the amount of 139 from Scotland. The Prince was pleased to hear it and will take good care of them in the Crim which it seems is the place of their destiny. A short time ago there came a ship load of raggamuffin Italians which had been enticed from Leghorn by an agent who being paid by the Crown at so much pr head I suppose was not very scrupulous, about the kind of people or how he obtained them. Some of them rose, killed the captain with the intention of returning, but were caught and brought in first I believe to Cherson, then to Actiar a port in the Crim. Among these was an Englishman who as soon as it was known that he was a Cole miner was set to search for cole in that Country. I found the poor fellow almost naked and living on 5 copecks pr. day the same as his companions had.

When I spoke of him to the Prince he promised him a good salary; and when I said he was almost naked, he ordered me to give him two hundred rubles to buy cloaths. This /I think proves no/ small degree of generosity as well as a favorable disposition towards us English. I gave the man and his wife 25 rubles each to cloath themselves. The 150 I was affraid to trust them with immediately.

Distill:

I before told you that the distillation of Malt spirits afforded one of the greatest subjects for improvement, I think I am now in a

[4] Samuel Bentham later obtained a sixth share in an estate in the Crimea, the main share of which was held by his friend, Admiral Mordvinov (M. S. Anderson, 'Samuel Bentham in Russia, 1779–1791', *The American Slavic and East European Review*, xv, 2 (1956), 171 and n.

situation very suitable to turn any improvement of that line to profit. But I want somebody to assist me in the management of it. It should be an Englishman it being understood always that a Scotchman would be still better. You know of course that the principal object is to save in fuel. If the construction of the Stills which you are acquainted with appears to be perfect enough or you can find out how to make them more so, I wish you would lay out twenty pounds in that way. The wood part it would not be advisable to have made there unless there is a good deal of work in a small space: but what is of copper and iron besides being better done would be cheaper there than here.

1. The vapour once condensed should not set off immediately for the receiver, and not be liable either to be again reduced to vapour by a superfluent heat, nor to run down again from whence it arose.

2. If the advantage of a woven (or spiral tube) over a straight one be that of compactness alone it perhaps is not worthwhile to be at the extra expence of workmanship to make it in that form.

3. Distilleries in this country are all at least that I have seen erected where there is a waterfall by the damming up of a river, so that the water runs through the condensing troughs. The fuel as well as materials are therefore transported a great way sometimes for the sake of acquiring this advantage.

4. The cold producible by evaporation is not applied to condensing nor perhaps is it so expedient as that of a fluid medium which is continualy changing. However it seems that without the necessity of a mechanical force to raise up water to supply the condensers, the business might be effected more commodiously by erecting the whole distillery in a floating boat or vessel so much immersed as for the circumferent water to serve for the cooling the condenser. This floating distillery might be at anchor in the. river which supplies it with ~~work~~ matter and facilitates the transport of its produce.

5. But where the subject to be distilled and the fuel are at too great a distance from such a river or lake then perhaps evaporation from a wetted coating must be employed for cooling the condenser. So that the construction of Stills or at least of distilleries must differ to be adapted to local circumstances.

Talk over these things with your freinds before you order the 20 pound's worth, which whether it will consist of one or more apparatus I need not go about to consider; persuaded that it would cost $\frac{1}{3}$ more here. New experiments however in which the work is out of the usual fashion may be much cheaper here.

The *King* will alter stills etc. to my experiments but he wont make new ones.

Maltmaking although the theory is very simple requires practical knowledge to be able to go to work with economy.

In the Crim it would be very advantageous to distill brandy from the wine as it would be free of duty. The botanist and I might do that together.

Kempel's contrivance is I suppose still secret.

Hydraulic rope I knew of.

The french Timber bending for Arches is insignificant whip syllabub stuff.

Air balloons I am tired of hearing of, but the imprint on Kacatchou may be usefull.

Essai sur le Commerce de Russie.

It is good for nothing any more than Guldenstadt's[5] which you wished to have but which I believe I declined sending.

Your new primum mobile[6] I think may be made usefull, but in another manner.

Microscope I wanted to give to Klangan at Barnaoul[7] in consideration of what he has given and what in future he may give me in the way of Nat. Hist.

Table and Kitchen Furniture I can say nothing about till I know for certain where and in what manner I am to keep house for myself. While I am at the Prince's estates it is probable I may have a Table etc. at his expence.

I desired you to bring me a pair of Gilt spurs but I fear the gilding will soon wear off better to be of yellow, gold-like-looking metal.

Fire Arms, none would be wanted particularly for any of the excursions which you mention, because whenever it is worthwhile to go where there is danger; there would be always Convoy. Yet as there are circumstances in which it is very expedient to have pistols, and as they woud always have their price here, if you have money to spare you might pick up second hand a brace of for the pocket, another for the saddle and even a third between those two sizes. If also the Guns you speak of bored in a new way have really so great an advantage over others. It would be good to buy one.

Portable Furnace. I should not much want if I have any body who is acquainted with the Construction of furnaces in general and even otherwise I have no immediate use for one. There is

[5] See letter 488, n. 8. [6] See letter 486. [7] See letter 445.

however no difficulty in having glass Vessels for the Prince has a glass house of his own at Kreetchoff.

Tools. Let me have mine as to all others I shall have a good provision from England through another channel without plaguing you.

Model of a Windmill a Steam engine and of any Machine applicable to this country there would be no danger in being at the expence of but I dont know that I can send you money for these things yet. Oil skin great coat ~~for yourself~~ one only made large enough for either of us.

Slitting Mill I want nothing of at present at least not immediately.

Oil Mills

The great pains you have been at in procuring me all possible information about oil mills cannot be of immediate utility as that speculation is not as well adapted to this part of the country where other fodure for cattle is so cheap.

Saltworks

Neither can Saltwork projects be put in execution here. However when I am at leizure, or rather when we are together a knot of us, we can put together what we know on that subject and after having made some models and drawn up directions for the use of an improved apparatus it may be turned to some account.

Nitre

The ground in this part of the country is excedingly nitrous and the exportation of Saltpetre which was till lately prohibited is now permitted.

Dingley's Saw Mill. Model[8]

If the model is compleat so as to show each component part in the Construction you may give as far as 10 guineas for such a one. By each component part being shown I do not mean that in all cases there should be as many pieces in the model as in the real mill; but that where one piece serves for many that the ~~part of~~ mode of 'construction' should be marked and the 'fastening' likewise. From such a model I could have a real mill made without the necessity of considering each part to invent the best mode of connection etc. which is a business which from my indecision and *thirst* for perfection makes me loose that is spend frivolously a

[8] See letter 101 at n. 2.

great deal of time. I dont care any thing about the neatness but a man who is capable and bestows pains enough to make a model so accurate, could not make it otherwise than neat.

All the letters you mention being sent me I have received.

Let me have one of the Copying machines with brass rolers, and a quantity of Paper Ink etc. necessary.

I.B.'s Money

As to your Money the produce of Malt-house,[9] I should be sorry you should lay it out in Annuity, but I would not take charge of it either: but I should wish and advice is that you should bring it here with you when you come to see me. I think you would find much better means of employing it here than at home; but you must see that yourself first. Ducats of Holland seem to be the best of all money to bring into this country particularly this part of it. These will here often fetch 3 rubles a piece, and a guinea would not procure you in credit through a Banker more than 6 rubles, you would gain therefore what you get more than 2 ducats in exchange for a guinea.

If we take a trip to the Crimea together you may like and find it advantageous to buy some land there. The use of buying is the having the choice of such as is at present in the hands of some of the Tartars who may wish to sell it. The Prince has promised to give me some as he would you likewise; but then we cant pick and choose.

Projet. Code.

As to the young man whom you seemed to think might be usefull to you. He is too school boyish and insignificant for me to court his freindship, and at the same time too insensible and inconstant to be capable of being of any use. He is a good natured boy who has nothing but Novels and plays in his head. I dont like at all that expression 'If the french be found tollerable.' Why not tollerable or rather good if corrected by a Frenchman who is master of his language and surely you will find one for that purpose. I hope you have almost done for it would be miserably vexatious if you were prevented from coming to see me at the end of the summer.

I cant help wishing there were no offer made to any Court. The having the work presented is sufficient to induce those to apply who are disposed to attend to the subject. At any rate do pray let me see the letters of offers before you send them.

[9] See letter 138, n. 8.

Ld S and Carew could assist you in desiring the English ministers at the different Courts to present the copies. Fitzherbert would require no such assistance. But I think it might be better that I should beg the Prince to present it. Still better if both were to present each a copy.

Code

I certainly before proposed to you the printing the french edition at Petersbourg. As I am not there it may be as well not. What would be the expence of a Printing press with a compleat apparatus of the very best types if possible such as Baskerville's. ~~I know nothing [. . .?] that.~~ How delighted the Prince would be to have a printing house at his Estate or in his Government where he might have printed superior editions of Classical and other books.

I do think we may be might[y] comfortable when you come if we get such a collection of clever people. There would be no objection to any of the peoples bringing females, if they be tollerable good housewives they wont be at all a charge. To be quite comfortable I think you should find a pretty house-keeper to put at the head of our table and to turn down the bed. The women here would not suit your Taste at all.

Dinwidder

As he wished to come could he only have his expences paid him, Send him by all means sounding him also whether he would accept of a salary of 40 or 50£ a year to be an assistant to me in my several undertakings, so as for him to consider his time at my disposal.

Henderson[10] I hope will come out also, but as to Partnership about the saltworks I can say nothing as yet. I must have done something to distinguish myself and must have set all my present business a going before there is any chance of my settling such an engagement as that of the Salt works with other people. I have told you that Distill: as it would be carried on where my business calls me affords the more immediate prospect of private advantage and ~~therefore~~ possibly ~~one or both~~ of Din: and Hend: might one or both of them come in for their part.

You must long ago have received a packet I sent you respecting some engagement with my friend Ribaupierre. I suppose also you ventured credit for 500 Rubles to furnish any persons who were

[10] See letters 543 and 556.

to come for that purpose with their expences. When I have your answer to that letter, I shall form a guess what I may expect from them.

Henderson's matches would never sell in this Country. There are perhaps half a dozen people who would buy a dozen of them out of curiosity, burn them all out at once, and never think any more of them: but I do not believe that any one person would make any use of them. I wish however you could persuade him to pay me a visit. A man of the extensive knowledge you represent him to be would not fail of finding some employment to suit him. He might bring his 2 mechanical girls or more of both sexes we could find work for them.

Mears.[11]

If he is engaged by the Minister I fear he will not be for me, at least not at present. He would be the Master Shipwright under orders of the Admiralty. I have nothing to do with the Admiralty. If he is not engaged by the Minister I dont suppose he would come to me because I cant give him a great Salary. Not more than 600 Rubles.

I.B.'s Visit

From Constantinople to Cherson you may get almost every day either in a vessel directly or by embarking first for Natolia and from thence either to one of the ports in the Crimea or to Cherson. At Cherson however you would have perhaps 3 weeks quarantine to make while the plague is on the Turkish Coast. By the greatest fortune you could be let off in a week. To enter the Crim 3 days quarantine and as a matter of favour you would be let pass from the Crim through Perekop without any quarantine. There are Vessels come from Marseilles straight to Cherson, but it would be a great chance to meet with one when you want it.

As however it is at Kreetchoff and not Cherson that you will find me, you will not I suppose think of the southern expedition at present. Besides it is very likely I should be able to accompany you that wayward. I could ask the Commission of settling the Botanist and his retinue and indeed it is probable that the Prince may desire me to take it and we may then go all together as far as the Crim. There if you or any freinds you have with you wish to Visit the Caban, Georgia or any of the Turkish territories all recommendations and assistance can be easily procured.

[11] See letter 501 and n. 3.

Cloaths.

I see no business you have at Petersburg at any rate none to frequent that Court and Societies there. Two suits for the season you will be with me is all you would want besides frocks, and they may be very plain.

If you are with me when the Prince comes and you should accompany him that would make no difference in dress. Two suits would be quite enough for the great hollidays, and at all other times you may dress as for dinner at Q.S.P.

A suit of Silk for Summer and Ratteen for Winter and one of cloth which would serve both would be sufficient for all seasons. Black breeches would serve for all. You might have 2 or 3 frocks for each of the two seasons. No rich waistcoats but neat ratten ones for winter and white or coloured cotton or linnen waistcoat and breeches for summer. This would be a complete reputable ex-Petersburg Wardrobe.

Wines etc.

The Wines drunk at Cherson are for the most part from the Crim or from the Greek Islands.

A Tenedos wine has much the taste and colour of Red port.

Sudac wine is a white /dry/ wine from the Crim as good for the table as can be desired.

There is a sort of wine from the Don which has much the taste and I think as good as Burgundy. The Prince prefers this wine of the Don and that of Sudac to all wines whatever.

But we have wines from all countries at all great dinners. Hungarian is given and no healths can be drunk without Champaigne, though at the same time the abovementioned wines are preferred for their taste. The dearness /alone/ of the latter keeps up the use of them. English beer also is much prized. Hydromel is also much used for common drink. But the Kislistchee is the best summer drink possible.

June 20th

As to trinkets which you might bring with you, for the purpose that you mention I dont know of any that it would be worth while. But these pocket books you mention are so cheap that you may bring 3 or 4 of them. 2. Needles of all the different sizes and even pins. 3. Two or three Penknives. 4. 3 or 4 Pocket Compasses of the size of watches to wear in a fob. I have seen them with a Hydrometer on the back. 5. Some Spirit Hygramters. 6. 2 bridles and 2 saddles for me one a handsome one the other plain, but I think plated rather than steel because of the rest. Remember that ideas of beauty here do not perhaps perfectly conform to the caprice of what may be the fashion of the day.

Cloaths for S.B.

You ask what my uniform is, If my portrait is arrived which I sent my father you have seen already. If not, it is a green coat with /scarlet/ red lapells, scarlet waistcoat with a broad gold lace and white breeches.

If therefore you shall any where meet with some remarkable fine Cloth of a grass green colour, and also some scarlet; buy me ½ a dozen yards of the former and a couple of the latter. If it be narrower than broadcloth, then a greater length to make up the quantity. A couple of yards of white cloth to match in fineness with the others, some white Kerseymere for undress waistcoat and breeches. These things you will perceive are not very essential. They are rather Coxcombish commissions but if you should meet with such articles ~~either at the London shops or should have some urge~~ there would be no extravagance as they would scarcely come dearer than an inferior sort here.

The lining of the coats is scarlet shalloon which should also match in fineness and short jacket uniforms which I wear in summer may be lined with scarlet silk matter.

I desired you in a former letter to bring 2 large and long Cloaks one of blue cloth the other of white. The white one may as well be without lining but the blue one had better be lined with a cheap kind of bath coating, white. I believe I advised you to bring for youself besides a red cloak, but this unless you are at Petersbourg may be dispensed with.

Shoemaker—Surgeon—Architect.

I gave you also some Commission about books. Could not you find a clever shoemaker who could come as a Servant—No dont think of it it is only here that /the same/ man will be cook shoemaker and bricklayer.

There are two other sort of people who if there came in your way a promising subject you might persuade him to seek his fortune here.

A Surgeon and Physician, and an Architect

The first must depend chiefly on his private practice with some very small Salary. But the other might perhaps get 1,000 rubles salary. and the building of a new Town or two, perhaps in the Crimea.

Not that the Prince has given me any directions about such a person: but I have no doubt but one who could show tallents would be employed. A Lover of antiquity would take a particular pleasure in restoring the beauty in the way of his art to a country where the Towns will retake their antient names. There may be some /fellow/ members of the Antiquarian Society at Edinburgh who would delight in the new building of Theodocia, for example. But such a man should be acquainted with the practice of building, Chemical as well as Mechanical and not to be too attatched to Antiquity to neglect the influence which the manners of the present inhabitants should have on their buildings. You may however mention this Idea to Anderson. Perhaps he may have some acquaintance it might suit, and I think the Prince would be pleased with a man who came out with such liberal views.

I cant help repeating my prayers that you would find a man who could serve me as Secretary, a limb of the Church would surely be most likely to have the necessary qualifications without that desire of engaging in other affairs which a laic would have. Wales or Scotland should have given such a man birth.

Yes the Navigation of the River Amur[12] is a subject I have long ago at my arrival from Siberia spoken of to the Prince. He at that time desired me to write down my observations and ideas about it and that he would give them to the Empress; but I insisted upon it I had nothing more to say than what was clear to every body and in this manner declined it in favour of my Observations on the Mines and Saltworks. He was however so intent upon it that when I went to him after my audience with her Majesty he asked me if I had spoken of it with her.

You know how advantageous the Russians find the Beaver trade by the way of Kamschatka under all the difficulties of the transport of naval stores to Ochotsk. You know also what a commerce the English ships with Cook made in that way without /their/ being /previously/ apprized of the value of the Skins.

The India Company and several private merchants have wished to fitt out Ships for this commerce, but the Hudson's Bay Company pleading their monopolizing Charter opposed all such attempts.

One Pillings[13] Assistant Astronomer on board the Resolution was questioned at the India house and had expectations of being sent

[12] This and the following four paragraphs of this letter were sent in copy by Bentham to the Foreign Secretary, Lord Carmarthen, about 16 July 1785, just before Bentham himself set out for Russia (Public Record Office, F.O. 97/340); see letter 536.

[13] Joseph Billings (b. c. 1758). In 1776 he was entered on board the *Discovery* and

there while there were hopes of permission. He had also offers made him by Private Merchants. At last when nothing was to be done in that Trade from England he came over last spring and entered into the Russian service with the view of being sent on such an Expedition under the Russian flag. His proposals were attended to but nothing will be fixed for him for this year or two and probably as matters stand at present not at all. Many people are ready to furnish Capital for such an Expedition and nothing is wanting but the leave. The leave is in effect given by the general liberty of Commerce but for greater certainty an express permission is required.

Now you are to know that for some time past I have had a great project for combining in one Expedition the effecting the Navigation of the Amur a trade with Japan, and a commercial intercourse between the Coast of America near Kamchatka and Canton. Sometimes my idea is only to be instrumental in the forming of such an Expedition at other times I have an irresistable itching to have the Conducting it. This however after I have tried my Shipbuilding Experiments and am better established in the Country and perhaps a little out of humour with the world, or impatient of a finishing stroke to Riches and reputation. To confess the truth it was with a view to this that I desired Cook's Voyages, which otherwise would not have been so very interesting.[14]

Such an assistant as you represent Skinner[15] to be for such a project would no doubt be desirable: but besides as you seem to have taken an affection for him I cannot but recommend his coming were it only as a Volunteer or Visitor and that he should spend some time with my friend Korsakoff.[16] He can no way have so

he sailed with her on Cook's last expedition. He transferred as an A.B. (age given as 21) to the *Resolution* in September 1779. He was commissioned lieutenant in the Russian navy in 1784, but not until August 1785 were all arrangements made for the eastern expedition he was promoting, which assembled at Irkutsk in February 1786 before completing the overland journey to Okhotsk, where the ships had already been built for its service. On his explorations, which went on until 1794, see *An Account of a Geographical and Astronomical Expedition to the Northern Parts of Russia... performed by Commodore Joseph Billings in the years 1785–1794, narrated from the original papers by Martin Sauer, Secretary to the Expedition*, London, 1802.

[14] When Cook's expedition in the *Resolution* and the *Discovery* explored Nootka Sound in 1778, members of the crews picked up sea-otter skins in exchange for articles of trifling value in barter with the native Indians and subsequently found that they fetched high prices, both in Kamchatka and at Canton (V. T. Harlow, *The Founding of the Second British Empire*, volume 2, *New Continents and Changing Values*, 1964, p. 419).

[15] See letter 493 and n. 2.

[16] Lieutenant Colonel Nikolay Ivanovich Korsakov (1749–88). He was killed by a fall down a precipice during the siege of Ochakov in 1788.

good an opportunity of studying Fortification and military concerns. Cherson to be new fortified and other fortresses in abundance all under his direction.

As to the french language he would have enough of opportunities here, and he might learn the german likewise.

Dont talk about the Contents of this sheet nor think about any part of it but what regards Skinner.

We have things enough to occupy us without extending our ideas so far.

Alas our Poor Uncle to be in such a state when there is little possibility of my ever seeing him. The more prosperous my circumstances are the more anxious I must be to see a man who has always been so dear to us.

I cannot help regretting that I cannot be Trustee for the younger daughter. Give me Pray a more particular account of both of them of their persons and their dispositions.

When I am more settled what should hinder their paying me a visit. My friend Korsakoff is exceedingly desirous of an English wife and I know none who would make a better husband. How happy I should be with such a connection. Dont think me mad for entertaining such a Project.

Dont distress yourself about what I said of the effect of Q.S.P.'s refusal.[17] It certainly served my enemies with matter for defamation at that time. But I flatter myself that my conduct at that time and the light my freinds set that matter in has left me little reason for regret.

[17] Jeremiah Bentham had been given an initial shock by the size of the final debts Samuel had incurred before the commencement of his salary in the Russian service. On 29 November 1783, O.S., Samuel had written to his brother: 'Sharpe has recieved a letter by this post in which he is informed of my father's having refused not only to pay for me but also to engage to pay it. This would be a terrible stick to me were it not that at present I am almost insensible to any subject misfortune but that of disappointment in my attachment. As it is the last assistance I ever will request of him I still flatter myself he will not refuse it me' (B.M. III: 462–3).

506

To Jeremiah Bentham[1]

6 July 1784 (Aet 36)

Whitchurch Hants July 6th 1784

Hond. Sir,

Last Sunday July 4th just as I had been venting to my Friends at Lincoln's Inn my Impatience in not having had any Letter from my Brother and giving some directions in Consequence, a Letter came,[2] as it is a very long one, by much the greater part belonging to other persons more properly than to me, and as I must answer it before I part with it, it may be a considerable time before you can see the Original and I have not had time to make any Considerable Extracts mean while I must beg you to accept this general Account.—

The date of it as to the time is April 7/18 so that it must have been long in coming, the place God knows where for it is not expressly mentioned all I can collect which however I do with certainty is that it is at an Estate of Prince Potemkins which is 30 Versts from another Estate upon the River Dnieper 8 Versts from Orsh[3] a Town upon that River 90 from Mohilew, the same from Smolensk (on the Dnieper) 70 from Vitepsk (on the Dwina) 600 from Riga which you know is at the mouth of the Dwina between 3 and 400 from Moscow towards the South and about 800 from Petersburg a Verst you know is just ⅔ds. of a Mile he was then but upon his way to Cherson and the Crimea.—

He begins his Letter with saying that since he set out on his present Journcy with Prince Potemkin he had formed a very strict Intimacy with his first Aid de Camp Lieutenant Col. Ribaupierre who is a Swiss by Birth but having Married into one of the principal Families here (the Bibikiffs) is become a Russian—He is a Man universally esteemed and high in favor with the Prince.—It seems, Sam says, that they two, himself and Ribaupierre, had long been disposed to make a better Acquaintance with each other but it was not till they became travelling Companions that they

506. [1] B.M. XXI: 288–9. Letterbook copy in an unknown hand.
The erratic punctuation was probably due to the amanuensis employed in writing the original—see Bentham's note to letter 513.

[2] Partly printed as letter 495.

[3] Orsha.

had an Opportunity what he (Sam) had seen of him was sufficient to dispose him to have the highest Confidence in his Integrity.—

My Brother tells me he /himself/ has got his Appointment of Lieutenant Colonel in the Army with his 1200d. Roubles a year and 100d. a Month for Table Money making in all 2400d. he had before talked of he is besides to have four Servants kept for him gratis and his travelling Charges are defrayed and to be defrayed. He speaks of his having sent you a present by Sea it consists of his picture drawn in his Military Uniform how he came by it he has left me to guess; I suppose the Prince in his Excursions is attended by a Painter as Count Strogonoff was, you may remember by him who made the drawing of the Amphibious Vehicle[4]—The post Summons me and I have only time for the present to subscribe myself

Yours dutifully and affectionately
J^{y}. B.

To Jeremiah Bentham Esqr.
Old Windsor House
Berks

507

To Jeremiah Bentham[1]

8 July 1784 (Aet 36)

Whitchurch July 8th 1784.

Hond. Sir

Having made a sort of half promise in my last,[2] I thought you would be disappointed if you did not receive something from me by this post. I have accordingly begun, but my eyes will not suffer me at present to proceed any further. Writing does not hurt me, but the reading Sams blind hand is very trying to me. Possibly I may be able to continue next post; but I cannot take upon me to

[4] B.M. XXI: 265.

507. [1] B.M. IV: 81. Autograph. Docketed by Jeremiah Bentham: 'Fils J^{y} Bentham / Lr. datd. Whitchurch July 8 1784.'

Addressed: 'Jeremiah Bentham Esqr.'

[2] Letter 506. Presumably the 'half promise' lay in the closing words 'for the present'.

give even a half promise. The post now goes out /hence/ and comes in hither every day. This convenient regulation began yesterday.

Yours dutifully and affectionately,
J.B.

You got back again the /French/ account of the Crimea[3] which I borrow'd of Maty,[4] and after returning it to him received of him again. As he himself had but borrowed it of Dr. Lort[5] (of Saville Row) I hope you have returned it to him again before this time.

508

To James Anderson[1]

12 July 1784 (Aet 36)

Whitchurch Hants. July 1784.

Dear Sir

In the first place let me acknowledge your favour of June 7:[2] it did not reach me here till the | |. I am sincerely concerned to hear that times are so bad in Aberdeenshire. I wish to God some little matter, it can be but little may be got to help them from the Russian employment,[3] if that should be obtainable: should /that/ be the case I am happy to have it in my power to say it is all your own: by the death of the relation[4] whose executorship has called me hither I have got a trifle which though nothing near equal to the trifle I had before, yet when added to that will set me a little more at my ease than I have been, and save me from the having recourse to such expedients as nothing but necessity would have driven me to.

With regard to the Queries, you have misapprehended the design

[3] Not identified.

[4] Paul Henry Maty (1745–87). At this time he was under-librarian at the British Museum.

[5] Dr Michael Lort (1725–90), F.S.A. and F.R.S., formerly regius professor of Greek at Cambridge and, between 1779 and 1783, domestic chaplain to the archbishop of Canterbury, Frederick Cornwallis.

508. [1] B.M. IV: 82–6. Autograph.

[2] Missing.

[3] This passage suggests that, in response to requests from Samuel Bentham made in accordance with his general knowledge of Potёmkin's ideas, Bentham had already been looking into the possibility of sending to Russia unemployed Scottish farm-workers from Anderson's estate.

[4] George Woodward Grove.

I had in troubling you with them, owing I believe to my not having sufficiently explained it. Far from expecting answers from you, if I had my wish about this matter it was rather that you should look them over with a view to see whether you could add any thing to the number of the questions. The use of them was to serve as a guide to my brother in the forming of the calculations which well or ill made would be necessary to determine the conduct of the undertaking he had in contemplation. Some of them are of a local nature, and could only be answer'd on the spot: if I looked for any assistance from you towards the finding answers for /any of/ them, it cou'd only be for a very few, such as those respecting the cattle, whether they could be worked at all while they were fatting, whether the oil-cakes gave them any bad flavour or other quality, whether by any and what means and in what time /etc./ that quality could be removed without prejudice to the accession of fat given them by the grains. I speak pretty much at random, not having any copy of the Queries by me. Whether the finding an accurate solution to a set of problems of that nature be an achievement commonly performed or not, you will agree with me I make no doubt, that the success of the undertaking cannot but depend on the approach that is made to such a solution: indeed the examples you have mentioned serve to prove as much.

I am vastly glad to find the apprehension I mentioned with regard to your eldest son is so far from having any foundation. I can easily believe the person in question is no extraordinary judge of characters, having since had occasion to observe him with my own eyes swallowing with apparently implicit faith the rhodomontades of some of the most shameless boasters I ever met with. He seems however to be a very civil inoffensive good kind of man: what he said was without the least degree of spleen, without any thought I am sure of its reaching you, and indeed I believe without thinking much about the matter. After what you have told me I cannot conceive what could have put such an idea into his head, unless it was /the/ observing your son employing his leisure hours in elegant amusements instead of mere boyish dissipation. He might look upon that perhaps as sufficient evidence of a predominant and exclusive affection for those amusements.

With regard to your son William, I cant think what it was led you to think I had an acquaintance with Wedgwood.[5] If I had, my endeavours shou'd not be wanting supposing you determined for such a measure: but I don't know that I ever saw him in my life.

[5] Josiah Wedgwood (1730–95), the porcelain manufacturer.

Were he disposed to take your son, I ~~rather question~~ do not very well see what there is in that business that should be likely very particularly to suit him: the ornamental branch, which is what you had in view I suppose as adapted to the imaginative genius of your son is in a manner given up, as /I was told, and indeed,/ had occasion to observe last year in looking over his collection. No more *vases* or things of that sort: nothing but teapots and such like useful furniture. Besides he would hardly I shou'd think like any body with a view to partnership without a premium much larger than it would be possible for you to spare: and you may imagine he would not wish for an apprentice that would be likely to set up for himself and rival him in his business. I should think too that were he disposed to take apprentices, a person so well known as he, and whose connections are so extensive must have been always fully provided.

As to the plating manufactory, I have nothing to say to you worth the reading. Is not the whole of their study confined to making the plated work look as much like what is made in solid silver as possible?

Well but now for some news. Last Sunday came a pretty long letter from my Brother. By far the greatest part is occupied with a project in which you are a party principally concerned: the whole of this I will send you either the original of or a copy: the rest is taken up wholly in commissions and dissertations relative to cloaths for myself and him. From the date you will observe it was impossible it should contain an answer to our plan of a perambulation employment for you. His last date is April 9/20: and my packet did not leave London till the 17th of that same month. I will now beg leave to send you to his letter:[6] what follows proceeds upon the supposition of your having read it.

The place you see is an out of the way kind of place: however its situation on the Dnieper gives it a certain though slow communication with the Black Sea, as its vicinity to the Dwina does with the Baltic. Rude as the country is, /a temporary/ an establishment there /on the terms in question/ is not to be looked upon as similar to a plan of colonization in America. On the latter place you have no fixed capital ready formed, no moveable capital but what you bring with you, no labour at command but your own, and for sometime your very subsistence is precarious and to seek. On that

[6] See letter 495, n. 1.

proposed you have a fixt capital, (such as dwelling-houses, barns, storehouses, mills etc.) ready provided, labour /such as it is/ without stint, and subsistance assured. The terms as far as I can judge seem to be highly liberal. I should hope *Ribaupier* is a man to be depended upon: you have already seen some proofs of my brother's wariness in that respect, and I have seen many more. The climate I should think must be much preferable to the best part of Scotland: both as being more to the south (for you will find it to the south even of Newcastle) and as being much more certain: the constant snow that covers the earth all the winter must be a great /and sure/ protection to such vegetables as will grow on it.

This project would combine extremely well with your perambulatory commission: Potemkin's own estates lying in the country in question, this would of course be one of the first countries he would think of sending you to. You will then be paid by government for pursuing a project which you may perhaps think it worth while to make your own. All interests concurring to favour the event of your appointment, Potemkin's as well as those of his two fellow-travellers whom I hope I may with some degree of truth stile his two favourites, I cannot but entertain pretty sanguine expectations of its taking place. If you think Burkit's hundred a year worth your acceptance, (which I should imagine you would, considering that all travelling charges, that is pretty near all charges will be defray'd besides) it will require no other effort on their part than the putting in your name in the room of Burkit's. In that idea I should think it might be not ill worth while for you to look out immediately for ingenious and trust worthy people in the capacities that would be wanted: a Mill-wright for the iron-work, another for the woodwork, and perhaps if a good *Tinker* and a good *Cooper* could be found for the Distillery-vessels, it would be no bad acquisition. It is hardly probable you could get all these people, even if the fund provided for their conveyance should be sufficient to include so many with their families: which you know would depend on the number of persons their families happen'd to consist of. But the more such associates we think about and try for, the more chances we have of succeeding in some instance or other. The distress which so great a part of Scotland labours under still, much to be lamented as it is in itself, may however perhaps prove favourable to, and receive a proportionable relief from this little plan of ours. In particular, some of your own tenants whom you had in view when you said you must turn them out you feared, and so reduce them to beggary, on pain of being reduced to that situation yourself, some of these I say might by means of this plan place themselves in a situation probably better than their former one, certainly widely different at any rate from that of beggary. All anxiety for subsistance would be at an end, and they would find themselves relieved from the drudgery part of their work by men who would look up to them as to a superior race of beings. The circumstances of the two Englishmen whom my Brother found contented and happy /on the Prince's estate which is but 20 miles from that in question/, insomuch that one of them had sent over for his wife /is such as/ cannot but afford a strong assurance to other adventurers: if Englishmen who have left a flourishing country as I believe that about Newcastle is find themselves the better by the change, how must it be with Scotchmen coming from a country which is in the situation you describe? An Englishman who wherever he is, is apt to be a discontented animal is I believe as remarkable for the difficulty he finds in accommodating himself to the circumstances of foreign countries, as a Scotchman is for the contrary facility.

The notion of converting a Millwright after the Mill is built into a Miller seems to me not a bad idea: the metamorphosis is surely not an unnatural one. The conductor of the Mill from having been the maker of it will be able the better to spy out from time to time what repairs are wanting, and the more timeously to apply them: if in his *Miller-state* he is paid pro ratâ, he will be interested in the strongest degree in the success of his labours in his *Mill-wright* state: and the comparative ease of his latter state will be a sort of *requiem* and reward for his labours in the former.—I wonder whether a good Mill wright would be able to copy any /improved/ ploughs or other instruments of husbandry which we might take over or send for from hence. Among those which I have seen at Sharp's the Ironmongers in Fenchurch Street London is one for levelling land that struck me as particularly ingenious. Suppose the surface of a field broken and render'd less fit for mowing, reaping etc., by little hillocks. When you have got it on a hillock by means of a particular manipulation, you make it bite as deep as you please, and it slices of[f] more or less of the surface of the hillock, which it carries in a kind of pan which by another turn of the hand, you discharge wherever you please into the next hollow: and the mechanism though I did not stay to examine it seemed simple. Let me recollect; you and I were once together and saw that with the rest.

All this while I should tell you that the *sine quâ non*, the credit on the Banker, is not yet arrived: but even if it were, and were the wished-for appointment from Potemkin come, I suppose you would hardly think it advisible to engage anybody to go over till you had been on the spot, and seen whether you should like to take any part in the management: but if you were clearly and absolutely determined not to think of it for yourself, then if with a view of serving any person whom you thought capable of undertaking such a charge you had a mind to turn it over /altogether/ to such person, I should have no objection: but in that case, my brother and I should not interest ourselves any farther in the affair, except that upon the credit of your recommendation, I would deliver over to the person in question what money I receive. In the event of your entertaining thoughts of taking a part in the concern, I think I should be disposed to approve the idea which he seems to entertain of /his/ having *one eighth*, leaving to your unlimited disposal the other three. The consideration for his share would be (1) the ground that he has already made, since it is upon the confidence Ribaupier has on him and of his /plans and/ recommendations that every thing turns: (2) the /degree of/ stability he would give to the engagement, by the apprehensions the other party would be in of violating it, supposing that contrary to my Brother's opinion of him he should find himself disposed so to do: (3) the support it might lie in his way to give it by solliciting any favours that might be thought advisible to apply to government for, or at least averting any discouragements. (4) the trouble he would have to take in the way of agency /for instance,/ by procuring any such articles as might be wanted from Petersburgh or from any other part of the Empire, by training servants /as he talks of/ to serve as interpreters etc.: Under this head may be included the share that I should take in the business in sending any articles that might be wanted from hence: or if I were out of the way, procuring others that would take that trouble: a business which might probably require /every now and then/ some little advances of money which in consideration of my Brothers having such an interest in the business I should not grudge to make. (5) his spending /with you/ what time would be necessary upon the spot in order to form the plan and begin if possible the execution of every part of it: for instance the erection of the mill or mills, the erection of the distillery house, the clearing of the river to make it navigable.

You cannot but be sensible, that to form a just estimate of the value of my Brother's contribution one must take into the account not merely the quantum of the labour to be bestow'd by him on this particular subject, but the time and labour and expence (amounting to many hundreds and I may say some thousands) and above all the extraordinary good fortune which have been expended in bringing him into the situation necessary to make him capable of bestowing in the way in question any part of his time and labour upon the particular subject in question. That, independently of friendship and social satisfaction it would be for your advantage to make it worth the while to a person circumstanced as he is to serve as a bond of union between yourself the Landlord, the Government there and this capital, is what I cannot entertain a doubt of your being sensible of. But as to the quantum of the share you should allow him, I mention what I have done rather because one must say something and because it seems to be that which he had himself more particularly in view, than that I am at all wedded to any such precise demand, or that I have made up my mind as to the reasonableness of it. My anxious wish on this as on every occasion on which we have any concerns together, that you would lay open your sentiments truly and without reserve: and from the experience we have had of each other I make little doubt of your believing me when I say that were I to enter into any agreement with you, and were I at any time to fancy I perceived on your part any symptoms of dissatisfaction with regard to the terms of it, from that moment, unless my suspicions were removed, it would cease to afford any satisfaction to me.

All this while I must own that glad as I should be to see you and my Brother connected together in some such way, and even in this out of the way place rather than in none, yet if the scene could be laid in the neighbourhood of Cherson, or what might be still better somewhere in the Crimea in the neighbourhood of some of the many ports there appear to be in that peninsula, it would be much more pleasing to me. There we should be as it were in the neighbourhood of Constantinople: a couple of days sail would be sufficient to waft us to that delightful spot. Through that channel we might have frequent and perhaps regular correspondance with Europe. The diplomatic body, and the Merchants of our own and so many other nations /could hardly fail to/ afford agreable and intelligent society. There we should find and from thence probably we might get, French Journaux, and English newspapers. There could be no doubt of his having at his command a little vessel either at his own expence or that of the Government, big enough to go anywhere in the Black Sea or even the Mediterranean on occasion. Four or 5 hands would be sufficient to navigate her.

One great convenience of the Russian plan for a large family like your's seems to be that being extendible at pleasure, if it would afford an eligible provision for any one member it would for all.

The notion of its appearing to be your own idea that my Brother should become concerned with you, and not his, seems to be a just one. Such a demand on your part could not but encrease the confidence entertained in him by Ribaupier, and to render it greater than possibly it might be, if it appeared that the engagement were of my Brother's seeking.

Were you disposed to engage in this plan and were the credit on the Banker arrived it would not be advisible I think to take any definitive step in it till we had /had another letter/ ~~heard~~ from my Brother ~~again~~ by which we should know more of his motions and destination, and in particular whether he had got any establishment at Cherson or in the Crimea.

When I sent you the Bibliotheque Economique along with the other books you may imagine I did not mean to guarantee the truth of the articles in them or even the value of them in any respect: /no more indeed do the Editors themselves, as they have the precaution in their Preface to observe. I thought/ it might prove acceptable to you as serving to give an idea of what has been done or said to have been done of late in that way in France and other nations on the Continent. As such I think it can hardly fail to have its value more or less according to the accidental fertility of the year. I mean therefore to take it in regularly.

I have just got transcribed for you an article from the Dijon Memoirs containing a description of a portable /it may be called a pocket/ chemical apparatus contrived by M. de Morveau, whom Kirwan in his new Mineralogy[7] stiles 'one of the first chymists of the age'. (Pref. p. iii) This frank will hardly hold it: but if there be room I shall send it by the next. I wrote about a fortnight ago to a person who is to be at Dijon to bespeak such an apparatus: but whether I shall ever get it or no, God knows.

My eyes grow worse and worse: this Executorship has almost done their business: for these two months past my work has been entirely at a stand: not a single stick done to it. I will tell you an idea which the consideration of my eyes put into my head within

[7] Richard Kirwan, *Elements of Mineralogy*, London, 1784. His reference was to Baron Louis Bernard Guyton de Morveau (1737–1816), a famous chemist, whom Napoleon made Administrator General of the French mint. The article referred to, 'Mémoires sur les Phénomènes de l'air dans la combustion', appeared in *Mémoires de l'Académie de Dijon*, i (1769).

these two hours while I was at dinner (July 11th) What to do with myself in the event of my being obliged to give up reading as I have done for these two or 3 days, I do not know. I have no relish for any thing that is commonly called pleasure. The conversation of my old friends that you know of, and of others that you don't know of, all conversation in short which does not bear a reference to my own or my Brother's pursuits, is become insipid to me. My own ideas are come no less so: for the task of invention has for some time been accomplished, and all that remains is to put in order ideas ready formed: to put them in order according to my notions of order, I must have them all before me at once: now that by me at least, is to be done no otherwise than by reading: to make sure of having omitted none, I must on every occasion have them before me in black and white. Well but 'Quorsum hæc tam putida tendunt Furcifer'[8]?—why to this, that it has come into my head that /perhaps/ the best if not the only good thing I could do for my eyes (for if I were to hang myself for melancholy they would be no great gainers in the long run) would be to go a begging to you at Edinburgh for some of your company. In that case the journey while it lasted would /serve/ pretty effectually to keep my eyes from poisoning themselves: and while I was with you my tongue and my ears might together perhaps make shift pretty tolerably to keep them out of harm's way. When I speak of going a begging to you for your company, I would not be understood to mean to go a begging to you for any thing else. It would be too much to have vagrants from England come to augment the famine. Therefore if I were to come, I should insist upon it as a condition sine quâ non that I should be permitted to make satisfaction for the damage I did. When I think of the social hours we have spent together in former days, and of the prospects we have in view, I can not help fancying that if you happen to have an odd corner in your home that would hold me you would not be averse to see me in it: but if I am mistaken /and you wish to get off handsomely/ you have but to tell me that you would be overjoy'd to see me, but you cant think of acceding to any such terms, and the matter is at an end. I mention this as a mere uncertainty: if I do visit you it will be with reluctant steps and with a heavy heart, as every hour I spend with you at this time and at that place I shall look upon as stolen from those which I hope to spend with you on a more agreable occasion elsewhere.

So I send you the original of my Brother's letter; that is as much

[8] Horace, *Satires*, II, vii, 21.

as I thought one frank would carry and as much as I thought would /be at all interesting/ to you. The rest consists of half a sheet to Burkit, answers to a former letter of mine, commissions for articles of dress etc. for him, and instructions for my own.

Adieu—ever your's

J.B.

July 12.

509

FROM FRANÇOIS XAVIER SCHWEDIAUER[1]

15 July 1784

Edinr. 15th July 1784

I am sorry I could [not] see you any more before my departure, my dear Bentham! I left the drawing of the fire engine to Mr. Schönborn[2] who will deliver it to you; he will likewise communicate to you what you desire to know about the code of laws etc. of Prussia—I got the Encyclopedia for you but the last volum will not be published before 6 or 7 weeks and then I shall [send] the whole for you to London.[3] If you can get the model (as you mentioned) of the Sawing machine, I go half the expences with you—Our Friend Anderson is setting out to the western Islands to morrow. I am glad, that his little book made so a good impression on the ministers, ~~this will be~~ If his plan should be adopted, it will [be] the most capital good for this country—Dr. Smith[4] with whom I am intimately acquainted, is quite our man, He is busy about a new edition of his wealth of nations. We have a Club here, which consists of nothing but Philosophers, Dr. /adam/ Smith, Cullen,[5]

509. [1] U.C. IX: 7. Autograph. The letter was forwarded on to Bentham at Whitchurch and bears two dockets: (i) 'This letter came from Clarkes this morning 22 July—J.T.' (ii) In Bentham's hand: '1784 July 15 / Swediar Edinburgh / to / I.B. Linc. Inn / Reced at Whitchurch July 23.'

Addressed: 'J. Bentham Esqr. / London / No. 6 Lincoln's Inn, old buildings.' Postmark: 'JY 16.'

Partly printed, Bowring, x, 136.

[2] Not identified.

[3] Probably *Encyclopœdia Britannica; or a Dictionary of Arts and Sciences compiled upon a new plan... with one hundred and sixty copper plates. By a society of Gentlemen in Scotland*, 2nd ed., 10 vols., Edinburgh, 1778–83.

[4] Adam Smith (1723–90), the economist.

[5] William Cullen (1710–90), physician and chemist. He became professor of chemistry at Edinburgh in 1755 and in 1766 professor of the study of physic.

Black,[6] /Mr./ M'Gowan[7] etc. belong to it, and I am also a member of it. Thus I spend once a week in the most enlightened and agreable, chearful and social company—The rest of the week I live in my house in the country where I am employed in Building a /manufactory;/ thirty workmen and labourers give a man employment enough, but as this will last only 6 or 8 weeks longer, I shall return to litterature and spend the next winter mostly among my dead Philosophical Friends, *perhaps* in collecting and printing their opinions on different subjects.—I hope you go on with your code, I wish to see it published. Adieu

Yours sincerely
Swedia'r

My direction, as I have nothing more to do with Physic, is simply thus:

Mr. Swedia'r
Edinr.

Have you read Voltaire's memoirs of his life written by himself,[8] I just got a copy of it from Paris; it is excellent, and great many anecdotes especially those about the King of Prussia I know to be true: the old scoundrel will not be much pleased to have his c'aracter so much exposed during his life time—

510

TO RICHARD CLARK[1]

16 July 1784 (Aet 36)

The matter you wish to consult me about is an affair of too much intricacy to be discussed by letters and at such a distance. Moreover it is a maxim in our family that what is not worth

[6] Joseph Black (1728–99), professor of medicine at Glasgow, 1756–66, professor of medicine and chemistry at Edinburgh from 1766.

[7] Not identified.

[8] *Mémoires de Voltaire écrits par lui-même*, London, 1784.

510. [1] U.C. CLXXIII: 57. Autograph. Docketed: '16th July 1784. Jeremy Bentham Esqr.'

Addressed: 'Richd. Clark Esqr. / Bridewell Hospital, London.' Postmark: '19/IV'. Stamped: 'WHITCHURCH'.

As letter 513 makes clear, Clark was inquiring about travelling in France. His letter is missing.

fetching is not worth having; whereupon we ground a practical rule of conduct which is, to make those who apply to us pay as dear as they can for what we know not how to refuse. Wherefore if my penmaker and his wife will come to me here at Whitchurch and make me a present of ½ a 100 of their best pens (such as this was before it was worn to the stump) I will Dr. Graham-like[2] give them a lecture gratis not on the art of propagating the species (which they seem to understand at least as well as I can pretend to do) but on the art of travelling in France, and Dr. Graham-like will pour out my whole soul to them. When discharged from the Hospital they may pass themselves on to Chertsey, where (knowing by experience that there are charitable people there) I make no doubt but they will find somebody or other that will have charity enough to take them in. Whitchurch is exactly 56 mile from London Chertsey being almost in the road, it cannot at most be more than 38 mile from thence hither. If your horses are worth saving from the dogs, set out in the cool of the morning 4 or 5 o'clock and they will make nothing of that distance. Here they may rest till they are tired of resting. From hence to Brighthelmstone through... (I forget the rout not having the road book before me) is 90 miles. From London thither is 60: so that you will but one easy days journey out of the way.

Jeremy Bentham Executor
Whitchurch and teacher of grown gentlemen
July 16 1784 and ladies to travel.

Here may be found trout-streams also very pleasant walks: a very good girl aged 22 whom I expect back from London the latter end of next week: item another aged 12, sister to the former, which latter is at a neighbours, till her sister returns:[3] also Stables which I could put horses in, who might live there if they could live upon air: lastly a field which they might run in, if a Quaker whom I have let it unto till Michmas would give leave. Answer me forthwith.

By your own shewing you are as idle as the days are long, and for some half dozen of them would be as well here as any where else. The pens should be made not from new quills, but from old office or Hospital pens worn pretty low: bring about half the quantity we may perhaps find the rest here: tho' we don't shine in quills.

[2] Dr James Graham (1745–94), a famous quack doctor.

[3] Anne Grove and her young sister, Susannah, daughters of the late George Woodward Grove.

511

To Jeremiah Bentham[1]

4 August 1784 (Aet 36)

Whitchurch Hants August 4 1784.

Hond. Sir

Since my last I have to thank you for two letters,[2] together with the franks which one of them announced.

You have been several times kind enough to offer me your assistance with regard to the settlement of my Uncle's affairs: there is one particular on which if you have time, and the employment be not disagreable to you, I should be much obliged to you for it. I mean the making an abstract of the title to the several parts of the Browning-hill estate; such an abstract it will be necessary to be provided with, in order to shew to any one who may be disposed to treat for the estate. I write by this post to order the copies which I have of the title-deeds to be sent directed for you to Q.S.P.: that you may know how to describe this parcel so as to distinguish it from others, the direction will be accompanied with these words 'From Mr. Bentham of Lincoln's Inn'. If it be agreable to you to undertake the job yourself, you will send orders to Q.S.P. to have the parcel transmitted to you wherever you are: if not, I will trouble to you to write a line to Mr. Browne, commissioning him to do the business, and to send accordingly for the parcel. In that case there will be no occasion to let him know that I had any other thoughts than that of putting the business into his hands in the first instance.

/If sold by Auction,/ What time do you imagine it would be necessary to allow betwixt the first advertisement and the sale? Supposing I got the first advertisement inserted in a week, might the Auction be so soon as Michaelmas? It might perhaps be a prejudice to the sale if it were delay'd till the fine weather were at an end.

I have now the pleasure to inform you that my eyes are considerably better than they were when I wrote last, though not so well as when I last saw you. I cannot yet afford to make use of

511. [1] B.M. IV: 96–7. Autograph. Docketed by Jeremiah Bentham: 'Fils J. Bentham / Lr. datd. Whitchurch Aug. 4, 1784.'

Addressed: 'Jeremiah Bentham Esqr.'

[2] Missing.

them for the purpose of mere chit-chat, nor in short to travel on any subject beyond the verge of necessity. I must therefore beg you to excuse my not taking the notice I might otherwise have taken of some of the contents of your two last letters.

I have a map here of the estate, but it was made so long ago as the year 1755: and therefore does not include above 155 of about 193 acres, which from some of my Uncle's papers I have reason to conclude there are at present. Hence it represents the estate as consisting of dismember'd parts which have been joined together or nearly so by subsequent purchases. I mean therefore to have the map completed and for that purpose have written to desire Mr. Mulford to enquire whether there is any body that could do it at Basingstoke. You could perhaps tell me of people in London, but to have a person down from London would be a great expence. By a receipt I have I find the making of this map cost but £4: it was done by a Thos. Blandy.

I am Honoured Sir, ever your's dutifully and affectionately

J^{y}. Bentham

You say nothing in any of your letters of the book which I wrote to you about the account of the Crimea which I borrowd of Maty[3]—I beg you would tell me in your next whether it is returned or no: if not, my credit will be quite gone.

512

From James Trail[1]

9 August 1784

London 9 Augt.

Dear Bentham

I received your Letter[2] with uncommon pleasure for I had almost despaired of ever hearing from you again, such an obstinate silence had you maintained not withstanding the repeated inquiries after your health and your commands—My satisfaction at seeing your Letter was indeed much abated when I found the cause of your not writing to be of so serious a nature—For gods sake do not expose your Eyes to any injury in so ignoble a service. If you will

[3] See letter 507, n. 4.

512. [1] U.C. IX: 8. Autograph. Docketed by Bentham: '1784 Aug. 9 / Trail Linc. Inn / to / I.B. Whitchurch.'

[2] Missing.

transfer your bureau to Town Wilson (if he is not become too great a man) and I will act as your commis and you shall use only the eyes of your understanding making us a pair of Spectacles to protect your mortal sight from all injury.

I fear much you are mistaken in your Law. I have been employed this hour in looking over all the abridgements and some of the Equity reporters and cannot find any ground to warrant you in refusing to /pay/ a debt of any kind till a year after the Testator's Death—By the Stat. of Distributions an admin, is not to distribute the residue until one full year after the Intestates death—It is a rule in Equity that an Exor is not compellable to pay a Legacy where no time of paymt. is mentd. in the will till a year after his Testrs. Death; But I find it said by some master of the Rolls 2 Atk 301 that tho' Exors have a year to pay Legacies it does not extend to Debts but they are liable to be sued the moment after the Testators Death—There is no form of a Plea for such a case /that I can find/ which is an additional argument agt. the existence of any such rule—I cannot pretend to be perfectly clear having run over the books in a great hurry but if I find any reason to alter my present Idea on the subject I shall give you notice. I have some recollection that you got this notable piece of Law from Wilson—As soon as he comes to Town which I hope will be tomorrow I shall question him about it and insist upon his writing to you if he can make good his position. Your commission about the papers to be sent to your father's shall be executed tomorrow—Tonight it was impracticable as I have not seen my Slave since I received your Letter.

I have read Memoires de Voltaire—They are entertaining and if not genuine are at least a /tolerable/ imitation of his manner—If I had been persuaded that they were authentic I am not sure but my expectations would have been disappointed in the perusal. There is nothing interesting and little of any thing except what relates to the King of Prussia.

I *admit* that Smith's book is in the press and that it has considerable additions—It will appear in 4 vols. Octavo—I cannot learn to what particular points the additions relate.[3] It will not be published in less than two months.

I hear of no public news but from the papers I need not therefore repeat what you see there. If the genl, advertiser is to be had at Whitchurch you will be entertained perhaps with /the/ account

[3] *Additions and Corrections to the first and second editions of Dr Adam Smith's Inquiry into the nature and causes of the Wealth of Nations* was published during 1784.

given in that paper of last Saturday of Fox's speech the night before.[4] I am told by those who heard it that it was equal to any he has ever made and with the uncommon advantage of being a reply to Pitt who has now given up the only remaining measure he had struggled for some time to maintain. The people in the City I hear are beginning to talk very freely of the inexperience and incapacity of their late favourite minister and Fox has given them great satisfaction by his temperate and discriminating opposition to such measures only as they have disapproved of. If Pitt should have as much to do next session I own I should not be surprized to see such a current agt. him as might affect his power—but he has got through all his Taxes having provided for the Interest of each even of that part of the debt which will not be regularly funded till next session—I cannot forsee that he will have any thing to do next session but to mend the high roads and enclose commons and make a parading speech about the produce of the sinking fund and the application of the surplus—

You do not say whether you have heard of your brothers further progress with Potemkin. He is certainly en bon train

Yours etc.
James Trail

Expect all your commissions in a day or two

513

To Richard Clark[1]

15 August 1784 (Aet 36)

Whitchurch Sunday Aug. 1784

The route from Rouen to Paris by water, that is chiefly by water, is by far the pleasantest I ever travelled in my life: but how

[4] On Friday, 6 August 1784, in committee of ways and means, the House of Commons continued discussion of a proposal by Pitt to issue stock instead of paying off directly government creditors holding navy bills. The principle and the details of his scheme were sharply criticized by Fox (J. Debrett, *The Parliamentary Register*, xvi (1784), 354–6).

513. [1] U.C. CLXXIII: 58. In the hand of an amanuensis except for the last two sentences and a few corrections in Bentham's hand. Docketed '1[] Aug. 1784. Jeremy Bentham Esqr.'

far you can make it suit you is what I have some doubt about. From Dieppe to Paris is by land, if one may believe the packet-boat-advertisements, which you may /see/ stuck up at the Corner of every Street, about One hundred and fifteen Miles. From Dieppe to Rouen is, if I remember right, about Six or Eight and thirty Miles on the way. This you must go by land at any rate. You will find no difficulty in hiring a Carriage of some sort or other, to carry you thither on moderate terms: at least I found none. Thus far at any rate it would be my advice to you to go; do not omit going to the top of the Cathedral, from whence you have a most extensive View of a most delightfull Country. From Rouan tis impossible you should find any difficulty in making your way by land. When the worst comes to the worst if you should not be able to hire a Carriage, which is what I cannot concieve, or should not chuse the Expence of travelling with Post horses, there is a regular Diligence which you may be sure of. I have some notion that since I was in France the Post furnishes Carriages as well as horses: but this I am not certain about. The Rout from Rouen to Paris by land I have never travelled: but be it ever so pleasant it can hardly come up to some part of that by water. With respect to this latter I will tell you all I can remember. From Rouan to Saint Ouen we went six of us, among whom /were/ two Men and their Wives, in an Open boat in the Evening, it was dark Night long before we reached Saint Ouen which is about six Miles. We were rowed by a man and his Mother whose skin was of the consistence of Parchment and of the Collour of Mahogany. At Saint Ouen we slept at a house which was none of the Most Magnificent nor the best provided; but however we got some Supper, and we Slept. In the Morning early we set off with a Carrier whom we expected to find and whom we found accordingly. With him we went, I think it was fifteen Miles; and by that fifteen saved as we were told about two hundred by water. We travelled on horses, such as they were: the rest of the Company, all the way: I about half the way: for our Complement of horses not being quite compleat, to accomodate a little boy who was otherwise to have rid before or behind somebody I gave him up my horse and walk'd or run by his side. Whether this would do for an Alderman and an Alder-

Addressed: 'To / Mr. Alderman Clark / Black Friars / London.' Postmark: 16 / AV'. Stamped: 'WHITCHURCH.'

The figure in the docket must be '5' as the 15th is the only Sunday in this month having a number in the teens.

For Bentham's correspondence during his stay in France in 1770, see *Correspondence*, i, 138–48.

woman I'll leave you to judge. Our /common/ object was cheapness, and my[a] particular one was Novelty we therefore made no enquiries after more expensive conveyances whether any such had we enquir'd after them would have been to be found I cannot pretend to say in the Middle of this Journey we stopt I think to take some refreshment it shall be called Breakfast or dinner as you Please at the end of it which brought us to the Water we found a Boat somwhat like a London Wherry but with a tilt to it it was pretty well filled by our Party which as I told You consisted of Six and a half with the addition of about five or Six more amongst whom was a common Soldier who was by trade a hair dresser but by behaviour and Sentiments as good a Gentleman as I ever saw his history and how he refused a present of a Crown which I and another would have had him take at parting You have heard from me I believe before now You will expect I should tell you the Names of the place at which we baited and of that at which we took water but unfortunately I have forgot them all I remember is that in the Country was in most parts of it the most entertaining and most Romantic for a Cultivated one I had ever seen and the Accomodation, though in a different Stile from what we have in England not displeasing on the left for considerable way at a great distance seen a chain of Mountains which seem'd as if cut by art into Mathematical Figures Vernon from whence our English Surname was one of the places we pass'd through and I believe one of those we baited at this I believe is the place you are brought to by your descent from a hill which dwells with me as exhibiting the most striking Scene of the whole journey when the Wherry landed us upon some place of which I have very little recollection it was dusk or I believe dark here again we found a carrying place /which saved us/ I believe about thirty Miles of water at the Expence of about a Mile and a half or a Couple of Miles of land the journey woud not have been very great if perform'd upon ten toes but we chose for Merriment sake to take what beasts the place afforded us. these were, Asses in plenty and one horse the Saddles of those who were design'd for Baggage were wooden Machines in the Shape of a W at the end of this carrying place we found a Stage house Boat which they call the ~~Call Yatcht~~ Galiotte it was in structure like the house boats You have seen at Oxford or

[a] [*Note in Bentham's hand*]: Stops and capitals are scarce with my amanuensis to whom I dictated: but my eyes which are very very bad will not permitt me to correct any further: you must divine the rest.

if You please bating every Idea of Ornament Magnificence neatness and convenience like one of your City Barges it was calculated to hold as I understood about two hundred people and it was crammed as full as it would hold /I thought myself in the Black-hole./ Our Company got all together at one of the Ends: a Grating parted us off from a company of Calves: at the other side of the Calves was a chamber which we might have hired I believe at a very moderate price, but the deamon of Oeconomy had posess'd us all. In this State-Chamber any two or perhaps half a dozen people might have been comfortable enough provided they could have contented themselves with sitting up all Night as we did or with lying upon Straw for my part I and another or two of the Company found our way up to the top of the boat and there we passed the time walking or sitting or lying down upon some trusses of Straw from which we were every now and then driven as trespassers what we lost in Sleep we got in Prospect sometimes we saw ten or a dozen Islands at a time many of them tufted with woods and Spangled with Stone Villages the Gal Yacht brought us at a good breakfast hour to some place I forget what. if it was not Saint Germain we found if I remember right Saint Germain in our Way, here our Voyages were at an end we got to Paris by about 2 O Clock in two Veheigles the one I believe what they called Pot de Chambre the other an humble immitation of a post Chaise the Pot de Chambre is a Vehicle more or less covered in which sit four or Six people all looking the same way My advice would be to you to go by all means to Rouen in the first Instance if you meant to try the way by water it would be best to take it in your return but if Your plan is to return some other way for instance by way of Flanders then it might be worth your while when at Rouan to enquire whether the inconveniences I have mention'd can be got rid of. If the fifteen Miles we travelled on horse back could be performed in a Carriage and if the State Cabbin of the Gal Yacht could be secured and if Mrs. Clark would Submit to the inconvenience of a voyage by Night if that should happen to be the time I would take upon me to recommend this way by water in preference to any other otherwise not as to the way from Rouen to Paris what I saw of Normandy was so pleasant that I can hardly suppose the road by land can be much otherwise on your return what say you to taking ~~Antwerp~~ Flanders in your way and Antwerp in particular if that should not betoomuch out of Your road Antwerp You know after having long enjoy'd a most flourishing existence has for about this Century past been dead and Buried but is now through the Merits and Mediations of its Saviour the

Emperor /at/ the eve of Obtaining a joyfull resurrection in prophane Language the River Sheld which made it a Port by Nature but had been blocked up by treaty is now begun to be opened again by the Emperor's fiat and the Acquiescence of the Dutch as it is writen in the Newspapers—

On the Sea between Brighthelmstone and Dieppe I sat upon deck all the time thinking I should be the better for the fresh Air whereupon I was sick the whole passage On my return by way of Calais I took to my hammock early and kept to it the whole time wherupon though the passage was remarkable tedious I had very little sickness I mention this for Mrs. Clark for as to You I remember very well that nothing Sickens You I need scarce observe to you that if Your return is deferr'd till the Weather gets Cold the return to Rouan by water would not do for her on that account.

In giving you all this information and good advice which is all that I can think of I am heaping coals of Fire upon Your head for in good truth You dont deserve it You write me a letter to ask it of me in Answer I ask you to come and fetch it but at any rate to tell me whether You would or no. Of this You take no Notice but take it, as I understand from M. Mulford, as a refusal. My reasoning was this. When he Answers me, which he cannot fail to do, he will tell me, either that he *will* come or that he will *not* come. In the first event, I have no need to Spend my Eye sight: my breath will answer the purpose: in the other event he shall have what he desires upon his own terms. This reasoning I think is not very unnatural: I should be curious to know what your's was. You surely could not think me serious when I stipulated for pens, or when I told you that according to the rule of our family, I meant to give you as much trouble as I could put you to. If you go to Paris, I should be vastly glad to hear from you from thence: perhaps I might find for you an odd jobb or two: a book or two to bring, or something of that sort: but when it is too much for you to give any answer to as cordial an invitation as was ever given from an old and intimate friend, how can I expect it? J.B.

514

From François Xavier Schwediauer[1]

14 September 1784

Edinr. 14th September 1784

Dear Bentham!

I have received yours last night;[2] and shall do according to your direction. If you had written some days sooner, I would have had a fine opportunity to send any thing to Petersburg; the Ship having left this place last friday.—The Encyclopedia[3] is in 9 volums bound, as I promised you, the 10th or last Volum is not yet published on account of the proprietors disagreement amongst one another—I shall send these 9 Volums with the first vessel, which sails from Leith to London under the direction you mention, because there is no probability of any other vessel going to Petersburg this Season. I have been exceeding well since I left you, and my work goes on very briskly; I shall spend this winter here, and arrange every thing in such a manner that I can go afterwards where I please—a fashion I am long accustomed to—I am obliged to you for your account of Kempel's[4] but wish you would be more explicit—I should be glad to get a drawing or a model of the Sawmill you speak of; or of the former, because I am sure of the effect of the latter and am uncertain (as yet) about the effect of that of Taylor's[5]—(always going halves with you about the expences)—I will mention to you in my next of a new /cheap/ and easy method of dissolving caoutichou, it is with Lord Dundonalds[6] tar obtained from Seacoals—I got some days ago a fine d—do—made of the same substance from Cayenne which I shall keep for some trial or other:—Mr. Adam Smith has published a new edition of his wealth of nations in 8° at Cadell: He is a very unprejudiced and good man I see him every week at least once, and we are upon a very friendly

514. [1] B.M. IV: 100. Autograph. Docketed by Bentham: '1784 Sept. 14 / Swediar Edinburgh / to / I.B. Linc. Inn / Encycl. Brit. / Caouchou / Mill-Models.'
Addressed: 'J. Bentham Esqr. / London / Lincoln's Inn no. 6.' Postmark: 'SE 15'.

[2] Missing.

[3] See letter 509, n. 3.

[4] Probably the inventor, Baron von Kempelen; see letter 471, n. 8.

[5] Not identified.

[6] Archibald Cochrane (1749–1831), 9th Earl of Dundonald, impoverished himself by unprofitable attempts to find industrial applications of chemical discoveries.

footing together; he was an intimate friend of the late David Hume and has the same principles. I am so as always

Yours sincerely
Swediar

515

From James Trail[1]

16 September 1784

London 16 Septr. 1784.

Dear Bentham

Wilson has so far relented that he has permitted me to write you some account of Lunardi's excursion with his air balloon.[2]—Fordyce[3] undertook to fill it with inflammable air and executed his part of the business with great coolness and success. He intended to have begun his operations on Tuesday evening about six o'Clock but was prevented by various accidents till 5 next morning so that he was obliged to make 10 Gallons of air in a second which exposed the balloon to be set on fire from the great heat produced by this rapid process. The ingredients were oil of vitriol and Zinck /with a great quantity of water/ and according to his calculations he was from £150 worth of each to collect a sufficient quantity of air, and at the same time to make as much white vitriol as would sell for £400—at the rate of £10 less per Ton than the market price. By this good management £100 will be gained by the process—About one o'Clock, the time fixed for the balloon to go off Lunardi became very impatient and was afraid the mob would have broke in so that Fordyce was obliged to humour him altho' he had not been able notwithstanding all his exertions to collect the quantity of air he wished—upon trial it was found that there was not enough to raise

515. [1] U.C. ix: 9. Autograph. Docketed: '1784 Sept 16 / Trail—Linc Inn / to / I.B. Whitchurch / Lunardi's Balloon Flight.' Addressed: 'Jeremy Bentham Esqr / Whitchurch / Hants.' Postmark: 'SE 16.' Newspaper cutting attached.

Printed, Bowring, x, 136–8.

[2] Vincenzo Lunardi (1759–1806), at this time secretary to the Neapolitan ambassador in London, was fired to emulate the exploits of the Montgolfier brothers at Paris the previous year, and secured financial backing from an Englishman, George Biggin (1762–1803). Whereas the Montgolfier brothers had filled their balloons with heated air, Lunardi arranged for his to be filled with hydrogen. The flight took place on Wednesday, 15 September 1784.

[3] George Fordyce (1736–1802), an eminent physician and chemist. See letter 84, and n. 6. For evidence of Bentham's intimacy with him see *Correspondence*, i and ii, as index.

the two Travellers with 25 pounds of ballast which obliged Biggins to get out and Lunardi set out by himself with about 30 pounds of ballast part of which he threw out almost immediately after he rose from the ground to enable him to clear a row of houses adjoining the artillery ground. We saw everything so distinctly and were so much satisfied with the safety of the attempt that it was by no means that awful or solemn scene that I expected. Everybody greatly interested but chearful and gay and in about ten minutes he was at such a distance that we could scarcely discover the gallery fixed to the balloon. It went at first north west and afterwards nearly due north and in about three quarters of an hour was out of sight of every person I believe in London—no certain accounts were received in Town of the conclusion of this voyage till this afternoon when two Letters one to Dr. Fordyce and the other to Biggins came from Lunardi written from Baker's house in Hertfordshire[4]—In these letters he says that after having been up some time he descended by means of one of his oars (the other he dropped by accident) till he came very near the earth and /by/ throwing out a small grappling he brought himself to an anchor in a large field where some men were at work. To these people he called with his speaking Trumpet and got some information which he does not specify—after leaving his Cat with them he threw out the remainder of his ballast and ascended again to a much greater heigth than he had been before. In his first voyage the Thermometer did not sink below 35 but in the second trip it fell down to 29. Some vapour had got into the balloon and being condensed fell down now and then upon him in drops but when at his greatest heighth these drops were frozen—He does not mention what brought him down a second time—It is thought notwithstanding his account the cause of his coming down both times was the waste of the inflammable air thro' the seams and perhaps the body of the Silk. The Oar was too small to have such an effect as he imputes to it. By his own conjecture he rose the 2d time to the heighth of 4 miles—but as he had no barometer (which was in Biggins pocket and forgot in the hurry) we cannot depend upon the accuracy of his judgement. He was up altogether 2 hours and 20 minutes and landed 3 miles beyond Ware in Hertfordshire where he was soon joined by Genl. Smith[5] and some other gentlemen who had followed him out of Town on horseback with whom he dined and went afterwards to

[4] William Baker (1743–1824), M.P. His seat was at Bayfordbury, near Hertford.

[5] General Richard Smith (1734–1803), retired from the forces of the East India Company, and at this time M.P. for Wendover.

Mr. Baker's house. In his Letter to Biggins he expresses his regret that he had not his company which he says prevented him from enjoying his voyage—but assures him he shall accompany him on the next—that the balloon shall be filled quite full and if then it will not carry two he (Biggins[)] shall go up alone—the balloon came safe to Town this Evening in Bakers caravan and was lodged amidst the acclamations of a great mob at Biggins's house in Essex Street—Fordyce had a very ingenious contrivance to lett out the inflammable air if it had been necessary. He fixed two silk tubes about the middle of the balloon which hung down, and in that position altho' open the light air could not force its way out, but by means of a rope and a pulley which went over the top Lunardi could raise up /either of/ the Tubes as high as any part of the balloon and then the air would have flowed out freely. It does not appear that he made any use of this contrivance—But it is a proof the principle is sound that the bottom of the balloon was open the whole time. Lunardi was child with the cold altho he had on a flannel shirt and drawers—We may expect to see him aloft again in a few days—We are promised besides an exhibition of a balloon from Lord Foley's garden on Monday next with which Col. Gardiner and Mr. Sheldon are to ascend.[6] Blanchard who went up in France has brought over his balloon and will no doubt perform some feats unless Lunardi has anticipated him.[7] He was in the artillery ground on Wednesday and endeavoured to turn everything into ridicule and at the same time to alarm the people who stood near the balloon while it was filling for their safety—he assured them the casks would certainly burst. He was so much attended to that several persons entreated the Prince of Wales who stood very near to retire—but he with great indifference desired his companion Tommy Onslow[8] who was uncommonly anxious to get him away, to retire himself if he thought there was any danger. Altho' the concourse of people was immense yet few in proportion came into the artillery ground; it is said not more than £400 was received for Tickets—

Yours etc.
James Trail

[6] This flight did not take place. Colonel Gardner was a member of a circle of balloon enthusiasts in London, which had the patronage of Lord Orford, Lord Foley, and the Duchess of Devonshire. Dr John Sheldon (1752–1808), an anatomist, was closely associated with this group.

[7] Jean Pierre Blanchard (1753–1809), the French balloonist. Sheldon seems to have acted as a sponsor of his visit to England and accompanied him on his first flight over English soil, which was made from Lochee's Military Academy, Chelsea, on 16 October 1784.

[8] Thomas Onslow (1754–1827), M.P.

516

From Samuel Bentham[1]

26 August/6 September–6/17 September 1784

Kritchoff August 26th 1784

A Courier has just now brought me a packet from Petersbourg containing some of your letters but I dare to say not all that were there; because Notman ~~is still~~ I suppose there and being probably in expectation of setting off every day I conclude most of my freinds /prefer sending theirs by him/ intrust him with my letters. I have nothing from anybody but Hynam. It is from him I receive your packets which were brought him by Tooke the Parson.[2] Never mind this if he did read it it cant be helped and I dont care.

It[3] is unlucky that the Packets were trusted to this Parson's Care. He is the most tittle-tattle man imaginable and he gave the packets to Hynam opened saying they were opened at the Custom house. Had there been only your packet of Letter VIII it would not have signified but there was XXV of last year containing your proposal to Payne[4] and many things which you must conceive it to be very disagreable should become the tea-table talk of my country men at Petersbourg. This vexes me much but as nothing that I can do can any wise prevent it the best I can do is to endeavour to forget it.

Only never trust anything with a *Parson* which can excite his inquisitivness.

In your correspondence about Mears[5] I cannot help observing that your stile was too *humble*. I see no reason for you to offer your *humble* service to any man. 'Il lui plairait de commander mes tres humbles services.' Is that an expression which any civility can require from an Englishman to a foreigner of whatever rank he may be when no ways in subordination to him. I know it is more than I should write to any one even in this country and though he be ever so much my superior. Yours of May from Whitchurch consisting chiefly of Extracts from Anderson. The pleasure I receive from the

516. [1] B.M. IV: 98–9. Autograph. Docketed by Bentham: '1784 Sept. 6 / S.B. Kritchoff / to / I.B. Linc. Inn / Received at Whitchurch Nov. 3 / Dams on Dnieper to be cleared. / I.B. to take S.B.'s money.'

[2] William Tooke (1744–1820), sometime chaplain of the English church at St Petersburg, and author of a number of books on Russia. See on him the note by A. G. Cross in *Canadian Slavic Studies*, III, no. 1 (1969), 106-15.

[3] This paragraph is scored through. [4] See letter 468. [5] See letter 501.

prospect of having one at least if not both the ingenious men which he speaks of, added to the hopes of seeing him and probably you this year, if not this Autumn dispells all disagreable thoughts about the Parson's Criticisms and in short delights me exceedingly. All that you tell me about /your/ coming is that it is more certain but more remote.

Septr. 6th O.S.

Mr. Notman the Englishman by whom I sent you some letters as far as Petersbourg and who at that time I thought might possibly go to England is this morning arrived here back again. It is by him I have been in long expectation of English letters which I supposed might have been kept at Petersburgh on account of so sure an opportunity. English letters however he brings me but one and that is from Mr. Carew written evidently before he had received or indeed could well have received one I sent him from the Crim. It had lain a long time in Mr. Fitzherbert's hands.

I believe I have already in a later letter acknowledged the receipt of your II sheet least I should not I will now give you all the dates of the letters ~~or different I have received~~ /of/ this year, some /of/ which as you will know came in company. I Jany. 2 II Jany. 15. III March 9th. March 26. April 5th 8th 11th or 12th. 28th. May 13th VIII July 7th (last date July 12th) so that between III and VIII there are no numbers.

I shall be very glad of the publication you speak of about sluices. The Empress has just ordered all the dams on the ~~upper part of~~ the Dnieper and on some other rivers communicating to it to be cleared away this year that the navigation from their very sources may be clear next spring. I may afterwards have occasion to shew as I now think that dams in some parts fitted with proper sluices besides being usefull as affording primum mobiles would facilitate the navigation.

I should even rejoice at the badness of your eyes if that should have determined you to come immediately at the finishing your executorship business to me here rather than to spend your time in Scotland as you seemed disposed. As you must have received my further proposals to Anderson I make sure that he is at least preparing to come. What you tell me of the state of his affairs must make a Salary of 1200 rubles i.e. £200 more material than I before thought it.

Sutherland says he sent you the credit for the 3000 rubles immediately but I doubt his exactness. /He told Notman so whom I had commissioned to ask about it for Sutherland never thought it necessary to but answer my letter./ Ribaupierre told me that the 500 was not sent so soon as he wished but however you must long have received it.

My present employment affords exercise enough for ingenuity of all kinds. You may be sure I should [be] glad of assistance of any kind for any of these establishments, and may be able to satisfy in, one way or other those whom I could find capable of affording it. Any of our freinds who would come and see me now might have all opportunities of having the satisfaction of putting their ideas in practice and the advantage to be derived from such experience might be looked for else where.

You for your part might try *jurisprudence* experiments in abundance. You might be as I am sometimes forced to be Legislator, Judge, Jury, and Sheriff.

I am all impatience to hear something final about the time of your coming and who you bring with you.

Anderson's East India grass seeds would please the Prince mightily.

Contrive that I should have a good quantity of elastic gum (Kooutchou) I have not a morsel left. The money I may be entitled to do what you please with for yourself as well as for me. I have just cancelled a part of a letter written above a month ago in which I had desired you to pay John Clark[6] fifty pounds out of the credit I have sent you and that I would replace it out of my Salary. Now however I think ~~there can~~ you may let that alone. If however he should be obliged to spend the winter in London, make him more comfortable in his manner of living and if he makes the journey proposed, let him have on my account what money he wants for that purpose.

[6] I.e. Bentham. See letter 491 and n. 3.

517

From Samuel Bentham[1]

14/25 September 1784

Kritchoff Septr. 14 O.S. 1784.

Your letter which gave me the news of our Uncle's death I received about a fortnight ago.[2] Notwithstanding I am much occupied I cannot get the better of my useless concern. It makes a breach in the plan of satisfaction and enjoyment which I had formed to myself on the prospect of visiting England. Your business of Executorship I make no doubt is a plaguing one to you. I am affraid of your being obliged to postpone your visit to me but I hope at any rate to see you this year.

I have within these few days taken upon me such a trust as with the continuance of my former occupations here will keep my invention ⟨in⟩ a constant *ferment*. I have the direction and the putting in order all the Prince's fabricks here. The great disorder in which all these establishments have been in of late owing to the mismanagement of the Colonel who had the direction of them induced me to offer and the Prince to accept my services. The great kindness he has shown me obliged me as it were to make him the offer, and the satisfaction he has expressed at my doing so makes me think little of the trouble I shall have. I must give you some account of my commission were it only that you might judge how far you could afford me any assistance. What a pity it is that I was not *Master of Arts*. . . .[3]

I cannot possibly write to my father by this conveyance. Let him know how busy I am.

517. [1] B.M. IV: 102–3. Autograph. Docketed by Bentham: '1784 Sept. 14/25 / S.B. Kritchoff / to I.B. Linc. Inn / Received at Whitchurch Novr. 3d. / S.B. Steward to Potemkin.'

Addressed: 'Jere^{y} Bentham Esq. / Lincoln's Inn / London'; readdressed: 'Whitchurch / Hants.' Postmark: '2 NO'.

[2] Missing.

[3] About twenty lines giving a list of the factories and workshops at Krichëv is omitted. See M. S. Bentham, *The Life of Brigadier-General Sir Samuel Bentham*, 1862, p. 78.

518

From Robert Hynam[1]

22 October/2 November 1784

St. Petersburg Oct. 22d 1784 O.S.

Sir,

I have only a few Mints. allowed before the Courier sets off which I employ in informing you that I recd. your favor of the 23 Sepr.[2] I think Mr. Sutherland[3] cannot deliver the Boxes as they are addressed to Prince Potemkin, however I have sent to Mr. Sutherland, and now wait for his Answer.

I had the satisfaction of receiving a letter from your Brother the 9th Instant—He is in good health.

Extract of a Letter from your Brother 'you know certainly before this that I have the direction of the Princes Fabricks here, it is only however that I may put them in a little better order probably a twelve month or so. I recd. a Letter to this Effect only this Morng.[4] so that I have as yet very little Idea of my pains and troubles.' The Letter was written at Kritcheff.

The Courier now waits.
I am Sir
With high Esteem
Your Most Obedt.
Hbe. Sert.
Rob Hynam

518. [1] B.M. IV: 116–7. Autograph. Docketed by Bentham: '1784 Oct. 22/Nov. 2 / For S.B. / Hynam Petersburgh / to / J.B. Linc. Inn / Quoting a Lr. of S.B.'s / dated Oct. 7/18 Kritchoff.'

Addressed: 'J. Bentham Esqr. / Lincolns Inn / London / To the care of the Revd. Mr. Smirnow.'

Endorsed on the back with a note: 'The Messanger who brought this Letter will be going back to Petersburg in 8 or 9 days, if Mr. B. has got any Letters to Send Mr. Smirnow will Send 'em in his own packet.' B.M. IV: 118–9 is a copy by Jeremiah Bentham, which is docketed by Jeremiah Bentham: 'original Recd. from Mr. Smirnoff / the 3d. Decr. 1784.' According to Samuel Bentham (letter 491, n. 2) Hynam was the empress's watchmaker.

[2] Missing.

[3] Richard Sutherland (1739-91), later created baron, the empress's banker.

[4] Samuel Bentham's letter to Potëmkin, offering to take charge of his industrial establishments, and the prince's reply dated 17 August 1784, [O.S.] are at B.M. IV: 108–9.

519

From François Xavier Schwediauer[1]

12 November 1784

Edinr. Nov. 1784

Dear Bentham!

I hope you have received the Encyclopedia by this time, I had since my last received letters from Riga that the Encycloped. /with/ Maquer's dictionary arrived there early in October and were immediately forwarded to your brother to Petersburg[2]—as there are many vessels coming ~~to Leith~~ from Petersburg to Leith early in Spring, I offer you to take the Encyclopedia back for the Same Price I Charged you for viz: 10£ 10s. and to pay the expences of the *retour*, if your brother will send it back to me in good condition under the direction *Dr. Swediau'r* ~~Edinburgh~~ *Leith to the care of Mr. Gavin Kempt mercht.*—It is a book which I should like to possess myself and thereby save you at the same time double and unnecessary expences.——

Lord Dundonald's[3] Process of making tar and volatile alkali from Pitcoals as well, as the Process of *Cort*[4] of converting cold short or so called Pig-iron into malleable good iron are both the most ingenious and at the same time the most useful discoveries made in chemistry this Century. Lord Dundonald was so kind to let me have a perfect sight of his whole manufactory and the Process, and of Cort's Process /an exact description/ was communicated to me by a man of great chemical knowledge, a friend of Cort's; but both these communications were made to me under the promise upon honour not to communicate either of them to any body else; if You, however, should be *really interested* to know the one or the other, I

519. [1] B.M. IV: 120–1. Autograph. Docketed by Bentham: '1784 Nov. 12 / Swediar / to / I.B.'

Addressed: 'Jer. Bentham Esqr. / London / No. 6 Lincoln's Inn / Old Buildings.' Postmark: 'NO/16' and '19/NO'.

Message added by the address: 'Schönborn writes me that he called Several times on you without finding you at home. Therefore if You call on him, let him know the days and hours when you are at home.'

[2] For previous references to the Encyclopædia, see letters 509 and 514. Schwediauer had obtained two sets, one for Bentham and another for Samuel, and now proposed to resume ownership of the second set.

[3] See letter 514, n. 6.

[4] Henry Cort (1740–1800), ironmaster, and inventor of the important 'puddling' process for purifying iron.

will endeavour to get leave to be dispensed /of my promise/ for one friend of mine—you may depend that Smith's new edition of the wealth of nations is printed; we are very good friends and he shewed me the book finished, but told me since that Cadell most probably will not publish it, untill all the people of fashion are arrived in London, and thus at once push a great Sale: this I find is a generally adopted Bookseller trick, and I think a very allowable one—There is not any other Philosophical news here, except a Book I am printing now, and which, I hope, will be finished towards the end of /next/ February or march, wherein among other Free Thinkers your name is most honourably mentioned,[5] for which I hope you will give me leave, on my arrival in London, to Kiss the nail of the great Toe of your left foot, for which blessing I shall be for ever

Your most humble, and
devout Servt. and Slave
Swediau'r

[5] Schwediauer was here referring to his compilation, *The Philosophical Dictionary; or, the Opinions of modern philosophers on metaphysical, moral, and political subjects (Compiled from the writings of the most eminent philosophers in Europe)*, 4 vols., London, 1786. He included in this anthology a number of brief passages from Bentham's writings, including passages from the *Introduction to the Principles of Morals and Legislation*, which was not published until 1789. These extracts are here itemized with the titles attached to them by Schwediauer and identified.

Vol. I, p. 353: The Difference between a Free and a Despotic Government [*Fragment on Government*, Bowring, i, 288].

Vol. I, p. 354: Resistance to Government [*Fragment on Government*, Bowring, i, 287–90: an amalgamation of several paragraphs with substantial textual variations].

Vol. II, p. 97: Legislature and its Omnipotence [*Fragment on Government*, Bowring, i, 288–9 with omissions and additions].

Vol. II, p. 192: Principles of the Monks, not a proper standard of Right and Wrong [*An Introduction to the Principles of Morals and Legislation*, in *CW*, pp 17–21].

Vol. II, p. 305: Mankind governed by Pain and Pleasure [op. cit., in *CW*, pp. 11, 34].

Vol. II, p. 306: Sanctions, or Sources of Pain and Pleasure, and their influence in Legislation [op. cit., in *CW*, pp. 34–7, with variations].

Vol. II p. 345: Pleasures and Pains, Value of their Kinds [op. cit., in *CW*, pp, 42–50 with some textual variations].

Vol. II, p. 358: Value of a Lot of Pleasure and Pain, how to be measured [op. cit., in *CW*, pp. 38–41].

Vol. III, p. 98: Promises, and their Obligations [*Fragment on Government*, Bowring, i, 270–2, omitting several sections].

Vol. III, p. 133: Proportion between Punishments and Offences [*An Introduction to the Principles*, in *CW*, pp. 172–4].

Vol. III, p. 136: Objects of Punishment [op. cit., in *CW*, p. 165 with minor variations].

Vol. III, p. 250: Origins of Right and Duty [*Fragment on Government*, Bowring, i, 292–3 with omissions].

Vol. III, p. 252: Standard of Right and Wrong [Apparently a summary of *Fragment on Government*, Bowring, i, 1–14].

P.S. I do not know whether I mentioned to you, that caoutchouc is not dissolved, as I was first informed in Lord Dundonald's Tar, but in a kind of ether prepared from this Tar by a process /invented but/ not yet discovered by Lord Dundonald who is one [of] the most ingenious chemists I know; what a pity that this man's projects /or rather imagination/ run constantly away with him, and thus deprive him of the real benefit, he could reap of his discoveries if he adhered to a more steady and prudent plan in the execution thereof —adieu.

520

From Jacques Pierre Brissot de Warville[1]

12 November 1784

Boulogne, 12th November, 1784.

For the services done to you, I shall, from time to time, have to ask others from you. In consequence of the new arrangements which I have been obliged to make with the government, I shall only be able to pass three or four months of every year in London. I am, therefore, obliged to abandon my London house. I shall tell you all this when I have the pleasure of seeing you. I thank you, beforehand, for all the interest you have shown towards me, and my misfortunes. Answer me here.

Project for the Translation into French of the best English Books on Constitutions and Legislation; and for the Translation of that of Mr. Howard on Prisons.

Some individuals, either opulent or instructed, but all desirous of promoting public instruction, are about to associate for the translation, printing, and circulation of the best books on Constitutions and Legislation. Some will give their labour, others their money. Mr. Howard's book on Prisons will be the first. Any individual undertaking it alone, and paying the expenses, would undoubtedly

Vol. III, p. 253: Right and Wrong [*An Introduction to the Principles*, in *CW*, pp. 25–9].

Vol. IV, p. 101: The Principle of Sympathy and Antipathy not a proper Standard of Right and Wrong [op. cit., in *CW*, pp. 21–33 with omissions].

Vol. IV, p. 290: The Principle of Utility [op. cit., in *CW*, pp. 11–16 with omissions].

520. [1] Bowring, x, 191–2. Docketed: 'Copied and sent to J. Howard, Friday, November 26, 1784.'

Bowring's rendering in English. Evidently incomplete.

be a loser. The reasons why good books are not translated in France is, that a Romance or a Journey has more attraction, and is more profitable. Two individuals, tolerably rich, are willing to subscribe a certain sum. Will Mr. Howard himself contribute, if their names, and the name of the translator, are communicated to him? I should have written to him; but from your intimacy, I hope you will propose the plan to him, especially for his own work.[2]

521

From Jacques Pierre Brissot de Warville[1]

30 November 1784

Boulogne, 30th November, 1784.

Your regrets on my future absence have much touched me. They prove your friendship. Mine is not less than yours; and sorry I am not to have better profited by your knowledge, during my stay in London. Next year I shall repay myself, for I shall spend three or four months in London, and see you often. If what you say is true when you quote Scripture, I may flatter myself to be much loved, for I have been cruelly persecuted. I read a part of your letter to my wife, who was enchanted with it, and who entreats to be recalled to your regards. Our child does well. These are my two consolations; for I have had many sorrows. Adieu, my friend—continue your friendship to me—write to me—employ me.—I am —I shall always be—entirely yours.

[2] Works on John Howard provide no further information about this correspondence. The first known translation of any of Howard's works into French is *Etat des prisons, des hopitaux et des maisons de force*, par John Howard, translated by J. P. Berenger, 2 vols., Paris, 1788. See L. Baumgartner, *John Howard (1726–1790) Hospital and Prison Reformer. A Bibliography... with an introduction by Arnold M. Muirhead*, Baltimore, 1939.

521. [1] Bowring, x, 192.

Bowring's rendering in English. Probably incomplete. A letter from Bentham referred to in the first line has not been traced.

522

FROM REGINALD POLE CAREW[1]

27 February 1785

Feb. 27. Park St.

Having just recovered from the Apprehensions of being burnt I shall spare you the Trouble of reading an apology for these late thanks for the interesting Communication of Your Brothers Letters.—I saw Mr. Frazer yesterday and took that opportunity of mentioning the Subject to him, he appeared disposed to talk upon it to his Principal.[2]

Blades is my Glass Grinder, but I shall desire to have the Privilege of making a Present to Potemkin and Co. of a Pair of Tumblers à la Tartare.

Mr. Rashleigh is in Town and I wish to fix some Day with You both for dining in Park Street—

I think Your Brother did well to wave to another the advantage of Steelmaking, lest he should literally himself have too many Irons in the Fire—

Mrs. Carew joins me in best Comps. who have the Honor to be very devotedly yours

R. Pole Carew

523

FROM THE MARQUIS OF LANSDOWNE[1]

17 March 1785

17th March 1785

Dear Sir

Mr. Symmonds of Cambridge whose character I need not mention to you is desirous of examining the Four Volumes on the

522. [1] B.M. IV: 138–9. Autograph. Docketed by Bentham: '1785 Feb. 27th / P. Carew, Park Street / to / I.B. Linc. Inn.'

[2] Fraser's 'principal' at the Foreign Office was now Lord Carmarthen. The subject of conversation may have been Samuel's letters about the Amur River (see letter 505 at p. 281 and letter 536, n. 2). Judging by the usual time required for mail to pass from Krichëv to London, the second of these letters, written on 14/25 January, might have just reached Bentham before this date.

523. [1] B.M. IV: 140–1. Autograph. Docketed by Bentham: '1785 March 17 / Ld. Lansdown, Berkeley Square / to / J.B. Linc. Inn / Introducing Symonds, Profess. of Histy. at Cambridge.'

French Finances which you have. I have told him that I would take the liberty of giving him a note which would not only introduce him to the Book but to what I am sure he would be more pleas'd to read, which is Yourself.

I am with great tru[th]
Dr. Sr.
Most sincerely
Yrs. Lansdowne.

524

From Samuel Bentham[1]

18/29 March 1785

Moscow 18th March 1785.

I have met here a Dr. Brown Physician from Carma[r]then South Wales from whom in the course of an intimacy which I have contracted with him I have heard of a man who wishes to come to this country and to be employed in some of the several ways in which I could employ him at Critchoff. I understand a Salary of 20 pounds a year with board and lodging would content him but it is necessary to advance him twenty five pounds to rig him out and ship him off. his name is George Benson an Irishman but many years in Wales. Dr. Brown has a wife and family at Carmarthen and has written to her to send off this said Benson with leave to draw on you for any sum not exceeding twenty five pounds. If he comes by way of London you will see him and may then give him what money within that sum there may be occasion for: but I have given him to understand that he will not have more than that till his arrival in Russia that is

Addressed: 'To Jeremiah Bentham / Esqr.'

John Symonds (1730–1807), a fellow of Peterhouse from 1753 (and who moved to Trinity College in 1772), became professor of modern history at Cambridge in 1771. For Bentham's further contact with him, see letter 527.

524. [1] B.M. IV: 142–3. Autograph. Docketed by Bentham: '1785 March 18/29 / S.B. Moscow / to / J.B. Linc. Inn / Reced. April 26th. / Benson. Tinfoil and Merc.'

Addressed: 'Jerey Bentham Esqr. / Lincoln's Inn / London.' Postmark: 'AP/26'.

Once again Samuel made use of his brother as an agent to obtain the service of subordinates at Krichëv; but in this case Dr Brown's recommendation was far wide of the mark, and during Bentham's visit to his brother Benson proved a sore trial to both brothers. See letters 578, 580, and 588. Bentham's papers include a copy of a letter from Brown at Krichëv dated 11/22 April 1785 to Benson, informing him about the arrangement (B.M. IV: 153).

at Riga where I shall supply him with further credit and means of continuing his journey.

I have spent a week here but am this moment setting off in my return, and as Dr. Brown is not yet come into business here and some general medical directions are very much wanted at Critchoff I have prevailed on him to go to pass a fortnight with me.

I hope to find Notman already returned[2] or at least some news from him.

I wish very much to have about five guineas's worth of tinfoil such as is used for looking glasses also about 20 pounds of Mercury.

525

From the Marquis of Lansdowne[1]

9 April 1785

Lady Lansdown presents her Compliments to Mr. Bentham—she is much oblig'd to him for the sight of some very fine Drawings, and begs to acquaint him that they are much too fine to be offer'd so lightly, and would if it is not taking too great a liberty advise him to keep them in some place free from dust, and at his return to get Mr. Cipriani to sort them, which she is persuaded he can do so as to make a very pleasing Collection of the best of them. With this view she returns them as they come with many thanks.

Lord and Lady Lansdown beg to assure Mr. Bentham of their best wishes for the success of his Journey and his safe return.[2] Lord Lansdown will be sincerely happy to have it in his power at home or abroad to prove his attachment to Mr. Bentham, and will expect him to be so good to remember his promise of writing to him. The

[2] James Notman had been in England, partly in order to recruit further staff for Samuel at Krichëv. See letter 528. He was a native of Newcastle, a quaker, and by profession a tanner. Potëmkin had taken him into employment, together with a currier, Matthew Robson, some time before Samuel Bentham arrived in Krichëv, with the object of establishing a tannery and leather manufacture. His trip to England had been thought of ever since the previous July (Samuel to Jeremy Bentham, 18/29 July 1784, B.M. IV: 91–2).

525. [1] B.M. IV: 145–6. In Lord Lansdowne's hand. Docketed by Bentham: '1785 Apr. 9 / Ld. (for Lady) Lansdown / Berkeley Square / to / J.B. Linc. Inn / Drawings returned attachment / professed—Letters offer'd / —Answer'd—sending back / the Drawings.'

[2] Bentham's plans to visit his brother in Russia were now firmly laid, although it was another three months before he finally set out on his journey.

Letters for Paris shall be forthcoming whenever Mr. B. fixes the time of his Departure.

Lansdown House.
9 April, 1785.

526

From Samuel Bentham[1]

2/13 April 1785

Critchoff April 2nd 1785.

I received a packet of letters from you a few days ago the last of which was dated Feby. 7th except that there were a few lines on the back of a letter of Notman's to his wife of the 11th.[2] These came by way of Riga the large packet came to Petersburgh by a Russian Courier and was dated Decr. 24th on the last sheet. I have answered your letter more fully by another conveyance but take the chance of sending off this by Riga in hopes of its finding you before you set out.

I am terribly affraid of your not having any answers to your letters to the Prince at least not in due time.[3] This might give you a great deal of uneasiness at the same time that it would put a stop to your journey. I wish exceedingly you could have contrived to

526. [1] B.M. IV: 149–50. Autograph. Docketed by Bentham: '1785 April 2/13 / S.B. Crichoff / to / J.B. Linc. Inn / J.B.'s letters reced. from Dec. 24 to Feb. 7 / Reced. May 17.'

Addressed: 'Jere^{y} Bentham Esqr. / Lincolns Inn / London.' Postmark: 'MA/[1]7'.

[2] Missing. The next sentence indicates that, as Samuel Bentham was now in the Russian service, Bentham could send mail through the Russian embassy in London as well as the Foreign Office.

[3] Missing. For acknowledgements of these letters see letters 529 and 531. In another note written about the same time, docketed by Bentham as dated 8/19 April 1785 but postmarked MA 23, Samuel commented in the same vein but more fully: 'The people you have engaged and every⟨thing⟩ you have done respecting the Commissions for Crimea I make no doubt would have pleased the Prince exceedingly, and I dare to say that he would give a good portion of land to both of us if we wish for it: but I am very sorry that you found it necessary to write to him about the business. It is not always that he is occupied about the prosperity of the Crimea. He had given the Commission for engaging people to me at a time when we were together on the spot. He ordered me credit for the money necessary in England. He expected at that time to have gone there again this spring probably he intended I should go with him and everything would have been settled. Were I to apply to him for an order for the payment of the Salaries of the people engaged by his desire he would certainly give it. but as to his doing any thing more for the forming his intended establishments that must wait till he has leisure, till he is in the humour for it.' (B.M. IV: 151).

have come yourself and have assembled your chosen here from whence when we should have settled the plans together they might have taken their departure southward with or without us, as circumstances should require.

I know there is a great deal of reason for the passing through the Southern provinces of France and in short If the Prince was occupied with nothing but the Crimea He could not but have been very much pleased at [the] zeal with which you have acted to contribute to his views; but I fear much that he for want of leisure to attend to the details in your letters may have found them troublesome and be displeased at the idea of my having desired you to write to him. I thought however that you would have collected from the manner of my writing to you on the subject of the Commissions for the Crimea, that as he would not fix the Salaries or terms of engagement himself at a time even when being on the spot the minutiae of the business would be more in season that it was not probable that he would like to be referred to about the choice of persons at any other time. He desired me to find those persons and he orde[re]d me credit for the furnishing the expences. He expected then to hear no more of it till the people made there appearance. It is done however now and you before this time either setting out in consequence of answers from him or what I fear is that the want of the degree of attention which you might have expected may have stopt you. I shall be very unhappy at hearing the latter to be the case, but will hope that nothing will prevent my seeing you some time or other this Summer. Such reflections as these joined to some trifling plagues I have had for these two or 3 days have made me so intollerably stupid that I scarcely know what I write.

I have not heard a Syllable either from Ribaupiere or the Prince about your letters to them.

I will send to Riga in time in case the state of the roads and other circumstances made it appear advisable to send horses from hence: but ⟨as⟩ I suppose Notman will come by sea as well as the rest and as there is a Soldier waiting at Riga for him I rather at present think it will be better to hire carriers from thence.

The idea of having Henderson the two Modellers and the people whom you tell me are to come to Riga to say nothing of the high educated dairy mistress, I must not indulge myself with least I should be disappointed.

Adieu and let nothing prevent our seeing one another this Summer.

527

From John Symonds[1]

28 April 1785

Trinity College, Cambridge
April 28, 1785

Dear Sir,

I should have answered your letter[2] much sooner, if it had not been for my staying to take an opportunity of one of my friends' going to London, that he might carry a dissertation, which I beg your acceptance of. It was written during the American war, and most probably never fell in to your hands. In 1761 and 1762 I read with particular attention the principal Greek and Latin historians, and had many points in view, among which was colonization, that was not a party-question before the stamp-act passed. When I answered my antagonist, who is a Scotchman, I had nothing more to do, than to have recourse to my notes; which soon convinced me, that something more than an honest inquiry after truth prompted him to misrepresent the writers of antiquity; and, in fact, he was soon rewarded by the Ministry with a pension of £200 a year, which he is reported to enjoy at this time.[3]

You may easily imagine, that, if I had taken it the least ill that you did not call upon me, I should not have sent you the pamphlet, trifling as it is; but I thought myself sufficiently obliged to you for the loan of the book relating to the edicts of Tuscany, which afforded me much information; and you would do me a great favour to inform me of any thing of that kind concerning any government in Italy, which has been published since 1770, should it have fallen in your way.

527. [1] U.C. IX: 4. Autograph. Docketed by Bentham: '1785 Apr. 28 / Dr. Symonds Cambridge / to / J.B. Linc. Inn.'

Partly printed, Bowring, x, 138–9. On the writer see letter 523, n. 1.

[2] Missing. This letter was evidently written in consequence of Lansdowne's letter of 17 March (letter 523).

[3] In 1778 Symonds had written an anti-ministerial pamphlet, *Remarks upon an Essay, entitled, The History of the Colonization of the Free States of Antiquity*, refuting a pro-government pamphlet published in 1777 by William Barron (d. 1803), professor of logic at St Andrews. Symonds's surmise about Barron receiving a pension is dubious. Barron's name was not on the list of secret service pensions handed over at the fall of North's ministry in March 1782 (Windsor Mss., cal. Geo. III, 4652) nor in other surviving accounts of secret service payments prepared by John Robinson, North's secretary to the Treasury, and preserved among George III's papers. More customary would have been a single *ex gratia* payment.

I am not a little flattered with the opinion you are so good as to form of my papers in Young's annals.[4] I intend to give him some upon the *moral causes*, and afterwards to publish them myself in a distinct volume with many additions, and shall I avail myself of your kindness in offering to do any thing for me in Italy. You will be able to inform me of some changes that have taken place, since the year 1770 when I left it; and to clear up some things which I did not observe in so explicit a manner as I could wish, though I did not lose much time during the long residence that I made there. Most of my friends are dead, who could be of real service to you. I shall certainly remember to give you letters for Cirilli[5] of Naples, and the Abbé Fortis[6] of Venice, whom you will find both instructive and agreeable.

As to modern publications upon the political Oeconomy of Italy, I know of none. When the Italians treat of this subject, they say little about their own country, but load their books with quotations from English or French writers. The best book that I have seen is the 'Lezioni del commercio o sia del Oeconomia civile' by the Abate Genovesi,[7] whom I knew very well at Naples; but nine tenths of this book, tho' useful, are general maxims, and not much is said of the civil or political Œconomy of Italy. I brought with me from Venice 5 vol. of the *Giornale d'Italia*, a periodical paper published by Grisselini,[8] which had sometimes tolerably good matter; tho' even that was too much charged with extracts from writers on this side of the Alps. Whether it has been continued of late years, I do not know; for I never could get any information about it from our London booksellers. I do not imagine, that La Lande will afford you the assistance you would wish to receive.[9] I recommended him to

[4] Symonds had contributed two papers in *Annals of Agriculture and other useful arts*, collected and published by Arthur Young, 46 vols., London, 1784–1815: 'Upon the Soil of Italy', iii (1785), 15–46, and 'Upon the climate of Italy', ibid., 137–66.

[5] Domenico Cirillo (1739–99), professor of botany and subsequently of medical pathology at the university of Naples and author of several important works in both fields of study.

[6] Alberto Fortis (1741–1803), naturalist and traveller, who had some personal knowledge of the eastern Mediterranean through which Bentham was planning to travel; in 1771 he had published his *Saggio sopra le is. di Cherso ed Ossero.*

[7] Antonio Genovesi (1713–69), philosopher and political economist, a lecturer at the university of Naples. His *Lezioni di commercio, o sia d'economia civile* was first published in two parts in 1766 and 1767, and republished in 1769 in an enlarged edition.

[8] Francesco Griselini (1717–83), traveller and writer.

[9] Joseph Jérôme Le Français de Lalande (1732–1807), a well-known French astronomer, was the author of many miscellaneous works as well as treatises on astronomy. His *Voyage d'un Français en Italie, en 1765–66*, was published at Paris in nine volumes in 1769.

our *young travellers*, in preference to the rest of the voyage-writers, because he has a *few* chapters upon the weights and measures, products, and manufactures of the several governments in Italy; but unfortunately these bear not the least proportion to the rest of his book; which is filled with dry and defective accounts of pictures, etc., unmercifully retailed from other writers.

It is very probable, that some business will call me to London next month; and should it take place, I will call upon you, tho' only for a quarter of an hour; as I must hasten hither to finish my lectures. Should I not go to London, I will not fail to send you the letters.

I am, Dear Sir.
with great respect,
yr obedient
humble servant
John Symonds.

Trinity College Cambridge
April 28 1785.

P.S. May I ask the favour of you to order yr. servant to carry the inclosed, when he goes into the City? If it is carried within a week, it will be time enough.

528

From Samuel Bentham[1]

29 April/10 May 1785

Critchoff April 29th 1785 O.S.

I can send you but a few lines now, and what I have chiefly to tell you is that Notman is arrived.[2] He has been here these 5 or 6 days but I myself was from home till yesterday. He brings me only one or two scraps of letters from you and one letter from my father. You must imagine the pleasure and delight it gave me to have such fresh certain and particular news of you all. When I asked him how old he thought my father looked to be; he said, about sixty. As for

528. [1] B.M. IV: 156–7. Autograph. Docketed by Bentham: '1785 Apr. 29/May 10. / S.B. Crechoff / to / J.B. Linc. Inn. / Farrier wanted.'

Addressed: 'Jere^{y} Bentham Esqr. / Lincoln's Inn / London.'

[2] On Notman see letter 524, n. 2. The friends he had recruited in Newcastle arrived about a month later (B.M. IV: 163–4).

you as I think you should give up all future pretentions for becoming Penny Postman you might as well be more sedate and /not/ make everybody race to keep your footpace. Poor Notman complains heavily of the fatigue you made him suffer.

He has brought nobody with him, but gives me all reason to expect his freinds everyday. As he came from Riga by Post he left a chest in which he had the patterns of cordage Sailcloth etc. to be forwarded by the conveyance which brings the other people.

I do not well understand Debraw's letter[3] which accompanied the razer but I fear that he had little reason to conclude that any steel when cast would be better than ordinary cast steel. I hope I shall have talked the matter over with him and even made the experiment before I can have any answer from you.

I have little doubt but he may have the malt spirit distillery upon the terms of receiving half the encreased profits for 10 years. Any new fabrick which may be found suitable to the estate may be engaged in on terms much more advantageous.

The box which Notman waited 3 weeks in expectation of and which you wrote of your having sent by the Coach he never received.

I hope you have somehow or other avoided any engagement with Robinson[4] and from what I hear of his character I shall be very anxious about your having taken so active a part in some of my commissions as to put it in his power to be very injurious to you. His friend the gardener[5] is said to be little better; but of him if he comes I can soon get rid of and at the same time oblige some acquaintance. All the other persons that I am in expectation of I dont doubt but I shall be well satisfied with.

As I may now find occasion to keep above an hundred horses for which [I] must answer and may use in every respect as my own, it would be of much importance to me to find an english farrier who at the same time that he would shoe or instruct others to shoe the horses much better than they are at present, might be entrusted with the expenditure of the corn and hay of which in other events I shall unavoidably be more or less cheated. Such a man by Notman's account I may possibly get for 20£ a year as I do not

[3] Dr John Debraw (d. 1788). Sometime apothecary to Addenbrooke's Hospital at Cambridge, Debraw was the author of one or two scientific works. On him see also letter 579 and note. His letter is missing.

[4] Not identified.

[5] This was probably the gardener named Roebuck, who turned up the following month, together with a trollop of a wife, in company with the four craftsmen and experts from Newcastle recruited by Notman. He was passed on into the employment of Prince Dashkov, who reported a year later to Samuel Bentham: 'Roebuck is still here, very much a burthen to me.' (B.M. IV: 301–2).

require that he should read or write. He will apply to his freinds for me: but should any such person by chance fall in your way do not decline engaging him. He might eat with my servants with whom he would not fare badly, but I think as far as 30$ a year enough wages.

Adieu it is 3 o'Clock in the morning I am writing this bit of letter and I have not my recollection well about me.

529

From Yakov Ivanovich Smirnov[1]

10 May 1785

Mr. Smirnov's Compliments to Mr. Bentham has recd. to days Post from Mr. Hynam the following: 'I pray you to Send a Line to Mr. Bentham and inform him I recd. his Last Letter for Prince Potemkin. The three former I also received. They were delivered to the Prince by Mr. Samborsky. You may add—the Prince expressed much Satisfaction, and has ordered them to be translated into the Russian Language. Mr. Bentham will soon hear from the Prince.'

Clifford Street
May 10th 1785

530

To Joseph Townsend[1]

12 May 1785 (Aet 37)

Lincolns Inn May 12 1785.

Dear Sir

Here am I still: how much longer I shall be here, I do not as yet precisely know: nor by what track nor by what ~~manner~~

529. [1] B.M. IV: 160. Docketed by Bentham: '1785 May 10 / Mr. S.B. and Pot / Smirnov Clifford Street / to / J.B. Lincs Inn / Quoting Hynam's reporting Potemkin's receipt of J.B.'s 4 letters.' Stamped 'PENNY POST PAID'.

Addressed: 'Mr. Bentham / No. 6 Old Buildings / Lincolns Inn / London.'

See letter 526, n. 3.

530. [1] U.C. IX: 10–11. Autograph, brouillon, with corrections. Docketed by Bentham: '1785 May 12 / S.B. and Pot. / J.B. Linc. Inn / to / Rev. Jo. Townsend Truro / Brouillon / For Miss Kirtland to go to a Wiltshire Dairy.'

/conveyance/ I shall migrate elsewhere. I am waiting for letters from Petersburgh: ~~which is like the countryman's waiting~~ /that is to say I am in the state and condition of your friend Horace's countryman who /kept/ waiting/ for the river to run itself dry. Thanks to my ~~stars~~ /sins/, I have to do with one of the most indolent men of one of the most indolent nations upon the face of God~~'s~~ /almightys/ earth. I write for him letter after letter about business purely his own. He, I am told, expresses much satisfaction: and how do you think he testifies it? You would suppose, by answering them: no such thing: he orders them to be translated out of my dog-French into Russian: for what purpose, or for whose use, I can't pretend to guess: not for his own most certainly: as he makes at least as much use of the French as of the Russ. However he talks of writing soon, and there the matter rests.

As for you, I will /almost/ venture to prophesy you will not quit ~~the land of~~ Tin /island/ in a hurry: the gnomes of Cornwall have ~~bound~~ /encompassed/ you with silver chains. I see the would-be Gulliver struggling to get loose: in vain, a swarm of little Pluto's keep fast hold of him by the heart-strings.

As to Sir Edward Bayntun,[2] I am much obliged to him for his good intentions: they are like Prince Potemkin's, of lasting stuff, not to be ~~demolished~~ /put an end to/ by performance. I should rather have said, for his declarations: which assuredly is full as much as I had any title to expect.

To come back to Milk maids. You gave me as your /decided/ opinion that no such animals would be to be met with, born in two countries at once. After great consideration and some enquiry, ~~I do believe~~ /am inclin'd to think/ you are in the right. Indeed I ~~knew but of~~ /never cou'd hear of more than/ one sort of being that ~~into and with /have been/~~ /is to be found/ in more than one place at a time, in any period of its existence. I think therefore I have done something in finding in /the person/ a Niece of my all ~~performing~~

Printed with incorrect date, Bowring, x, 139–40.

Miss Kirtland was (allegedly) the niece of the horticulturist, Henderson, whom Bentham had engaged to take to Russia with a view to his entering into Potëmkin's service (see letter 531). For further reference to her Wiltshire visit see letter 534. It is evident from this letter that Bentham was hoping to receive instructions from Potëmkin how to arrange his journey; and the only reply he is known to have received from Potëmkin (letter 531) confirmed that he was expected to come by the southern route unless this presented difficulties.

[2] Sir Edward Bayntun Rolt (1710–1800), 1st bart., of Spye Park, near Chippenham, Wilts. The reference to him remains unexplained; both this and the beginning of the following paragraph indicate that Bentham had received a letter from Townsend which is now missing.

capable Scotchman an intelligent well-bred young /gentle/ woman of about 25, who to the theoretical merit of having imbibed sound chemical principles from her Uncle, adds the practical requisite of having been born and bred in a Cheshire Dairy. You will say that is doing the business but by halves: true: but it would be more than half done, if I could get her regenerated in Wiltshire. Now how to bring about this good work? of my self /you know/ I can do nothing: ~~I can pretend~~ to the /art/ of regeneration ~~no more /I can have no more pretend~~ I make no more pretensions/ than to its simple ~~forerunner~~ prototype. But you, my venerable friend, are alike an adept in both: the ~~one is~~ /last/ your ~~choice~~ /pastime is,/ ~~the other is /and~~ the first/ your trade. Now then how shall I contrive to pay you: for everyone must live by his trade: and yours is ~~not~~ none of those which ~~people dont~~ /men are wont to/ live the worst by. ~~I wont pretend to pay you but put it into your hands~~/ Don't /be wicked now and/ think that I mean to propose to you/ to pay yourself by ~~making~~ /intermixing upon this occasion/ your pastime /with/ your trade: that would be curtailing you of a syllable, without making you a jot the richer: besides that my commission does not extend quite so far: /and [*several words crossed out*] sacred as the precedent is, it is possible she might have her scruples about acting/ the part of Ruth, though you were to be her Booz. I mean to pay you more liberally in your own coin. Pewsey, I am told, or the near neighbourhood of it is a second Canaan; don't be angry, I speak of its produce, not of its inhabitants. The ditches instead of mud are filled with milk: and the footpaths instead of gravel are cased with Cheese. You ~~must~~ /can not but/ know plenty of your *ouailles* or of their *commeres* who out of ~~courtesy~~ /Christian Charity/ aided by the moderate application of a more substantial motive would undertake this pious work. The process ~~would~~ /need/ not take up above a week: and any recompense you thought adequate, two or three guineas suppose, would be chearfully bestow'd. But what /you will say, is/ become of the Levites there ~~you'll say~~ all this while? Have a little patience. I have a piece of Malachites—(Ye heavenly powers! what a piece!) fit to make a breast-plate for the Angel Gabriel. ~~Indeed I know not but that it might~~ /Who can say it may not/ have served heretofore to that use? Stones you ~~know~~ /tell us/ have fallen from heaven before now and ~~this for aught I know~~ /why may not this/ may be one of them? Sure nothing half so beautiful ~~was ever~~ /could ever have been/ dug out of the earth. This /jewel/ my fair Cheese-maker, who ~~I am told~~ /I understand/ is a fossilist to boot, shall bring down in her lap, and deposit with pious gratitude in the sanctum sanctorum of Pewsey. To this ~~all~~ /shall/ be added about 50 or 60 specimens of Siberian ores: sent over by my Brother in days of yore as an earnest of better things to come. True it is these were put up in a bundle with your direction to them before I had thought of Pewsey in any other light than that of a place in which I had spent some pleasant hours, and might possibly, at I know not what distant period, spend more. But the handling of so much wealth hath made me mercenary: and I have vowed a vow, /a tremendous irrevocable vow,/ that your eyes shall never behold a single grain of them, unless wafted to Pewsey by that enviable conveyance.

When you see Lord Lansdown, you will hear of a great pie which was cut up at his house, and in which, alas! alas! I full well know, my reverend friend would have rejoiced to have had a finger. I cried out with a loud voice, where is he? They answer'd me and said, three hundred miles off, even in Cornwall: too busy and too wise, to leave mountains for ~~an~~ /horse-loads/ chip-bond-boxes. What could I do? There is an hour for pies as for other things. The hour of this pie was come: it had been kept till it ~~could be kept~~ /would keep/ no longer. But what hath kept, keeps still, and will have kept when pyes and custards are grown stale (how does my little custardophagus?) is the /sincere/ regard and esteem with which I am

/Dear Sir/ Your obliged friend and humble servant If /at this distance/ you can assist me, /I beg leave to propose/ the best mode of doing it that ~~you should send me~~ /in your answer to me/ you should inclose a letter addressed to the discreet matron ~~you make~~ /whom you honour with your/ choice of, ~~which~~ that I may forward it to her. The lady's name is Miss Kirtland. At any rate I beg your immediate answer, that other measures may be taken if this should fail.

531

FROM PRINCE POTËMKIN[1]

23 May/3 June 1785

Monsieur,

Je dois vous remercier pour les soins que vous vous etes donné dans l'execution des Commission dont vous avez bien voulu vous

531. [1] B.M. Add. Mss. 37520, fos. 34–5. A letter-book copy in a clerk's hand, followed by an English rendering.

For Bentham's concern to receive approval of some sort from Potëmkin, particu-

charger pour moi; le tems ne m'a pas permi de donner plutôt une resolution touchant les Objets dont vous me parlés; mais maintenant Je vous prie d'engager Monsieur Henderson a accompagner ces Gens a Petersburg, au cas que le trajet par la Mediterranée parut plus penible, d'autant plus qu'ici nous ferions les Arrangements necessaires et convenables, et que J'aurai beaucoup de facilité à les faire transporter par terre en Tauride.

Soyes persuade de ma reconnoisance pour toutes vos peines et de la Consideration distingué avec laquelle, J'ai l'honneur d'etre,

Monsieur,
votre tres humble Serviteur,
Prince Potemkin.

St. Petersburg.
le 23 May 1785.
A Monsieur
Monsieur Bentham—
a Londres.

532

From the Marquis of Lansdowne[1]

13 June 1785

Dear Mr. Bentham

Come and break fast here on Wednesday at nine o'clock and you'll meet a Frenchman who may be of use to you, as he is just come from making almost the same Tour—and I shall be happy to take your further commands.

I am
Most Truly,
Yrs.
L.

Monday.

larly about the route he was to follow, see letter 530; and for Henderson, see letter 543, n. 5.

532. [1] B.M. IV: 161–2. Autograph. Docketed by Bentham: '1785 June 13 / Ld. Lansdown, Berkeley Square / to J.B. Linc. Inn.'
Addressed: 'To Jer. Bentham Esq.'

533

From the Marquis of Lansdowne[1]

23 June 1785

Dear Mr. Bentham

Ld. Townsend certainly expects you at ½ past 3—I would call upon you, or carry you, but I am to go home from the House of Lords with Ld. Townsend[2]—This will give you an opportunity with Lady Townsend and Mr. Beresford[3] which I dare say you will make the most of—He lives on the left hand of Dover Street about the middle his name on the Door.

I want to see you about your Letters—
I am most Truly,
Yrs.
Lansdown

Thursday, 3 o'clock.

534

From Joseph Townsend[1]

25 June 1785

My very dear Sir

I crossed myself a thousand times when I saw the Breastplate. Had you never told me whence it came, I should have known that it belonged once to the Angel Gabriel. I am happy that it fell to Earth and happier still that it found the way to Pewsey. I never saw anything half so resplendent. With it there came a Magnetic Cristal of Iron of a most peculiar form, a non déscript, which I value

533. [1] B.M. IV: 166–7. Autograph. Docketed by Bentham: '1785 June 23 / Ld. Lansdown, Berkeley Square / to / J.B. Linc. Inn.'

Addressed: 'To Jer. Bentham Esq. / Lincoln's Inn.'

[2] George Townshend (1724–1807), 4th Viscount Townshend, a general in the army. He had been Lord Lieutenant in Ireland, 1767–72.

[3] Ann, Lady Townshend, née Montgomery, was the sister-in-law of the Irish politician, John Beresford (1738–1805), who had married her sister, Barbara.

534. [1] U.C. IX: 12. Autograph. Docketed by Bentham: '1785 June / For S.B. and Pot. / Townsend / to J.B. Linc. Inn'.

Addressed: 'Jeremy Bentham Esqr. / Lincoln's Inn / London.' Postmark: 'Pewsey / 27 IU.'

Partly printed, Bowring, x, 139–40. In reply to letter 530.

highly. Most of the Specimens are numbered and refer to some Catalogue. I wish you had copied out the Inventory: as many of the Substances are new to me—I was much disappointed, in not finding here my amiable Guest and fear by the shortness of her /stay/, that her abode was not agreeable.[2] I hope Solitude was her only objection to this Mansion and wish to persuade myself that my Housekeeper was not defective in attentions.

Have you seen a book lately published and now on sale at Rivingtons St. Pauls Church yard and at Taylors 56 Holborn called Dairying Exemplified by J. Warmley? This book professes to teach the Art of Cheese Making peculiar to every County. I shall depend upon hearing from you before you quit the Kingdom.

Ever most sincerely yours
Joseph Townsend

Pewsey 25 June 1785

535

To Horace St Paul[1]

5 July 1785 (Aet 37)

Lincoln's Inn, July 5th, 1785.

Dear Sir,—I take shame to myself for not having taken an earlier notice of your favour of the | | last.[2] The case is, I am preparing for a *demenagement* longer and more formidable than your's. My Brother has been for this twelvemonth past commanding a Batallion quartered at Prince Potemkin's estate at Krichof in White Russia. In a fortnight's time I hope to set out in my way to join him by way of France, Italy, Smyrna, Constantinople and Crim

[2] Subsequent events indicated that Miss Kirtland, like Henderson, was not what she professed to be, and that she neither had nor intended to have any interest in cheese-making. See letter 556, n. 1.

535. [1] George Grey Butler, *Colonel St Paul of Ewart, Soldier and Diplomat*, 2 vols., London, 1911, i, pp. cxxi–cxxii.

After a period of service in the Austrian army, Colonel Horace St Paul became friendly with Lord Stormont during the latter's term as British ambassador at Vienna (1763–72). In 1772, after retiring from the Austrian service, he was appointed secretary to the embassy at Paris, where Stormont had just been appointed ambassador, and during Stormont's absences he remained in charge of the embassy. He retired in 1776 and thereafter resided at Chertsey until, in 1787, he moved permanently to Ewart, which he had purchased some time before. For his earlier career and his early contacts with Bentham and his friends see letter 325, n.16.

[2] Missing.

Tartary. My baggage is already on board the Mary Frances, Capt. Ro: Brine, which sailed a week or ten days ago for Nice, Genoa, Leghorn and Smyrna. I shall join the vessel the latter end of next month at Nice. Have you any commands for Paris?

Your removal from Thorpe removes the only reason I had for regretting the little chance there is of my ever reassuming my habitation in that place. If it was a mortification to me t'other day to see your card instead of the writer thereof, how much greater was it to be obliged, as I was more than once, to pass the door, I mean Mr. Langlois's,[3] without the possibility of sparing a few minutes to see whether you were not there!

Mr. Wilson is gone his circuit, after which he pays a visit to Aberdeen; his connection with Thorpe is I believe pretty well at an end, as well as mine: he begins to pick up guineas and reputation: he has lately lost his father, and got a brother-in-law. Douglas made about £3,000 by the Elections.[4]

I am much honoured and obliged by the place Mrs. St. Paul is pleased to keep for me in her remembrance. Excuse this hasty scrawl, and believe me to be with the truest respect and regard,

Dear Sir,

Your most obedient humble servant,

Jeremy Bentham.

P.S. I send your books, all but a small pamphlet which I hope will follow.

[3] Probably Benjamin Langlois (1727–1802), M.P. for St Germans, 1768–80. Langlois had been at Warsaw in the suite of the British envoy extraordinary, Lord Stormont, during the years 1756–9, and he became under-secretary of state when Stormont was appointed to the northern department in November 1779. Like St Paul he belonged to the circle of intimate friends which Stormont had built up during his long diplomatic career. For earlier reference to his contacts with members of Bentham's circle see letter 339.

[4] Bentham's friend, Sylvester Douglas, specialized in cases concerning controverted parliamentary elections, which were tried before committees of the House of Commons. The fees such barristers could command were lucrative.

536

To the Marquis of Carmarthen[1]

16 July 1785 (Aet 37)

Russian Project for opening the Amoor etc. J.B. to Ld. Carmarthen

Lincoln's Inn July 16th 1785

My Lord

Since I had the honour of laying before your Lordship the intelligence contained in my Brother's letters[2] relative to a project of the Russian Court for the effecting the navigation of the vast River Amoor which empties itself into the sea of Tartary, I have heard of the mercantile expedition which is fitting out from *hence* for attempting a Furr trade with China from King George's Sound on the Western coast of North America.[3]

536. [1] Public Record Office, F.O. 97/340. Autograph.

Francis Godolphin Osborne (1751–99), by courtesy title Marquis of Carmarthen until, in 1789, he succeeded his father as 5th Duke of Leeds, was Foreign Secretary in the younger Pitt's first ministry from 1783 till 1791. He had been one of Bentham's contemporaries at Westminster (Bowring, x, 31).

[2] This opening sentence indicates that earlier on the same day Bentham had had an interview with Carmarthen, probably in connection with his obtaining official letters of introduction to British envoys at the capitals through which he would pass during his now imminent journey to Russia. With a view to advancing his brother's affairs he had taken the opportunity to supply Carmarthen with copies of extracts from two of Samuel Bentham's letters relating to his interest in the Amur River and the Pacific trade. For the first of these, see letter 505 at n. 12. The second, briefer, extract from a letter dated 15/26 January 1785 (B.M. IV: 135–6) ran: 'I have now taken to Shipbuilding again with fresh spirit and am in hopes in the course of the summer to have tried some interesting experiments. Perhaps I may be able to make shift without the assistance of any Shipwright; but I am in great want of a rigger. I do not forget my Amur project, some of my Ship building experiments are subservient to it, and I am in hopes you will find me some assistants. Should I be engaged in any other kind of employment more agreable than such a distant expedition, I should still wish to have a hand in promoting it, and might possibly have the direction of it. Two or three young men who might become usefull on such an expedition if you happen to meet with such who are disposed to seek their fortune in this country I could get made Officers in my Batallion.' These copies immediately precede Bentham's letter in the Foreign Office file and are dated 16 July 1785, both at the head and also in explanatory footnotes supplied by Bentham.

[3] For the formation of the King George's Sound Company and the preparations for this undertaking, see V. T. Harlow, *The Founding of the Second British Empire*, volume 2, *New Continents and Changing Values*, 1964, pp. 419–25. P. I. Kabanov, *Amurskiy Vopros*, Blagoveshchensk, 1959, pp. 32–7, makes brief mention of Russian activities around and beyond the Sea of Okhotsk during the eighteenth century but has no reference to the expedition led by Billings alluded to here (see letter 505 and n. 13).

If however in other respects his Majesty were disposed, as your Lordship seemed to think he possibly might be, to view the Russian project with a favourable eye, I must confess I see nothing in the British enterprize that should forbid an Englishman from wishing to see his Majesty's assistance extended to the projects of his Imperial ally upon the plan which I ventured with all deference to suggest.

If I mistook not, your Lordship made no difficulty of acceding to the following propositions:

1. That the Russian enterprize, were the Court of Petersburgh to make a point of it, might unquestionably be carried into execution without the assistance of any hands from England.

2. That, were such assistance *imagined* to be necessary it might /at any rate/ be obtained, by offers the nature of which would be to dissolve the connection of the persons employ'd with his Majesty's service.

It seems to follow

3. That if on the other hand the expedition were to be carried on with the assistance of Officers under leave of absence from his Majesty, and by that means still remaining under his Majesty's dependence, such Officers might, for the purpose of any subsequent use which it might be proposed to make of their experience for the benefit of this country and of his Majesty's service, be consider'd as having virtually been employ'd all that time under his Majesty's command. Looking back to England as their country and to his Majesty as their patron, they would in effect be inspectors paid by Russia to give *us* information of *her* proceedings and achievements.

'But', it may possibly be said, 'would not the object of the Russian expedition be likely to interfere with ours?'—From what I understand at present I must confess I can see no sufficient ground for entertaining any such apprehension. The latter being fitted out by mere traders, with no other than mere commercial views, will confine its course to the track indicated by that trade.[a] The former, having for its main and probably for its sole object the extension of Geographical knowledge, and the occupation of some port calculated to facilitate at some future period the navigation of those as yet unknown seas, and in particular to facilitate by that means the communication between Kamshatka and the less remote parts of the Russian Empire, seems much more of a nature to contribute in the character of an expedition of discovery or otherwise to the *promotion* of any trade which may be attempted by us in that part of the world than, in the character of a commercial project, to interfere with and prejudice that trade.

As to the River Amoor, according to the maps the mouth of it is situated in Lat. 54, seven degrees of latitude beyond the spot pitched upon for the utmost limit of the British enterprize.[(a)] And as to this point your Lordship will be pleased to observe that as far as appears from the intelligence I have hitherto received, neither the views of the Empress nor of her Minister Prince Potemkin have as yet extended to any thing farther than the effecting the navigation of that vast river and of the adjacent seas. The combining with this expedition of *discovery* an enterprise of *trade* is nothing more than a random project of my Brother's own, grounded on the then supposed improbability of any such undertaking's being set on foot from hence.

If then that navigation should prove impracticable, we should be but as we were: if practicable, it must be by means of harbours or other convenient stations, of which we as well as they might have the use.

Even allowing that the Russian project of discovery would end in the extension of the trade on Russian bottoms, and that that trade would be of more disservice than service to our own trade in that part of the globe, yet, taking for granted /as above,/ that it would be in the power of Russia to carry on her enterprizes without us and in spite of us, it may deserve consideration whether good policy should not afford us motives for doing what depends upon us towards insuring her good offices in that part of the world, and at any rate averting any ill offices of hers, to which any change in her dispositions might chance at any future period to expose us. It is proposed, I understand, to leave at King George's Sound a Mate with a few men to strengthen and extend the intercourse with the Natives. If then the Russians were so inclined, there will hardly, I believe, be a doubt of its being in their power, to crush this infant settlement, and *that*, if they thought it necessary, by such underhand measures, (such as instilling jealousies into the Natives, raising quarrels apparently accidental among subordinates, and the like) as would leave us no ostensible grounds for calling them to account. Small as their present force is upon those seas, there is no doubt, I believe, of its being more than sufficient for such a purpose, indepen-

(a) I understand it is not proposed that the ships King George and Queen Charlotte should stretch in any part of their course further North than lat. 47.

dently of any accession of strength that might be derived to it from the opening of the Amoor.

With a view to any such mischance, the arrangement proposed, might, I should humbly conceive be of advantage to this country in two ways:

1. As tending to restrain them by the ties of gratitude from so much as conceiving any sentiments to our prejudice.[(b)]

2. At the worst, as a means of enabling us to counteract with greater advantage the operation of any such adverse sentiments, if any such should happen at any future period to be entertained.

In a general point of view, I should humbly conceive that it can not but be of advantage to us that that powerful nation should be confirmed as much as possible in the habit they seem to be in of looking up on every occasion to this country for assistance; and that every measure that can tend to rivet them in that sort of dependency may in so far at least be regarded as worthy our adoption.

Upon the whole I flatter myself your Lordship will join me in opinion that whether or no it be *their interest* to *receive* that sort of assistance from us, it is at any rate *our* interest to *lend* it them: and that if they can be made to fancy it would be of use to them, the advantage of such an arrangement would be much more unquestionable on our side than on theirs: and lastly that all this holds equally good whether it be or be not likely that their interests in that part of the world should clash with our's.

His Majesty's known love of science, and the particular favour he has been pleased to extend to those branches that are connected with enterprizes of discovery, afford a further hope, that an arrangement of this sort might afford my Brother, and any other of his Majesty's subjects who might come to have a concern in it, an occasion of exerting their humble endeavours to render their services *personally* acceptable to their Sovereign. If, for the promotion of any branch of science or with any other such views as may be expected from his Majesty's wisdom, he were pleased to honour them or any of them with any special instructions or commands, I need scarcely beg of your Lordship to imagine with what zeal they would of course embrace the opportunity

(b) That considerations of that kind are not wholly without their influence upon nations, the reception given by the very nation in question to Captns. Clerk and Gore will I trust be thought sufficient to demonstrate.

of endeavouring to shew themselves not unworthy of such his gracious notice.

I have the honour to be, with all respect
My Lord
Your Lordship's much obliged
and most obedient humble Servant
Jeremy Bentham.

The Rt. Hon. the
Marquis of Carmarthen
etc., etc., etc.

537

To the Marquis of Carmarthen[1]

16 July 1785 (Aet 37)

Lincoln's Inn July 16th, 1785

My Lord,

I take the liberty of inclosing in a separate paper a letter[2] which your Lordship will be pleased to make such use of as may be proper.

If it had been your Lordship's business that I was delaying instead of my /own/, I should have had many apologies to make, or to speak more truly, I should have taken care not to /have/ given occasion for any. I find I have still a fortnight good, and within that time shall hold myself in readiness to receive any commands which your Lordship may have to lay on me.

I suppose your Lordship has heard that *Pillings* or *Billings*[3] the person mentioned in my Brothers letters is just set out on an expedition of discovery; not by water but by land, which is expected to take him up some years: and that advice has lately been received at Petersburgh that the Chinese have cut off all intercourse with Russia; a measure which may probably enough have some influence on the Amoor project, though in what particular way it may perhaps be difficult to pronounce.

537. [1] Public Record Office, F.O. 97/340. Autograph. Docketed: 'Lincolns Inn July 16th. 1785. / Mr. Bentham.'

Addressed: 'To / The Marquis of Carmarthen / etc. etc. etc.'

[2] Presumably letter 536.

[3] See.letter 505 and n. 13.

I have the intelligence about Pillings, accompanied with several details, from an intelligent person just arrived from Petersburgh. But I suppose your Lordship is already in possession of every thing belonging to it from a more authentic source.

I have the honour to be, with the highest respect My Lord
Your Lordships much obliged
and most obedient humble Servant
Jeremy Bentham

538

From the Marquis of Lansdowne[1]

late July 1785

Dear Mr. Bentham,

I had a Head ach yesterday and the Day before, which made it impossible for me to write—I send you all which I have been able to write to day—I have desir'd the Abbé Morellet[2] to give you Letters for Lyons and Marseilles, as he has very good connections in both places—I have desir'd Monsr. Rayneval[3] to give you one for the French Ambassador at Constantinople—You must take your chance about Dijon and Genoa /and Montpelier/—tho' I dare say Monsr. Rayneval will give you Letters for them if you can find a proper moment to ask him—I will take my chance of to morrow's

538. [1] B.M. IV: 168–9. Autograph. Docketed by Bentham: '1785 July / Ld. Lansdown Bowood / to / J.B. Linc. Inn / letters of introduction.'

Printed Bowring, x, 148. This and the next letter both immediately precede letter 540 and can be attributed to about the last week of July.

[2] André Morellet (1727–1819), law reformer and political economist, an associate of Diderot and the encyclopaedists. Lansdowne had met him in Paris in 1771 and invited him to come and visit him in England early in the following year, and thereafter maintained a constant friendship and correspondence with him. As the translator of Beccaria, Morellet was already known by reputation to Bentham, who, in 1778, had written to him sending copies of *A Fragment on Government* and *A View of the Hard-Labour Bill* (letter 250; see also letter 249, n. 1). This letter, unlike those sent on the same occasion to other French scholars, had failed to draw a response (letter 267).

[3] Joseph Mathias Gerard de Rayneval (1746–1812), *premier commis* in the French department for foreign affairs from 1774 to 1792. During the autumn of 1782 Vergennes on three occasions had sent Rayneval as his personal representative to conduct with Lansdowne the crucial preliminary negotiations which laid the foundations of the Peace of Versailles of 1783 by which the American war of independence was ended. During these meetings Lansdowne and Rayneval established a cordial relationship. Nevertheless, according to Bowring's information, Rayneval gave Bentham but a cold reception when he passed through Paris and furnished a letter of introduction to Count Choiseul, the French ambassador at Constantinople, merely saying 'that the bearer was held in estimation by Lord Lansdowne' (Bowring, x, 149).

Post finding you with three Letters, one for Rouen, another for Monsr. Torryel,[4] a celebrated lawyer at Paris, and another upon my own account to the Abbe Morellet.

I beg to assure you that you go with the affectionate good Wishes of all this Family. Lady Lansdown and Miss Fox desire [me] to mention theirs particularly—My last advice to you is upon no account to be taken in to stay among Barbarians—They can make you no offer worth your acceptance, except they were to name you Embassador to China—I own that would tempt me. Come back soon, and bring your Brother with you, if he does not get a provision ample enough to live upon here in a few years, and as well secur'd as the Bank of England—In the mean time get into no Intrigues to serve either English or Russian, no not even with a handsome Lady, if any Politicks should be mix'd with it, for I have said in all the material Letters, that I would be answerable for every part of your Conduct publick or private.

The Abbe Morellet may possibly offer to carry you to Monsr. Rayneval—but in your place, I wd. go alone—but Don't say I advis'd you to do so.

I have told Sir H. Mann[5] that you would write me an account of his health.

I will send you a Line for Blankett[6] in case you meet with him.

The Post is going and I must deferr the rest till to morrow.

I am very Truly
Yrs.
Lansdown.

539

From the Marquis of Lansdowne[1]

late July 1785

The bearer, Captain Williamson,[2] appears to me a very intelligent person. He has been last year at Constantinople, and the Greek

[4] Not identified.

[5] Sir Horace Mann, 1st bart. (1701–86), who had been British representative at Florence since 1738. By this time he was in failing health.

[6] On Captain Blankett, see letter 398, n. 4.

539. [1] Bowring, x, 148–9.

This is clearly the continuation which Lansdowne promised at the end of his previous letter (538). Both are acknowledged together in letter 540.

[2] Perhaps John Williamson, appointed lieutenant R.N. 1774, commander, 1780, and captain, 1782.

Islands; and I thought it might be agreeable to you to make his acquaintance, which has made me desire him to call on you.

I hope my servant told you, as I had not time to write as I intended, that we would have kept the *Voyages de la Grèce*,[3] to be bound, before we sent them; but, as you will carry them on board ship, I thought it might be agreeable to you to have them half-bound in some fashion of your own, that might make them more portable.

I hope you will have the goodness to present a sword from me to your brother, which you must pass for your own, to avoid the custom-houses through which you pass. Although a Russian colonel, I hope he will accept an English sword. I do assure you, that we are all (Miss Fox included, who is sitting by me) concerned for your going, independent of the loss of your company, which we always have considered as a resource, when the interested and the factious deserted us. We are apprehensive that you will lend yourself to some plan which interested and ignorant people may open to you; and after detaining and robbing you of time—which may be more reputably, at least, if not more usefully to yourself employed—may desert you. This observation applies equally to your brother's situation. I told Count Woronzow[4] that I meant, if I had continued in administration, to have placed him in some advantageous situation here. Count Woronzow knows him, and wishes to see you. If you please, make use of my name to him.

I am obliged to write in great haste, because Captain W. and a good deal of company are by, and waiting for it.—Ever yours,

Lansdown.

[3] Marie Gabriel Auguste Florent Choiseul-Gouffier, *Voyages Pittoresques de la Grèce*, Paris, 1782. A second volume appeared in 1809.

[4] Count Semën Romanovich Vorontsov (1744–1832) succeeded Simolin as Russian minister in London in 1784. He was a brother of Princess Dashkova, with whom (as with her son) Samuel Bentham had become acquainted after his return from Siberia at the end of 1782.

540

To the Marquis of Lansdowne[1]

c. 31 July 1785 (Aet 37)

My Lord

I have been perfectly oppressed of late with so many repeated marks of your Lordship's kindness. The Count Choiseul-Gouffier's Voyages are certainly so much the better and more convenient for not being bound up.[2] Your Lordship ~~has certainly~~ must have a high opinion of my honesty to trust me with so magnificent a sword (as that I am to carry to my Brother). I hope[3] /it will come out/ to come of as clear as Mr. Roger North who in his life of his Brother the Lord Keeper Guildford, to shew how ~~honest and~~ trustworthy he was tells us of the ~~honour~~ his being appointed cash-keeper to keep ~~the half crown his~~ fees his Lordship received when counsel and of the alarm he took at having a piece of round glass ~~tumble~~ fall out of his pocket for Fear his brother should suspect him of having convey'd thither one of the half-crowns which he had got /earn'd/ that morning by making motions of course.[4]

It will do me Knight's service on my /travels/ way through France and Italy I shall make it glitter in the eyes of every lady I meet that they may ~~ask me who I~~/ give me a pretense/ to tell them who I had it from. But as to the Russian Colonel, I ~~fear~~ doubt the chance of reaching him may be much lessened by the circuit it will have to take.

Capt. Williamson[5] left town earlier than he at first expected, so that ~~I had not quite so much opportunity of proffer~~ I did not have quite so much /advantage/ as I had hoped ~~to have done~~ by of the opportunity ~~your Lordship had your~~ /Lordship's kind attention thence/ the goodness to throw into my ~~hands~~ way.—I have not yet

540. [1] B.M. IV: 170–1. Autograph. Draft with many corrections. Docketed by Bentham: '1785 July / J.B. Linc. Inn / to / Ld. Lansdown Bowood / Thanks for Choiseuils Voyages Sword etc.'

This letter acknowledges both letters 538 and 539, particularly the second. Passages at the end appear good ground for attributing it to about the last day of July, a few days before Bentham's departure on 6 August on the first stage of his journey to Russia.

[2] See letter 539, n. 3.

[3] The rest of this paragraph is scored out.

[4] See Roger North, *The Lives of the Norths*, 3 vols., London, 1890, i, 117, para. 131.

[5] See letter 539, n. 2.

found time nor perhaps if the truth were ever known assurance enough to profit by the word your Lordship /was pleased/ to drop in my behalf at Count Woronzoff's.[6] Your Lordship is certainly at the bottom of a very flattering letter of introduction which the President Fischer[7] has been kind enough to offer me of his own accord to the Conte de Montacute[8] Governor of Leghorn. The President is /by this time/ set out on his return deeply regretting the combination of untoward incidents which deprived him of the opportunity of profiting /so much as he could have wished to have done/ by the /Abbe Morellet's/ recommendation ~~he was happy enough to obtain promise the Abbe Morellet to your Lordships.~~ By my carelessness I let slip an opportunity I think I might have had /without much difficulty/ of getting letters from a Genovese /Marquis/ to whom it fell in my way t'other day to show some little civilities, a man of quality highly spoken of by President Fischer and the Conte de Kersaint[9] which will be the greater loss as Genoa is a place I shall have to spend a week or ten days at without having access to a creature there unless perhaps it be the British Consul whoever he may be.

I think now to set out /for Paris/ within ten days, and within that time shall hope to receive the last and greatest marks of your Lordship's /goodness partiality to me./ ~~kindness which will never fail to meet with corresponding gratitude in the breast of one who has the honour to be with the truest respect and attachment~~

I have the honour to be

My Lord etc.

Linc. Inn July 1785

My Lord

I have received at different times letters for the following persons (I feel some compunction at the thoughts of having given so much exercise to hands so much better employed in wielding the reins of government)/I am in haste, I go./ Do not measure the

[6] See letter 539, n. 4.

[7] Perhaps Johann Bernhard Fischer, a Prussian state councillor and Commissary for husbandry in the province of Anspach; he was a member of various agricultural societies. On him see *The Correspondence of... Sir John Sinclair of Ulbster*, 2 vols., 1831, ii, 371–2.

[8] Not identified.

[9] Count Gui Pierre de Coetnempren Kersaint (1742–93), a French naval officer and political writer.

depth of my respect or the strength of my gratitude by the length of my letter but believe me to be

Your Lordship's most devoted

J.B.[10]

541

To Jeremiah Bentham[1]

7 August 1785 (Aet 37)

Brighthelmstone Sunday Aug. 7.
12 o'clock 1785.

Hond. Sir,

Having a few minutes to spare I cannot employ them better than by devoting them to your amusement. I am here on the point of embarking on board the | | Captn. Burton for Dieppe. I arrived here yesterday by the Coach at about 6, and should have found the intermediate time hang rather heavy on my hands, had it not been for the agreable woman who is sitting opposite me, a Mrs. Holdham wife of Mr. Holdham, whose name was Shuttleworth, which /being a younger Brother of my old friend Bob S./ he changed for his mother's estate.[2] Her husband lives at a place called *Sochez* or

[10] The sheet on which this draft is written also contains the following unexplained financial calculation.

Principal	75 – 0 – 0
Interest at 4 pr. cent viz 3£ a year for ten years from May 13th 1775 to May 13th 1785	30 – 0 – 0
Do. from May 13th 1775 to July 13th 1775 being two months	0 – 10 – 0
Do. from July 13th to July 19	0 – 1 – 0
	£105 – 11 – 0

541. [1] B.M. IV: 174–5. Autograph. Docketed by Jeremiah Bentham: 'Fils Jeremy / Letter datd. Brighthelmstead / Augt. 7 1785.' Copy by Jeremiah Bentham, B.M. IV: 176.

Addressed: 'Jeremiah Bentham Esq / Queens Square Place / Westminster.'

[2] Bentham's travelling companion was Elizabeth, née Whitmore, second wife of the Rev. Charles Edward Holden (1750–1821), who was the fourth son of James Shuttleworth and Mary Holden and who formally took the name and arms of Holden in lieu of Shuttleworth in 1791. Robert ('Bob') Shuttleworth (d. 1816), Bentham's contemporary at Westminster School, was James's eldest son and in 1775 succeeded to the family estate of Gawthorpe, Lancs.

Sauchai or some such name 5 miles from Dieppe with a Mr. Wynne[3] brother of a Sir | | Wynne with whom they are upon a visit till they can suit themselves with a house. An accident which befel this lady and myself in common at the Coach office at Charing-cross threw us into the same vehicle the stage-coach instead of the Post-Coach alias Machine which we had both paid for, and as she is a pleasing well-bred woman, I at least have no reason to repent the change. I was denied admission into the Machine in which I had taken a place paying the whole passage, and I was glad, at the expence of a person who had a still worse title than myself, to get admission into the Stage Coach in which I had not taken a place. During the wrangle the Machine drove off, and I thought myself fortunate in being able to lay an embargo on the Stage-Coach, till the Usurper a dirty Barber, could be turned out. I know I had a right to take a Post-chaise at the Coach owner's expence, but I did not care to load myself with that charge trusting for my indemnification to a lawsuit which I should not be in the way to superintend.

The rest of the company consisted of a Mr. Bourgeois a perfumer I think he is in the Hay-Market a very decent intelligent useful man, and three Maid-Servants who came down to prepare a house for the reception of Lady | | who /is/ expected here to-day. Mr. Bourgeois having found a friend here whom he was to meet, and the Maids being gone upon their business, Mrs. H who had been disappointed by some accident of a gentleman whom her husband had engaged to conduct her, was not sorry I suppose for want of a better Cavaliere Servante to put herself under my protection. We went to the play and supped ~~tete a~~ together, I was going to say tête a tête, which would not have been true, as the tête a tête was spoilt by one of the aforesaid Maid-servants whom she had engaged to be her bed-fellow, and who came in at the time that was presented to her, before we thought of going to the play which does not finish here till very late. In justice to truth and to the Lady I could do no less than tell you who she had for a bedfellow, lest you should suspect anybody else.

The play-house is much prettier and the performers much better than I could have expected: the women in particular a very decent set, at the head of whom figures Mrs. Wilson,[4] the rest almost all of

[3] Unidentified; possibly the younger brother of Sir Watkin Williams Wynn, 4th bart. (1748–89), of Wynnstay, Denbighshire. Sauchay is a village about five miles to the east of Dieppe and about the same distance from the coast.

[4] Mrs Wilson, née Adcock, entered upon her career as an actress in the early 'seventies and married the actor, Richard Wilson. She died in 1786. *The Castle of*

them either act or look well, or both, and even sing well: the men but so-so: indeed they are in every respect *over-womaned*, the females being so numerous that two of them in the Castle of Andalusia (that was the play) took the men's parts.

Mr. Stanhope[5] (Ld. Harrington's brother) Mrs. H tells me is pulling the devil by the tail at Dieppe—/over/ hearing two Bailiffs who had just been arresting a friend of his mention his own name he had just time enough to make his escape from them in slippers in a cock-boat, sacrificing the place he had under the Prince of Wales. Mr. and Mrs. Smith[6] who went over about a year ago with their ten children in the hopes of living upon £7 or £800 a year returned ⟨t'⟩ other day after spending 2,000—A part of it went in law expences on account of the young gentlemen who were for boxing their french companions a l'Anglaise.—

I have no time to read over this scrawl, though I have some doubts whether you will find it intelligible. The Coach-business was such a Chaos that it would have taken two sheets of paper to unravel it.

I left orders for Cox[7] to be sent to you and saw it put up for that purpose—likewise Pole Carew's Mss[8] under cover to you.

The lady, at least if she be like some I know, will think I have been sacrificing rather too long to duty at the expence of politeness, I can therefore no longer defer subscribing myself

Dear and Honoured Sir
Your's ever
Jeremy Bentham

Mrs. H's husband was round the world last time with Capt. Cook. Sailing ⟨is⟩ /or rather was/ his profession, but it is still my old friend Bob Shuttleworth's passion—You remember him at Westm School. He is going out again soon in a Yatch that cost him 3,000 gorgeous with mahogany as King Ahab's house was with ivory. The

Andalusia, in which she was performing on this occasion, was a comic opera by the Dublin actor turned dramatist, John O'Keefe (1747–1833).

[5] Henry Fitzroy Stanhope (1754–1828), younger brother of Charles Stanhope (1753–1829), 3rd Earl of Harrington. At the end of 1782 he had joined the party of Charles James Fox, which enjoyed the patronage of the Prince of Wales, and in consequence he had lost his seat in parliament at the general election of 1784.

[6] Not identified.

[7] Archdeacon William Coxe (1747–1828), the historian, had recently published *Travels into Poland, Russia, Sweden and Denmark. Interspersed with historical relations and political inquiries. Illustrated with charts and engravings*, 2 vols., London, 1784.

[8] See also letter 571. The nature of this manuscript is not known. Presumably it related to Carew's common interest with Bentham in penal reform.

three brothers are sometimes good friends, sometimes fighting, and Bob calls his servants to turn his brother Charles Shuttleworth out of doors. He (Bob) has settled £300 a year upon an old mistress whom he renew'd acquaintance with since his marriage and went off with to Paris for six or seven months. A French man has since made her an honest woman. Bob had originally 20,000 a year. He sold an estate t'other day for 25,000£.

542

To Jeremiah Bentham[1]

17 August 1785 (Aet 37)

Paris, Wednesday Augst. 17. 1785.

Hond. Sir,

I scribble in haste from Mr. Pattle's[2] Country house at Argenteuil, formerly the House of the Marquis du Chatelet, and Residence of Voltaire, present Mrs. Villette, Mr. Pattle, Captn and Mrs. Brook and Mr. Roger Metcalfe,—Mr. P. has been venting a multitude of obliging Reproaches against you for not writing to him,—I dined with him on Saturday last, the day of my Arrival, and the next day, after which a large posse of us went to see the Count d'Artois *Bagatelle* at | | about a league from Paris.

I send you some Specimens of warm Cloathing—for the Extremities, you will let me know at a future period, which you like best, I can find some method or other of supplying you,—They go by favor of Captn. and Mrs. Brook—a pair of Stockings of Vigogna Wool for Understockings when your Legs are cold, a pair of Stocks, Do. a pair of Gloves, Do.—a pair of Beaver (the Smooth) and a pair of rabbit-fur the rough striped ones—I get into the Lyons Diligence on Friday at Midnight, the 5th day at 6 o'Clock we are to be at Lyons, the last two days by Water.

542. [1] B.M. Add. Mss. 37520, fos. 41–2. Letter-book copy.

[2] In 1775 Samuel Bentham had stayed for a short time with a Mr Pattle at Paris (letters 143 and 144, notes) during his sojourn in France. Presumably this was the same man. The other persons mentioned in this letter remain unidentified. Captain Brooke is stated to be Pattle's son-in-law in a letter Pattle sent to Jeremiah Bentham dated 28 August 1785, announcing that Brooke would bring over to London the gifts mentioned in this letter; but further letters to Bentham senior seem to indicate that their transit was slightly delayed and then effected through the good offices of other army officers (B.M. IV: 188–9, 192–3, 194–5).

I met your Friend Dr. Keary[3] here on Sunday who made the most affectionate Enquiries after you.

I am
Dear and Hond. Sir,
Ever Yours
J.B.

P.S. Roger Metcalfe is the best natured most useful Man to me imaginable.

543

To Jeremiah Bentham[1]

16–17 September 1785 (Aet 37)

Genoa Sept. 17 1785 Friday

Hond. Sir

I reached Nice this day sennight a little before noon, and had immediately the pleasure of receiving through the hands of Sr. R. Herries's[2] correspondent there a fresh proof of your paternal care in the promise of a letter of introduction from M. Simolin to the Russian Ambassador at Constantinople[3] upon my arrival at that place. I wrote to you from Brighthelmstone Sunday the 7th August. I wrote again from Paris Sunday the 14 of August: but as the last mentioned letter was to go by Capt. Brooke[4] whose departure I found afterwards was not to be so speedy as I at first expected,

[3] Not identified.

543. [1] B.M. IV: 196–7. Autograph. Docketed by Jeremiah Bentham: 'Fils Jeremy B. / Letter datd Genoa / 17 Septr. 1785.'

Addressed: 'Jeremiah Bentham Esqr. / Queens Square Place / Westminster / Angleterre / Viâ France.' Postmark obliterated.

Friday was 16 Sept.

[2] Sir Robert Herries, Kt. (1730–1815), a partner in the London Exchange Banking Company, which handled his invention 'the circular exchange note', prototype of the travellers' cheque. In association with the Hopes of Amsterdam the company had a network of agents and exchange facilities extending all over Europe and into the Levant.

[3] Yakov Ivanovich Bulgakov (1743–1809), a professional diplomat and by long standing a personal friend and political associate of Potëmkin, who was largely responsible for his appointment to Constantinople, where he served from 1781 to 1789 (after the declaration of war in August 1787 he was confined in prison). He was a faithful exponent of Potëmkin's policy of intimidating the Porte by constant threats; for an instance see letter 557, n. 1.

[4] See letter 542, n. 2. In this passage Bentham mis-stated the date of it.

it is possible you may not have received it before you receive this. I sent you by the same channel some antipodagrical cloathing for the extremities such as are not to be had in England. On Monday the 8th of August about 9 o'clock in the morning I reached Dieppe after a tolerable passage of about 18 hours, sick whenever I stirred, easy so long as I neither spoke, thought, nor stirred. I found difficulties getting from Dieppe to Rouen greater than I expected. I did not leave Dieppe till Thursday morning 11th and then I travelled /en *franc-etrier* as the phrase is/ on Post-horses with a Courier not behind me as you would suppose, but before me, for so ordereth the Law. I reached Rouen by dinner time and set off the next day after dinner about 3 o'clock /in the Mail-diligence/ for Paris, travelled all night and got thither by about 8 o'clock in the morning, when I found Mr. Henderson and his nieces as I expected.[5] On Saturday morning immediately after the midnight of the Friday (it requires some care to describe so ambiguous a time) we set out all four of us in the Lyons Diligence by way of Sens Auxerre and Châlons: the price 100 livres to Lyons, table and bed included, but exclusive of 2 great crowns to Coachmen and one to Postillions. We reached Chalons on Tuesday by dinner-time; then /and there/ migrated from land to water and got to Lyons by Wednesday afternoon. On Friday morning (26) we embarked on board the Diligence d'eau which falls down the Rhone for Avignon. At the latter place we thought to have got a carriage for Montpelier: but we happen'd to meet with an opportunity of that kind at Pont St. Esprit a place where we stopped to sleep the 2nd day (Sat. 27) about 24 or 25 miles short of Avignon. This carriage was a vile old rumbling Coach which with the same 3 horses brought us to Monpelier by way of Desmoulins and Nismes on Monday evening 29th. On Tuesday at noon I alone set out for the port of Cette about 20

[5] From Paris onwards Bentham was continuously in the company of Henderson and the two Miss Kirtlands until the party reached Constantinople. Nothing is known of Henderson save what is revealed in the course of this correspondence. Bowring understood him to have been recommended to Bentham by 'Mr Playfair, the brother of the late professor'. From the occasional references to him in Samuel Bentham's letters it appears as if he skilfully impressed Bentham with a smattering of scientific knowledge, until he came to be regarded as a paragon who would fill with success the place of manager of the botanical garden which Potëmkin wished to establish in the Crimea; while Miss Kirtland would be fully competent to set going a dairy and cheese manufacture. Close association on shipboard was to reveal Henderson as a less reputable person than Bentham had realized: the elder Miss Kirtland was no niece, but Henderson's mistress and a trouble-maker—as Bowring afterwards learned from Bentham, 'a thorn in Bentham's side, and a rod of iron over Henderson's head' (Bowring, x, 149, 151). But the full shortcomings of Bentham's protégés were not revealed until after Henderson took up his post in the Crimea (see letter 556 n.).

miles distant in the mail-diligence a tolerable kind of four-wheel chaise which I had all to myself, in order to enquire for vessels for Marseilles or Nice; met with none that I cared to trust to and returned by the same conveyance at midnight, and travelling in the night got back to Monpelier on Wednesday morning (31st) between 5 and 6 o'clock. Our carriage from Pont St. Esprit to Monpelier cost us 2 louis besides a great crown to the Coachman: my jaunt to Cette and back again a most amusing and agreable one in a thousand respects cost me /for the vehicle/ but a great crown besides a voluntary fee of 1d. to the driver. On Thursday the 1st instant Sept: we set out from Monpellier for Marseilles in another vile rumbling Coach (spring-less like the first) dragged a snail's pace by three mules. We went by way of Aix, crossing the wooden bridge from Tarrascon to Beaucaire, and by that means leaving Avignon unseen to our left, and afterwards Toulon to our right. We reached Marseilles on Sunday 4th about noon, found the sea-conveyances from thence too uncertain to be depended upon in our circumstances, and accordingly on Tuesday 6th set off by land in a third rumbling vehicle called a *Diable* which notwithstanding its name was less incommodious and jolting than either of the two former. In this Diable we were drawn by horses again not by mules and went now and then at the rate of between 4 and 5 miles an hour instead of going constantly at that of two. The Mule-carriage from Montpelier to Marseilles cost us 3 louis and ½ a one to the Coachman: the Diable 7 louis with the same fee. We took the Diable optionally to leave us at Antibes the 3rd day or carry us on for another guinea by land to Nice the next morning. On the Wednesday afternoon between Vidalbon[6] /where we dined/ and Frejus where we slept the Diable played us a slippery trick: in crossing a bridge happily not a very high one I should rather have called it a water-course, the Driver through carelessness overturned us into the ditch on the left hand which happily proved a dry one. Miss Kirtland was bruised all down the left side, but is now pretty well recoverd. Mr. Henderson got a violent contusion in his right arm, which for a time threatened to be dangerous and is still very troublesome. I, having the upper-hand in the jumble rent my garment a little but scarcely scratched my skin. As for the youngest Miss K. having the same advantage it cost her nothing but a scream. We reached Antibes however on Thursday the 8th (Sept.) and finding in our shatter'd condition a sea-conveyance more eligible we engaged that same evening a chaloupe or /open-/

[6] I.e. Vidaubon, 43° 26′ N., 6° 26′ E.

row-boat manned by a 3 men and a boy for three great crowns and embarked about 7 on Friday morning, and weathering it out all night got into Nice harbour about 11 on Friday[7] forenoon. The Mary Frances, as we found reason to apprehend by a letter we received at Marseilles, had sailed for this place some days: but this we were in no pain about, being sure of a felucca from Nice to this place at any time, and if necessary on to Leghorn. After staying the term we wished viz. from Friday to Monday[8] last at Nice, we accordingly embarked in a vessel of that sort, and coasting all the way enter'd this port on Wednesday morning. We had then three hours to wait for the ope⟨ning⟩ of the Health-office before we could be permitted to land. The Felu⟨cca⟩ was a Row-boat manned with 11 men and a little boy of whom 8 row'd at a time. The ordinary price is 5 louis, but by the friendly industry of M. Giraudy a Merchant at Nice to whom we were directed to apply by Capt. Brine, we got it for 3 louis exclusive of ½ an one to the Crew. A Felucca is an open boat provided only with a tilt and Mattresses to lie on.

Saty. 18.[9] in the afternoon—

We are now on the point of embarking on board the Mary Frances for Leghorn. We have been treated here with much civility and friendship by M. Cassarena[10] Minister from the Landgrave of Hesse Cassel to this Republick. Mrs. Cassarena mentioned Mr. Jackson of the Post office as a gentleman with whom they were intimate. I thought you would prefer a full though dry journal to scatter'd and general remarks. I may possibly enclose a piece of a letter which you will see was intended for another person but not sent.[11] Almost everywhere in France in the course of the journey we eat at Tables d'hote whereby we saved half the expence and mixing with the people of the country, observed their manners—Dinner cost 40 sous a head: supper bed included, 45 sous. Nothing could exceed the civility we always met with from the company. As to the Innkeepers they take no notice of you, any more than the Shopkeepers of whom you buy. I am in a bad writing humour as you will perceive but too plainly, but there is no help for it.

[7] Here Bentham, confused in his chronology, first wrote 'Satur' and then over-wrote 'Friday'.

[8] 'Friday to Monday' is a correction from 'Saturday to Tuesday'.

[9] Saturday was the 17th.

[10] Not identified.

[11] Letter 544.

544

Begun to the Marquis of Lansdowne but sent to Jeremiah Bentham[1]

17 September 1785 (Act 37)

Prices of the Wine called Côté-roti at Condrieux in Dauphiné the place of its growth, as stated by M. David, master of the Inn called the Eau de la France who is also a Wine-Merchant, and professes to have served the Duke of Gloucester and 600 English families. N.B. If his wine is as good as his dinners, whoever deals with him will have no reason to repent it. The following particulars were collected in answer to some queries that had been proposed by a gentleman who lives at Paris.

Price of the wine per *barrique*: each barrique containing from 240 to 250 bottles; the bottles somewhat larger than the English ones.—Red wine of 5 *feuilles* over five years old /the oldest and best he has on the spot/ 10 louis the barrique do. of the last vintage, 8 louis—White wine 2 louis less than the red.

Carriage from Condrieux to Lyons, 7 livres: from Condrieux to Paris, 40 livres the barrique.

Duty at Lyons, 33 livres: do. at Paris, 70 livres. N.B. These are the droits d'entrée which wines going to England by another route, for instance that of Marseilles would not have to pay.[2]

My Lord—On board the Lyons Diligence d'eau between Condrieux and Thyons Aug. 26 1785

The above is the result of what I could collect in the course of about an hour's stay I have been making at Condrieux, part of which was taken up by the necessary operation of dinner, and other

544. [1] B.M. IV: 198. Autograph. Docketed by Jeremiah Bentham: 'Fils Jeremy B. / Letter datd. Genoa / 19 Sepr. 1785 / being the Appendix to one datd. 17th Sepr. 1785'.

Bentham began this letter on 26 August 1785 and intended it for Lord Lansdowne, but he eventually decided not to send it to him and added it to the packet sent to his father from Genoa three weeks later (see letter 543 at n. 11). He himself misdated both letters and his father followed the errors in the docket: his packet was dispatched from Genoa before sailing on Saturday, 17 September.

[2] For the system of internal tolls and customs charges which obtained in France in the years before the Revolution, see J. F. Bosher, *The Single Duty Project. A Study of the Movement for a French Customs Union in the Eighteenth Century*, London, 1964, pp. 1–24. Bentham's informant was apparently referring to the *octrois* levied upon goods entering or leaving various towns and cities in France and applied to the financing of local administration and charities.

part by the survey of a very simple and ingenious mechanism by which boats are made to cross the Rhone in both directions by the mere force of the current without any other moving power. I never saw it applied in England or any where else, though it certainly might be any where where the current were tolerably strong, as well as here. I write upon deck in the water-diligence from Lyons to Avignon in the midst of all sorts of interruptions, dogs barking, horses kicking, officious Frenchmen chattering, rain dropping, women's eyes clamouring for attention, which as your Lordship can not but know is more interrupting than all the other interruptions put together. The scenery of this voyage might find employment not unworthy of Lady Lansdowne's pencil. Prejudice apart, the banks of the Seine I can not help confessing to be superior to any thing I have seen in England: and the Rhone is I believe universally allow'd to have the advantage over the Seine. If the French could do, or to speak more candidly, if the government in its wisdom would allow them to do as much for themselves, as Nature has done for them, nobody who could come here would stay in England. Look which way you will, you may see the iron hand of monopoly crushing improvement in the bud. So long as the Grand Monarque is every man's Waggoner and every man's Postillion, if the communications from place to place should be carried on upon a footing of tolerable convenience, the persons concerned must act without a motive. The vehicle I was convey'd in from Rouen to Paris was either a prototype or an imitation (if an imitation a very humble one indeed) of our English Mail-Coaches. The distresses I suffer'd in it were such, that out of pure spite, I can not help insulting the French upon every occasion with the comparison. The greatest was a compound fracture in the blade of the Russian Colonel's sword. Paris supplied a new blade not distinguishable from the former; and I flatter myself that in the eyes of a judicious metaphysician the identity of the object will not be destroy'd by the reparation If any friend of mine were to propose taking a pleasurable excursion in this country I would beg him as he tender'd his own comfort to take a list of the things he should provide himself with before he crosses the channel: and, bating eatables and drinkables and a very few wearables indeed, this list would contain all the portable conveniences of life. Fifty Coaches to serve as Fiacres have lately been imported /into Paris/ from Liverpool at 60 guineas apiece. Nobody who for love or money can get one of these English Coaches will darken the doors of a Parisian one. It is rare however that they are to be met with for ordinary occasions: they are generally engaged for the wedding-feasts of the Bourgeosie: which as your Lordship knows are in this country celebrated with great parade. If the English goods which were bought up with so much avidity were worth nothing when they got here, or if the money which a part of them were perhaps bought with were not to be had for commodities as commodities are for money, or if it is right to take money out of the hands of a husband man or any body else in order to put it into the pocket of a clumsy manufacturer, the French may not have been much in the wrong in their late rigorous tho' polite prohibition of English goods. I am, ever your Ldship's most devoted

J.B.

[*Added at top of page*]

Septr. 18th 1785 P.S. to J[h]Bentham Esqr.

I saw yesterday a letter from Algiers dated 26th August which speaks of a peace with Spain as an event no longer probable.

A letter from Tripoli dated 1 July says 2138 persons being 1/5 of the inhabitants had died there of the plague in 14 days. Another day had carried off 238 being 1/40 of the remainder.

Pray send [*several words crossed out*] these letters to the Lord Mayor,[3] desiring him when he has done with them to forward them to Mr. Mulford.

545

To Jeremiah Bentham[1]

23–30 September 1785 (Aet 37)

Florence Friday Sept. 23 1785

Hond. Sir

We sailed from Genoa on Saturday afternoon the 17th instant. A little before I embarked I sent a letter for you to the Post Office. My orders were that it should be put into the French post: but that being shut, my servant put the letter into the Genoese Office which he found open. This Genoese post goes by way of Turin and

[3] I.e., Richard Clark.

545. [1] B.M. IV: 199–200. Autograph. Copies, B.M. XXII: 289–300, and Add. Mss. 37520 fos. 57–70.

Addressed: '[name obliterated] / London / Angleterre.'

Bentham began this letter on the 23rd and finished it on 30 September.

Flanders: but though it sets out on the Saturday night letters sent by it do not reach England so soon by three days as those sent by the French post, though the latter does not set out till the Monday after. We came to an anchor at Leghorn about 10 o'clock on Tuesday morning (the 20th). We found the lodging so dear at that port that after having looked about us a little and examined all the Inns we determined to return and sleep on board for that night, which was all the Captain would allow us. As he keeps shop on board of ship, it is necessary he should have it clear to receive his customers. Mr. Henderson's arm growing rather worse than better, and being so bad as to render the jolting of a carriage dangerous, it was determined that I alone should go to Florence. I accordingly filled a little /leather/ trunk with necessaries for the journey and got a boat called to take me from the ship to the Key (which is about ¼ of a mile) about 8 o'clock, being the time when a carriage, for which I had agreed with the Post-Master, was to meet me. *Diis aliter visum.* In handing the trunk to the Water-man, my Servant, like a careless blockhead as he is, quitted it before the Waterman had so much as touched it, and in it dropped into the Sea. In it were all my pecuniary resources and some of the most valuable of my cloaths. I immediately gave over all expectation of seeing any more of it, unless by great chance with the help of divers, when to my no small surprize it rose and the Waterman catching hold of it, convey'd it safe into the boat. Upon examining it I found the contents not so badly drenched as I expected: however there was not a single article that did not come in for its share. You would have imagined the expedition at an end, for the day at least: so did I; and accordingly sent soon afterwards to countermand the carriage. However by dint of four hours hard labour in unpacking, wiping, and repacking, every thing was replaced in the trunk in a state of tolerable driness before 12: and by 1 I got into the carriage. From Leghorn hither by the shortest road is 7 posts, making 56 miles: the Post-master said it would take me 9 hours: however it took me near 11; for it wanted but little of 12 when I reached the Inn from which I write, viz: Meggot's in the Street called Fondaccio di Spirito Santo or Holy-Ghost's-Ditch. You are not to judge of this ditch from Hound's ditch or Shore-ditch or any /other/ of our London Ditches: it is a very handsome Street, and Sr. Horace Mann's house which is a truly noble one forms a part of it. This venerable Nestor has been half a century out of England, 40 years of which he has been Minister to this Court.[2] His Nephew, Sr.

[2] See letter 538, n. 5.

Horace Mann Junr. the great fox hunter and Foxite has also been here ever since May.[3] It has been my suttling house till now and will be ⟨till⟩ my return which must be tomorrow evening at the farthest for before Sunday noon the Captain gave me to understand he should set sail. I snatch a few minutes to write thus much on my return from the evening *Conversatione*. What shall I tell you about of all the curiosities animate and inanimate that I have seen or shall see: of the old stock of Churches Palaces, Statues and pictures, which I care almost as little as I know about, of my friend the Abbé Fontana's[4] /Botanical/ garden in wax not distinguishable from nature; or rather of the Old Pretender and his newly-acknowledged daughter the Dutchess of Albany,[5] of Lady Craven and her friend Mr. Vernon,[6] and of Mrs. Piozzi and her loving spouse?[7] A world and all about /some of/ these things, /and all these persons/ could I tell you were I at your elbow /after dinner/ at Queen's Square Place, and you should give me an extra glass to pay me for it. The *soi-disant* Dutchess was bred, and I believe born, in France, of I know not what Mother: she went by the name of Madame d'Albany: upon his divorce /or separation/ from the Princess

[3] Sir Horace Mann, Kt. (1744–1814), of Linton, Kent, who succeeded his uncle as 2nd bart. in 1786. During the last few years of his uncle's life, he spent part of almost every year with him at Florence. As M.P. for Maidstone in the parliament dissolved in March 1784, he had acted as an independent country gentleman rather than as a partisan of C. J. Fox.

[4] The Abbé Felice Fontana (1730–1805), court doctor to the dukes of Tuscany, professor of philosophy at Pisa, director of the museum of natural history at Florence, and author of several works on medicine and science. Bentham had met him in 1779 (letter 325 and n. 30).

[5] Charlotte, the so-called Duchess of Albany (1753–89), was the illegitimate child of the Young Pretender by his mistress, Clementina Walkenshaw, who had left him in 1760 and retired with the infant to the abbey of Meaux. In 1780 the Pretender, deserted by his wife, the Countess of Albany, took Charlotte to live with him in Florence, where she became a great favourite.

[6] Elizabeth, Lady Craven (1750–1828) was the second daughter of the 4th Earl of Berkeley. She married, first, William, 6th Baron Craven. They separated in 1780, and she spent a number of years abroad, in the course of which, subsequent to the date of this letter, she formed a connection with the Margrave of Brandenburg-Anspach, who, in 1791, immediately after her husband's death, married her and settled in England. Her letters to the Margrave describing a tour she made through the Crimea in 1786 were afterwards published as *A Journey through the Crimea to Constantinople. In a series of letters to... the Margrave of... Anspach*, London, 1789. Henry Vernon was a great nephew of Admiral Edward Vernon (1684–1757).

[7] Hester Lynch Thrale, née Salusbury (1741–1821), widow of the Southwark brewer, Henry Thrale (d. 1781), married 2nd in 1784 the Italian singer, Gabriel Mario Piozzi. Living in Italy during the years 1784–7 they became members of the 'Della Crusians', a group consisting originally of English people in Florence, later joined by various Italian patriots. In November 1785 they published the *Florentine Miscellany* a literary collection containing many poems in sympathy with the cause of Italian nationalism.

of Stolberg his wife, her Father sent for her here where she has been living with him ever since, and created her Dutchess of Albany. /She is Countess of Albany they say by creation of the King of France./ I have seen her three times; once in her coach in the street yesterday at the Comic Opera and this evening at the serious. She is a good comely young woman rather nearer 30 as I should conceive than twenty: the lady I think her most like of all our female acquaintance that I happen to recollect is Miss Dyer.[8] If I could persuade her to marry me your eldest Grandson would be a Duke: but as he would be but a sort of a Duke Humphry I believe I may as well let the matter drop, the rather as she is good-natured enough to accept of a ride in young Sir H's phaeton whenever he asks her. At all times when I have seen her she has ⟨been⟩ accompanied by an Irish Lady a Mrs. O'Donnel or O'Connor I don't know which, some ten or 15 years older than herself. I saw the poor old gentleman her Father at the Comic Opera yesterday, and got a perfect view of him. Sr. H. as you imagine never visits *him*, notwithstanding his acquaintance with the daughter. He looks in years but to my eyes has nothing of that Scottish appearance which I forget who had found in him a pretty many years ago. He goes by the name of the Count of Albany. Mrs. Piozzi and her *caro sposo* I saw at Leghorn: they were just rising from dinner in a room I had occasion to cross upon looking for lodging at an Italian Inn the sign of the Golden Cross. They both looked grave and seemed as if they had not much to say to one another: however I hear he makes her a very good husband and shews her great attention. The acquaintance began in Ranzzini's where Piozzi used to find an open table. He was a very low kind of an Abbé, born and bred at *Milan*: his brother keeps a Chandler's shop there at this present writing and by the kindness of his fortunate relation a much better one since the marriage than befor. They have taken a house in that capital and furnished it: they lived in it for some time, and some notice was taken of them by some good families. Finding however that the respect shewd was all paid to Mrs. Piozzi as an Englishwoman and that the fond Shepherd in spite of the alliance could not get any /of it/ to his share, they left their house for a time at least and took to rambling, but it is thought will not be long before they return again. She in conjunction with a Mr. Parsons,[9] a Mr.

[8] Jeremiah Bentham's acquaintances included a Thomas Dyer, the father of Sir Thomas Swinnerton Dyer, 8th bart. (letter 138, n. 14). His eldest daughter, Mary Elizabeth Charlotte, was born some time between 1770 and 1775, and died in 1805.

[9] William Parsons (d. 1807), from Chichester, was a member of the 'Della Crusians' and contributed poems to the *Florentine Miscellany*.

and Mrs. Greathead,[10] and I believe one or two other English have just been printing at a Florentine press, a collection of Miscellanies chiefly in verse, and chiefly if not wholly in English. Some of it consists of Musick. It is said but 150 copies are struck off, and none sold. I just got a glimpse of it: the ⟨names⟩ front the title-page.

Friday Sept. 30 3 o'clock.

I write now on board the passage boat from Leghorn to Pisa. I left Florence a little before midnight on Saturday last, and, travelling all night, reached Leghorn again before 10 according to the strict orders of the Captain who assured me he should sail by /Sunday/ noon. Instead of that it is not absolutely certain that he will sail tomorrow evening though to make sure I must be on board by that time. In the mean time I have got a furlough to go to see Pisa which is about 15 miles from Leghorn, and if possible the famous baths which are about 4 miles farther. Mr. Henderson /and the ladies/ had been to Pisa while I was at Florence. As he went by water, his arm was no hindrance. The fare is but ~~threepence~~ 4½. I take my ragamuffin of a Servant, as I did to Florence. I engaged him at Nice, at the recommendation of a Dr. Metcalf[11] (an old acquaintance of Lind's) whom I found there /intending to take him on to Crichoff;/ but he turns out so indifferently that I shall discharge him before I go on board. I understood from a Swede who was at Constantinople so late as June last that I have some chance of getting a good servant there. I have written to a Merchant there a friend of Mr. Grays[12] and agent of the Prince's to look out for one. My letter, I am informed, will reach Constantinople in a month by way of Vienna. If you write to me soon after you receive this, there will be little doubt of your letters reaching me before I leave Constantinople: at the worst it will follow me to the Crim. I saw yesterday a London Chronicle so late as the 13 instant. I hear that Admiral Mackenzie our countryman is no longer in the Crimea:[13] he is replaced however by a Count Suchotin,[14] who is well known here (at Leghorn) as a great friend of the English, and one who detests the French. You must excuse sudden transitions: time is

[10] Bertie Greatheed (1759–1826) and his wife Anne, also members of the 'Della Crusian' circle and close friends of the Piozzis.

[11] Not identified. [12] Not identified.

[13] Admiral Thomas Mackenzie (d. 1786) joined the Russian navy as a midshipman in 1765 and rose rapidly in rank, becoming rear-admiral in 1783.

[14] Vice Admiral Yakov Filippovich Sukhotin (d. 1790), commander-in-chief of the Black Sea fleet 1783–5.

pretious, and pen and ink and paper likewise. We have executed all our Botanical business to our satisfaction. I was the more particular in a former letter concerning the mode and expence of travelling, on account of my Lord Mayor, who seemed desirous to obtain information of that nature. I would by no means advise him to think of travelling in France without his own carriage the freight of which will cost him less than the hire of a villainous vehicle that would reduce him and Lady M. to the state of two Mummies before they had travelled the length of Paris. Pray tell Mrs. Browne that I made a point of accepting a dinner from Mrs. Perkins. She has a very handsome agreable house with a good garden to it so situated as to answer the purpose of town and country house and she keeps her carriage: she gave me a magnificent dinner tête a tête. She talked much, and seriously as I am apt to think, of a visit to England next Spring: her wishes if she has any that way will be powerfully seconded by Mr. Joseph, who professes a violent affection for his Mistress's native country. At Pisa, live for the present as man and wife a man who *calls himself* Mr. John King, and a Lady who really is Countess Dowager of Lanesborough in Ireland.[15] I dined in company with them one day at Leghorn. I heard ⟨...⟩ at Florence. According to Sir H.M. he is a Jew Usurer. He put me ⟨...⟩ proper forms of Synagogue law a Jew ⟨...⟩ had, and has since been married twice over to this Lady Lanesborough. His Jew-wife with her four children is lately come over to reclaim him. Lady Lanesborough's jointure is said ⟨to be⟩ about £600 a year: and it is said he has about as much; if so, probably in annuities *per autre vie*. The acco⟨unt⟩ he gave of himself to Sir H. is, that he was the Author of some letters in a newspaper signed *Neptune* (I think it was) for which Charles Fox obtained a verdict against him for £1000: to avoid payment he made himself a bankrupt, but paid his Creditors, he says, 20s. in the pound. He is now under an injunction not to leave the country, for debt. He tried t'other day to persuade Sir H. to get the injunction taken off and to lend him money; you may imagine with what success; especially considering the party embraced by Sir H. Jun. who is the acting man. Lady L. tried Ld. Pembroke[16] on whom she had certain claims: his answer was if she would discard that fellow, his purse was at her service; but not otherwise. What a situation for a Lady of her quality! She is a

[15] Jane, Countess of Lanesborough (1737?–1829), the widow of Brinsley Butler, 2nd Earl of Lanesborough, 'married' after his death in 1779 Jacob Rey (d. 1823), a Sephardi Jew who had changed his name to John King.

[16] Henry Herbert (1734–94), 10th Earl of Pembroke.

decent well-looking woman seemingly about 35: as far as I could judge from the little I saw and heard of her, has much the behaviour and appearance of a woman of fashion. He is a forward chattering fellow seemingly about the same age. Neither France nor Italy have agreed with me extraordinarily well. Since I have been in Tuscany in particular I have felt an indescribable kind of lassitude and numbness which seemed almost to take away the use of my limbs. I think now however it has pretty well left me. I know not what to attribute it to, except the heat: and yet the heat as such was not troublesome to me. At this moment contrary to all expectation rain is falling, and I have neither great coat nor *parapluie* with me to keep it off. It is dropping on the paper, and I fear will contribute to make the writing illegible. We have been all living at Leghorn in the oddest way imaginable, sleeping only at our lodgings, eating altogether at a Merchants of the name of *Violet* to whom we had an ordinary letter of recommendation from Mr. Cassarena of Genoa. I found my company established in that way on my return from Florence. Mr. Griffiths the young Surgeon who went round with Capt. Brine forms part of it; having nothing else to do he has determined to seek his fortune in the Crimea.

The post from Vienna to Constantinople sets out twice a month, the 2d. and the 18: it takes from 15 to 17 days. It will be easy to learn in London what time a letter takes to go from thence to Vienna. I find the time as well as manner of our getting from Constantinople to the Crimea is likely to be very uncertain, any of my friends therefore if they have any thing particular to say to me need not scruple directing letters for me at the Ambassador's at Constantinople for months to come. For any thing of consequence as late as the last day of Feby. to speak at a venture, but a duplicate should be sent to Krechoff at any time after the arrival of this letter. I saw at Sir H.'s a Mr. Greenland (Augustus Greenland)[17] who is travelling with his daughter said to be a very accomplished girl. He is I believe an Atty: my Brothers if so, must know him. He seemed desirous of possessing Sir H. with an opinion of his intimacy with Ld. Camden:[18] but it did not get him a dinner at Sir H.'s while I was there. I don't know that I saw Lady Craven. I had a pretence to call on her from having seen her beautiful little boy,

[17] Augustus Greenland (d. 1803) was a solicitor, a deputy-teller of the exchequer, and an acquaintance of Mrs Piozzi.

[18] Charles Pratt (1714–94), 1st Baron Camden, a former Lord Chancellor and a political associate of Lord Lansdowne in the 1770's, now held the office of Lord President of the Council in the younger Pitt's administration.

Keppel at Mr. Pattle's (Mrs. Villette[19] and she are great friends) and I was to have taken a letter to her but that the post was preferred as being more certain, as it proved. I pursued her to two places but missed of her in both. She /and Mr. Vernon/ received a friend of mine in a bedchamber as the custom is, and the bed was supplied with two pillows and other duplicates.

[*Added on the back*]: I shall have I suppose at least 400 lb of luggage.

546

To the Marquis of Lansdowne[1]

27 September–1 October 1785 (Aet 37)

Leghorn Tuesday Sept. 27. 1785.

My Lord

I have been informed here that a considerable part of the produce of the Italian market is smuggled into England by way of Dunkirk; and in particular that 1000 ton of Zante Currants, and 12000 lb of Bologna Crape (the duty upon which latter /article/ according to my informant is 35s. 6d. pr 1b) was smuggled that way /from this port/ in the months of October, November and December last. I have this from a Mr. Adge an English Merchant who has been settled at this port these twenty years. He said he had several times entertained thoughts of writing a letter of information on this subject to Mr. Pitt: and intimated that he should have no objection to pass an examination before a Committee of Parliament or any other competent authority in England at any time. Whether this forwardness is grounded solely in public spirit, or whether it is to be attributed in any degree to personal pique or mercantile jealousy or any other private motive /are points/ concerning which no adequate means of judging have as yet come in my way. On the one hand in all that I have heard him say on the subject I have not perceived the least trace of any thing that savoured of acrimony against individuals, nor indeed did individuals come at all in question: and as far as I am qualified to judge, he has all the appearance of a steady, sensible man, totally devoid of

[19] See letter 542 and n. 2.

546. [1] B.M. IV: 201–3. Autograph. No address or docket.

After receiving this letter Lansdowne passed it on to Jeremiah Bentham (see the latter's introductory remarks to his letter-book copy at B.M. XXII: 387–90).

acrimony. On the other hand the persons in whose company I have found him are very odd whimsical characters, of unpolished manners, composing a /very small/ set who I observe live much among themselves, and with whom the others as I am informed will not associate, but for what reason I have not learnt.

At Genoa I heard some particulars relative to the manner in which the bullion is carried out of Spain; for instance from Barcelona. The Spanish proprietor is at the trouble and risk of sending it as far as 14 leagues out to sea to a longitude and latitude agreed upon. There it is taken up by a foreign vessel, suppose an English one: the Captain has 1 per cent, only for /only/ carrying it from Barcelona to Genoa. My informant was a Captain Simpson a Scotchman commander of a little Brig called the Susannah: the vessel is his own and he has had no other home for several years. English vessels he says are so much preferred in the Mediterranean to French, that though when he came into a port, I think it was that of Genoa, he found three French vessels waiting for a loading, he got his own vessel full, and left them empty as he found them. Upon asking him the reason of this difference he said it was owing to the bad reputation of the French in point of probity: if valuable goods such as silks were put on board them, the Masters would embezzle more or less of the cargo, getting the crew to join in a protest importing that the missing part was thrown over board by reason of bad weather. So unpopular he says are the French in Barcelona, that a Frenchman can hardly show his face in the streets there without being insulted. The Revenue-laws there seem to be still worse executed in that absolute Monarchy than under our mixt and limited government: the /very/ Master of the Custom-house had been, (he said) on board of him to smuggle.

I happen'd to dine today in company with a Mr. John King as he calls himself, and the Countess of Lanesborough in Ireland, who pass for man and Wife. The account that I heard of him from good authority at Florence where he has also been, is, that he is a Jew money-lender or rather was while he had money to lend, for now he is more disposed to borrow—that he repudiated a Jewess he had to his wife, according to the Jewish Law, which however good it may be in the Synagogue is I doubt of no great force in such a point in Westminster Hall; that since then he has been actually married to Lady Lanesborough, and *ex majori cautelâ* more than once. They are now upon their shifts, attempting to borrow of every body they meet: amongst other persons her Ladyship applied to Lord P. on whom, it is said, she had claims better imagined than explained:

his answer was, that his purse was at her service, provided always that she would first turn away her Jew. The account he gave of himself to Sir H. was that he had an action brought against him by C. Fox for a libel signed *Neptune* I think it was, in one of the London Newspapers; that he had a verdict against him for a thousand pounds, to free himself from which he got himself made Bankrupt, but paid 20s. in the pound. He has for some time since been a sort of prisoner at large (whether by the seizure of his effects or by the equivalent to a *ne exeat* I have not learnt) for debts contracted here: to free himself from this thraldom he made application to Sir Horace to intercede with government without any pretence that I could learn. The merit upon which he grounded his pretensions to favour on the part of Sir H. was no other than this libel: whatever favour he might find in the sight of Sir H. the Uncle, a libel upon Charles Fox was not very well calculated, as your Lordship may well imagine, to procure him much in the sight of Sir H. the Nephew, or to give much efficacy to the request of a loan with which the other application was accompanied. He is a forward prating fellow, by no means devoid of the talents /naturally/ connected with assurance: as to Lady Lanesborough, a pleasing well-bred woman, one can not but be concerned to see a woman of her quality reduced to such a state of degradation. Here also is or at least was three or four days ago, Mrs. Thrale-Piozzi. I saw her on Tuesday at the Croce d'Oro an Italian Inn sitting in a balcone tête-a-tête with her caro sposo. They are on the point of returning to a house they have taken at Milan, where his Brother keeps a Chandler's shop, the stock of which has been much encreased by the bounty of his English Sister-in-Law. *She* has been received I understand in some good houses there as an English-woman, but nobody but his Brother the Shop-keeper will take any notice of *him*. It was this circumstance drove them from Milan, to which place *ennui* now forces them to return. Piozzi however it is said makes her a very good husband. They in conjunction with a Mr. and Mrs. Greathead, and a Mr. Parsons, and I believe one or two more, have within these few days treated the Florentines with a literary curiosity. It consists of a miscellaneous full-sized octavo volume printed in Florence, chiefly if not wholly in English, the greatest part if not all of it in verse, and some of it set to Musick. The names of the Authors are opposite the Title-page: 150 copies printed off, but none sold. I heard at different times a few extracts from it, in all which the ball of /mutual/ compliment was bandied about without mercy: but as it seemed to me the poetry by no means bad for those who love poetry which unhappily is not my case. I laid diverse plots for getting a copy to deposit in a library to which I am much obliged: but Time, the grand frustrator of plots would not permitt me to bring any of them to maturity. From what cause I know not, even Sir Horace did not get so much as a single copy. I saw his poor Ex-Majesty, and a pleasing young woman with him, his lately acknowledged natural daughter, the Dutchess or as some call her Countess of Albany; the latter title she is said to have from a King whose titles are of rather better currency than her Father's, the King of France. I saw not the Grand-Duke nor any of his family; they were not at Florence. I am sorry to say, neither did I see Lady Craven: I had a pretense for accosting her, and accordingly pursued her to two places but in vain. Every body knows she is accompanied in her travels by a Mr. Vernon, an officer, I believe he is, in the Spanish service: a gentleman who paid them a morning visit told me he was received in a bed-chamber in which was an unmade bed, provided with two pillows and other articles in pairs.

I arrived at this place on Tuesday 20th inst. set off for Florence the next day; got to that capital by midnight and set off /on my return/ much about the same hour on Saturday. The three days I staid there I lived, lodging excepted, at Sir Horace Mann's. Of a multitude of English travellers that were at Florence, I saw none at Sir Horace's except a Mr. Greenland for a few minutes; the civilities of Sir H. were such as bespoke his deference for the letter of which I had the honour to be the bearer. I travelled all night by special injunction from the Captain for fear of losing the ship, and on my return had the mortification to find I might have staid four or five days longer.

I have not yet had the pleasure of seeing Captain Blanket: he was expected here on his return from escorting the King of Naples, but is now said to have gone in quest of a Pirate that has done some mischief in the Archipelago.

Oct. 1. On board the passage-boat from Pisa to Leghorn.

I expect to sail this evening for Smyrna. It will probably therefore be a considerable time before I shall have any farther opportunity of testifying the respectful attachment with which I have the honour to be,

My Lord,
Your Lordship's most obedient
and much obliged humble Servant,
J.B.

P.S. According to Mr. Adge no seizure was ever made of the /Leghorn/ articles smuggled by way of Dunkirk as above. To my question how he accounted for this uninterrupted success his answer seemed a very natural one, viz: that the goods in question not being of the number of those commonly known to be smuggled, passed without suspicion; if questioned the Master would say he was bound for London or some other port, and nobody could prove but that he meant to pay the duty.

I take this opportunity to confess a theft, piously intending to make restitution by return of the Mary Frances, which however will hardly be before March. Among the books I last borrow'd from your Lordship's library I purposely omitted returning 2 /out of the 8/ Volumes of De La Landes' Voyage d'un Francois en Italie[2] viz: the 2nd and 8th. I enquired for it all over London in vain. I was told it was at present out of print: but that a new edition with additions was expected very soon. Out of these two circumstances laid together, your Lordship's mercy will I hope pick out a double excuse.

547

TO JAMES TRAIL[1]

1 October 1785 (Aet 37)

Oct. 1. 1785 On board the Passage boat
from Pisa to Leghorn.

Count Verri, Author of the Meditazioni sulla Economia Politica, is retired from Milan to Rome.[2] He had begun a general history of Italy, and even printed 15 or 16 Sheets of it, but partly through indolence, partly through timidity, alter'd his mind, called

[2] See letter 527, n. 9.

547. [1] B.M. IV: 204. Autograph. The address has been heavily blocked out, save for 'Angleterre'. A copy of this letter made by Jeremiah Bentham (B.M. IV: 205–6) is docketed: 'Copy of a Letter from Mr. Jeremy Bentham to | | /dated on board the Passage Boat from Pisa to Leghorn, 1st Octr. 1785/ The original being Transmitted by the Marquis of Lansdown from Weymouth to J.B. Senr. at Cheltenham the 13th August 1786 inclos'd in a Letter to him from his Lordship, datd. the 11th Augt. 1786.' Bentham senior also noted that his son's letter had been postmarked 24 October. The addressee is identified as James Trail in George Wilson's letter of 24 September 1786 (letter 576). Another, letter-book copy by Jeremiah Bentham, B.M. Add. Mss. 37520, fos. 71–5.

[2] Pietro Verri (1728–97), economist, a native of Milan, who held various offices concerned with finance in his native duchy. His *Meditazioni sulla economia politica* was published in 1771.

in the Sheets and burnt them. This I had from Tomaso Masi Book seller and Printer at Leghorn, by whom the Sheets were printed. I see an answer to Verri's book, petulant and violent—it promises so ill I don't know whether I shall encumber myself with it. I saw and bought a violent sortie against the Roman Law, against which I am still more violent by an anonymous author so old as 1772. Masi told me it was by a Count Castellamore of Turin,[3] who was obliged to fly his country for it: he retired to Venice where he lives still.

Upon enquiry about the masked myrmidons[4] I was informed by a man too low and too ignorant to be partial, who had travelled all over Italy that in Tuscany and the Venetian the custom had existed time immemorial: he remembers it in Tuscany long before the /accession of the/ present G. Duke. I saw such a mask at the Comic Opera at Florence, but none at the serious which is at a different house. At a Public Concert in the Play-house at Leghorn, I saw none. In the gardens of the Palazzo Pitti it is true I saw nobody: I was there from ½ after 12 to 2: which certainly can not be the general hour for walking. Near the gate sat a /Military/ Officer, stationed apparently as Centinel. The sight of me though evidently a foreigner did not appear to excite in him the smallest curiosity. However young Sir H.[5] told me that the G. Duke/and his Ministers/ was infected to a great degree with that sort of curiosity. One of them took notice to him once of his being seen with an Opera girl from Naples whose name I have forgot: 'true', says he, 'I keep her, and what is that to you?' He speaks with great contempt of the G.D.[6] and says the people hate him and he them. Upon enquiring for grounds, after as close an examination as I could take with decency, I could not find any so much as alledged, but the trifling one abovementioned. I have enquired of high and low, malecontent and neuter, and can hear nothing of any place to answer the purpose of a Bastille, nor any trace of any coup d'autorité whatsoever, except that there are houses of correction where des jeunes gens dereglés are shut up upon application of their friends, but not so as

[3] Count Giacomo Ugo Bottone di Castellamonte was the author of *Saggio sopra la politica e la legislazione Romana*, published anonymously in 1772.

[4] This matter remains unelucidated. It appears that Trail may have believed the ducal government to depend upon the services of a particularly nefarious secret police.

[5] The younger Sir Horace Mann. See letter 545, n. 3.

[6] Leopold (1747–92), grand duke of Tuscany, 1765–90, subsequently the Emperor Leopold II. He was the younger son of the Empress Maria Theresa, and brother to the Emperor Joseph II, whom he succeeded in the Austrian dominions and the imperial title.

to be inaccessible. The Police is so well kept, with scarce any apparent means that theft is scarce ever heard of, and robbery never. As for murder it is entirely out of the question. Compare this with the accounts given by your Cousin of the roads in a neighbouring state. [*Several lines crossed out*]

Of my little abridgement[7] neither of the Sir Horace's had ever /so much as/ heard. They both treated it with the greatest contempt, especially the old one who is almost childish, who said he had never heard any thing of any monopolies suppressed by the G.D. or any thing else done by him that was worth notice, and seems to labour, without /directly/ saying so to make me believe that not a syllable in it was true. Afterwards after he had made some enquiries, he said he found it was nothing but an Index to the Laws of that period (as if it pretended to be any thing more) and admitted that the facts mentioned in the notes were true. After that an Abbe Mori[8] whom I met with twice at Sr. H.'s table (an intelligent young man he seemed to be) told me the name of the Author which I enter'd immediately on the title page but do not now recollect. He was the G.D.'s agent at Paris, but is since dead. His R.H. if he does not do well must at least be allow'd to do much. Every year produces a Folio Volume of edicts not much less voluminous than ours. I saw them in the shop, a goodly show: They are at any rate to be had for money which is not the case in Genoa. Not so much as the State Printer keeps a copy of his works. There is an 8vo edition of the G.D.'s laws (I suppose the general and *not-temporary* ones) from I know not what period to I know not what other. Will you believe me when I tell you that I rummaged all the capital bookseller's shops for it at Florence without success? It is printed forsooth at Sienna; and might perhaps be got from thence at some uncertain time; perhaps in some weeks perhaps in some months; for as to any regular communication between any town and any other in this small and *well-roaded* state, there is none. The same observation I was told by an Italian may be applied to all Italy. No: not even between Leghorn the port, and Florence the capital. English and Italians join in assuring me there is not a chaste married woman in all Tuscany, you may venture to extend the observation to all Italy. Those who disapprove of the suppression of prostitutes will naturally be disposed to attribute the former fact to the latter

[7] *Indication sommaire des reglemens et loix de son Altesse . . . l'Archiduc Léopold, Grand Duc de Toscane par ordre chronologique, depuis 1765 jusqu'à la fin de l'anée 1778. Avec des notes.* Brussels, 1779. For Bentham's mention of his acquisition of this volume, see letter 370 at n. 11.

[8] Not identified.

operation as its cause: but as far as I can understand the supposed effect existed long before.

I fear I must conclude already. The bark is just at Leghorn, and I expect to sail this evening for Smyrna. If I get a reprieve, I may possibly *treat* you with a little more: for I will not give into the stale and insincere supposition, that my communications such as they are are in any danger of being otherwise than welcome. I wish I could have done more to testify with what truth and affection I am

Ever your's

J.B.

You will see a good deal of this is not for every eye [*two lines crossed out*] One of the causes I heard assigned for the unpopularity of the G.D. indeed the only specified cause besides those above, is his disbanding a number of troops, suppressing a number of offices, and as is supposed, laying up money. In short his great Vice is the Virtue we are aiming at in England. But the Abbé Fontana[9] for works equally ⟨...⟩ useful, admirable wax imitations of dis ⟨...⟩ has Carte Blanche with regard to Expence. Hospitals and seminaries of Education are endow'd, and a vast and encreasing family of Princes and Princesses maintained. The Emperor, another Miser, has given another boundless order to the same Abbé and his assistants for the use of his Chirurgical schools.

I have recovered this from the water. Adieu
I sail for Smyrna 6 o'clock.

548

From Joseph Mathias Gerard de Rayneval[1]

15 October 1785

À Fontainebleau le 15 8th 1785

Je suis aussi étonné qu'afligé, Monsieur, que le pacquet que je vous ai addressé à Nice poste restante ne vous soit pas parvenu;

[9] See letter 545, n. 4.

548. [1] B.M. IV: 211–2. Autograph. Docketed by Bentham: '1785 Oct. 15 / Rayneval Versailles / to / J.B. Constantinople.'

For the writer see letter 538, n. 3.

je l'avois cependant fait porter exactement. J'y supplie en vous envoyant ci-joint le duplicata de la lettre que M. le Cte. de Verg⟨enne⟩s[2] écrivoit à notre Ambassadeur. J'espère, Monsieur, que vous me pardonnerez une faute qui n'est pas mon ouvrage, et que vous rendrez toujours justice à la Sincerité des Sentiments avec les quelles j'ai l'honneur d'être, Monsieur, votre très humble et très obeissant Serviteur

De Rayneval

M. Bentham.

549

From Anthony Hayes[1]

27 October 1785

Sir,

Conformable to your desire, I spoke last Night to Sir Richard Worsely,[2] concerning his facilitating matters to render the Passage on board the Impl. Ship, in regard to conveniency as Satisfactory as circumstances will admit, to the Gentlm. and Ladys, who resolve to proceed by that opportunity to Consple and the Crimea, and he desir'd me to let you know, with his Compliments, that he would with great pleasure do everything that lays in his Power, in regard to the use of the Cabin, or other matters to oblige the Company on board, and to serve them in every thing that lies in his Power, and which he told me he had confirmed to the Captain

[2] Charles Gravier, Comte de Vergennes (1717–87), the French minister for foreign affairs.

549. [1] B.M. IV: 214. Autograph. Docketed: '1785 Oct. 27 / Smyrna / Consul Hayes Smyrna / to J.B. ibid. / Sir R. Worsely ready to accomodate etc. on board / the Imperial vessel.'

Anthony Hayes (d. 1794), a British merchant at Smyrna, held the post of British consul there from 1762.

[2] Sir Richard Worsley, 7th bart. (1751–1805), of Appuldercombe, Isle of Wight. He had been travelling abroad since the spring of 1783 and was now proceeding by way of Constantinople to Russia. Bentham crossed his path several times in the next few months, and came to consider him 'haughty, selfish, and mean' (Bowring, x, 153). One reason may have been the unexplained but clearly resented failure of the arrangement to which this letter refers. According to Worsley's travel journal, he arrived at Smyrna on 21 October and left on 2 November on the sloop *Diana*. His journal provides no further explanation of the matter (Worsley Mss. 24, pp. 59, 65, Yarborough Collection, Lincolnshire Archives Office, Lincoln).

who call'd upon him this morning. I have the honour to be with great Truth and Regard

Sir
Your most Obedient
and most humble Servant
Anthony Hayes

Smyrna Thursday
Morning 27th October
1785

550

To Jeremiah Bentham[1]

11 October–25 November 1785 (Aet 37)

P.S. Constantinople Nov. 25. Friday evening. This letter consists of two sheets. I have no time to read over either of them

On board the Mary Frances at Sea Tuesday Oct. 11 1785

The business of the day has been the passing the streight which separates Sicily from the peninsula of Italy, and a finer day for it it was impossible to have had. It is the only day I have been alive since we left Leghorn. We slackened sail last night for fear of being caught in bad weather in the night time in a narrow sea which is flanked /mostly/ by bold shores /especially/ on the Italian side, and is not always in so peaceable a state as that in which we found it. The streight is neither /quite/ so narrow nor so long as I expected to find it. Everybody however agrees that at the narrowest it can not be more than a league and it continues at nearly the same width for some miles: a sufficient length to exhibit an infinite variety of objects on both shores within a very discernible distance.

550. [1] B.M. IV: 207–8, III: 456–7. Autograph.

Addressed on the second sheet: 'Jeremiah Bentham Esqr. / Queens Square Place / Westminster / Angleterre.'

Begun on 11 October and dispatched from Constantinople on 25 November. It appears that Bentham sent the account of his journey in two parts, one to his father, the other (letter 551) to John Mulford, and that his father then reassembled the whole before making a complete letter-book copy (B.M. XXII: 313–60). This copy has been used to supply words now obliterated in the original, but the order in which the story is there told is an artificial one created by the rearrangement of parts of Bentham's letters to his father dovetailed in chronological order with the contents of the letter sent to Mulford. Here the letters have been printed separately, as originally sent. Another letter-book copy of the whole exists at B.M. Add. Mss. 37520, fos. 76–145.

On the Sicilian side the only town that presents itself to view is the remnant of Messina: with the assistance of glasses and in some places without we could plainly discern a multitude of stately buildings not yet recoverd from the ravages of the Earthquake. Some of them appeared in a condition of transparency, the roofs being off, and the windows void of glass, if ever they were provided, which the generality of the buildings in this warm /region/ seem not to be, with that luxurious accommodation. Many were plainly to be seen propped up with shores. Brydone I think speaks of the principal range of buildings that lines the Key as being semicircular and extending a matter of a mile.[2] If so I doubt the devastation must have been vast indeed, for this superb range has at present but little curvature in appearance though the distance from which we saw it would not be more than half a league, and I should not guess the extent of it at more than ¼ or ⅓ of a mile. It is still, however, a very considerable town, and the environs of it for miles at each end are richly spangled with villages. A great number of the houses and other buildings both in the town and in the villages have sprung up since the earthquake. On the Calabrian (Italian) shore the towns though not so large are more numerous; the shore on this side especially very bold and the ground thrown, probably by earthquakes of a date infinitely ~~beyond~~ anterior to all history or even pretended history, thrown into a thousand romantic forms. The general altitude of the coast seems to be two or three times as considerable as that of Dover Cliffs, and in several places within ⅓ or ¼ of the summit you see a town stuffed into a cleft in a rock or stuck upon the point of one. What they do for /fresh/ water the Lord above knows; not the least drop have any of us been able to discover in all Sicily, though we have had views more or less near of little less than ⅔ds of its circumference, nor in all that part of Calabria, though that part of the peninsula outstretches the Island pretty considerably. As for Etna we have seen it in three several directions from so many different sides of the Island, reckoning the short portion which forms the streight as one in addition to three longer ones which alone are taken account in the general idea of its form from which it obtained the surname of Trinacria[3] in addition

[2] Patrick Brydone (c. 1736–1818) in 1773 published in two volumes *A Tour through Sicily and Malta. In a Series of Letters to William Beckford*, describing explorations he had made in 1770. Exceedingly popular, by 1780 the work had gone through six editions or reprintings in England and had been translated into French and German. Much more recently, on 5 February 1783, the area around the straits of Messina had been devastated by a fearful earthquake, in which 12,000 people were thought to have died.

[3] To the ancient Greeks Sicily was known as Trinacria.

to its other appellations. The side which fronts you as you approach the island from the gulph of Genoa is that from which Etna is at the farthest distance, yet though the sea is skirted all long with lofty mountains, Etna is plainly seen on the other side overtopping them all. When an observation by a quadrant shew'd it at 66 miles distance, we could plainly see the smoke issuing from it in torrents which though at that vast distance they seemed to be slow must have been of vast rapidity to exhibit any motion perceptible at such a distance. Considering how large an island Sicily is, how many mighty states it contained in classic times, and how considerable a figure it still makes on the map, I could not help wondering to observe that by far the greater part of it if not the whole could be taken by the eye not only in the course of one day's navigation, but /in great measure/ at one view. From this and other specimens that have occurred in the course of this short part that has already elapsed of our short navigation our little globe has lost a vast deal of the space that it had been used to fill in my conception. At one and the same view for instance, I could take in all the little islands you see marked on the map under the name of the Lipari Islands, together with a small part of the Italian shore nearly as far North perhaps as Naples, and one of the sides of the Sicilian triangle. In like manner one and the same glance presented us with Corsica, Sardinia and the corresponding part of the Italian peninsula. Of the Lipari Islands Strombolo ought to have treated us with an illumination: it is said to be generally in that state: unfortunately it happened to have nothing better to entertain us with than /a little/ smoke, of which we had got a quantum sufficit from Etna. We however got a reasonable whiff of sulphur from one of its neighbours. On both shores the country seemed to be cultivated wherever it was level enough to admitt of cultivation. As to Scylla and Charybdis, all our diligence could not discover any objects that exhibited any traces of having been ever endued with any of the properties attributed in days of yore to those celebrated bugbears. Brydone I think has very satisfactorily accounted for their disappearance. The streights however from other causes are not always without their danger: the narrowness of the passage, with the shallowness of the water in some parts in the Calabrian side these circumstances added to the accidental conflicts of winds and currents are sufficient to produce that effect without the help of monsters. As it was we saw and traversed a number of little spots which at a less favorable conjuncture /I was told by the learned/ might have been dangerous whirlpools. These were little smooth spaces which in the midst of the gentle undulations that composed the main surface of the stream were distinguishable like so many ponds. A faint eddy playing round them kept them from /yielding to the impulse and following/ the direction of the circumambient waves.

Oct. 16. Sunday. 1 o'clock.

We are at the moment a little short of the Island of Cerigo[4] viz: to the South-west of it, near enough to see with the naked eye the roads and the houses if there were any. The Island belongs to the Venetians: whether it has at present any inhabitants we are as yet in doubt: if there are none, the bad neighbourhood it is in, viz: that of the Maniotes,[5] as bad thieves as their forefathers the Lacedemonians, is enough to account for the depopulation. Our present situation affords another example in support of the preceding observation relative to the unexpectedly great extent of a Sea-view. I can now see at one and the same time three of the four promontories which divide and terminate the Morea (viz: Capes Gallo, Matapan and Cervi).[6] The island of Cerigo lying between the Ship and Cape Cervi, the island of Ovo[7] a small island about 2 leagues a head not marked in my map of Europe, and to the right (the South) the Island of Cerigoto, and further still the great island of Candia, the ancient Crito, a tantalising object /of/ which I must content myself with a distant view. To the Morea we are near enough to distinguish all the inflections of the coast /to the bottom of both gulphs:/ but we are so far advanced to the East that I question whether at the present instant Cape Gallo be any longer visible, or whether it be not by this time completely eclipsed by the interposition of Cape Matapan.

Captain Brine who is a most dexterous harpooner has just been striking a Pilot fish with an instrument called a Grainge. In shape this fish is as much like to a trout as to any fish I can think of: its colour greyish streaked with blue 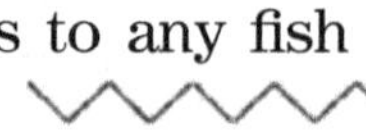 /zigzag/ in the manner of tent-stitch: it is a fine-flavoured fish with very little bone

[4] Otherwise Kithira, south of Cape Malea.

[5] A Greek people, descendants of the Spartans, settled in the central mountainous area of the Peloponnese, who fiercely maintained their independence against all comers. In later days a section of the Maniotes living round Cape Matapan became notorious for their piratical activities.

[6] The terminations of the three great promontories jutting southwards out of the Morea are capes Gallo (Akritas), Matapan (Tainaron) and Malea, which Bentham called Cape Cervi. It is not clear what he reckoned as the fourth cape not then in view.

[7] Ovo lies a little to the north of Cerigotto (Andikithira).

in it. In size they seem to run from about ½ a lb to a lb. The Grainge or as it is sometimes called in the plural the Grains is an instrument somewhat like Neptune's Trident except that instead of three prongs it has six all barbed like the Devil's tail, and the handle about 8 foot long. The handle being made fast to the ship with a long line the operator may without danger of losing the instrument quit his hold when the depth at which he sees the fish requires him so to do. Out of 8 strokes which the Captain has had occasion to make at these little fish within these few days but one missed the mark, though several times the fish were almost the length of the instrument under water. It was not without surprize that I found the fish when taken out of the water of the colours above described. When seen through the water which itself was blue, the blue streaks on the fish appeared brown. At another time the Captain made a stroke at a sucking-fish and hit him, but the fish got off. The sucking-fish is a fish much larger than the Pilot: the latter is so called from his escorting the ships from port to port, for when a fish of this sort once approaches a ship he seldom leaves her: the sucking-fish attaches himself to some part of the ship, generally the Rudder. The Pilots are the only fish we have caught: but we have seen at different times a number of porpoises, several squadrons of flying fish pursued by Dolphins, a few blubbers, a sea-snake, and a sleeping turtle. The latter we had formed designs upon, but lost sight of her before we could get out the boat. The Sea-snake I had a full view of as it was playing about the rudder. We supposed it about 8 or 9 feet long.

Wednesday Oct. 19.

Yesterday the Captain, Mr. Griffiths[8] and I paid two visits, both uninvited. The first was on board a Ragusan, which was about a mile a head. After the usual salutations when we were come alongside of him, he invited us on board to drink a glass of wine: it was about ½ after 11, we accepted his invitation, tasted his Ragusan wine which to me seemed pleasantly like Burgundy, better than any of the variety of wines we have on board, but was held very cheap by my companions. I found amongst the men's provisions some black bread as dry as biscuit of which I begged a small piece to gratify the curiosity of the Ladies. He had a couple of iron guns four-pounders which he took the first occasion to let us know were English, of which he would have been glad to have obtained a far-

[8] He is described above as a young surgeon (Letter 545, at p. 361). According to later account, he was a debtor on the run (Bowring, x, 150).

ther supply, if we had had any to spare. He had others, but they were counterfeits, of which therefore in contradiction to the common quack warning there was no need to beware. He had not a single article on board except provisions and /small/ arms of which latter he had a plentiful store of his own country manufacture, both swords and fire-arms. He said he was bound for Smyrna and talked of looking out for a lading, but did not say, nor did he seem to have settled with himself what it should consist of. He had not a scrap of any thing like a chart on board: a [*word crossed out*] very obliging offer which our Captain made him of lending him /a chart/ or even giving him a copy of one was received but coldly. All we could say to him to persuade him to come on board and dine with us was without effect. All circumstances laid together our Captain could not help entertaining suspicions of his being one of those roving gentry who it seems are not uncommon among his race (the Sclavonians) who are in utrumque parati, either to take in freight or to plunder as the time serves. He was a fine, tall, stout, athletic fellow, with a fine physiognomy and a noble pair of whiskers. His vessel was quite a new one, and if he told us true had been out from Ragusa but a short time. If time were to be had for wishing for, I would attempt a description of the Cabbin and its furniture. The most remarkable article was an old man we found sitting in it with great gravity. The skin of his neck which was of the colour of mahogony was pleated longitudinally /in the hinder part/ into folds of the length of one's hand and the thickness of one's finger. From his gravity and silence we took him for a Turk, but upon enquiry were told he was a Greek. The Captain says, that conformation of the skin of the neck is common to a greater or less degree in the Levant. I think I have observed traces of it in ancient busts.

Our second and last visit was on board a Venetian who was about as far astern as the Ragusan was a head. I might as well have observed before that it was almost a perfect calm, or we should not have bestow'd so much time as must otherwise have been lost in visiting. From him we obtained some very interesting intelligence. To our first question, where he came from, his answer was from the Coast of Barbary. You may imagine we were in no great hurry to lessen the distance between him and us, till an answer to a farther question assured us that the port he came from was 200 miles at least from Tripoli, the focus of the plague. This port is marked Bengazzo[9] in Roux's Carte de la Mediterranée published at Marseilles in 1764 in 12 sheets. In the Map of Europe I left with

[9] I.e., Benghazi.

you which though the latest and perhaps the best English map of Europe extant is I am sorry to say a woefully incorrect one, no traces of it are to be found. You may conceive it however to lie on the East part of the gulph of Sidra between Bernic and Cape Razat. Upon hearing this, and being assured that there was no symptom or any indisposition of any kind on board though he had been a fortnight or more at sea, we made no scruple of complying with his invitation. From him we got the first distinct intelligence of a Pirate that had for some time been infesting the Levant. She was first heard of about 3 months ago (the middle of July). /In the compass of about 2 months/ she had taken in all seven vessels, 2 Ragusans, 3 Venetians and 2 French, the crew of all which ships were all massacred to a man. She carried 16 guns and 200 men: being a Pyrate professed, she hoisted black colours. Her crew were Dulcingnol Turks. At last about 40 days ago she put into Tripoli: the government of that state having received advice concerning her /by Circular letters/ from the Grand Signior's ministry at Constantinople seized her in that port. The crew if I understood right were /to be/ sent to Constantinople to take their trial. During her cruize a Venetian ship had fought her for 7 hours and obliged her to sheer off. Our host himself had had the bad luck to meet her, and the good fortune to get clear. /It was to the South West of the Isle of Candia:/ He was going from Joppa or Jaffa port in the Holy Land to Smyrna with I know not what lading, and a company of upwards of 100 *Hadgias* passengers, Turks who had been on their pilgrimage to the tomb of their prophet at Mecca from which meritorious circumstance they take their denomination. His crew were no more than twenty or thirty strong /and he had but 6 three or four pounders/, but he had some spare small arms and the Hadgers being all or most of them armed, with their arms bright and in good condition, all together made a respectable appearance. To put the better countenance upon the matter they all came upon deck together resolved to sell their lives as dear as they could, knowing the enemy they had to deal with, and having no hopes of quarter. The stratagem if such it can be called succeeded to well, that the Pirate whose cruelty seems to have been tinctured with a proportionable share of cowardice, sheered off without firing a shot, or so much as haling. /It was no longer than 33 days ago that/ Our host left Smyrna, to which port he was now returning. There had then been no plague for a considerable time: this, added to the capture of the Pirate, you may imagine, was no bad news to us. On our entrance into the Cabbin, our host presented us with some wine and some dates and presently after one of his people brought up and presented to each of us a live sprig of sweet Basil in flower. The Wine was sweet, and to my taste excellent; we were told it came from Zant. The Dates though smaller were to my taste preferable to any of the few which at different times I have eat in London. These came of course from Barbary and seemed to be part of the regular stock of /the ship's/ provisions. Upon our begging a handful to take to our ladies, he insisted upon our carrying off a good parcel to the amount of 3 or 4 pints. Over the Cabbin in a large wooden cage was a bird which Captain Brine said was a kind of partridge such as they have in the Isle of Rhodes. Upon a cursory glance it seemed to me in size and colour more like a Guinea-fowl. After some pressing the Venetian Captain accepted our invitation, and came off with us in our boat to dine with us. After Tea, Capt. Brine and Mr. Griffiths escorted him home in one of our boats, and as the vessels were by that time almost close together, the Ladies took the opportunity to gratify their curiosity, and brought off the remainder of the Basil in the pot in which it was growing. At parting the Venetian saluted them with all his guns. What made the visit on board of him the more interesting was an idea that was started of engaging him to take us from Smyrna to Constantinople, and from thence under Russian colours to the Crimea. The feasibility of assuming such colours and obtaining the privilege which they confer seemed to be agreed on by both the Captains. The Venetian seemed to lend a favourable ear to the idea, said if he took us he should not charge us much, but took the matter *more Batavico ad referendum.* He seems a good honest plain kind of a man with a beard the length of which seemed to be more owing to negligence than to fashion. One piece of furniture we observed in his cabbin an English waiter of the Pontypool kind, the only article he had that was English, and the only article as he politely observed that was worth any thing. The national vanity could not receive a more ample gratification than at the incense offer'd to it by this rough Venetian Sailor, who declared with /much/ energy and apparent sincerity that he knew of nothing in any way that deserved the name of good but what came from England. At ~~leaving~~ the conclusion ⟨of our⟩ first visit we were accosted by a lad of about 20 in very tolerable English who said he had served on board an English ~~vessel~~ man of war I forget what for about 5 or 6 months, and would have been very glad if Capt. Brine would have taken him: he made no other complaints, but said he had not seen a morsel of meat for a week past. Our table yesterday happend to be not quite so well served as it is commonly: neither fruit pye nor pudding. We had however some excellent pease-soup, a fine piece of salt-beef, a chicken-pye and a haunch of mutton venisonified with sweet sauce. What luxury this to the frugal and spare-dieted Venetian! He eat however but sparingly, and all the temptations of Capt. B.'s well-stocked Cellar were insufficient to prevail with him to exceed the strictest limits of sobriety. I don't know which of the Captains it was that proposed to the other to keep company during the voyage: the proposal if not made was at least cheerfully accepted by the Venetian and in consequence he has several times slacken'd sail that he might not get a head of us. We are a protection to each other, especially we to the Venetian: for scarce has any instance been known of a /Mediterranean/ Pirate's venturing upon an Englishman: this mutual security is more particularly of use in going into the ports, which the barbarity of the inhabitants renders in many places more dangerous than the waves from which they appear to offer an asylum. I have not yet told you because we have but this instant learnt ⟨that⟩ the name of our friend's ship is the San Nicola (St. Nicholas) and his own Giovanni (John) Patareschi or some ⟨such⟩ name. We are now trudging together (8 o'clock P.M.) near enough for us to see and hear our neighbours at their prayers. We have been mutually toasting one another with Music; if ours was but so so theirs, Italian as it is, was infinitely worse. We have been all day long in a situation tantalizing at least to me rambling amidst a labyrinth of islands, without landing on any one. I have just been viewing with a glass an odd hill like a sugar-loaf /thick/ spangld with buildings from top to bottom, and crowned with one which from its superior size and commanding situation I should suppose to be a Castle. This was on the Isle of Serphanto[10]

Friday Oct. 21.

This morning Capt. Brine treated us with an excursion to the Isle of Scio:[11] the company, Mr. Griffiths, Mr. Schneider, (a Russian merchant of German extraction whom we took in at Leghorn) the Venetian Captain, young Jack (Randal) whom you saw aboard, and myself. We got into the boat about 10, and were on board again a little after 2: it took us about an hour and a half to row thither, and about an hour to sail back. Our landing was upon a fine sandy beach, about a mile from a town which we clambered up to as fast as our legs would carry us over a road in some places steep and

[10] I.e., Siphanto (Sifnos), one of the more westerly islands of the Cyclades.

[11] Chios, or Scios, south of the entrance to the gulf of Smyrna.

every where roughen'd with loose stones. The name of the town I could not collect with certainty, Laddea, or Taddea, or Thaddea. A description very exact or copious cannot reasonably be expected from 1½ hours stay part of which was taken up in merchandizing, and other part in herborising. A beautiful palm not above 100 yards from the landing was the first object that interested us before we came near enough to take part in the animate scenes that exhibited themselves as we approached. We found 2 or 3 houses close to the shore, in the neighbourhood of which were 7 or 8 persons variously occupied. Two Boys we took for our guides, through the intervention of the Venetian Captain who spoke the modern Greek with fluency. The streets such of them as we saw, and we were told they were the principal, were about the width of the narrowest part of Shire-Lane: the houses built of such sort of stone as the soil underneath afforded, without a particle of mortar, seemed in general to be 2 stories high: in many places the upper story of a house of one side of the street was connected with the correspondant story of the other side by an arch: and the spaces thus cover'd in seemed in some of the streets to be equal to that which was left uncoverd. The windows were holes left in the walls: glass we did not see an atom of in the whole town: yet every house had some ornamental carving in the stone-work over the door, elegantly designed and neatly executed, without /attempting/ however to imitate flowers or any other production of Nature. The rooms were as small in proportion as the streets were narrow: we did not go into any of them, but from such glances as we could catch as we walked on we could discover no other furniture but a few stools. All the people we saw were Greek: we were told there was scarce a Turk upon the island: one of the first persons we observed was a most comely venerable old man with a long curling beard as white as snow: I could have fancied him one of the 7 sages. The young women were several of them very pretty: a good set of teeth and black eyes were by no means rare amongst them: in particular we observed a girl seemingly about 9 or 10 years old with eyes of the deepest black we had ever seen. All the people viewed us with attention, none with displeasure, and most of them with remarkable complacency: many of them asked what countrymen we were, and the intelligence of our being mostly English seemed to give very general satisfaction: *'callos'*, *'callos'*, that's well, that's well, was the word they made use of to express it. Some of the women threw us down flowers from the upper story. An old woman took hold of my hand and kissed it: then offerd me hers. I thought she meant to have the compliment returned: I accordingly took hold of hers and was lifting it up to my lips when a kind of laugh on her part as well as on that of the bystanders, together with the word *denari*, Italian for money, advertised me of my mistake. This was the only sign of begging we any of us observed. I made the best signs I could to get her to understand I had none of their money about me, which was the truth, and she was satisfied. The Captain bought to treat the Cabbin with some almonds raisins, melons, and oranges, some of the latter as ripe as you have them when they first come in in England, others in a state of sowerness fit for punch. It cost him in the whole about a crown including porterage and guides. Fresh grapes, pears and peaches we could hear no tidings of: a woman offer'd him half a dozen indifferent looking apples for 4 *paras*: (you know what a para is) about a half-penny a piece. This he refused as exorbitant: I begged him to lend me the money that I might buy them: but as before this time he had spied a breeze which summoned us on board again with all possible expedition, he could not allow me time to compleat the bargain. Not a creature we saw had any such thing on as a stocking: a few of the best dressed among the men but none of the women had slippers: shoes and their appendage buckles nobody expects on a Greek island. Few of either sex but had /some sort of a/ linnen garment; but generally ragged and dirty, and universally coarse. A little valley by which we returned afforded some pretty little gardens: in which I saw more flowers cultivated as such than I had observed, a few palaces excepted, in France and Italy put together. French and African marigolds made the most conspicuous figure. We saw besides tobacco in flower and in seed, the egg-plant in fruit, the purple kind such as is eat under the name of *aubergines* in the South of France and under the name of | | in Italy, Oranges, Lemons, Olives, Jujubes (a paltry fruit a little like a very small *date*) /various sorts of/ melons, and pumpkins, not to mention Blackberries which were growing wild there as with us. We saw Mulberry trees and Almond trees; but no fruit on either: the fruit being all gathered in as well as from the fig-trees. The Mulberries I suppose are cultivated for silk: and when that is the case the tree is so checked by the continual depredations committed on its leaves that you seldom see any fruit: indeed the fruit of the sort which is cultivated for the sake of its leaves, is white and good for little. Cotton we saw in the houses, but none growing; some women presented us with some pods of it: picking it seems to constitute the chief occupation of the inhabitants. I observed a man with his hands stained blue. Upon enquiry I learnt as I suspected that he was a Dyer. I should have wished to have peeped into his Dye-house; but we were then hastening back, and it was a considerable distance behind us. In one of the Streets we saw one side of a Chapel which was in ruins: not from age, however, though it seemed far from modern; but /as we supposed/ from violence. The inside was coverd with paintings al fresco, chiefly portraits of Saints; with legends which I had no time to attempt decyphering: the letters were capitals which upon a hasty glance seemed like the antient: the numerals however which we observed over the doors of private houses were not the antient Greek, but the Arabick, as our's are.

Saturday Oct. 22 11 o'clock.

I am writing in the midst of a storm: the wind being right against us we were forced to turn tail on Smyrna about 3 hours ago: we are trying to make a harbour called Olivier on the Island of Metelin.[12] The Capt. is grave we are in some danger.

Oct. 22 ½ after 11 A.M. in continuation.[13]

I have no objection to this storm; we shall see an Isle the more for it and if we don't go bump ashore we shall soon be at our ease. As God's mercy will have it we have got for our *infans portus* not only /our friend/ the Venetian but a little Caichi which is before him. Spring and I have the Cabbin to ourselves; there is better to do upon Deck: I have just been up to take a peep: the land on all sides I imagine would loo⟨k⟩ beautiful if the storm would but give us leave to steer it. Our foretop sail has just been blown to rags: but who cares? We have just given the go by to a dangerous rock that sticks itself up right in the middle of a very narrow part of the entrance; and are now out of all danger. This harbour is an enormous long one, running up the country like Portsmouth but infinitely narrower; upon an average perhaps about the width of the Thames at Westminster Bridge; but the Lord knows: for I am now in the Cabbin, and I am but a bad judge of distances: We are in no want of company: Capt. B. has already pointed out to us a

[12] The *Mary Frances* was being driven north-west out of the entrance to the gulf of Smyrna towards the island of Lesbos (Myteline).

[13] The double sheet, B.M. III: 456–7, starts here. In Jeremiah Bentham's copy of this letter the text runs on without a break, and there seems no reason to alter this arrangement (B.M. XXII: 330). The storm caused Bentham's ship to take refuge in one of the havens in the island of Lesbos.

Frenchman and a Russian. What makes the loss of a sail dangerous at some conjunctures is that if you have no sail by which you can give a motion to the ship in a different direction to that of the the wind you draw before it like a log and must go bang against the shore or any object that lies in the way without the possibility of helping yourself. We had plenty of thunder and lightening last night, some of the flashes fell very near the ship, I was waken'd by the crash. At one time there was such a rattling upon deck I thought it had been from hailstones as big at least as marbles. I was afraid I should have heard of mischief done to the crew: upon enquiry it turned out to be mere rain without a single hail-stone: the rattling was owing to the size of the drops and the violence of the wind.

Oct. 23 A.M. Sunday.

A Mr. | | Clerk to | | a French house at Smyrna has just been breakfasting with us and from him I have picked up the following particulars. His abode is on board the French ship now in the harbour: he left Smyrna [*two words crossed out*] 22 days /ago, has been here ever since/ and thinks to be back again some time this week. His business is to collect Oil, the only merchantable produce of the Island. His house sends it to Marseilles there to be manufactured into Soap. Though the best in the Archipelago it is not used for eating, though it might be were not the Leghorn oil as much better as it is nearer hand. This Greek [oil] must /be bought here/ very cheap to make it worth while to send for it from such a distance into an oil country. His dealings are with the Aga who commands the Island. He farms the Revenue from the Grand Signior for 600 purses a year. The principal branch of it is the Tithe of the Oil which he takes up in kind. If Tithes in England are a grievance, in Mitelin, as may be imagined they are a much greater. In England the Farmer chooses for the Parson: here the Parson chooses for himself. By dealing with this great Improprietor, the Frenchman therefore, if this German clerk of his is to be believed, skims the cream of the best oil that is made in Greece. To the burthen of the English Farmer, these poor Greeks add that of the French Peasant; after the choicest of their produce has thus been taken from them they have the amusement of carrying it themselves on board the ship which carries it off. It comes in sheep skins with the wool in the inside: I saw a skin which I suppose was one of them hanging up in a distended state on the Isle of Scio. By this then there must be a considerable loss: but the loss comes not to the

Aga nor to the Merchant, but to the Farmer for the Merchant pays for no more than the quantity emptied from the skins into his own barrels. Whether the service is part of the duty legally annexed to the tax or whether it is an exaction wrongfully imposed by the present Aga I have not learnt. As to the Aga himself, all he has to do with the Oil, as may be imagined, is to strike the bargain for it and receive the money: but he has two Brothers who condescend to take a more personal concern in it. These Gentlemen execute the office of /searchers,/ tasters, garblers, and whippers in: the Greeks stile them the pair of Devils. If such they are they are according to this German, who speaks upon 7 or 8 years experience the proper sort of gentry to deal with these descendants of the pretended virtuous Greeks: for they are well matched he says by the Turks, and nobody else could deal with them. If this be true it is no more than what is to be expected: such as the Government is such, making allowance for the time which moral causes take to operate, must be the people.

Did I tell you? (no I believe I did not) that we shall find the plague in Smyrna? We heard this unwelcome news on Thursday last (the 20th) from an English vessel that had left that port the Monday before, the William, Capt. Cook. It did not break out however till after he had got his bills of health: it came as he heard from Constantinople; another crumb of comfort for us. The wind being at that time contrary our Captain and Mr. Griffiths took a cruise in the boat, and fell in with this vessel which at their setting out, the Captain and he did not know to be our countryman. To sweeten this bitter intelligence they brought off a present of fruit for us, consisting of figs, pomegranates etc, and a few fresh grapes. The pomegranates are here what I think they must be everywhere, vile, insipid trash.

Not only the sail I mentioned but all the other sails of the poor Venetian went to pot in the storm of yesterday: it would cost him to replace them with new ones, our Mate says, not less than $40 or 50. If they were such as [we] use, it must be a good deal more; for the Capt. estimates the one sail he has lost at between 30 and 40 $. As the disaster might perhaps be owing in some degree to the Venetian's good faith and complaisance in waiting for us to shew us the way into a harbour which to him was familiar and to us new, Capt. B. thought he could do no less than to lend him a suit to carry him to Smyrna. He accordingly sent /them/ off with half a dozen men to put them ~~up~~ on this morning, and consequently during the time that operation took up, which might be a couple of hours, we had to wait. We have been under way for some time for Smyrna with a fair wind, and are now out of the harbour. This unexpected expedition put an end to a scheme which had been settled last night for an expedition over land to Mitilene the capital. We were to have gone Mr. Griffiths, Mr. Schneider and myself with Mr. Henderson's French-Italian Servant whom he brought from Nice, and the Venetian captain. Mr. Griffiths speaks good French and a little Italian—the Venetian speaks Greek fluently. It is about 1½ hours journey, the Venetian was to have procured us horses from a Village which he shew'd us. This fair wind a North one came unexpectedly and for us loungers very spitefully. The Captain had made up his mind to the being obliged to stay several days for the weather to settle; and with all his anxiety not to lose time, he would not have sailed this morning had not he seen other vessels preparing to set him the example. These companions of our's proved to be a Turkish vessel, a Venetian, and one under Russ[ian] colours manned with Greeks /and Sclavonians/, with only one Russian on board /a common sailor./ This latter we visited yesterday afternoon, the Captain, Mr. Griffiths and Mr. Schnieder and I, at the desire of Mr. Schneider, to whom in his quality of a Russian subject such a visit was more particularly interesting. It proved to be a Polacea two months from Taganrog (at the farther end of the sea of Azof) loaden with corn for Smyrna. The Captain who was a Greek was not on board: we therefore did not go on board ourselves: What was still more agreable to me we /landed and/ made a little excursion into the country, first on one side of the harbour and then on the opposite. I picked up some plants one of which a pretty shrub with quinque-foliated leaves was new to me. It had no flowers, so that we could not determine its genus but what was better it had seeds of which I took care to lay in a good stock. /P.S. It turns out to be the Vitex Agnus-Castus/. In one group on rocky ground close to the water's edge I found Oleanders Mirtles one of the sorts of Mastick Tree which grows every where, wild vines and a pretty kind of reed about 10 or 11 foot high, and the five finger-leaved /anonymous/ shrub above mentioned. Further up we saw the arbutus in fruit, a few of them were ripe and were not unpleasant to the ⟨taste⟩ I made a pretty nosegay of some tall elegant heaths of several sorts that were cover'd with beautiful flowers. Mr. Griffiths in the mean time picked up close to the water a substance which proved a curiosity. It was a piece of bitumen about the size of one's fist with shells encrusted on it. Its lightness shew'd it not to be a stone: and upon being held to the candle it melted and shew'd itself to be a combustible. This discovery might have been an interesting one, had we had time to pursue it. I find no mention made of any such thing in any of the topographical books I have at hand. There may be plenty of it for aught we know. I was not by when it was picked up. Except on here and there a rocky spot the ground was every where planted, chiefly with olives, under which nothing but a few ugly and common weeds will grow. We found a pear tree seemingly wild the fruit of which though rough and sharp was eatable. I saw another old pear tree which had been /lately/ grafted after the manner of crown grafting. It was pleasing to see /even this slight/ instance of the union of skill and industry. Human creatures we saw none, except a few stragglers from the different vessels like ourselves. I could not learn from either the Venetian /Captain/ or the French Merchants Clerk that any part of the Island the capital included affords any sort of manufacture even of the coarsest kind, or any article which one could wish to buy, except ordinary provisions. The Bullocks here are said to be small seldom weighing above lb 400. On coming out of the harbour we saw four Swans flying at a great heighth. Some islands near Smyrna are said to be crowded with them to an incredible degree.[14]

Wednesday Nov. 9th.

On board a Turkish Caïk from Smyrna to Constantinople. E. of the Island of Metelin.

We anchored at Smyrna Tuesday fortnight Oct. 24. We embarked this Turk Friday last Nov. 3 /a little after/ midnight, and immediately set sail. A deal of time in arrear for journalising—I must e'en omitt for the present the transactions at Smyrna.[15] The few moments I can snatch for writing in the midst of all manner of embarassments would otherwise be consumed in recollecting. Previous to our embarkation we took a farewell supper with Capt. Brine. The two Mr. Lee's and Capt. Seward of the Smyrna in the Levant trade were of the party to take

[14] Up to this point Jeremiah Bentham's copy is practically identical with the letter as sent. In the next dozen or so lines there is some variation of phrasing, though not of substance, preliminary to the interpolation of the greater part of Bentham's letter to Mulford (letter 551).

[15] No account by Bentham of his stay at Smyrna between 24 October and 3 November has survived, and possibly he failed to carry out his intention of writing one. Memoranda of the kind mentioned by Bowring (x, 150b) have not been found. While there he unwisely published the fact that he was empowered to engage British subjects for the service of Russia, failing to realize the intensity of Turkish feeling after the Russian annexation of the Crimea (Sir Robert Ainsley to the Marquis of Carmarthen, 10 December 1785, copy, Public Record Office, F.O. 261/2).

leave. The little wind which blows pretty regularly off land at midnight brought us no farther than a league or two beyond the Castle. The next day at noon /Saturday today 5th Novr./ between calms and contrary winds we found ourselves no farther on our way than off Fochia Nova,[16] a place considerably within the gulph of Smyrna. The wind not only contrary but violent, at least in the estimation of Turkish Navigators, determined the Captain to seek shelter in the harbour belonging to that little town.[17] The same causes detained us there till yesterday morning; /Tuesday Nov. 8.,/ we left it with a fair wind /at 6 o'clock./ The wind from a scarce perceptible breeze swelled gradually to a pitch which would have been the delight of an English Captain, but struck terror into the soul of Sacristi Osman Reis. He sought shelter between the Asiatic main and two or three islands too small to be marked on your map of Europe. This morning when at our rising we expected to find ourselves off the Dardanelles, we found ourselves at Anchor but a few leagues beyond /the southern extremeity of/ our old acquaintance the Island of Metelin. By our conjecture, the Imperial vessel which we ought to have been on board of ⟨is⟩ by this time at Constantinople. We sailed from Fochia in company with several vessels all which have distanced us and are long ago out of sight. To Turkish unskilfulness our vessel in particular adds the misfortune of a lading by much too deep for it: what would be cowardice in another may in ours be no more than prudence. The Captain besides has the candour to acknowledge his own people worse sailors than even the Greeks.

You will be curious to learn the situation of us poor Christians among these votaries of Mahomet. Our Vessel upon the largest computation is but 80 tons: upon the smallest not more than 60: yet being very shallow it is at least ⅔ the length, and more than the breadth of the Mary Frances: though laden to extremity, it draws not more than 7 feet water. Our crew consists of 15 men besides the Captain: we have 24 passengers on the deck, all Turks; besides 18 young Negresses (slaves) under the hatches.[18] Bugs, lice and fleas, of each a moderate provision: Maggots about twice the length of a

[16] Yenifoça, on the Asiatic mainland coast about forty to fifty miles north-west of Smyrna, near the entrance to the gulf.

[17] Chronologically the next part of Bentham's account is given in the first and larger part of his letter to Mulford (letter 551). This follows accordingly in his father's letter-book copy, breaking, however, the order of the text in Bentham's original letter.

[18] Here once more Jeremiah Bentham, in his letter-book copy, broke into the text of his son's letter to interpolate the fuller description of the party on the Turkish caique contained in the first part of letter 551.

meat maggot, out of number. The catching of these last as they crawl over the wainscoat our cloaths, our persons and our provisions, forms no small part of our necessary occupation. Mr. Schnieder and Mr. Griffiths have a small cabbin between them at the head: with a kind of oblong box big enough to hold Mr. Schnieder's servant on one side of it. At the stern we have a larger Cabbin for Mr. H the two ladies and myself: with two such boxes one on each side. This Cabbin which is a hole about 11 foot wide, 8 deep and 4 foot 2 or 4 inches high serves as a common-room for the whole half dozen of us and as a Bedchamber for the Ladies: the 2 boxes serve Mr. H and me for bed chambers. A stratum of boxes serves me as a bedstead: on that I lay the mattress belonging to my cot. I squeeze in through a square hole just big enough to receive my body: it requires no small exertion to turn my head one way and my feet the other so as to lay myself at full length: this task accomplished there may be at the outside /utmost/ from 6 to 8 or so inches between my head as I lie and the tester of my bed or the cieling of my bedchamber, call it which you please. As to the dining room to account for the heighth of it, you must consider that the passengers for whose use it was calculated sit with their legs folded in under them like Taylors, and know no such things as chairs. Being a bran-new ship and this her first voyage the Cabbin looked neat /enough/ at first when decked out with a ⟨hand⟩some carpet, and another /spread/ double over it by way ⟨of a⟩ sopha: but this tempting appearance was much changed when upon taking possession of it we found the carpets taken up and the greatest part of the space filled up by the multifarious assemblage of boxes hampers /bags/ sacks and baskets that were necessary for the containing of our provisions, together with such parts of our baggage as are in most immediate use. Our provisions are mostly cold: but the Captain /agreed to/ allows us the occasional use of his kitchen, upon our giving him a solemn promise not to introduce into his ship an atom of any thing that could come under the denomination of pork. Of the construction of the habitable part if such it may be called of the vessel it is impossible to give a satisfactory description without a drawing: This cabbin of our's which forms the principal part of it has no windows looking to the sea, the roof of it forms a sort of quarter deck: over it moves the helm, and here in the open air the Captain with his mess-mates make their meals. The vessel projecting aslant over the water gives room /at this end/ for a tier of oblong boxes rising one above the other the whole breadth of it; the lowermost, a little wider than a man's back is broad, serves the Captain for a dormitory, and occasionally in a fit of laziness for a dining room. Those above are too narrow to serve for anything but shelves and lockers. They are ornamented with rows of tassels and minature balustrades. The Cabbin table, adapted to the posture of the guests for whom it was designed, is raised but two or three inches from the floor: the low boxes and parcels which serve us instead of chairs giving us a sort of mean elevation between the Turkish and the Christian mode, my camp-stool reversed gives a suitable elevation to the table. A piece of broken earthen ware /which I found on the shore at Fochia/ forms a candlestick much preferable to the filthy ricketty brass one to which it has succeeded. Considering the ships size the number of passengers you will acknowledge is not small: in the ⟨evening⟩ when they are stretched out at their length to sleep it is difficult to find a place to set one's foot on in passing from one end or one side of the ship to the other.

Thursday Novr. 10 9 at night

Here we are still stewing up in a little hole of a harbour not above 1½ leagues from our former station. The wind has /not only/ been fair but the weather mild ever since yesterday afternoon: but we Turks have no idea of sailing by night. We kept our considering caps on this morning with the /fairest wind and the/ finest weather reflecting that as the weather had once been bad it might be so again: at last at about 11 we made a desperate effort and got out of our former station: we came here /at ½ after 12/ why ⟨would⟩ you think? because in case of foul weather ⟨there⟩ might be no port to run into before dark. ⟨In the⟩ mean time Here we are to lounge till the next ⟨morning⟩ as we have been lounging all the after⟨noon⟩ when we are ready to go tomorrow the weather may have become foul and the /fair/ wind gone. Having nothing else to do we have been on shore on the island we happened to be nearest to, one ⟨of a⟩ numerous cluster between the great island of Mytelene and the Asiatic main. Some of our crew have counted as they suppose a dozen: the chart of de Choiseuil's which is the latest and I suppose the best map of these parts gives 3 or 4. On the ⟨isle⟩ in question I saw no inhabitants but one m⟨an⟩ who was ploughing with a pair of oxen close to the shore. His habitation was a square building with a flat roof cover'd as it appeared with earth The whole island is broken and rocky, this plowing operation seemed to have been the first experiment that had been made on it /perhaps/ for ages, amongst us we traversed the whole island and can be pretty sure of there being no other habitation than that of this Robinson Crusoe. He appears however to have some occasional visitors as Defoe's had. Two of our party had guns and found plenty of partridges of the beautiful Lesbian kind; but too shy to be killed: I sprung a hare. Plants we found none but what we have found every where. The shore yielded pumice-stones and pieces of spunge. Several other vessels we found already put in from the same prudential reasons as governed us. Even one or two Greek, tho' they had not the depth of their loading to plead as we have. Even in the smoothest sea the water comes in at our scuttles /scuppers/, and we have no vent to let it out at. The next port we are to try for if wind and weather permitt is one called Papa /Baba/ or Pawpaw /Bawbaw/[19] if ever we reach that, which /on the supposition of our having/ our choice of wind we expect to do in a day, the Captain promises us a safe sea to the Dardanelles: till then we have nothing but Scyllas and Charybdis's to encounter with. Every body has lost all patience, except myself: out of a spirit of contradiction I keep mine. With little or perhaps no exception the Asiatic main rises boldly from the Sea. Here and there we catch a town or part of a town seated on the summit of a rock. The absence or presence of a Minaret shews whether it belongs to the Faithful or to *Gyaurs* (Infidels). At 12 this day Thursday /10th/ we had a pretty distinct view of Jundadass or Jundadussi[20] a pretty considerable Gyaur town inhabited by Greeks. Better eyes than mine pronounced the houses distinct from each other and flat roofed.—N.B. A Minaret is a round tower which answers the purpose of a Belfry. It is attached to the Mosque to which it forms a constant appendage, but does not communicate with it. At about ¾ of the heigth is a hole for a door-way opening out into a circular balcony, in which the Sexton, *Iman* I think he is called makes his rounds to call the people to Church. The Balcony is just big enough for the man to walk round in, the door-way for him to go out at, and the sha⟨ft of the⟩ Column to receive a stair-case for him to crawl ⟨up by⟩ He who has seen one Minaret has seen all.

Constantinople Friday Nov. 25 1785.

The post sets out this evening. It is expected to reach London in about 30 days. The thread of my history is continued in a letter of this same date to Mr. Mulford.[21] I have desired him to forward it

[19] The town of Baba and the cape of that name, the most westerly point in Asia Minor, lie just north of the island of Lesbos.

[20] Not identified.

[21] Letter 551.

to you, all but for a sheet which I suppose he will tear off as it is relates solely to some Turkish pipes, a specimen of Jerusalem Soap, and other such trifles which I have sent him. Capt. Brine has promised to bring you on my account ¼ of a quintal of Virgin Raisins and another of Virgin Currants. The Turkish quintal is 122 of our pounds. I hope you will find them enough to furnish you with plumb puddings for Sunday's dinners /every Sunday/ till I return to partake of them. These sorts I am told here are not to be bought in London: as to figs you could buy them [as] good there as here. You will hardly see Capt. Brine before April. I fear we shall be obliged to finish our journey by land. Mackenzie after all is still Admiral at the Crim.[22] Here as well as at Smyrna I found my brother's old friend and Fellow Traveller Mr. Eaton[23]; he is to the last degree friendly and obliging. A most pleasing and intelligent man; I hope to see him at Crichoff, perhaps, conduct him thither. There is a little of the plague, but no great matter. My dear Father.

Adieu!

[22] On Mackenzie, see letter 545, n. 13. The remaining part of this letter is mostly illegible, and a text which, however, appears to vary slightly in phrasing, is supplied from the letter-book copy.

[23] William Eaton, a merchant based at Constantinople, had considerable commercial knowledge and interest in the Levant and the Black Sea region; in 1798 he published his well known *Survey of the Turkish Empire.* At this period he had already passed some time as Dutch consul at Basra, had entered into a trading partnership at Constantinople in 1776, and was beginning to explore the possibilities of trade in the Black Sea lands (M. S. Anderson, 'Samuel Bentham in Russia, 1779–1781', *American Slavic and East European Review*, xv, 2 (1956), 160 n.; E. I. Druzhinina, *Severnoye Prichernomor'e v 1775–1800 gg.* (Moscow, 1959), p. 144). Samuel Bentham met him in St Petersburg in 1780 (*Correspondence*, ii, 429, 454 n., 460 n., 466 n., 483 n.). Eaton tempted him to visit Constantinople and the two set out together; but if Samuel ever toyed with the idea of entering into partnership with him, a few days on the road soon made him change his mind. Eaton, so he told his brother, 'is the man worst calculated for commerce or business in general unless it be to manage the Turks, that you can conceive. He understands everything very well but can do nothing... a man of a great deal of learning, but very little of the knowledge of the world.' Eaton, moreover, had 'picked up a playhouse girl whom he has married and by whom he is at present entirely governed... a woman who without sense to see either his interest or her own or even any passion which can induce him to pursue any one object to please her makes him however to submit to every whim of the moment.' Samuel was glad to part company from Eaton at Pultava and make his own excursion to Kherson to see the new shipyard (B.M. III: 74). Letters 560 and 563 form a sole known exchange of correspondence between Jeremy Bentham and Eaton, indicative both of Eaton's conversable temperament and his curiosity about the commercial possibilities of the Rumanian principalities.

551

To John Mulford[1]

5–8 and 25 November 1785 (Aet 37)

Transactions at Fochia from Sat. Nov. 5. to Tuesday Nov. 8th.

The /little/ harbour of Fochia[2] is bounded on the North by a point of land in the shape of a pear, connected with the mainland by the stalk. On this peninsula stands the town: it is walled round, and covers the peninsula exactly, leaving no room for gardens. The streets are in this little town, as in all the others I have seen in the Levant, Smyrna not excepted, exceedingly narrow, and the houses small and of a ruinous appearance. The little hovels that go by the name of Shops, are here as elsewhere in the Levant collected together in streets, distinct from those which are occupied by the somewhat bigger hovels that serve for dwelling-houses. Some of the latter are occupied by men, who if the report of one of the towns-men may be credited may pass for wealthy, by comparison with the general run of Turkish fortunes: he mentioned several who might be worth from 2 to 3,000 piastres, that is from 200 to 300 £St. a year. As a proof that there was wealth in the place, in spite of the total absence of every external sign of it, the author of this intelligence, no less a personage than a Greek Barber, asked our Interpreter whether we had any watches to sell, offering himself as a purchaser /for his own use/ for any thing in that way not exceeding 100 piastres = 10 £St. value. This however must have been at least twice as much as his shop could be worth in the estimation of any country, stock and furniture included. Whether all this wealth was amassed or pretended to be amassed by the mere exercise of his profession, I did not learn. Four paras about 2½d I found was the ordinary fee: for thus much was taken of our Interpreter who was too poor in appearance to be expected to be generous, and too well acquainted with the country to be imposed upon. This pay, if a man had full business might afford some savings in a country where

551. [1] B.M. IV: 215–16, 217–18. Autograph. The first sheet bears the address: 'John Mulford Esqr. / Basingstoke / Angleterre.' Postmark: 'DE/24'. The second sheet carries no docket or indication of position but is placed with the first on the basis of the internal evidence. It cannot belong to Bentham's letter to his father (letter 550), since the two sheets of which Bentham stated that letter to consist are accounted for.

[2] As Bentham stated that his vessel put in at Yenifoça (p. 387, above), it is presumably this place that he was referring to here and not the town of Foça a few miles to the south of it, further up the gulf of Smyrna.

wants are so few, the stile of living so simple, and necessaries so cheap. Mutton we found about 1½d a lb: bread, nearly as much as there is in a twopenny loaf for a halfpenny.

We were eager to get on shore, all hands, in order to make a comfortable dinner upright and in fresh air. We thought we had found an excellent place for the purpose in a half enclosed space with a large oblong stone at the further end, rough indeed and of coarse materials, but in other respects not unlike the marble slabs you have in England for side-tables. A burying ground was near adjacent, but there was a road between. We had spread out our provisions, and already made some advance in our dinner, when the appearance of a number of Turks who by this time had collected together with visible marks of dissatisfaction in their countenances, shew'd that by some means or other we had given umbrage. They said something to me, which of course we did not understand: all we could do was to call to our old interpreter who happen'd to be at some distance, but hobbled up to us as soon as he could. Through him we learnt that the slab had something sacred in it, which they apprehended would be profaned by our repast. We immediately assured them that pork formed no part of it: this we were enabled to do in Turkish by a sentence we took care to be provided with (Dômooz yok boorda)[3] in order to convey a similar assurance to our Turkish Captain who had /exacted/ it as a condition precedent to our admission into his vessel. At this they seemed to be in some measure satisfied: but lest the satisfaction should fail of proving compleat or universal, we thought it best to change our quarters, and accordingly removed to a broad low wall which though it formed part of the fence which half encompassed this sacred stone did not seem liable to the same objections. A Mohometan Algerian, who /had/ come into the port a stranger like ourselves, accepted without hesitation our invitation to join us in a glass of wine: an invitation, which we /have/ found some reason to think there are few Turks but would accept, some with more some with less ceremony: some only in private, some in the face of their comrades without scruple. At present the chief effect of the precept seems in this as in other instances among us, to give a zest to the violation of it. As to the sacred stone the reason of its possessing this quality became apparent enough the next day, when we saw the body of a child laid on it for a considerable length of time, while a sort of funeral service was performing previous to its interment.

What shall I give the preference to, the description of this

[3] I.e., *domuz yok burada*, there is no pig here.

funeral, the Greek inscriptions, the aqueduct, or the visit to Achmet Effendi? For the inscriptions I had not far to look: against you pay a visit to Fochia I will tell you where you may find them. As soon as you have enter'd at the gate which is nearest the beach, turn short upon your right hand: at the end of a winding lane you will find yourself in an irregular kind of area, which being about big enough to swing a cat in bears about the same proportion to the adjacent /streets and/ houses as Grosvenor or Cavendish Square may do to the streets and houses in their neighbourhood. About the center of this area stands a kind of pedestal which fronts you as you enter from the /above/ lane: the side which then fronts you faces the West nearly: on that side is an inscription in Greek capitals, which I have copied in part, and which another opportunity at a proper time of day would I believe have enabled me to compleat. I say at a proper time of day: for it was only in the afternoon when the sun shone full upon it, that I could get a tolerable view. A few feet to the right of this, stood a similar pedestal, in a direction at right angles to that of the former, and accordingly nearly facing the South. This had also an inscription on it, but considerably shorter consisting only of 4 short lines, the words of which I made out I believe pretty exactly, though the total import will I believe be difficult to decypher without the assistance of collateral information which has not fallen within my cognizance. I will subjoin it by way of a rebus with which you may amuse any of your antiquarian friends. I understood from the people of the place that not long ago each of these pedestals had a statue on it, which was carried away by some Franks like ourselves. This tradition agrees very well with the import of the inscription
ΦΛΕΙΜCΤΡΑ | *ΤΗΝ* ⋮ *ΦΙΛΟΣΟ* | *ΦΟΝ* ⋮ *ΣΤΕΦΑ* | *ΝΗΦΟΡΩΝΤΕ* |
These marks | shew where the lines end: the dotted marks ⋮ shew where I imagine the words end: the *Σ* in the third line being obliterated by a crack in the stone is supplied by my conjecture. The general import I take to be that on this pedestal stood the statue of a /nameless/ philosopher: the rest is open to conjecture which I have /at present/ neither room nor leisure nor sufficient learning to discuss.[4]

The time I was employ'd in decyphering or rather endeavouring to decypher these inscriptions was much circumscribed by the

[4] As it stands the text of this inscription appears corrupt. A possible suggested reading is:

ΠΑΛΑΙΣΤΡΑ ΤΩΝ ΦΙΛΟΣΟΦΩΝ ΣΤΕΦΑΝΗΦΟΡΩΝΤΕ

i.e., 'the academy of the philosophers and the winners of prizes'.

necessity I was under of having the old interpreter at my elbow, and the annoyance I met with from the people of the place, particularly the children who came in crowds to stare at the stranger who was busying himself so seriously about such insignificant nonsense. Amongst others however came an old man of a genteel appearance, who after putting some questions to me and receiving such imperfect answers as I could give him through the medium of our old man who spoke no language that I had the least smattering of except Italian, gave me to understand that he knew of another inscription, and that if I would call on him some other time, (for he was then going to prayers) he would send a man with me to shew me the way, and should then be glad to hear my sentiments about it. To enable me to carry on this conversation a little less imperfectly I determined to endeavour to engage the company not only of this old man, but of Mr. H's Nissard Servant who speaks French and Italian with equal facility. To find a time in which the leisure of these three persons could be brought to coincide was no such easy matter: on Monday afternoon however the business was accomplished: and I got admission attended by my two interpreters into the house of *Achmet Effendi*, that was the old gentleman's name, who I had learnt in the mean time was a man of the first quality in the place. The apartment into which the door open'd from the street was neither more nor less than a stable, in which however there happen'd at that time to be no company of the four-footed kind: from thence went up something between a ladder and a staircase which open'd into a pretty spatious hall of the same dimensions as the stable, rather /upon the/ antique, but upon the whole not ill fitted up. In the upper part of the room, being the farthest from the staircase and nearest the windows, which I can assure you were glazed sash-windows though not of the lightest workmanship, on an elevated platform cover'd with matting and some carpeting, sat the master of the house. His first salutations over, upon a sign from the old gentleman I stepped on the platform and seated myself by his side: 3 or 4 little boys, one tolerably dressed, the others dirty and shabby, crowded round us as if they had been at home: one or two of them I believe were already with him, others enter'd along with us: what relation if any they bore to the old gentleman I did not learn. My two interpreters remained on the area below, sometimes standing, sometimes kneeling as convenience dictated. I found him with a printed book by his side which I found was to make the subject of our conversation. It proved to be a general system of Geography in Arabick written by a man of the name of Khatib Chelibij[5] and printed at Constantinople in the year of Mahomet 1125, which, speaking at this distance from all books that could ascertain the matter I imagine is not widely distant from the year 1720 or thereabouts of our Æra. Upon my expressing my surprize at seeing a book printed at that metropolis, where I should not have expected that either the capacity of the people or the disposition of the ruling powers would have been favourable to such a performance, he told me it was printed by a French Renegado who went there to settle. It contained a number of Maps, upon a small scale and rude as might be expected from the place and time. On one he shew'd me the signs of the Zodiack telling me how many of them there were. I asked him what he made the number of the planets, meaning to introduce Herschel's discovery of a new one[6]: He answer'd, *nine*: and went on to shew me other things, not having patience to enter into any discussions relative to the number. He afterwards turned to the map of Europe, for the purpose of shewing me the track taken by the Russian fleet in its passage to the Mediterranean: a subject which I should little have expected to find him touch upon of his own accord. Instead of coming from Petersburgh through the Baltic he made them come from Archangel or thereabouts North about: in other respects his conception seemed to be just enough. He spoke of the publication of this book as an æra of importance to the Ottoman empire: before that time, it was impossible for the Grand Signor to have any tolerable idea of what was going forward in his empire: since then if he hears of a rebellion, he turns to the book, and sees where it is: if he orders troops to quell it, he turns to his book again and sees which way and how far they have to go. Speaking of the Mariner's compass he acknowledged it to be a most useful and fortunate invention: imagine why: because of its use in navigation? no: but because by the help of it the faithful are enabled to turn their faces exactly to the right spot when they are saying their prayers. This spot, understand, is that on which Mahomet's tomb is situated. You have probably heard of a prophecy the Turks have, relative to the approaching dissolution of their Empire: I found Achmet Effendi possessed with this idea: he

[5] Mustapha ibn Abdulla, known as Katib Çelebi or Hajji Khalfa (1609–57), a noted scholar. Among his works *Jihānnumā*, a work of geography giving an account of lands discovered since the fifteenth century, published at Constantinople in 1732 (in the year of the Prophet 1145, not, as Bentham states, 1125), was a landmark in Ottoman scholarship.

[6] The astronomer, William Herschel (1738–1822) had discovered the planet Uranus in 1781.

alluded to it in the course of the conversation: but Mr. S. having by that time joined us, and the discourse taken another turn, I could not examine him /on that subject/ as I wished to do. He seemed little disposed to attend to any thing I offer'd to communicate to him relative to European customs or European learning: indeed it was easy to perceive that the object of the interview was on his part not to gain information but to display importance. In this view after proving his learning by the exhibition of this book, he thought proper to prove his wealth by the display of a pair of ear-rings which he sent a servant out for while I was turning over the book: they consisted each of them of 3 or 4 ~~diamonds~~ pearls in so many drops, of some size but of very bad colour and uncouth shape. What was singular enough, though his eyes seemed weak with age, he was so extremely near-sighted as not to be able to read unless the book was almost in contact with his eyes. This proved a sad obstacle to /so much of/ the conversation, as /related to the book as it/ was absolutely impossible for him and me and the interpreter to have our eyes on it at a time. He invited me to smoke a pipe with him: upon finding me decline it, and hearing that it was not much the fashion in my country, he sent for some /dried/ raisins, and a kind of cake they make in Turkey of grapejuice boiled down with flour, both which he said were the produce of his own estate. I took what I thought proper, and upon our taking leave (Mr. Scheider was at that time of the party) he insisted upon our carrying away with us what was left. I can not say but that I was a little di⟨sapp⟩ointed by the unexpected appearance of Mr. S.: for by ⟨tha⟩t means I necessarily lost in some degree the command of the conversation, and missed a number of particulars which I was preparing to collect. At length the old gentleman observed to me that it was time I set out on my way to the piece of antiquity he had been speaking of: for if I staid there till it was dusk, I might stand a chance of falling into the hands of some evil-disposed people who might use me ill. He accordingly sent for the man who was to be my guide: and Mr. S. though unacquainted with Greek and incurious of antiquity, chose to bear me company. Before I took my leave of the Effendi, I asked him whether he knew of any antiquities of the small kind such as seals or coins or medals that were to be met with in that neighbourhood: his answer was that on the morrow he should be ready to talk with me on that subject: but that for the present, the hour was come and he must go to prayers. He had informed me that besides the antique stone I should see there had been another not far distant: /from/ which a Frank (I think he said a

Frenchman) had (with his consent and assistance, I think he said) cut off so much as contained the inscription, and carried it away. Upon reaching the promised curiosity I found it was nothing but a /large/ stone which had been taken with a few others to form the mouth or upper part of a well. It was laid on its side, and so situated that what at present is the bottom of the stone is worn on the outside perfectly smooth, in such manner that two or three of the first letters of every line are lost beyond redemption. In the rest the hand of the sculptor is with difficulty if at all to be distinguished from the hand of time. Light failing and company pressing, I had time only to copy a few detached letters, and one entire word which however seemed to afford some clue: the completion of this atchievement I must leave to some future antiquary of more learning and more leisure. This well that you may know where to find it is called *Kartal Kuiusu* (pronounce *Kooeoo-soo*).[7] It may be about ½ a mile from the town: in go⟨ing to⟩ it you pass by a good part of the *aqued⟨uct⟩*. This aqueduct is of very rough workman⟨ship⟩ and manifestly enough of no very great an⟨tiqui⟩ty. I am ashamed to say I have learnt neither its origin nor its termination nor its author. I was told /upon enquiry/ that it had no particular name: but that it was called by the name given in that language to Aqueducts in general, Su-yol-lu (Soo-yol-loo)[8] literally *Street of Water*. It cons⟨ists⟩ of a chain of /stone/ arches, higher or lower according to the inflection of the ground, but no where that I saw above 10 or a dozen feet high, bearing a kind of ⟨...⟩ed trough or water-course of the same rough workmanship and materials. The dimensions so small as to afford very little room for water; hardly so much as is afforded by one of our wooden water-pipes. In general it may be observed that these aqueducts which in some places are monuments of elegance and magnificence are every where monuments of ignorance and unskillfulness: as such I look upon them rather with disgust than pleasure even upon the superb modern one of Monpelier. As to the inscriptionified well this was to have been revisited and the promised minature antiquities enquired after on the morrow: but on the morrow God Almighty sent a wind which blew us away from Fochia and our projects with us. Of[9] the passengers that are not of our party the three most conspicuous characters are an old Walachian, Thomas Morat by

[7] I.e., *kartal kuyusu*, the well of the eagle.

[8] I.e., *su yolu*, water-way, aqueduct.

[9] The text of fo. 217 commences here. Below the last sentence on fo. 216 a line is drawn above a final passage added on 24 and 25 November, which is here printed in its chronological order below.

name, a Student of Divinity, understand Mahometan Divinity, and a man who is the proprietor of the Negresses. The first of these is an interpreter appointed by Providence for our use: he is the channel and the only channel of communication except a very imperfect grammar, between us and our Mahometan Ship-mates. He speaks amongst other languages, German, Italian, and Turkish: this last in perfection, having been used to speak it from his infancy: he is by birth a subject of Hungary. He calls himself a Merchant; and says he has a house at Vienna. In the course of his travels he has been at Constantinople 4 or 5 times. The object of his present expedition however was not merchandise, but devotion: what think you of a pilgrimage to Loretto? He set out from Vienna, and made his way /to Loretto/ across Italy, sometimes on ship-board sometimes on foot: from thence as a more easy means of returning he availed himself of an occasion for Smyrna: when he is at Constantinople he will make his way to the mouths of the Danube, and so home. He has all the externals of the most wretched poverty; bread only to eat, and not enough of that; and for apparel rags crawling with vermin which he makes no scruple of cracking in the face of the world with as much composure as his Turkish neighbours. Yet he speaks of himself as continuing for his amusement, the expedition to which devotion had given birth: and he is to stay at this and that place on his route, longer or shorter, according as he finds them more or less agreable to him. This is not out of pride; for he shares with thankfulness the repast of our servants. The student of Divinity is a young Moor, seemingly about 19 or 20, who is going to Constantinople to be one of 2,000 who are brought up to the Church there, or if you please the Mosque, at the public expence. He was looked upon as a good Scholar, that is he could read, and write a good hand, and had with him some Manuscripts of his own copying. But I found that they were all in Turkish, that he understood nothing of the Arabick, that his stock of divinity, setting aside the Koran, which he was not disposed to shew, consisted of nothing but a Cathecism and a few homilies, and that he had never so much as read any books on any other subject. Yet if a *Giaur* like myself (so the Mahometans call all who are not of their persuasion) might be allowed to judge, I shou'd suppose him not ill qualified to make a conspicuous figure in his profession, for he chaunted forth his oraisons five times I think it was in the 24 hours with great fluency and with an audible voice. A great part of the discourse seemed to make its way through the nose, in a manner that would have led anyone who was not in the secret to suppose he had been mocking somebody with the intention of making his but as ridiculous as possible. As to the Slave-holder he must have been a man of substance, for these 18 wenches were all his own, and he expected to make from 30 to 50 lb stg. a head of them at Constantinople. Some of these young ladies, Mr. Henderson who had had slaves of his own, knew by their filed teeth to be Cannibals: One of them he found by some marks in their cheeks I think it was, to be of quality, probably of the blood royal, but gentle and simple, they were one and all, if any faith is to be given to external indications, by far the happiest set of people in the ship. From day to day there was nothing among them but playing and singing and laughing, and even such dancing as their confined situation would permitt. Their proprietor seemed to be a very gentle master, and to make use of hope as his instrument of government, instead of fear. As often as there has been any debarcation for any length of time, these young ladies have gone on shore to take the air, as well as the rest of the company. The notion they have been taught to entertain is that whoever buys anyone of them is to marry her, and that they are all of them to be great ladies and ride in their coaches, or do what is equivalent.

Tuesday Novr. 15th: On board the Maria, Capt. Newman in a bay off *Kvèmed* on the Asiatic coast at the entrance of the Sea of Marmara.[10]

Here are we all of us, except our Russian mess-mate Mr. Schneider, by a most fortunate and unexpected revolution which makes us amends for all the distresses out of which it has deliver'd us.

On Friday the 11th at 8 in the morning we left the station described in my last in the paragraph dated Thursday the 10th. At 10 o'clock at night we made the town of *Baba* situated on the Cape of that name, the westermost point of Asia.

On Saturday the 12th at day-break we made the Island of Tenedos[11]: at 11 A.M. the /great/ Island of Lemnos was visible on our left, though to an unexperienced eye not easily distinguishable from a cloud. We never approached near enough to get a much clearer view of it.

On Sunday the 13 at 3 o'clock in the afternoon we enter'd the Dardanelles with a fine wind.

On Monday morning the 14 between 4 and ½ after 6 we were obliged or thought ourselves obliged to lose 2½ hours of this

[10] Now Kiemed.

[11] Otherwise Bozcaada, about thirty miles north of Cape Baba.

precious wind to stop at a place called Lepseg[12] on the Asiatic side to lay in a stock of bread for the Turkish part of our passengers whose provisions were pretty well expended. We Christians not having the same necessity to plead had not the option given us to go ashore. Lepseg /or Lampsa/ on the Asiatic side is nearly opposite to Gallipoli on the European, but not so considerable a place. We now set sail again, shaping our course for the Isle of Marmora which not being above 7 or 8 leagues off we expected to reach it in a few hours. Man proposes, God disposes. At about 2 we were still several leagues short of that island when the wind shifted to the northward and came off in strong puffs. Porpoises to the amount of some score at a time, some of them within 7 or 8 yards of the vessel by their unwieldly gambols had prognosticated the storm. Having been buffeted for an hour or two in our endeavours to reach the island we at last gave up the attempt, put the ship about, and ran /back/ for our lives into the nearest port which proved to be that from which I date. We had all the ingredients of a storm, thunder lightening and hard rain. The temperature from moderate became bitter cold: the deck was all in a puddle: the poor unshelter'd Turks were wet to the skins. The Captain was /frightened/ out of his wits. His awkward sleeveless crew were pulling and hawling some this way some that way all confusion. The experienced amongst *us* pronounced our condition dangerous. The rolling made me squeamish. I crawled to my hole in search of sleep, my usual recipe against sickness: but the extreme cold which pinched my feet allow'd me but a small portion of this pleasant remedy. At 7 the ship anchored and then our company assembled in our great cabbin and took a cheerful dish of tea. On Tuesday the 15th, the first object that saluted my eyes after I had crawled out of my hole was a Turkish Caic wrecked upon a rock within a few score yards of us. It seems she had been our consort for a little while, and led the way at the entrance into the bay. A /very/ narrow ledge of rocks projected /to/ a considerable distance from the shore. She perceived the danger time enough to warn us, though not to escape it herself. The crew are saved; but the vessel and a great part of the cargo will probably be lost. The shore is strew'd with bullock's skins filled with oil, which at a little distance we took for dead fish.

After breakfast Mr. Henderson, Mr. Griffiths and myself, attended by the Interpreter, went ashore to look about us and recruit our stock of provisions which as to every thing but biscuit

[12] Now Lâpseki.

and a little fruit was pretty well expended. We got some goats' flesh just killed, some jerkt mutton, and some fine onions and some eggs with a few bottles of tolerable red wine at about 7 farthings a bottle, but our Turkish competitors had reduced /our portion of/ meat to a small pittance. Our motions being necessarily govern'd by the destination of the boat, we returned aboard to dinner. Besides a few Caïcks /that were moored closer to the shore along with us/ we had observed from the first a Frank ship at anchor a little farther out. We heard different accounts of her: some said she was a Venetian, others a Greek under Russian colours. Some of the company had started the idea of paying her a visit in order to pick up intelligence, and in particular to inquire whether she was bound for the Black Sea. I came into it immediately. On our return from shore I summoned the rest of the company, I mean the male part of it to carry the idea into execution. Mr. H. declined; Mr. G. complied with reluctance: Mr. S. the Russian was well disposed. I contrived to hale a very small boat belonging to /one of/ the Caïcks that would but just admitt 2 persons beside the boatman. Mr. S. seeing Mr. G. and myself both in readiness could not be prevailed upon to take either of our places. When we were come close alongside we perceived a gentleman who we took for granted was the Captain in a red lapelled coat with a fur cap on such as we had seen worn by Venetians. We accosted him in our broken Italian with *come sta Signor Capitano* etc.: his answer was, Gentlemen, we are countrymen, I perceive. He proved to be the Captain Newman of whom we had all of us heard honourable mention, and in particular for his experience in the navigation of the Black Sea. We made known to him our situation, he offer'd us immediately in the most generous manner and in a way that precluded a refusal a passage to Constantinople (whither he was bound) for ourselves and our whole company bag and baggage. We returned on board our prison without delay: the glad tidings were an excellent sauce to a good dinner. He sent his boat for us according to appointment; and here we are as happy as released Jail-birds, all but our Russian friend, who to our great astonishment would neither share in our joy, nor in the good fortune that had given birth to it. The Captain had sailed from Alexandria the | | last, with nothing but salt for lading: to crown our satisfaction, he informed us that he had left at that port, bound for Constantinople and from thence for /Sebastopolis in the Crimea/ the very port we are going to, a good vessel, commanded by an intelligent civil Frenchman who had been his mate: that he supposed her already sailed: but without waiting for her, he supposed he should find little difficulty in finding us at Constantinople some other ship equally eligible for the same port. Here the Ladies have a spatious state-room to themselves: and we three men share with the Captain a cabbin considerably larger than Capt: Brine's.

Thursday Novr. 17. 10 at night.

We are getting under way for Constantinople: the Turk has been gone this hour or two: our Captain, an experienced veteran /to save useless labour/ would not stir till the /wind and/ weather promised steadiness. The cold has confined the ladies all along on board; as want of curiosity has done the Captain. We men took advantage this morning of the boat's going ashore to go likewise in order to settle some matters with the Turk Captain. Cold and slight indispositions sent my comrades back again /immediately/ by an accidental conveyance. I staid on shore till the return of the boat which was about ½ after 1. We had embraced a similar opportunity yesterday morning: but a caution on the part of our old interpreter, *Morat*, suggested as I supposed by weariness, had deterred my comrades from venturing into the Turkish part of this little town /or rather village/: they were jealous, he said, of strangers; and intimation had been given him, he said, that we should not go there: they complied for that time. I yielded to the sense of the majority with reluctance. This morning finding myself and free I determined to employ the time that was allotted me in exploring as much as I could both of town and country. I have found no reason to repent my resolution. I soon explored the utmost limits of the former, and pursuing a road which skirts the river at the bottom of a beautiful narrow vaile, I came up unexpectedly after about ¼ of an hour's walk with a noble fragment of antient architecture: it consists of two entire arches part of /either/ a bridge or aqueduct which appears to have stretched /from a steep hill that skirts the road on one side/ across the present road and so across the river on the other side to the opposite bank. Its commencement at the hill is still visible and almost entire: the 2nd arch is at least 30 foot high: the first, of course not so high. Farther descriptions would lead me to too great a detail.

I will rather mention a short visit I made to the Asiatic main which I forgot to take notice of in its place. It was on Friday Novr. 11th. We had just dined. We obs⟨erved⟩ the boat getting ready, and upon enquiry were told it was to go on shore for water. We made haste to take advantage of the opportunity. Being the last who received intelligence of it, I was the last in readiness. Mr. Henderson, Mr. Griffiths and Mr. Schneider and the eldest Miss Kirtland had already stepped in to the boat. [*Sentence crossed out*] Upon approaching it I found Mr. Henderson Mr. G. and Miss K. stepping out again: it seems the crew had opposed their entrance, and one of the Turks had shoved Mr. G. back in a rude manner. Not knowing at the time what had passed I jumped in. The Turks used words and gestures the import of which seemed to tend rather to dissuade me, and one of them, the same who had pushed Mr. G. made signs that there were a rude set of people on shore who would seize us and cut our hands off; an argument which had been made us[e] of on a former occasion to reconcile us to the refusal they had given to a similar request. However as their behaviour to me had nothing of incivility or displeasure, and Mr. S. on my proposition had consented to be of my party, I determined upon keeping my station, and so I did. The truth is, I put no great faith in their plea of danger: concluding it to be suggested by their unwillingness to be troubled with a large company, who might detain them longer than they wished: an unwillingness which the diminution of the company would lessen if not remove. When we came near the shore, I found there was no landing dry-shod: I accordingly pulled off my shoes and stockings and waded with the crew. Mr. S. whether his heart failed him, or he did not care for the trouble of dressing and undressing, could not be prevailed upon to follow me. After spending some time in examining the stones and shells upon the beach, I advanced into the country, using no other precaution than to keep within sight or hearing of some of the crew that had gone on shore. At last I came to the spot where they were filling their casks; it was a stone well at about ¼ of a mile or more from the sea. /Upon coming up with [them]/ I observed two or three men whom I knew to be strangers standing round the well with two others whom I took to be /as they proved to be/ of our crew. Accosting them with /one of/ the Turkish forms of salutation, I was received with civility and expressions of satisfaction: but the same fellow who had before made signs while in the boat to warn me of having my hands cut off happening to be there, repeated them upon my coming up and turning to the strangers laughed and said something to them by which I perceived he had informed them of the bloody account he had given me of them in order to avoid being troubled with my company. I laughed with them, and said in Turkish, 'No, no: Turks are good sort of people.' After this explanation I made no scruple to wander to a distance. My curiosity was soon gratified with the sight of a fine Oak of an appearance different from any I had seen before. A quantity of /undecay'd/ leaves which lay under it on the ground seemed to indicate that it had been threshed: a Turk stranger seeing me stop to consider it at a little distance picked up one of the acorn-caps and brought it to shew me: it was scaly, like a fir-cone; and on the outside as large as a moderate sized tea-cup. I intimated to him that the present was incomplete, without the acorn: he looked afresh and gleaned up two or three which he presented me: with his search and my own I collected about 8 or 10 in a growing state which I intend for England. I then crossed a large field in order to examine a plough which I saw at the other end with a pair of oxen reposing on the ground: it was, as might be expected, of the rudest construction, without a wheel. The ploughman who came up soon after had in his hand a stick, one end of which terminated in two pointed crooks  of unequal lengths, which he made use of to prick the cattle with; the other in a kind of small trowel or spatula,  the use of which appeared to be to clear the ploughshare when clogged with earth. A part of this field was neatly planted with a very low slender twig which from the very few /imperfect/ leaves that were to be found on it I could not at first make out. A countryman coming up to me, by pointing to the plant and then to my shirt, made me understand it was cotton. I found afterwards by conversation with some Turks on board that the sort of acorn was well known in the country under the name of Palamoot or Balamoot, and the cups of it used /in the preparation of/ shoe-leather. The same man or another (for I found a difficulty in distinguishing these uncouth figures) had afterwards the civility to inform me of a nearer road to the boat which in the meantime had quitted its station, and to apprise me of its approaching departure. Thus ended my adventures among the bloodthirsty Turks.[13]

Constantinople Thursday Nov. 24. 1785

The post sets off tomorrow. I must snatch a few moments to conclude this. We anchored off the city on Sunday the last the 20th,

[13] Fo. 218 ends here. The remainder of the letter is the passage added by Bentham on what was left blank of fo. 216 and its verso upon his arrival at Constantinople. Bowring's account of Bentham's visit to Constantinople (x, 152–6) appears to be based largely on conversations and on notes which have not been found in Bentham's papers, and its details are probably suspect—for instance, Bentham was only there for three weeks, not five or six as indicated by Bowring.

but at 4 or 5 miles distance from the port: the same day the Captain went on shore alone. We had been becalmed in sight of Constantinople ever since Friday morning. On Monday Nov. 21 Mr. G. and I came on shore: we took boat at about ½ after 12: it was [*two or three words crossed out*] manned by three Turks, who took directions from the ship where to land us. The current which always runs out from the Black Sea being much more than a match for the little wind which there was in our favour, we were near two hours before we disembarked at Pera, the French suburb which lies on the furthermost side of the harbour. The necessity of eluding the force of the current which ran as supposed at the rate of 4 miles an hour, kept us close in all the way with the shore: this gave us a very near and advantageous view of one side of the vast triangle (for such is the figure of the city of Constantinople) the Seraglio included which forms of itself a town of no inconsiderable dimensions, containing as is supposed not fewer than 10,000 people. But paper gets scarce: I must dismiss descriptions and details. I dined on Monday (Nov. 21) with Duke Humphry[14]: Tuesday (Nov. 22d) with our Ambassador[15]: Wednesday (Nov 23d) with the Imperial Minister[16]: Yesterday (Thursday Nov 24) with a mad French Jeweller who perhaps may be of more use to me than all their excellencies. Yesterday morning I saw from the French Ambassador's palace the /public/ entry of the Venetian[17]: a confused and ridiculous scene. Here as at Smyrna I found Sir Rich. Worsley: I wished him at the Devil, God forgive me, or what would have come to the same thing with his wife. But for him I should have been lodged at Smyrna with the Consul and here with the Ambassador: but Sir R. /and his painter Mr. Reve⟨ley⟩/ coming first

[14] I.e., to go without dinner.

[15] Sir Robert Sharpe Ainsley Kt. (later 1st bart.) (?1730–1812) was British ambassador at Constantinople from 1776 to 1794.

[16] Bentham had been provided (see Bowring, x, 152) by his acquaintance, Baron Raigersfeld (see letter 370 at n. 15) with a letter to Herbert, the imperial internuncio at Constantinople. Baron Peter Phillip von Herbert Rathkeal, the son of an Austrian officer who had been taken prisoner together with his family during the Bosnian war of 1757, had been released by the Turks on the representations of the Jesuit, Father Francis, who educated him and several other youths at Constantinople in like circumstances with a view to their joining the order with special qualifications for work in the Near and Middle East. Herbert thus acquired an excellent grounding in oriental languages; but for a career he chose the Austrian diplomatic service, in which he served at Constantinople for most of his life. In 1779 he was promoted to be imperial internuncio, a post which he continued to hold, save for the interruption of the war of 1787–91, until his death in 1802.

[17] The French ambassador was Count Choiseul-Gouffier (see letter 539, n. 3). Cavaliere Girolamo Zulian was accredited as Venetian minister to the Porte in April 1786.

have been first served.[18] To these two his Excellency adds a 3rd guest, the Hon. | | Cadogan[19]: so that his spare room, he says, is compleatly taken up, otherwise, as he had the politeness to assure me, he should have insisted on me taking up my quarters at the *Palace*. Nothing can be more friendly or obliging: he offer'd at the first interview to fit up for the company I have with me the Infirmary belonging to his palace, or to furnish an unfurnished lodging of which he had heard we had the option. Adieu.

552

To the Marquis of Lansdowne[1]

25 November 1785 (Aet 37)

Constantinople,
Friday, November 25, 1785.

My Lord, Capt. Richard Brine of the *Mary Frances*—the ship which brought me from Italy to Smyrna—expects to be in London again by the latter end of March. He has promised me, if possible, which he thinks it will be, to take home for me a he, and two she goats of the Angora breed. Should they arrive safe, I hope Lady Lansdowne will do me the honour to accept of them, and that Bowood, in addition to its manifold luxuries, will in due time afford a stock of comfortable muffs, such as her ladyship, as I understand, has sometimes not disdained to wear. Should the breed prosper, I may perhaps, upon my return to England, become an humble suitor for a part of the progeny, in the view of trying how they may succeed in some northern part of Scotland, where their sequestered situation may the better secure them against admixture, and where the coldness of the climate gives the wool of the country a degree of fineness, which, according to my friend Dr. Anderson, is superior to any produced in the southern parts of our island. I wish I could

[18] For Sir Richard Worsley, see letter 549. He arrived at Pera on 15 November (Worsley Mss. 24, pp. 70–1, Yarborough Collection, Lincolnshire Archives Office). Willey Reveley (d. 1799) accompanied Worsley on part of his travels in the capacity of draughtsman and expert on architecture, but parted company with him at Constantinople and went to Italy. Bentham tried to tempt him to come to Russia (letter 557, n. 1), and after 1790 had dealings with him about architects' plans for the panopticon.

[19] Charles Henry Sloane Cadogan (1749–1832), eldest son and heir to the 4th Baron (later 1st Earl) Cadogan.

552. [1] Bowring, x, 156–7.

Bowring misdated the letter 'November 14', but the only Friday in November on which Bentham could have sent a letter from Constantinople was the 25th.

have had a better security than the promise above-mentioned for the arrival of those animals; but there were none to be procured, not even seen at Smyrna; they are to be had, if at all, only by the caravans, which travel but now and then, and take a fortnight's journey to go from Angora to that part.

Smyrna affords two sorts of grapes, the one of the raisin, the other of the currant size, which from a property which is common to them, and to the maiden *berberines* we have in England, have received a similar denomination. I have heard them called by Christians, virgin raisins; virgin currants, by Jews; eunuck currants, eunuchs. If neither appellation should be deemed so conformable as might be wished to the laws of delicacy, the blame must be at the door of the first authors. I can hear of no other epithet to distinguish them by. As the ideal imperfection to which they owe their name is generally looked upon as no small perfection with reference to the use we put them to, I have taken measures for sending to England a few plants of each sort, in hopes of your Lordship's doing me the honour to give them a place at Wycombe or Bowood, leaving it to your Lordship's ingenuity to rebaptize them in such manner as may be deemed most proper before they are introduced to the notice of the ladies; and that the learned at your Lordship's table may be the better enabled to pronounce whether they are worth a place in either garden, I have taken the liberty of addressing to your Lordship, by Captain Brine above-mentioned, a small specimen of each contained in two *drums*, as they are called, which have been filled under my own inspection, and marked by me V.R.L., the other V.C.L.: each drum contained, as near as could be contrived, 1-4th of a quintal, Turkish, equal to 30½ lbs., English. I should not have thought of troubling your Lordship with such trash, but that I was told at Smyrna that they never found their way to England but in the shape of presents; the stock not being abundant enough to send to market.

I landed at this port on Monday last, the 21st instant; I found the ambassador full of friendship and politeness, as might be expected from the letter I was honoured with. He would have insisted on my quartering myself in the palace, had not the spare room in it been completely preoccupied by Sir R⟨ichard⟩ W⟨orsley⟩, his draughtsman Mr Revely, and the Hon. Mr Cadogan. The two former come from Egypt: the latter is going thither; and for the purpose of the expedition, is nourishing a pair of whiskers, which, respectable as they are in an Asiatic point of view, form an odd mixture with a garb in other respects completely English.

What with the remonstrances of friends, the want of pilots, and the inconveniences or rather dangers of quarantine, the fruits of Russian management, I believe I shall be obliged to finish my tour by land: the return of a Moldavian princess, sister to the reigning prince, promises safety as far as Jassi, and perhaps society.[2] Before I set out on the expedition, if ever I should set out, I shall not fail to turn to a book of instructions given me by a certain noble friend, with as much devotion as Peter, Jack, and Martin did to theirs. Therein shall I find *totidem literis*, if not *totidem syllabis*,—'cut the coat according to thy cloth,' and, moreover, in the words of the seer, 'metiri se quemque suo modulo et pede.'[3] In the mean-time, to cut off all occasion of scandal, I think it meet to declare and to protest that the princess, being of fit age and experience to make a prudent choice, hath for some time past committed the charge of her household affairs unto a man, by nation a Greek, of goodly stature, and of a ruddy countenance; and, moreover, that with my knowledge and acquiescence, a certain young English surgeon[4] is soliciting to be intrusted during the course of her journey with the care of the health of her Moldavian Highness.

553

FROM LOGAN HENDERSON[1]

25 November 1785

A quantity of rare seeds are just come from Petersburgh by last nights post in all about 350 dift. parcels. Many of them from China and Siberia to be delivered to a Gentleman of this place, I have requested they may not be sent away for this evening that you may see them if you can spare so much time I have had a very difficult job to collect the parcels from the Vessels and customhouse and I am sorry to observe they are not all come to hand however

[2] See letter 554.

[3] The first of these references is to Jonathan Swift's *Tale of a Tub*, where Peter, Martin, and Jack represented respectively Roman Catholicism, Anglicanism, and Nonconformity. The final Latin quotation is from Horace, *Epistles*, II, vii, 98.

[4] In the British ambassador's account of the departure (letter 556, n. 1) the surgeon is named as Griffiths, who had been one of Bentham's travelling companions on the *Mary Frances*. It appears as if at this time Griffiths had decided to accompany Bentham and try his fortune in Russia; but after the failure of this attempt to travel in the cortège of the Moldavian princess, he seems to have gone off independently (see letter 563) and there is no further mention of him in Bentham's correspondence.

553. [1] B.M. IV: 220. Autograph. Docketed by Bentham: '1785 Dec. [*sic*] / Constantinople Henderson / to / J.B. ibid.'

I have got 23 parcels of yours here and hope to have the remainder on sunday morning.

I should be glad to know if you are to Sleep here this night; as your bed is ready for your reception I suppose you will will not like to trespass too far on the hospitality of Mr. Humphries[2]

Friday 4 o'Clock 25 Novr. 1785.

554

To Richard King[1]

4–7 December 1785 (Aet 37)

Constantinople Decr. 4 1785

Sir

I write this to beg the favour of you to send me a copy of the translation of the Abbé Spalanzani's works[2] lately published—You

[2] According to Bowring's account of the travellers' stay at Constantinople (x, 154–6), Bentham, Henderson, and the two women of the party were all lodged with a British merchant of the name of Humphreys. However this passage seems to indicate that the party had taken accommodation elsewhere, which corresponds with Bentham's explanation (p. 407) that Ainsley had offered to furnish for him an unfurnished lodging of which he had heard; the passage also suggests that Bentham himself had hospitality from Humphreys for the first three or four days after his arrival at any rate, and as his relations with Miss Kirtland were not cordial he may well have remained there till his departure on 10 December (cf. the end of an account from an anonymous informant quoted by Bowring (x, 156): this may have been Maria James, the future Mrs. Reveley, best known in the name of her second husband as Maria Gisborne—see ibid. 251).

554. [1] B.M. IV: 221–2. Autograph. Docketed by Jeremiah Bentham: 'Mr. Jere[y] Bentham / Letter from him to Mr. Rd. King / datd. Constantinople / 7th Decr. 1785.' Further docket in the hand of Jeremiah Bentham: 'Jan 31 1786. Mem. I deliv'd the within mentioned Books to Mr Cazalet to be sent to Constantinople by Captn. Bourne who was to set sail next Saturday.'

Addressed:'To Mr. King / Six Clerks Coffee House / Chancery Lane / London / Angleterre.'

Copies in B.M. XXII: 361–3 and B.M. Add. Mss. 37520, fos. 146–9.

Richard King was a business man who acted as Bentham's agent during his absence in Russia and handled the dispatch of various consignments of goods to both the Benthams.

On a blank leaf of the letter Jeremiah Bentham wrote the particulars: 'Dissertations / relative to the / Natural History / of / Animals and Vegetables / Translated from the Italian of the / Abbé Spallanzani / Royal Professor of Natural History in the University of / Pavia, Superintendent of the Public Museum, / and Fellow of various learned Societies. / To which are added / Two letters from Mr. Bonnet to the Author / And (to Each Volume of this Translation) an Appendix / The first containing a Paper written by Mr. Hunter F.R.S. / And the Experiments of Dr. Stevens on Digestion; the Second / a Translation of a Memoir of Mr. Demours and Mr. Debraws / Paper on the Fecundation of Bees / in 2 Vols. / London printed for J. Murray No. 33 / Fleetstreet / 1784.'

[2] Abbé Lazzaro Spalanzani (1729–99), an Italian naturalist, became professor of

may get it on my account of Mr. Whieldon Bookseller in Fleet Street.[3] Let it be sent to Messrs. Cazalet Merchants /in London/ whose address I cannot give you, but as they are people of great eminence you will easily find them by a Directory.[4] Let it be put up in two covers: the innermost directed 'To his Excellency Sir Rob. Ainslie Ambassador from his Brittanic Majesty to the Ottoman Porte Constantinople' The outermost 'To Anthony Hayes Esqr. his Brittanic Majesty's Consul at Smyrna' and on one side 'To the care of Messrs. Cazalet by the earliest conveyance.' Let it be bound and letter'd if there are any copies to be had in that condition time enough: if not, in boards.

I expect to set off from hence for Russia by land on Wednesday next Decr. 7. We take advantage of the departure of a Moldavian Princess, sister to the reigning Prince, for Jassi his capital.[5] The Ambassador has had the goodness to introduce us to her Highness for that purpose. She has an escort of twenty of her Brother's horse who came here to convey his tribute to the Porte: a protection without which it would be altogether unsafe to travel that route unless it were with a Courier whose pace would be too quick to be supportable to any body not inured to such an exercise. No ships will cross the Black Sea from hence till the latter end of March or beginning of April. From Yassi to Olviopol or Olviopli is about 400 miles. This is the frontier town between Turkey, Poland and Russia. There, in consequence of a letter that went to my Brother by the last courier[6] [*several words crossed out*] last Saturday sennight, I expect to hear from him, and it will depend upon his answer whether I go round by the Crimea without him, or whether I go straight to him at Crechoff. Lest I should not have time to write to my Father, I will beg the favour of you to forward this to him, and on that supposition shall proceed. I have desired my brother if he can to send a carriage and horses for me to Olviopol, and at all events a letter, for which according to the course of the

Greek at Reggio in 1754 and professor of natural philosophy at Modena in 1760. He was the author of many learned works, including the one cited.

[3] Whieldon and Butterworth, booksellers, 43 Fleet Street.

[4] Cazalet and Cooke, merchants, 6 Austin Friars.

[5] The reigning prince of Moldavia at this time was Alexander Mavrocordato (1754–1819), member of a leading phanariot family at Constantinople and previously Chief Interpreter to the Porte until his appointment dated 1 January 1785. In December 1786 he fled to Russia, where he passed the remainder of his life. He had two sisters, Sultane and Roxandre: it is not known to which of them reference is made here (Emile Louis Jean Legrand, *Généalogie des Maurocordato*, Paris, 1900, pp. 20–1).

[6] Missing. Samuel Bentham mentioned receipt of it in a letter to his father of 6/17 January 1786 (B.M. IV: 237–9).

posts he will have sufficient time. If this letter goes without my mentioning any thing to the contrary it may be concluded that we go with the Princess on Wednesday next. The Princess expects to be at Yassy in 20 days from the day of her departure: but it is thought the journey may take 25 if the roads are bad as most likely they will prove at this time of the year: the distance is 572 computed miles.

Wednesday Decr. 7th 1785 5 o'clock

The Princess is set out: so is our party in a coach given us by the Ambassador, from whose house I date this—I set out this instant to over-take them with a Janissary. They go no farther this evening than Ponte Piccolo, about 10 miles distant.

555

To Alexander Hendras Sutherland[1]

8 December 1785 (Aet 37)

To Mr. Alexander Hendras Sutherland Merchant in London

Pera near Constantinople Decr. 8th 1785

Sir

At thirty days after sight please to pay on this my first bill of exchange ~~please to pay~~ second not paid to the order of Messrs. John Humphreys and Sons sixty pound sterling /value received/ and place the same to the account of his Highness Prince Potemkin for

Jeremy Bentham

555. [1] B.M. IV: 223. Autograph. Docketed by Bentham: '1785 Dec. 8 / Constantinople / J.B. Draught / on Sutherland / for Potemkin / Brouillon.'

A. H. Sutherland appears as a Russia merchant in the London directories of this period, first in Old Broad Street and later at 11 New Broad Street. He was a brother of Catherine II's banker, Richard Sutherland.

556

From Logan Henderson and Willey Reveley[1]

8 December 1785

Dr Sir

As I find it impossible to proceed on our journey with this carriage and bad road I have with great reluctance resolved to

556. [1] B.M. IV: 224–5. Autograph. Docketed: '1785 Dec 8 / Constantinople / Henderson Ponti Piccolo and Reveley / to J. B. Palais d'Angleterre / Impossibility of continuing journey.' Addressed: 'A Monsr. / Monsr. Bentham / au Palais d'Angleterre / à Constantinople.'

This letter explains the breakdown of Bentham's plan for himself, Henderson and the two Miss Kirtlands to travel as far as Jassy in the train of the Moldavian princess. It may have been received by Bentham while he was on the road in pursuit of the rest of the party. Sir Robert Ainsley wrote a detailed explanation on 10 December to Lord Carmarthen: 'Mr Bentham, in company with Mr Henderson, his two Nieces, and a young English Surgeon named Griffiths, proceeded for Moldavia the 7th instant, in the Suit of a Lady, Sister of the reigning Prince, to whom I personally introduced, and, in the strongest manner, recommended the Party. This mode of proceeding, proposed by the Russian Envoy, on account of security, was judged impracticable in this Season of the Year, unless attended with a portable House, and a number of Workmen; all which, independent of an Escort of twenty four Men, had been provided for the Princess. The journey was nevertheless undertaken, rather than risk the Navigation of the Black Sea, or incur delays. I accordingly provided them with one of my own Carriages of the Strongest kind made at Vienna. But, the attempt proved unsuccessful. The Coach, overloaded with Baggage, was in fact too much for Six Horses in Such Roads.' Having received pressing messages from Samuel, Bentham decided to hurry on without his heavy baggage and catch up the princess's party, leaving Henderson and the two women to make their way to the Crimea by sea (Public Record Office, F.O. 261/2).

The abortive departure produced a slight contretemps. Before learning that Henderson had had to turn back, Bentham, and William Eaton (an English Levant merchant with whom Samuel Bentham was already acquainted—see letter 550, n. 23) to whom Bentham had revealed the amusing secret, disclosed that Henderson had a mistress, not a niece, and that the whole English community at Pera had been deceived (Bowring, x, 155). In the sequel, as Eaton afterwards wrote to Bentham, 'Mr Henderson and the Ladies took things very easily, but the latter received no more visits nor Invitations' (letter 563). Either Henderson did not realize who had revealed his secret, or else he bore no ill-will, for he later corresponded both with Bentham and with his father.

To the general surprise (for navigation in the Black Sea was supposed to be halted for the winter), Henderson and his party reached the Crimea early in February (letter 566). His journey was probably arranged—as Ainsley surmised it would be—by the Russian ambassador. Henderson was certainly a plausible ne'er-do-well, who imposed successfully on Bentham, and on Ainsley also. On his arrival he immediately entered into a thirteen-year contract with Potëmkin's representatives to manage a botanical garden, whilst Miss Kirtland was to run a dairy and undertake the making

return to Constantinople, every one of our traces broke soon after we set out, and afterwards part of the Carriage gave way, so that it was 12 at night before we arrived here, the Horses are incapable to perform the task. the Princess has 8 horses at least and 12 in some of her carriages they were also broke and she did not set out till late this morning. She has got a House ready to set up on the road in case of accidents which she hourly expects and she has got workmen with her for that purpose they were employed all last night repairing the damages of the days Journey. It would lead on to further expences to attempt to proceed on our expedition. I have taken care to leave direction that the Coach shall be attended by the Janisary back to Constantinople ~~but have~~ tomorrow morning but ~~have brought~~ /shall take/ your portfolio to be deliverd to yourself, and your sword. Every thing else I hope will be safe.

I am

Yours etc. L. Henderson

Ponto Piccolo
8 Decr 1785

N.B. We are obliged to return by water as the Coach can not carry us back, it will take 10 or 12 hours without us

Sir

Having been consulted on the possibility of going the journey, it is my opinion that without a temporary house and workmen to repair the carriage (all which the Princess carries) it is an impossibility and therefore the attempt would be madness.

I am with great respect yr humble: sert

Willey Reveley

of cheese. But eighteen months later the administrator of Tavrid oblast indignantly informed Potemkin: 'They receive their salaries, they live at their ease, and they have done nothing in return.... Henderson has not planted a single blade of grass and mamzel has not made a single cheeze.' He described them as 'shameless imposters', engaged in covering up their ignorance of their callings (E. I. Druzhinina, *Severnoye Prichernomor'ye v 1775–1800 godakh*, Moscow, 1959, p. 136 n.).

557

To Jeremiah Bentham[1]

10–28 December 1785 (Aet 37)

Journal of my journey from Constantinople to Crichoff begun Saturday Decr. 10. 1785.

At about 11 I left the Stable at a place called Givani Serai viz: the abode of beasts /or Horse repository/ at Constantinople. Dr. ⟨Bartol⟩ozzi a Physician settled at Jassy had the kindness ⟨to⟩ accompany thither cross the water from Pera, and staid with me to serve as interpreter till I set out. I reached Ponte Piccolo[2] at 40 min. after 1.P.M. My train consisted of 1. my Janisary Ahmet whom his Excellency had appointed to attend me till I should over-take the Princess. 2. A Turkish attendant /on horseback/ to take charge of the Janissary's horse and wait on him on his return. 3. Mr. Schneider's servant Ludwig whom I had borrow'd of his master to wait on me till my arrival at Ovliopol where I expect to meet a messenger from my Brother. ⟨4. The⟩ pack-horse for Mr. Schneider's baggage. 5. Another pack-horse for my own baggage. 6. A guide on horseback to take charge of the above horses and my own to and from *Bucharest* for which place they were engaged. In all 5 horses engaged for Bucharest with a guide: and 2 with another

557. [1] B.M. IV: 226–9. Autograph. Copies, B.M. XVI: 30–42, B.M. XXII: 366–76 and B.M. Add. Mss. 37520, fos. 151–81.

Bentham dispatched this journal from Bucharest to Henderson, presumably in the care of the returning embassy janissary who had looked after him on his travels through Turkish territory (letter 562, p. 446). Henderson wrote to Jeremiah Bentham on 20 January 1786 reporting its arrival at Constantinople and promising to forward it by the next post (B.M. IV: 234).

Sir Robert Ainsley was glad to see Bentham go. He reported on 10 December to Carmarthen: 'It is difficult to imagine the eclat given here to Mr. Bentham's Party, which both French and Russians, though from very different motives, affected to denominate the English Colony. The former visibly aimed at irritating the Turks with exaggerated account of pretended Services rendered by Gt. Britain to the Enemies of this Empire; whilst the others, in view to intimidate the Porte, avow them all, and even suppose as much more as they can get People to believe. Indeed, Mr. Bentham was very imprudent in publishing at Smirna, as well as here, that he is empowered to engage British Subjects for the Service of Russia; and I am credibly informed, that he actually proposed a hundred Pounds Yearly, with Prince Potemkin's protection, to a British artist here, who rejected the offer. I have kept this intelligence, as well as my remarks, to myself, but was no ways displeased at Mr. Bentham's departure.' (Public Record Office, F.O. 261/2). Possibly the artist whom Ainsley mentions was Willey Reveley.

[2] Küçuk Çekmece, on the coast of the Sea of Marmora.

guide /retained together with the Janissary/ for an indefinite time untill we should over-take the Princess.

Ponte Piccolo, in Turkish, *Cutchuk Checkmije* is a little town /lying between a/ hill and the bridge from whence it takes its name. As the hill slopes towards the bridge /in going from Constantinople/ you see no appearance of the town till you are close to it.

At Ponte Piccolo we staid no longer than about ⟨half an⟩ hour to refresh the horses. We set out at about 10 minutes after 2. At about ½ after 3 we crossed a bridge called by the Janissary if I understood him right, *Hir ahouet* deresa[3] At ¼ after 5 we reached Ponte Grande, in Turkish *Buyuk-chickonzje*[4] where we slept instead of Silivria,[5] the place which the Janissary had led me to expect we should reach at the end of the first day.

We took up our quarters at an immense *Hahn* (Inn) not much less as it seemed than Westminster Hall. I am sorry I did not pace it to take an exact idea of the dimensions. Here as elsewhere we saw several parties of Turks grouped round the arched fire-places which are ranged at regular distances along the side walls of these Inns, which are built almost all of them upon nearly the same plan. Parallel to each wall runs a range of low mangers which are so many boxes of a form nearly cubical in which the chopt straw, the only provender I have yet seen given to the horses, is thrown. The bottom of these mangers is level with the inner area on which the horses stand to feed: the top of them is level with the above mentioned range of fire-places: the intermediate space forming an elevated plat-form, which being equal⟨ly⟩ open with the interior area below affords no other circumstance than those of position and elevation to distinguish the apartment for human travellers from the stable. Here I expected at first entrance we should have taken up our quarters on the bare ground: but was agreably disappointed when upon following the Janissary up a narrow blind staircase, cut as it were, out of one of the side-walls, the same through which the entrance is, I found myself in a little room, without indeed either chair or table, for even dwelling-houses furnished *à la Turque* know neither of these conveniences, but warm, or at least capable of being made so, by a charcoal fire, and decently enough covered with matts and meagre sofas. Below instead of windows it had /only/ window shutters, shutting closer than in a room of Turkish architecture could have been expected: but above each window-shutter

[3] Not identified.

[4] Büyuk Çekmece.

[5] Silivri, on the coast of the Sea of Marmora, about forty miles west of Constantinople. After this point Bentham's route lay inland.

was a small glazed window à la Turque, that is composed of small oval panes enclosed in massy woodwork. Its warmth it ow'd in great measure to its being without a fire-place, which forced me to have recourse to the unpleasant and unwholesome expedient of a pan of lighted charcoal in the middle of the room. Our Supper consisted of 1. a kind of sallad composed of a kind of white root, it might be a turnip for ought I know, pulled into narrow strips, seasoned with indifferent oil and vinegar and garnished with about a dozen black olives. 2. a dish of flat-fish, flounders or somewhat like them fried, I know not whether in /suet/ or oil, /hog's lard it would not be/ but at any rate very good. 3. Pilau or Pilav: a dish which when announced to me, as it was with emphasis, by the Janissary, I had expected to have found composed of rice and meat, but which /has/ turned out hitherto both there and elsewhere to consist of nothing but rice, too much greased with but indifferent oil or suet.

Sunday Dec. 11.

We left Ponte Grande at about ½ after 5 in the morning, long before the dawn of day. At about 40 mins. after 7 we passed through Comburgas[6]: at 50 mins. after 8, through Aidos[7]: at about ¼ after 11 we came to Silivri, after leaving a place called *Kiflick* or *Chiflick* about 2 or 3 miles to the right. Silivri is a pretty considerable town: I counted in it 5 minarets at a distance. It stands close upon the sea: some of the houses are built upon a perpendicular rock that overhangs the water: others within the enceinte of a pretty large castle in Turkish condition that is ruinous.

Between Aidos and Silivria I observed at different places along the sea-shore a number of large birds, the bodics considerably larger than those of crows, and their wings when extended at least twice as long. By their /hooked/ bills I should have supposed them carnivorous, of the eagle kind, if I had not seen them sitting in great friendship with a flock of mag-pies, intermixed as I believe with small birds. They were so tame as to suffer our company to approach them to /I suppose/ within ten yards distance, and dogs to within five. Upon the dogs coming up with them and barking /at/ them they took wing, but flew heavily and sat down again at a few yards distance. Near the town at entering it we saw flocks of

[6] Kumburgas.

[7] This and a number of other places, left without annotation, have not been identified.

sheep, with goats feeding amongst them promiscuously. In one or two of the goats /above/ the ground of the hair which was snuff-coloured projected a considerable quantity of white, not less I should suppose than 1½ feet in length, as if they had been of the *Angora* breed. The faces of the sheep here as elsewhere in Turkey different from the English, and much prettier. We left Silivri at about 12, after ¾ of an hour's stay, about ⅓ of which delay was owing to my having stepped aside to take a peep at the above-mentioned old castle, to the great discomposure of the careful Ahmet, in whose vocabulary curiosity is synonymous to folly. Here and there fragments of white marble pillars with capitals of Corinthian architecture, or at least like Corinthian, betoken⟨ing⟩ better days. The castle is comparatively modern, being crowded with embrasures for cannon. I saw no appearance of a garrison.

Coming out of Silivri we crossed a bridge of 32 arches with a big causeway at each end: the architecture too good for Turkish but too fresh for Grecian or Roman.

At 20 mins after 3 we came through a small town the name of which I understood to be *Kenich*: about ½ an hour before we had for the last time lost sight of the sea of Marmora, the coast insensibly tending to the left, and our course to the right. From Ponte Piccolo our course had been all along near the Sea, and in some places close to it on the very sand. I think it is at Silivri that the streight over which the bridge is thrown joins the sea with a salt-water lake, which seemed not less than 4 or 5 miles square.

At 5 /minutes/ after 4 we came abreast of a conical hillock which from its steepness and regularity seemed to be artificial: if such, it must have been no inconsiderable work. Qu? to what use? It wanted trenches to give it the appearance of a camp. It seemed to be about ¾ of a mile from the road on the right hand: a part of it, scooped out facing the road, affords a retreat for cattle.

At 20 minutes after 6 we arrived at *Chorli*,[8] where we eat and took up our quarters for the night. I say *eat*: for /it seems/ the Turks like the Greeks of old make eating but once in the 24 hours, and that is in the evening. This suits me very well with the addition of a few dishes of coffee at the first halt, which I accompany with a good luncheon of bread. The abstemious Ahmet refuses every thing but a single dish I should say thimble-full of coffee without bread. It would take at least 2½ of these thimble-fulls to make a reasonable English cup: he is much scandalised at seeing me drink 4 or 5 of them together. He says I shall hurt myself, and recommends wine

[8] Çorlu, some twenty-five miles west of Silivri.

in preference. If in this particular he does not follow his own prescription, his abstinence is the result of taste and not of a religion: for now and then he takes a moderate glass of brandy without scruple or grimace. In truth this honest Mahometan seems to have no more religion about him than a Christian: the Captain of the Turkish Caïk was everlastingly at his prayers: this man never.

At Tchorli or Chorli our apartment consisted of a small room looking into the stable, provided with a mat, and over that some ragged carpeting a couple of still more meagre sophas and a fire-place: instead of glass the windows were of oiled paper. In this dog-hole we had a magnificent supper consisting of Dolmah, Yahané, Queue-esta, Pourusa, and Uzum-turchiza. Of the 3 first two were a kind of hashes; the other a kind of forced-meat balls with a little onion: the greasiness of some of them was corrected by a lemon which Ahmet squeezed into all of them alike. Uzum turchiza is a dish composed of grapes stript off the stalks, and drenched in a liquid composed of water, sugar, a little vinegar, and something which gives it a kind of pungency like pepper: I imagine it to be the Capsicum: the grapes being plumped up by the fluid are improved in consistence if not in flavour. The table-apparatus which is much the same at one Inn as another, I must /defer the description of till/ I am more at leisure.

Next morning Monday Decr. 12th we left Tchorli, at 40 minutes after 5. A little after 6 we passed a bridge called Tchorlisi-Queuesili, consisting of 5 arches, with two smaller ones over them these last I suppose are to give vent to the water in case of a high flood: the stream at present is small and shallow, /so much so that we forded it./ Between each pair of arches is a jettee: the architecture /though fresh/ seems too well contrived and neatly executed for Turkish. At 10 mins past 8 we crossed a bridge /of 6 arches/ called Arganae. The architecture neat and regular like the other: this too is furnished with jetties. The masonry seemed fresh, particularly the mortar: the stone /very spongy/ seemed composed in great measure if not entirely of shells.

At 15 minutes after ten, we came abreast of *Carasteran*.[9] The road does not enter the town, but leaves it about ½ of a mile to the right. Close by the road between it and the town is an area encompassed with a mud-wall little more than breast-high and nearly circular. Here in this inclosure we found entertainment such as it was for man and beast: hay and coffee both, which we partook of in

[9] Büyuk Kariştiran.

company with ⟨4 or⟩ 5 other travellers. In one line [...?] between the road and the town stand 3 pretty acute quadrangular truncated pyramids: whether they have any thing to do with the conveyance of water I could not learn. I could discover but one minaret in the town. About an hour's ride short of the town I observed a number of mushrooms in appearance like the English.

At ½ after 12 I observed at a distance on the left such another conical hillock as that above mentioned. On a nearer approach, the Janissary made me take notice of it and called it *Pilou-tepefa.* I imagine therefore there is some tale that hangs by these hillocks. Does 'tepefa' mean *hill*? *Pilou* is the same word by which they call the Turkish dish made of rice etc. About 2, we came abreast of three other such hillocks which we left to the right. He called them or one of them Un-quieue-tepesa.

At 15 minutes after 2 we reached Bourgas or Bulgas,[10] where we slept. Having heard this spoken of as a place where the pipe-bowls of red clay somewhat like Wedgewoods which are so universally made use of by the Turks are manufactured, Dr. Bartolozzi at my request had desired the Janissary to remember to shew me the manufactory: I took care to remind him of it; accordingly he was ready enough to make me observe what I could not have avoided observing, the shops in which they were exposed to sale. But all my contrivance was insufficient to make him understand that what I wanted to see was not the places where they were sold, but the places where they were made. At one time I thought I had succeeded for having amongst other signs described a wheel as one of the machines which I supposed might be employ'd in such a manufactory: a shopman to whom I addressed myself made signs that he understood me and that if I would stay a while till he went somewhere my curiosity should be satisfied. When at last he appeared again and I expected him to beckon me to follow him to the /manufactory/ I found to my no small surprise and disappointment that his /errand/ had been not to pave the way for my reception any where but to bring a parcel of pipe-bowls with wheels attached to them one on each side. Of this clumsy appendage what can be the use? The man made signs as if they were to enable the smoker to glide the pipe with greater facility upon the floor on which the length of the tube obliges him to rest it. I saw I think about 7 or 8 shops appropriated solely to the vending of these implements with a very few others of the same kind of ware. Ahmet suffered me to go into a few others to buy some figs etc: which gave me a view of the

[10] Lüleburgaz.

greatest part of the Bazar (quarter for shops) but either through laziness or prudence forbid my going any further. I was therefore oblig'd to repress my wishes of exploring the town which from the apparent wealth of the shops and the number and size of its mosques promised to be considerable. The windows of our apartment here too were of oiled paper: We had for supper a sallad composed of chopped onions and a couple of the Turkish hashes abovementioned; and for desert some excellent grapes. I could get a near view of no more than one of the Mosques which seemed full as large as a moderate sized English Cathedral. I saw a pretty considerable Gunsmith's shop.

Tuesday Decr. 13.

We left Burgas at 40 minutes after 6: at 2 o'clock we reached Kirk Eglisi,[11] and there ended our day's journey. About an hour's ride from Burgas we entered a kind of forest, composed of Pollard and underwood Oaks thinly scatter'd interrupted with the Rhamnus Palinurus; about 3 or 4 hours afterwards we passed through a Village with one Mosque, called if I understood Ahmet right, Atabeyla. Here were some cabbage fields, producing some good sized cabbages, several cart-loads of which we had seen travelling towards Burgas, from 16 to 20 miles distant: to get seed from Atabeyla, where the market for cabbages can be but small, and sow them at Burgas where it can not but be considerable, would be too great an enterprize, too refined a speculation for a Turkish husbandman.

At Kirk Eglisi the Inn we put up at was of a construction quite different from that /of any/ we had ever seen before: ranges of apartments built round a quadrangular area, like many Inns in England particularly in London: the ground floor, stables: the first floor lodging-rooms: a few lumber-rooms a story higher: here we got a room, to appearance at least upon a par with any of the rest, full of windows glazed, so to speak, with oiled paper which at first might have been tolerably transparent, but by repeated patchings had become in most places opake: so much so that it was with difficulty I could see to hold a pen at noon-day. In this dungeon above ground I was doomed to pass little less than two days. The day of our arrival neither of us had proposed to stir: for though we have had fine moons, Ahmet will never hear of taking

[11] Bentham rendered a corrupt form of Kirk Kilisi, now Kirk Lareli. From Lüleburgaz his route followed a generally northward direction.

the benefit of them: he chooses rather to set out early in the morning, when it is pitch dark.

Wednesday Dec. 14.

Upon our rising I proposed to Ahmet according to my agreement with Dr. Bartolozzi to wait that day for his arrival with the Russian Courier: but Ahmet would hear of no such thing: but some delay happening in the picking up of our baggage, so that it was broad day-light before we were in readiness, he alter'd his mind and refused to stir: not on account of the abovementioned engagement of which he had been apprised in good Turkish by the Doctor, and to which he had promised to conform, but because there was no place where we could get a lodging nearer than Canara, and Canara was not reachable before sunset, so that we should be in danger from highwaymen, who would shoot us and so forth, as he made me easily understand by signs.

Thursday Decr. 15.

This morning every thing was in readiness in good time, and I expected every instant to set off: when a fresh incident intervened to retard our departure. On the Tuesday I had observed high words between our 2 grooms or horse-leaders, Mahmud and Hassan. By this morning it had proceeded to such a heighth, as to render it necessary for us to part with one of them: for Hassan had declared, that if Mahmud went farther he would not. The untoward event ⟨rendered⟩ two operations necessary: one was to go before the Magistrate to settle the dispute; the other was to look out for another man and horse to replace Hassan who was dismissed. Ahmet took with him my servant, I know not why, for he made no use of him as an evidence: it would have been more interesting to me to have been witness to this specimen of Turkish justice: but I knew nothing of the transaction till all was over. I now thought I had a good plea for staying this one day more for the Russian Courier: which would have brought us to the utmost extent of the time desired by Dr. Bartolozzi: my remonstrances however were without effect: for it seems though 8 o'clock was too late, ½ after 10 was not so: accordingly out we set.

At 20 minutes after 1, we passed Evekli,[12] leaving it about a stone's throw to the right. Of this place at the distance of 4 or 5 days I recollect nothing. I think I saw one *minaret* in it, and but one.

[12] Now Evikler, about eight miles north of Kirk Lareli.

At ½ after 3 we reached Cojabarla /or Cojatarla/[13] a Bulgarian village: and there we took up our quarters for the night. I asked how many hours we were short of *Canara*[14]: the answer was, two: and in fact the next morning we reached it in 1½ hour. Yet to Canara he would not go, notwithstanding he had mentioned it as the only place that would afford a lodging: but chose rather to put up at a hut which gave me the first taste of Bulgarian accommodation. Neither this nor any of the 4 other Bulgarian houses I have *now* slept at (Monday Dec: 19) are Inns; but private houses into which we have obtained admission by negotiation and promise of *Bakshish* (present) which would have been backed as I understand, if necessary, by legal force. The covering of this our resting-place was thatch; walls and floor, mud: cieling and windows, none: door, one and that too many: for light, a chimney of vast diameter and about a foot above the lowest part of the roof, answer'd the purpose of a window. Yet this seemingly inclement mansion was not without its comforts. The instant of our entrance two very neat cotton carpets fresh as if they had never been used, large enough to cover the greatest part of the room, though they were each doubled, were, one upon another, spread upon the ground: the /earthy/ composition of which the floor and the walls were made, though it might without impropriety be termed *mud*, may in a favourable point of view be consider'd as a kind of *stucco*, which if it may be depended upon for duration, I don't know whether I should not prefer to any stucco, I have seen: it forms a smooth even surface, perfectly free from cracks: the colour, a /most/ pleasant /uniform/ light brown, shewing no spots, and in that as well as other respects infinitely preferable in my eyes to the dead white which colours the walls of the meanest houses in England, and of some of the most magnificent in Smyrna and Constantinople. Our dinner-supper consisted of 1. Hushmilch. 2. Bulgarian pilaw. 3. a couple of barn-door fowls. This Hushmilch if I have got the name right is a kind of pancake, composed of flour and Caymac i.e.: clouted cream. At different Bulgarian tables I have observed it to assume forms considerably different, but all of them palatable: here and at another place where it was least good it formed a kind of thick pudding, rather heavy with lumps of unchanged *caymac* still perceptible on the surface: in another place it formed 5 or 6 very thin sheets perfectly distinct from each other, and the two lowermost

[13] Probably Kaibilar, now Strandzha, just within the present Bulgarian frontier, N.N.W. of Kirk Lareli.

[14] Now Kanara, just within the Turkish frontier.

crisp like pye crust, with no traces of the caymac, if that indeed were the oleaginous ingredient, perceptible: another time, it formed a kind of thin striatic substance of the crispness of a poor pye-crust, free from greasiness, and in this last form it suited my palate best. Bulgarian Pilaw instead of rice, is made of wheat, soften'd by boiling, and enriched with some kind of unctuous substance, whether caymac or some kind of fat I could not tell, hardly butter, for at this place I saw none of the implements necessary to such a kind of manufacture. I believe this kind of pilaw or something like it is called in England, *firmity*, from the Latin *frumentum* or the French *froment.* /Here as elsewhere among my Bulgarian hosts/ the fowls and the bread were equally extemporaneous: the one passing from the barn-door to the pot or spit, the other from the flour-bag to the oven, in the interval between the guest's first appearance and his sitting down to table.—Pardon me, my dear Father, for whose amusement this scrawl is principally designed, pardon me, I am sure you will, for entering thus minutely into the details of my bills of fare. Cut off almost entirely, during the course of this my tedious peregrination, from every opportunity of intellectual intercourse, my relations must be proportionably confined to the little incidents that have come within the cognizance of the senses. As a father no incidents that have been connected in a manner however trifling and transient with my *bien-être*, can fail to interest you: and as a man of speculation, you will be the less disposed to contemn these seeming trifles, when you consider that, in a political view, amongst the most important of the features by which the condition of a people can be depicted are those which relate to their subsistance and the arts by which it is supplied: and that, from knowing how a traveller like myself has fared in a few weeks, some conception may be formed of the manner in which a considerable part of the subjects of this vast empire fare for their whole lives.

Friday Decr. 15.[15]

We left Cojabarla this morning at 15 minutes after 7: in exactly 1½ we reached Canara which is called a 2 hours' journey. Yet our pace, exclusive of stops, is not more than a very moderate horse-walk: so that from the best judgment I can form I should not suppose that a Turkish hour's journey can exceed 3 miles. It may be set down, I think, as equivalent to a French great league. Here I observed a number of Buffalo calves living in great friendship with a flock of magpies, who sat perched 5 or 6 at a time upon

[15] Friday was December 16.

their backs. The alliance had I believe, like most others a mutual interest for its basis: for the birds seemed to be picking something, vermin /I suppose/ of some kind or other, from the hides of the beasts: if this conjecture be well founded, the principles of attraction on the birds' part is evident enough: but by what means the calf could be made sufficiently sensible of the interest he had in the connection to submit with the patience he did to such close visits from so numerous a company, I must leave to the corps diplomatique of Constantinople, with the assistance of some of the learned Dervises who, according to the Arabian nights entertainments, are skilled in the language of birds and beasts, to determine. Similar alliances may, for aught I know subsist in England: but if they do, they have never happen'd to fall within the sphere of my observation.

At 45 minutes after 12 we enter'd another Bulgarian village called *Faki*.[16] Here it seems this day's journey was to end. I was the less concerned at the delay inasmuch as I had understood from Dr. Bartolozzi, that if he failed of meeting with us at *Kirk-Eglis*, it would not be difficult for him to overtake us before we had left Faki. We thus waited half a day at Faki, but no Russian courier, no Italian Doctor came. The Dr. knows the road having often travelled it. He speaks Turkish like a Turk. If he enquired after us, how could he have missed us? Mr. Schneider was to have come by the same conveyance. If not after his friend how could he fail enquiring after his servant and his baggage? I left at our Inn at Kirk-Eglis an open letter directed à M. M. le Dr. Bartholozzi, ou a quelque autre Cavalier qui ce soit dans la compagnie du Courier Russe: giving the Master of the house to understand in the presence of the Janissary etc. that it was for the *Courier Moscov*: a term that I had heard frequently from all their mouths. As for Ahmet, either from laziness or design he has constantly abstained from all enquiries and all steps that would tend to effectuate the junction: once upon my uttering the words Ah! Courier Moscov! Courier Moscov! in a tone calculated to make him sensible how much I had it at heart, he repeated the words after me with petulance, and followed them by two or three sentences which from his tone and countenance were evidently expressive of no small degree of dissatisfaction.

Our hosts of this night consisted of a middle aged man three women and 2 young children. These people live in a great state: for besides the open portico which seems to preface all Bulgarian

[16] Umur Faki, now Fakija, about fifteen miles north of Kanara, on the upper course of one of the rivers running into the gulf of Burgas.

houses, his house had two rooms in it, one within another: the outermost was abandoned to us *three*: the family retired to the innermost, where the cookery was performed: the evening before that operation must have been performed at a neighbour's house, for I saw nothing of it in our own. How and where our 2 Turk Grooms have fared I have never known: except that once when we were very coldly lodged, the servant who happened to have seen them told me their quarters were better than our own. The ladies, to judge from their apparent ages, may have been grandmother, mother and daughter: the middle-most, wife to the gentleman of the house: she, still not uncomely: the youngest, beautiful. Her age seemingly about 16, but still more her maiden bashfulness, bespoke her unmarried. Impelled by motives, stronger, if any body chooses to have it so than mere curiosity, I took an early opportunity of paying a visit to the inner apartment, where I found the 3 ladies together, with 2 little children; dirty, squalling, and diseased. Of these last I took a sort of notice which if I must confess the truth, I believe I should not have taken, had it not been to warrant my taking a similar notice of a part of the family that was more agreable to me. To improve the acquaintance, the two elder ladies took occasion to insinuate that a compliment of a para apiece to the two young folks would not be unacceptable. I could not choose, as may well be imagined, but oblige them at so cheap a rate: respect for beauty prevented my insulting their fair sister; who had not been comprised in the intimation, by a similar compliment. Perhaps the insult might have been forgiven; but it is no /great/ wonder, I believe, that habit should act in such a case before reflection had time to modify it. I feared that a present suitable to the age of the receiver and the fancy of the giver might have been deemed an attempt to purchase. I soon found by experience what I might have surmised from reason, that Bulgarian delicacy did not shew itself in that shape. I strolled soon after into another house where there was no gentleman, but more ladies and more children. After I had gratified my curiosity awhile /in the/ examination of the apartment and its furniture, and maintained a sort of conversation by a few scatter'd words eked out by nods and smiles, I was made to understand that these young folks had as little objection to *paras* as the others: the readiness with which this intimation was complied with encouraged the elderly ladies (for such they were) to take off the mask: and I now found that the reputation of injustice would be incurred, if matrons were to be denied an attention that had been paid to children. Corrected by this lesson, by the time that leave was to be taken of our hosts, I had learnt to regulate my notions of honour by the Bulgarian stile: Upon that occasion the ladies of the family were ranged in a row, the youngest, as it happen'd, nearest to me. I had provided my waistcoat pocket with a stock of *paras*: and I now found an unsuspicious opportunity of repairing my former failure: I must confess however to my shame that my mode of distribution was still so far from being conformable to the laws of equity that before my hand had reached that of the eldest lady, my funds were exhausted, and instead of paras I was forced to entreat her acceptance of an apology. If any body should wonder at my scribbling thus diffusely, let them know that I am at this instant in another Bulgarian palace, rioting in the enjoyment of such a scribbling apparatus as no Turkish Inn has ever afforded me: a low corn measure, made high enough to sit upon by a cushion such as there is no want of: and another higher corn measure for a table, big enough to hold several papers, with a good candle raised, by a convenient though odd shaped earthen candlestick, almost to a level with my eyes. Before I dismiss the subject of *paras*, I will e'en add for the sake of truth, how ill soever it may accord with poetical prejudices in favour of rustic manners, that I have seldom if ever quitted a Bulgarian house but opportunity has been taken behind the Janissary's back, to intimate that the fowls, or the wine, or some other part of the entertainment has been forgotten to be paid for: this of course has produced an appeal to the Janissary: upon which appeal the insinuation has as constantly been retracted. Fear it may be said, /and not truth/ has been the cause of the retractation. What gives me the satisfaction (shall I say?) of thinking otherwise is that my servant talks a little Bulgarian and understands it better; a language of which the Janissary does not understand a syllable: sometimes my servant himself has been the channel through /which/ the intimation has been convey'd: and yet in no instance has any attempt been made so much as by whisper or gesture to urge the plea of *duress* either to him or me. As constantly has the master of the house, according to what seems to be the *etiquette* follow'd us a few hundred yards from his door in order to receive a parting present from the Janissary's hands. Taught by this experience, if now any application is made to me for *paras* on the score of justice I refer it to the Janissary, by saying, 'Yenghichery para': which reference though I have been alone has been submitted to without remonstrance or apparent dissatisfaction. To do justice however on both sides to our Bulgarian hosts, I have found them I think without exception cheerfully civil and attentive: enduring with wonderful good humour a torrent of abuse which the Janissary is perpetually pouring on them without cause. Let me add likewise to the credit of the honesty or the prudence of one of them, whose name it is a pity I have it not in my power to immortalize, that a neat /English/ iron spoon as much superior in value to their wooden ones as a silver one is to that, having been left behind by the servant was brought after us to the distance of a quarter of a mile. To policy or some such motive I must allow its share, because, lest the particular present expected according to this theory from me, should be *merged* in the general present expected from the Janissary, care was taken by the man who brought it to give it not into the hands of the Janissary, or of the Bulgarian who according to the etiquette above-mentioned was attending him, but into mine.

Shoomly or Choumli Tuesday Dec. 21. 5 o'clock P.M.[17]

I have just got out of a scrape, which I shall not easily forget. I have heard of such things as drubbings, and now I know by experience what they are. I had been taking a short turn in the town with *Osman* (so his name is it seems, not Hassan) a very civil good creature, to attend me. Before I re-enter'd my Inn, I stopped at a Mosque which is just opposite to it. The Mosque was open: the good Musulmen ⟨were⟩ at their devotions. I waited on the outside at a respectful distance, /not only/ without the door, but without the place where the slippers were deposited. The Minaret was close on my right hand. I had no idea of ascending it: having /often/ heard that such liberties were not to be taken. A young man came up to me, and touching me at a time I was looking another way, pointed to the Minaret, and made signs to me to go up. I thought him very civil, and imagined that Shoomley being a very large town, probably from its size a place of trade, and formerly in the hands of the Russians might have worn off some of its religious prejudices: I was consulting /with myself/ whether to accept of the invitation, when he renew'd it in a pressing manner saying, Eida, Eida, Eida. I accordingly went up: my Turkish attendant staid below. I passed some minutes in the gallery at top in great tranquillity, surveying the town below me. I counted 12 minarets and do not imagine I saw all: I think the town cannot be less than a mile square if so little. I was just coming down, when the appearance of two men climbing the narrow cork-

[17] Otherwise later known as Shumla, or Shumen, and now Kolarovgrad. Tuesday was 20 December.

screw necessarily stopt me. From their gestures and manner of speaking though not uncivil, I concluded their errand was to hasten my descent: One of them immediately went ⟨down again⟩. I followed him, leaving the other to follow me. I had not got down above half a dozen steps when I felt a stick which one of them had, in size and shape exactly like our Constables' staves, poking at me from above. I cried out to let him know he hit me, imagining it to be an accident: this only produced a repetition of the blow, with a phrase of obloquy, which left me no doubt of its being intentional. I made what haste down I could with my Turkish Jack-boots: but my descent was necessarily retarded by the man who preceeded me: however the narrow spiral form of the staircase pre⟨ven⟩ted the stick above me from acting with much effect: and luckily there was nothing harder than a few hard words below me. This however was not the case /in the street/ below: a crowd was collected, and amongst them more sticks than in my confusion I had leisure to count. One of the hardest and most deliberate blows I felt proceeded from a tall fat man, who from his handsome dress and appearance ought to have been a little above the level of such prejudices, or at least more temperate in his manner of giving vent to them. I ran in confusion, first one way then another not knowing which way to turn myself for some time nor recollecting in the hurry the blind entrance that led to the Inn, a volley of hard words with now and then a blow pursuing me. Defence would have been madness: parly was impracticable. I did what I could by groans and deprecating gestures to move their pity and put a period to the storm, as I was running in this manner here and there, I spied at the same time, the entrance of the Inn and the Janissary coming out as if to meet me. His appearance seemed to cover my retreat: for they followed me no farther. They certainly did not mean me any serious mischief: for none of the blows fell upon my head: fortunately in addition to a coat lined in the arms with thick flannel, I had two great coats on: and now at 2 hours distance I feel but 2 of the blows one on my right arm, the other on my left shoulder. I hear my imprudent conductor who ought to have prevented my accepting such an invitation, shared in some degree my fate. I understand from the Janissary, that the Janissary has been to the Aga, and that the aggressors are to suffer by the *Lex talionis*. If so, I am sorry for it: as it may tend to stimulate revenge, and because those who dealt the blows are not I believe the most to blame. I have a notion the young fellow who invited me is a Greek, and gave me the invitation out of unprovoked malicious sport, only to bring me into a scrape. Being in the gallery at least ten minutes, I must have been observed by numbers, some of which I saw were staring at me, but this I imputed at the time to no other than the general cause my being a stranger.

Shoomley perfectly astonished me by its unexpected vastness: considering its inland situation and inconsiderable celebrity, I am afraid to say I know not how to think ⟨it⟩ less than Smyrna. Its position is picturesque. The country round about to a very considerable distance not only highly cultivated but parcelled out into small and neat inclosures up to the tops of overhanging mountains, bespeaks the security of property and the accumulation of a large capital. Yet here the Russians had quarters in the last war if I am rightly informed by my servant, who says he was here at the time in the service of an officer of that army. The town has or at least once had the pretension of being fortified. Over a /wretched/ mass of boards that seems to have been intended for a drawbridge we crossed a /dry/ ditch which a man might hop over (I believe I speak without hyperbole) and a mud wall which he might step over. It is to serviceable fortifications what a baby-house is to a habitable house. If Shoomley had been of Romulus's building, Remus might here have had his joke. This place is at least 4 good hours from Chingy,[18] the place of our last night's lodging. We came through 8 or 10 Bulgarian Villages, the least of them capable to all appearance of affording as good quarters to sleep or bait at as any of the 5 we have lodged in. Yet would not Ahmet notwithstanding my request stop for a moment at any one of them, though /this was the/ longest day's journey we had made, and though he had baited on former occasions when the journey was scarce ⅔ds so long. Distance called 6 hours has taken us but 4½; and so in proportion: but this, called sometimes 10, sometimes 11, took us by night watch, 9½ or rather more.

Bucharest Dec. 28. 1785.

I arrived here the day before yesterday: I set off the day after tomorrow. The gaps in the above journal I shall endeavour to fill up and send off the sequel at a future opportunity: possibly the quarantine at Olviopol may afford me more time than I could wish. This place is interesting and the civilities of the Russian Consul and Imperial Agent render it agreable.

[18] Now Chenge, seven miles south of Shumla.

558

To James Lee[1]

c. 8 January 1786 (Aet 37)

1786 N.S.
Jassy in Moldavia Jan. | | 1786.

Dear Sir

About the beginning of Novr ~~I left~~ being on the point of leaving Smyrna I charged Capt. Ri. Brine of the Mary Frances with a packet containing from fourscore to 100 different sorts of seeds collected /at physic gardens and elsewhere/ in the course of my travels in France, Italy, and /in/ Levant, /also some plants of Raisins and Currents without stones,/ of which if I do not mis-recollect I gave you advice by the post. About a month ago I left in the hands of Mr. James /an English/ Merchant at Pera near Constantinople another packet containing some Asiatic acorns that I thought might possibly be new and about 6 or 8 sorts of seeds from the northern parts of China sent /amongst others/ by Mr. Dimidoff[2] of Moscow to /a gentleman at/ Constantinople. They were /the only/ part /I could find time to preserve out/ of a collection of about 300 many of which, as far as my imperfect acquaintance with Botany enables me to judge I imagine to be little if at all known in England. I imagine it will not be long before I visit Moscow, and I shall then not neglect to make acquaintance with Mr. Dimidoff, whose great wealth and passion for Botany /may/ afford /to/ his /friends such/ opportunities of making collections from the Northern parts of China and other unexplored regions bordering upon or included in the Russian Empire as perhaps are hardly obtainable through any other channel. I have provided such a present as I hope will be acceptable to him, and if I meet with him my endeavours shall not be wanting to bring you and him to a correspondence.

The purpose of the present letter is to desire you to send on my

558. [1] B.M. IV: 232 (the first half of a double sheet, the other part of which contains letter 559). Autograph. Draft, with corrections. Docketed (with reference to both letters): '1785 Dec. [*sic*] / J.B. Bucharest / to / Bulgakoff Pera / idem / to Lee Hammersmith / Brouillons.'

James Lee (1715–95) had been established since 1760 as a nurseryman at the Vineyard, Hammersmith, in partnership with Lewis Kennedy. He was a correspondent of Linnæus, part of whose works he translated into English under the title *Introduction to the Science of Botany*. Letter 568 is his reply.

[2] See letter 399, n. 4.

account to Mr. Bulkakoff the Russian Envoy at Constantinople as compleat a collection as can be obtained in London of /seeds of/ all sorts of /plants/ seeds particularly /kitchen/ garden seeds as will live in that climate where there is now and then some frost but very little, without hot-house or green-house. Seeds of trees and shrubs should be included, except such American seeds as are not to be had without extraordinary expence. Kitchen Garden seeds /such as pease, bean etc./ should be sent in such a quantity as will afford a small plate at once to /be/ served as a specimen upon table. Let them be divided into classes tied up in several bundles, such as Kitchen-garden seeds, flower-garden seeds—/deciduous/ shrubs—evergreen shrubs, and trees. As for such fruit-trees of which the goodness depends upon grafting, it will hardly be worth the while. I have told him that I would desire you to put upon each paper not only the English and Linnean names, but the French /whenever/ you happened to be acquainted with it. The case is he has a high opinion of a French gardener he has lately engaged from the King's Botanical garden at Paris, and I want /to wean him from this predilection to let/ him to see what we in England are acquainted with and possess. Ships from London to Constantinople are very few and I fear not seasonable: to Smyrna they are more numerous and possibly some may be in season for the next sowing time. /(Direction for Smyrna)/ I have told him that I would desire you immediately upon receipt of this /and due enquiries made about ships/ to write him a line telling him whether he may expect to receive the collection this next season or whether he must wait till the season ensuing. Send what catalogues you can get marking such plants as you are possessed of or can procure. He as well as other men of eminence in Constantinople are fond of gardening, but it is hitherto in the formal meagre French stile: if they can be brought to look up to England as the center of perfection in gardening, they may send to us for plants of all sorts, and your name I have taken care shall not be unknown. You will be surprized when I tell you that ~~except peaches, apricots, figs, pears,~~ very few of our fruits grow or are even able to be met with at Constantinople. As this order comes not from Mr. Bulkakoff by whom it was totally unlooked for, but purely from myself who have no favour to ask of him and have nothing to actuate me but my love for Gardening and old England, unless you will give me leave to add my regard for you, and as I have been at some expence /as well as trouble/ in making the collections above-mentioned, and the mere expence of seeds will to you be little or nothing, I shall take for granted that if they come to hand[3] you will not expect payment for this order: if otherwise send me the Bill and as soon as I know the amount of it I will send you a draught on my Banker for the discharge of it. If you think I have given you or am likely to give you an equivalent, I should be glad you would send a similar collection /in my name/ to our own Ambassador there, Sir Rob. Ainslie. A few of our best sorts of Potatoes should not be forgotten, as they prize a very indifferent sort they have there. Finding an excellent sort of Radishes t'other day at Bucharest the capital of Valachia: as mild as our best though bigger than my two thumbs. I thought that capital might perhaps afford varieties we are not possessed of. I accordingly made a collection /for you/ of about 15 or 20 sorts which are all the place affords. I send them from hence along with this through Mr. Bulkakoff leaving him to choose the best of 3 or 4 channels which I suggest to him. Brusa a place within reach of Constantinople affords, I am told, a remarkably large peach or apricot I forget which: I wish you had it. Perhaps if upon sending the above-order'd collection you were to ask him or his gardener they would get some plants and send you.

I am told from good authority that the transparent apple is neither a fable nor a casual disease but a permanent variety as good to eat as to look at, and is to be had in great perfection at Moscow: if so, I will strive hard but I will get you a few plants of it. But as such an enterprize would unavoidably be attended with expence, I should be glad to know to what expence if any you would go for it.

Having observed in you a liberality not manifested by others in the trade, I have confined my correspondence to you, that the benefit of it, if any, may be yours. Direct to me at Crichoff to the care of Messrs. Hey and Zucherbuher Merchants in Riga.

559

TO YAKOV IVANOVICH BULGAKOV[1]

8 January 1786 (Aet 37)

A Jassy le 8 Janvier 1786 N.S.

Jaloux de votre jardin /monté/ à la Françoise, et de votre Jardinier François, je voudrais bien voir si l'Angleterre ne se trouve

[3] The rest of this paragraph is written as a series of insertions in the margin.

559. [1] B.M. IV: 233 (see letter 558, n. 1). Autograph. Draft with corrections. On Bulgakov, the Russian ambassador at Constantinople, see letter 543, n. 3.

pas assez riche pour ajouter /faire quelque addition/ à [vos] fonds. Pour en faire l'expérience j'ai donné ordre à /M. Lee à Hammersmith près de Londres/ un de nos plus savants Jardiniers-pepiniéristes d'envoyer à la première occasion à l'addresse de V.E. un recueil complet de tout ce qu'il peut se trouver de semences /en Angleterre/ à Londres qui puisse convenir au climat de Constantinople. D'après l'expérience que j'ai eue de son exactitude et de son savoir-faire je ne doute nullement qu'il ne remplisse /parfaitement/ la commission. Ne sachant /connaissant/ pas d'autre canal aussi sûr, je prens la liberté d'envoyer ci-jointe la lettre que je lui ai écrite à cet effet,[2] priant V.E. de vouloir bien faire ensorte qu'elle se trouve incluse à la première occasion favorable dans l'enveloppe de M. l'Ambassadeur d'Angleterre. Pour reveiller d'autant plus l'attention de ce Jardinier je prens la liberté de lui adresser par ce même canal un petit paquet contenant le recueil de toutes les semences potagères et autres que j'ai pu trouver à Bucharest. Si le vaisseau Anglois que j'ai laissé à Constantinople n'est pas encore parti, ce sera-la meilleure occasion pour le lui faire parvenir en tems pour la saison prochaine; c'est à dire avant la fin d'Avril: si non il faut que je prenne la liberté de remettre au bon plaisir de V.E. ou de l'envoyer par la route de Smyrne, ou bien, si cela se peut, ce que j'ignore, sous l'enveloppe de M. l'Ambassadeur d'Angleterre. Je soupçonne pourtant que ce dernier canal seroit trop à chargé pour être emploié, quelle que soit la partie sur laquelle devoit tomber le fardeau.

~~Je saisis avec plaisir cette occasion de remercier~~

Quant au recueil de semences à l'usage de V.E. j'ai donné ordre que sur chaque papier au nom Anglois de la plante on joigne en Latin le nom technique d'après le systême de Linneus et même le nom François pour peu que la connaissance que je sais qu'il a dans cette langue l'admis à même de la marquer. Au reste cette dernière précaution se sera trouvée superflue au cas que votre jardinier se trouve pourvu de la traduction Françoise du Dictionaire de Jardinage de Miller, hors qu'un Jardinier François seroit bien blamable de ne pas avoir. Quant à l'autre il sait bien le tems où le recueil doit arriver pour être à tems pour la saison prochaine: /les semailles prochaines/ et je lui ai dit d'écrire à V.E. pour lui marquer si cela sera possible vu les occasions /assez peu fréquentes/ que presente le commerce d'Angleterre avee Constantinople, ou bien s'il faut que l'envoi soit remis au printemps de l'année suivante. En tout cas dès que ~~le pacquet /cet recueil/~~ cet

[2] Letter 558.

envoi [sera] parvenu aux mains de V.E. je le prierais de vouloir bien m'en faire donner avis par une ligne addressée à moi à Crichoff la [*several words crossed out*] /près Mohileff ou bien prés Mtislaff dans la Russie blanche./ Partout où je puis me trouver elle ne manquera pas à m'atteindre.

Je saisis avec plaisir cette occasion de remercier encore V.E. de ses ~~bontés~~ amitiés, et de vous prier Monsieur de me croire avec le respect le plus sincère ~~de votre Excellence~~ le très humble et très obligé serviteur

J.B.

560

To William Eaton[1]

8 January 1786 (Aet 37)

Jassi Sunday Jany 8th 1786

Dear Sir,

While at Bucharest, where different necessities obliged me to spend eight days, I bought two skins, one red, the other yellow, both good, but the red in particular excellent: it was of a rough grain, such as I have seen employed in a few instances for the richest Bindings for Books in England; I was told it was Goat skin, manufactured at Russchuk on the Danube. The red I was asked four piasters for, (a Piaster is about 3s./6d. or 4s.//). They took two and an half owing to the good offices of a faithful Conductor I had with me; for the yellow they asked, I think it was, two piasters, and took 70 Paras (the value of a Para is about an English Half Penny). I passed through Rushchuk, but did not know of this manufacture till afterwards. At Bucharest also there is a House or two houses together where I saw them manufacturing red Leather, but the specimens I saw of it at the Shops were very different from the other, and much inferior, and I found the manufacture there was in so little account that but few Persons, out of many I questioned, knew of its existence. I happened to stumble upon it accidentally as I was lounging in the neighbourhood of the Post established for the Quarantine, at the foot of the Hill which you

560. [1] B.M. XXII: 308–312. Letter-book copy by Jeremiah Bentham, headed: 'The following is a Letter from J^{y} B. to his Friend Mr. Eaton, a Merchant at Constantinople and by him forwarded to —— Bentham Esq. to the Care of Sir Robert Herries & Co. Bankers in London.' Printed, *The Slavonic and East European Review*, XXIX (1950–51), 67–72.

Professor A. Vianu of the university of Bucharest kindly provided information on a number of the persons mentioned in the following footnotes.

descend abruptly as you approach the Town, when you are at that Post, pursue the right hand Road of Two into which the Main Road there divides itself, you will find the Manufactory at about a quarter of a mile distance, still in the Suburb, before you reach the Town, you may know it by the Skins you may probably see hanging up in different states. Upon Entering the Manufactory I observed a Man pounding in a Trough a vegetable substance that to all appearance had been a leaf, but in the State in which I found it, was reduced to small fragments, tho' not yet to powder. The finer it was rendered, the more it approached in appearance to the powder which under the name, I think it is, of Al Hanna, or Hina, is used all over Turkey for covering the Women's nails red; accordingly the Nails of the Man whom I saw pounding it were died not red indeed, but, as might be expected, of a deeper colour resulting from continued use, a sort of a dirty blackish brown. This colouring substance I was told every where comes from Egypt, probably it is already known as well to Botanists, as to Theorists, who knows but that after all it may be nothing but Madder, which I have never seen but in a growing State. If not and if it be a Plant as yet peculiar to Egypt, we could first import it into England and then grow it in the West Indies.

You and I know also of a certain Utopia where it may be cultivated. I brought off with the consent of the People a small Specimen of the Drug used at Bucharest which I mean to experiment upon, and confront with the *Hoanna*, of which I have also made provision. The Bucharest Drug is apparently pure, but my *Hanna* from the weight of it must be largely adulterated with Sand. Having no tongue to speak with, I could not ask for any of the leaf, in its more perfect state; To you, my good Friend, who to the Gift of Tongues unite chemical Science, and Zeal and industry to apply it to curious and interesting subjects, to you, it would be easy to possess yourself of this valuable Manufacture at *Rushchuk* the Seat of its perfection; a day would be sufficient, but if it were a week, I believe you will agree with me that it would not be misemployed, a short visit afterwards to the Bucharest Manufacture would perfect you by shewing you the Circumstances upon which its inferiority depends. At Rushuk, as elsewhere, the Turks I imagine are too ignorant to be jealouse, Manufactures, like Plants, they look upon as nailed to the Soil; what hitherto has been, according to them, always will be; if by way of introduction you have a mind to make a purchase bring a Skin of each sort at the Prices above mentioned, or thereabouts, and when you bring them to Critchoff, I will take them off your hands and thank you; at Rushuk and Bucharest together you will be able to fill up to advantage the Interval between one Russian Courier and another: for that purpose in addition to the Letter you will have from the Russian Envoy[2] to the Russian *Consul*[3] there at Bucharest you will do well to get one from the Internuncio[4] to the Imperial Agent[5] at Bucharest, the latter is a Man of industry and extensive knowledge; cultivate him as I did, and he will communicate to you as he did to me, his Manuscript Observations on the State of the Ottoman Empire, of which you may possibly know as much as He, and his observations relative to the political and politico-œconomical State of the Provinces of Walachia and Moldavia in particular, of which you can know nothing but from him. His history of the transmigration of the Sheep from Transilvania to Walachia if he has consigned it to paper by the time you reach him you may confront with what you may have learnt relative to the same Subject in the Neapolitan State.

I copied the Titles of all his Manuscripts, finished and in Embrio, had I had time he would have permitted me to copy any part of them. I did make an imperfect Extract. To give you your *cue* I tell you in confidence that his good qualities are tinctured with a certain *hauteur* which might be spared; as an instance, I submitted to accept from him an excellent dinner in preference to the equally excellent dinner of the Russian Consul, where I was sure of a Welcome, upon an Invitation so little flattering as 'voulez vous diner ici aujourdhui?—si vous voulez, vous etes le maitre.' Some have accordingly given him the Name of Joseph 3d, and in consideration of his method of treating the Transilvanians that depend on him, the *agent a coups de Baton:* by his own account you would suppose the reverse to be the case; to reconcile the two, conceive him to be fond of governing and making liberal use of both engines, reward as well as punishment. He and the Russian are good Friends at least as to the Exteriour, as I can testify, but

[2] Y. I. Bulgakov.

[3] Ivan Ivanovich Severin. He was Russian consul general in the Rumanian principalities from 1783 until the outbreak of war between Russia and Turkey in 1787.

[4] On Herbert, the imperial internuncio, see letter 551, n. 16.

[5] Ignatz Stephen Raicevich, a Ragusan, a tutor in the household of Alexander Ipsilanti, Prince of Wallachia, 1774–82, and Austrian agent at Bucharest, 1782–7. After the outbreak of the Russo-Turkish war, he retired to Italy, where the book which Bentham had seen in manuscript was published as *Osservazioni storiche, naturale e politiche intorno la Valachia e la Moldavia*, Naples, 1788. It soon appeared in French and German editions.

others say, as I suspected at bottom They were as Caesar and Pompey; that they should see one another and that often is necessary, or they would be as Robinson Crusoe, for other European Society they have none save Monsieur de la Rose (French Secretary to the Hospodar) and his wife, and M. Weber, a German Maitre des Langues, and his young Wife, in so much that, including the other, Each can have at most but a Triumvirate: as for the Walachians they are Vegetables. I saw for Example at the Agent's an Oak of great dignity and bulk proportionable, a *Brancovan*, who to the quality of a Walachian Boyard, adds that of Prince of the Holy Roman Empire; some exceptions however there are, and These, the Country considered, not a few. There is for instance a Constati (Constantine) a young Greek of 22, or 23 brought up at Constantinople, 2d Ecrivain de la Cour dans le[6] department des Comptes, a place, they say, of some profit and importance. He speaks good French and reads English, which he learns from Weber, and of which he is passionately fond, I met him at the Italian Theatre, (what think you of an Italian Theatre at Bucharest?) an Enterprize of his own; an Englishman being a black Swan in that Country, He was, or affected to be overjoyed to see me, he returned me in his Carriage, for at Bucharest as at Petersburg every Chimney Sweeper has his Carriage; I expected he would have given me Victuals, which for curiosity sake I would have gladly eat, he, however would not, possibly because he had none to give, or because it is with him as I had heard it said of those half Turkeyfied Christians, that the best among them have nothing decent to eat Victuals with or to lay them upon; accordingly neither Caesar nor Pompey ever get any at Bucharest but from one another. By him or otherwise you will find two Europeanized Boyards, the young Princes Cantucuzem.[7] He avowed himself one of four or five Sectators of Helvetius, his fellow Disciples he would not confess, but I suspect these two to be of the number, possibly the Son of the Hospodar[8] may be another, I was to have waited on this latter by appointment; but at that late period of my Stay, business more urgent prevented me. The Hospodar himself I should have seen, but real Sickness rendered him invisible.

[6] 'les' in Ms.

[7] The brothers Cantacuzino were John and Nicholas, sons of Prince Raducan Cantacuzino (d. 1774) who had raised a Wallachian regiment to support the Russians in the Russo-Turkish war of 1768–74. Raducan and Nicholas (1763–1841), who eventually became a major-general in the Russian service, are both noted in the *Russkiy Biograficheskiy Slovar'*.

[8] The hospodar, or prince, of Wallachia at this time was Michael Sutsu. He had three sons, Gregory, Ivan and Alexander. Presumably the first of them is meant here.

Besides its Leather Manufactury Bucharest has its Glass-house which affords a tollerable Crown Glass, still cheaper than the Cheap Bohemian Glass which abounds here. Fire wood almost for nothing —Building in Brick proportionably cheap, notwithstanding the immense quantity of materials employed in Waste. What a situation for Hot Houses! and yet hot houses as little known as Ice houses in Arabia; I don't know how they manage it but both Caesar and Pompey have most enviable Cooks; I wish but without hope I could get the fellows to [desert] them for Kritchoff.

To compleat the *Carte du Pays a votre usage*, the Agent is fond of English books, the Consul of English Colifichets,[9] I made him happy by the present of a small Dram bottle I had cased with leather.

Should room be vacant and letters strong enough it will be infinite comfort, and some saving, if you can get a Sleeping-Hole in either of their houses. That of the Consul for whom alone I had provided Letters being full, or soi-disant full of Mr. Willis,[10] the Valet de Chambre thrust me into a vile vaulted Dungeon above Ground, without Table, Chair, air or light, furniture of every kind, the most necessary of all, not excluded, though the Dungeon was a Story high, were absolutely wanting. For this Dog-Hole he extorted from me a Piastre a day, pressing me for it with a premature and impertinent anxiety lest the Master of the House, to whom he allowed only a Part, as the Man himself told my Servant, should be before hand with him; he tryed to make me pay for a day more than I had it for, and to oblige me although there were corn Coffee houses in plenty, he chose to furnish me himself at the price of half a Piastre with Breakfast of Coffee, with a little Milk and butterless Bread for which 7 or 8 paras would have afforded a reasonable profit. The Consul of his own accord, after regretting for formsake that the only Spare Apartment in his House was full of Mr. Willis, told me that the Servant would provide me with a Lodging and with Coffee for my Breakfast, the same Consul after the departure of Mr. Willis told me that his appartment was kept for the reception of an unnamed expected Guest who never came; the Same Consul a little before my departure quitted abruptly and without apparent Cause the Room where he and I were alone, immediately upon which enter'd the said Valet de Chambre figeting about as if on posture of doing something and doing nothing; finally the same Consul, upon my having suffered the favorite to figet out again, and undisturbed, reenter'd *solus*, and having asked leave to give me a

[9] I.e., trinkets.

[10] An English merchant travelling to the Crimea (see letter 562).

piece of advice, told me a Certain Walachian Merchant, called a Spravinek, at Fokshan in consequence of a general recommendatory order which the Hospodar, on his (the Consul's) account had presented me with, would give me food and lodging on my passing through that Town, whereupon he Counselled me, *pour mon nom*, to make a present of a piastre to the said Spravinek's Servants; laying all these circumstances together I must own myself to have been uncharitable enough to conclude, that the Spravinek was put but for an Example. I had originally destined for my industrious Proveditor a present amounting to something more than the money I found afterwards he had fleeced me of; ashamed to push aside a begging Box so plainly held up to me by a hand that had in other respects had treated me hospitably, but still more alarmed at the Idea of being taken for a Dupe, I remained inexorable. I offered a present of a few piastres to another Man of the Consul's train who had bestowed much time on me, and beat down Shopkeepers for me with disinterested Zeal, and done me other real Services, yet with all the persuasion I could use, and I used much, I could not get him to take a farthing. This Man's name is Michael or Mikeli, a Venetian born, he keeps a Billiard Table and a Confectioner's Shop at Bucharest; He serves the Consul with Confectionery, and whether for protection, love, or money, disdains not though a reputable housekeeper, to dress the Consul's Hair, and upon extraordinary occasions, wait on him at Table his Sister born in Germany is married to the Italian Physician Bartolozzi, whom you saw with me at Pera, for whom at his entreaties I waited a day at Bucharest and with whose Company for my Sins I was encumbered from thence hither.

When you pass through Bourgas, fail not, if possible, to see the manufactury of Wedgwoodian ware; I saw the result in plenty, but for want of a Tongue could not see the operation.

I saw the Russian Coffee house keeper, Confectioner at whose house we breakfasted once, giving immense Prices for paltry Flowers out of Season, pray inform yourself of the particulars, and bring them with you, an Establishment at Constantinople would I think be an excellent speculation for an able or even for a tollerable English Gardener.

Dr. Bartolozzi told me, he found by a Conversation he overheard between my Janisary Ahmet and the Horse keeper at the Eivanserai that the former allowed the latter only 22 piastres a horse, instead of 27, which he took from me; if it be material for our Embassador to have honest Men about him rather than Rogues, this may be worth enquiring about; as likewise | | piastres which he withheld out of the 20 which I paid for Horses from [*half a line blank*]

Upon the supposition of Mr. Henderson's pursuing his Journey | | fail not, if you have opportunity, to lay me in suitable terms [*a line left blank*] most excellent of all other Excellencies tell him that in Walachia some | | have been found, but they are in the hands of the Imperial Agent, who prizes them too much to part with them; also as I am told in Moldavia; but these are in the hands of a Boyard-amateur of this place. I have endeavoured | | particulars, but as here I am most unhappily situated for every kind of Information, I fear it will be in vain.

Superstition has kept me from Thursday last to this day (Monday Jany 9th) my Polish Wagon which I bought dearly of the Consul must now be put upon a Sledge. The concurrence of two sorts of workmen is unhappily necessary. Greek feasts tye up the hands of the one, one day Latin those of | | another day | | Rammed into a filthy dog-hole 10 feet square with two filthy Jews and my Servant besides incessant Visitors, I am undergoing Jewish justice suffering for Sins which are certainly not my own; but I am in hopes of changing a shivering Stench for pinching Frost in the Compass of three hours.

What will you give me for my Chance of recovering the odd Volume of the Dizn de Chemin?[11] When you blame me for this Scrawl pity me for writing mostly on my Legs without tollerable pen or Ink, convenient light or Chair or Table. Shew it to Mr. Henderson as a proof of my existence, for which his prayers are sincere, whatever they may be for my prosperity, send it afterwards I beg of you, changing the Direction to my Father, you are politico-Œconomist good enough to know how Things of no Value acquire one by mere change of place—perhaps his Excellency may lend his Enveloppe—

Adieu believe me your's, most truly

Jeremy Bentham

[11] *Sic* in MS. Possibly a copying error for 'Dict. de Chemie'.

561

FROM — SCHNEYDER[1]

c. 9/20 January 1786

J'espère qu'on ne vous fera point faire la quarantine de cette coté-ici, puisque on a connoissance de votre arrivée et que pour cette raison le domestique du Médecin a été chez vous, j'en parlerai au Major, demain matin, envoyé[?] après-\demain quelqu'un pour vous donner avis à ce sujet tout depend de la rivière la quarantine ne vous fera aucun obstacle. Patientez-vous dans Votre Retraite et croyez moi toujours à Vos ordres

Votre Serviteur
Schneyder

561. [1] B.M. IV: 321. Autograph. Docketed: '1786 / Schneyder Olviopol / to / J.B. Bohopol.'

The date attributed to this letter is suggested by Bentham's statement that he reached the frontier town of Bohopol on Monday 5/16 January 1786 (letter 562 at n. 8).

Schneyder was a Russian merchant of German extraction, who had boarded the *Mary Frances* at Leghorn (see letter 550 below the heading, 'Friday Oct. 21'). He subsequently accompanied Bentham's party on the Turkish coaster on which they took passage from Smyrna to Constantinople. He did not join them in the transfer to Captain Newman's ship, on which they completed the last part of that journey; but he renewed his acquaintance with Bentham at Constantinople, and when Bentham's plan to accompany the Moldavian princess to Jassy fell through, he himself on 9 December entered into a formal agreement with Bentham about the journey to the Russian frontier at Olviopol. By this agreement Bentham was given the services of Schneyder's servant, Ludvig, who was to travel on ahead in his company with some of his master's baggage, and various charges for horses were divided between them (B.M. IV: 230, not dated, but drawn up the day before Bentham set out—10 December). Although Bentham's further narrative of his journey (letter 562) makes no mention of the fact, evidently Schneyder had caught up with him either before or at the frontier and, knowing his way round the quarantine regulations, had crossed the frontier to Olviopol ahead of him. Bentham himself was admitted across the frontier about 12/23 or 13/24 January.

562

To Jeremiah Bentham[1]

6/17 January–10/21 February 1786 (Aet 38)

Bohopol Jany. 16. 1786

I have within this hour, my dear Father, received your letter of the 4th of Novr.:[2] and though I hope to be the bearer of it myself as far as Crechoff, which will be its most expeditious if not nearest route, yet having a few hours if not days, of necessary leisure, I can not employ the present moment better than by sitting down under the first impressions to acknowledge the pleasure which yours afforded me. The letter that puzzled you never passed through the hands of Mr. Mulford. I mention this that you may let him see it by the first opportunity. As the time of its reaching you would be uncertain, I made use of a 3d person to convey to my Brother with speed, such part of its contents as it might be material he should be informed of.[3]

You do not mention your having received the parcel I sent you from Paris by Capt. Brook: it contained stockings, gloves, etc of Beaver and *Vigogne* wool. I thought I had mentioned it in one of my letters by post, besides one which was to accompany the parcel.

As to the news about the Prince's appointment it might have been good, had it been true; it might have been /true/, and may at any time if he pleases but was not then whatever it may be. So said a person at Constantinople who if it had been true could not but have known. (P.S. After all it actually is true: the reason of its being denied to me as late as Dec. by the Russian Envoy at Constantinople is perfectly inconceivable. Feb. 16th.)[4]

Against you revisit Bath, the seat of chitchat and gambling, I will give you an instruction by which you may make a fortune. Whenever you see /in a newspaper/ an article from Petersburgh, lay

562. [1] B.M. IV: 240–3. Autograph.

Addressed: 'Jere[h] Bentham Esq. / Queens Square Place / Westminster / London.' Postmarks illegible. At the foot is added: 'Direct for either of us at Critchoff to the care of the Postmaster at Riga.'

The head of the letter is misdated; see n. 8. Partly printed in *The Slavonic and East European Review*, xxix (1950–51), 73–6.

[2] Missing.

[3] The letter to which this passage refers appears to be missing, unless, as seems probable, letter 551 is meant.

[4] This is a later insertion, a day or two after Bentham had arrived at Krichëv. It is not clear to which of Potëmkin's appointments he was referring.

2 to one, /if/ from Constantinople, 5 to one, that it is not true. At the latter place I amused myself with reading accounts of I know not what commotions at a time when they were as quiet as Lambs: and every body concurred in assuring me that it was rare to find an article purporting to come from that capital that had a syllable of truth in it. If such be the case in this enlighten'd age when correspondences are so abundant and so publick, and where Falshood as it should seem could not tread a step without feeling Detection at its heels, how must it have been in days of yore when printing was unknown, and how uncertain must be the lights that can be derived from even the most rational and best attested histories?

All this while you are wondering where I am—You must have some patience before you can collect the first intelligence which a man usually obtains from his correspondent. From Maps and Gazetteers, even the freshest and most particular you would look for it in vain. Know then that *Bohopol*,[5] the place /village/ from whence I date is in that part of the Ukraine (as we /choose to/ term it, though by the inhabitants themselves it is termed *Granitz*)[6] which remains to Poland: yet so that into Turkey could I cast forth one shoe, and into Russia the other. Spread out before you your map of Europe, as I do mine which is its fellow. In Little Tartary you will find a river named *Bog*, joining the Dnieper at Oczakow. We call it here the *Booh*, but you in England being free may stile it as you please. To the right of this river you will find one without a name running into it near a place called *Ponowa*:[7] it is almost eclipsed by the daubing which is intended to mark the division between Little Tartary and the Polish province stiled in the map Poldolia. This river is called here the *Sinyuka* or *Shinyuka*. Bohopol is situated in one of the angles formed by the junction of these two rivers. By the *Bog*, it is separated from the Turkish territory: by the *Shinjuka*, from the Russian. On the Russian side stands a little village or to speak by curtesy a town called Olviopol or Olviople: on the Turkish side another called Holla....The Russian⊞ may contain about 150 houses; the Polish about

⊞The Russian town is compact: the Polish, scatter'd: the Turkish still more so. In the Russian post there is a Colonel with 200 men [...?] the Polish a Lieutenant with 12: in the Turkish, no [...?]

[5] Bohopol, together with Olviopol, and Holla to which Bentham made reference later in this letter, all of which were situated about the confluence of the Bug and the Sinyukha, have become the present Russian town of Pervomaysk.

[6] Russian—*granitsa*, frontier.

[7] Not identified.

threescore: the Turkish about as many. Olviopol seems to have been the parent of the other two: it owes its birth to a cause to which so many others have owed their depopulation, /I mean/ the Plague. The Russians in consequence of the treaty which put them in possession of that part of Little Tartary, which lies between the Bog and the Dnieper, established on their side of this central spot, a post for the observance of the quarantine. Through this place pass all letters between Petersburgh and Constantinople: at this place the /Russian/ Courier who sets out once a fortnight from Constantinople, stops, at the Quarantine house: he /there/ leaves his bag, which after having been fumigated and so forth, is forwarded by another courier through the Russian Empire, and returns himself to the capital from whence he came.

At this same *Bohopol* I arrived yesterday evening. (Monday Jan. 15.)[8] after dusk: in anxious expectation of answers to 2 out of 3 letters I sent to Sam, by so many successive couriers, from Constantinople. A thaw which just now, as my ill star would have it, has destroy'd the snow-roads all around, and deluged the ice of the Sinjuka, render'd a passage across that river either for Myself, or for a Messenger, difficult: the police of this town render'd it impracticable. This morning I found means to send a Messenger with a letter to Major Poulevitch the Russian Postmaster inclosing two letters of introduction from so many different persons in Constantinople and Bucharest: the messenger brought me not a letter from Sam which I much expected, but a letter from you which assuredly I did *not* expect. Disappointed of necessaries, I have got a luxury to console me. I proposed to him in my first, and more particularly in my second, to send somebody to Olviopol to meet me: now have I got between 7 and 800 miles to travel alone, in a wild country, of the language of which I know not a single syllable. Under these circumstances it would be cruelty to you to send off this letter before I reach Crichoff if ever I should reach it. Not a creature established at Olviopol understands either French or English; so my old fellow-traveller Mr. Scheider informs me, in answer to my French note to Major Poulevitch. But his track coincides with mine at least as far as Kremenchuck, which is about 120 miles on my way. There he tells me I shall meet with people who have French tongues in their heads, and thither he invites me to bear him company, which I shall most gladly do. There too I shall fall in with Sam's route in his way between

[8] Monday was 16 January by the Gregorian calendar, by which Bentham was still reckoning at this time.

Crechoff and the Crim in the south with Prince Potemkin: as he staid there some days he must have made acquaintance on an advantageous footing with the Governor and so forth. Now you see the other side of the picture: so that all things consider'd, whatever you may be, I am as easy as an old shoe.

Before you fold up your map do but look at a place called there *Konicepole*: (it should be Konietzpol.) Why this most beggarly of all beggarly villages I ever saw, and which never could have been anything better, should be honoured with a place in the map of Europe, /in preference to at/ least half a dozen /much bigger/, which I saw within the space which the name of it occupies upon the map, is more than I can conceive. /It had hardly more hovels than there are good houses on Pye-nest Green./ In *fact* it is within *3* miles of the *site* of Bohopol: whereas it is *represented* as if at least *20* miles distant. The same error is copied into a Russian map of the province of New Russia (in which /lies/ *Olviopol*) of the year 1779. To the left of the *Bog* you will see a river called *Rodeme*, with an R; instead of Kodime, with a K, as it should be. It does empty itself into the Bog, but, if my information here is just, at more than six miles distance from the junction of the latter with the *Sinyuka*.[9]

Before this reaches you, you will have received, I hope, a letter of mine from Yassi to Mr. Eaton at Constantinople, as I particularly desired him to forward it to you.[10] From Bucharest I had already sent a kind of imperfect journal, contained in one or two large sheets I forget which to Mr. Henderson, with a similar request.[11] (It was one folio sheet and one quarto). At present therefore what remains is that I account to you for my appearance at this place.

At Bucharest I met, as my letter from Yassi informs you, Mr. *Willis*, an English Merchant who from Constantinople went to settle in the Crimea. In his journey from thence he had passed thro Olviopol: for through that place every traveller from the Crimea or from Cherson to Moldavia and so on to Constantinople is obliged to pass. This you will observe is a great *detour*: the political causes above hinted at concur with the want of bridges and other physical causes, (but I know not as yet in what proportions) in rendering a nearer approach to the sea impracticable. From Yassi to Olviopol,

[9] The Kodyma, a right-bank (western) tributary of the Bug, joins it a few miles upstream from Pervomaysk.

[10] Letter 560.

[11] Letter 557. In a letter to Jeremiah Bentham dated from Pera, 10 January 1786, Henderson stated that this had just reached him and would be forwarded by next post (B.M. IV: 234).

there are two routes; one through the Turkish territories, the other, higher up, through the Polish. The former is the most ordinary route; it is that which the Couriers pursue. The other would scarcely be adopted, but for the sake of avoiding the quarantine to which travellers through the Turkish territory are subjected whenever the plague is known to exist in Constantinople. At Constantinople and the environs that calamity prevailed at the time of my departure (so my passport from the Russian Envoy testified) to a considerable degree: but it was then understood that in the Polish territory near to Olviopol itself it was still more prevalent. This account was confirmed by Mr. Willis: it was his opinion therefore as well as the Russian Consul's that I should be obliged to take the route of Bessarabia (which is the name of the Turkish province) subject however to any counter advice which the Russian Vice-Consul at Jassi might from maturer information think fit to give me. At Jassi the Vice-Consul informed me that the quarantine with regard to Poland was /already/ taken off: and that by pursuing that route I should obtain three advantages: 1st, a shorter cut, 2. the saving the expence of a Janissary (which is necessary for every Frank who travels any where in Turkey) and 3. the escaping of the quarantine. Between that part of Moldavia and the Polish territory the only communication is through *Soroka*[12] which is separated by the river *Dniester* from *Chekanofka* on the Polish side. For Soroka or for *Checkanofka*, though the least of those two paltry villages is equal to ten *Konietzpols*, you would search in vain: but you will find two points marked *Zampól* and *Cherinoe*: Soroka and Chekanofka may be conceived as lying between those two points. From Yassi to Soroka there are post-horses stationed all the way: at Soroka or at Chekanofka which like *Stroud* and *Rochester* may be considered as one and the same town, I should meet /he said/ with Carriers who would take me on to Olviopol, ~~the Vice Consul~~ he supposed for about 5 or 6 Roubles. From Yassi to Soroka they compute 12 Polish miles: whereof each is /reckoned/ equivalent to 10 Russian Versts. This would make 120 Versts, and from Soroka to Olviopol he conjectured there might be about 200 more: total 320. Ten versts should make a trifle more than six English miles: but by observation of the time compared with the rate of travelling, I am clear that one of these Polish miles can not make so little as eight English. Between Yassi and Soroka there are 5 posts; including that at

[12] Now Soroki, in Russian Moldavia, situated at 48° 08′ N., 28° 12′ E., on the right bank of the Dniester.

Yassi: the third post is at a place called *Belch*:[13] the only station, which can be dignified with the appellation of a village. If the name ofends you, cut 'it' out; and please to remember *I* am *not* its Godfather.

On Monday Jan. 9th my Waggon being at length mounted on a sledge I bade adieu to Jassi after dusk: the snow being deep and the track not as yet harden'd by use, we dragged on heavily, seldom more than a foot pace, with frequent interruptions. At the rate of 4 miles an hour we ought to have reached the first post by about 10 or 11: I had /all the way/ 6 horses, understand, paying but for 4, whether altogether according to custom, or partly through favour, I did not clearly comprehend. After toiling some hours, how many I know not, (for except when I have gone to bed I have scarce ever thought to wind up my watch), at length we stuck outright: luckily, we were within 4 miles of the post. After struggling an hour or two to no purpose, and breaking a reasonable quantity of tackle one of the two postillions set out for the post in quest of a reinforcement: he returned about daybreak with /a 3d postillion and/ 5 supplemental horses in addition to the 6 we had before. The same scene of whipping, and shouting and lifting recommenced, and with the same success. The additional cattle seemed rather to have diminished than augmented our effective strength. By whips composed of a short stick and a piece of slender pack-thread such as you would tie up half a dozen books with, no impression capable of lasting beyond the moment could be made. If then the /three/ postillions had been perfect timists, with Dr. Burney to lead them, instead of honest *Ludwig* (which is my Polish Servant's name) the effective strength to be collected out of the 11 horses would have been equal to that of 3; but as it was seldom that any two were struck together, or, when struck, pulled in the same direction, how many fractions of a horse our total effective strength amounted to for a constancy, is a problem which I must leave to the Royal Society /to solve/. Of the sleevelessness and stupidity and ignorance manifested upon this and other similar occasions by the honest Moldavians, no man whose travels have been confined to England and the countries which come next to England, can form a tolerable idea. Of all which, having neither implements to operate with nor tongue to speak with, I was obliged to be an inactive spectator, and, as impatience would have been useless, I chose to be a patient one. The country, though bare and wild and unenclosed, is not so desert as not to afford here and

[13] Beltsy, 47° 44′ N., 27° 51′ E.

there a miserable hovel with a good stock of stout horned cattle: some such habitations, though not in sight, were fortunately at no great distance. Fortunately also the experience of the superior virtue of oxen at a dead pull had made its way into Moldavia: in process of time 4 of these cattle were procured and these, added to two of our best horses, at the first effort drew me out of *limbo.* I reached the post house at about 10 or 11 o'clock of the Tuesday morning (Jan. 10.) Here I eat a morsel of bread, and made a dish of milk-less Coffee in a tin pot I had bought at Bucharest: the only refreshment I had taken except a slender meal of the same sort, since Sunday about noon: and what I was much more in want of, I got a recruit of hot water for my feet in an earthen bottle I had brought from Jassi. Please to understand in a parenthesis that in all the shops of that metropolis, /though populous enough to contain between 3 and 400 places of worship of which about 70 parochial/ no such implement was to be purchased as a *cork.* I was obliged to have recourse to the Vice-Consul's generosity who gave me 4 of different sizes, but so expensively, though clumsily, fitted up with rings and caps and buttons and wires, aping at an immense distance our English ones, that I was ashamed to take them. What made the hot water expedient the more necessary is, that /since I have left Bucharest/ ~~in this part of the world~~ I have found the hearths every where raised a foot or two above the ground, as if on purpose to prevent the application of artificial heat to the lower extremities, the only parts which with me stand essentially in need of it.

A little before dusk I arrived without any material accident at *Belch*: the posthouse offering wretched accommodation and diseased inhabitants, I went a little out of the road in quest of a private house; much against the will of honest *Ludwig*, who though very studious to serve me in his own way, has /proved/ a constant enemy to every kind of eccentricity. By bad *accommodations* take care you do not understand as in England /want of a separate room or/ bad provisions or even none, for none /did I expect or wish for/, but a smoaking chimney, or an imperfect door, or a door opening immediately upon the fire place, in the one room which constitutes the house. I was shewn to the house which appeared to be the best, and which proved to be occupied by a Jew: Dealer and Chapman as all Jews are, but in what particular articles I could not learn: for *Ludwig* is an enemy to all *impertinent* curiosity, and with him *all* curiosity is impertinent. In this palace, for such it was in comparison of the ordinary Moldavian houses, I was as well received as I should have been at a post-house. And now would I fain paint to you this Jewish house and this Jewish family, as I would every house and every family I have visited since I left Constantinople, and so I could, if I had time: but I shall ruin you in postage, and at this rate we shall never reach /even/ Soroka. Here I made an Anti-Jewish meal of Yassi Sausages; Christian neighbours furnished a plate to put them on. I left *Belch* about 7 at night and after an exact repetition of the former night's scene, the oxen excepted, reached Soroka Wednesday morning at 11.

Soroka being the /last/ Moldavian town, there consequently end the Moldavian posts. As it was through Poland that I was thenceforward to travel, I thought the Polish town the best spot for enquiring concerning the means of travelling. Not to leave my baggage unguarded or guarded by strangers. I thought it a point gained when I had prevailed on honest Ludwig to engage the Moldavian postillions to cross the river to Chekanofka. I had no sooner crossed it than I was stopped by a Polish Centinel unarmed, who declared that the colonel's order forbad my advancing any further. Passports were produced, but in vain, and all explanation refused: I desired to be introduced to this Colonel: this too was impracticable. In the course of the altercation, understanding I spoke little or no German, 'what business then,' says he, /'can he have/ to travel?' A piastre dispelled this and every ⟨other⟩ difficulty, and I soon found myself at the 'Colonel's' quarters. He there informed me that /according to orders/ a quarantine as against travellers from Moldavia was there in force: but that as he, all circumstances consider'd, apprehended no danger, he would not send me to the quarantine house but /station me at large in/ better lodgings, from whence if I would wait with patience, he hoped in the course of two or three days to have it in his power to dismiss me. The conversation was carried on sometimes through the medium of Ludwig, who comprehended French but very imperfectly, sometimes immediately in Latin. He had got the length of several sentences, and still I heard nothing of myself, but a great deal concerning I knew not what 3d person under the title of *Magnificus*. Whatever pride your son might have conceived at finding himself to be the personage dignified by so high-sounding a title would have been much lower'd by a question that was soon put to him whether since he had denied himself to be a merchant, was not Magnificus a Drawing-master or a Player. The firm and possibly rather disdainful tone with which I thought it advisable to answer these and other such questions in the negative operating on him as an evidence of truth, he betook himself to his apologies, begging I would not take amiss what he said, observing that questions of that nature were necessary preliminaries, and concluding that being now perfectly satisfied that I was what my passport purported me to be, an English Gentleman, he could not think of assigning me any other quarters than his own house. His momentary suspicions to the contrary had been founded he said on something that had been dropped by my servant whom he understood to have said that I was /actually/ a Drawing-Master. I have my conjectures relative to the ground of this mistake, but it is not worth while to state them here. He then introduced me to his Wife, a good pretty young woman, with whom his honey moon seemed still to be in the full, though it had already lasted above six months. His name is Dunakefski: he acknowledged six and twenty: (very young thought I for a Colonel, but of that hereafter). He is a subject of the Emperor being a native of *Cracow* in Austrian Poland: he had spent 10 years he said in the service; the first 4 or 5 in the K. of Prussia's, the rest in that of Poland.—I have set you down in this house:—how shall I bring you out of it? I must pass over Madam Dunakefski's Jew Men-mantua-makers, her female visitants, my visit with ⟨the family to⟩ a neighbouring gentleman of the name of *Callinski* /⟨my devotions⟩ at the Greek church,/ and my transactions at the Custom-house. One incident however I will mention relative to my visit. One of the sons, a young man seemingly about one and twenty, talking a little Latin, kept himself near me, standing by the sofa on which I sat. Observing him constantly in that posture, I asked him why he did not sit? upon which, after looking round him with marks of hesitation, he set himself down in the place I made for him. I soon found that in compliment to me he had broke an etiquette—Guess why he could not sit? because his mother was in the room. Present this, with the traveller's best respects, to the present Clerk of the Rules, and the future Chancellor, who knows but it may lessen your bill from the Upholsterers?

I had not been above 2 hours at Chekanofka before I was ⟨informe⟩d by the Colonel, and I believe truly, that ⟨by ord⟩ers received since my arrival, the quarantine was totally taken off. I was therefore at full liberty, but horses remained to be procured. Upon talking with the Collector of the Customs he had mentioned by conjecture about 6 roubles as a likely price for 4 horses either all the way on to Olviopol, or a part of the way, I forget which: but his conjecture seemed to be a random one not grounded on experience or any specific information. Ludwig could not meet with any one who would undertake for the whole journey, which he was informed was 18 (= 144) miles. Several indeed were willing to undertake for the first stage, which is 3 (= 24) miles at a place called *Miaskoofka*:[14] but they all concurred in demanding 1½ florins equal to a trifle more than 9d a horse per mile, and as the snow they said was deep and the road steep and mountainous, none would undertake it with fewer than 10 horses. I was informed through the same channel that the cattle were but indifferent and that it being a feast *holiday* time as usual amongst some or all of these people it was uncertain how soon if at all this requisite number could be collected. After several conferences on the subject, the Colonel interfered, telling me a person whom he could depend on and who had six stout horses for whose sufficiency he could answer was willing to let them for the three miles for as many ducats. This made 54 florins. The other proposal amounted to 45. The enormity of this demand /concurred with other circumstances in/ exciting some suspicion: but I had already had experience of the inefficacy of undisciplined numbers: and for so small a difference as 9 florins equal to about 4s 6d, prudential considerations, if no other, seemed to forbid the rejection of an offer coming from such a quarter. In short I accepted it: he then said, if I would then deposit the money in his hands the bargain was made, and he would forward the money to the proper hands and be answerable for the event. I thought this a little odd, but I complied. Other incidents relative to this negotiation I must e'en pass by: such as his labouring without effect to prevent my visiting the *Collector*; and my labouring, I believe with a little effect to make him believe that that visit had no ⟨reference⟩ to him.

About 2 o'clock of the day after my arrival (Wed. 12th) I set out for *Miaskoofka*: dinner seem'd to have been hasten'd that I might share in it. We parted with many professions of friendship on his side; and many farewells and bows and acknowledgements on mine. I was surprized at the splendor of this hired equipage: 6 fine horses that would not have disparaged an English carriage decently caparaisoned, and driven by 2 smart postillions, with an outrider bearing a long pike. I asked Ludwig, whether he knew whose they were: he said he had asked, and nobody would tell him: but thus much he knew by the circumstances of the pike-man, that the owner could be no other than a gentleman, or if you please, a nobleman. As Noblemen in that little spot could not be plenty, our suspicions concurred in fixing on the Callinski family. Not long after

[14] Not identified.

he spoke to the Postillions, and then he told me they confessed that their master was no other than mine host. Admitting payment to be due for accommodations proffer'd by hospitality, he would have been no loser had he lent his horses instead of letting them: 4 or 5 pound of extraordinary fine raisins in a place where raisins of no kind were to be had for money, an English letter padlock which he stripped my cloak-bag of, in exchange for a trumpery one of the country, a pair of Leghorn hare fur gloves which *Madame* wheedled me out of after *Monsieur* had attempted it in vain; these articles, trifling in England, Leghorn and Smyrna, but every one of them matchless in Chekanofka: these presents, you will think, if weighed against the entertainment of a day to which no addition appears to have been made on my account, might have been sufficient to turn the scale of obligation in my favour. Honest Ludwig repulsed a similar attack with better success. *Madame*, smitten with a bauble she saw hanging to his watch, would have begged it of him: his offer of parting with it for the 6s or 7s it had cost him in Leghorn was rejected: but pleading servitude and its attendant poverty, he was at length excused. After all my friend the Colonel, as his Soldiers called him, and as he himself suffer'd me to stile him all along, turned out to be neither more nor less than a Lieutenant of horse. So Ludwig, who having served in armies recognised him by his uniform, and knew this very man three years in his present rank, informed me, but with his usual simplicity not till after my departure. His command, render'd lucrative if Ludwig's information speaks true, by horse-jobbing; and his wife, who brought him two villages to her fortune: these resources, if he had had no others than his pay, should have set him above the disgrace of plundering travellers under the mask of hospitality. Let Mr. Mulford thank his star that his 7–foot pipe-tubes did not make the tour with me by land: Madame Dunakefski (for this noble young lady without a breach of the fashion smoaks) would not have failed to grasp at them: and who could have wrenched any thing out of so fair a hand?

After all I saw no cause to regret the forced preference I gave to the Commander's cattle: for it was not without some difficulty that in about 5 hours his six fine horses under able management, dragged me to Miaskoufka.

Here the difficulty of getting horses recommenced; nor could it be overcome till the next morning (Fri. 12. Jan.)[15] about 3 or 4 o'clock when I set out with 6 horses for Cheechelnik.[16] The 5 or if you please

[15] Friday, 13 January.

[16] Not identified.

the 40 miles between Miaskoufka and that town took me till near the same hour in the afternoon. Here as at Yassi, Religion intervened and put a spell upon me. From one side of the Polish Ukraine to the other not a Christian horse ever stirs without a Jew-Broker to give him motion. Before such an animal could be ferreted out, tho' no time was lost in hunting him, the Sabbath had begun: and it was not till the afternoon of the next day (Sat. 13th)[17] that *Ludwig* after tugging all night long, tore a leaf out of the book of *Mortimer* and held up to the view of the astonished inhabitants of Chechelnik the doctrine of *'Every man his own Horse-broker.'* I arrived at *Savran*,[18] a stage of equal length, travelling as usual in the night, by 2 o'clock the next morning (Sun. 15 Jan.) There by good fortune, though not without Jew assistance, in the compass of 2 hours I got horses for *this* place.—From Chekanofka even unto Bohopol, a space of not less than 144 miles not an Inn have I entered that has been in any other hands than those of the race of Israel: a people by inbred filthiness the worst qualified, and by religious scruples, one should think the least disposed, to engage in such a business. Would that our good friend, his late Lordship,[19] were s-itting beside me (he knows what I mean) I would relate to him at full length and in piteous sort my entertainment among these Iewes. He and I, in reading of the scrapes they /used to/ get into in Hollingshead, have often joined in lamenting their hard ⟨me⟩asure: enlighten'd by experience and familiarized with vicarious punishment, I am now satisfied that the sufferings of the forefathers were no more than a just retribution for those which the children have inflicted on me. *Qui fit Mœcenas*, that in all Poland, (for it is the same in other provinces as in this) a man can not get a rag to cover him, nor a piece of black bread to eat, /nor a beast to carry him,/ nor a hog-stie to lay his head in, but he must have a Jew to help him to it?—O but (cried an old Polish Latin-talking gentleman-traveller to whom I gave a supper at Miaskoufka) they *have* a head!—'Yes,' replied I, 'but it is a lousy one.'—If such is the superiority of Jewish heads, what are native Polish ones! I have a theory less disgraceful to the body of the nation. These interlopers form the *tiers etat*, standing in the gap between a people of Lords and a people of slaves, in a country not inviting enough to allure better capitalists.[20]

[17] Saturday, 14 January.

[18] A village at the confluence of the river Savranka and the Bug, 48° 09′ N., 30° 04′ E.

[19] I.e., Richard Clark, who had been Lord Mayor in 1784–85.

[20] The earliest instance (one in print) of the use of this word noticed in the *O.E.D.*

Before I take leave of Chechelnik, it would be ingratitude not to commemorate a Russian Major, of the name of *Bibicoff*: he redeemed me out of Jewish Purgatory, and entertained me with the politeness of a gentleman and the cordiality of a friend. He has been stationed there these two years by the Admiralty at Cherson, purveying wood from the demesnes of Prince Lubomirski;[21] (who by the bye has a not inelegant palace built within these 4 or 5 years in the middle of the town, but locked up, /his family being absent/ and invisible in the inside.) Over night, as an article of news, *Ludwig* had apprised me of his existence: it struck me immediately, in spite of Ludwig's controuling judgement, that a Russian officer serving in an inferior rank within the sphere of my Brother's connections might be willing as well as able to be of use to me. ⟨Finding no⟩ station in the Inn ample enough to receive my narrow bed, except the State bedstead, a kind of portable trough, littered with chopt straw, which /I had just seen/ the Landlady empty of two children, to receive me, I abandoned this luxury to my faithful attendant, leaving him to bask in the straw inhaling the fumes of Judaism, and in spite of his remonstrance retired to a cleanlier place ⟨in the⟩ Stable. There, climbing up into my waggon ⟨and⟩ wrapping my pelisse around me, ⟨I had⟩ as perfect a night's sleep as ever I enj⟨oyed at⟩ Lincoln's Inn. He objected a frosty night ⟨and⟩ imperfect roof at least fifty foot high in the company of cattle: but I had already had more than one night's sleep on colder nights without any other roof than that of the Waggon, and I am *Gulliver* enough to prefer *Houhyms* to *Yahoos*. In the morning having taken a breakfast of Yassi bread and Yassi Coffee, with some rich Chicken ⟨broth⟩ poisoned by a Jewish pipkin, I dragged *Ludwig* with me to the *Majors*: he was not yet stirring, but returning a while after to the charge, I found him visible. He detained me to dinner, while he bestirred himself with great zeal to find out horses for me, though eventually without effect. The company consisted of his wife, a Clerk called in Russian stile his *Cancellier*, and I know not what Russian visitor: a little Italian, of which our stock was equally slender, enabled him and me to maintain some sort of conversation. At parting, he gave me of his own motion a letter to a person in authority at Savran to find me horses, and another of general recommendation to a dependant of his /here/ one Licoka, a Jew,

is by Arthur Young in 1792. An instance of its use as early as 1764 in a Russian official document is noted in E. I. Druzhinina, *Severnoye Prichernomor'e v 1775–1800 gg*, Moscow, 1959, p. 67.

[21] Not identified.

with whom /having a room to myself,/ I am much better lodged than I could have been at any other home either here or at Olviopol.

Crechoff Feb 10/21. I arrived here after a variety of unexpected and unfortunate delays, this day sennight: and now I may without scruple make use of the first opportunity for sending off these two sheets of my history. The joy produced by the re-union of your two sons after a separation of 5½ years may be left to their father to conceive. This paper will scarce hold anything more: but it will not be long before you have another. Take in the mean time a very general sketch of the events which filled ⟨up⟩ the long interval betwixt the first and the last dates of this long letter. After crossing the Sinjuka through a deal of dirt and with a deal of difficulty, I reached Olviopol the 6th day I think it was after my arrival at the opposite shore. I had then 4 or 5 days more to kick my heels alone at the Quarantine House. My journey from Olviopol to Kremencheck took me 4 days of which one was spent amusingly enough at St. Elizabeth[22] at the house of a rich old farmer of the Brandy duties. There, as indeed at Olviopol, I found myself treading on what to me was much better than classic ground: ground on which Sam had trod, in the company you know of.[23] At Kremenchuck I had the good fortune to meet with Lieut. Col. Fanshaw[24] and Col. Chevalier de Ribas.[25] The former has the only remaining one except Sam's of the ten independent Batallions. The other, half an Englishman by the mother's side, ⟨has⟩ a Regiment of horse. I happened to have a letter of introduction to Gen. Sinelnikoff the General of the Province,[26] but Fanshaw told me, and as I had reason to think truly, that the best introduction

[22] Not identified. Probably Yelisabetgrad, about half-way between Olviopol and Kremenchug.

[23] I.e., in the company of Potëmkin.

[24] Lieutenant Colonel Henry Fanshawe (1756–1828), *alias* Fensh, under which name he and members of his family appear in the *Russkiy Biograficheskiy Slovar'*. He came of a landed family in Lancashire, had risen to the rank of colonel in the 1st regiment of footguards, and, after the end of the American war of independence, sought adventure and opportunity in the Russian military service. A few months after Samuel Bentham received his military rank and command of an independent batallion of chasseurs, Fanshawe was given a similar command with the same rank. He eventually rose to the rank of general in the Russian service, at various times held the governorships of Kiev and of the Crimea, and became a senator.

[25] Don Jose de Ribas-y-Boyons (1749–1800), born at Naples, the son of a Spanish father and a French mother (so identified in F. A. Golder, *John Paul Jones in Russia*, New York, 1927, p. 53 n.). He had been introduced into the Russian service some years before by Count Orlov.

[26] Ivan Maksimovich Sinel'nikov (d. 1789). He was Potëmkin's chief assistant in the government of the namestnichestvo of Yekaterinoslav and was governor and officer in charge of the building of the town of that name.

I could have had was the relation I bear to Sam. I had there the satisfaction of hearing of his existence after ½ a year's interruption of all intelligence. I was detained there a fortnight by a rascally Major who pretended to wait for nothing but passable roads to set out for Dubrovna a place of the Prc⟨'s⟩ within a post or two of Crechoff, and who after all left me in the lurch. I was obliged in his stead to take up with one of a small party of Sam's batallion whom my good stars had sent to Kremenchuck some months before. From Kremenchuck to Crichoff took me from Thursday night to Tuesday /last/ inclusive. And here for the present I must end.[27]

563

From William Eaton[1]

12 March 1786

I was going to refer you to a letter I wrote about a Month ago but on turning over a few pages of my memory I find it was conceived but never brought forth. I received your letter from Jassy it suffered a delay in being sent to your Father for want of his address at last it went recommended to the Care of Herries /the/ Bankers. We were all sorry for the drubbing you got, but we admired your impassionate and Philosophical relation of the circumstances. I thank you for the directions about the road and shall inquire about the Manufactory. The Herb you describe is most certainly hanna or kna they use oil and mild-vegetable-Alkaly in dying with it.

Here follows the history of Pera. Mr. Henderson and the Ladies took things very cooly, but the latter received no more visits nor Invitations. Upon the whole we might both of us have held our tongues, but we are neither of us men of the World, tho' perhaps

[27] Some of the chronology of the last part of Bentham's journey can be established only approximately, and he appears to have over-estimated the periods he spent at the frontier and at Kremenchug. If he stayed ten days at Bohopol and Olviopol, he resumed his travels on 16/27 January and reached Kremenchug on 19/30 January. These dates are uncertain; but his statement is categorical, that he left Kremenchug on 29 January/9 February, and reached Krichëv on 3/14 February.

563. [1] B.M. IV: 248–9. Partly in a clerk's hand, partly autograph. Docketed: '1786 Mar. 1/12 / Eaton Constantinople / to / J.B. Crichoff.'

Addressed: 'a Monsieur / Monsieur Jer. Bentham / Gentilhomme Anglois / à Kritschef.' Also bearing addresses in Turkish and Russian. In front of the address, 'N.62' has been inserted in a different hand.

Replies to letter 560.

not the worse for it. The Ambassadour told to Mr. Revely and to Others and Mr. Revely to all the World that you had given a bad Acct. of the learned Doctor G.[2] and was violently affronted with me for having presented him. A week afterwards he told the same to me and then accused me of having betrayed his Secret ten days before he intrusted me with it. Consequently I am out of his *good Graces*. The Doctor produced a Number of documents to prove he was no Knight Errant and He became a favourite: he is gone to Aleppo to perform some desperate operation: it is said he goes thence to the East Indies with Major Morrison. Mr. Henderson with the Ladies sailed hence with a French Captain to the Crim some time ago. Some time before they went I lived in your room not having room at Mr. ~~Jackeens~~ /Jacquins/ to finish some drawings for the Russian Envoy. I now keep the whole House. Mrs. Eaton is still at Smirna as the season is now so far advanced I intend going with her to Charson and thence to Petersburg making Krichef in my way where I hope to find you. Neither Mr. Henderson nor the Drogoman since his departure has been able to recover the 20 Vrs. of the Jew. | | The shape of the henna leaf, much resembles Senna, it grows in Bombay wild.

The Ambassadour took no notice of the discovery mentioned in the first part of my letter, tho' he doubtless was vexed at it. It is thought Sir Ricd Worsely will succeed him in the Embassy. Mr. Humphreys[3] was not pleased at your having fixt the exchange for him he says you should have given him a credit for it upon your Banker: he says he loses by the transaction I have no news here that can in the least interest you At Alexandria there has happened a very disagreable Affair to the Franks. Murat Bey has seized the Cattle and demands a large *Avania* of the Franks who have refused to pay it: and have sent an express hither. The Ministers Conjointly have made a Strong representation to the Port, and some Turkish men of War are to be sent down, which probably will put things in Order again. The Capt Pashaw is omnipotent. There is a new Vizier who was formerly in his Service I am anxious to hear of your having finished your journey and found your Brother in perfect health: pray make my Compliments exceptable to him: Assure him of the great pleasure it would give me to see him, and that I shall not go thro' that part of the Country without

[2] Presumably Griffiths (who was a surgeon, not a doctor). On him, see letters 550, n. 8 and 552, n. 4.

[3] For Humphreys, see letter 553, n. 2. Bentham's bill of exchange drawn in his favour is letter 555.

waiting on him. Thus far by an amanuensis. Pray tell your brother. At Venice an immense quantity of /Glass/ beads of all kinds are made and other cheap glass manufacturies, which are sent to the East Indies by the way of Aleppo, Egypt, etc: great quantities go to Persia and thence to Bokara Tartary etc. a great quantity goes to Petersburg. This would be a matter of great consequence. I can procure him people at a very cheap rate who can establish him these *fabrics* if he will tell the Prince of it and let him lay his commands on me. I believe a Russian minister could not get these people so well as I could, besides I know some and have been applied to. More matter with my next. In a day or two I shall know which way I go for I shall have an answer from S. Petersburg.

We have had strange weather winter and hard winter and summer in the same week: lately I have heard little of the plague but since you went we have had some weeks a good deal.

Believe me with the greatest esteem and affection
Dr Sir
Y. ms. O. H. Servt
Wm Eaton

12 March
at Pera
1786.

564

To Richard Clark[1]

17/28 March 1786 (Aet 38)

Direct to Col. Bentham now and hereafter in English to the care of the Postmaster at Riga.

J. & S. B. to R.C. Crichoff March 17/28 1786

Inclosed is a letter[2] which we should be much obliged to you to convey into Q.S.P.s hands, without any body else's knowing of his having received it. Pray treat us with an answer telling us how things go on there, and any other intelligence publick or private that happens to occurr to you. You will neither wonder nor growl at finding this a short letter, seeing that all the long ones are as

564. [1] U.C. CLXXIII: 59. In Jeremy Bentham's hand. Docketed: '28th March 1786 J. and S. Bentham.' Postmark: 'AP 28.'
Addressed: 'To / Mr. Alderman Clark / London.'
[2] Presumably letter 565.

much yours as they are any body's else. At leaving England I (J.B.) gave orders according to your then Lordship's[3] permission that my books or some of them should be convey'd to your said Lordship's garret, I have your said Lordship to thank for very many civilities shew'd me by sundry Merchants at Smyrna and Constantinople. All were very civil, several friendly but a Mr. Ensly[4] whose name was not on the back of my letters but who is a partner in the house in which Mr. *Morier*[5] is a partner, having formed a plan to impose upon me, and being detected and disappointed was very angry at his disappointment as is natural to suppose and as I was informed by third persons though as to myself I did not happen to see him afterwards. An Italian Skipper having mentioned to others a certain price he meant to ask of me to take me and mine from Smyrna to Constantinople, my countryman Enslie, unasked by him interposed in order to persuade to give about double the price, pretending great friendship and zeal to serve me, and certifying that this double price was unreasonably low.

565

To Jeremiah Bentham[1]

17/28 March 1786 (Aet 38)

Critchoff March 28/17 1786.

Hond. Sir,

You wished my Brother to get Money; He is now in a way of doing so. He has lately told you from Riga of the fortunate Completion of his Contract, and of the use he was making of the Capital it produced by bandying it about the Country.[2] It is gone to

[3] A reference to Clark's tenure of the office of Lord Mayor of the City of London.

[4] Not identified.

[5] Isaac Morier (1750–1817), a merchant of Huguenot descent, born at Smyrna, where he was engaged in commerce. He was later naturalized in England and a number of his descendants had distinguished careers.

565. [1] B.M. IV: 250–1. Copy by Jeremiah Bentham. Docketed: 'Copy / Fils Jeremy / Letter dated Critchoff / March 17/28 1786.' Another letter-book copy at B.M. XXII: 400–1.

[2] For the general situation at Krichëv and the activities of Samuel Bentham, into which Jeremy Bentham found himself occasionally drawn, see Ian R. Christie, 'Samuel Bentham and the western colony at Krichëv, 1784–1787', *The Slavonic and East European Review*, xlviii (1969–70), 232–47. Samuel Bentham informed his father on 6/17 January 1786 (B.M. IV: 237–9) that he had entered into a ten-year contract to run a number of Potëmkin's manufactures at Krichëv, including leather, glassmaking, a smithy, a millwright's establishment, and a rope-walk. About 20,000

Krementchuck, and Cherson under the joint Care of honest Benson,[3] and a Russian Officer, and we now begin to expect the return of it every day. This simple mode of turning the Penny will of course be pushed as far as it will go; but whatever becomes of this, there is no want of others; the Possession of some Capital having put him upon Enquiries into the several possible means of turning it to account. He finds that there are *various articles* of Commerce, which, without interfering at all with his Fabrics, promise a still easier and more considerable Profit, not only the Rate of Profit is much greater than in England, but the Returns are proportionably more speedy: what is more, they are more secure, as it will be in his power so to manage as not to sell but for ready money, or such security as in point of safety is equivalent to it.

Clerks and Agents He gets for nothing, or for as little as he pleases, among his officers and others under his Dependance, and his Battallion-Horses serve for Carrying the Goods to the best Market,—Which they may as well do as stand idle in the Stable.

Thus it is that without the Reproach of being /called/ a Merchant, He has better means of Carrying on Merchandize than if he were one.

I will give you an Example or two of the Advantages that are to be made by ready money. The Hides that he has taken of the Prince, as Part of the Stock of the Leather-Fabric, to the number of 2, or 3,000, cost one with another, a Ruble a Piece, (i.e. 100d Copecs), now by sending from Market to Market, he is buying as good for 50, or 40 Copecs—Tar, the Prince's Steward would give him or anybody 20 copecs a Pood, ready money, for the Rope Fabric, taking at that rate, between 3 and 4,000 Pood a year, now he finds it may be had a few Poods at a time for 15, or even so low as 10 Copecs a Pood; and He only waits the Result of the Enquiries He is making into the Quantity of Poods that can be got at this lower Price, in order to contract for supplying the article at the higher. Wax, when he was at Riga, he found the Merchants there paying for, at the rate of 13 Rix dollars a Pood; now in this Neigh-

rubles was advanced as a loan in connection with these undertakings; and Samuel, then at Riga, reported: 'My business in coming here was to change into Ducats 19,000 Rubles, which I had just received all in silver money. These Ducats I send into another part of the Empire to change again for Rubles, by which I am sure to gain 5 or 6, and perhaps as far as 10 p. cent in the course of a month or six weeks.'

[3] George Benson, an Irishman formerly engaged in the linen trade in Ireland, but for long out of business, and on his beam-ends in Wales, was the protégé of Dr Charles Brown of Carmarthen, who had visited Samuel Bentham at Krichëv in 1785 and secured an opening for him there (letter 524). For his later adventures see letters 578, 580, and 588.

bourhood he finds this to be had at 10, or 9½ Ruble a Pood, and a Rix dollar is worth more than a Ruble by about ¼th.—Now the Carriage from hence to Riga would not amount to half a Ruble a Pood were he to hire Carriers which He has no need to do—here there would be a Gain of 60 p. ct. upon the Supposition that the Riga Price continues the same, at the time by which He can send Wax (which will be the latter end of May,) and as That we believe is by no means a fluctuating article, if the profit of it should not quite come up to the above, can hardly fall greatly short of it.—Accordingly He is taking Measures to secure all the Wax he can.

There may be full half a dozen or more other Articles equally promising which I must omit either because the Information we have been able as yet to obtain relative to them, is not as yet full and precise enough, or on account of the difficulty of extracting it from him, amidst his incessant avocations.

As a number of returns may be made in the Course of the year, if you could contrive to let him have £500 in addition to what he has there seems little doubt of his being able to make Cent per Cent of it.

He has been selling Cloth at a Profit, although he has been cheated to such a degree by Capper (whom he then employed, and whom, you may be sure, he will employ no more) as to be made pay more than the retail Price.

He is told that the Custom is, in that Trade, to give Twelve months Credit and that the wholesale Price of Broad Cloth, that sells retail for 18s., cannot at most be above 14s., now then, if you can contrive to get it at twelve months credit, and send it over here, he is pretty sure of selling it at a Considerable profit, and absolutely sure of selling it at no loss; in the latter event, when the worst comes to the worst, He will have the money to play with for 7, or 8 months, and still have time enough to remit to you the money before the time came for you to pay it. It will be partly for Cloathing the officers of his own Battallion.

It may be ordered in the following way; Benson, for the purpose of taking such Parts of the Concerns as it would not be creditable for my Brother to appear in, is to be set up in a kind of Shop, which has been purchased for that purpose, a decent House the Price for the Fee simple of which is about 120 Rubles, that is about £30.

You may therefore speak of Benson as a Person whom either on his own Account, or on account of his being under the Coll's protection you wish to serve, and order the Cloths as for him, and in his name answering yourself for the Payment of it in such manner as may be required.

The Proportions should be ⅖s of the number of yards, *Green*, the Same of *White*, and ⅕ of *Scarlet*—The Green should be a Grass-Green (as you see by the Coll's Uniform) whether it be this or that Shade, do's not much signify—The Shalloon shod, be Scarlet matching exactly the Scarlet Broad-Cloth, it should be the finest there is or nearly so.

If it happens that the whole account should come to a little more or less it will not be material. I mention this, that you may not think it necessary to break a Piece—a small Inferiority in goodness would be no Objection if made amends for in Price, for instance 2s/ a yard.

Direction for the Cloth, to be sent to Riga

To Mr. George Benson at Coll. Bentham's/Critchoff/

To the Care of Mr. Christian Trompovsky at Riga.[4]

My brother is at my Elbow, and joyns me in the assurance that we are

Hond. Sir,

Your dutiful and affectionate Sons

J^y and S Bentham.

566

To Jeremiah Bentham[1]

30 March/10 April 1786 (Aet 38)

Crichoff $\frac{\text{March 30}}{\text{April 10}}$ 1785[*sic*]

Hond. Sir

The game of battledore and shuttlecock with Dutch Ducats has answered for this once rather better than we expected:[2] but there does not seem to be any great probability, though there is some, of its being soon renew'd: the country is poor and the market (to change the metaphor) is soon stocked. Honest Benson and his Russian guide arrived on Saturday last and brought back the

[4] The total bill for the cloth amounted to £583 6. 9, and payment of £500 on this account was not made until July 1788. The consignment was shipped in June, together with the tools which Bentham ordered in his next letter (letter 566) which, including packaging, cost £42. 4. 8½ (B.M. XXII: 402–3).

566. [1] B.M. IV: 147–8. Autograph.
Addressed: 'Jere^h Bentham Esqr. / Queens Square Place / Westminster / London.'
Letter-book copy, B.M. XXII: 398–99.
[2] See letter 565.

needful. They had been gone about 7 weeks: we expected them in about 3: we had charged them to write: no letters from them had arrived, nor though written have arrived yet: such is the miserable state of Russian post! A letter of the Governor of Ecatherinoslav from Kremenchuk to Sam was 7 weeks on the road. What /would/ you have felt if you had been in our case? We felt nothing at all, as we had other things to think about in plenty.

This post I take but little room having but little time: of the thousand things I could tell you, what shall I tell you in that time. Since we have been here I have paid but one visit and that was to a General Bandre about 8 versts off: the nearest neighbour we have except some people of inferior note in the very town. What struck me most was the tables and chairs all made of fineered work very neatly executed by a peasant of his own whom he had got instructed for that purpose. These fineering peasants are not uncommon in Russia: I intend to make Sam have one of them before I have done with him. Prince Dashcoff has one that executes flowers and landscapes in this manner: we must send him an apprentice. We have but one visitor Prince Dashcoff who left us about a week ago having staid with us about as long. We expect in about a month about a dozen of his Peasants which are to work under our English Joiners Smiths and Gardeners in order to learn those businesses, ~~kept~~ maintained all the while at Dashcoff's expence, and are to be detained by Sam as long as he thinks proper. Another Russian Friend of Sam's has begged of him to take any number of *his* peasants for the same purpose. We shall take about a dozen, with a few girls perhaps for other businesses. By Benson we got a letter from Mr. Henderson by which we learn that he arrived to our great surprize in the Crim so early as in February: his letter is of the 7th of March: another letter sent by post three weeks before is not yet arrived.[3]

We are going to be great Farmers; a spot with many capabilities, pretty already and susceptible of further beautification: some hundred acres of grass land in good order and regularly overflow'd: horses for nothing: Men some for nothing, and others for next to nothing: many thousand loads of Dung likewise for nothing: a navigable river deeply indenting and almost surrounding the estate, these with others I have no room for, are pretty strong temptations. We are now busy in measuring and surveying: by the next post or next but one we shall know and then you shall know a little more of the land than we do at present.

[3] Both Henderson's letters are missing.

Dashcoff's regiment is just order'd to Kiev where it will probably be stationed for a year or two. This /town/ is about midway between this and the Crim: a halfway house. He tender'd me a promise to stay here 5 years. I accepted on condition of his spending as many weeks with us in every year, which he agreed to: but you know what materials promises, especially such promises, are made of. He is to revisit us in September; we are too busy to make visits: My great apprehension is Sam's being order'd away to the Crimea, where indeed his Batallion is expected. We made it the /great/ Prince's interest to prevent this. I hope he will understand his interest and pursue it.

Sam would be much obliged to you to bespeak the following articles to be sent as soon as possible to Messrs. Pearson, Huhn, Trompovski and Wale Russia /Riga/ Merchants (They live I cant tell where the Directory will tell you—Alderman Clark has it) directed for Col. Bentham to the care of Mr. Trompovsky at Riga

From Mr. Buttal's Ironmonger

Files	Vices	
3 called Rubbers—1 Bastard weight 6 lb. each—1 Follow whereof —1 smooth	6 of about 40 lb. weight 4 of about 50 lb. 1 of about 72 lb.	1 Cucumber cutter 1 pair of Snuffers of the sort which are an improvement on ⟨...⟩, clearing ⟨...⟩ themselves by the ⟨...⟩ same motion ⟨...⟩ opens them. ⟨...⟩ they are made by ⟨...⟩ A pair I saw cost 15.
1 Gross of 12 inch files 1 Gross of 16 inch do. cut no coarser than the 12 inch ones	1 the largest one there is, supposing it not much to exceed 112 lb.	

½ dozen Bricklayers' Trowels and two of each sort of Plaisterers trowels with one hammer of each sort used in these trades.

We wish much for a plan of Metcalf's hoggery: the buildings and the mode of feeding them: you wished for an errand /thither/ here is a special good one.[4] The Prince had some hundreds of hogs with

[4] During the spring of 1786 Dr Charles Brown visited Jeremiah Bentham in London and exchanged news about the colony at Krichëv, and took upon himself to deal with this particular query. On 17 June 1786 he wrote to Jeremiah Bentham: 'Though Mr. Benson's Letters do not contain any Intelligence of Consequence with which you are not informed...yet knowing how anxious you as a Parent must be to be informed of every minute Particular relative to your Son, I thought it might be satisfactory to you to learn from Benson's Account that the Colonel and the Director general of the Prince's Estates are now upon the best of Terms....I have wrote a long Letter to the Colonel [*missing*] in which I have given some Hints about the Distillery and have explained my Sentiments pretty fully upon the Hoggery and how far the Method observed at Bromley can be adapted to the Severity of a Russian Winter' (B.M. IV: 262–3).

many cows here fed with the grains from the Distillery: but a great part died from bad management. For £60 or £70 or thereabouts Sam is offer'd a quantity of grains that will keep 100 Cows in a year and 200 hogs: but he will not embrace the offer unless he can correct the acidity of the grains, for the stuff they distill the brandy from here is little better than vinegar. This however we shall attempt.

Blue broadcloth the *Navy colour* or thereabouts: 2 *pieces* to be *substituted* to as many of the *green*, or if that is too late *sent* after them.

[*In S.B.'s hand*]:

I Samuel Bentham am alive and alive like, will this do for the Tontine[5] or must I swear it?

567

TO JEREMIAH BENTHAM[1]

28 April/9 May 1786 (Aet 38)

Crichoff $\frac{\text{May 9th}}{\text{April 29th}}$ 1786

Hond. Sir,

Not a day, I suppose, has passed since my arrival, but we have been imagining you here, and even hatching random projects for realising our imaginations; but true it is that we little dreamt of our being so near the accomplishment of our hopes, as we find ourselves to have been by your Letter of the 14/3d March [2] received on fryday last, the second of Two which we have received since my last. Unfortunately at the present Conjuncture, circumstances are

[5] The principle of the tontine, a type of life insurance, was that the investor staked his money on the chance of his own life (or that of a nominee) enduring for a longer period than those of other persons involved in the speculation. Subscribers were divided into age-groups, and the annual interest in respect of each group was paid to the survivors, the longer-lived of whom might profit considerably. The system was used to raise government loans, and was also operated privately.

567. [1] B.M. IV: 258–9. Copy by Jeremiah Bentham. Docketed by him: 'Copy / Fils Jeremy / Letter datd. Critchoff / April 28 / May 9 1786.' Also docketed under the date heading: 'Recd at Finchley 13 June 1786.'

An extract from this letter appears in Jeremiah Bentham's letter-book, B.M. XXII: 391.

[2] An incomplete, undated copy of part of this letter is at B.M. IV: 322. Jeremiah Bentham contemplated setting out about June on a visit to his sons.

not so favorable to such an Expedition on this side of the water as on your's. Barracks have been a long time preparing, and are now compleated for Sam's Batalion at Sevastopol the new Port in the Crimea, and Col. Fanshaw's Batalion is Ordered thither, as he himself told Benson; it was expected that Sam with his Batalion would soon succeed him for a time, in the way to their final destination. In effect, since then Orders have come from the Prince; transmitted through General Haskin,[3] who commands at that Town, requiring my Brother to put himself under the General's Command, under which Command he accordingly is at present. We have been in hourly expectation of the Prince in his way to his Government for a considerable time; but that expectation though confirmed, is rather retarded than accelerated by a Letter of his, an exact Copy of which is here subjoyned. When ever he do's come, it is looked upon by every body as a matter of course, that He will take Sam, and wish to take me, with Him, making Trips here and there, out of the main Road, to do business or see Relations, and stopping at every place an uncertain time. Whether under such Circumstances a Visit to Critchoff would be likely to answer to you both, and to my Mother in particular, must be left to you to determine. I rather imagine, you will think it advisable to defer setting out till you have heard from us something more determinate relative to my Brother's destination.

I thank you kindly for your News about Lord Cornwallis, the D. of Richmond's Motion, Hastings Affair etc.[4] except that I am a Stranger to every Atom of English news that is of later date than some day in November; at Riga my Brother received a promise from Mr. Trompovsky of a regular Supply of news-Papers, one of which, I believe, is an English one. Unfortunately they were to come through the Channel of a Friend of Trompovsky's who lives between This and Riga, and we have seen nothing of them yet.

This (Tuesday) is the first day for sending Letters by the Post since fryday when we received your's as above mentioned.

[3] Not identified.

[4] In February 1786 Charles, 2nd Earl Cornwallis had accepted the government's invitation to become governor-general of Bengal. The Duke of Richmond was at this time head of the Ordnance Board and a cabinet minister. His proposals for fortifying the naval bases at Portsmouth and Plymouth at considerable expense had been thrown out by the Commons at the end of that month (Alison G. Olson, *The Radical Duke*, Oxford, 1961, pp. 81–5). Edmund Burke took the first step in the Commons towards the impeachment of Warren Hastings on 17 February. (*The Correspondence of Edmund Burke*, volume v, *July 1782–June 1789*, ed. Holden Furber, with the assistance of P. J. Marshall, Cambridge, 1965, p. 259).

Ayton, our Gardener, is Nephew to the King's Gardener at Kew,[5] and was brought up under him.

With respect to Sam's Journey to Riga, They travelled post; all in Kibitkas, the only Winter Carriage used in Russia. These were Three of Sam's, one of the Prince Dashkoff's, He and Sam, went in One, Benson with the Money in another, my Brother's upper Servant, and the Prince's in another.

I found the Military Instruments transferred to Prince Dashkoff, and I was glad of it. It would have been all out of my Brother's Pocket, and a Master to teach them would have Cost £40, or £50. Dashkoff has a Capital Master, and my Brother can at any time send a sufficient number of men to learn of him, at little or no Expence. This Plan I shall promote.

We had begun and almost finished measuring the Land in the Peninsula, called Zadobras,[6] but the melting of the Snow and consequent overflowing of a considerable Part of it obliged us to suspend our Operations; as soon as the waters have subsided, which, had it not been for some unusual heavy rains they would have done by this time, we think to finish. A Description, without a Plan would convey a very imperfect Idea.

The following is a Copy of Prince Potemkin's Letter to my Brother.

Monsieur, Je ne vous envoye aucun Ordre relativement aux demandes du votre Lettre de trois Mars de cette Année. La raison est, que comptant bientôt partir, j'aime mieux différer la décision de ces Arrangemens jusqu'à mon arrivée à Critchoff. Je vous prie donc de m'attendre et d'être persuadé de l'entier dévouement, avec lequel j'ai l'honneur d'être parfaitement, monsieur

votre très humble et très obéissant serviteur
Prince Potemkin.

St. Petersburg
le 1/12. Avril l'année 1786.

[5] The king's gardener was William Aiton (1731–93), who became manager of the botanical garden at Kew in 1759, and who, at his death, was succeeded in his post by his eldest son. John Aiton's parentage has not been traced. He appears to have been the son of an unidentified younger brother of William Aiton whom the historian of the Aiton family, confusing him with his father, reports as having been employed, presumably later in his career, in the botanical service of the Russian Tsar (William Aiton, *An Inquiry into the Origins, Pedigree, and History, of the Family, or Clan, of Aitons in Scotland*, Hamilton, 1830, pp. 38–40). On him see also letters 604 and 613.

[6] The correct form of this name is Zadobrast, but Bentham normally omitted the final 't'. Presumably it was not clearly sounded in local speech.

Sir,

I do not send you any Order relative to the Questions in your Letter of the 3d of March last, the reason is, that imagining I shall set out very soon, I chuse rather to defer the determination of those arrangements till my arrival at Critchoff. Pray expect me then, and be persuaded of the entire /attachment/ *devotion* (devouement) with which I have the honor, perfectly to be,

Sir,

your very humble and obedient Servant

Prince Potemkin

St. Petersburg

The 1st April 1786.

568

From James Lee[1]

14 June 1786

Dear Sir,

I recived, and have sent your orders[2] as soon as a ship could be found, but should have wished you had given more Early intiligence as I am afraid you can do nothing with the seeds till nixt springe, we could not procure you any Tares owing to the lateness of the season having applyed in vain in all the London markets, and as the casks was measured to contain them, we was obliged to fill them up with two additional Bushels of Rygrass. Grass seeds was never so scarce as it is this Season, being nearly Double the price that it is in Common years. in regard to the plants it is impossible to send them at this season, they should either go early in the Spring or Autumn, and we shall endeavour to send them at a proper season.

The Package consists of 2 Casks marked Coll. B. Directed to the care of Mr. Trompovsky at Riga

No. 1 Contains	No. 2
80 lb. Red Clover	20 lb. Field Turnep
80 lb. White do.	2 Bush: Hors Beans
4 Bush: Rygrass	20 lb. Field Turnep
	80 lb. Saint foine

I recived your letter from Constantinople[3] and one from Mr. Henderson at the same time, but have had no opportunity of

568. [1] B.M. IV: 260–1. Autograph. Docketed by Bentham: '1786 June 3/14 / Lee Hammersmith / to / J.B. Crichoff / seeds sent.'

Addressed: 'Col. Bentham.' [2] Missing. [3] Letter 558.

sending the things you ordered and must defer them till new seeds are saved. have heard nothing of Captain Brine he is not yet araived in the port of London.

I am well acquainted with Mr. John Aitton he is an ingenous man and a good gardner, I suppose the best you have in Russia. I beg you will make my Compliments to him and Mr. Henderson.

In any future orders that you send let it be in time, and it shall be punctually executed. and if you have any opportunity of collecting Seeds, I will endavour to make a proper return for them. I particularly want seeds of *Rhodadendron Daurecum*, *R. Chrysanthum*, and *Azalea lutea*, I am Dear Sir with great regard for self and Co. your obedient humble servt

James Lee

Vineyard Hammersmith
June 14 1786

569

FROM RICHARD KING[1]

14–23 June 1786

Invoice of Goods Sent by Order of Mr. Jeremy Bentham directed to Col. Bentham at Crichoff in White Russia to the Care of Mr. Trompowski at Riga by favour of Messrs Baring and Co from Rich[d] King June 14 1786.

Stamp'd Paper Ornaments

Lot	£	s.	d.
1—2 Large Scroll Vases and 2 Ram Head Vases @ 1/– each		4.	0.
2—2 Snake Vases @ 6d. & 4 Flower Pot at 4d.		3.	4.
3—2 Smaller Scroll Vases @ 8d. 2 Pedastal @ 6d.		2.	4.
4—2 Pr. Griffins @ 1/6, 1 P. Sphinx @ 1/4		4.	4.
5—2 Pr. Medalions @ 8d., 2 pr. Bacchus & Appollo @ 8d.		2.	8.
6—6 Patres No. 5 @ 2d. each & No. 6 No. 11 2 each 1 Doz. No. 10 @ 12d.		3.	0.
7—1 Doz. Do. No. 40 @ 1/– 6 No. 42 @ 16d.		2.	4.
8—1 Doz. Do. No. 12 @ 1/– 1 doz. No. 43 @ 8		1.	8.
9—1 Pr. Empr. & Empress of Russia @ 18d.—1 Drapery Vase 8d.		2.	2.
10—6 Star Patres 6d. 12 Small Sort No. 45 @ 4d.			10.
11—6 Corn Swags @ 4d.—6 Corn Drops for Do. @ 2d.		3.	0.
12—8 Yds. Second Size Husks No. 84—4 Yds. Next Size 55 @ 6d.		6.	0.
13—1 Yd. Border No. 3, 4, 5, 6 @ 6d. p. yd.		2.	0.

569. [1] B.M. IV: 280–1. Docketed by Jeremy Bentham: '1786 / R. King London / to / J. B. Critchoff / Invoyce / Goods sent by Polly / ⟨Capt.⟩ Dixon.'

Addressed: 'Col. Bentham / at Crichoff / au soins de Maitre des Postes / a Riga For Jeremy Bentham Esq.'

	£	s.	d.
14—5 Yds. No. 7 @ 4d.—1 Yd. No. 9 @ 5d.		2.	1.
15—5 Yds. No. 10 @ 4d.—1 Yd. No. 11 @ 3½d.		1.	11½
16—1 Yd. No. 31 @ 6d.—1 Yd. No. 25 @ 6—1 Yd. No. 96 @ 6d.		1.	6.
17—1 Yd. No. 18 @ 5d.—1 Yd. No. 68 @ 5—1 Yd. No. 38 @ 4d.		1.	2.
18—1 Yd. No. 16 @ 6d.—1 Yd. No. 28 @ 5—1 Yd. No. 29 @ 4d.		1.	3.
19—1 Yd. Tulip Husks at 8d.—6 Yds. Beads at 2d.		1.	8.
20—4 Yds. Small Leaf Border No. 45 @ 2½			10.
21—2 Patres No. 1 & No. 2 @ 4d.—1 Pr. Scrolls 6d.		1.	2.
22—6 Vine-Leaves @ 2½d.—1 Yd. No. 86 @ 4—1 Yd. 69 @ 4d.		1.	11.
23—1 Large Hollow Glass @ 6—1 No. 46 @ 2½			8½
24—1 Large Husk No. 53—1 Yd. Bead No. 58 @ 2½d. Larg Size			8½
25—2 Doz. Ribbon knots @ 18—1 Yd. Null'd Borders. No. 30 @ 3		3.	3.
A Small Packing Case mark'd S.B.		2.	0.
	£2 ,,	16 ,,	3.

Cheese

	£ s. d.
1 Cheshire cheese	
1 North Wiltshire	1 . . 6 . . 1½
52 lb. @ 6d.	
Case SB No. 1	1 6
	£1 . . 7 . . 7½

Tin Copper & Pewter

Tea Urn		1 . . 16
2 Oval Dishes	@ 5/6	11
2 Ditto	@ 4/6	9
2 Ditto	@ 3/6	7
2 Round Do.	@ 5/6	11
2 Ditto Do.	@ 4/–	8
2 Ditto Do.	@ 3/–	6
		£4 8

Carried forward

Brot. forward.		£4 . . 8 . . 0
2 Doz. Soup Plates @ 16/–		1 . . 12
6 Doz. Flat Plates 14/–		4 . . 4
8 only were found[2]	2 Oval Dish Covers	9
	2 Ditto Do.	8
	2 Round Do. @ 3/6	7
	3 Ditto Do. @ 3/–	6
1 Tea Kettle—1 ditto		10
2 Melon @ 3/–		14
2 large do		
2 Round Pewter Turins		1 . . 8
Case S.B. No. 2		5 6
		£14 . . 11 . . 6

[2] These words added in Bentham's hand.

Brushes

		d
1 Painter Cornr. Brush		1½
1 ditto		2½
1 ditto		3½
1 ditto		5
1 ditto		7
1 ditto		8
1 ditto		9
1 ditto		10
1 ditto Ground		11
1 ditto Do.		5
1 ditto Do.		6
1 ditto Do.		9
1 common Tool No.	1	1
1 ditto Do.	2	1½
1 ditto Do.	3	2
1 ditto Do.	4	2½
1 ditto Do.	5	3
1 ditto Do.	6	3½
1 ditto Do.	7	4
1 Sash Tool	1	2½
1 ditto Do.	2	3
1 ditto Do.	3	4
1 ditto Do.	4	5
1 ditto Do.	5	6
1 Small Flat Brush		5
1 Cloth Do.		1 . . 4
1 Large Oval Do.		2 . . 3
6 Tooth Brushes		6 . . 0
		£0 . . 19 . . 7½

Musick

Nicolais Trios	10. 6
Sonatas 3	10. 6
5	10. 6
7	10. 6.
9	10. 6
10	10. 6
	£3. 3. 0

Cutlery

12 Pr. Real Camwood Knives and Forks best London Blades —	14. 0
2 Rule Hunt of ditto	4. 0
	18

Bridle Ornaments

A Sett of Tips Chased	6. 0
Large Nose Ornaments Do.	3. 6
Ditto for the Breast	3. 6
	13. 0

Corks & Silver

6 Plated Mounted Corks	6. .0
6 Silver Ditto	9. 0
6 Setts Silver Cruett Tops	1 . . 16.0.
	£2 . . 11

Seeds

1 Peck Sanfoin	1. 6
1 Quart Turnip	1. 6
1 Pint Carrott	6
Bag	6
	4. 0

Books

Youngs Annals of Agriculture	13.
Essays on Hogs etc.	2.
Farmers guide	12.
Tour in Ireland	14
Millers Gard'ners Dictiony.	4. 1. 6
Builders Price Book	2. 6
2 Latest Price Current	1.
Dossies Agriculture	19.
	£4. 8. 6

Stationary [*sic*]

3 Qr. Cartridge Paper	4.
2 Qr. Blue Royal	4.
3 Qr. Blue Demy	2.
Small Almanack	2.
1 Box Colour'd Wafers	1.
1 Box White ditto	6
4 Pieces Tape	4
	15. 6

Coach Ornaments

2 Large Double Cyphers J. B. Wrought	2. 4. 0
1 Large ditto S.B. do.	1. 2.
6 Doz. Silver Screws to fix them on with	7. 6.
1 Pr. Plated Octagon Lock Handles	16. 0.
	£4. 9. 6.

lb. Sweet Meats	
8½ Tamarinds @ 1/6	12. 9.
5 Preserved Ginger 3/–	15.
	£1. 7. 9
China and Earthenware	
2 China Quart Bowls	6. 6
2 Black Tea Pots	3. 6.
23 Pt. Black Bowls Wedgewood only 2 instead of 23[3]	13. 0
	1. 3.
2 Bottles soy	10.
	1.13
3 Butter Patts	1.
3 Tin Canisters	1. 6
Packing Case S.B. No. 3 with a Small Case in it and Cord	10. 6.
in the case Case are	
9 Reviews from Mr Wilson	
Recapitulation	
Stampd. Paper	2.16. 3
Ornaments SB	
Cheese and Case SB No. 1	1. 7.11
Tin Pewter & Copper and Case SB No. 2	14.11. 6

		£ s. d
Brushes		19. 7½
Books		4. 8. 6.
Stationary [*sic*]		15. 6
Musick		3. 3. 0
Cutlery		18. 0
Bridle Ornaments		13. 0
Corks and Silver		2.11.
Seeds		4.
Sweetmeats		1. 7. 9
China & Earthen Ware		1. 3.
2 Botts. Soy		10.
Coach Ornaments		4. 9. 6
2 Butter Patts 3 Tin Canisters		2. 6
Packg. Cases SB No. 3 and Cord		10. 6
		£40.11. 3
Spallanzani's Works sent to Constantinople		12.
		41. 3. 3
White Pumice Stone 2. 3.	23 @14—	2. 1. 4½
Red Bole	25	4
Cask BD		4
Cartage to Custom House		2. 3
Porterage SB & SB No. 3		3
		2.14. 7½
		£43.17.10½

Dear Sir

As Near as I could, I have sent you According to your Orders of wch. the Fore ⟨going is⟩ an Invoice; I could not get 1 Doz. of Dishes in 2 Similar Nests without waiting ⟨...⟩ Making, therefore have sent 6 Oval and 6 Round. I have sent 6 Corks plated Mou⟨nted⟩ because I met with 6 Silver Mounted very Cheap I sent them; the Silver Mounted ⟨are⟩ Commonly 2s each, these are packd in the Teapots. The Caster Tops in the Canisters w⟨ith⟩ the Seeds. Plated things of this kind are not worth having the Difference in the price being so very little. I sent Round Turins as they are much cheaper than Oval and you did not order which; The Bridle Bitt I have not sent as I was order'd not to send it till somebody comes out, who as you may learn by my last will not be of my sending; if you please the Bitt may be sent when I send the Book of Architecture.

[3] These words added in Bentham's hand.

The Goods are Shipped for Riga in the Polly Capt. Robt. Dixon Consigned to Messrs Pierson and Co. by Messrs Baring and Co Merchts No 6 Mincing Lane London. The Cases SB No 1 of Cheese and No 2 of Tin etc. were packed by the People of whom I Bought the Goods. The Cases SB and SB No 3 I packed myself not caring to trouble Messrs Baring with so many little Articles: as I had no orders for Ensuring them, they are not ensured. Besides your orders there is a Cask of Pummice Stone and Red Bole Marked BD to be Charged to your Acct by Order of Dr. Debraw; there is likewise another little Box marked JD and directed to Mr. Trompowsky, this I suppose will be open'd by him and the Contents deliver'd to the Owner Dr. Debraw, it is his French Pamphlet Sword Belt etc. Mr. Greenly has sent me a Bill for Dinners etc. 1 . . 19 . . 9 Another is come from the Lamplighter 14s one from the Carpenter for little Jobbs in Chambers 8s one from Mr Wilkes Printer at Winton for Advertising Baghurst Estate for Sale by private Contract 1 . . 12 . . 0: this last I have engaged to pay. Mr. Baron's Clerk has called on me to inform me that some repairs are Wanting to the House in Southampton Buildings pray is Mr. Bulmer's *under* Lease a Repairing Lease or not? I should be glad of your instructions herein. In the Meantime with my Best Respects to the Col

I am Dear Sir
Your most Obdt Humble Servt
R. King

June the 23rd 1786

P.S. Applying to Messrs Baring and Co for Better Information about Hogs Bristles they desired me to send you the Enclosed. Two Cyphers JB I find are a Sett for the Chariot, one on each Side; and one SB for the Phaeton to be fixed on the Back Pannel.

570

To Jeremiah Bentham[1]

16/27 June 1786 (Aet 38)

Critchoff June 16/27. 1786.

Hond. Sir

This goes by a private opportunity which occurs for Riga from whence we desire it to be forwarded by the first ship. The

570. [1] B.M. IV: 282–3. Autograph. Docketed by Jeremiah Bentham: 'Dated Critchoff June 27/16 1786 / Recd. at Queen's Square Place / Saturday 5th May 1787.' Addressed: 'Jeremiah Bentham Esq.'

inclosure directed to Mr. Carew you will be kind enough to convey to him.[2] It accounts for and in part supplies the deficiency he accused me of. Pray what papers accompanied his manuscript which you deliverd to him? Was there not the copy you took or a part of it, and some continuation of it by another hand?

As Beattie's letter afforded you some amusement, I embrace this opportunity of sending you a copy I have got taken for the purpose of the draughts he had preserved of some more of them.[3] I might be worth rather more to you, perhaps than as it is, could I employ my time in the same manner: but besides giving my Brother an helping hand my own business goes on as briskly as ever it did at Lincoln's Inn: the sooner it is done the sooner you will see me which if not late in the autumn will I hope be early in the winter: so that upon the whole it may be as well to you I should work on like a good boy, as be idle and write pretty letters.

[2] See letter 571.

[3] Robert Beaty, a sailcloth maker and hemp worker from Newcastle, was one of the two British settlers at Krichëv most liked by Jeremy Bentham. The copies of Beaty's drafts which he inclosed to his father have not been found, but the first-mentioned letter, dated 18 February/1 March 1786, does survive in copies made by Jeremiah Bentham (B.M. IV: 246–7, 323–4, and XVI: 384). Parts of it are of interest for the impression of the milieu in which Bentham now found himself. Beaty wrote: 'From the receipt of my Mother's Letter in December I have the satisfaction to know, that...you would hear of my safe arrival at Riga on the 2d of June and finally at Creichoff on the 20th in good health, after travelling 500 English miles in something less than seven days. Since that time in the Course of the Summer several other English People have arrived and with us that went from Newcastle, and those there before makes our Number, Wives and Children included, about Twenty.

'Colonel Bentham received us very graciously and I and J. Bell were sent to live with J. Notman at the Coll's Country House while Two Rooms were fitting up for me at the Sail-tuck Factory, so that it was the latter end of July before I got started with my business when I shifted to the Factory, and had Four Russian Boys allotted me to instruct, who had been some kind of Hucklers before. These are yet under my Care, and all my present Employment is making up their work and attending our Hemp-beating, at a kind of rude Mill constructed for that purpose six or seven years ago: so that I have little to do but walk about at present, therefore have time enough for my old amusement of writing which you may be sure I do not forget.

'One of the greatest difficulties I have found here, and I beleive it has been so with the rest, was my Ignorance of the Language; I thought it at first a Collection of the Strangest Sounds that ever invaded my Ears, but by the help of Industry however and application I have got a slight knowledge of it and feel myself on that account a great deal easier.

'I have likewise in my Dealings with the Jews, from whom we buy almost all the Necessaries of Life, got some German words, and likewise some French ones from my own Grammar, to know the Russ is hardly enough here; for though the Jews speak it they speak it very badly and are always blabbering out Their own Lingo. This consequently brings one acquainted with the German of which their Language is a Dialect and is spoken by them through all the extensive Provinces of Poland. The heterogeneous mixture of People here is surprising consisting of Poles, Jews, Russians, Germans, Don Cossacs and English....' He continued with further details about language, climate, and current prices.

For fear of accidents I will not omitt acknowledging by this opportunity the receipt of yours of May 6th,[4] though my acknowledgment of it by the post will I expect come sooner to hand than this. I have heard nothing from Mr. Mulford, who you say in a former letter talked of writing to me. You do not say expressly, but you give me reason to conclude that you communicated to Ld Lansdown some at least of the letters I wrote in the course of my travels. If so you had as good let him have the whole, /if you have not already/ including that addressed to Mr. Mulford which I desired him to communicate to you and which I dare say he has communicated to you accordingly; also that which you mention your having received from Mr. Eaton to whom it was addressed. The messenger is going off, and I can add no more. The letters we have received from you since my arrival here are of the following dates

1785 Decr. 29
1786 March 5
March 24
...This not at hand countermanding the notice of your intended visit.
May 9[5]

571

To Reginald Pole Carew[1]

17/28 June 1786 (Aet 38)

Dear Sir,

By a letter I received a short time ago from my Father, I find you have a charge against me of breach of promise for not ~~returning~~ accompanying /by a fair copy/ the return of the manuscript ~~you were kind enough to lend me~~ the use of which my importunities extracted from your kindness. If you since the return of the original, you happen to have cast an eye over it, I fear you have ere this found out a still heavier charge, I mean the (omitting to

[4] Missing.

[5] All these letters are missing.

571. [1] B.M. IV: 285, 284. Autograph, with corrections. Docketed by Bentham: '1786 June 17/28 / J.B. Critchoff / to / P. Carew London / Brouillon / Sent by Trompovsky Riga by S.B.['s] horses to go by sea.'

For the dispatch of the original see letter 570. The original, copied, as Bentham mentions, by an amanuensis, who may have been Beaty, is not among the Carew papers at Antony House and the papers mentioned in it are not identified.

return) disappearance of a part of the original itself. Whether what I have to allege in exculpation will be deemed a valid one, I cannot ~~pretend to say,~~ /must be left to yourself/ but at any /rate/ it is /highly/ incumbent upon me to confess and account for the omission, if I cannot justify it. [*several words written and crossed out*] ~~The smallness of the hand the irregular arrangement of the pages,~~ Several circumstances concurred in rendering me unwilling to put it out in the ordinary way to an hackney writer, as I might have done by a paper of less value. The difficulty of decyphering it, owing to the smallness of the hand and the /casual/ irregular arrangement of the pages, and the novelty of many of the terms contained in it: the danger of its being lost or injured by carelessness; or pirated by ~~knowing avarice~~ rapacity if consigned to the hands of an unknown quill-driver /besides a considerable part of it being in French /[...?]/ was an additional obstacle not overcome./ These considerations concurring with your kind indulgence were the reason of my detaining it from day to day in hopes of fresh opportunities of perfecting the copies which had been begun and carried on /at chance/ opportunities by different hands on whom I could depend, of which number my father as you know was one. Before I went a copy was taken ~~of I believe~~ /of the greatest part if not/ the whole except 3 or 4 pages of the English, and the 11 or 12 pages ~~of which~~ /in/ the French intimately blended with the English in the same paper. A very few days before my departure an opportunity /or a chance at least offerd/ happend for the first time of getting the French copied by a Frenchman who writes an extraordinary fine hand and who was then /employed on/ writing ~~constantly~~ in the presence of a person on whom I thought I could depend in every respect. I delivered it accordingly into the hands of that person accompanied with a request that as soon as the copy was completed he would convey both to my father which was just by in a cover ~~which~~ with a proper direction which I left with him for that purpose. In the mean time I had got a ~~copy which~~ person who I think writes a fair hand to begin a copy /from my father's rough one corrected as far as it went by me/. I intended /it/ for your use. I forget now how it happen'd that that copy which circumstances did not permitt me to get compleated ~~happened not~~ to accompany the original and my father's rough copy when disposed /consigned/ of by me to the hands abovementioned I took care however to send it to this same persons in a cover in which I desired it to be added to the rest of the manuscript I had left with them /directed to my father/ ~~for the purpose which they knew.~~

The original all except a ~~piece or two~~ /scrap loose paper or/ of which presently, I find learn by my father had found its way to you by his hands: but great was my surprise when some time after my arrival at this place I found here the above mentioned /fragments of a/ copy in the cover in which I had sent it; and accompanied with the abovementioned fragments of the original. I now embrace the first opportunity that has occurred of sending you this one and the other: and having now got a copy written of the above fragments of the original I have thereby the satisfaction of /having secured/ the contents ~~out of the reach of the~~ against the dangers of the sea. Whether the /first/ rough copy was compleated or if not how far it was carried down I have not yet had the means of learning, though I expect /in a few weeks or so/ to see a person who can inform me. The bulk of my baggage and amongst the rest a Secretaire which contains some of my Papers, though sent for from home are not yet arrived from the Crimea to which country they were taken from Constantinople.[2] Whatever parts /if any/ of the copy are not among those papers went or at least were to go to my father along with /that part of/ the original which you received. ~~If any other~~ /Whatever other/ parts ~~than what you now receive the copy~~ of find their way hither I can and will get copied by the same hand who wrote what I ~~now~~ send you now. I am sorry to think that this /tedious history/ ~~I have~~ which I know not how to shorten should after all be so far from being as satisfactory as I could wish and you are entitled to expect. To account for it, not being more so, you will forgive I hope my putting your patience so much further to the trial as to represent to you that this danger of missing the ship which after all—I did miss at the first place of rendezvous obliged me to precipitate my departure from England /delayed and distracted by/ amidst a variety of concerns of which the preparations for my journey were the least important. Of two of the opportunities which chance threw into my hands, had the one continued a few days longer or the other presented itself a few days earlier, I might and I trust should have fulfilled my undertaking to a tittle. Throwing myself upon your candour, or if you think it more proper, upon your indulgence, I remain with the truest respect and regard

Dear Sir

Your much obliged

H.S.

J.B.

[2] In fact Bentham seems never to have received this consignment all through his stay in Russia—or, if he did, only when he was packing to come home—for Samuel

Potemkins C° desires his sincerest thanks for your present of the tumblers a la Crimean. The same evil genius that cheated him of the first has vented his spite upon the last, /both/ which were demolished in their way from Riga, tho' not so utterly but that they have served for patterns of several we have had made. He would beg your acceptance of a sample out of courtesy, but that your Custom-house forbids it, and to tell you the truth, the best metal which the materials here obtainable have allowed us to make is still so muddy that we are ashamed to show it.

Mr. Rashleighs wants we have not yet been able to find any opportunity of supplying. We treasure them up however with care, and possibly an expedition we project towards Moscow towards the close of the summer on the course of which we think to see Dimidoff may afford us the means of doing something.

572

To Jeremiah Bentham[1]

19/30 July 1786 (Aet 38)

Critchoff July $\frac{30}{19}$ 1786

Hond Sir

Last Fryday, July 26/15, we were favour'd with your Letter of June 8/19,[2] which is all we can say to it, unless we were to say a great deal more than there is room for here. The Originals, of which you sent the Copies, came at the same time. No letter yet from Dr. Brown. Many thanks for the Parliamentary Intelligence. The Newspapers have failed us for the last three weeks, (i.e. three posts) but I hope they will come at last. It is owing to the Governor of Riga's dilatoriness.

The affair which gave rise to the Renconter, related in the succeeding Letter[3] by one of the Actors, is a long story, of which

Bentham wrote from Kherson in September 1787 that it had not yet come to him there from its port of arrival in the Crimea (letter 600).

572. [1] B.M. IV: 286–7. Copy by Jeremiah Bentham. Docketed by him: 'Mr. Jeremy Bentham / Copy Letter from him / datd. Critchoff July 19/30 1786.' Other copies, ibid: 288–9, 290–1. The greater part of this letter is also in copy in B.M. XXII: 392–4, with the opening sentences detached at fo. 408.

[2] Missing. In the letter-book copy its date is given as '19/8' (B.M. XXII: 408).

[3] Count Mellin to Samuel Bentham, 10/21 June 1786. A copy in the hand of Jeremiah Bentham is at B.M. IV: 264–5, followed by several other copies and English renderings in succeeding folios. Mellin has not been further identified beyond the information here given by Bentham.

I have neither time nor room to give more than a short Abridgement. Count Mellin is a Livonian Nobleman about three or four years older than my Brother. He commanded, and for ought we know, still Commands an Independant Batallion, like that of my Brother's, but which is upon the point of being reduced upon Prince Dashkoff's getting a Regiment given him as a sort of reward for the Intelligence he had brought from the Crimea of the Conquest of that Country; Part of Count Mellin's Corps was draughted off to be incorporated with that Regiment.

Dashkoff's general Character is That of a most accomplished and very honourable young Man, but too free in his speech, and overun with Vanity. My Brother's acquaintance with Count Mellin commenced at Krementchuck on his return from his Tour with Prince Potemkin. The Quarrel had even then risen to a Challenge, which had been given by the Count to the Prince Dashkoff, and a Duel would have taken place then and there, had it not been for I know not what Interruption occasioned by Prince Potemkin's precipitate and unexpected departure for Petersburg upon Genl Landskoy death[4]—Prince Dashkoff, upon taking the Command of Count Mellin's Men, had conceived some hasty and groundless notions to the disadvantage of the Count's behaviour in the Command; these notions he had been spreading as inconsiderately as he had taken them up. Upon being questioned concerning them by the Count, he would neither retract his Charges, nor could he make them good. Till the Catastrophe He had all along shewn a backwardness not suitable to the Character of a Military Man, to give the Count what is called a satisfaction—My Brother, together with some other of his Friends, had been earnest with him, from the first to the last, either to fight the Count, or to beg his Pardon, or to do both. The Consequence of the Calumny had been ruinous to the poor Count, he had lost a good deal of his reputation, was in danger of losing his Batallion, upon which he had spent a considerable part of his fortune, and had actually lost his Mistress, a Lady of large fortune, to whom he had been in a manner engaged.

A remarkable Circumstance is, that the Count after his disappointment at Krementchuck,—knowing my Brother's Intimacy with the Prince Dashkoff, wrote, notwithstanding, to my Brother, to beg of him to be his, the Count's, second in this Duel; upon his declining it he persisted notwithstanding, and came to Critchoff

[4] Aleksandr Dmitriyevich Lanskoy (1758–84) died on 25 June 1784 O.S. Potemkin was urgently concerned to ensure that the successor in Catherine's favours was his man and not a tool of his enemies at the Russian court.

from Krementchuck on no other Errand, but in vain, as you may well suppose.

Time is as scarce with me here as ever it was in London; to conciliate my business with your Amusement, I send you underwritten, Copies of two Letters, One from me to Prince Dashkoff of this date,[5] Part of which will save me the writing the same things over again to you for the history of the other.[6]

Your's most dutifully
and affectionately
Jeremy Bentham

To Jeremiah Bentham Esq.,
Queen's Square Place
Westminster

573

TO PRINCE DASHKOV[1]

19/30 July 1786 (Aet 38)

July 19. 1786

Yesterday's Post brought my Brother a Letter from Count Mellin; we had got hold of some others which, at another time, would have been interesting, I happened to open That; the first sentence which I communicated to him, before I went on to any other, rivetted the attention of us both to that Letter, and every thing else was flung away. The result drew Tears of Joy into his Eyes: from the Beginning of that unhappy Affair, He now own'd to me, he could never think of you with that pleasure, nor behave to you with that cordiality, that he had done before; now he turned crazy the other way, now nothing would serve him, but he must scamper away to Kiow without any other business upon the face of God's Earth, but to kiss you and hug you, and all that, because you had been a good Boy, and so forth. I, who happened to

[5] The letter to Prince Dashkov is printed as letter 573. The other is Count Mellin's letter mentioned in n. 3.

[6] The salutation and address appear only in B.M. IV: 290–1, which omits the first paragraph.

573. [1] B.M. IV: 292–5. Copy in the hand of Jeremiah Bentham. Another copy by him, ibid: 296–9.

be nine years older than his *High-Nobleship, observed to him—that all that was very pretty, and might have been feasable at another time, but as matters and things then stood, would be impossible; It was but the day before that having learnt from Countess Scavronski,[2] who called here in her way to Petersburg, that the Prince of Princes had given up his Intentions of coming here, it was but the day before, I say, that having received this Intelligence some days before, That my Brother, urged thereto, by diverse and sundry weighty Causes and considerations, had written to the Prince for leave to repair to him at Petersburg as soon as possible; forgetting that, and not choosing to be reminded of it, all hands were set to work in his Noddle to forge Pleas for going to you; He could find other business by the way, it was not above 300d Versts, he could get there by such a time, be back by such a time, and so on; I had before begun to represent to him that by all this straining, to the destruction of a thousand affairs he has upon the Anvil here, all he could get, would be the seeing you a very few weeks sooner than he would otherwise; for he had learnt from the Countess that you persevered in your Intentions of treating us with a sight of you in your way to Petersburg in September. However I left him the last word, knowing he would come to himself again after the first Spirt was over and his Eagerness had time to cool upon his Pillow. My Brother was going, after Dinner, taking four or five of his officers, upon a day's Visit to a *Pole's*, who has no Name and who lives fifty or sixty miles off, I don't know where. *His merit* is, that hearing that since Prince Dashkoff had left us, I was in want of a Bear to keep me Company, he had declared with great Vehemence, that he would give orders to his Huntsmen and Bears should be forth coming if any were to be found in Poland.

For all this I should have gone without my Bear, had it not been for the Prince's Huntsman, who with less Zeal, having had better success, brought me three months ago a beautiful young †Midwid who to the great grief of his disconsolate Master, and a numerous Tribe of Friends, died a few days ago, of a wound he received in a Duel, he had fought about a month before, with a Wolf more bloody-minded and obdurate than ‡Count Mellin.

*The literal Translation of a Lieut-Colonel's Title in Russ.

†The name of a Bear in Russ.

‡with whom Prince Dashkoff had been fighting.

[2] Yekaterina Vasilevna (née Engelhard), a niece of Prince Potëmkin, was the wife of Count Pavel Martinovich Skavronskiy (c. 1757–93).

Taking the Will however for the Deed, this merit of the Pole was to be rewarded, in your Country way, by turning in five or six hungry Green-coats at a Time, to eat him out of house and home.

We were just rising from Dinner, when in came a Man from Count Soltikoff,[3] the Major General, telling us that his Master was at Critchoff, where he proposed to stop a night in his way from his Estate at Viasma to Krementchuck, where, they say, he is to command under Hekin.[4] The Intelligence changed for the present, the Trip to the Pole's into a trip to Critchoff, whither my Brother repaired forthwith, leaving me here to write you a line upon the presumption that Soltikoff may be the bearer of it the greatest part of the way if not the whole. Along with it, I suppose will go another, which was given to some People, whom my Brother had occasion to send to Krementchuck some weeks ago, but who brought it back t'other day not having passed your way.

I don't go to any of your Pole's; for I don't see any body, nor go any where; consequently I shan't go to Petersburg with my Brother, nor even with you; having nothing so much at heart, I should say, having nothing else at heart but the finishing a Scribling Job I want to dispatch out of hand, that I may leave this blessed Country, where there is not a Printing Press within 500d miles of one, meaning however to scramble back, some how or other after a reasonable time.

If there should be time we shall send you a copy of Count Mellin's Letter; not that you deserve from us That or any other Token of Remembrance, are you not a Shabby Fellow to let Countess Scavronski go away (to whom, by the by, you gave a grand Fete, it seems, and so forth) without sending us a single Line; notwithstanding that before she left you, your Affair with Mellin must have been over, of which however she did not say a syllable.

In short we have not had a Line from you since you have been at Kiow, nor, I think since that scrap of one from Dubranka,[5] notwithstanding the numerous and weighty Commissions with which we honoured you.

As to the Six Horses you were to have taken us in to buy of you, my Brother says, you may keep them to feed Crows with; He is become very uppish since the purchase he made t'other day, at

[3] See letter 441, n. 13.

[4] Not identified.

[5] Dubrovna, or Dubranka, was the other, and larger estate, which Potëmkin owned in this region. It lay north-west of Krichëv, in the vicinity of Orsha.

Starodub,[6] where he bought seventeen, including two Mares, which would not disgrace Hyde Park, and which, were it not for their Sex, would match extremely well with a Pair of very good coach Geldings he bought of the poor old disgraced Provotel.§

Your Man, Maxim, turns out very well, and the Beatings that were destined for his use, are all laid up in Lavender, to be given to your man Simeon, who we understand, from the Doctor,[7] has a Constitution that will absorb them all, and as many more as any body would be at the trouble of administering, without exhibiting any visible effect.

As to the Survivor of your unfortunate Pair, Sam feeling himself out of the reach of English Laws, has looked into his mouth, in spight of English Proverbs, and declares, that altho' there are worse horses in the world, yet that the principal merit he has, results from the Consideration of his Master, and of his Master's name, which he bears with great Meekness, and without any of his Master's vanity.

All this while, in the name of wonderment, what is become of your dozen ¶Musick Boys, who were to have been here in Six Weeks from the latter End of March, and of whom we have not seen nor heard any thing now in the middle of July. Madwinoffs have been here, I dont know how long, these two or three months; *we* have sufferred cruelly and deplorably for the want of your's, having cut out our work in expectation of them.

I say *We* all along, like the Fly upon the Wheel—Sam said, just now, with a malicious grin, as who should say, 'This will put him upon his mettle; ask him, how it is, he manages his People, that they won't obey him?'

§Russ for Steward, vizt the Prince Potemkin's Steward at Critchoff, he has another above him at Debranka, wch is the principal Estate.

¶The Peasant slaves are called Mujicks or Moojicks which signify litterally a Petty Householder.

[6] A town some hundred or more miles south-east from Krichëv, at 52° 35′ N., 32° 46′ E.

[7] See letter 528, n. 3.

574

PRINCE DASHKOV TO SAMUEL AND JEREMY BENTHAM[1]

13/24 August 1786

Kiow the 13th of August
1786

To Both

Here is money but 450 Roubles only, Tis all I have at present in my possession.

The death of the poor horse I bemoan

It was the best Beast since Rosinante's time that ever was shod.

The Port wine I received and give you my best thanks for it. There were but *60* bottles only. To Your Shame be it told that You send things without cognisement.[2] The least scrap would have done and the wine had come safe but on the Contrary I was happy to take what was given not knowing how much there should be.

Green Caps you shall not get because there is no green leather here nor is it possible to get any from Poland. The Same with Coins,—the same with horses.—

AppleCake was never made here I will however get you Some Fruit trees and Sweet meats you shall get no Sooner than next month. No more for the present.

N.B. The men are long a coming but what is delayed is not lost. All in good time like Sancho's Island

---

To Jeremiah Bentham individually

Pray is your Crazy Brother already gone to Petersburgh? It is very like him indeed what you describe in your Epistles that he wanted to Come here with a thousand projects more and ter-

574. [1] B.M. IV: 301–2. Docketed by Bentham: '1786 Aug. 13 / Pr. Dashcoff Kieff / to / S. and J.B. Crichoff.'

[2] Samuel Bentham received a similar rebuke from his friend, Vice Admiral Mordvinov, in command at Kherson, for failing to include a bill with a consignment of tools which had been sent there (17/28 October 1786, B.M. IV: 310–1). In both cases the fault was not, as his Russian friends supposed, his lack of business sense, but the failure of his agent at Riga, Christian Trompovsky, to send invoices when the goods were dispatched to Krichëv (see letter 585).

minated the whole with a nap. Happy it is for you that there is no /printing/ press near you for to judge by the poor Stuff you write /to me/ of that you would burthen the public with, it would but serve to make your friends blush and lull all there to Sleep. Mind that.

Thank You for Mellin's Letter,[3] It is pretty near the Truth.—Tell Honest Benson he is a puppy for not writing with the Port wine. As ~~for~~ to a future Cargo I will be very thankful for it provided it be accompanied with a rescript. Cloth I cannot at present talk of, as I have not the most necessary ingredient for it.[4] In September I shall come myself to Kritcheff with the primum mobile of all things and there will settle those matters with him.

Your honest Englishman is still a waiting I beg pardon for delaying him these two days. Adieu.

May the Lord in Heaven repair Your Judgements and make you wiser is the sincere wish

of your faithful friend

As this side of the Sheet is better adapted to writing I have a great mind to continue. Well then Roebuck[5] is Still here very much a burthen to me. pray be so kind to send his Cloaths with the first opportunity. He owes a Jew 2 or 3 R which I beg Sam: to pay and let the Cloaths come as soon as possible.

In September I go to Petersburgh. Your foolish brother would do much better to wait for my arrival to Kritcheff and then we would go together. But in this as in all things I resign myself to the will of the Lord of Lords

Adieu

[3] See letter 572, n. 3.

[4] I.e., Dashkov had no funds with which to pay for the cloth Samuel Bentham had supplied him for the clothing of his regiment.

[5] The rascally gardener whom Samuel Bentham had unloaded upon him the previous year (see letter 528).

575

From Richard Clark[1]

31 August 1786

A great event has happened in the family of Q.S.P. Mr. Abbot is married to a lady with a fortune (as I hear) of £60,000.[2] I never heard a syllable of the business from either Mr. or Mrs. B., and the newspaper is the only channel through which I am informed of the marriage. I hardly know what public events to relate to you, as I conclude you receive some English newspapers. The sale of the Prince of Wales's stud has made a great noise; but as his debts are put into a course of payment, I hope they, as well as the nation's, will be honourably discharged.[3] It has been long apprehended the King of Prussia's death would occasion great commotions in Europe: that event has happened,[4] and now things seem to go on as quietly as ever. The emperor's brother[5] has just arrived—but whether on business or pleasure is to me a profound secret. What do you intend to do with the Turks? Since the doctrine of Mahommed has been so heartily drubbed into your head and shoulders, I suspect you have some predilection for the circumcised. I have no wish to see Constantinople added to your empire, which, I think, is as large as can be well managed by one sovereign; but I wish a respectable kingdom could be carved out of the Ottoman dominions; and I should not have the least objection to placing the Princess of Moldavia, and the gentleman who accompanied her highness from Constantinople, at the head of it.[6] The Board of Trade is going to be revived, and Lord Hawkesbury

575. [1] Bowring, x, 162–3.

[2] Farr Abbot's marriage to the wealthy Miss Pearce of Abingdon Street, Westminster, took place on 13 July 1786.

[3] By the summer of 1786 the debts of the Prince of Wales, incurred largely in connection with the Pavilion at Brighton and the rebuilding of Carlton House, amounted to over £250,000, and since George III declined to come to his assistance he decided to dismiss his household, sell his stud, and live like a private gentleman (*The Correspondence of George Prince of Wales, 1770–1812*, ed. A. Aspinall, i, 214 and correspondence for 1786 *passim*).

[4] Frederick the Great of Prussia died on 17 August 1786.

[5] Leopold (1747–92), grand duke of Tuscany, brother of the Emperor Joseph II and his successor (1790–92) as the Emperor Leopold II.

[6] The 'gentleman' is of course Bentham himself, whom Clark still apparently believed to have followed the original plan arranged for him at Constantinople of travelling in the train of the sister of the hospodar of Moldavia (see letter 554 and n. 5). Evidently the estrangement hinted at at the beginning of this letter had prevented Clark from receiving news of Bentham's adventures.

(late C. Jenkinson) is to be at the head of it.[7] The members of the board are not to receive a salary, as such, but will possess sinecure places which can't be well abolished. His lordship, for example, is made Chancellor of the Duchy of Lancaster. You may recollect that I have been remarkable for a number of road adventures. A few days ago, as Harry Russell and myself were going in a post-chaise to make a visit below Dorking, we were overtaken on the Epsom road about twelve miles from town, between one and two in the afternoon, by two gentlemen on horseback, who eased us of some cash and our watches. Mr. Russell's, unfortunately, was of gold, with a chain and seals of the same metal. I shall be glad to know where you are, and what you are about. Let me know the value of land in your neighbourhood, and whether there is any pretty snug farm, well wooded and watered, with a pretty snug house upon it, which you could recommend as a country retreat from the noise and bustle of London. I am informed that government has just determined to send off seven hundred convicts to New [South] Wales, under convoy of a man-of-war, where a fort is to be built, and a colony established, and that a man has been found who will take upon him the command of this rabble. Major Semple[8] is to be of the party,—a gentleman who has given proofs of his dexterity to the Marquis of Lansdowne, also downwards to ladies' maids and hackney coachmen. These wretches are to be furnished with a twelvemonths' provision, seeds, etc., and then must shift for themselves. I forgot to take notice of an event which, for a few days, alarmed the country,—an insane woman offered to present a petition to the king, and, at the same instant, made a blow at him with a knife; she was instantly secured, and, after several examinations before the council, was sent to our hospital of Bethlem where she is like to spend the remainder of her days. She told me nothing could prevent a deluge in the kingdom, but restoring the blood; and that the only way to bring that about, was for the Prince of Wales to make her a mother.

[7] Charles Jenkinson (1729–1808) was created Baron Hawkesbury on 21 August 1786, appointed chairman of the Board of Trade on the 23rd, and made chancellor of the Duchy of Lancaster on 6 September.

[8] James George Semple Lisle (b. *c.* 1759) was a celebrated confidence trickster. He evaded the sentence of transportation recently passed upon him. See his autobiography, *Life of Major J. G. Semple Lisle, Written by himself*, London, 1799, and *The Northern Imposter; Being a Faithful Narrative of the Adventures, and Deceptions, of James George Semple, commonly called Major Semple…*, London, 1786. See also letter 583.

576

FROM GEORGE WILSON[1]

24 September 1786

I could give very good reasons for not having sooner answered your letter from Crichoff of 29th May, or 9th June;[2] but it would take some time to state them. As to our silence before that, you will recollect that we had reason to suppose that you desired to hear from neither of us, and that it was, in a manner, settled, before you set out, that we were not to correspond, because you found yourself involved in too many engagements of that sort already. Your letter from Leghorn[3] we did not consider as any departure from this plan; but only as an infliction of your revenge on Trail, for his and his cousin's calumnies against the Grand Duke. I say this by way of justification, and by no means with any spleen; for, I do assure you, I have felt great yearnings towards you since you left this country, and vehement longings for your return. If I had the advantage of a title, I should, no doubt, have found it easy, as Lord L. has done, to see your letters to Q. S. P. on my own terms. Trail received, on going to town last Friday, a scrap of paper from you, desiring an account of the new taxes;[4] and before he returns, will do what he can to supply you: I am not sure that any supplement to Burn will come down low enough;[5] but you will at least have a little table of taxes, published by Kearsley.[6] Trail had before sent you by Mr King, The Debate on the Sinking Fund, and Report of the Committee,[7] Baring's Principle of the Commutation Act,[8] Plan for settling the Black Poor

576. [1] Bowring, x, 163–4. Incomplete (see letter 584, n. 11).

[2] Missing.

[3] Letter 547.

[4] Missing.

[5] The most recent (15th) edition of that great work of reference, Richard Burn's, *The Justice of the Peace and Parish Officer*, had been published in 1785. Its appendix lists the statutes; but there is no record in the British Museum catalogue of supplements giving the text of these.

[6] George Kearsley, London publisher. He produced Annual Tax Tables, but the British Museum has none of earlier date than 1794.

[7] *The Debate upon the establishing a Fund for the Discharge of the National Debt, Wednesday, March 29, 1786, To which is added, the Report from the Select Committee, relating to the public income and expenditure, March 21, 1786*, 1786.

[8] Francis Baring (1740–1810), M.P., an eminent London businessman, a member of Lansdowne's political circle, and by this time a recognized authority on questions of trade and finance, was author of *The Principle of the Commutation Act established by Facts*, London, 1786.

near Sierra Leone, by Smeathman,[9] who is since dead, and, I suppose, the plan with him; Character of Lord Sackville, by Cumberland,[10] Correspondence between Lord Macartney and General Stewart,[11] Burke's Charges, and Hastings' Defence,[12] and Maty's Reviews, down to August, inclusive.[13] Newspapers we cannot send you; because they go to Scotland, to my sister, who, by the by, is very well, and has a son nine months old. While you are making Fermes Ornees in a country which is not to be found in our maps, other people here are invading your province of a reformer. There is a Mr. Paley, a parson and archdeacon of Carlisle, who has written a book called Principles of Moral and Political Philosophy, in quarto, and it has gone through two editions, with prodigious applause.[14] It is founded entirely on utility, or, as he chooses to call it, the will of God, as declared by expediency, to which he adds, as a supplement, the revealed will of God. But notwithstanding this, and some weak places, particularly as to oaths and subscriptions, where he is hampered by his profession and his past conduct, it is a capital book, and by much the best that has been written on the subject in this country. Almost everything he says about morals, government, and our own constitution, is sound, practical, and free from commonplace. He has got many of your notions about punishment, which I always thought the most important of your discoveries; and I could almost suspect, if it

[9] Henry Smeathman (d. 1786), author of *Plan of a Settlement to be made near Sierra Leona, on the Grain Coast of Africa*, London, 1786.

[10] Richard Cumberland (1732–1811), government official and dramatist, had served at the Board of Trade under Lord George Germain (1716–85), 1st Viscount Sackville, and was his friend and admirer. On Sackville's death he published his eulogistic *Character of the late Lord Sackville*, London, 1785.

[11] *The Papers and Correspondence from July 16, 1783, After the Return of Major General Stuart to the Presidency*, London, 1785. This was one of the publications put out by Major General James Stuart (d. 1793) in defence of his conduct while in command of the East India Company's military forces in Madras presidency after he had been suspended from the command by the governor and council and hustled on board a homeward-bound ship. In June 1786 Stuart fought a duel with Lord Macartney, who had been governor at Madras at the time of the incident, and severely wounded him.

[12] *Articles of Charge of high crimes and misdemeanours against Warren Hastings Esq.... presented to the House of Commons on the 4th day of April 1785, by the Right Hon. E. Burke*, London, 1786; *The Defence of Warren Hastings... at the Bar of the House of Commons, upon the matter of the several charges... presented against him in the year 1786*, London, 1786. Burke's charges marked the beginning of his crusade against the Indian administration of Warren Hastings, which led in due course to Hastings's impeachment (see P. J. Marshall, *The Impeachment of Warren Hastings*, London, 1965).

[13] Paul Henry Maty (1745–87) began the publication in January 1782 of the *New Review*, dealing particularly with foreign publications. It ran until September 1786.

[14] William Paley (1743–1805). His book was first published in 1785 and went into a second edition in 1786.

were possible, that he had read your introduction; and I very much fear, that, if you ever do publish on these subjects, you may be charged with stealing from him what you have honestly invented with the sweat of your own brow. But, for all that, I wish you would come and try; for I am still persuaded, my dear Bentham, that you have, for some years, been throwing away your time; and that the way in which you are most likely to benefit the world and yourself is, by establishing, in the first place, a great literary reputation in your own language, and in this country, which you despise. But all this had been said often enough already, and it is needless to tire you with it any more. Paley's book is written in a clear, manly, simple style, and he reasons with great accuracy. I meant to have copied and sent you an inquiry of his into the guilt of a drunken man who kills another, and the quantum of punishment that ought to be applied to him, which is as exhaustive and correct as if you had done it yourself, and, if I may say it without offence, less formal and prolix. But I have forgot it, and have not now the book by me. He has added, unnecessarily, a treatise on political economy, which he does not understand. You will see by the papers that there is a large subscription to erect a statue to your friend Howard,[15] who is now making a tour of the Lazarettos for the plague in the Levant. Jonas Hanway, another of your fellow-labourers, but at some distance, is dead.[16] Government are going at last to send the convicts to Botany Bay in New Holland; the Hulks being found, by sad experience, to be academies for housebreaking, and solitary confinement to any extent, impracticable from the expense of building. These colonists are not to be turned loose there; but are to have a government established over them, and some troops left; notwithstanding which, I much fear it will end in the ruin of the Friendly and Society Islands, which they will undoubtedly attempt to reach if they can either get or build ships; unless, indeed, the colony should expire, which is not unlikely, as, to 600 men there are but 70 women, and those probably not the most fertile. Will you have a few convicts for the Crimea? We have been reading here Cook's last voyage, and are very desirous to know what is become of our good friend Major Behm, and whether our court ever interested itself to procure him any preferment.[17] Tell us also, how far we may rely on De Tott's account

[15] John Howard, the prison reformer.

[16] Jonas Hanway, the philanthropist. He died on 5 September 1786.

[17] Major Magnus von Behm was governor of the Russian territory of Kamchatka

of the Turks.[18] Eden went to Paris by no other revolution than that of his own principles, which came about more suddenly and with less pretext than any in this reign.[19] He is to be a vice-treasurer of Ireland in the room of Lord Walsingham, who goes to Spain. It is universally believed that the French Commercial Treaty is settled; but the articles are not known: probably they will make some noise, as they cannot but touch some of our dearest prejudices. There is also an agreement about the mutual recovery of debts in France and England. It seems their courts have not been open to us, as ours are to them. Sir Gilbert Elliot is, I hope, by this time chosen for Berwick. The election was to be last Wednesday, and he was pretty safe.[20] Douglas is well, and increasing in fame and wealth.[21] Trail has left Ainge, and is now a complete and accomplished draughtsman, waiting for instructions. I am going on, or rather, standing still as before; for though I shall get rather more this year than the last, it is owing to accidents, and not to any regular or permanent business. There are great changes in the King's Bench this year. Davenport is dead,[22]—Tom Cowper dying,[23]—Jack Lee paralytic,[24] and John Wilson[25] a judge by the death of Nares.[26] By each of these events I get a step, as the soldier did when the general was

in 1779 and gave generous aid to the members of the Cook expedition when they put in there for provisions. Returning that summer to St Petersburg he brought to Europe the first news of Cook's death at Hawaii. See also p. 517.

[18] François de Tott, *Mémoires du Baron de Tott sur les Turks et les Tartares*, 4 vols., Amsterdam, 1784. An English version was published in 1785.

[19] William Eden (1744–1814), M.P., later 1st Baron Auckland, with whom Bentham had had some correspondence in 1778 (letters 238–41). After the fall of the Fox-North coalition ministry in December 1783 Eden had been one of the most vehement opponents in the Commons of Pitt's administration; but he was a government careerist by nature, opposition had no charms for him, and in December 1785 he made his peace with Pitt in return for a post as special envoy to negotiate a commercial treaty with France. His conduct was widely regarded as ratting among those whose sympathies lay with the Foxite opposition.

[20] Sir Gilbert Elliot (1751–1814), 4th bart., a strong supporter of the Fox-North party, was deprived of a seat in parliament at the general election of 1784. He was returned duly elected at the by-election for Berwick on 21 September 1786.

[21] Sylvester Douglas.

[22] Thomas Davenport (1734–86), M.P., serjeant-at-law, 'a very creditable person in his profession', died on 25 March 1786.

[23] Thomas Cowper, barrister, and recorder of Chester, did not die until 25 July 1788.

[24] John Lee (?1733–93), M.P., one of the close associates of the late Marquis of Rockingham.

[25] John Wilson (1741–93), barrister, was appointed a puisne judge in the Court of Common Pleas on 7 November 1786 and knighted on the 15th.

[26] Sir George Nares (1716–86), a judge of the Court of Common Pleas since 1771. He died on 20 July 1786.

killed. Bower[27] is to have a silk gown;—so probably will Law,[28] and Chambré,[29] if he pleases. Erskine is at the head of the K.'s Bench decidedly,[30] and Mingay[31] almost before Bearcroft.[32] Thurlow has been at death's door, and is not well yet.[33] Lord Mansfield still Chief-Justice, but unable to do the business.[34] Thompson[35] is Accomptant-general by the death of Anguish.[36] All this you don't care about; but I have no news but law news.

577

MEMORANDUM[1]

18/29 December 1786 (Aet 38)

Account of Packets sent to Riga by the Serjeant along with Mr. Benson and Mr. Palmer.

December 18th
1786

[27] Foster Bower (1748–95), barrister. He was appointed a K.C. on 27 June 1787.

[28] Edward Law (1750–1818), later 1st Lord Ellenborough and Lord Chief Justice. Called to the bar in 1780, he became a K.C. in 1787.

[29] Alan Chambré (1739–1823). He had been called to the bar in 1767, but seems never to have taken silk. He became a serjeant-at-law and a baron of the exchequer in 1799.

[30] Thomas Erskine (1750–1823), a close friend of Fox and Sheridan, one of the most brilliant barristers practising in the King's Bench, was kept out of high legal office till late in life only by his political connection.

[31] James Mingay (1752–1812), K.C.

[32] Edward Bearcroft (1737–96), M.P., a K.C. He became Chief Justice of Chester in 1788.

[33] Edward, 1st Baron Thurlow (1731–1806), the Lord Chancellor.

[34] Lord Mansfield (1705–93), Chief Justice of the Court of King's Bench, retired in 1788.

[35] Alex Thomson, a Master in Chancery.

[36] Thomas Anguish (1724–85), accountant general of the Court of Chancery, and a Master in Chancery since 1763. He died on 31 December 1785.

577. [1] B.M. XVIII: 242. Only phrases in round brackets are autograph. Docketed: '1786 Dec. 18/29 / Contents of the packets sent to Riga for England by Benson and Palmer.'

Bentham evidently regarded this sheaf of letters as exceptionally important. They covered four major topics, three of which materially concerned his brother and the fourth himself. When Samuel Bentham was suddenly called away from Krichëv in mid-December 1786 by Potëmkin, he had two rows on his hands, one with George Benson (see letters 578, 580 and 588) and the other with Doctor John Debraw (see letters 579, 580 and 593). The consequences might be serious, for both men might engage in damaging intrigues against him—Benson had openly threatened to do so—and Jeremy Bentham was anxious to forestall this as far as possible. Samuel Bentham was also in difficulties through Trompovsky's dilatory discharge of his duties as agent. He required funds which Trompovsky was withholding and also invoices for goods received which he had resold without as yet knowing what charges he himself

No. 1 To Mr. Trompowsky to be read first[2]

2 J.B. to Mr. Trompowsky general Letter

No. 3 First breach with the Doctor Written Oct. 4 (with his Oration by Beatty)

4 Dr. D.'s History.[3] Also Collonel Bentham's and Dr. D.'s Contract. (In this were no. 24 and no. 25 the d.'s shameful letter of ult 6 and his advertisement)

5 History of the Riga Smiths, with their proposals and agreement to return.

6 Correspondence between Dr. D. and Mr. B.

A Letter for Dr. Brown Caermarthen England[4]

A Letter to Alderman Clark London[5]

A Letter to Geo. Wilson Esq., No. 13 Lincoln's Inn, London[6]

One to Walter Sharp Esq., British Consul, St. Petersburgh

A parcel of Leathers Numberd from Robson

To Jeremiah Bentham Esq., Queens Square Place, London[7]

Dr. Anderson, Coats near Edinburgh

Monsieur Malartie[?] Paris

Mr. King London, including one to Mr. Payne[8] Copy of the Pamphlet on Inspection house.

578

To Christian Trompovsky[1]

18/29 December 1786 (Aet 38)

The old man's history is briefly this. The summer before last Dr. Brown of Caermarthen an English Physician spending some

would have to meet for them. This was probably the subject of letter no. 2 in this list which is missing, but the contents of which are partly explained in letter 585 (see also letter 593). In addition to these matters Bentham himself was concerned to send two copies of the manuscript of his letters on the Panopticon to England by separate conveyances to safeguard against loss—one direct to his father and the other to his agent in London, Richard King (see letters 582 and 585)—and he was anxious that George Wilson should give help over some points which he was unable to clear up for lack of printed materials at his hand (see letter 584).

Those letters listed in the memorandum which are not identified in the following footnotes have not been traced.

[2] Letter 578. [3] Letter 579. [4] Letter 580. [5] Letter 583.

[6] Letter 584. [7] Letter 582. [8] Copies in letter 582.

578. [1] B.M. IV: 447. Autograph. Draft with corrections. Headed in pencil by Bentham: 'J.B. to Tromp. Benson.' It is clearly a draft for 'la petite lettre' to

time at Crichoff mentioned this Benson as a man whom he might /probably/ find ~~means to make use of useful~~ /an use for/ in some shape or other, and whom⊞ it would be charity to take. ~~He was My Brother accordingly wrote to me to furnish him~~ Benson ~~was~~ understanding that he was to have a living at least was very glad to come. He came to me with scarce a coat to his back. I supplied him /according to my Brother's desire/ with £18 which according to Dr. Browne's calculation would be necessary for him, and I think nearly as much again which according to Benson's calculation was also necessary. His own account to me was that he was an Irishman by birth and had /once/ had some concern I don't know what, in the linnen manufactory: that about 14 or 15 years ago he had had with a Major General Philips[2] such a quarrel as made his own country no longer tenable to him: that he muster'd up £500 /with/ which he came over to Caermarthen in Wales. There he had been lingring ~~upon his £500~~ without any employment whatsoever ~~till he had tired out every body's hospitality~~ till every farthing of his money was spent and every body's hospitality as well as generosity tired out into the bargain: and in this condition ~~my~~ Dr. Brown's letter found him. When I have told you that he has been all along compleat Master of my Brother's house ~~having all sorts of keys in his possession~~ that his great evil and even great complaint has been the not having enough to do for the copying now and then a letter and keeping such indifferent accounts as he is able to keep have filled up but a small proportion of his time, that he had never received an unkind word or even look either from my Brother or from me nor made any sort of complaint of either of us to either of

⊞ as he was in absolute want of bread, besides being over head and ears in debt. By my Brother's consent the Dr.[3] wrote to him accordingly.

Trompovsky referred to in letter 585 and so can be identified with fair certainty as letter no. 1 in Bentham's memorandum (577).

For the origin of George Benson's connection with Samuel Bentham, see letter 524. By the autumn of 1786 he had become thoroughly disappointed and discontented with his lot, and his growing insubordination built up to an open row in mid-December, as a result of which he was summarily dismissed and packed off to Riga on 18/29 December with the party carrying all the mail detailed in 577. His delinquencies are also related with other and fuller details in letters 580 and 588. Jottings for an upbraiding letter to him dated 16/27 December in the handwriting of both brothers are at B.M. IV: 312–3.

[2] Major General William Phillips (?1730–81). He had reached the rank of colonel in 1772 about the time this incident occurred. He was on active service in North America from 1776 onwards and he died in May 1781 while on service with Cornwallis in Virginia.

[3] Dr Charles Brown.

us, you well know at least as much as is necessary to enable you to judge of the temper and character that could dictate two letters[4] /of his/ copies of which I enclose.

After his ~~reception~~ /receipt/ of my Brother's answer to them his behaviour as I understood from half a dozen witnesses was still more frantic than ever you /could have seen/ the Drs.[5] All the execrations /all the terms of reproach/ the language furnishes were ~~vented against~~ /bestowed upon/ me and my Brother. ~~all the terms of repr~~.... My Brother did not love the smell of powder: he would follow him and call him to account—he would go to the Prince and make complaint against him: he would go to the Empress—he would go then to Mr. Pitt to complain of me.* With all this madness cramming every thing into his trunks that took his fancy: refusing to give up things that had been lent him, and conveying his packages out of the house at night by stealth.

When they had been a whole night at the Drs. then he was ready to have them search'd by any honest man, by which, as he declar'd he meant to exclude every one of the English here.

My Brother all the while, you observe on his journey. I three miles off at Zadobras. But from the reports made me I expected for some time I should have had my life to defend against a mad beggar to whom I had never given the shadow of an offence.

The Dr. this morning in conversation with my man Beattie affected to speak slightingly of Benson: Whether any of the Drs. politicks were lurking behind this /language/ I do not know.

*He would publish everything he knew of both our letters.

579

To Christian Trompovsky[1]

18/29 December 1786 (Aet 38)

To Tromp. unfinished

I don't know whether you know that the lending of the money was without any instructions from my Brother who had only sent

[4] Missing.

[5] Here, and below, 'Dr.' indicates Dr John Debraw.

579. [1] U.C. xcix: 63. Autograph.

Draft, partly in pencil, written in columns and very difficult to decipher, on the back of a sheet of notes concerning the civil code. The document is dated and its context established by the memorandum printed as 577, which also shows that a letter based on this draft was actually sent.

it to be changed and was entirely Bensons doing who however is altogether free from blame, as he acted for the best and made /in lending the money/ a bargain which would have been a good one had it been adhered fulfilled as he had all the reason to think it would.

[...?]

Good to consult with as a Phy. and to be laughed at as a but: but entirely unfit to be trusted to as a manager or a friend.

Ushaka not bad [...?] [...?] S.B. had [...?]

Ushaker necessary

1. Fuel there
2. Glass house which Dr. was to improve

4.

S.B. still with [...?] to those [...?] on the Ushaka scheme

1.

S.B. has said nothing to recommend the place

2.

He knew of S.B. [...?] cleared out a place for his furnace at Critchoff

For other references to the money matters raised at the beginning of this letter see letters 585 and 593.

Dr John Debraw (d. 1788), at one time apothecary to Addenbrooke's hospital at Cambridge, and a man of very considerable medical talent and wide scientific interests, seems to have crossed Bentham's path early in 1785, when Bentham was scouting for assistance to send to his brother at Krichëv. At one time Samuel Bentham thought Debraw might take over a contract at Krichëv for the production of malt spirits (to Bentham, 27 March/7 April 1785, B.M. IV: 151–2); and somewhat later a letter in which Debraw discussed the properties of steel, presumably in connection with experiments which Samuel then had in hand, passed between the brothers (see letter 528). However, Debraw's journey to Russia was a speculative venture and not under any firm arrangement with Samuel Bentham. He arrived at Riga some time early in 1786, stayed with Samuel's agent, Christian Trompovsky whom he cured of a near-fatal illness (letter 593), and during the late summer and autumn of that year paid a prolonged visit to Krichëv, the unpleasant consequences of which are related here. His attitude towards Samuel's English workmen was short-sighted and tactless (see Ian R. Christie, 'Samuel Bentham and the western colony at Krichëv, 1784–1787', *Slavonic and East European Review*, xlviii (1969–70) pp. 244 and 246). Also he proved so difficult to deal with, that Samuel would contemplate no arrangement with him except a complete transfer to him of responsibility for the glasshouse at Ushaka. This he declined. After leaving Krichëv early in 1787 Debraw soon established a name for himself in southern Russia in his professional line. In 1788 he was appointed first physician to the Russian army, but the patent of his appointment did not reach Kherson till after his death. 'Had it come before it would no doubt have saved his life', Samuel wrote, 'for he died more of disappointment than anything else.' (To Bentham, 12/23 October 1788, B.M. IV: 489).

The enclosures mentioned in the course of this letter are missing.

3.

On going to Ushaker he tried to dissuade S.B. from building his house [...?] [...?] Ushaker

If the Dr. is to be believed, you Riga folks /not only/ were very loth to part with him but expressed /since his departure have expressed/ their wishes to have him back again. If so, I wish to God you had him or any body else, so that we were but rid of him.

1

D.'s asking for his letters.

2

D.'s not sending the medicines, not withstanding his sincere regard for Tr.

3

D.'s desiring power over the Adjutant

3

D.'s stay at Riga not owing to his regard for T. but respect shewn him by the Ushaka etc.

4

D. cannot have any hopes only [...?] on the expectation of being bought off.

5

D.'s want of perseverence? Ex. [...?] water glasses at Riga [*rest indecipherable*]

So far in general which proves only one dissatisfaction. Now for a few /half a dozen/ out of a thousand particulars which may serve to shew the grounds of it

First as to /such of/ the concerns now subsisting in which he has any interest in it

That there is a want of discipline and order among the workmen is but too true; the causes⊞ are /partly/ the most deplorable want of money owing to the untowardly circumstances you are already apprised of partly to confess the truth or at least what appears to me such a want of steadiness and resolution /firmness/ on the part of my Brother.

My hopes or rather my wishes were that by the Drs. assistance, who does not want for principle and positiveness at least the want might in some measure be supplied.

⊞ antecedent to the Drs. arrival were

Neither his assistance in that respect is likely to be of much use; a paper herewith enclosed will contribute something towards enabling you to judge, if it be worth the reading, which perhaps it may be for the joke's sake. It contains a specimen of the Drs. discourse to the men immediately upon his arrival, and was brought me to my no small surprize by one of them after a multitude of misgivings and apologies as you may imagine.

You must know I have nothing to do with the men in general, not interfering in the least in any of my Brother's concerns, except hearing now and then what he ~~wishes to say to me~~ /himself makes me hear/ and holding a pen for him as you see. But this man having attracted my attention by his [...?] for literature, had conceived a sort of attachment for me.

Next as to the projected concerns projected, which the Drs. talents were (to set a going) were to be the ground of.

My Brother seeing what nobody could avoid seeing that the Drs. interference in the concerns at Crechoff itself could do (nothing but harm to both of them) no good to either of them, and could not but continue to do /what it/ as they have done all along hitherto to speak mischief /to my Brother/ as it was well possible for any man's interference to do, had very early formed a wish to see the Dr. transfer himself to *Ushaker* a village about 26 miles off where the Glasshouse is with /upwards of 30/ 27 men attached to it.

For that same reason my Brother had studiously avoided throwing out the least hint to him about the matter; having found out from the suspiciousness of the Dr's temper that the sure way to prevent his embracing any measure however reasonable and even necessary, is to express any desire to see it embraced. He thought that the nature and purpose of the engagement between them, the evident necessity of /the measure/ both for the Drs. advantage as well as his ~~as my Brothers (I mean upon the supposition of his feeling himself able or conceiving it necessary to appear to feel himself able to make good any part of his professions)~~ (that /either/ the /some such/ considerations as these /added to/ on the pleasure of /independant power/ (making himself troublesome) must sooner or later to bring him to propose the same, thing and so it proved. He accordingly on Saty last (my Brother being then at his Cottage at Zadobras /where we live/ 3 miles from Crechoff,) wrote my Brother a letter of which I enclose a copy.

As soon as my Brother's concurrence was given ~~which it was instantly in the fullest manner~~ the Drs. note was as entirely changed. Difficulty was started after difficulty and the whole was as compleatly unsaid as it had been said before. The idea of inconsistency would have abashed and brought round some men: this idea, as you who know him may conceive, and as my Brother foreknew /saw/, only exasperated the Dr. The scheme /his own scheme/ and every part belonging to it was treated in terms as 'ridiculous and absurd'.

* In[2] the course of their conversations ~~my Brother had said to him~~ the Saturday /Friday/ morning last my Brother had said to him (with his usual mildness) that while he was at Crechoff he was only as a ~~guest~~ visitor in which capacity he was always happy to see him there or ~~elsewhere~~ anywhere else but that in any other capacity he neither was nor /from the nature of his concerns/ could be nor attempted to be of any use (to either of them) that Ushaker was the only place in which he could act in the character of the man of business. This passed off at the time without much animadversion on his part.* In the evening, what was our surprize, when as my Brother and I were sitting at Zadobras in my room in stalked the Doctor, and with the countenance of a man out of Bedlam demanded a pass for Riga, for which place he declared himself resolved to set out the next morning.

My Brother's answering that it was neither in his power nor his wish to hinder him from going to Riga or anywhere else where he thought proper, but expressing some little surprize at his taking so suddenly so extraordinary a step, and observing that matters stood between them it might not be improper to come to some little adjustments previously, he gave us to understand immediately, that he had no meaning but to come back, and that something very terrible to my Brother was to be the consequence of the visit excursion.

Finding this threat producing a little stare on our part and a little smiling without ~~the~~ any part of the apprehension it was destined to excite, his tone was alter'd. He was ill had got the Ague enclined to vomit but brought up nothing. ~~He took his leave After receiving my Brothers assurances that the~~

~~Upon being asked~~ To the [...?] as to the ground of this ~~sudden~~ extraordinary resolution, the ~~alleged as the only~~ [...?] and the only answer was that expression /my Brother had spoken of him as a visitor/ of my brother as above mentioned: explanations were offered but none could be received. After having been detained for some time by bad weather, and engaged by me to talk

[2] The passage between stars is scored through.

about indifferent things, he took his leave. My Brother foretold immediately upon that there would be no going to Riga and so it proved, for that the illness was only an escapement, and so it seems / Ever/ for since that he has been ill to my Brother, though /without/ his servants seeing anything of this matter. He has been too ill to come to as he had otherwise offerd to do to Zadobras: much more to go to Riga: tho not too ill to go to General Banders /which from Crechoff/ is about twice the distance of Zadobras.

580

To Charles Brown[1]

18/29 December 1786 (Aet 38)

Dear Sir

We had the pleasure of receiving your kind letter[2] much about the time I believe, in which it ought to have been received. I wish I could have added that I answer'd it at the time at which it ought to have been answered. I waited /have been/ for events in hopes that some odd section in the chapter of accidents might turn up that might enable me to answer it in the way we all wish. To be sure there was a middle course to take which I might and ought to have taken viz. the acknowledging the receipt of it immediately as you desired and taking the earliest opportunity of giving you at least what payment might be afforded by our thanks. ~~Sefton, though the Dr.~~[3] ~~chose to bring him with him here by post instead of letting him go by water with his wife and daughter, is however here, and being here remains in my Brother's service. My Brother therefore will allow the Dr. so much as Sefton's coming here would have cost had he gone by water as at first designed:~~ [*two lines illegible*] ~~this trifle therefore he is enabled without doing himself injustice to add to the other trifles which he allows you.~~ But though I have taken upon me the high office of Secretary, I do not in every instance give his business quite so much dispatch as a less uppish one might give:

580. [1] B.M. III: 470–1, IV: 448, 444–6. Autograph. Faint pencil heading by Bentham: 'I.B. to Dr. B.' Draft with corrections.

Dated and the context established by Bentham's memorandum (577). There is further reference in letter 588 to a letter based on this draft having been actually sent.

[2] Missing; referred to in a letter from Charles Brown to Jeremiah Bentham of 17 June 1786 (see letter 566, n. 4).

[3] Debraw. Bentham added in the margin: 'for his own accommodation'. Nothing is known about the workman, Sefton, save that he was still at Krichëv in the late summer of 1787.

pleading in excuse that that office might of itself if compleatly conducted nearly fill up a man's time, and I have enough scribbling of my own to fill up the four and twenty hours if they could all be spared for it. Turning over just now some other letters which stand in the same predicament yours presents itself and gives me a severer twinge than the rest: and so I have plucked up resolution at last to break silence.

In answer to your kind enquiries about our situation (I say *ours* for shortness) it is chequer'd like most other people's: and consists as yet more of hopes than anything else. /The burning of Our/ Smith's shop burnt in the summer put us to some expence and threw that business a great deal back as you may imagine. This very day we have the pleasure of learning that the Glass-house at Ushaker has shared the same fate. This is the end I suppose of the Glass-house business which from delays and difficulties in getting clay for the furnaces and other inconveniences has hitherto rather been a burthen than a gain. The tannery has likewise undergone sad delays from similar causes: ~~which could~~ but it is now we flatter ourselves within a month or two of being compleated, and in the mean time we have got between 2 and 3000 hides in of one sort or other, some of which are coming out every day. Mean time we have great orders at great prices: and when compleatly stocked we have reason to expect that it may produce 10,000, 15,000, or even 20,000 Rubles a year. My Brother has hit upon a very singular new and I think important /though simple/ idea in Architecture which is the subject of a course of letters I have just finished for my Father which it is not improbable may find their way to the press. This you will say belongs more to your head of the *dulce* than the *utile.* Another that I hope will come under both heads as well as under that of the *honestum*, is a new and very strange idea in ship-building, which having obtained full powers he is carrying into execution with all his might. If it succeeds to the degree in which according to received theories and experiments which have already been made of it though in a much less perfect state than that to which it has been brought to now, it ought, it will, effect a great revolution in inland, nay we hope even in maritime navigation. It is as simple in its conception as the other architectural one, though in its application it requires a combination of contrivances.

The architectural idea ~~consists in nothing but~~ /in the plan of what we/ call an Inspection-house is that of a circular building so contrived that any number of persons may therein be kept in such a situation as either to be, or what comes nearly to the same thing to seem to themselves to be, constantly under the eye of a person or persons occupying a station in the centre which we call the Inspector's Lodge. You will be surprised when you come to see the efficacy which this simple and seemingly obvious contrivance promises to the business of schools, manufactories, ~~Hospitals and all sorts of~~ Prisons, and even Hospitals, if one may venture to say so to an adept. The ship-building idea might be given in a single word: but even that word must be suppressed considering the channels through which the letters may have to pass.

Amongst the plagues I must not omitt a two-legged tormenter something between the knave the fool and the madman whom I have done my brother the kindness to introduce to him in the quality of chemical projector for which he is well enough qualified in point of knowledge though of nothing else.[4] He offerd himself to me in London and as ~~his situation~~ he was glad ~~made him content~~ to come without that security which you know it was not in my power to offer, I thought it was no ill turn I had done my brother by encouraging him to come here: He was moreover an able medical practicioner in every branch if any faith is to be put in former character or the signal successes that have attended him here. In every other respect my Brother and I think we characterise him to one another pretty compleatly in a very short phrase by saying he is just as opposite to /another Dr. we know/ as one man can be to another.[5] As folly and /even/ madness are not incompatible with a considerable share of cunning, what you will be sorry to hear is that he has found enough of the latter quality to enable him to poison the mind of poor old Benson.[6] [*Sentence crossed out*] Of this alliance one of the effects is that this poor fellow has so far forgot the good advice you gave him as to send my Brother verbal messages telling him when to come to him and when not to come: and so far forgot his discretion /without the privity of my Brother or me/ as to communicate to the Dr. copies of which he Benson had been employd to take of letters of mine to my Agent in which happily there was nothing that I should have cared about though it were published at Paul's cross.

When first I reached Crichoff which was in february last, nothing could be more good-humoured than he was ~~more obliging~~ more

4 Debraw.

5 Brown had sponsored Benson's engagement at Krichëv, and this and the following passages establish him as the addressee beyond doubt.

6 Added in the margin: 'the only Englishman to whom he has not rendered himself ~~of our little colony amounting now to 25~~ at once odious and ridiculous among 25 souls which our little colony at present consists of reckoning the sex that have none.'

obsequious, more faithful or more contented.[7] I mean as towards my Brother and me for he had had his quarrels with most of the English and had well nigh drove a very able work man out of the service. God damn me was the usual salutation language to them tho chiefly out of zeal to my Brother in whose service he did not think them sufficiently alert. At our first interview he told me of his own accord without any question of mine to introduce the subject he expatiated with great warmth on the happiness and comfortableness of his situation behaving to my Brother and speaking of him in terms expressive of the strongest mixture of affection and respect.

You[8] would naturally suppose from this that there had been some previous misunderstanding some previous supposed ill usage on my Brother's /part/ previously complained of, and unredressed: some harsh treatment given or at least harsh language used: some promises or at least hopes given on the one part and eluded on the other: some explanation required with regard to him on the one side, and /eluded/ refused on the other. No not a shadow of anything of this sort. General and indiscriminate invectives against ~~all sorts of people~~ /everybody else/ that came in his way, English workmen, Russian servants, and Russians in general were indeed frequent enough: but as all along there was the appearance of great attachment to my Brother, all this /was/ passed off by /my Brother/ with now and then a smile and now and then a good-humoured observation: ~~looking upon~~ these as little blemishes in a character in other respects laudable /a worthy one/: on a sudden we were surprised with a letter from the Dr. (whose constant residence was at Crichoff while we were more frequently at the farm 3 miles off) speaking of an occasion he had to send /a special messenger/ to Riga, and mentioning Mr B.'s earnest desire to be that messenger that he might go from thence to England. My Brother being otherwise engaged I went to Crichoff to see what was the matter with /the old man/: imagining too that as he and I had always been upon the best terms, not the shadow of a difference or complaint /or unkind word or even look/ on any occasion whatsoever, he might possibly unbosom himself to me with /rather/ more freedom than to the Colonel. When I came, I soon found a concert between him and the Dr. with whom however at that time I ~~had had no more disagree-~~

[7] This paragraph is contained in B.M. IV: 448. All but the first sentence is scored through.

[8] B.M. IV: 444–6 begins here. The first two sentences, down to 'anything of this sort' are scored through.

~~ment than~~ /was upon just as good terms as with/ Benson: each ~~making~~ way leaving the other alone with me in a manner which could not have happened without previous intelligence. My object being to sooth, my address /as you may imagine/ was /at least/ as friendly as /upon that occasion as it had been on any/ other: he began upon the high ropes, with big look and a low voice, and so he continued as long as ~~I had patience to~~ he thought proper without the opposition or interruption from me. There was nothing for him to do—he could be of no use—nobody minded what he said no more than if he had been a dog—he was put to servants work—he did not choose to be made a slave of any longer—Dr. Brown had told him that he was to ~~make a great fortune~~ /do great things/ that he was to get enough to make himself comfortable the first year. That as he saw no prospect of any thing of that sort nor of his being of *use* in any way, a phrase he most dwelt upon, he wished to get out of the country as soon as he could—he did not like the country and he would not stay in it upon any terms, especially /after/ what Sr. Rich Worsley (who had been on a /month's/ visit to us)[9] had just told him of the laws of the country according to which any man who struck an officer was to suffer death. This indeed seemed to be the greatest of all grievances standing in the way of the /notion/ he had ~~conceived for thrashing any body~~ /formed of the propriety of/ his thrashing any body who should incur his displeasure: an English liberty which seemed more valuable in his eyes than any ~~thing~~ /idea/ of gain to which however he is not in other respects insensible. Upon my asking him which I did not venture upon without much submission and apology whether he had formed any plan of life to be pursued upon his return to England: his answer was ready, that Sr. W. Mansell[10] when he saw him in London had offer'd /to get/ him a place of £50 a year, which his honour and so forth forbadde him to accept. This may be true: but if it was I rather wonder I did not hear of it at the time.* It came out either then or afterwards that, unknown to my Brother, /without my Brother's knowledge/ he had offer'd his services both to Prince Dashcof and to Sir Richd.: both of whom declined the offer, as you may imagine, /but/ without mentioning it to my Brother. In conclusion he would go to Cherson

*as ~~his honour~~ the principle which forbad his acceptance of the offer did not forbid his mentioning it.

[9] Sir Richard Worsley stayed at Krichëv from 7 August to 5 September 1786 (Worsley Mss. 24, pp. 183–4, Yarborough Collection, Lincs. Archives Office).

[10] Sir William Mansel (1739–1804), 9th bart., of Ischoed and Woodstone, at this time M.P. for Carmarthenshire.

to try to get the money if my Brother chose it, but that done, no consideration should keep him a moment in the country after the first ship was ready to sail. This money was some money which my Brother had sent him to change from Ducats into other money and which not being able to find chapmen for he had trusted the Admiralty with who were not able to pay it till a long time after they had engaged. /With this proposition/ My Brother, partly as a means of expediting payment,† but still more to get rid of a man who had worked himself into such a humour, afterwards closed. Since then not having been at Crichoff, nor he at Zadobras from whence I write, I have never set eyes on him.‡

As[11] to the servitude he complained of it consisted in his doing those little offices about a house for which he is but⊞ fit and for which he had himself sollicited, keeping keys, bottling of wine, a talent in which he valued himself, and the like. On the other hand he dined constantly at my Brother's table except when unknown to my Brother he chose to slip out of the parlour to go and dine in the kitchen with the /termagent English/ Housekeeper after the reconciliation of the original and most bitter enmity which had prompted him to supplant her in the power of the keys. A grievance which though /not/ much insisted upon weighs perhaps almost as much as any of the rest, is the name of *Starik* by which he is called. Starik means the old man, and is a term of respect rather than otherwise: just as Batushka, father is, an appellation by which an inferior addresses a superior though ever so much younger than himself. The same persons who have called him Starik /in speaking of him to my Brother/ have at the same time /spoken of him as/ the Colonel's Uncle: a notion my Brother has found pretty generally prevalent, and which may assist you in judging which is most likely that he has been oppressed with bad treatment or spoilt with good.

† [*In margin*]: Traligin[?] went with G.B. to Riga—came back tete a tete with Dr. D.

‡ [*In margin*]: He chose his own serjeant S.B. broke him so B. complains

⊞ [*Very illegible marginal note*]: Never declined anything except ordering her Brought her into the parlour to drink tea and Coffee to Officers never without entreaty.

Perfect master of the house command of everything and refused himself and her nothing Sent off Bell dressing nice cuts for themselves Sir disused in language and letters.

[11] This paragraph is scored through.

~~Among~~ /To/ the /male/ seducer ~~must no~~ I have mentioned I believe we must add another /at/ whose power you will be the less surprised when you learn that it was a ~~woman and she rather young than old though not~~ thing with a cap on and though none of the most beautiful yet rather under than above the middle age. In plain English a termagent Cook-Housekeeper, another pretty present of mine to my Brother, who had given me that commission and I was obliged to put up with Hopson's choice having little time to choose. Her tongue had made her the terror of all my Brother's people English as well as Russians, and of none more than old Benson, whose antipathy to her produced the only exception my Brother found to his obsequiousness: he would do any thing else but begged no commission or orders might be given him that would oblige him to communicate with her. My Brother used to rally /him/ sometimes, expressing his ~~wish~~ /regret/ that ~~a better understanding might~~ some sort of unison could not be established between them, no matter how cemented, as a means of taming her savage nature. Sure enough at last this union did take place, how cemented nobody knows, nor is it worth while to enquire. From that time every thing /belonging to her/ was angelical: an observation could not be made about the meats being done too little or too much but the blood would fly up into his face. No sooner was my Brother's back turned but he brought her into the parlour to dine: there the happy pair would feast upon the tid-bits: while another Englishman, a reputable master of a vessel who had been put to board at the Housekeeper's table was left to dine by himself on scraps and offals.

As to the servitude he complained of it consisted in his doing those little offices about a house for which he is best fit, and for which he had himself sollicited, such as keeping keys, bottling wine ~~and the like~~ a talent on which he had much valued himself, and the like: to the great displeasure of Mrs. Housekeeper whose unfitness he lost no occasion of holding up to view to justify his invasion of her province. His other business consisted in keeping the books,⊞ paying the workmen their wages, and now and then copying a letter or two for me or my Brother. All together /however took up so small a portion/ bore so small a proportion to his time,

⊞ as well as he could keep, which you may imagine were /not very/ but ~~indifferently~~ extraordinarily.

that ~~his great evil~~ as he has not the good fortune to have a turn for any kind of sedentary amusement his great evil, and even his great complaint was the want of occupation. With all this grievous servitude he has been more Master of the house my Brother says, than he himself has: having the command of every thing, and refusing ~~himself~~ nothing either to himself or since the coalition to the fair object of his regard. It now is beginning to come out that while they have their tea and coffee regularly officers find /have found/ a difficulty in procuring either, and that when my Brother /has been/ out of the way, hours incommodious to them have been chosen for meals that the Master and Mistress of the house might not be importuned with unwelcome company.

But enough of this tittle tattle. Let me add only one particular concerning which if you think it worth while to ~~be at the trouble of a~~ bestow a letter upon the subject my Brother would be glad to ~~recieve some information from you~~ be informed. Upon his mentioning t'other day his leaving some debts and his anxiety to clear them off, my Brother ~~asked him~~ took the opportunity of asking him what they might amount to. He answer'd £150. My Brother would be glad to learn what you know of that matter, as likewise as near as you can recollect, what sort of intimations you gave him of the advantage he might expect to reap by coming here. I am Dear Sir with the sincerest regard

etc. J.B.

581

To Jeremiah Bentham[1]

18/29 December 1786 (Aet 38)

The Cloth has all found Purchasers, and is packed up to be sent off: But the Scarlet is much complained of; It is said to be very thin, not Man's Cloth but Woman's Cloth. The Money is to be paid upon the delivery; and as soon as received we shall send it over to you. That however can hardly be these three months on account of the distance.

581. [1] B.M. XXII: 408. Copy in Jeremiah's hand with the heading: 'The following is a Copy of a Note inclosed in a Packet of Letters dated Critchoff 29/18 Dec. 1786 and received at Queen's Square Place 23d March 1787.'

For the purchase from England of this cloth see letter 565, and for the difficulties about collecting payments in Russia letter 574.

582

To Jeremiah Bentham[1]

18/29 December 1786 (Aet 38)

Crichoff Decr. 1786.

Hond. Sir

I think it was in August last that I wrote last to you.[2] The last I have of yours is dated so long ago as June 20th.[3] I fear, shall I say, or I hope that in the long interval some letter or letters may have been destined for us, and miscarried, as has been the case before. I wonder whether a small packet sent to Mr. Pole Carew /under your cover, by Sea/ in answer to his message through you ever came to hand.[4] If for some time past you should have thought me a scanty correspondent that will not be the case now: for besides this you will receive 20 letters at once. I am not yet quite decided whether to enclose them under this cover. On the one hand I could wish to save you the enormous expense of postage for what you may think not worth it. On the other hand as I send another copy to Mr. King I mean to double the chance of safe arrival by postponing one copy a post or two, and I have reasons for wishing that one might go to any other address than his. When first I sat down to write I intended but one letter, to which I intended no other publicity than what you might think fit to give it, by communicating it to your Brethren of the Magistracy for whose use it was designed. But when I came to see the extensive applicability of the idea, I saw no reason for confining the communication to any one set of men. I therefore send instructions to Mr. King for the publishing of his copy. But as the letters are addressed to you, I have

582. [1] B.M. IV: 314. Autograph. Docketed by Jeremiah Bentham: 'Fils Jeremy / Letter accompanying / a Plan of An Inspection / House or House of Correction / Dated Crichoff Decr. 18 1786 / Recd. at Q.S.P. 23d. March 1787.'

A fragment follows on the next folio (315), copied by Jeremiah Bentham:

Crichoff, White Russia Decr. 18–29. 1786.

I observed, t'other day, in the St. James Chronicle an Advertisement of a Pamphlet, on the Subject of a County Workhouse therein spoken of as projected for the County of Middle[sex]

It occurred to me that the Plan of a Building, lately contrived by my Brother for purpose in some respects similar and wch. under the name of the Inspection House or The Elaboratory He is about erecting here might afford some Hints for the above Establishment, I have accordingly obtained a Drawing which I here inclose.

Subsequently amended this formed the opening of letter I of *Panopticon* (Bowring, iv, 40).

[2] Letter 572. [3] Missing. [4] See letters 570 and 571.

no right to make any such use of your name without your leave. You will therefore stop the publication if you think proper or strike out any part in which you yourself are mentioned or alluded to. If you thought fit you might have stars in the room, or if the passage be long, give notice in a note of such erasure: or, if you thought it better you might say the manuscript was illegible, provided the words omitted were but few /but I hope and am pretty confident there is nothing in the letters that will incline you to make use of this power./ You will likewise make any addition by way of note or otherwise, which you may think proper, provided it be in your own name, or in the general name of the Editor. All I stipulate for is that I may not be made to say any thing that I do not say, however trifling the alteration, and how much better soever it might be than what I do say: for it would be impossible for you to judge at your distance, how far such alteration might quadrate with our views here. As some part of the letters bear relation to the subject of Penitentiary-houses, and I have not the Act that passed on that subject to turn to, only a copy of my own Views of the first H. Labour Bill, I have written to Mr. Wilson to beg of him, if he has leisure to add more notes, if necessary, by way of correcting any /erroneous or imperfect ideas/ which I may have given of the state of that concern.[5] I have likewise begged of him, if he thinks proper, to take upon him the office of Editor, for the purpose of correcting the press etc.: if not, it may as well go to Payne at once. I know not how far Mr. Wilson's avocations will permitt him to take any part in it: but if he should, you will I dare say have the consideration to take up as little of his time as possible with discussions relative to a subject which can not be expected to be so interesting to him as it is to Sam and me, and we flatter ourselves will be to you. Possibly, out of compliment to you, your brethren of the Magistracy might be for making it /their/ request to you that the letters may be printed: if so, there may be no harm in their understanding that the impression is in consequence of such request, nor in inserting the form of words in which they signify it. I will take care that any number of copies you please shall be at your command.

I received a kind letter t'other day from Alderman Clark[6] who informs me more particularly than the papers did of Far's marriage, but tells me that there has been scarce any intercourse between you and him for a long time, but without hinting at any assignable cause. In answer to what I had said to him in a letter which I told you of, intimating that I took for granted he saw all the letters to

[5] Letter 584. [6] Letter 575.

you which gave any account of my travels, he speaks as if he had seen but a part and that not without difficulty. Pray be so kind as to send him the whole bundle for a fortnight at least: you will not be the poorer. I must not neglect friends who have deserved well of me; if they can not get intelligence of me any otherwise than immediately from myself I must be obliged to write separate letters to them all, and consequently have so much the less time and the less matter to write to you. I think you got from Mr. Mulford a letter I sent him in continuation of the sort of sea-journal sent to you; continuing among other things the account of my stay at Fochia in the gulph of Smyrna:[7] that will I hope go to the Alderman with the rest.

Copy
To Mr. Rich. King

Sir

I enclose herewith some papers to the amount of 44 pages together with | | sheets of drawings, which I will beg the favour of you to deliver to Mr. Wilson, or if he should not be in London to Mr. Trail: or if neither of those gentlemen should be in town or soon expected, then to Mesrs. Payne with the letter on the other side. If Mr. Wilson or Mr. Trail return you the copy declining to have any concern in the publication, in that case also you will deliver the copy and letter to Mesrs. Payne. But if either of them accepts the trust, then you will deliver, to the person so accepting, the letter for Mr. Payne. By this same post or perhaps a post or two later I propose to send a fairer copy to my Father.

Copy
To Mesrs Payne Booksellers Mews Gate London.

Crichoff White Russia Decr. | | 1786

'Gentlemen Please to publish on my account the pamphlet herewith deliver'd, being a series of letters from me to my Father on the plan and uses of a newly-imagined kind of building called an Inspection-house. Number of copies, form, type, mode of printing, price etc. at your discretion: allowing my father to strike out any parts, or even stop the whole if he thinks proper: with liberty to him to take as many copies as he pleases, reserving however a hundred to be drawn for on my account by Mr. Richard King of the Six Clerks' Coffee House, Chancery Lane. Unless you advised otherwise,

[7] Letter 551.

I should be glad the paper were had at Mr. Chapman's and the printing performed by Mr. Hughs.'

As we can only afford one set of drawings, we send it you. You will do as you think best about the publication of it. The ground plan of the upper story of the Cells being somewhat different from that of the lower, my Brother had he thought of it in time would have represented the upper upon half the circle.

Copy of a memorandum I took of what I was told at an exhibition of the rejected plans for the Penitentiary-houses.

Sixty-five Plans were given in to the Supervisors: and of those rejected 15 were exhibited by subscription among the Authors. I forget what were the prizes given to those approved of. I believe £150 to the 1st, £100 to a 2nd, and £50 to a third. But I do not know whether there were 3 prizes or only 2.

Decr. 17. The day before yesterday Sam was obliged to set off for Cherson: but I expect him back in three weeks. Could he have staid a day longer we should have given you references in the drawings. But the Messenger who takes this as far as Riga can be kept no longer.

583

To Richard Clark[1]

19/30 December 1786 (Aet 38)

Crichoff Decr. $\frac{19}{30}$ 1786.

I. and S.B. to R.C.

We thank you much for your kind letter,[2] congratulate you on your increase of family, and hope to see Miss one of these days an Alderwoman as well as her Mama.

The main purpose of this letter is to tell you of my writing to Q.S.P. by this same post desiring him, pressing him, to let you have all my letters for at least a fortnight. Wilson of whom he is more jealous being in the same predicament as yourself with regard

583. [1] B.M. IV: 317–8. Autograph. Docketed: '30 Decr. 1786 / Messrs. J. & S. Bentham.'

Addressed: 'To / Mr. Alderman Clark / London.' Postmark: '1A/30'.

[2] Letter 575.

to the difficulty of getting a sight of those invaluables, I must beg you to cut him a week out of your fortnight if you get it. I mean to write to you but shortly: having occasion to write long letters by this same conveyance to Wilson as well as to Q.S.P. about ~~a pamphlet~~ a series of letters of mine to Q.S.P. /about an invention of Sam's/ which may possibly see the press. Wilson I dare say will either shew you my letter to him or give you a full account of the contents. If he should not shew it you you will not be surprised, as I don't know that the contents will be confined solely to my own affairs and Sam's. If the thing is printed, you will have a copy sent you, that is to say, may it please your worship I sollicit with all respect your worship's acceptance of a copy.

Major Semple took in every body at Petersburgh except Sam who suspected him from the first and cautioned Sir J. H. against him but in vain.[3]

It is not impossible that you may have seen all the letters of mine which Q.S.P. had at the time, for though long /in general/ they have not been numerous. As to making it matter of favour, you know that is his way in every thing: the legal right must be in him, neither is it in my power to *pluck* it out of him.

584

To George Wilson[1]

19/30 December 1786 (Aet 38)

Crichoff, December 19–30, 1786.

My dear Wilson.

Great comfort to get a letter from you at last;[2] but some chagrin to find I have been destroying the better part of my life, as you pretend to do your vacations. I had ordered horses for England, to take triumphant possession of the throne of Legislation, but finding it full of Mr. Paley, I ordered them back into the stable. Since then, I have been tormenting myself to no purpose, to find out some blind alley in the career of fame, which Mr. Paley's magnanimity may have disdained. After all, I have been obliged to go a-begging to my brother, and borrow an idea of his, which I have

[3] See letter 575, n. 8.

584. [1] Bowring, x, 165–8. B.M. IV: 319–20 is a copy of parts of this letter, docketed by Jeremiah Bentham: 'Fils Jeremy / Extracts of his letter to Mr. Wilson / Dated Crichoff Dec. 19/30 1786 / Reced. from Mr. Wilson 3d. March 1787.'

[2] Letter 576.

dressed up with a little tinsel of my own, and now send to London as a private venture *Parve, nec invideo sine me liber ibis in urbem.*[3]

I think the effect of your good advice to me, is—commonly much snarling and growling at first, and obedience at the last. You and Trail passed sentence on my Introduction to a Penal Code, *alias* Principles of Legislation, *alias* I don't know what besides, and there's an end of it. I think you have told me more than once, that if it were possible for my scrawl to be tolerable in any shape, it would be in that of letters. I have accordingly given that form to my twopenny-halfpenny pamphlet, consisting, I suppose, from 150 to 200 pages. The hero celebrated is our Sam: for the hero to be addressed, I have taken Q.S.P. as Boileau took his gardener. The origin of this choice was, that when I first sat down, I meant nothing more than a private, or, if you please, a semi-public letter, to be shown by him to anybody that would condescend to look at it: more especially his worshipful brethren, the Middlesex Justices, to whom it more particularly belonged, as you will see. As it grew upon me, your *dictum* confirmed me in my choice. Being a sort of Flying Castle, or, to speak more to the times, an air-balloon, it sweeps over all sorts of ground. Amongst the rest, it passes over the ruins of the poor old Penitentiary house. There I have occasion, or, perhaps you will say, no occasion, to fling a stone or two once more at Goliah Eden.[4] This you will be sorry for, as before, for the same reason that David's brethren were for David. On the other hand, if you happen to think any of them give him a twinge, you will be glad, because Goliah is a Philistine. There are great bets here which carries it—private friendship or party spleen: to be sure, what we should be glad to see, were it possible, is that they might shake hands and divide stakes. Now for a little job for you and (or) Trail, which I have taken care to leave you both at the most perfect liberty to take in hand, or let alone as you have a mind. I have not here the Penitentiary House Act which passed;[5] nor anything belonging to that affair, but my own view of the hard [6] Labour Bill. Consequently, I have been forced to proceed altogether upon the ground of the said View, whence divers undesigned misrepresentations may have arisen. What I want, is some charitable hand to take the Penitentiary Act, and, by a few notes at the bottom of the

[3] His Panopticon letters. The tag may be an adaptation from Martial's *Epigrams*: 'Vis commendari sine me cursurus in urbem, Parve liber, multis, an satis unus erit?' (III, V).

[4] I.e., William Eden.

[5] 19 Geo. III, c. 74.

[6] 'hard' in B.M. IV: 319–20. In Bowring, 'first', which is clearly incorrect.

page, correct such misrepresentation for the benefit of the unlearned reader. These notes might be prefaced and accounted for by some such advertisement as this:—'At the request of several of the Author's friends, one of them has added a few notes for the purpose of correcting some undesigned misrepresentations of the danger of which he was aware, but which the distance of his situation rendered unavoidable.' You may then disavow in what terms you please all combination and confederacy, etc. Treat me as cavalierly as you please, for which this shall be your sufficient warrant. If, in any shape, I have done said Goliah, or whom ever else it may concern, any injustice in point of fact or argument, redress the wrong, adding or not adding, that it was at my desire. If you and Trail want leisure, or resolution, turn the business over to anybody else that may vouchsafe to meddle with it. I avoid sending it to you, that if such should be your pleasure, you may avoid dirtying your fingers with it altogether. I send it to King, at the Coffee-house, with instructions to him to give you notice of its arrival, and make legal tender of it to you, or either of you, that you may do about it as you please. If, like old surly Northington, you please nothing, he will put it into Hughes' hands to print, and, I believe, into Payne's to publish. It remains for the learned to determine whether it were best in 8vo. form—for the faint chance of being bound up by a few people with the poor View of the Hard Labour Bill; or in 12mo., in which case it might make a bindable book of itself. Two or more architectural drawings will accompany it; but as they are mere outlines, anybody may execute them, and the expense can be but a trifle. Perhaps the publisher will manage that. Alderman Clark had once a protege in that line of the name of Sharp. If he is not dearer than other folks, which Payne, I suppose, could tell, if it were worth asking, which it hardly can be, this Sharp might as well be employed as anybody else....

If out of compliment to Q.S.P., the Justices should be for having it published, and signify their desire in proper form, I suppose there can be no harm in the printing of their order containing such desire....

Whether you take any part or no in the publication, tell me in due time, in perfect sincerity, what you think of it, as well of Sam's architectural idea as of the puffing and the collateral matter of all sorts which I have added to it; tell me also, as far as you can collect, what other people say of it, if they say anything. Perhaps, to give the thing two chances of arrival, I may take measures for the two copies being sent from Riga at a post or two's distance.

A possibility upon a possibility, is that we may pay England a visit in the course of the summer in a vessel of Sam's invention, manned by a part of his battalion. If so, it will be from Cherson, or a port in the Crim; and perhaps we may make a point of pushing for England without touching anywhere in the passage. In that case we want to know whether, plague or no plague in the Levant, we should be obliged to perform quarantine. You could tell us by looking into the acts, or otherwise. There is no knowing beforehand, whether it will bear the sea or no; but a small trial will soon show. Perhaps though it did not at first, it may at last. At any rate, it can scarce fail to be of use for inland navigation. We shall know, as soon as rivers are open, what it is worth; and if it answers expectation, we shall have to take out a patent for it in England, and I shall have a puffing pamphlet to write to show the advantages it has above all other vessels imagined or imaginable, from which it differs as much as a house upon the inspection principle (my string of letters will tell you what that means) does from common houses. If it ever reaches England by sea, it will be scarcely less of a raree-show than the air-balloons. If it bear the sea, and the event demonstrates the received theories to be just, it should go near to supersede all other sorts of vessels, and it would have the strangest consequences with regard to trade and politics. It has already been tried, and answered as far as it has been tried: doing in its infant state what no other vessel could have done. But a regular course of experiments, whereby alone can be taken the exact measure of its utility, in comparison with others, cannot be made till the rivers are open again: in the meantime, the great improvement has been hit on to which he trusts for its bearing the sea. In the meantime, he has *carte blanche* for maturing the experiment; and very busy a-building we are. It is very foolish for me to run on in this manner: but it would have cost me more pains to stop than it was worth being at. At any rate, I have given one—yes, two answers, amongst more that might be given to the question, what Sam is doing? Other inventions he has of the mechanical kind, some finished, some finishing, which, if he comes to England, may perhaps form part of his cargo.

You have received, I hope, a paper, which frightened, I suppose, the man that gave it you. I hope you quieted his fears. After one passage of it, the writer ought not by good rights to have sent it you, as he writes me word; but he tells me he had just received a kind letter from you, which made him sell his soul to the devil in hopes of pleasing you.[7]

[7] Not elucidated.

Q.S.P. is so jealous of you that I have no hopes of getting you a sight of my letters by scolding him for his backwardness with regard to you. But as Alderman Clark makes similar complaints, I shall beg of him to lend them to the alderman, and write the alderman to lend them to you.[8] I give Q.S.P. the power to prevent the publication altogether, or to add anything to it which he may choose to add, either in his own name, or in that of the editor; as likewise to strike out anything, either whole passages, or words, supplying the place with stars, or saying the manuscript was illegible in that part....

Of the accuracy of De Tott's account, I can tell you nothing certain. Some said that it was true, others that it was a lie, or exaggeration. I had no opportunity of cross-examining people. The diplomatic people and the Franks live very much among themselves, and have very little opportunity of knowing what is going forward among the Turks on the other side of the harbour. The account I could give you of the authenticity and verity of Habins' publication would be about equally satisfactory.

Major Beym[9] does not deserve the honour of your inquiries. He got at the time at least ten times the value of what he gave, and which he took care to set down to the public account. In the first part of his journey home, for instance, at Irkutsh, (where Sam heard of him, and drank some of the rum he had left there in presents,) he could not find terms to express his sense of the astonishing generosity of the English. As he advanced nearer Petersburg, his note lowered, till at last he came to complain of neglect and ingratitude. Sam, firing at this, sent him a message, recommending it to him to change his note back again, if he had not a mind to find himself contradicted to his face. Sam wrote particulars to Sir James Harris at the time; but his recollection of the matter is now very imperfect. Besides swords and watches, and other things, of which the value was known to the donors, he received those valuable sea beaver or otter skins, of which the value was not then so fully known, to the amount, as Sam thinks, of some hundreds; at any rate enough to make an ample fortune to him. Sam thinks he got, besides a gold snuff-box from Sir J. H., besides a magnificent piece of plate, with an inscription, which the Admiralty sent him, and which he offered to sell to Prince Potemkin, at whose house Sam saw it,—Sam thinks he got 600 of those skins; but does not pretend to any sort of certainty, except with regard to the general result.

[8] See letter 583. [9] See letter 576 at n. 17.

To speak seriously of Parson Paley, I should not have expected so much of him, from the account given of a part of the work in one of the nine reviews of Maty's, which I received by Trail's grace. People were surprised to see how green my eyes were for some time after I received your letter; but their natural jetty lustre is now pretty well returned.

You have no need to breed mischief in my family by pretending affection to Sam. He never rebels against my authority, but he takes credit for your alliance. He has cut out some of the best passages in my pamphlet, on pretence that you would have done so if you had been here. Hang it, I shouldn't care if you were, for you could not be a greater plague to me than you are now at fifteen hundred miles distant.

Sir R.W.[10] has a notion that Pitt means to reduce the rate of interest from five to four. Tell me what you hear about it; were it true I should like to give him a piece of my mind first. I have arguments against it *ready cut* and *dry*: the former epithet you may have some doubt about; the latter you will not dispute. You know it is an old maxim of mine, that interest, as love and religion, and so many other pretty things, should be free.

Code was going on at a very pretty jog-trot, till Sam's inspection-house came upon the carpet, not to mention his new model of ship-building, and his other whimsies. Fighting Sam and you together is bad enough, but correcting three copies taken by ignorant people is intolerable. In a few days I hope to return again to duty. The day has abundance more hours in it at Crichoff (or rather at our cottage three miles off, where I now live altogether) than anywhere in England. I rise a little before the sun; get breakfast done in less than an hour, and do not eat again till eight or nine at night. Trail with his three and a half lines is a shabby fellow, unworthy of my notice.—Sir W. Jones![11] how came he to return from the E.I.? Give me his history.

Could you get me any lights respecting the following points?—1. Expense of the ballast lighters per man, per annum. 2. Expense per man of the New Zealand expedition. 3. Expense per man per month in prison before sent there.

[10] Sir Richard Worsley.

[11] Sir William Jones (1746–94), the orientalist, who had been judge of the high court at Calcutta since 1783. This reference to him indicates that Bowring's text of letter 576 is incomplete.

585

To Trompovsky and Co.[1]

18/29 January 1787 (Aet 38)

Mess:rs

Je viens d'apprendre que M. Chr. Trompovski n'étoit pas à Riga quand le paquet que j'avois envoyé d'ici à son addresse (par un Serjeant de mon frère qui escorta M. Benson avec la servante) ainsi qu'une lettre détachée, y arriva. J'écris la prèsente pour vous prier au cas qu'il ne soit pas encore de retour d'expédier ici les choses que vous avez sous votre garde pour mon frère, avec la plus grande diligence, coûte qu'il coute. J'ai reçu une lettre de mon frère où il parle dans les termes les plus forts de la détresse où l'on se trouve à cause du retardement /si inespéré/ qu'a éprouvé ce convoi. Il se trouve de plus très embarassé faute de n'avoir encore reçu de votre maison le compte qui les regarde. /Je prie l'affairé ou autre personne quelleconque qui dans l'absence de M. Trompovski a la direction principale des affaires de la maison/, ~~Je vous prie aussi~~ d'ouvrir le paquet susdit pour en sortir des lettres qui s'y trouvent destinées pour la poste, à la réserve d'une addressé à M. Walter Shairpe à Petersbourg, laquelle, étant devenue inutile au moyen d'une autre que j'ai reçue de lui, peut être mise au feu. Je prie l'affairé ou autre personne quelleconque qui dans l'absence de M. Trompovski a la direction principale des affaires de la maison de vouloir bien prendre lui-même la peine d'ouvrir ce paquet, et de le refermer aussitôt sans rien dire de tout ce qui se trouve, avant d'en avoir parlé à M. Trompovski. Entre autres lettres pour l'Angleterre il se trouve un paquet bien gros addressé à *J. Bentham Esq.*, etc. à Londres, et un autre à *M. Rich. King* à la même Ville.[2] Si c'est M. Trompovski qui lit la presente, il aura la bonté de suivre les instructions ci-devant données à cet égard. Si non, je desirerois que celle pour *M. Bentham* fût expédieé par la première poste avec les autres lettres, à la reserve de celle pour M. King que je désirerois qu'on detînt une poste, ou même deux, si ce dernier servit le moyen de prendre la chance d'un autre paquebot que celui qui devra

585. [1] B.M. IV: 330–1. Autograph. Fair draft with a few corrections. Docketed by Bentham: '1787 Jan. 18–29 / J.B. Crichoff / to / Tromp. & Co. Riga / Also / March 24/4 A[pril] / Letter by S.B. / referring to this / pressing again for / the account desiring / it in 3 weeks at furthest / on account of intended / departure for Cherson / and mentioning the / non-arrival of the / Tea and Rice /.'

[2] I.e., the two copies of his Panopticon letters.

prendre la première lettre de la Hollande en Angleterre. La raison est, que ces deux lettres contenant des *duplicatas*, je voudrois doubler ainsi les chances de leur arrivée. Que si M. Trompovski étoit attendu bientôt à Riga je désirerois que la lettre pour M. King fut expédiée tout de suite, et que celle pour M. Bentham fut détenue à sa place (l'ayant laissé ouverte pour être vue de M. Trompovski) pourvu que la détention ne passât pas les deux postes. Quant à la petite lettre pour M. Trompovski qui accompagnera le gros paquet je prie celui qui lit la presente de l'ouvrir et d'en rendre public le contenu à sa discrétion, puisqu'il ne s'y agit que de ce M. Benson dont il peut importer que le caractère et les procedés soient connus.[3] Je vous prie de vouloir bien me donner une réponse au plutôt possible (Anglois ou François c'est égal) et de me croire

Mess:$_{rs}$
votre très humble Serviteur
Jérémie Bentham

Le Pr. P. a détenu jusqu'à présent mon frère, mais je l'attends à tout moment de retour de Cherson et de la Crimée.

Articles commissionés dans la lettre à M. Trompovski. Je vous prie de les joindre aux choses que nous attendons d'Angleterre, ou si celles-ci se trouvent déjà expédiées d'en faire un convoi séparé, et de l'expédier au plutôt possible.

Harengs cruds salés	1 barrique	On les attend à Cherson avec impatience à cause de l'arrivée de l'Imperatrice et que l'on en sache ici la prix lors de leur arrivée ou avant
Porter Anglois	1 barrique	
Bière Angloise	do.	

Thée Suchong	8, 9 ou 10 livres
Thée Verd	2, 3 ou 4 livres
Ris	½ poud ou 1 poud

1 Marteau pour accorder	pour le clavecin au cas qu'il n'y en a point déjà envoyés avec cet instrument.
1 suite de cordes	

To Mr. Trompovski

If you mean my Brother and I should see the Newspapers you must direct them to him. The Dr.[4] has had some this fortnight, but whether he means to let us see them is yet a matter of doubt.

[3] See letter 578.

[4] Dr Debraw.

586

To George Wilson[1]

9/20 February 1787 (Aet 39)

Zadobras, near Crichoff,
February 9–20, 1787.

My Dear Wilson,

In my last which went from hence the latter end of December,[2] but which I doubt was rather late in coming to you, I mentioned amongst other things a project of my brother's which, if successful, would require a patent, begging the favour of you to tell us whether a caveat would answer in any, and what respect, the purpose of securing to him the property of the invention in the meantime.[3] As it was necessary for him to send a model to Petersburg, we find it is beginning to make a noise: and there are various channels through which the idea seems likely to have already reached England in its unfinished state. We have, therefore, judged it advisable, to run the hazard of the post, for the sake of giving you a general intimation of it, under the notion that some such intimation may be necessary for the purpose of taking out a caveat, which, if it will answer the purpose, we will beg the favour of you to get taken out as soon as possible. The single word *vermicular*, is sufficient to give a general idea of a leading principle. The vessel consists of a string of barges to any number, each individually of the simplest construction, and capable of being connected or disconnected at pleasure. The modes of connexion have given a good deal of exercise to his invention: for inland navigation there is but little difficulty: any mode almost will do; but the difficulty lays in adapting it to sea service—a difficulty which, though he believes everybody in England who knows any thing of what sea is, will look upon it as insuperable, he is not without hopes of overcoming. Two barges upon this principle, the one of three smaller links and the other of five larger ones, were built and made use of in the course of last summer. The former was used only in plying about upon this river, from one part of our dominions to another. But the larger was sent down from our Soz (Soje) into the Dnieper, and so down as far as Kremenschuk, (about

586. [1] Bowring, x, 168–71.

[2] Letter 584.

[3] The reference to the caveat was omitted from Bowring's text of letter 584, nor was it included in the extracts which Wilson supplied to Jeremiah Bentham (B.M. IV: 319–20).

midway between Kiev and Cherson,) about 800 or 1000 miles. Laying out of the account stoppages, which the business required to be made at different places, the voyage was performed in eighteen days, a degree of expedition much exceeding anything that had ever been known. Sam and I, and Sir R. Worsley,[4] went down in it about one hundred versts, (sixty or seventy miles.) According to the received theories, the length of a vessel makes no difference in the resistance it meets with in pushing through the water. This, I suppose, may hold good with regard to the greatest differences in point of length, that can ever subsist upon the present plans: if it hold good in strictness, and with regard to any length, the velocity might be increased to infinitum, by adding sails and oars, so that you might get a boat, which, like Jupiter, would require but four efforts to get from one end of the world to the other. Back-breaking, which is the death of so many vessels upon the ordinary plans, is prevented, you see, by the division of the whole into *vertebræ*, as short as can be required. The mode of connexion thought of for the sea is now practising upon a vessel which, under the name of the Imperial Vermicular, is building here, for the faint chance of her majesty taking a fancy to set foot in it. A barge has been built for her at Smolensko, and another for the emperor, and sent down to Kieff; but they are so clumsy, that there are great doubts whether they will be deemed fit for service. In this imperial vermicular, the joint is such as to render the vessel flexible in all directions: the tail (stern) of each intermediate link is concave and adapted to a corresponding convexity in the head (stem) of the link behind.

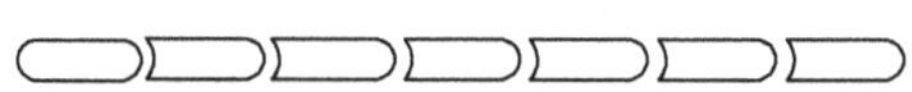

The enabling them to play up and down as well as laterally, is performed by a contrivance which I am not able to describe without drawings, and which would be difficultly apprehended without a model. Suffice it to say, that by means of an iron bar playing upon rollers in a horizontal groove, the links are kept from striking one against another, at the same time that they are capable of being allowed to pitch and roll in every direction. This has the inconvenience of requiring some good carpenter's, as well as smith's work. Upon further reflection, my brother has conceived what he looks

[4] Sir Richard Worsley had spent a month at Krichëv during the summer of 1786. Of the trip down the Sozh, made on 13 August, he noted only that it was made on a barge of 'new construction'. It is probable that Samuel Bentham had pledged him to secrecy about his new invention. The current carried the vermicular along at about five versts an hour (Worsley Mss. 24, pp. 183–4, Yarborough Collection, Lincolnshire Archives Office).

upon as a more commodious mode of connexion, as well as more secure mode of fastening by nothing but ropes and wood; and the convex and concave terminations which required some work, he now looks upon as unnecessary, even for sea service. He is accordingly building two other vermiculars, which are nothing but a parcel of oblong boxes, such as every one can work at who is capable of handling an axe—that is, every man in Russia. As such a vessel cannot be governed by the tail, it must be governed by the head, and the head link is accordingly adapted to that purpose. There are other contrivances for rendering the serpent flexible or inflexible at any joint, as occasion may require. The above-mentioned are on Sam's own account. The prince's peasants are just about to be set to work upon a vermicular of a hundred links, which, if it has so many, will be just a verst—that is, two-thirds of a mile long. This is to fetch Crimean salt from Kremenschuk, to which place it is hindered by waterfalls from getting all the way from the Crim by water. Another, of a few solid links, is to try the experiment of sending wood to the Crim, where it bears an immense price: the timber alone costing more than the ship it is destined for would cost when completely built at Petersburg. Timber, at present, travels very expensively and awkwardly by sea. Sam flatters himself that his mode of navigation will admit of a considerable saving in the article of men in comparison with the common one, as well as in the articles of workmanship and materials. When you go over as Judge to the E. Indies, let him have the honour of building a vermicular for your conveyance. Should it be a calm, he'll row you all the way faster than the wind could blow you. I wish I could know, for example, what the ordinary rate of expedition is at present in the London fish trade, and what advantage would be likely to be had, if that rate could be increased in any given degree, for example, doubled. I believe, at present, the fishing smacks are stopped every now and then at Gravesend waiting for the tide. A vermicular shall catch them for you out at sea, and row them up to Oxford, dropping a link wherever there is a market. I doubt they will smell rather strong at that rate before they come to the end of their voyage, unless one can persuade them to live a little while in a cage with or without fresh water. I will leave it to your imagination to extend the idea to the thousand applications, belligerent as well as pacific, to which ours extended it some months ago. We intend you for the command of an expedition to storm Paris with; and pray do not let a foolish tenderness prevail with you to leave anything there alive. You will conclude for or against the patent according as you think it more likely to do good by securing the invention in this unformed state, or harm by publishing it. Mr. Williams, Alderman Clark's partner, has taken out patents: if the connexion still subsists, nobody better. I have all along understood that the taking out a caveat costs but a guinea; but this, I suppose, does not include the solicitor's fee. A few words, I imagine, is all that is necessary, or even usual; just enough to serve as an index to the invention.

I am grudging every instant of the time I am fooling away in writing stuff and nonsense to you, and the much greater time it takes me to consider which I shall say to you of the thousand things I should have to say to you if it took up no time. I am writing letters to *you* abusing Pitt for being about to reduce the rate of interest, and abusing the world for limiting the rate of interest at all.[5] I am marginal-contenting[6] *Essai sur les Recompenses*[7] about the size of Beccaria's book, with Voltaire's Comment added to it. It was begun to serve as one of the divisions of my great French work; but I found it detachable, so I swelled it out a little, and send it you to do what you will with it. It touches upon all the possible applications of the matter of reward, ordinary and extraordinary. I want the Report of the Commissioners of Accounts bitterly; but want must be my master. I pull down the church in it *inter alia*; but the church will have been settled, as well as the rate of interest reduced, before it gets to England. All I have to say on the civil branch of law is marginal-contented and ready for reading, were you but here. It is a preceding introductory book. There is a Frenchman of the name of Allix,[8] whose business it is to teach French. Alderman Clark, by whose means I knew him once, knows, I suppose, where to find him. Him I should like to have to correct the press, and expunge solecisms. A parson would not do, because perjury subscriptions are abused, and the emoluments of ecclesiastics reduced to what they themselves set them at by Curacies. If Hughes' correctors understand accents and so forth, as a Frenchman would, I would take my chance for solecisms, if such a thief as Allix could not be had for the value of five guineas. I mention Allix thus early, because his lodgings may perhaps be unknown to the Alderman by this time, and it may take some time to find him out.

I am distracted to know what to do about staying here or

[5] A reference to the gestation of the *Defence of Usury*.

[6] A reference to Bentham's practice of running an abridgement along the margins of his works.

[7] The material which became the *Rationale of Reward*.

[8] Not identified.

returning. Here I can work double tides; but every now and then I am non-plussed for want of books. London is infested with devils. If I knew of any such lodging-place as Thorpe, where I could be *perdu* till my book was printed, without being known to anybody to be in England, besides you and Trail, and honest Mr. R. King, whom I could depend upon for not betraying me, it might be a means of my returning sooner than I should otherwise. I would change my name and pass for a madman, or a bankrupt. I can sleep without a bed, and live without victuals. The only article of luxury I should be puzzled by the want of, is a two-legged animal who lies down without a bed by the fire and keeps it in all night, with power for me to get up at any time and kick him out of the room. A rush-light, with a fire ready laid in my bed-chamber, would be but an indifferent *succedaneum*.

Pray get from R. King a packet containing securities of mine: open it and give me a list of them, (there are but few,) and keep them in your custody. In particular, tell me whether amongst them is a Tontine *debenture* on my life, and whether it appears therein up to what time the interest has been received.

This day three weeks the empress passed through Crichoff, in her way to Kieff. Besides Russians, there were F.[9] H., and the French and Imperial Ministers. Lord Carysfort[10] was not of the party, as was expected. Poor F., who is ailing, having got something the matter with his liver, was sadly sick of the excursion. The same company, the same furniture, the same victuals: it is only Petersburg carried up and down the empire. Natives have too much awe to furnish any conversation: if it were not for the diplomatic people, she would have been dead with ennui. Dr. Rogerson, the E.'s physician, attended her of course: no other Englishman of the party except a young officer, adjutant to one of the generals. Five hundred and fifty, I think, was the complement of horses provided here. The most extraordinary part of the cavalcade were no fewer than thirty washerwomen. A large wooden house, under the name of a palace, had been built here as at every other station, for the purpose of furnishing her a night's lodging. Sam was not in the way, being then upon an expedition about the vermicular business to Cherson and the Crim, from whence he returned but Saturday. Neither was the

[9] F. signifies Alleyn Fitzherbert, the British minister at St Petersburg. H. is not identified: it is possible that Bowring has here incorrectly represented part of a contraction of Fitzherbert's name.

[10] John Joshua Proby (1751–1828), 2nd Baron Carysfort, a budding diplomat. He later became British minister at Berlin in 1800 and acted unofficially at St Petersburg in 1801.

prince,—for it was he that Sam was dancing after. Sam saw some of them in his way home through Kieff. I was, of course, much inquired after, which I chose rather to be than seen: being at the farm here a few miles from Crichoff, I escaped regal notice. The streets through which she passed were edged with branches of firs and other evergreens, and illuminated with tar barrels, alternating with rows of lamps, formed by earthen-pots filled with tallow and a candle-wick in the middle. So I was told, for I had not curiosity to go to Crichoff, either before or after, nor have I been through these three months.

God love you. Answer this as soon as you receive it, and tell me the news, particularly what projects of all kinds are said to be in agitation.

587

From George Wilson and James Trail[1]

26 February 1787

You have now made a reasonable visit to your brother, and on your own account you are doing nothing there which may not be done at least as well here. I have, therefore, some hope that you will be induced to return by a shorter and more certain mode than that of your intended ship. It is not because Trail and I disapproved, that you abandoned your Introduction, your Code, your Punishments, etc. The cause lies in your constitution. With one-tenth part of your genius, and a common degree of steadiness, both Sam and you would long since have risen to great eminence. But your history, since I have known you, has been to be always running from a good scheme to a better. In the meantime, life passes away and nothing is completed. I don't know why I talk thus, unless, because at this distance I may do it with safety; for, except the satisfaction of discharging so much spleen, I expect no good effect from it. I do very much wish, for many reasons, that you would come home; and am sincerely of opinion that your worldly interest absolutely requires it. If your father should not be wrought on to alter his will, there is great danger of his squandering his fortune. I understand, that not long ago he purchased a house for Mrs. B. to live in, after his death, which house they are now tired of, and

587. [1] Bowring, x, 171–2. Fairly certainly incomplete. The first passage indicates that this is a reply to letter 584.

want to sell. He is just now beginning a great building in his court, to look into the park, everything being down except the screen. In short, there are new whims every day, and all of them expensive. [*A paragraph added by Trail*]

I join most sincerely in Wilson's entreaties, that you would return soon to this country; and for other reasons besides the very weighty ones which he has mentioned. Our ministers, as they have little to do abroad, seem to be full of schemes for domestic improvement. Pitt has just introduced a plan for consolidating the customs, and which he is to extend to the excise and stamp duties.[2] The state of the poor laws has excited a good deal of attention. Gilbert, who has undertaken to reform them, is utterly incapable; but the information he has been enabled by the legislature to collect, may be useful to wiser heads.[3] The Protestant dissenters are at work to get the Test Act repealed, and they entertain good hopes of success. Fox, and other leading men, have promised their assistance. Pitt owes so much to the dissenters, that he cannot oppose the measure.[4] The people are certainly become more enlightened in their notions on commercial subjects. The French treaty is not only popular among those classes of manufacturers who expect to derive immediate benefit from it; but it is generally approved of throughout the nation.[5] Lord Lansdowne sometimes says it is a pimping imitation of one of his great schemes—at others, that it is a very good treaty—and then, again, that it is a ruinous measure. I have heard nothing of late about reducing the interest of money. Soon after the conclusion of the war, it was a subject of conversation; and the landed gentry, who had found great difficulty in borrowing even at five per cent., were said to be very anxious to have the rate reduced. But since it has fallen of itself, and may be expected to sink still more, I think the subject has died away.

[2] This long overdue reform in the financial administration came into effect in May 1787 under the Act 27 Geo. III, c. 13 (see J. E. D. Binney, *British Public Finance and Administration, 1774–1792*, Oxford, 1958, pp. 109–10).

[3] Thomas Gilbert (?1719–98), M.P. He was the author of an important poor law reform Act in 1782, and he continued, both in parliament and by the medium of pamphlets, to campaign for further improvements in this branch of administration.

[4] The proposal for repeal of the Test Act in favour of Protestant Dissenters was made in the House of Commons on 28 March 1787 and was supported by Fox, but not by Pitt since he felt that, as the king's minister, he could not do so without the approval of the bishops, whose advice was sought and given in the negative. Three further attempts in the ensuing three years were also unsuccessful (Stanhope, *Life of William Pitt*, 4 vols., London, 1861, i, 336–8; B. L. Manning, *The Protestant Dissenting Deputies*, edited by O. Greenwood, Cambridge, 1952, pp. 217–18.).

[5] The Anglo-French commercial treaty negotiated by William Eden in 1786. For the mixed public reaction to it see John Ehrman, *The British Government and Commercial Negotiations with Europe, 1783–1793*, Cambridge, 1962, pp. 62–6.

588

To Charles Brown[1]

early March 1787 (Aet 39)

Zadobras $\frac{\text{Feb.}}{\text{March}}$ 1787

Dear Sir

~~About the latter end~~ Some time in of Decr. went from hence a letter of mine to you mentioning /amongst a variety of other things/ Benson and his discontents; requesting the favour of you at the same time to state what you know of his debts, and /what you recollected/ of the expectations you held out to him as inducements for coming here. The paper in the margin of which I am writing, and which contains literal copies of two letters of his to my Brother and one of my Brother's to him will speak for themselves. My Brother, the day or the day after he wrote his, set off for Cherson, without having seen Benson as you may imagine.

After his receipt of my Brother's letter, his behaviour as I understand from ~~half a dozen~~ several witnesses was like that of a man ~~escaped~~ /broke loose/ from Bedlam. All the execrations, all the terms of ~~reproach~~ /abuse/ the language furnishes, were bestowed /not only/ upon my Brother but upon me, who had never /seen him nor/ interchanged a line with him since the conversation mentioned in my last—'My Brother did not love the smell of powder: he would follow him /to Cherson/ and call him to account—he would go to the Prince, and make complaint against him: he would go to the Empress—he would go to Mr. Pitt, and complain of me. He would publish every thing he knew of ~~both~~ the letters and all other concerns of us both.' (With all this madness, ~~packing up~~ filling his trunks without witnesses, and cramming every thing into them that he ~~took his fancy~~ /thought proper; such as sheets and bedding and I dont know what besides: for he had been ~~for he had the keys of every thing~~ used to have the keys of every thing and you know yourself the bare condition in which he came/: refusing for a long while to give up Things that had been lent him, and conveying his packages out of the house at night /as it were/ by stealth. When they had been a whole night at his friend the Drs., then he was

588. [1] B.M. IV: 339–40. Draft, mainly in Jeremy Bentham's hand, but with one or two notes by Samuel. This forms a sequel to letter 580. See also letter 578.

ready to have them searched by any honest man: by which, as he declared, he meant to exclude every one of the English here. My Brother, you will observe, all this while on his journey. I, three miles off at Zadobras. But from the reports made me, I expected for some time I should have had my life to defend.)[2] against a man to whom I had never given the shadow of an offence.

For some days he persisted in declaring his resolutions of following my Brother to Cherson: but as his fair friend was bound for Riga, it was prophesied that that attraction would prevail, and so it proved. He set off with her about ten days after my Brother's departure.

You will observe that in his /first/ letter, though full of ill humour [*some words crossed out*] he does not so much as pretend any cause of complaint against my Brother. No more has he ever, by word of mouth. His only grievance was, /as you will see,/ an expression charged upon me, and which I have a notion did once fall from me amongst many more expressions of regard in speaking of him to his friend the Dr. If I do not misrecollect, it is a pretty exact copy of an expression of yours applied to the same subject. He had taken care, however, before he wrote that letter to take the fullest vengeance which his tongue would enable him to take of any injuries he might have received. He ~~told the English here~~ gave people here to understand in the most express terms that my Brother's affairs here were in a bankrupt state, advising them to look to themselves and to get what they could of him as fast as possible: and my Brother found that he had given similar accounts to all his friends to whom his recommendations /and countenance/ had procured him access. The cloth you find alluded to was some cloth /to the amount of between 5 and 600 £s worth/ which my Brother had got over from England upon his credit, in the view of putting a little money into Benson's pocket,[3] and if ~~the first experiment succeeded~~ he found it likely to answer making it the ground of a trade which might serve in time to set him upon his own legs. A rough sort of calculation was made according to which my Brother was to receive such a price to indemnify him for the freight, duty, carriage and all other expences, and all above that was to be Benson's own, he not standing to any of the risk. I forget what it was computed his profit would amount to: I think something nearer fifty than forty pound.

[2] Alongside in the margin Samuel wrote: 'All within the brackets may be left out as conveying suspicions too harsh to be expressed without proof, however much appearance favours.' The rest of the sentence is added in the margin.

[3] See letter 565 and n. 4.

Customers were accordingly found for it at /the price proposed/ amongst my Brother's friends. When my Brother came to speak with them, he found that Benson before he set off for Riga had written them letters, telling them the cloth was his, and forbidding their paying for it to my Brother.

In addition to the ~~other sums~~ 200 Roubles mentioned in ~~my Brothers~~ this letter of my Brothers to him and the 50 Roubles he had to pay for him to Col. Korsakoff,[4] I find he has received on my Brothers account the following sums:
1785

May 3	Advanced by J.B. in discharge of	Mrs. Brown's draught—	18 .. 12
20	By	do. in London as by G.B.'s receipt—	6 .. 8
31	By	do. as per do. . . . —	13 .. 0
			38

This is exclusive of his expences from Riga to Crichoff and ~~I believe~~ /if I am not mistaken of the 10 guineas which/ of his expences from London to Riga he acknowledges besides 10 Roubles laid out for articles of dress at Riga the second time of his being at Riga and I think my Brother says he spent other money of his besides in the same way /of which 90 roubles appear in the books which B. set down against himself/[5] but of this I am not sure. Since his arrival at Riga he has transmitted a more particular account of the R. 300: how far it is satisfactory to my Brother I do not know as since his return from Cherson and the Crim where he ~~went with unexpected~~ /had a long/ while to dangle after the Prince the little time we have had together has been taken up by subjects of more immediate necessity.

~~I now close~~ From what you have heard of the old man's language concerning my Brother before the ~~quarrel~~ breach, you /may/ judge what it is now at Riga.

I now close this disagreable subject, remaining ever with the truest regard

Dear Sir

I don't know whether it is worth adding that for some time before the date of this letter of his he had so far forgot the good advice you gave him as to omitt in his letters those customary forms of

[4] Probably Lieutenant Colonel Nikolay Ivanovich Korsakov (1749–88).
[5] This insertion is in Samuel's hand.

respect which even ~~among~~ as between equals nothing short of the most perfect familiarity ever dispenses with.

Note the effect of the footing on which he was received by ~~any~~ persons in authority at different places through my brother's recommendation some of whom having the title of *Prince* contributed not a little to turn his brain.

My Brother thinks it was the countenance shown him by

P.S. My Brother who has read over this at Critchoff sends it me back with the following note on a passage on the first page.

I answer, that I should not imagine his having taken any thing to signify to which he could not bring himself to fancy he had something of a title. But not only bedding but sheets and towels he certainly took away without asking leave as I was told by plenty of witnesses. His pretence would be that they were what he used and had ~~been sufferd~~ to put his mark in without any notice having been taken of it.

589

From George Wilson[1]

24 April 1787

I have received your two letters of the 9–20, February and March.[2] Why the first was enclosed to your father, you best know. The consequence of it was, that after keeping it a week, he sent me, not the letter, but information that he had it, for the purpose of obliging me to open it in his presence. I was accordingly obliged to read great part of it to him, and had much difficulty to conceal the rest. But reading it is not enough. I have been forced to promise to copy for him all I have read; and the copy he will put in a book which he has entitled *Epistolœ Benthamianœ*, consisting of your letters and Sam's, mixed up with his to Lord Lansdowne, Alderman Clark, Dr. Brown, etc., and their answers.[3] He was much offended at having himself no letter in that packet of a later date than December, which should, indeed, have been a reason with you for not enclosing mine to him. But his anger as to this point, seems to have subsided since the receipt of your letter of March.[4] He has at

589. [1] Bowring, x, 172–3.

[2] The first of the two letters mentioned is letter 586. The other is missing.

[3] This is now B.M. XXII. This letter did not get transcribed in it.

[4] Missing. Only the cover of Jeremiah Bentham's copy of this letter is now known to exist. It was later used for the draft of one of Jeremiah Bentham's business letters (B.M. IV: 341).

last given me a reading of the collection of your letters, which are entertaining, and in many parts interesting; but I think in other parts, it appears that you were working hard to make out a letter which you had no pleasure in writing. With respect to your inspection pamphlet, he seems inclined, since your last letter, to publish it, but with his own corrections and alterations, which are to be communicated to me to-morrow. I shall endeavour to delay the publication till the arrival of your answer to my letter of 27th February.[5] I hope you have since received one from Trail and me, of about the 12th March. We are so well convinced from this experiment, of the difficulty of publishing for an author at such a distance, on account of the alterations which even the lapse of time may make necessary, to say nothing of other circumstances, that we are resolved, I mean Trail and myself, to have no concern in the publication of any other work which you may think proper to send over. We have another reason for this resolution, and that is, that being fully convinced of the necessity of your return, for the reasons mentioned in our two last letters, and which still subsist, we think it fair to use this species of distress which accident has put into our hands. It gives us great pleasure to learn that you have so many things in forwardness; and we think the subjects are such as will do you credit, but we are not quite reconciled to the French language, or the form of letters. As to the rate of interest, no proposal has been made in Parliament to reduce it, nor have we been able to learn that any such intention has been entertained by Mr. Pitt, or any other great man; so that whatever applies to the alteration, as to this time particularly, you will have to alter. This circumstance alone, might satisfy you of the advantage of being on the spot, if you write on subjects relating to this country. I think you had your intelligence from Sir R. Worsley. The subject of interest, is, however, of great importance at all times; and you can say a great deal about it which has never yet been said. It is at all times sufficiently in people's minds to make it interesting; and perhaps new doctrines concerning it, will have more weight that they do not appear to be published on the spur of the occasion. We are, therefore, very desirous that you should publish, but not till after your return.

[5] Wilson here referred to letter 587, which, in the only text available, Bowring's, is dated 26, not 27 February. The reference to 'reduction of the rate of interest' in letter 592 shows that Bentham had received that letter, but in the text of letter 592 as preserved by Bowring he made no rejoinder on this point. Wilson's and Trail's letter of 12 March (see next sentence) is missing. Possibly it gave rise to the third paragraph of letter 593.

I have little news to write; and if I had, perhaps I should withhold it, by way of an additional distress. But, to use the words of a great author—'it is a busy age, and everything teems with improvement.'[6] Our Customs are consolidated, and in three weeks our ports will be open to the French. The crownlands are in a way of being sold. Great materials have been collected for a revision of the Poor Laws, which, in other hands than Mr. Gilbert's, might be turned to profit. The House of Commons have given a great blow to the ecclesiastical courts; and I think people begin to be more and more convinced of the mischief of tithes.[7] Indeed, on all points of political economy, there is an evident change in the public opinion within these ten years, which may be in some degree owing to the circulation of Smith's book, but still more to the events which have happened in our political and commercial connexion with America, to the utter disgrace of all the old thrones. In Ireland, there are great schemes of police going on, and a new system of education just announced in a long speech by Mr. Orde;[8] and all this time you are living in a cottage in White Russia, ignorant of everything that is passing in the world, unless when Sir R. Worsley gives you some misinformation. The dissenters have failed in their attempt to get the Test Act repealed, but the division was respectable, and they are not discouraged. They are very angry with Pitt, whom they will probably no longer support as they did at the general election. Priestley has written him a letter, a printed one, I mean, full of rage against Pitt, the Trinity, and the Church Establishment—clever enough, and very bold, but very indiscreet, and certainly prejudicial to the cause.[9] They are founding a college at Hackney, which is to rival and overthrow Oxford, and Cambridge; but I fear they have

[6] Wilson paraphrases the opening sentences of the Preface to Bentham's *Fragment on Government:* 'The age we live in is a busy age, in which knowledge is rapidly advancing towards perfection. In the natural world, in particular, every thing teems with discovery and with improvement' (Bowring, i, 227). On the public events referred to in the following lines see the notes to letter 587.

[7] A Bill for the prevention of vexatious suits in ecclesiastical courts was going through its stages in the House of Commons during April 1787 (*The Parliamentary Register*, xxii (1787), 59–60, 90–1, 127–32).

[8] The speech outlining proposals to foster education in Ireland made by Thomas Orde, chief secretary to the Lord Lieutenant, on 12 April 1787, is reported in *The Parliamentary Register: or, History of the Proceedings and Debates of the House of Commons of Ireland*, vii (1787), 486–96. Although the scheme was approved, the death of the Lord Lieutenant, the Duke of Rutland, and the withdrawal of Orde, caused it to lapse (W. E. H. Lecky, *A History of Ireland in the eighteenth century*, 5 vols., 1913, ii, 512–14).

[9] Joseph Priestley, *A Letter to the Right Honourable W. Pitt... on the subjects of toleration and Church establishments: occasioned by his speech against the Repeal of the Test and Corporation Acts... the 28th of March 1787*, London, 1787.

not heads to effect that good work.[10] They are violent zealots in their way; and one article in the constitution of the new college, is, that all the professors shall be dissenting parsons. Several eminent men among them have refused to subscribe on account of that clause. I know nothing of the history of the late transactions in France; but we are told that their land-tax is to be given up, and that at present, all credit, public and private, is at a stand.[11] Not being a citizen of the world, I hear the miscarriage of improvements in France with great philosophy. There is a navy officer, whose name I forget, who has invented a pump which works by the motion of the ship, without men, and he is now gone out in a frigate to try it. Notice is given by Mr. Minchin, of a motion with respect to the criminal law.[12] Our fleet for Botany Bay, is, I hope, sailed to-day—they waited for a wind, and it is fair. Your father has heard of an *Atlas de Commerce*, by Le Clerc, Père and Fils, and a book of maps of Russia, etc., published last year in France, which are said to have great merit, and he is trying to get you a copy.

590

To William Pitt[1]

late April 1787 (Aet 39)

Krichoff 1787

Sir

I suppose you may have received before now a /printed/ copy of my Brother's letters on the subject of a particular kind of building contrived by me for the purpose of keeping persons of any

[10] Hackney College was founded in 1786 to meet the needs caused by the closing of Hoxton Academy in the previous year. In 1787 it was established in permanent quarters at Hamerton Hall. It lasted until 1796 (H. McLachlan, *English Education under the Test Acts*, Manchester, 1931, pp. 246–55).

[11] The reference is to the abortive proceedings of the French Assembly of Notables (February–April 1787), which refused to avert national bankruptcy by accepting wider systems of taxation and the abandonment of aristocratic privileges of exemption.

[12] Humphrey Minchin (c. 1727–96), M.P. He gave notice of his motion on 4 April; but when he moved for leave to bring in a Bill on 27 April, Pitt suggested delay till more parliamentary time was available and the motion was withdrawn.

590. [1] B.M. IV: 442–3. Autograph. Docketed by Bentham: '1787 / Panopt / J.B. Crichoff / to Hon. W. Pitt London / Not sent / First intended proposal.'

The three material pieces of information which give some indication of the possible date of this draft are: (1) Bentham sent the copies of the Panopticon letters to Riga for onward transmission to England towards the end of December 1786 (letter 582);

description under the eye of an Inspector. Lest you should not, I have directed another copy to accompany this ~~letter~~ address.

Since then my Brother's ideas of the advantage with which the principle might be applied to Penitentiary-houses or other prisons, an application which /otherwise/ would hardly have attracted my attention, has so far operated on my mind, that if any such use should be thought of being made of it in England, I could almost wish to lend my hand to the accomplishment of such a business.

/If I do not deceive myself/ The reception given to some late successful projects seems to hold out to the nation /a general assurance/ that while power remains in the hands it is in at present, novelty will not be a conclusive objection to any plan which appears to have utility to recommend it. If in your judgement this of mine comes /should come/ under that description, and it appears /should appear/ to you that, as to so much of it as relates to the disposal of Convicts, /the execution of/ it would stand any the better chance /of success/ for being in the hands of the contriver for the execution of it being put into the hands of the contriver, the satisfaction of putting ~~to the test of experience~~ my own pretty sanguine conceptions to the test of experience, would be a powerful temptation to me to engage in an undertaking, of which, if crowned with success, the utility might be render'd so extensive.

Inventions in the mechanical line, of which, such as they are, I have some stock, are my chief amusement here; and the opportunities, which my situation affords me, of carrying them into practise, form one of the principal ties which attach me to this country.

In the course of these amusements, the nature and circumstances of some of the people I have to deal with has led me to pay a particular attention to the means of making work go forward in ~~unskilfull~~ unexperienced or otherwise unskilfull hands; in which view various mechanical contrivances have occurred to me adapted to the several natures of the different kinds of work. This circumstance forms the ground of a conception I am disposed to entertain, of being able to ensure a comfortable subsistance to any such convicts

(2) Samuel parted from Bentham at Propoysk on his way to south Russia on 22 April/3 May 1787 (letter 591); (3) on 25 May/5 June 1787 Bentham wrote to his father asking him not to let the letters go to press till he returned to England (letter 593). The most likely date for this draft seems to be after sufficient time had elapsed to enable the letters to get to England and be sent to press and before Samuel left for Kherson. The draft is in Bentham's hand but was intended for Samuel, and it seems likely that it may have been discussed between them. Accordingly this draft is placed at the end of April, but it might have been drawn up at any time between January and May.

as might be disposed to embrace it after the expiration of their terms.[2]

With these views I think I could content myself to exchange the command of an independent Batallion of 900 honest Russian soldiers, who in the natural course of things must shortly be augmented to a Regiment of 2000, for that of even a smaller number of British malefactors: provided it could be done, without descending too low from that line of service which in this country is /the/ most honourable ~~(and which in the highest degree of it confers rank superior to any other.)~~ and is the /regular/ road to the highest situations.

And it is by such means, that, ~~if furnished with~~ in a course of time, if furnished with proper seconds, such as might be found without much difficulty in England, though scarcely to be found here, I would not absolutely despair of bringing these establishments, like the Post-Office, to furnish /something of/ a revenue rather than consume one instead of consuming one.[3]

To silence the envious, if my situation gave any room for envy, I could always compare whatever reward I got for my invention, to that which Perillus got for his.[4] And I would desire to be no better off than he was if the persons themselves whose punishment was the object of it for whose punishment it was designed, did not find themselves the better for it /the invention/ as well as me.

After making the sacrifice I have been offering to make to the desire I feel of giving what security the zeal of the projector himself might afford to the success of /a project/ an experiment, of the importance of which I am more and more convinced, the more I think of it, it is saying less to assure you To the offer I have thus taken the liberty to make I beg leave farther to add, that should you happen to know of any other hands in which you think the conduct of /the plan/ could be placed with /more or equal/ advantage ~~to which you would prefer the trusting it~~ I should be happy at all times to afford any additional assistance which I may be thought capable of ~~affording rendering~~ yielding at this distance.

I have the honour to be, with the highest respect

[2] Below this line a pencil line is drawn across the page. Pencilled above it on the right is, 'To p. 3', and below it in the left margin, apparently referring to the next passage, 'From p. 3.'

[3] Below this is a pencil line and the pencilled direction, 'Back to p. 2'. The following portion of text down to, 'To the offer I have thus taken the liberty...' is scored through.

[4] Phalaris, proverbial for his cruelty as tyrant of Agrigentum in the fifth century, B.C., burnt his victims alive in a brazen bull; its efficacy was first tried out upon its inventor, Perillus.

591

To Jeremiah Bentham[1]

4/15 May 1787 (Aet 39)

Zadobras near Crichoff /Monday/ May $\frac{4}{15}$ 1787

Hond. Sir

I am now alone. Sam is before this, I hope, at Kieff, or in his way from thence to Cherson. I left him /on Thursday sennight/ at Propoisk, a town upon the Soje about 40 miles from hence by land, but double or treble the way by water, pursuing his course on board his new-invented *Serpentine* or *Vermicular* Barge, whichever you please to call it. Of this barge you will expect some description. It consists of 6 different boats, connected together by a particular mechanism, so as to form but one, but pliable in every direction in the manner of a snake. Each boat /or link as we call it/ is 42 feet in length: consequently the length of the whole is 252 feet. The two head-links are taken up entirely with oars: as is the fore-half of the 3d, and the whole of the sixth. In the first link are 36 oars: in the 2d, 40: in the rowing part of the 3d, 20: in the 6th 24: in all, 120: besides two at the head of the head link, and as many at the tail of the tail-link, to answer the purpose of rudders. There are 2 ranks of rowers on each side: consequently 4 are seen of a row when you look across the boat. The /back/ half of the third link, and the whole of the 4th and 5th, constitute the habitable part of the barge; which I must lose no time in telling you, is destined for her Majesty's use, if she will vouchsafe to set foot in it. The breadth of this habitable part is, throughout, $\overset{F}{13}.\ \overset{I}{5}$ in the inside: on the outside, from the bottom of the windows, the breadth is continued on each side $\overset{F}{1}.\ \overset{I}{8}$ which breadth forms a plat-form or foot-board for people to walk on in passing from the head-rowing-links to the rowing link at the tail, behind the habitable part: /consequently the extreme breadth is about 16 – 9./ From this foot-board to the floor of the rooms in

591. [1] B.M. IV: 347–50, 368, 363. Autograph, except for fo. 363. Docketed by Jeremiah Bentham on fo. 350: 'datd 4/15 May 1787 / Reced. 12 July 1787 / of Mr. G. Wilson who recd. / it the 10th July.'

Addressed: 'Jeremiah Bentham Esq. / Queen's Square Place, Westmr. / London.'

For further reference to fos. 368 and 363, see n. 3. 4/15 May 1787 was a Tuesday. B.M. XXII: 409–12 is Bentham senior's letter-book copy of the first part of this letter, corresponding with B.M. IV: 347–50.

depth, and from the side of the rooms to the side of the boat, (that is the breadth of the foot-board) in breadth, forms a space all along, which, opening into the rooms, affords a continued range of cupboards on each side. Height of the rooms, 7. 4 in the middle: 6. 7 at each side: the difference is occasioned by the form of the roof which of course is a little arched for the sake of strength, that upon occasion it may bear a man. The front room (occupying only the hinder half of the /3d/ link on which it stands, forms an *anti-room* for attendants: That immediately behind it, occupies the whole of the 4th, and forms the *dining-room.* Of the 5th link the front half forms a *drawing-room* or *dressing-room*, which-ever you please to call it, into which Her Majesty, with a select party, may withdraw from the dining-room: behind this drawing—or dressing-room is the *bed-chamber*, with two cabbins for attendants, and other conveniences. The place for the bed is an alcove taken out of the breadth and occupying the middle part of that breadth, just at the hind part of the link: fronting it is a very neat cabbin-stove in the English taste made on purpose. The whole length of the rooms is filled with windows on each side, separated only by pannels of 6 inches wide. Height of the windows 3 foot all along: width of each window 2½: to each window 4 panes; the wood-work very light. The windows draw up and down; and there is a blind to each of them that does the same. Between the anti-room and the dining-room there is necessarily a space of 2 or 3 feet /or more/ to give room for managing the junction/ [*About two inches left blank and a note interpolated*: 'I had left this space vacant, for the purpose of attempting something in the way of drawing, but I can make nothing of it'.] of the two links: so for the same reason, is there between the dining-room link, and the link which contains the drawing- or dressing-room and bed-chambers.

A little short of the extremity of the first link stands a half-octagon platform about 4½ above the rowers seats: on this my Brother stands /to give orders/ with a speaking trumpet, of which you may imagine there is some need, as the length of the whole barge is above ¼ as long again as that of your garden. A semi-circular rail cover'd with scarlet cloth and standing on three pillars /rising from the platform/ serves for his support. Fronting this platform, at the other end of the barge, is a platform somewhat similar for the same purpose.

The 3rd, 4th and 5th link being left out, the 1st 2nd and 6th form a purely rowing-boat: in that case her Majesty may seat herself on a sopha towards the stern formed of /a neat kind of/ platted work, red edged with chocolate colour (the colours of Wedgwood's ware) with cushions of stuffed leather.

I wish you may be able to make any thing of this general description: for drawing, I have neither skill nor instruments. It cost my Brother three days hard labour to make a representation of it in paper, something betwixt a model and a drawing,[2] to give the Prince some idea of it, when he follow'd him in the winter to Cherson and the Crim, as mentioned in a former letter. This drawing he wished much to send to you, as it would have been possible to have done, in a letter: and I had taken it at one time for that purpose: but his thinking of an occasion which might occurr of producing it before her Majesty etc. put by the sending it for the present. His intention was then to endeavour so to do through the channel of Mr. Fitzherbert upon their return: but I know not but you may have a powerful rival in the Grand Duke, who having heard of the barge, has desired to have some kind of representation of it, though my Brother is not yet acquainted with his Imperial Highness's pleasure.

Of the mode of junction I know not how to give you any tolerable idea. I do not perfectly understand it myself, the mechanism being mostly concealed by the structure of the parts. The stern of the head link, for example, is concave: the head of the 2nd link is convex, fitting exactly into that concavity. In the concavity, between the upper edge of the boat and the water, runs an horizontal groove. The connection is formed by an *iron bar* which is fixed in the 2nd link, turning /playing,/ I believe, there round a perpendicular fulcrum, and running upon friction rollers in the horizontal groove in the breech of the first link. The length of the bar is broken /divided,/ as it were, by a hinge, which lying horizontally, parallel to the horizontal groove, of course gives room for (that part of the bar that is not fixed) the end of the bar opposite to that which is fixed, to play up and down according to the motion of the link /boat/ into which it is inserted by means of the horizontal groove. The hinge is just perceived, as you look down between the two links /boats:/ and the diameter of it forms, I think, all the interval which there is in general between them, but they are capable upon occasion of being let out to I /don't/ know what distance: I believe a foot or more. All the other links are connected in the same manner. Instead of a long-boat the barge has a 24-oared boat of one link, but in other respects constructed upon the same principles: 6 rows of rowers in length: 4 in breadth: being very

[2] This 'model' is at B.M. XVIII: 320.

shallow (drawing very little water) it goes with great swiftness, notwithstanding its great breadth: being so broad, it is as steady as *terra firma* and will turn round like a top that sleeps, without changing its situation. There is likewise a four-oared boat /not much unlike/ our common wherries. As to the great barge there had been no opportunities of trying its swiftness nor can there /have/ been till it gets fairly into the *Dnieper*: The *Soje* is so full of short turnings, and shoals, and stumps and branches of trees projecting some above the water others a little way below the surface; the inundation not being yet over, nor the natural bed of the river ascertainable. One of the turnings I observed was so short as to form much less than a right angle: my Brother thought not so much as half such an angle: It was curious to observe the barge bending itself to that form: had it been inflexible, it could not have passed the turning.

When the /construction of the/ barge was too far advanced to admitt of any alteration, my Brother thought of another mode of junction much more simple than the foregoing, and consequently, if it succeeds much preferable. He took with him a vessel of 3 links constructed upon this principle, and which he hopes will live in the Black Sea. The ends are quite square like those of a box, and the junction is effected by two ropes crossing one another /thus/ ╳ one end of each rope in one link, and the other in the contiguous link. Beams slide out, I can't recollect how, to keep the two links asunder when and at what part it may be found necessary.

Dimensions of the Sea-Vermicular

		F. I.				
Breadth		14 0	Thickness of the planks at the	Bottom	0. 3	The timbers 8 inches square. The bottom and sides connected by Dove-tailing
Length of the	Middle link	34 6		Sides	0. 2½	
	Fore and Aft links	36 6		Deck	0. 2	

This serves for the present voyage as a sort of tender to the great Imperial Vermicular, containing some baggage, with Washerwomen and other followers of the floating camp.

Besides the above, there is another experimental vessel upon the same simple plan but much larger in its dimensions designed only for fresh water and calculated chiefly for the conveyance of timber.

It consists of 5 links, 3 of them hollow, and the other 2 solid composed of timbers packed up together into a mass of the /same/ breadth as the hollow links, and designed to sink in the water to the same depth. These solid ones being built at a different place from the others, I did not see them.

		Feet
Breadth of all the links		32
Length of the	Middle link	70
	Fore and aft links	51

The hollow links were to hold planks. It was not in readiness to accompany my Brother, but was to set off after him from a place at some distance from hence as yesterday.

Of the number of oars to these vulgar-vessels I can not speak with any certainty, my attention having been so much taken up with the Imperial one. The actual number was limited by the number of hands that could be spared: but double rows could be stow'd the whole length, the habitable and stowage part being under deck.

I should never have done if I attempted the describing all the subordinate contrivances: for these vessels differ from all others in almost every particular that can be imagined. For example instead of one large mast as in common, 2 slender masts forming a triangle with a thick rope that stays them. Of the two rudders which the Sea-Vermicular and Timber-Vermicular are each provided with one at the head the other at the tail, in one I forget which the staff is set down in the middle of the broad part, thus ⊥ instead of the side, as in common rudders thus ⌊. This was for a reason which Sea-men will readily apprehend, and which I apprehended at the time but have since forgotten.

The great principle upon which the advantage expected from this construction in point of swiftness depends is, that according to a maxim /my Brother says/ received by all shipbuilders theoretical as well as practicable, a vessel meets with no sensible retardment from its length. But by increasing the length you may increase indefinitely the number of rowers and consequently the moving force: while the increase of length, as far as the above maxim holds good makes no sensible addition to the resistance. What sets limits to the length on all plans of construction hitherto known is the ~~capacity of the~~ vessel's capacity of hold⟨ing together⟩ without falling to pieces by its own weight, /which is called *hogging* by sea-men./ My Brother does not know that any body before him ever put two rows of rowers close together on the same side. They row without interfering with one another in the least.

Of the particulars contained in the above description scarce any were furnished me by my Brother. His attention was sufficiently taken up partly by an ague, partly by the conducting of these unexampled and untried vessels, with a crew perfectly raw and unexercised, through a navigation render'd as dangerous by sunken or projecting stumps as a sea-navigation by sunken rocks. When I embarked he had had his ague about 10 days: and he was so weaken'd by it as to be unable to stand, and sometimes to speak, even when the fit was not on him: but in the course of the time I staid with him on board, which was 2 days and 2 nights (for he was kept waiting one day for the men's provisions) I had the satisfaction of seeing him considerably strengthened, and I hope the ague gone. When he was incapable of business, which was the case for several days every thing was either at a stand or going wrong: nobody capable of supplying his place, in a business so new and so much his own. Fear of being distanced by the Empress, hurried him away in this condition before the fitting up of the habitable part was finished. He took a number of the hands aboard with him for that purpose: and they were working as much at their ease as on dry land. The hold given to the wind by the necessary heigth of the habitable part above the water was a great difficulty to contend with in a stormy part of the year, through so confined and winding a chanel, renderd only the more dangerous by spending itself occasionally, at this season of inundation, over underwoods and sand banks. Poor Burkit was sadly out in his *two* stories for a species of vessel, which must indeed have *one*, but for which *one* is almost too many.

It[3] is now /almost/ a twelvemonth since your two sons have heard a syllable from their father: and this is neither the first nor the second time of their expressing their concern they feel at so unprecedented /distressing/ a silence. My letters on the Inspection-House /at length/ I was in hopes could have been favoured with some notice.[4] If they have failed of giving you ~~satisfaction~~ /pleasure/

[3] The rest of the original of this letter is missing. The next three paragraphs are recoverable only from Bentham's draft of the final portion of it, which he docketed (with what, perhaps, was the actual date of dispatch): '1787 May 11/22 / J.B. Zadobras / to Q.S.P. Q.S.P. / The rest a description of the Imp. Verm.' (fo. 368). The text of the draft continues, but the fourth paragraph of this last part of the original letter is recoverable from an extract copied by Jeremiah Bentham, docketed by him: 'Copy of Part of a Letter from Mr. Jeremy Bentham / to his Father / Dated Zadobras near / Crichoff / May 15/4 1787 / Recd. 12th July / about a Remittance / intended to be sent by / his Brother Lieut. Coll. [Bentham]' (fo. 363). A further letter-book copy of this last passage by Jeremiah Bentham is at B.M. XXII: 408v, where the month of dispatch is incorrectly rendered as 'March'.

[4] See letter 582. A marked interruption in the receipt at Krichëv of letters from

they have failed of one of their main objects. ~~I have advice~~ of the arrival of the rough copy I have advice: I have no tidings of the fair copy (accompanied by a private letter) addressed to you: except that we heard of its being sent from Riga. /Willing to double the chance of its safe arrival and under a notion for the sake of security against sea-risk/ Thinking that a purpose might be answer'd by it at Riga we gave permission to Mr. Trompovski to detain your copy (which was the only one that could be offerd as legible to persons not particularly interested in it) just so long as might be necessary for the two copies to go by different packets. This was a sudden thought /idea/: ~~I know not as yet~~ If your copy has miscarried ~~I have occasion to congratulate myself of be glad I did the idea~~ the idea it was a lucky one: if not, perhaps it may have proved otherwise.

In the course of last summer I sent /to Riga/ a packet /for you/ which we desired Mr Trompovski to forward by Sea.[5] ~~It contained~~ The contents were besides a letter for you, one ~~it contained~~ a fair copy of /such/ part as I had been able to get copied of Mr. Pole Carew's manuscript with a letter of apology to him in answer to his message through you. ~~of the receipt~~ Of this packet I have never had any tidings since.

~~This goes with a~~ I send by this same post under cover to Mr. Wilson[6] a pamphlet in defence of Usury desiring him to send it to the press, or to keep it till he sees me, as he thinks fit.

Zadobras near Crichoff May $\frac{15}{4}$ 1787.

Of[7] the money for the Cloth, and the Iron Ware, I am sorry to have nothing more satisfactory to tell you now than in my last.

Jeremiah Bentham may have been due to the growing deterioration in the relations between Trompovsky and the Benthams. Possibly this was the chief reason why Bentham dispatched this letter via Pleshcheyev at St Petersburg, together with his packet of the same date to Wilson (letter 592) inclosing *A Defence of Usury*, which he wished Pleshcheyev to correct in one or two particulars before forwarding it (see letters 593 and 595).

[5] See letters 570 and 571.

[6] Letter 592.

[7] Jeremiah Bentham's copy of the extract representing the final portion of the letter begins here. In place of the first ten words in his copy Bentham's draft reads: 'Of Fludyer's and Buttal's money'. Otherwise there are only unimportant variations of wording between the draft and the copy. A final sentence in the draft not reproduced in the copy runs: 'I have suffer'd too much about this cloth business to be at all disposed to take a part in any similar one in future.' The firm of Fludyer, Marsh, and Hudson was one of the leading firms of clothiers in London, with large west-country connections. Jonathan and Thomas Buttel were ironmongers in Greek Street, Soho.

Part of it we had been expecting according to Promise for two or three months past. The whole is perfectly safe, but the difficulties of Communication in this Country, which is inconceivable, has prevented it's being sent as yet; Sam has by this time I hope been at one or both of the Places from whence it is to come. When he sends it I believe it will be through Mr. Shairp. I have taken every precaution for the punctual remittance of it wch. anxiety could suggest: Written Instructions to Sam, Letters to Friends where he is going, to remind him of it. It will, I believe, be sent directly to Petersburg from Kieff or Cherson without passing thro' this Place, and consequently without my knowing of the sending it till after an uncertain Time. I mention this that you may not be surprised if you shod. receive future Letters from me without any further mention of it. Money which had been originally allotted for this purpose was applied, without my knowing how the matter stood, to defray the unexpected Exigences of the Imperial Vermicular which otherwise must have been abandoned when It was half finished, and by that means the whole of the Expence thrown away. If the Experiment succeeds, Sam hopes the Principle may be applied with advantage to the purpose of Inland Navigation in England, in which Case he would take out a Patent.[8]

592

To George Wilson[1]

4/15 May 1787 (Aet 39)

Crichoff, May 4–15, 1787.

My Dear Wilson,

I send for your edification, a Defence of Usury and some other enormities.[2] Abuse it and keep it, or abuse it and print it, as to your wisdom may seem meet. Don't let Trail see it or hear it (the blasphemous 14th letter I mean) till he has submitted to have his

[8] At the end of fo. 363 Jeremiah Bentham added the note: 'Mm. The original Letter, of which the above is a true Extract was received by us at Queen's Square Place on Thursday the 12th July 1787, J[h] B.'

592. [1] Bowring, x, 174–5.

[2] *A Defence of Usury* was published in 1787, despite Wilson's threat (letter 589) not to see any more of Bentham's work through the press. The 'other enormities' were the 'Defence of Projectors' and the proposed dedication. As printed it consists of thirteen letters: the 'blasphemous 14th letter' mentioned immediately below was evidently deleted.

hands tied behind him, for fear of mischief. Douglas's phlegm might be trusted, but he is Attorney-general by this time, and has not time.

Don't let any very flagrant absurdities go for want of correction or erasure: false or dubious law I don't so much care about, provided you correct it or clear it up in a note. What I send you at large is only the middle; the condemned head and tail I send you only the contents of: somewhat of their history you will find in margin of said contents. The chapter on Blackstone[3] I give you full power over. Sam, as often as he considered it in the abstract, was for suppressing it, because Blackstone is dead, and its harping on the old string, etc.; but as often as he heard it read over, which he did two or three times, he laughed so heartily at the parody that he could not bear the thoughts of parting with it. You see there is nothing at all ill-natured in it, and as it adds a considerable strength, I think, to the argument, I should be rather sorry it were out. My greatest scruple of conscience is whether *Jockeyship* is really used in the sense in which it occurred to me, and in which alone it can be admitted, viz., for the sin of *selling* a horse at a high price. You may call this confined subject, flying at small game: but, with submission, I don't think such a confined subject stands, as such, a worse chance for being read than a great system. As for the form of letters, it was written in this form before the law against letter writing was promulgated; and the Defence of Projectors could not have been conducted in any other way with near so much advantage. If you do print it, don't let it linger; but send it to the press quickly, that it may begin the sooner to lay in a little stock of reputation for me against I get home. When that part that relates to the reduction of the rate of interest was condemned upon what you told me of that measure's being laid aside, I was sadly puzzled for a long time how to introduce the part which you now see. I give you, on the other leaf, a various lection, which I wrote to humour Sam, who wanted something to be said to give folks to understand that I did not stay here, as some might suspect, to intrigue to get into this service,—an honour which I have most certainly taken no steps whatever to obtain, nor would accept of were it offered me.

The intimation given that these ideas of mine about usury are of old standing, as I dare say you and I recollect they are, was a piece of selfish prudence, which you will think vain. There is one Playfair who published, just before I left England, a trumpery book in 4to,

[3] *A Defence of Usury*, 1787, letter IX, 'Blackstone considered', pp. 84–93; Bowring, iii, 14–15.

called the Interest of Money Considered.[4] Nine-tenths of it is bad writation about the origin of society, and so forth: the other tenth is a perfectly vague and shapeless proposal for relaxing the rigour of the anti-usurious laws in favour of projectors; yet without any argument in it, or any other idea, but that vague one thrown out in almost as general and vague a way as I have stated it in. I understand it has been well enough spoken of by several people.

That you may not plead scruples of conscience, take notice that I give you full power to make all manner of alterations, additions, and subtractions to any extent you think fit.

PROPOSED DEDICATION.

'Dear——

It was because he had a fancy for it that Ovid, as he himself certifieth, wrote his Metamorphoses. It is for the same reason I write about usurers, whom I have a fancy, and that you know not a new one, for metamorphosing into honest men. I have a fancy for addressing myself to you on this occasion, rather than to the world (at large.) I have a fancy for sending you these letters, rather than wait a few months, and be myself the bearer of them, when the visit, which, though to a brother, your friendship styles a long one, is at an end. I have a fancy for staying here, to pick, in not unpleasing solitude, this dry bone, instead of plunging into the passing vortex, and retracing the course of the Borysthenes, to stare at crowns and diadems.'

The egotism and pertness of the above, will prevent, I suppose, your giving it place. But do with it as you list.

When I wrote it, I had not as yet hammered out the introduction which you see.

Don't wait to correct the work before you write me word whether it is to see the press or no: that you can tell me within a few days after you have received it.

Sam is gone in pursuit of the empress in his serpentine or vermicular barge, of which I have given some account to my father.

I stay here partly to wait for him, partly to wait for my things, the bulk of which, whatever you may think of it, I have never yet been able to get from the Crimea.

[4] Probably William Playfair, *The Increase of manufactures, commerce and finance, with the extension of civil liberty, proposed in regulations for the interest of money*, London, 1785.

593

To Jeremiah Bentham[1]

25 May/5 June 1787 (Aet 39)

Zadobras near Crichoff $\frac{\text{May 25th}}{\text{June 5th}}$ 1787.

Hond. Sir

On Friday last I received a letter from Mr. Wilson,[2] inclosing one from you to him of the 15th of April.[3] The pleasure which the sight of a line under your hand would have afforded under other circumstances could not but be much alloy'd, by the proof it afforded me that the silence, under which your sons have so long been suffering, is not owing to any disinclination to writing in general, but to some other cause which it would be of no use for me to attempt to guess at. I derive from it however this intelligence, which to me is very material and decisive, viz: that what inclination you appear to have to publish my letters on the Inspection-house is grounded not on any personal satisfaction such a publication would afford you on your own account, but on the anxiety you conceive to subsist on my part to see it take place for some purpose or other respecting us or one of us. *In my last, which went from hence this day fort-night by way of Petersburgh under cover to Mr. Plescheјeff,*[4] I told you that the hopes of their giving you pleasure was one of the main objects I had in view in writing those letters. Whether those hopes have been fulfilled in any respect is more than I have any means of knowing. I have however learnt enough to extinguish most perfectly whatever desire I had originally and do accordingly write this for the express purpose of begging and entreating that they *may on no account go to the press till we meet*,[5] an event which

593. [1] B.M. IV: 371–3. Autograph. Docketed by Jeremiah Bentham: 'Original Letter / of / Mr. Jeremy Bentham / datd. Zadobras near Crichoff / June 5/May 25 1787 / Reced Augt. 28 1787 / Vermicular.'

Addressed: 'To / Jeremiah Bentham Esqr. / Queens Square Place / Westm. / London.' Postmark obliterated.

B.M. IV: 438–9 is a draft in Bentham's hand with some corrections and differing somewhat in phrase from the letter as sent; it is docketed: '1787 J.B. Zadobras / to / Q.S.P. Q.S.P.' Jeremiah Bentham's letter-book copy is B.M. XXII: 413–4, which omits most of the first paragraph containing his son's upbraidings.

[2] Letter 589.

[3] Missing.

[4] Letter 591. The words 'this day fortnight' seem to confirm that that letter, although dated 4/15 May 1787, was not actually dispatched till 11/22 May.

[5] In fact, *Panopticon; or, The Inspection House*, was not to be published until 1791.

as far as depends upon my wishes and intentions can not be many months distant. I know not how soon I may set out on my way home: *if it is not within these two or three months, at any rate it will not be later than till the winter roads are formed.*

In my last, as abovementioned, I gave you a *pretty full account of my Brothers* Vermicular Barge or rather *Vermicular Squadron*, with which *he set off about a month ago* to overtake the Empress. I have no tidings of him since.

Mr. Wilson tells me that you are anxious to know if B.[6] who you have learnt has behaved ill, seduced by D.[7] has affected S.'s connection with a house you mention. The state in which that connection stands at present is as follows: About the latter end of last year I sent a considerable sum for ducats as before: authorising T.[8] to retain what was due to him as per account deliver'd. D. coming to Riga with a recommendation from T.'s partner and a great medical reputation very deservedly obtained from an extraordinary chirurgical cure performed during the voyage, and finding T. brought to death's door by a lingering disorder, was received into his house, and fitted him for a matrimonial engagement there, which he has since consummated in breach of a prior one at Edinburgh. The method T. took to recompense D. was to discharge with S.'s money what debts D. had contracted there for cloaths and other such personal expences, on pretence of the agreement T. had drawn up between D. and S., the purport of which was that if upon his coming to Crichoff they should engage in any joint undertaking (which they have never done) or that D. gave any assistance in certain parts of his then subsisting concerns (which he has never done) D. should have a certain share of the profits. *T. was at the same time authorised to retain what might be necessary for the expences of the cargo consigned to him by Mr. King. He accordingly retained a sum about equal to the prime cost promising at the same time an immediate account by the then next post, which account has never yet arrived, though written for 3 or 4 times since, in the most friendly but the most pressing terms; alledging the distress S. would be in for want of the information contained in it in respect of the settling accounts with people at Cherson etc. No answer to all this*: however Mr. Wilson's letter inclosing your's and directed to the Postmaster at Riga came through that channel with their compliments on the cover. The method taken by the house which S.

[6] George Benson.

[7] Here and subsequently 'D' signifies Dr Debraw.

[8] Christian Trompovsky.

quitted for this to make the Connection answer[9] to them was by Charging as paid at the Custom house money which was not paid, to the amount I think it was of about half as much again as was really paid. This was discovered by D., the false charges deducted and S. has the account here article by article. A great failure /there/ by which T.'s house were considerable sufferers, may help to account for this behaviour. As to B.'s, his was altogether unaccountable: it vented itself in conduct expressive of the highest degree of rage and malice in return for unsated kindness, without so much as a previous complaint: but by this no pecuniary loss has been sustained. B. denies that D. had any Share in influencing him: Whether truly or no is neither easy to be known nor worth knowing. B. we hear has been well received by the Govr. at Riga on the score of Countrymanship and a plausible appearance and address. All these Circumstances together cut off in a manner our Communication with Riga. I could not take shipping there without having my intention (according to the general Law of the country) made public there 3 or 4 weeks before my departure: and all that time I should be kicking my heels at an Inn there at least /twice as dear/ again as the dearest ⟨...⟩ D. is gone off to Kieff and that way in pursuance of an invitation given him upon the strength of his reputation for insanity which seems to have originated in the behaviour produced by the notice taken of him on account of his professional merit at Riga. The diverting themselves with characters of that ⟨sort⟩ forms a favourite amusement with some people. If you have a mind to be a Defendant in an action for words you have nothing to do but to let the contents of this get to the knowledge of your Russia merchants. With about two months ⟨...⟩ close employment, neglecting every thing else, I could give you an ⟨history⟩ of these pretty incidents and some other similar ones, full enough to afford a tolerable satisfaction to your appetite for ill news.

Crichoff is just sold. What change, if any, this event may make in S.'s situation it would be to no purpose for me to pretend to guess, at this distance from all sources of intelligence. The Jews, not liking their purchasers, have been talking about making up a purse to enable S. to try to buy up the Town itself with a small district round it, the purchasers it seems not liking this part of their bargain: but all that remains in darkness.

[9] Perhaps owing to faintness in the original the following passage has been traced over by Jeremiah Bentham. Samuel Bentham had withdrawn his business at Riga from the firm of Hey and put it in the hands of Pierson, Huhn, Trompovsky and Co. about the end of 1785 (B.M. IV: 237–9).

I could have wished to have known about the House of Correction for Middlesex; whether the Inspection plan, to which in itself I suppose you have no objection, came time enough to be proposed for that purpose which was the original and at first the only occasion of my letters—

594

To Jeremiah Bentham[1]

14/25 June 1787 (Aet 39)

Zadobras near Crichoff June | | 1787

Hond. Sir

If the description I sent you 5 or 6 weeks ago of my Brother's Serpentine Barge etc., and the account of the short voyage I took with him in it on his way to Kieff, Kremenchook and Cherson, have reached your hands,[2] you can not but have felt some impatience to hear further tidings of his adventure. It is now for the first time in my power to afford you some sort of intelligence, though very imperfect, coming through a Russian medium, and not directly from himself. On Saturday last I received a visit from one of my Brother's officers who, /taking Notman for interpreter/ brought with him a letter he had received the Thursday before from the /Batallion/ Surgeon who accompanied my Brother. The letter was dated from Kremchook May 23/June 3. My Brother ~~with his~~ in the Grand Barge arrived it seems at Kremenchook the 8th day after his departure from Monasteroc where I embarked; consequently the 7th day from Propoisk, where I left him. *Eighteen* days, the time in which the same voyage was performed last autumn by an ordinary experimental barge of his construction was a time much shorter than that voyage had ever been performed in before. In his way to Kremenchook he passed of course by Kieff: there he learnt that the Empress had left that place, travelling by land, but two hours before he arrived there. Accordingly he staid there not a

594. [1] B.M. IV: 376–8. Autograph. Dooketed by Jeremiah Bentham: 'Original letter of / Mr. Jeremy Bentham / datd. Zadobras near Crichoff / June 23/14 1787 / recd. Augt. 28 1787.'

Addressed: 'To Jeremiah Bentham Esqr. / Queen's Square Place / Westminster / London.'

Jeremiah Bentham's letter-book copy is B.M. XXII: 415–8. This has supplied some words, printed in square brackets, which are now illegible owing to damage in the original. Another copy, B.M. IV: 380–2.

[2] Letter 591.

moment, but pressed on for Kremenchook towards which place he was informed she had bent her course. Thither he must have arrived /a day or two/ before her: for she it seems did not arrive there before May 3/14. There however he found the Prince: who had been residing there: that being the seat of his government, during the time she spent at Kieff. There ends all I can tell you about dates. The Prince was mightily pleased with the invention: and as a proof of it, had declared his intention of having barges built forthwith upon the same plan at four places, Petersburgh, Cherson, Kremenchook, and Dubrovna, which you know is the estate he has still in the neighbourhood of Crichoff. Between the 3d and the 9th, he embarked on board, and fell down the river to a new town which is building about 120 versts from Kremenchook, under the name of Ecatherinoslav (Catherine's glory, if I do not mistake). They went at the rate of 12 versts (8 miles) an hour. The vessels that had been built by the Admiralty for the Empress's use during her progress could go no farther than half way, on account as was said of their being so much exposed to the wind, by reason of their heighth above the water. At Ecatherinoslav they found the Emperor, who came on board.[3] One date more I can give you: which is, that on the 9/20 of May the Empress set out, still by land, for Cherson, and with her the Prince, and with him my Brother, and with him the Adjutant, the rest of his officers staying behind at Kremenchook with the Grand Barge. The Tender, destin'd for an experiment on the Black Sea, was of course distanced by the Grand Barge, but arrived afterwards at Kremenchook and is since gone on to Cherson. It does not appear all this while that the Empress has ever been on board my Brother's Barge, nor even her own; but it is not to be concluded that she will not, as her stay at Cherson is to be but short, and she is to return to Kremenchook. The men on board the Barge have had a rare time of it. The Prince soon after he came on board order'd them 300 Roobles, and 50 more before he disembarked: the Emperor also, and many other people made them presents. As the hands that row'd the vessel were thus treated, it seems not an unnatural conclusion that the head which planned it will, at the long run, not go altogether unrewarded. The letter speaks much of the caresses bestowed on him by all the great folks there. Amongst his visitors it mentions by name Field Marshall Romanzoff[4] (the

[3] Joseph II of Austria had been invited by Catherine II to join her tour of South Russia. After he had made a preliminary visit to Kherson, the two sovereigns met at Kremenchug, and Joseph accompanied the empress on her royal progress to Kherson and the Crimea (A. G. Brikner, *Potëmkin*, St Petersburg, 1891, pp. 91–9).

[4] Count Pëtr Aleksandrovich Rumyantsov (1725–96) was one of the leading Russian

conqueror of the Turks you know) and Count Chernicheff[5] who you also know is at the head of the Admiralty. My Brother, I am sorry to find, has been labouring under a very indifferent state of health. The surgeon speaks of him as being on the mending order, but not yet well. However that he can not be very ill appears by his exposing himself to the fatigue of a land journey of some hundred versts in attending on the Empress to Cherson. That it should be his wish she should not see his Barge till his return from thence I can easily conceive: by what I saw of it, it could not well have been finished in the inside at the time (May 9/20) she left Kremenchoock on her way to Cherson. But I can not so well account for her not having been in all this time so much as on board of her own barges. The Prince is particularly pleased it seems with the 24-oared boat which I described to you in my letter of April/May | | and never goes on the river in any other vessel. What is surprising, and a little alarming is, that in all this time neither we here, nor so late as May 23/June 3 had they at Kremenchoock any tidings of the great Serpentine vessel which set off from hence as I informed you about ten days after my Brother. I suppose it must have got aground ~~at some~~ or otherwise met with some stoppage at some place considerably distant from any post-town. I am not at all surprised at my Brother's not writing: circumstanced as he is, he would hardly have found time to write had he been well, but as there were several Englishmen with him on board I rather wonder that none of them have scrawled a line to their friends here. My great dependance was on *Beatty* who /went/ on board the last mentioned Serpentine. The name of the new estate the Prince has bought near Kremenchook is *Smolianchina*: the town included in ⟨it⟩ Smolian it is on the P[olish side of the Dnieper]: about 60 versts if I understand aright lower down than [Kremenchook] The news is that the Tannery is to be removed from this place [to Smolian that is] in plain English a great building which is but just compleated [is to be left to the] new Polish landlords, /who can make no use of it/ and another built in its place. This same [transportation, says the] news is to be performed upon the Glass-house: an operation the one [half of which has been] performed by a fire that burnt it to the ground 5 or 6 months ago. [The Prince is] much pleased with some Potatoes of English race that my Brother [took with him] from this place: and talks of having the whole Potatoe produce [of his farm, (which] may

military commanders during the Turkish war of 1768–74. From 1764 he held the post of governor of Little Russia.

[5] Count Ivan Grigor'yevich Chernyshëv (1726–97). See letter 488, n. 4.

amount perhaps to about a dozen acres) sent from hence, [as soon as they] can be taken up, to plant Kremenchook with, upon a large [scale. The bat-]tallion, it is understood, is to move that way-ward, but whether [this autumn or] not till the ensuing spring is not known. All this indicates [a final farewell to] Crichoff and Zadobras. —Prince Dashcoff, I hear, is removed [from Kioff to Mohilev] in this neighbourhood [and] instead of his regiment of two [batallions has got] a Grenadier Regiment which consists of four.

I have scarce left myself room to thank you for your letter which arrived here on Friday sennight.[6] Since then there has been one post gone out from hence, by which I only have written to acknowledge the receipt of it; but I had little stomach to write then, at a time when the very little intelligence I could give you of my Brother was worse than none. An officer had passed through the place a few days before, who had seen him on board the barge, I don't know where but brought no other news than that of his health, of which he gave a very unfavourable account. After congratulating *you* on the being able to speak of *your* indisposition in the preter perfect tense give me leave for fear of the future and in return for the good advice you have been giving me, to remind you of the law-maxim *Cui libet in suâ arte credendum est*: in plain English, I am sorry to hear you are not so obsequious to Mr Welch's advice as you ought to be consistently with your opinion of him, and as your family would wish. Many thanks for your news: it went onwards by means of an accidental opportunity forthwith towards Kiev and Kremenchoock etc. and perhaps on account of its freshness may have proved news to Mr. F. The Inspection-House was not begun *here*: nor, as you see, is it like to be. I have no later news from England. P.S. I wrote to you this day fortnight through Trompovski's house through which channel I write now.[7] I am sorry to say your letter which you mention of 16th March never came to hand.[8]

[6] Missing.

[7] This passage, written at the top of the first page of this letter may refer to a missing letter, since it seems unlikely that Bentham, for fear of accidents, would have sent via Trompovsky and Co. his previous known letter of 25 May/5 June (letter 593), in which discreditable things had been said about Trompovsky; and that letter had been written not a fortnight but three weeks before.

[8] Missing.

595

From Sergey Ivanovich Pleshcheyev[1]

14/25 June 1787

Gatchina Grand Duke's Seat 45 versts
from Petersbourg Juine 14th 1787.

I very luckily came for a few hours to town, when I received your little box with letters. Being obliged to return to Gatchina, I had only time enough to read over your refference page 27th, as it was a post day, I immediately hasted with it to the post master general, and recommended it to his care: So, be easy on that score, your packet, by this time, is travelling in Prussia in its way to England, wrapt up in a fresh cover and addressed to *Mr. King Six Clerks Coffee house, For George Wilson Esqr.* I must acknowledge to you that it is with some hesitation I determined myself to part with it so soon, and nothing but the utility, which you, and Sam may reap, from its being under press without delay, could overbalance the eager desire I had to read it attentively, the table of contents, which I run over in very great haste, has given me an idea of your work, and the strength of argument, which I perceived in some places, makes me think it a very valuable production.

I thank you for the copy of the letter to your father,[2] which gives so circumstantial a description of Sam's vermiculars. My intention is to translate it into Russ for the perusal of the Grand Duke. I am astonished there is no mention made of this curious invention in the reports, which General *Pustchin*[3] has from time to time made to the Grand Duke about the state of Galleys and other vessels, prepared for the Empress's Journey.

You have been misinformed about the necessity of standing a month in the Gazette when one is to leave this country; it is true, the publication is to be repeated three times, but all this takes up no more than 9 or 10 days. If you determine yourself, as I hope you will, to shape your course to England through Petersbourg, it would be even necessary to stop that number of days to prepare yourself for your departure and to see the things worth your notice, was it

595. [1] B.M. IV: 383–6. Autograph. Docketed by Bentham: '1787 June no day / Pleschejeff Petersbourg / to / J.B. Crichoff / Received Monday June 28 / Answered next day June 29/July 10. Aug. 12/23 / Reced reply dated / July 29th.'

Bentham's reply is missing, as is also his original covering letter. For the contents of the box, which Pleshcheyev forwarded, see letters 591 and 592.

[2] Letter 591. [3] Admiral Pëtr Ivanovich Pushchin (1723–1812).

but to have merely an idea of the place and of the things done in it: as for being unknown, nothing can hinder you to observe as rigid an incognito as you please; you could endoss another name, and live either in the tavern, or at my house, without discovering yourself to any soul living. As for publishing the notice of your departure during your absence, it is quite impossible.

I cannot blame you for not engaging in any service; there is so much dependency, slavery and intrigue in all the services, that a person, who knows the real value of freedom, quiet and honest dealing, will never be dazled with the āparent advantages, which foolish ambition ever exagerates. Your familly circumstances are such, that you stand in no need of selling your liberty, and ease of mind from a motif of lucre; your father is old, his death must procure you a positive establishment: in regard to your literary reputation, it is already established on permanent basis; so that your *amour propre* if it is not an unbiass'd one, can be securely at ease and enjoy satisfaction, which few people are doom'd to taste. As for our Sam's position, it must be view'd in a different manner, he is a *cadet*, whose fortune and reputation are grounded in labour and perseverance, he must long fight the battle ere it brings him the comforts, he aims at. and for that reason I love to encourage his fondness for scheeming and projecting.

You wish to see my book translated into german. I do not know if any body has undertaken that task, but de la Coliniere the french minister's Counselor of legation has put it into french, which I intend to publish next winter when we come to town for good and all. I should be glad to see my book in English[4] and incorporated with that of Mr. Beaty's,[5] whose association as a man of abilities and known to the studious world, will do a great honour to an obscure, barbarian author such as I am.

I am very impatient to see your french work on legislation and hope to have a copy of it as soon as it is published. I would give it into the hands of my select Russian friends, and see what they say about it. in regard to what you say about the terms of borrowing money in Russia, instead of 6 I put 5 per cent, which is the rate fixed by law at the opening of the new bank last year, the rest is perfectly well stated, the correction I made on page 27th is word for word as follows, marked wth. red ink.

[4] Pleshcheyev was referring to his *Obozreniye Rossiyskoy Imperii* (Survey of the Russian Empire), which had been published in 1786. It was published in London in an English translation made by Y. I. Smirnov in 1792.

[5] Not identified.

—'In the country, in wch. I am writting the whole System of laws on this Subject, is perfectly inefficacious. The rate fixed by law is 6 per cent: many people lend money; and nobody at that rate: the lowest ordinary rate, upon the very best real Security is 8 per cent: 9 and even 10 upon such security are common. /Six or/ Seven may have place, between relations, or other particular friends: because now and then a man may choose to make a present of one /or two/ per cent to a person whom he means to favour. The contract is renewed from year to year; for a thousand roubles, the borrower in his written contract obliges himself to pay at the end of the year one thousand and sixty /fifty/ Before witnesses, he receives his thousand roubles: and, without witnesses, he immediately pays back his 20 /30/ roubles, or his 30 /40/ roubles, or whatever the sum may be that is necessary to bring the real rate of interest to the rate verbally agreed on.'[6]

I have picked up some Gazettes and send it you according to your desire; as for a dictionary in which the Russ stands before, there is no such a thing in the Empire of all the Russias. if there ever appears one, you shall instantly have it.

If Sam is return'd from his excurtion, pray tell him that I insist on his acquainting me on what footing are at present all his fabricks at Krichoff, since, we are told, the prince has sold it to a polander for 900,000 roubles.

God bless you both

596

From George Wilson[1]

14 July 1787

Dr. Smith has been very ill here, of an inflammation in the neck of the bladder, which was increased by very bad piles. He has been

[6] The passage, as corrected by Pleshcheyev, occurs towards the end of letter VII (Bowring, iii, 12). The words and figures appearing as insertions in the text are his red-ink corrections.

596. [1] Bowring, x, 173–4.

This is evidently only an extract, for Bentham's reply (letter 598) indicates that the original included some discussion of the *Defence of Usury*.

There is no evidence that Pitt made any effective use of Adam Smith as an adviser at this time, and in any case Smith's illness probably precluded him from any such activity (information communicated by Mr John Ehrman).

cut for the piles, and the other complaint is since much mended. The physicians say he may do some time longer. He is much with the ministry; and the clerks at the public offices have orders to furnish him with all papers, and to employ additional hands, if necessary, to copy for him. I am vexed that Pitt should have done so right a thing as to consult Smith; but if any of his schemes are effectuated, I shall be comforted.

597

To Jeremiah Bentham[1]

13/24 July 1787 (Aet 39)

Zadobras near Crichoff July Tuesday 13/24 1787

Hond. Sir

Since our last Post-day I reced. from my Brother Two thousand Rubles—accompanied with a short Letter datd. Krementchuck July 5/16.[2]

The Prince was just then come on board the Vermicular (it was then ½ after 4 in the morning) in order to fall down the River a second time in his way to Cherson where my Brother was also to attend him this second time.

But now with regard to the sending the money to England as soon as the remainder can be collected in, of which my Brother was in hourly expectation.

A difficulty occurs which must wait your decision, I give you his representation of it, which is all I know about the matter.

In the last winter the Exchange was such that a Pound Sterling might be had for *5* Rubles; now it could not be had under *6*. This, you see, makes £20 per cent difference. He speaks of the difference as periodical, assuming as an event that may be relied on, the Exchange returning to, or near to the Point at which it was last Winter. The *6* is without doubt greatly more against Russia than the

597. [1] B.M. XXII: 419–20. Copy by Jeremiah Bentham, with a note under the date '(Reced. at Q.S.P. Septr. 20, 1787).' An incomplete copy with variants is at B.M. IV: 363v–364.

[2] B.M. IV: 387–8. Samuel wrote. 'Half past one o'Clock at night and the Prince is just come on board Vermicular to sleep, that we may set out by daylight without waking him. I am in a hell of a humour not having yet received a farthing in payment for Verm, and still worse from hearing that the Exchange is terribly unfavourable for remitting, in the winter a pound £ might be bought for five rubles and now you must give six for it 20 p. ct. difference. Have you no means of raising the money till winter or of stopping Q.S.P.'s claims till then'.

par or Medium Rate; but how much I have no means of knowing. I think the medium rate has been looked upon as about 5¼ or 5½; at least on one or other of those footings the Englishmen's wages here have been reckoned.

With this information I submit the matter to your decision, sincerely regretting the delay which the waiting for that decision renders unavoidable. In the mean time the following is the Plan which I shall recommend to my Brother to pursue. In three weeks from the date of his Letter he says he is to be here by appointment to settle some matters with the Prince's Steward | | and | | and he means to ask leave to go immediately from hence to Petersburgh, then will be the time for him to take the money thither, and after consulting with Mr. Shairp[3] there about the time of remittance lodge the money with him, giving you advice of his so doing through that Channel: if the result of that Consultation should be in favour of an immediate remittance, such remittance will take place of course, if otherwise then it will rest with you to draw for the Money (which you will be authorised to do) at the time and in the manner you think proper. Had I even determined to send what money is come to me at all events without waiting for your decision, I know not of any prudent Course I could take to send it by any speedier means than that of my Brother's Journey to Petersburgh.

The Post master here is described to me as a raw Lad of about 17 or 18 years of age having not a penny of his own whereby he might be responsible. There is a method of remitting money by Post upon paying per Centage: ½ p. Ct. is the Rate between some Places and Petersburgh, and probably were it practicable, That would be the rate here, but here I am told it is not practicable; nor do I know of any place that I think I could depend upon for that purpose nearer than Mohileff which is about a hundred miles off; thither therefore should I have sent for that purpose, were it not for the reasons above stated, by the Special Messenger, an Englishman, who brought me the Money from my Brother at Kremenchuck.

I had thoughts of setting off (from hence) during the Course of the Summer but my Brother with much earnestness insists on my not leaving this Country till he has seen me. This request which I cannot refuse complying with, postpones my departure to a Season when a Journey by Sea would be far from agreable, and not altogether safe. I think therefore of setting off as soon as the winter Roads are formed in a Kibitki, a Cradle or Vehicle which People

[3] The British Consul.

use as far as Holland. That, I reckon will be about the beginning or middle of November.

In my last I gave you to understand that the Empress was to take Kremenchuck again in her return to Cherson. This, I imagine, was my Interpreter's misconception: from Cherson She went to review her Army at Pultoway,[4] and from thence to Petersburgh where She has been arrived, I dare say, long ago.

I question whether I have yet thank'd you in my Brother's name for your kind offer about the Maps and Atlas de Commerce—He will have an opportunity of availing himself of it before I see you.

598

To George Wilson[1]

16/27 August 1787 (Aet 39)

Crichoff, Aug. 16–27, 1787.
Tuesday.

Dear Wilson,

Last post-day, Friday 12, I received yours of July 3–14.[2] You have received, then, my Defence of Usury. You think you shall approve of it. You inform me of the imminent danger it is in of losing the appearance of whatever merit it may possess by delay. And *yet*—spite had almost said *therefore*—you delay it,—delay it till *I* don't know when, still less *you*. No, you have *not* delayed it: I accuse myself of injustice in attempting to believe you. Yet my anxiety not to see week thus flung away after week, makes me force my mind for a few minutes to this improbable supposition. Send it, then, if you have any desire to acquit yourself of breach of confidence, or I, any power over my own,—send it somehow, anyhow, to the press. I wish it were possible for me to devise the least coercive form of words that would be sufficient to produce this very simple effect: no others would I use,—but those indeed I would use at any rate....

If you think it wants correction, which you want either time or inclination to give it, send the part in question, which comes within

[4] Poltava.

598. [1] Bowring, x, 175–6.

[2] Letter 596, which is known only from the text provided by Bowring, who omitted Wilson's comments on the *Defence of Usury.*

a narrow compass, to some publishing lawyer with a fee. But this unknown Mercury must not speak for me: what he says must be in a note of the editor's—not in the text—yours, or Trail's, or Douglas's, who, the more you would say for me, the more I should be obliged to you. But even that is not at all necessary. All I am anxious to avoid is the plying the public with false law: the being seen to be ignorant or mistaken in points of law at 1500 miles distance from all sources of information, gives me not the least concern. I have no opinion-trade to spoil.

'To Mr. —— to peruse the enclosed paper for the press, and state in form of notes of the editor what, if anything, may be necessary for clearing up the points of law therein referred to, | | guineas.' There is a form for you to save your trouble, and obviate, if possible, that uncharitable fund of scruples and difficulties of which your imagination is so fertile.

'The author being at a distance from all sources of legal information, and disappointed of the revision to which he had trusted with respect to matters of that nature, the present editor begs those circumstances may be considered.'

Corrigenda if you please—not otherwise. Date—The letters were began, I think, in February or January, finished in April. If you think there will be any use in putting either of those dates instead of the one they bear already, do.[3]

In the short chapter on compound interest, strike out, 'It makes frequent pretences of hating letters, but its hate is as inconstant as its love.'[4]

In the chapter on Champerty, strike out the passage beginning 'You would tell me I had caught,' and ending 'but this is not a place to plant it in.'[5]

If you have an opportunity, tell Douglas how much I should be obliged to him for any part he might be disposed to take in it. He had once the kindness to say, 'Don't send your French to the press without my seeing it,' and I the bluntness to reply, 'I can have no confidence in *your* French.' The vacation, I hope, will not be over before this reaches you. On the other side an order for Hughes— lest you should think it necessary that an advertisement be inserted, if

[3] The first letter was published under the date 'January 1787' and the last two with the subscription 'March 1787'.

[4] Letter XI. The passage was evidently deleted.

[5] Letter XII. The passage was evidently deleted.

necessary, that is, if your refusal makes it so; but subject to your correction.

A thousand ways have I turned and twisted my imagination to squeeze out means of obviating the host of impediments apprehended on the part of yours; several of the condemned letters I had written before this. The event will show with what success.[6]

It is possible I may be set out on my return before an answer from you can reach me; but as that is quite uncertain, don't let it hinder your answering.

Sam is not come back yet, but I expect him every hour.[7]

Anderson had had the kindness to offer, even in the form of petition, to take charge of anything I might wish to publish in my absence. One of the condemned letters was to him for that purpose. I gave up that scheme for uncertainty of success and certainty of delay. He may be dead, ill, occupied, etc.

When you see Ald. Clark, thank him for the letter I had the pleasure of receiving from him the other day.[8]

With this goes a letter to King, enclosing Tontine power-of-Attorney and Certificate.[9]

599

To Richard King[1]

16/27 August 1787 (Aet 39)

Dear Sir

Mr Wilson tells me that you are very uneasy at not hearing from me—that you complain that I have never acknowledged the

[6] See letter 589, in which Wilson informed Bentham that Sir Richard Worsley had misinformed him about an intended lowering of the legal maximum rate of interest. Possibly this is what is referred to here.

[7] In fact, as Bentham learned on 9 September, his brother was detained at Kherson indefinitely (B.M. IV: 395–6).

[8] Missing.

[9] B.M. XXII: 421 is Jeremiah Bentham's letter-book copy of the Tontine certificate: 'I the Revd. Euthemius Sowarsk Minister of the Parish of St. Parascivia in the Town of Crechoff in White Russia Do hereby Certify that Samuel Bentham Youngest Surviving Son of Jeremiah Bentham, by Alicia his first Wife was living at the said Parish the twentieth of April last present and is still living as I believe though not now here. Witness my hand this 17th August 1787, Euthemius Suwarski.' It was enclosed in letter 599.

599. [1] B.M. IV: 440–1. Autograph. Draft with corrections. Docketed by Bentham: '1787 / J.B. Zadobras / to / R. King / London.'

This letter was sent with the letter to Wilson of 16/27 August 1787 (letter 598) and is therefore of the same date.

receipt of a cargo of goods which you sent me, and that you are very anxious that your account with me should be settled; because it might be a great prejudice to your family, if either you or I should die while things are in their present state. The ground of this uneasiness I must confess I do not /perfectly/ apprehend. I wish you had rather stated it yourself in your own words, informing me at the same time of the precise things you wished me to say in order to remove it. Whatever it is that you wish me to do for that purpose you have a perfect right to call upon me to do and my readiness to do it is proportioned to my acknowledged sense of your right.

The cargo of goods in question being a cargo chiefly of iron ware for the use of my Brother /to the amount according to your account of 392.2.3½/ I acknowledge the receipt of, and they were I dare say according to the invoyce for I never heard him say any thing to the contrary. I had perfect confidence as well as he in your acting with zeal and propriety in the execution of any commissions /of that nature/ you might accept from either of us: that confidence is ~~not at~~ in no respect impaired by the result of the commission just mentioned: this is all I can say, my Brother being at a distance, and I no judge of the articles nor having ever seen or concerned myself about them. I advised you of the arrival at the time, by a letter which appears to have miscarried. But if the things themselves had never reached us here, would you have incurred any risk on that account?

As to the settlement of an account, current as our's, I do not very well apprehend what you wished me to do for that purpose nor how such an account can well be settled till we meet, which I hope will be ere many months are at an end. It is not improbable but I may be set out before any answer from you can arrive. [*Line crossed out*].

I should be much obliged to you for my acct. and your account with Sir Rob. Herries as soon as you can conveniently let me have it. I want it, and ought to have applied for it before for the settling of some accounts here.⊞ It is so short, that if you have not got it. Be pleased also to send the continuation of my account current till the present time.

I ~~enclose~~ return you the Power of Atty. for receiving the Tontine money filled up, likewise the Certificate.[2] I wonder they would not accept of my hand-writing which is so well known to them, as

⊞ I propose to set out as soon as the winter roads are formed, possibly before: but do not let this prevent your writing.

[2] See letter 598, n. 9.

sufficient evidence. For proof of my Brother's being alive they accept of the declaration of my Father grounded on his sight of a letter of my Brother's.

600

FROM SAMUEL BENTHAM[1]

2/13 September 1787

Cherson Sept. 2/13.

For all this money will be wanting, horses must be bought, hides for the leather fabrick and Iron for the works. I know not what success I shall meet with but I send by this opportunity a pressing letter to Popoff[2] to induce him to pay the bearer what the Prince owes me, if he refuses it I shall make one more attempt on the Prince and then ask leave of absence or dismission whether it be war or peace, and try my fortune at Petersburgh. As I shall probably have to give up my batallion ~~therefore~~ I do not know how I can leave any men at Creetchoff unless it be four as denchiks[3] or servants and three more with an under officer for the present at least under pretense of guarding my things which from the circumstances of my detension I could not at present transport. At any rate I hope all the Potatoes will be dug up and the most necessary work done before this reaches you. Could a Vessel of some kind be procured it would certainly be well to send potatoes to Chremenchuck as also every thing superfluous: but as there is little chance of that if Leather fabrick continues then all the potatoes which can not be sold at a good price in the winter should be planted in the spring and for this purpose a piece of land hired if Zadobrast is taken away.

600. [1] B.M. IV: 397–8. Autograph. Docketed by Bentham: '1787 Sept. 2/13 / S.B. Cherson / to / J.B. Crichoff / Reced Sept 9 / N.B. The Express left Cherson Sept 4.'

This document is in sequence to fos. 395–6, also from Samuel, which form a complete letter on their own, of a date three days earlier, ending with the word 'Adieu'. Nevertheless both sheets were sent together by Samuel and received together by Bentham on 9 September, and the abruptness of the commencement of fo. 397 seems to be explained by the fact that it constitutes further thoughts on the last part of fo. 396, in which Samuel asked his brother to send as much leather as possible from Krichëv to Kherson. Much of the letter in folios 395–6 is quoted by Bentham in letter 603 and is therefore not included in its place here.

[2] Vasiliy Stepanovich Popov (1743–1822). He was Potëmkin's confidential secretary and chief subordinate in the execution of his policy of developing the resources of the south of Russia and the Crimea (E.I. Druzhinina, *Severnoye Prichernomor'e v 1775–1800 godakh*, Moscow, 1959, pp. 14, 28).

[3] *Denshchik*, batman.

The scarcity of corn and the great demand for it will probably make a great price for potatoes last year they sold from 4 to 8 rubles the chetwert at Chremenchuc. If /Leather Fabrick/ ~~Zadobrast~~ is to be abandoned this winter then to be sure they must be sold at any rate.

I know nothing against the Swede's honesty although he is apt enough to lye.[4] When I had thoughts of going to England this winter I intended to take him with me. As to his wife she is a nuisance and I know not what to do for her but as he would probably like the journey he would find means of disposing of her. The two girls who are with you I should not like to give up. If they are to be bought ten rubles for each will secure the property of them Jacob Pauvolitz[5] may manage it, but if Gallinsky wont sell them, then give the commission to one of the officers to steal them and ~~bring~~ send them here.

While Zadobrast is not given up I suppose you will stay there till you have finished your work: but will you not come here to see me at least before you set out for England? Why not spend the winter here. You may be retired as well as at Zadobrast and as to any apprehensions of danger from an attack of the Turks that is what should they intend it there will be warning enough for you to march off bag and baggage. Your things are not here yet, but will be soon, but I shall not send them from hence till I hear again from you. What is to become of Aiton? If he is disposed to stay in the country he may get his Salary or a greater in many parts. If you write to Pleschejeff he can find him employment and oblige somebody at the same time. The bricklayers also may certainly be provided for. This one has lately been ill or I should have found him employment. As I suppose the glass-making German has nothing more to do at Ushaky he may be sent here by which means I may get out of him some of the money he has cost me. He has tallents that may turn to account here.

The millwright I suppose is dismissed.

If I fix myself here and Zadobrast is not given up, I must have a baydac of some kind or other built during the winter to bring all manner of things from your part of the world here, and till then almost all my things may remain. Horses I can scarcely do without therefore such things as I am in want of might be brought by them. I cannot however recollect any thing that I can be said to be much

[4] On this man, Du Bark, see journal 615, n. 4.

[5] Yakov Pavlovich Tsetvich, a subaltern who had been acting as agent or business manager for Samuel during his absences from Krichëv. He appears in an equivocal light in Bentham's account of events preceding his departure homeward (see memorandum 611).

in want of therefore the horses might be loaded with leather packed up in Cabitkys. I would like to have the company of Korsakoff and his bay companions, but if your reciprocal freindship should not admit of a separation I will content myself as I can. If you come here you should come in the carriage, but otherwise I can do without it.

I had while at Chremenchuc improved in my amphibious vehicles so as to adapt them to military carts. I left some of my people and wood to construct one at Fenshaw's I have lately heard that it had been shewn to the Prince much approved of and that similar were making for all the four batallions of chasseurs of which this is now the second. It is however by accident only that I heard this as nobody gives me any notice of it directly.

You must not forget that the chance of my giving up my batallion should be kept quite secret least under a security of being no longer under my command Vokt and others should be utterly regardless of my interests.

I send you some Pamphlets and what newspapers I could lay hands on. I have also sent all papers of accounts and letters of business

601

From Prince A. B. [V?] Vyazemskiy[1]

early September 1787

Еремеи Ивановъ or Ивановичъ

Si je n'ai pas eu le plaisir de vous répondre plus tôt,[2] prêtés vous en à Monsieur frère, qui de tous les Anglais de ma Connaissance est assurement le plus flegmatique et le plus indécis. je vous assure Monsieur que je lui ai demandé plus de vingt fois quand il enverra ma Lettre, et c'est toujours des réponses de Normands. voilà assez sur cette matière.

Je suis très fâché de ce que vous n'avés pas voulu venir voir

601. [1] B.M. IV: 411–2. Autograph. Faded and the ink 'spread' in places and hard to decipher. Docketed by Bentham: '1787 Sept. / Pr. Wiasemsky Cherson / to / J.B. / Zadobras.' The Russian heading reads: 'Jeremy Ivanov or Ivanovich' (the third word is English 'or' and not in Russian characters).

This letter was written not later than 4/15 September 1787, since it arrived at the same time (see letter 603 at n. 9) as Samuel's letter of 2/13 September, which left Kherson on 4/15 September and arrived on 9/20 September (letter 600).

For the possible identity of the writer, see letter 442, n. 2.

[2] A missing letter from Bentham to Vyazemskiy is indicated here.

notre célèbre ville de Cherson, surtout pendant qu'elle a été embellie par la présence de deux têtes impériales, j'avoue que je consens[?] très facilement qu'un hom̄e qui vous ressemblerait d'après les idées que je me suis fai[tes] sur vous ne doit pas faire grand cas de tous ces titres fastidieux, mais c'est que mon propre intérêt était fortement lié à vous voir un peu de curiosité car cela m'aurait mené à faire la connaissance d'un hom̄e que j'estime déjà beaucoup par relation indirecte, je vous avés préparé la Chambre la plus isolée de ma maison, et la table la plus grande que l'on a pu trouver dans toute la ville, c'était d'après les renseignements de votre frère. ma fem̄e qui vous fait bien ses complimens se faisait aussi une fête de faire votre connaissance. elle ne vous écrit pas elle-même parce qu'elle a la fièvre depuis un mois, et que j'écris ceci de la chambre de Mr. Bentham. dans les circonstances actuelles cela ne serait pas honette de vous inviter venir ici, un hom̄e qui s'est devoué aux intérêts du genre humain qui prend sa cause en main et qui tâche d'alleéger le poids qui l'opresse de toute part ne doit pas venir assister au spectacle des maladies frénetiques de ce même genre humain, qui va s'égorger sans rime ni raison pour le plaisir de deux individus qui ne se sont jamais vus ni ne se verront assurément pas, et cela pour avoir quelques pouces de rubans jaune, rouge, bleu etc. cela ne devrait pas être le langage d'un de ces forcenés nom̄és guerrier, mais com̄e cette Lettre est adressée à un *sensible man* j'ai dû me dépouiller de mes préjugés et suivre la dictée de la raison, mais si je suivais celle de mon Cœur, je vous aurais toujours invité avec bien des instances à venir ici, à fin que je puisse vous assurer de vive voix de l'estime et du respect avec lequel je suis pour toujours

Monsieur
Votre très h. et très ob. Ser.
A. B. Wiasemsky

Je vous envoie un journal Ency. où j'ai vu qu' [*three words illegible*] à Londres vous rendait publiquement justice, et trois brochures qu'on m'a envoyé de Paris. je vous prierais de me renvoyer les dernières.

602

To John Farr Abbot[1]

12/23 September 1787 (Aet 39)

Zadobras near Crichoff Sept. 12/23 1787.

My dear Far

I have just been telling your Mother, as how and as when I have been hearing of your having committed matrimony. Much about the time that you were recommending that holy state by your example, the thread of my lucubrations had brought me to an humble proposal for the encouragement of it in the only way in which such a connexion ought to be, or can stand in need of being, encouraged by rendering it easy for those who do not find it sit easy on them, to shake it off. The idea itself is rather antient, as antient for aught I know, as Adam and Eve, but the arguments I have brought in support of it, are of such strength, take my word for it, as must impress conviction upon the judgement of every unprejudiced person, who may think it worth his while to listen to them. Whatever you may think of them, I am in no doubt of meeting with readers, whose feelings will bear due testimony to their merit. As far as I hear, however, I have but little chance of finding either you or Mrs. Abbot of that number: so that if I get any thanks from either of you, it must be by bespeaking them, which I do by these presents, of which take notice.

I have been wishing your Mother a whole rabble-rout of Grandchildren, but that was only a way of speaking. I hate squalling as much as I love Musick. I hear from an old Gentleman of our acquaintance, that my new Sister has a pretty finger ⟨which⟩ he invites me to come and admire: and that is the one part of her person, a man, who is not her husband, can have unlimited indulgence for admiring, any acquiring of children to you would only be so much loss to me. I never yet knew any good, and have often known much mischief, come to Musick, from women's having brats, whatever may be the case with other kinds of harmony.

The world says, to use a Johnsonian expression 'you give good

602. [1] B.M. Add. Mss. 36524, fos. 25–6. Autograph. Endorsed on the first page in pencil: ' Jere'.

Printed, Bowring, x, 177–8. A few words now indecipherable in the Ms. have been supplied from Bowring's text. This letter was dispatched through Alleyne Fitzherbert at St Petersburg under cover of a letter to Fitzherbert of 14/25 September (see letters 604 and 619).

fowls': I rejoice to hear of it: I scarce know of any greater merit in such a world as this, than that of giving good fowls: it gives me a great respect for you. I have been rubbing up my epicurean ideas as well as I can, to enable me to worship your fowls: 1500 or 2000 miles journey will, I hope, give me some appetite for them. Amongst the many additional oddities I have, I dare to say, contracted in this my hermitage, is that of eating nothing but bread and butter till about 9 at night, and then not caring what I eat, nor much whether I eat any thing or no. But I never was better in health in my life, and I /rather/ increase in flesh than fall away.

Remember me affectionately to Charles. He is taking great strides, I make no doubt, towards the top of his nasty prostitute profession. I will not pretend to wish that families may be ruined for his sake, any more than that Turks may have their throats cut for Sam's: all I can wish is, that if Turks must be killed, Sam may have some share in the killing of them: and that if Christians must be plunder'd, Charles may have a good finger in the plunder pie.

I am, Dear Far.

Your's and his very truly
Jeremy Bentham

John Far Abbot Esqr.

603

To Jeremiah Bentham[1]

14/25 September 1787 (Aet 39)

(Duplicate)

My dear Father

Since the last post that went out from hence arrived an officer of my Brother's despatched by him express from Cherson with

603. [1] B.M. IV: 399–400. Autograph. Marked, 'Duplicate'. Docketed by Jeremiah Bentham: 'Mr. Jeremy Bentham / Letter datd. Critchoff Sept. 25/14 1787 / with an Extract of a Letter / from his Brother the Lt. Coll. / to him datd. Cherson / Augt. 30th O.S. Sept. 10th N.S. 1787.'

Addressed: 'To / Jeremiah Bentham Esqr. / Queens Square Place / Westminster / London.'

For the circumstances of the dispatch of this letter and others accompanying it, see letters 604 and 619. The other copy, sent by a different channel, is not now in Bentham's papers.

letters of which the following is an extract. N.B. The Officer left Cherson the 5/16 instant, and arrived here the 10/21.

Cherson $\frac{\text{August 30}}{\text{Sept 10}}$ 1787[2]

'You will no doubt have heard before now that war is already commenced here: by the Turkish fleet which lies at Ochakoff' (Oczacow in the maps) 'attacking two Russian ships which lay at anchor near them. It was on the 5/16 of this month that the Russian Minister was conducted to the Seven-Towers, and on the 17/28 the Turks made their attack. Their fleet at Ochakoff consists of 4 ships of the line of 66 guns, 3 frigates of 26 guns, 3 sloops, 10 Gallies and a Bomb-vessel. One of the Russian Vessels mounted 40 guns: the other 12. As you may imagine, the Russian Ships did not lie long at Anchor when attacked by such a superiour force, but setting sail directed their course as fast as possible up the Dnieper. The large ships of the Turks were afraid to follow them, no doubt on account of the shallowness of the channel.' (N.B. The Dnieper is said to have been never known to be so shallow as this year). 'however their ten galleys and bomb-vessel were dispatched to secure the prize. Fifteen versts' (10 miles) 'they accompanied the Russian ships, keeping up as brisk a fire as their strength would permitt: but towards dusk the Russians outsailed them, after having killed a great many of their men, and disabled two of their vessels, which, we have learnt ⟨sunk⟩[3] with their guns in them after their return. On board the Russian ships, three men only were killed. Their Commanders have been promoted for their gallant defence.

At Gluboka,[4] which is about half-way to Ochakoff, we have one 64 gun ship, and a frigate: the former of which can not take in her guns, or at least cannot sail with them in, for want of water. Besides these, there are half a dozen transport vessels, /into/ which we are endeavouring to put some guns. We have here at Cherson seven Gallies, in which the Empress and her suite came from Kieff: and 8 barges which accompanied them carrying provisions, carriages etc. With such materials we are endeavouring to compose a fleet, not

[2] The original letter is B.M. IV: 395–6 (see letter 600, n. 1). Bentham omitted a final section concerning the dispatch of some of Samuel's possessions and trade goods to Kherson, and he interjected a number of parentheses. For an account of the naval engagement described by Samuel Bentham, see R. C. Anderson, *Naval Wars in the Levant, 1559–1853*, Liverpool, 1952, p. 319.

[3] Word illegible in Bentham's letter supplied from Samuel's original.

[4] I.e., 'the deeps'—the deep channel at what came to be known as Shirokaya, below the bar which made Kherson itself unusable by large vessels.

to defend ourselves against, but to make an attack upon, the Turkish Squadron at Ochakoff. Perhaps indeed we may add 2 or 3 fireships, which, if they don't burn our enemies may at least serve to light us to our attack. In this business I flatter myself I am a principal agent: the fitting out the Gallies and small vessels from hence, and the finding commanders for them is my more particular business. Four of the Gallies are commanded by Englishmen: one who had been acting Lieutenant in England came here to enter into the service before the war broke out: two more Captains of Merchant-ships /here/' (Hall and Love) 'who upon the war's breaking out offer'd their service: and the fourth, Captain Bell whom I was not sorry in this way to get off my hands. They have all (Englishmen like) much eagerness in the cause.' (Love I know nothing of. Hall had been mate to Capt. Newman who took me up at Kiemid on the Asiatic coast,[5] and was at that time master of a vessel Newman had been buying at Alexandria in Egypt. The Bosphorus being renderd impassible and the trade of the Black sea suspended by the war, these people were of course to seek for employment. Bell who had been master of a vessel at Newcastle was one of the people engaged there by Notman. Bell was a Quaker as well as Notman: but my Brother's pious zeal had render'd him a convert it seems to war and orthodoxy. Were this service properly represented to the Archbishop of Canterbury, I should humbly hope it might be thought not altogether undeserving of a small token of his Grace's approbation. The post would carry a pastoral letter, though not a consecrated sword. Charles, I think, is well at Lambeth—But I would not be too intruding.)

'I am detained here at present, by an order from General Souvaroff,[6] Commander in Chief here, in consequence of Mordvinoffs[7] representations of the need he had of my assistance at this critical time.' (Col. Mordvinoff is first member of the board of

[5] See p. 402.

[6] General Aleksandr Vasil'yevich Suvorov (1729–1800), the most outstandingly successful Russian military commander of the last quarter of the eighteenth century and the man chiefly responsible for Russian military success in the field during the Russo-Turkish war of 1787–91. On him see P. Longworth, *The Art of Victory. The Life and Achievements of Generalissimo Suvorov, 1729–1800*, London, 1965.

[7] Suvorov's dispatch to Samuel Bentham, no. 91, dated 27 August 1787, headed 'Order' runs: 'From your knowledge of Admiralty business, and on the request of Rear Admiral Mardvinoff I require you to remain at the Admiralty here till further order, of which I have informed his Highness.' (Two copies in English, B.M. IV: 401 and 402). Suvorov's letter to Potëmkin of 27 August requesting confirmation of this step, and Mordvinov's application to Potëmkin dated 20 August to have Samuel attached to his command, are in *Materialy dlya istorii russkogo flota*, vol. xv, ed. Veselago, St Petersburg, 1895, pp. 511, 45.

Admiralty) 'They have both made their reports to the Prince' (who since the Empress's departure has been at Kremenchook the capital of his governments) 'who has written to Mordvinoff that I may be made to belong to the Admiralty.'—

'I[8] had, while at Kremenchook, improved in my amphibious vehicles, so as to make them answer the purpose of military carts. I left some of my people and wood to construct one at Fanshaw's.' (An English Lieut-Colonel who commands such another Batallion as Sam's.) 'I have since learnt that it has been shewn to the Prince, and much approved of, and that similar ones were making for all the four Batallions of Chasseurs, of which mine is now the second.' I had already heard of those amphibious pontoons from two officers of my Brother's who arrived here from Kremenchook about 3 weeks ago. The remains of his Batallion except two officers and 15 men marched this day sennight for Kremenchook in consequence of a sudden order from the Prince issued doubtless on the prospect of the war, and received here about three weeks before.

By the same conveyance comes a letter to me from Prince Wiasemski repeating the invitation (mentioned in my last) to go and spend the winter with him at Cherson;[9] seconded by an observation of my Brother's that though the Turks are not far distant, a siege is not very probable, and at any rate there would be warning time enough for me to decamp.[10]

But at the same time comes a letter from my father dated Aug. 8th,[11] desiring to know whether I ever mean to see England again during his life. My answer is, that I am preparing for a visit to that country with all possible expedition: and that I hope in the course of a fortnight to be on the wing. The season of snow-roads would have been a much more convenient one for travelling: but the dispersion of the greater part of the English, especially of those who are more particularly attached to me (Aiton and Beattie) would render my stay till that time much less comfortable than it has been hitherto. The sudden breaking up which is the unavoidable result of my Brother's indefinite imprisonment, added to the circumstance of the change of ownership in the estate, throws the whole weight of his business into hands not the best qualified for, and much averse to such a task.

What you have now read will I make no doubt be looked upon as

[8] The next three sentences were extracted by Bentham from Samuel's letter of 2/13 September (letter 600).

[9] Letter 601. Bentham's 'last' letter to his father mentioning the original invitation is missing. See n. 12.

[10] In letter 600.

[11] Missing.

sufficient reason for passing over in silence most of the topics touched upon in your double-letter. As to your pecuniary requisition I answer it in the best and indeed only way in which I could answer it, viz. by a draught on Mr. King. The events of war have thrown back, as you see, the fulfillment of the expectations given in my letter of a fortnight or three weeks ago,[12] to an uncertain period. That fulfillment depended upon payments of money which it may perhaps require personal sollicitation to obtain, though due from and promised by persons perfectly and instantly able to fulfill such promise. In the mean time the 2000 Roobles mentioned in my last have been or will have been distributed among persons to whom more was due, and whom otherwise I must have seen some thrown into jail, others starving before my face. My great apprehension was, lest the affair of the cloth should have appeared in your ⟨eyes⟩ mere pretence for getting the money back, unaccompanied /from the beginning/ with any intention of replacing ⟨it⟩. Laying all circumstances together, I can not but apprehend your finding some diffi⟨culties⟩ in avoid to make a change for the worse in the exterior of your appearance. Under the ⟨circum⟩stances, the generosity with which you acquiesce in the disappointment, ⟨makes a prop⟩er impression on me. Rather than that should happen /the greatest part of/ whatever income I possess [*line crossed out*] is most perfectly at your service. One room, somewhere not far from town, will hold me as well as a thousand. Whether there be a bedstead in that room is a matter of great indifference. Featherbeds I have long had an irreconcilable quarrel with: curtains I have quarrel'd with and discarded since I came to Russia. I am, how little reason soever there may be for it, a somewhat prouder man than when I left England, and as my pride is not grounded upon wealth, poverty would make no abatement in it. I have lived in great luxury, and in great simplicity: in the latter much more to my comfort than in the former: nor is there any luxury which would make up to me for the pain of being forced from occupations to which I am attached into company for the conversation of which I have no relish.

It is not now worth while reckoning up how many letters of mine must have miscarried, in some or all of which the cloth was mentioned, betwixt that of July which you acknowledge, and the Inspection-house letters—One if not two in which Sir R. Worsley was mentioned who staid a month with us. With the account of the

[12] Missing. Presumably Bentham was referring to a letter to his father sent about the same time as letters 598 and 599. The previous known letter relating to this financial business is letter 597 of 13/24 July, which cannot be meant here.

duel went a copy of a letter I had been writing to Prince Dashcoff, which as far as it went would have served for our history as well as one addressed to you. A packet to you by Sea much about that time inclosing one to Mr. P. Carew appears also from your silence to have miscarried. It contained nothing more material than a copy of his own papers as far as I had been able to get it taken, with a letter to him stating why it was impossible for me to transmitt it to him before my departure.

One of these duplicates I reckon to send through Mr. Fitzherbert: another through Mr. Cum⟨min⟩ Merchant /at Riga/ a connection of Aiton's wife's, just found out by me.

Whichever duplicate comes first to hand, you may if you please send to ask of Ld. L. whether he has received a letter from me: if not, then you may tear off the first half sheet of this and carry or send it him. I write to him to the same effect.[13] But a letter to him stands a worse chance than one to you. I enclose in one of these duplicates a letter for my Mother. I write by way of Petersburgh to Far.

To Mr. Richard King of the Six Clerks Coffee house Chancery Lane London.

Crichoff in White Russia Sept. 14/25 1787

Sir

At fourteen days after sight pay to Jeremiah Bentham of Queens Square Place Westminster Esquire or order on this my first bill of exchange (second not paid) fifty pounds eleven shillings and seven pence £50. 11. 7 (value reced.) on account of Your's

etc. Jeremy Bentham

604

To Alleyne Fitzherbert[1]

14/25 September 1787 (Aet 39)

Sir

Though the principal part of the intelligence contained in the following extract can be no news to you, yet /on account of/ ~~as~~

[13] Of this letter to Lansdowne only a fragmentary rough draft is known (letter 605).

604. [1] B.M. IV: 407. Autograph. Draft with corrections. Headed above the greeting: 'J.B. To Mr. Fitzherbert Petersburgh by post Crichoff Sept. 14/25 1787 enclosing 1. a letter to Q.S.P. covering one to Mrs. B[entham]. 2. another to Mr. Abbot.' Docketed:

~~there are some of the circumstances it contains~~ some particulars /it contains/ which may not have come to you through other channels, but more on account of the relation they bear to my Brother in whose fate you take so kind an interest, I thought it might possibly prove not unacceptable to you. It was brought me on the 10/21 instant by an officer of his who left Cherson on the 4/15.[2]

~~I do not know whether~~ I believe you staid long enough to know that an account of the expence of the Vermicular Barge had been asked for and the money order'd. You will not look upon it as an event incredible that that order remains still unexecuted. The express above-mentioned took a /letter which my Brother says was/ very pressing letter to ~~Colonel~~ Popoff from whom the money had it been obtained was to have been brought hither /hither where in truth there is no small need of it/. None came: but as Popoff was pronounced /known to be/ ill and invisible to every body the disappointment is not quite so discouraging as if the letter had been received by him and either not answerd or answerd in the negative.

The breaking up of things here affords such an opportunity to any body who wants a Gardener, as has never yet offer'd itself in Russia. John Aiton[3] whom I thought myself fortunate to get for my Brother from Scotland at so low a salary as £80 a year, is nephew and was some years foreman to Aiton the King's Gardener at Kew. I question whether ever ~~Gardener~~ man ever had so /complete a gardener's/ education: for besides /breeding him up/ at Kew which may be reckoned the first school in the kingdom, his Uncle sent him to serve successively at Lee's the Nursery-mans, a man of particular eminence in his line, Mrs Southechs[?],[4]the Duke of Northumberlands,[5] and the Princess Amelia's,[6] and I don't know what other places. These opportunities have not been thrown away upon him, I look upon him just as far as I can judge he is a compleat master of his business: I have just that sort of superficial knowledge ~~I have the fondness I have~~ for gardening and botany ~~has given me that superficial knowledge which~~ may enable /a man/ to form some judgement of the abilities of ~~a man~~ one who knows more. He has likewise ~~both~~ here /as well as/ in England had some experience in

'1787 Sept. 14/25 / J.B. Crichoff / to / A. Fitzherbert Petersburgh / Also J.B. Crichoff / to / Ld. Lansdown London.'

The letter to Mrs. Bentham is missing. The draft of that to Lansdowne is letter 605.

[2] I.e., a copy of the information in Samuel Bentham's letter of 30 August/10 September, similar to that reported by Bentham to his father in letter 603.

[3] On Aiton, see letter 567, n. 5.

[4] Not identified.

[5] Hugh Percy (1714–86), 1st Duke of Northumberland.

[6] Princess Amelia Sophia Eleanora (1710–86), the 2nd da. of George II.

the farming line. To say he is sober, is only saying he is a Scotchman; and with regard to his honesty my Brother's long absence has afforded me such occasion to observe it as does not lie within the compass of ordinary experience. He has a wife who being bred in a farmer's family understands I believe, pretty compleatly the dairy business, and might on that account prove a valuable accession to the family of any one who were disposed to engage her husband. He leaves my Brother with regret, and it is with regret I part with him: indeed I would not have parted with him so soon had I staid some time longer as I thought to have done till I heard of my Brother's being thus impounded. He refused some time ago £100 a year which was offer'd him by my Brother on the part of the Prince to go to the Crimea.

Before I close this packet /letter/ I don't know whether I may not take the liberty of troubling you with one for England. The contents being of some consequence to my Brother and me I send a duplicate by way of Riga but can not trust to that Channel having lost by means of it ~~I believe~~ more than half a dozen letters since I have been here. I ~~shall not~~ /have no need to/ trespass so much further upon your politeness as to beg an answer: hoping to shape my course homewards through Poland and Germany ~~before any could arrive~~ in about a fortnight's time.[7]

~~You will excuse I hope my having written~~ I wrote to Mr. Pleschejeff /likewise/ about the Gardener ~~to the same effect, I thought~~ as a means of doubling the man's chance. I send him off when I go myself. Going with horses of my brother's it may /take him/ a month perhaps ~~before he arrives at~~ /to get to/ Petersburgh.

Of the Vermicular-barge money a part was wanted to help discharge the arrears due to this man and the other English. They bear their disappointment with a patience and good humour which touches me very sensibly.

[7] Bentham's departure was in fact delayed by the action of one of his brother's creditors (see letters 607–11).

605

To the Marquis of Lansdowne[1]

18/29 September 1787 (Aet 39)

Crichoff in White Russia Sept. 18/29 1787

My Lord

The commencements of war, how trifling soever in themselves, derive an importance from the events to which they lead. It is partly this consideration, partly that of the kind interest your Lordship takes in what concerns the writer of a letter I have just received, that I take the liberty of troubling you with an extract.

After the extract follows the list of the fleet—[...?][2]

We have it here, that not only the Emperor joins the Russians, but likewise the Kg. of Prussia who it is said has a body of troops already in Courland on their march to co-operate some time or other with the Russian armies.[3] The Poles, it is said, have assembled or

605. [1] B.M. IV: 407v. Autograph.

Draft with corrections, written on the same sheet as letter 604. The original has not been found in the Lansdowne Mss.; but the extract preceding the list of the fleet was probably the whole or part of the extract from Samuel Bentham's letter which Bentham sent to his father in letter 603. Lansdowne did receive the letter, which was sent by way of Cummings (or Comyns) and Co. of Riga (see letter 619).

[2] Jeremiah Bentham's copies of his son's letters include (B.M. XXII: 424v) a 'List of the Russian naval force in the Black Sea as it stood in Jany. last (1787)'. It seems probable that it is another copy of a list sent in this letter to Lansdowne. It runs:

Building at Cherson	At Taganroc	At Sebastopol in the Crimea
1 of 80 Guns	4 40 Gun Frigates	3 of 66 Guns
1 of 66	4 Transports	2 50 Gun Frigates
2 50 Gun Frigates		9 40 Gun Frigates
		6 Armed Ships
		8 Transports

N.B. The 80 Gun ship, That of 66 Guns, and one of the Frigates were launched while the Empress was at Cherson. That of 66, is That called in the S.B.'s Letter the 64. The 80 Gun Ship, it appears from the above Letter and from Verbal accounts is not at Cherson; I suppos'd She has joyned the Main Body at Astopol.

according to an Instruction dated at Petersburg Nov 18/7 The number of Recruits Ordered is as follows

For the Artillery	3700	This instruction though printed is secret. Copies are sent to the Governors General, Commanders of Garrisons, and Generals in employ.
For the Fleet	18000	
For the Army		
Total	90000	

[3] Austria was pledged to involvement in the war as the ally of Russia, but Prussian policy during this war was dictated by jealousy of Russian expansion, and the court

are assembling an army of observation of 30,000 men. /The Venetians, we likewise understand, accede to this wonderful alliance/ ~~But of this you have certainly much prompter and more authentic intelligence.~~ Our notion is that the Porte has been forced into this war by the populace, who had seized or attempted to seize the heir-apparent. But of all this you have certainly much prompter and more authentic intelligence. ~~What a fertile field for speculation!~~

Last winter I attempted to trouble your Lordship with one of my never ending letters. Laying circumstances together I am inclined to think the attempt did not succeed.[4]

After a struggle between the opposite attractions of Cherson and London I think before many ⟨days are at⟩ an end, to set my face homewards, having my course most probably through Warsaw and Berlin and I hope it will not be very long before I have the honour of testifying in person the sincere and respectful attachment with which I am

606

To Cummings and Co., Riga[1]

22 September/3 October 1787 (Aet 39)

Crichoff in White Russia Sept. 22d 1787

Sirs

Though I have not the pleasure of your acquaintance, I take the liberty of recommending the bearer John Varey, a Bricklayer and Plaisterer late in the service of my Brother L.Col. Bentham to any good offices he may stand in need of /at your hands./ He is a very honest worthy young man, and during his residence here has behaved himself much to the satisfaction of my Brother (in whose absence I write) and of every body else. He is very apprehensive lest the regulation about giving notice of departure should detain him beyond the time of sailing of the last ships. In that case, the nature of his business affording no employment during the winter season, he would be in danger of finding himself destitute of every

of Berlin engaged in diplomacy hostile to Russia. Plans for the Venetians to conquer the Morea and give up their territories on the eastern Adriatic coast to Austria came to nothing, and the Venetians did not join in the war.

[4] No such letter has been found in the Lansdowne Mss.

606. [1] B.M. IV: 410. Autograph. Draft. Docketed by Bentham: '1787 Sept 22 / J.B. Crichoff / to / Cummings & Co. Riga / Re J. Varey.'

In letter 619 Bentham spelled the name 'Comyn'.

means of subsistance, that is, in other words, of being kept to starve. To prevent such a misfortune, if, in the event of his not being able to meet with any employment, you would be kind enough to advance him on my account any sum not exceeding a Rix dollar per week, /as long as he remains without employment/ from the time of the departure of the last ships of this season to that of the first ships of the next, I am setting out for England by land in a few days, and as soon as arrived, which I expect will be in about six weeks shall hold myself in readiness, with thanks and punctuality to reimburse your correspondent in London any sums so advanced by you as soon as as often as advised.⊞

I am, Gentlemen
Your most obedient humble servant
Jeremy Bentham.

⊞ The house of Pierson, Huhn and Co. having been hitherto my Brother's correspondents, I should not have attempted giving you this trouble, but for the very extraordinary behaviour of Mr. Christian Trompovski who ever since Novr. last has been detaining a large sum of money of my Brother's in his hands, promising an account and rendering none, though he has been informed over and over again that, independently of the money, the want of the account itself is productive of very great loss and inconvenience.[2]

P.S. Please to direct to me Queen's Square Place Westminster. I give Varey at a venture a letter to the Governor stating the case, in order that he may get a pass if possible, notwithstanding the general regulation.

607

To Governor General Pëtr Passek[1]

13/24 October 1787 (Aet 39)

à Zadobras près de Critcheff ce 13 Oct. 1787

Monseigneur

Etant ici en visite chez ~~mon frere~~ le Lieutenant Colonel /mon frère/ ~~chef de Batallion dans le service de sa Majeste~~ je me trouve

[2] See letter 593.

607. [1] B.M. IV: 416. Autograph. Draft with corrections. Docketed by Bentham: '1787 Oct. 13 / J.B. Zadobras / to / Gov. Gen. Passek Mohileff / Sent by Beaty Oct. 14 / By him deliver'd Oct. 15.' All dates are O.S.

dans une circonstance fâcheuse qui m'oblige de ~~recourir a la justice de~~ m'addresser à V. Excellence. Je ne sais quel marchand a obtenu /de la Haute Justice de Mohileff/ à la charge de mon frère /une Ukase/ fondée sur des prétentions que j'ai les plus fortes raisons de ~~croire mal-fondus~~ /regarder comme peu solides:/ mais sur lesquelles ~~je ne prétens pas occuper v. Excellence~~ /je passe comme ne me regardant pas/. Sur ce fondement tel quel, hier est venu ici le Capitaine Ispravnik de Cherikoff qui m'a fait signifier que j'avois moi à satisfaire sur le champ cette demande au montant de deux cent et tant de Roubles; ~~et mon repos~~ /et de ce que je m'en suis excusé/ il m'a fait savoir que j'étois au arrêts. En meme tems il a mis le scellé à des effets à mon frère, entre lesquels se trouve /tout ce qu'il y a de/ la provision pour la nourriture des ouvriers qui servent dans les fabriques du Prince Potemkin qui sont sous la direction de mon frère. /Lui il/ est absent au service où son devoir l'appelle: moi, je n'ai la moindre liaison avec ses affaires. Je ne crois pas qu'il y ait pays au monde où l'on condamne les absens sans leur avoir donné la faculté de se faire entendre encore moins /où l'on arrête/ un étranger innocent pour les dettes d'autrui. J'ai ouï dire que le pretexte sur lequel on s'est fondé pour s'addresser à moi c'est que j'ai vendu des effets à mon frère. Il est vrai que j'en ai vendu quelques uns au montant de deux ou trois cent roubles; tant par ce que son déplacement les lui /avait/ rendu inutiles, que pour payer ses gens ~~que je trouvais autour de moi~~ /dont je me trouvais entouré/. Il est egalement vrai que j'ai emploié à ce même effet cinq /ou six/ fois autant de mes propres deniers dont une grande partie est allé payer ce /même/ marchand, dont en consequence j'ai vu le contrat qui a été dechiré en signe d'accomplissement par devant témoins. C'est pour cela que je me vois traite en criminel sans en être départi

Pëtr Passek (1736–1804) owed his advancement to his connection with the Orlovs and his participation in the conspiracy of June 1762 which led to the deposition and death of Peter III and the accession of Catherine II as reigning empress. In 1772 he was appointed governor general of the two White Russian provinces annexed from Poland by the First Partition.

This is the first of a group of documents relating to an attempt by Samuel Bentham's former business manager, subaltern Yakov Pavlovich Tsetvich, to secure, before Bentham left Russia, the payment of 280 rubles which he claimed to have advanced to two merchants who were supplying bark to the tannery which Samuel had entered into contract with Potëmkin to manage. A copy in Russian of Tsetvich's undertaking to the merchants, made by Beaty, is at B.M. IV: 422 (memorandum 611, n. 4) and a French translation of it at fo. 394. Bentham, who was just about to set out for England, found himself threatened with arrest when he refused to make immediate payment. He suspected Tsetvich's claim to be false (pp. 589–90). With this letter he sent a formal application for relief, together with an attestation concerning his arrest, to the regional court of justice at Mogilëv (letter 608). The conclusion of the affair is not recorded in his surviving papers.

ni de faits ni de paroles du respect le plus profond que l'on peut témoigner pour tout ce qui porte les caracteres de la Justice. Je soupire ~~apres mon~~ de me rendre chez moi où les affaires les plus pressantes m'appellent. Chaque heure peut ajouter à l'outrage que j'ai /déjà/ souffert /des dommages/ irréparable. Dans ces circonstances j'ose supplier de la Justice de V. Excellence /un/ passeport ~~en plus vite /necessaire~~ pour moi et un domestique/. Mes effets se trouvent indistinctement mêlés avec ceux de mon frère, pour trancher l'affaire il a été longtems question de tout saisir à la fois: /pour le moment/ on s'est laissé fléchir; mais si les voyes de fait ont cessé, les menaces existent: et je me refugie auprès de V. Excellence, tant pour ne pas être plus prisonnier, que pour ne pas mourir de faim dans un pays étranger. Pour la punition des coupables, je ne m'en mêle pas, c'est l'affaire de la Justice du pays, et non pas la mienne. La protection de l'ambassadeur de son pays est le refuge naturel de tout etranger qui se croit lesé: ~~suffi c'est la a elle que je m'addresse~~ Mais /celle/ ~~l'assistance~~ de V. Excellence comme plus prochaine ~~convient il autant [...?]~~ seroit plus prétieuse: et ~~la sentiment de mon~~ les hautes qualités de V. Excellence jointes aux droits que j'ai de les voir se déplacer en ma faveur, me la fait regarder comme certaine.

608

To the Regional Court of Justice at Mogilëv[1]

13/24 October 1787 (Aet 39)

В Могилевское наместническое правление
отъ иностранца Ермолая Бентана
покорнеишее доношение

В сходственность из Могилевскаго наместническаго правления ЕЯ ИМПЕРАТОРСКАГО ВЕЛИЧЕСТВА указа Чериковскому земскому исправнику Гну Манжинскому которои получа сеи указъ наложилъ на особу

608. [1] B.M. IV: 413–4. Copy. Docketed by Bentham: '1787 Oct. 13 / J.B. Zadobras / to / Mohileff Justice Court / Rapport in Russ / Drawn up for me by Gen. Bandre at his house at / Nijni Oct. 13 (Thursday) / Copy taken by Serjt. / sent on Friday morning 14 / by Beaty. / Delivered by him Saty. 15.'

Thursday was 14/25 October 1787. General Bandre was the Benthams' nearest neighbour of any social consequence. B.M. IV: 422v is a version of this letter in French, with one or two omissions, which, in view of the way in which it follows the Russian construction in places, was clearly made from it by one of Bentham's friends for his information.

мою арестъ; равно жъ и оставленнои в деревне Добрости могазеинъ для кажевных фабрикантовъ, которые доволствуютца изъ онаго могазеина, запечатававъ Онъ Гнъ Манжинской своеи печатью, а в случае таковыхъ обстоятелствъ дабы не могли претерпевать кажевныя фабриканты какого либо изнурение, которои арестъ наложенъ за долгъ брата моего служащаго в россиискои службѣ Екатеринославскаго егарскаго корпуса во второмъ баталионе подполковникомъ Самуилы Ивановича Бентона; а какъ я из своего краю приехалъ сюда единственно для свидания з братомъ моимъ, и по темъ причинам нахожусь в здешнихъ местахъ; к тому ж ежели какие либо претензіи касающияся до брата моего то должно к нему писать и с нимъ иметь дело а не со мнои, того ради Могилевскаго наместническаго правления покорнеише прошу в таковых случаяхъ меня яко чужестранца защитить и наложеннои на особу мою арестъ равно ж и некоторые смешанные мои вещи между братнинами, к тому жъ и запечатаннои могазеинъ повелеть освободить, а за таковыя мне приключившияся озлабленїи я не оставлю писать к находящемуся при ЕЯ ИМПЕРАТОРСКАГО ВЕЛИЧЕСТВА дворе аглицкому посланнику; а какъ я имею отсуда скоро отъезжать в свои край, для чего и їмею ожидать скореишеи резолюцый; к сему доношению иностранецъ Ермолай Бентома руку приложилъ

В Могилевское наместническое правление,
отъ иностранца Ермолая Бентома
покорнеишее доношение

Октября | | дня
1787 года В Могилевѣ

Enclosure

Свидетельство

1787го года октября | | дня мы ниже подписавшияся свидетелствуемъ в томъ что когда Чериковскои земскои исправникъ господинъ Манжинскои приехавши в Задобрость, иностранцу Ермолаю Бентому наложилъ арестъ, с темъ приказаниемъ дабы означеннои Бентома никуда не могъ с того места отлучитца причемъ были, и подписуемся;

Translation

To the Justice Court of the namestnichestvo of Mogilëv
From the foreigner Ermolay Bentan
a most humble submission

In pursuance of a ukase issued from her Imperial Majesty's Justice Court of the namestnichestvo of Mogilëv to the captain of police of Cherikov district, Mr. Manzhinskoy, he, upon receipt of this ukase, placed my person under arrest; in like manner, he, Mr. Manzhinskoy, sealed with his seal the store which has been left in the village of [Za]dobrost'[2] for the leather workers, who draw their supplies from this store, but in face of circumstances of the kind

[2] The error is by the Russian copyist. The name should read, Задобрости, 'Zadobrost''.

that have arisen, in order that the leather workers should not suffer deprivation of any kind; and whereas this arrest has been made because of the debt of my brother Samuila Ivanovich Benton, who is serving as a lieutenant-colonel in the second battalion of the Ekaterinoslav corps of chasseurs; and as I have come here from my own country solely to meet my brother and am staying in these parts for these reasons; and furthermore if there are any claims of any kind concerning my brother, then he should be written to and business had with him and not with me; on this account I humbly pray the Justice Court of the namestnichestvo of Mogilëv in these circumstances to extend protection to me as a foreigner and to give orders for the arrest put upon my person to be cancelled and similarly for certain belongings of mine which are mixed up with those of my brother, and in addition the store which has been sealed up, to be released. And on account of such vexations as have been inflicted upon me I shall not fail to write to the English ambassador accredited to the court of her Imperial Majesty; but as I shall soon leave here for my own country, for that reason I shall await the speediest decision. To this submission the foreigner Ermolay Bentoma has set his hand.

To the Justice Court of the namestnichestvo of Mogilëv
From the foreigner Ermolay Bentom
a most humble submission

October, 1787 the | | day At Mogilëv

Enclosure[3]

Testimony

1787 October the | | day we the undersigned bear witness that when Mr. Manzhinskoy, the police captain of Cherikov district, came to Zadobrost', he placed the foreigner Ermolay Bentoma under arrest, with the order, that the aforesaid Bentoma could not betake himself anywhere from this place, on which occasion we were present and we subscribe ourselves.

[3] B.M. IV: 415. Copy. Docketed by Bentham: '1787 Oct. 13 / At Zadobras / Attestations of / J. Notman / and / R. Beaty / testifying the arresting of / J.B. by the Captain Is / pravnik of Cherikoff / Oct. 12 / This form was drawn up / by Lavrenti as dictated by / his Master Gen. Bandre / at his house at Nijni Oct. / 13 / Copy taken by Sergt. / signed same day by / Notman & Beaty at Zadobras / and sent to the Mohileff / Justice-Court along with / J.B.'s report by Beaty / Oct. 14 and by him presented.'

609

From Governor General Pëtr Passek[1]

16/27 October 1787

Государь мой

Сожалѣю что не могу писать къ вамъ по францускy, причина сего есть та, что секретарь штата моего францускoй Экспедиціи нынѣ отлучился. Я велелъ зделать нужныя выправки относящїяся до дѣла вашего, и будте уверены что коль скоро будутъ оныя произведены, не оставлю прозбу вашу безъ справедливаго удовлетворенія, и поданія вамъ, такъ какъ чужестранцу защищенія, и возможнаго пособія. ежели только дело ваше есть справедливо не сумнѣваитесь нимало въ полученіи справедливой отъ меня помощи. я между тѣмъ посылаю при семъ письмо мое къ Гну здешнему губернатору Энгельгардту, которой на сихъ днях будетъ въ Черикове, рекомендуя оным разсмотреть дело ваше и доставить вамъ законное защищеніе. вы сіе письмо вручите Гну губернатору, или прежде пріезда его въ Чериковъ отправте к нему.

въ протчемъ пребываю
вамъ Государь мой
охотнымъ слугою
Петръ Пассекъ

октября 16о дня
1787 года

Translation

Sir,

I am sorry that I cannot write to you in French. The reason is that the secretary of my staff of the French department is at present away. I have given orders for the necessary enquiries concerning your affair to be made, and rest assured that so soon as they have been carried out, I shall not leave your petition without just satisfaction and without providing protection for you as a foreigner and all the help possible. Provided only that your affair is just, have no doubt whatever that you will receive just succour from me. Meanwhile I send herewith my letter to the local governor, Governor Engelhardt,[2] who is going to be at Cherikov shortly, recommending in it to investigate your affair and give you the protection that the law affords. Hand over this letter to the governor or dispatch it to him in advance of his arrival at Cherikov.

Meanwhile I remain,
Sir,
your eager servant,
Pëtr Passek

October 16
1787

609. [1] B.M. IV: 419. Docketed by Bentham: '1787 Oct. 16/27 / Passek Mohileff / to / J.B. Zadobrast / Russ original.'

A reply to letter 607. A version in somewhat eccentric French is at B.M. IV: 418.

[2] See letter 610, n. 1.

610

To Governor Nikolay Bogdanovich Engelhardt[1]

18/29 October 1787 (Aet 39)

a Zadobras près de Critcheff
le 18 Octobre 1787.

~~Votre Excellence~~
Monsieur

La lettre ci-incluse[2] m'a été envoiée par le Gouverneur-Général. N'entendant pas la langue Russe, je l'ai malheureusement ouverte au lieu d'une autre qui m'étoit destinée. Cependant avant d'en avoir compris un seul mot, je suis revenu de ma méprise, que j'espère que Votre Excellence aura bien la bonté de pardonner comme involontaire; et ainsi que d'être ~~assure que~~ /persuadé du respect inviolable avec lequel/ j'ai l'honneur d'être ~~avec un respect inviolable~~

De Votre Excellence
le très humble Serviteur

611

Memorandum: Bark Contract[1]

18/29 October 1787 (Aet 39)

Procès au sujet du Contrat pour l'Ecorce. Critchoff Oct. 1787.
~~Sur mon refus de payer~~

Le 12 Oct. Mercredi est venu à Zadobras M. le Capitaine Ispravnik de Tcherikoff accompagné du sous-Lieut. Jacob-Pavlitch Tsetvitch ci-devant homme d'affaires de Lieut. Col. mon frère.

610. [1] B.M. IV: 420. Autograph. Draft with corrections. Docketed: '1787 Oct. 18 / J.B. Zadobras / to / Gov. Engelhardt / supposed at Cherikoff / Inclosed to Postmaster of Cherikoff.'

The addressee was Nikolay Bogdanovich Engelhardt (fl. 1756–91), who became vice-governor of Mogilëv in 1779 and was appointed governor in 1780, a post from which he finally retired in 1791. He may have been kin but does not seem to have been a close relative of Potëmkin's brother-in-law, Vasiliy Andreyevich Engelhardt.

[2] From Governor General Passek to Engelhardt, referred to in letter 609.

611. [1] B.M. XVII: 20–25. Autograph. Draft. Docketed by Bentham: '1787 Oct. / Bark Law Suit / J.B.'s. Case.'

This is the fullest account in these papers of the affair of Tsetvich's claim. It was evidently prepared in connection with the investigation to be carried out by Governor

~~Outre ce Jacob Pavlitch il y avoit present~~

~~Entre dans ma chambre, le Capt Ispravnik se trouvent~~ Ils sont entrés ensemble dans ma chambre où j'étois avec le nommé Robert Beaty Travailleur en Chanvre: et peu après y sont entrés pareillement le nommé Jacques Notman Maître de la Tannerie, et un Serjent qui est ici comme un des Denchiks[2] de mon frère.

Par l'entremise de ces trois personnes, tous les trois servant de leur mieux comme interprètes M$_r$. l'Ispravnik m'a annoncé aussitôt qu'il avoit sur moi une demande de 280Ro à cause d'une somme pareille qu'il disoit dûe à un certain Marchand Russe de la part de mon frère, et que j'avois à le payer sur le champ.

Comme il persistoit toujours à exiger à cette demande une reponse instantanée, ~~oui~~ voulois-je payer ou ne le voulois-je pas? ma réponse ne pouvoit être autre que negative.

Pour repondre au désir que j'ai temoigné en même tems de savoir surquoi une demande qui me paroissoit si étrange étoit fondée, on m'a produit quelques feuilles d'écriture Russe sur papier timbré que l'on m'a dit être une Ukase de la part de la Haute Cour de Justice à Mohileff, soit à moi addressée, soit où il étoit question de moi de je ne sais quelle manière.

Aussitôt j'ai prié avec bien des instances copie de la dite Ukase avec quelque peu de temps ne fut-ce que trois ou quatre jours pour m'en faire expliquer le contenu et pour déliberer sur ma réponse.

La réponse a été, qu'on n'avoit aucune copie à m'en laisser: et que ce ne seroit qu'une formalité inutile.

La prière que j'ai faite la-dessus pour qu'on voulut bien sur mon reçu me laisser l'original de cette procedure, pour que j'en pusse en faire faire copie au plus vite m'a été pareillement refusée.

Après les instances les plus pressantes et réiterées de ma part on a consenti par manière de faveur à me laisser faire prendre sur le champ avec les faibles secours que j'avois des copies de quelques morceaux dont je m'étois emparé de cette procedure et des pièces qui y avoient rapport. Pour abréger, M. l'Ispravik toujours en faisant éclater son impatience du retard que je lui occasionnais, avoit même la complaisance de prendre la plume

Les pieces ~~ainsi~~ dont j'ai ainsi obtenu copie sont

1. L'Ukase même.[3]

2. Un billet (recité par la dite Ukase) de la main de Jacob-

Engelhardt (see nos. 609 and 610 above) and was written on, or up to, 18 October. The end of the text indicates that a final portion is missing. Bentham's papers do not contain any information about the last stages of the business.

[2] *Denshchik*, batman.

[3] Missing.

Pavlitch ~~sur lequel~~ qui faisoit comme il me sembloit une des pièces sur lesquelles se fondoit cette Ukase.[4]

3. Une lettre [...?] munie d'une signature, qui m'a parue ressemblante à celle de mon frère, laquelle lettre on m'a dit avoir la valeur d'un acte de procuration ou plein-pouvoir à lui Jacob Pavlitch donné par mon frère.[5] Je crois, sans pouvoir l'assurer que de cette lettre ainsi que du billet avant dit il y avoit copie couchée en forme d'appendice à cette Ukase. Pour l'original, je crois qu'il se trouvoit dans les mains de dit Jacob-Pavlitch, et que c'est lui qui l'a produit.

Comme j'avois beaucoup entendu parler d'un contrat en forme passé entre Jacob Pavlitch et le marchand au sujet de cette même affaire, j'ai demandé où étoit ce contrat; à cela Jacob-Pavlitch ~~a produit~~ m'a fait voir pour la première fois un papier qui il disoit être cela. J'en ai aussitôt prié ~~copie~~ permission d'en faire faire pareillement copie: cette permission m'a été refusée. Mais Jacob-Pavlitch m'a promis de m'en faire une lui-même et de la donner

[4] B.M. IV: 422. Docketed by Bentham: '1787 Aug. 13 / Jacob Pavlitch Tsetvitch / to / Russ Merchant / Note engaging for the 285 Ro. / over and above the Contract / price. / Copy taken by Beaty Oct. 12 / by assistance of Jac. Pavlitch in / presence of the Capt. Ispravnik / of Cherikoff, when he sealed up the effects etc. at Zadobras.' it runs:

1787 года Августа 13го днеи при ращете по контракту о поставкѣ коры на аглицкой Кожевной заводъ купцы Петръ Яблочниковъ Инохй Араповичъ заверiнй мною что о притенаю свой за покупной лес в Поронѣго помѣщика в двустахъ восемдесатъ рублехъ за прибитйм̃ъ господина подполковника Бентома будетъ удоволствований случае ж ево неприбетя въ Кричевъ то емаютъ бить удоволствований оний от мня въ чемъ и подпесался на подленой.

подпоручикъ Яковъ Цетвичъ
Секретарь Дмитрй Добранскiй

Читалъ Регистреторъ Иванъ
Бурсковъ

B.M. IV: 394 is an inaccurate version in French described in Bentham's docket as 'Traduction literale dictee par M. de Ludvig a J.B. le 22 Oct. 1787.' The note reads: '1787 August 13, at the making up of the account on the contract concerning the delivery of bark to the English leather workshop, the merchants Petr Yablochnikov [and] Inokhi Arapovich have been assured by me that their claim against wood purchased from the landowner at Poronego for 280 rubles will receive satisfaction on the arrival of lieutenant colonel Bentom, or in the event of his not coming to Krichëv they will receive satisfaction from me, and to this effect I have put my signature on the original document.

Second-Lieutenant Yakov Tsetvich
Secretary Dmitri Dobranskiy

Perused, Registrar Ivan Burskov.'

At the time Tsetvich signed this note Samuel Bentham was on the move between Kremenchug and Kherson in attendance on Potëmkin but was expected to return shortly to Krichëv (see letter 598). In the French version (B.M. IV: 394) the name of the place at which the wood was purchased is rendered as 'Voroniko'.

[5] A copy of this in Russian, made partly by Beaty and partly by the Russian captain of police, is at B.M. IV: 346, and a second copy, made from this, immediately precedes it at fo. 345.

pour moi au ci-devant nommé Beattie, le lendemain: mais jusqu' aujourdhui 18 Octre cette promesse a été sans effet. Je ne sais rien encore du contenu de ce contrat que par des rapports vagues. On peut s'imaginer quelle instruction pourroit tirer d'un instrument Russe lu à la hate ~~a~~ à l'homme qui n'entend pas cent mots de Russe: mais /seulement/ j'ai eu le tems de remarquer que cet instrument se trouvoit dechiré comme auparavant j'avois ouï-dire qu'[il] a été en signe d'accomplissement, l'instrument du contrat donné par ce Jacob-Pavlitch à ce marchand Russe.

Restoit encore une partie considérable des écritures qui se trouvoient sur le même amas de papier timbré sur lequel ~~se trouvoit~~ /étoit/ l'Ukase. Il y en avoit je crois ou deux ou trois feuilles. On m'a dit que c'étoit là la supplique du Marchand. Je ne sais pas s'il y avoit autre chose. J'ai insisté toujours avec la même pertinacité pour pouvoir faire faire copie de même de cette supplique: mais la patience de M. l'Ispravnic étoit lassée, et mes prières se sont trouvées infructueuses.

J'ai le malheur d'être dans l'ignorance la plus parfaite de la Jurisprudence Russe. Je me flatte de ne pas être dans une ignorance tout-à-fait si parfaite de /la Jurisprudence Justice naturelle et universelle/ ce que la Jurisprudence est ou devoit être dans tout pays.

Je proteste done contre cette procédure comme contraire à cette Justice pour plusieurs raisons: et je soumets très respectueusement à la consideration de mon Juge quelconque les allégués /points/ suivans:

1. Qu'on n'a pas dû me faire cette demande de 280 Roubles ni aucune autre, ne me laissant dans l'impossibilité de savoir ou de conjecturer si et pourquoi cette demande pouvoit être juste: mais que cette demande avoit dû être accompagnée d'une copie de l'ukase sur laquelle elle ètoit fondée ainsi que des pièces sur lesquelles /la Cour/ on s'étoit fondée pour lâcher cet Ukase: et qui ~~avant tems convenable~~ préalablement à toute réponse de ma part, delai convenable auroit dû m'être accordé pour /déliberer sur/ le contenu de la demande: lequel délai auroit du être d'autant plus long que les difficultés où me mettoit ma qualité connue d'étranger d'en chercher l'explication, étoient manifestes.

2. Que dans ces circonstances l'arrêt qu'on m'a annoncé ne peut être regardé que comme un outrage aussi injustifiable qu'inutile. Si la saisie qu'on a fini par faire des effets de mon frère a été légale c'est ce que j'ignore, et ce ~~qu'on~~ /de quoi ou comme je ne peux qu'ignorer une chose, de laquelle on/ m'a refusé les moyens uniques et néces-

saires pour /former une opinion quelconque./ ~~juger. Ce qui est constant c'est qu'on n'a jamais pretendu que cette c'est moi qui ai rien fait pour contracter celle pretendue dette.~~ Mais légale ou illeé\gale elle suffisoit, comme on a reconnu, pour obtenir /effectuer/ le but proposé. C'est done aà cela qu'on auroit dû se borner; au lieu de commencer par infliger une punition personelle sur un individu qu'on ne pretendoit pas même avoir ~~été pour rien~~ en aucune part à contracter la prétendue dette.

Là-dessus pour finir, on m'a repeté la demande de ~~une~~ ma réponse finale à la question, voulois-je payer ou ne le voulois-je ~~payer~~ pas:— et comme mon ignorance absolue sur la justice qui pouvoit avoir une pareille demande à moi addressée, restoit toujours la même, ma reponse a été comme auparavant négative.

Pour répliquer à cette contumace on m'a fait savoir aussitôt que j'étois aux arrêts. La prière que j'ai faite d'un délai de trois ou quatre jours pour chercher des explications des communications tronquées que j'avois obtenues, et des conseils a été refusée. J'ai demandé seulement permission d'aller consulter un ami qui ne se trouvoit éloigné que de quelques versts et qui j'offrais de nommer:—pareil refus—sous ce pretexte je pourrois m'échapper.

J'ai compris presqu'aussitôt qu'il s'agissait de faire saisie de tous les effets qui se trouvoient à la place. J'ai demandé s'il agissoit de saisir les miens aussi bien que ceux de mon frère. On m'a dit peut-être que non: mais qu'il falloit que j'en fisse instamment la distinction en faisant voir d'un côté ce qui étoit à moi et de l'autre ce qui étoit à mon frère. Cette séparation instantanée étoit impossible. [*Several words crossed out*] causes sur lesquelles il ne vaut pas la peine de s'appesantir en avoit rendu le mélange si complet, qu'il m'eut falu des heures pour ne pas dire des jours pour le débrouiller: pour ne ~~pas parler~~ rien dire des papiers dont la séparation présentoit des difficultés induicibles.

Après bien des pourparlers j'eus la joie /enfin/ de voir M. L'Ispravnik se contenter du contenu de deux *Oumbars:* dans l'un dequel se trouve le fruit de la moisson et dans l'autre tous les instruments d'agriculture et de jardinage.

Voilà pour ce qui me regarde personellement: mais comme des effets [de] mon frère absent se trouvent saisis, et que le préjudice que ~~cette saisie ne peut que resulter de~~ cette saisie ne peut qu'apporter à ses affaires ne peut m'être tout-à-fait indifferent, j'ose supplier ~~de la part~~ /l'attention/ de mon Juge pour les ~~soupeons moyens~~ /raisons/ que j'ai cru voir pour ~~la~~ soupçonner ou qu'elle est indue

/elle meme/ ou au moins que la demande qui l'a fait naître est mal-fondée.

Si je ne ~~parle~~ peux parler que des soupçons dont le fondement est précaire, ce n'est que mon malheur et non pas ma faute. Cette incertitude a deux causes principales.

1. L'un est le refus susdit qu'on m'a fait des moyens ~~necessaires pour juger pieces~~ faisant le fondement de la demande: et nommément de la supplique ou demande du plaignant le marchand Russe.

2. L'autre est l'infidelité et la prévarication de Jacob-Pavlitch cet ~~hemme~~ emploié soi-disant fondé de procuration ~~de la part~~ du Lieut. Col. mon frère, qui au lieu /d'aider/ de defendre son principal, ne rougit pas d'emploier ouvertement tous les moyens imaginables pour lui nuire. Mais il faut que je revienne /séparémment sur le sujet de cet homme/ sur son sujet ci-bas. Mais c'est ici un sujet sur lequel je me dispenserois volontiers d'insister à moins que cela ne soit jugé necessaire.[6]

Voici donc le jugement /l'opinion, les doutes/ précaire que j'ai pu former d'après les lueurs imparfaites que les dés[a]vantages susdits m'ont permis d'attraper.

La demande du Marchand a pour fondement original un ~~contrat~~ accord qui s'est fait entre lui et Jacob-Pavlitch au nom de mon frère pour une certaine quantité d'écorce propre à tanner à raison de 8 copiques par poude; duquel accord il s'est dressé acte qui je crois être le même que j'ai vu dans les mains de Jacob Pavlitch comme ci-dessus.

Or je crois que ce contrat a /été parfaitement/ accompli de la part de mon frère et tout l'argent qui étoit dû là-dessus payé pour les raisons suivantes:

1 iere Que lors ~~du dernier~~ de ~~une~~ certaine avance que j'ai fait de mes propres deniers à Jacob Pavlitch, et il ~~qu'il disoit~~ me l'a dit que c'étoit le dernier qu'il avoit à me demander à cet effet. C'étoit une somme de 525 Ro. le jour étoit le 12 Aout: C'est par l'entremise ou du Tanneur Notman ou du jardinier Aiton ou de tous les deux qu'il m'a fait cette déclaration. J'ai compris ensuite de Notman que le Marchand ~~doit~~ se trouvoit en même tems à la maison: que l'argent par moi delivré à Jacob Pavlitch a été sans désemparer passé au Marchand: qu'en consequence le papier sur lequel étoit couché le contrat /signé par Jacob Pavlitch/ a été ~~delivré~~ rendu par le Marchand à Jacob Pavlitch pour être déchiré en signe d'accomplissement comme on m'a dit que c'est la coutume Russe: et que ce déchirement a eu lieu aussitôt: aussi le papier qui m'a ~~fait~~

[6] This sentence is added in the margin.

voir/laissé entrevoir/ Jacob-Pavlitch comme ci-dessus m'a t'il paru dechiré, en plus d'un endroit. Il faut savoir que je ne l'ai vu que dans ses mains sans l'avoir eu dans les miennes.

2. Que la quantité d'écorce reçu répond ~~assez exactement~~ aux sommes d'argent dont le payement est reconnu. ~~Je tiens~~ Pour cela je m'en rapporte au Tanneur Notman.

Ce qui est dessus je ne crois pas que le Marchand le nie: on dit que tout en admettant le contrat originaire il se fonde sur le billet posterieurement donné par Jacob-Pavlitch. Le sens de ce billet si on me l'a bien expliqué est que après la ~~passation du contrat~~ /la coupe d'une partie de l'écorce/ le proprietaire actuel quel qu'il soit du domaine de Critcheff ayant fait defense de coupes ulterieures le marchand s'est vu obligé d'obtenir permission pareille chez ~~quelque~~ /je ne sais quel/ autre Seigneur terrien: et que pour cet effet il a été obligé de payer la somme dont il s'agit de 280 Ro.

A ce pretendu payement je ne peux pas me defendre de le soupçonner d'être simulé: et quand même il se trouvoit véritablement arrivé, il ne me paroit que celà devroit suffire pour autoriser le procedé qui a eu lieu contre mon frère.

/A qui me suit là/ Je le soupçonne d'être simulé pour /ce sont/ les raisons suivantes.

612

From Nikolay Kokhovskiy[1]

22 October/2 November 1787

Милостивыи Государъ мой
Еремей Ивановичъ

Майстеръ которой хорошо делаетъ кибитки боленъ; посланная жъ присемъ когда вамъ понравитца то я сочту за мое удаволствіе. Приложенное

612. [1] B.M. IV: 425. Autograph. Docketed by Bentham: '1787 Oct. 22/Nov. 3 / Kokofski Ghoneli / to / J.B. Zadobras / with Kibitki.'

Sir Richard Worsley recorded in his travel journal that, early in September 1786, in company with Samuel Bentham, he visited 'the seat of Col. Michalevitch, nephew to the Governor of the Taurica', where a country house was being built, and, later that day, 'Mr. Kokofski's, the elder brother of the family, a very worthy man who has the misfortune of being blind' (Worsley Mss. 24). Both houses were near Nikopol, near the boundary between the two gubernias of Mogilëv and Smolensk. Possibly the former of these persons was the writer of this letter. The Kokhovskiys were one of the prominent landed families in this region. At this time V. V. Kokhovskiy was governor of the Crimea (E. I. Druzhinina, *Severnoye Prichernomor'e v 1775–1800 gg.*, refs as index) and command of the troops there was held by his brother, Count Mikhayl Vasil'yevich Kokhovskiy (1734–1800) (ibid., 120 and 142, Worsley Mss. 24, and *Russkiy Biograficheskiy Slovar'*).

This evidence of continued preparations for Bentham's journey home seems to

присемъ писмо, когда вы будите въ лондонѣ пожалуите верно доставте Господину Шевалье Ворслейну чемъ меня много обяжите.

За выраженіе какъ къ вамъ надписывать въ лондонъ писмы покорнейше васъ благодарю: это мнѣ будетъ составлять пріятнейшѣе удаволствіе; а особливо когда и вы примите трудъ извещать о себе. По примеру взятому отъ васъ прилагаю записку какъ надписывать писмы ко мнѣ, равно и Господинъ Шевалье Ворслейнъ если захочетъ темъ одолжатъ, то по такой надписи мы верно оные получать можемъ.

Впротчемъ рекомендую мѣня в благосклонное содержаніе съ искреннаю усердностію и почитаніемъ пребуду навсегда

Милостивыи Государь мой
Вашъ
Покорнейшей слуга
Николай Коховский

22 октября
1787го года
Холмъ

Извините что къ вамъ пишу по-руски; потому что секретари мое таперь въъ смоленске

Translation

My dear Mr. Jeremy Ivanovich,

The craftsman who is skilled at making kibitkas is ill; but if you are satisfied with the one I have sent you herewith I shall count it a pleasure on my part. When you get to London, be so good as to deliver the inclosed letter safely to the Chevalier Vorslein[2] and you will greatly oblige me.

I thank you most humbly for telling me how to address letters to you in London; that will be a very great pleasure to me; and particularly if you will take the trouble to give me news of yourself. Following your example I inclose a note showing how to address letters to me; similarly, if the Chevalier Vorslein is willing to do this favour, then we shall receive them safely with such a superscription.

For the rest I commend myself to your favour and shall always remain with sincere zeal and respect

My dear Sir,
Your
most humble servant
Nikolay Kokhovskiy

22 October
1787
Kholm

Excuse me for writing to you in Russian; the reason is that my secretaries are at present at Smolensk.

indicate that the vexations of the lawsuit referred to in the documents immediately preceding had been brought to a satisfactory conclusion.

[2] Probably Kokhovskiy's version of 'Worsley'.

613

From John Aiton[1]

22 October/2 November 1787

2 Nov N.S. 1787

Sir

Yesterday I received the clover seed, for which I received payment. I don't know how you will like your Kibitki, but it appears to me to be a very good one. Mr. Kakovsky behaves exceeding well to us hitherto, I endeavour to give him all the satisfaction I can. I have drawn a plan of a pinery for him, and a Peach house, and also altered the plan of a peach house, that was almost finished before I arrived here. I am now engaged with drawing a plan of an Orchard which he intends incloseing with a Brick wall all round; it [is] a square field about 240 Sargines[2] in length, and as much in breadth, another plan I have to draw which is partly round his house, a kind of pleasure ground, which I believe will complete my Month, at which time I intend, if sledgeroads to set out for Petersburgh,[3] if not sledge roads I must wait untill the[y] come.—you mentioned in your letter of forcing another 25 my way, which I will be very glad if it is in your power—Mr. Kakovsky says he will have nothing for his Kabitka I told him he might have what instruments he pleased to its value, he did not say he would, nor would not, so I fancy it is left entirely to yourself. I would have ⟨wr⟩ote something more, but the horses was put to the Kabitka before I knew any thing of it—I am Sir Your humble servt. John Aiton.[4]

613. [1] B.M. IV: 426. Autograph. Docketed by Bentham: '1787 Oct 22/Nov 2 / John Aiton / to / J.B. Zadobrast.'

[2] *Sazhen*, an old Russian unit of measurement, equivalent to seven feet.

[3] In September Bentham had written recommending Aiton to the good offices of the ambassador at St Petersburg, Alleyne Fitzherbert (letter 604).

[4] At the bottom of the letter Bentham wrote: 'Sent the 25 R note 27 Oct. by return of Messenger.' Aiton and Beaty were the two employees at Krichëv most attached to Bentham (letter 603), and in Aiton's case Bentham's strong amateur interest in botany, illustrated in the following document (Bowring, x, 178–9), was a further bond of attraction.

List of Seeds gathered in 1787, near Crichoff, in the government of Moghilev, in the province of White Russia, N. Lat, 54, and communicated to Dr Anderson, Dr Trail, Dr Pitcairn, Dr Fordyce, Mr Aiton, and Mr Lee

A

Plants growing in a very shady situation at the skirts of woods:

No. 2. Habit somewhat like a Cowslip. Flowers purple,—in a very shady situation, some of them red on the same stalk.
No. 1. Anemonoides.—Corolla 5 ad 7 petala alba—lineis viridibus distincta.—Folia cordata amplexicaulia.
No. 1. Id. 7 petala vice 5 petala.
No. 3. Corolla 5 aut 6 petala—alba—rosacea.—Folia ovato-oblonga. Planta humilis.
No. 4. Fumaria,—a variety with white flowers.
No. 5. Fumaria,—some of it *probably* a variety with white flowers.
No. 6. Andromeda.—Folia Kalmoidea caulis summitatem arcuantia.
No. 7. Orobus,—an vernus?

B

Plants growing in a situation not much shaded, though near the skirts of woods:

No. 1. Low plant, with awl-shaped leaves, and a spike of purple flowers.
No. 1. A variety of it with red flowers.
No. 2. Vicia spicae 5 aut 6 unciali,—planta per elegans, c. 1786. Non reperio in 1787.
No. 3. Rubus humulis,—bacca quadriacinâ.
No. 4. Cheiranthus flore lurido noctuolente.
No. 5. Lilium Martagon, flore nutante carnicolore maculato.
No. 6. Campanula flore magno cæruleo.
No. 7. Campanula flore magno albo cærulescenti.
No. 8. Spartium.
No. 9. Lathyrus flore luteo, foliis binatis.
No. 10. Hawkweed, hairy-leaved, trailing. — Flower brimstone-coloured.
No. 11. Planta Antherici facie? Spica sparsa. Caulis longus. Radix fibrosus. Folia graminea. Flos non visus.
No. 13. Anemone flore albo sub-lanuginoso.
No. 12. Flos labiatus partim flavus partim rubescens. — Folia superiora purpurea.

C

Plants growing in a mossy swamp:

No. 1. Willow-leaved, with globular tufts of yellow stamina, and no apparent corolla.
No. 2. Rush-leaved, with globular tufts of white stamina.
No. 3. Cyclamen flowered myrtle-leaved, creeping plant, growing midst mosses in swamps.
No. 4. C. Impatiens,—a variety, with a yellowish flower almost white.
No. 5. Frutex humilis. Corolla lagenoides. Calyx nullus. Folia ovata glauca subacida.
No. 6. Rhododendron? Folia Rosmarinidea. Flores verticillati albi. Planta tota odora.

D

Plants growing in a very dry soil and sunny exposure:

No. 1. Trifolium flore luteo.

E

No. 1. White strawberries, remarkably large, from a gentleman's garden.
No. 2. Planta incognita, sub-humili sepe apud Bentheim collecta.—Spica circiter 12-uncialis.—Flos non visus.
No. 3. Seeds of I forget what plant.

N.B. For want of leisure, books, and instruments, the botanic characters were not attended to. The ground for looking upon them as new, is their appearing such to an experienced botanical gardener, bred up under the king's gardener at Kew, and in other capital gardens in the neighbourhood of London. The names or descriptions here given, however loose and untechnical, it was presumed would be more satisfactory than none.

614

FROM SAMUEL BENTHAM[1]

early November 1787

The Bearer of this Captain Pustoshkin (Семенъ АфонасьIвичь пустошкинъ)[2] is a Captain Lieutenant in the fleet which gives the rank of Major in the army. He is sent from hence by Mordvinoff to take possession of and continue the works in the Rope Fabrick which somehow or other the Prince after having sold as you know has made a present of to the Admiralty here. I have given him powers to stop the *plein pouvoir* given to J.P.[3] and though I cannot require of him to take any very troublesome part in my affairs: yet every thing relating to the dispatching my effects I make no doubt he will arrange according to your desire or to such instructions as I give him. What I am most disposed to do at present is to take away all my private effects and then as I am pretty well clear of all the English workmen to give up the leather fabrick and all stock of tools and materials relating to any of my former concerns to the Prince's steward that he may dispose of them as he thinks proper, but I shall wait for an answer to this from you or some account from Mr. Pustoshkin in case he does not find you. I have written to Notman about the sending off my things.

Sefton and Frederick have no excuse for their behaviour. I never received any letter from them nor had any reason to believe them in want.

With a handful of Vessels we drove away the formidable Turkish fleet from Ochakoff had they staid a few days longer I hope we should have destroyed the greatest part of them.[4]

614. [1] B.M. IV: 391–2, 389–90. Autograph. No address or docket.

This letter must have been written after Samuel Bentham had heard about the legal action taken against Bentham on 12/23 October and before news reached him of Bentham's departure for England on 19/30 November. As the journey from Kherson to Krichëv seems to have been covered within a week by couriers at this time of year (cf. letter 600, n. 1), a date around the beginning of November (N.S.) is indicated. At that time the naval news mentioned by Samuel (see also n. 4) would not have been stale.

[2] I.e., Semën Afonas'yevich Pustoshkin (1759–1846), who became in later life an admiral and a senator.

[3] I.e., Yakov Pavlovich Tsetvich.

[4] Samuel Bentham's observations can only refer to the naval engagement of 14–15 October 1787, which followed immediately upon the crushing defeat of the Turkish assault upon Fort Kinburn. An advance by Russian vessels in the Liman, in an attempt to encircle units of the Turkish fleet, was followed

I have at least an opportunity such as I could not expect of trying my war experiments. Vermicular however has not credit enough with me for war purposes to risk a trial, especially as there are other ideas less doubtfull.

The Prince is arrived I mean to press him but with little hopes of success.

If possible let me see you

Adieu.

Dont plague yourself with an Interview with Tromp's partners in London. Interest will get the better of all your arguments.

Inspection House The Bricklayer will talk about in England. It is the most valuable of our Projects.

Vermicular for inland navigation however should by no means be neglected.[5]

Inspection house papers I have mislaid or by mistake sent to you.

Q.S.P. is indeed all kindness much beyond what we could have reason to expect, and I am happy in the idea of being able /to/ remit the sum independent of the Prince. I would wish however defer doing it as long as possible that is till I have assurance of my having no further hopes from the Prince.

I would advise you to take of Mr. Pustoshkin 1,500 rubles the sum *I owe you* and change it into ducats as well as you can in your neighbourhood.

Here ducats fetch as far as 3 rubles and 25 copeks.

There was some money I think laid out in the Irish Tontine in my name how is it that no certificates from me has been required for so long time?

I hope you will require ample satisfaction for the impudent judges daring to arrest you.[6]

I have no means of doing any thing in form with respect to the discharge of De Bark, but I cannot conceive that you have any thing to fear on his account. He as your servant with a Passport or certificate from any body else with whom he is represented as

by an action fought mainly between light units of both sides. The Turkish fleet withdrew to the open sea and then retired to Constantinople for the winter (R. C. Anderson, *Naval Wars in the Levant, 1559–1853*, Liverpool, 1952, pp. 319–21).

[5] The point merits emphasis here, that Bentham returned to England charged to exploit both Samuel's inventions as a joint enterprise on the part of them both. While virtually nothing about vermiculars occurs in his later correspondence (this, after all, was not his line of country), the Inspection House was to engross a great deal of his time and energy, as his papers for the years from 1790 onward clearly show.

[6] This sentence is evidence of a missing letter from Bentham to his brother, written some time shortly after 12/23 October 1787.

having lived must be sufficient. But if you have any difficulties from thence, you would have none from hence.[7] I have settled with Pustoshkin that when any body or any thing is dispatched from Kreetchoff to this place for me, they shall be directed to call at Maslinokoff's, a Merchant who has a sugar-fabrick in Chremenchuck, so that in case the Kamenka[8] plan takes place I shall send a letter to this Maslinokoff at Chrem[en]chuck with directions about their changing their road. I would wish to have both the girls sent here and have commissioned Pust: accordingly at any rate Mat's sister.

Say all that can be said to the Privitel[9] and Gen Bandre for their Kindness and make the best excuse for my not writing myself.

In case of accident I have sent you a blank Poderagnis[10] signed by governor of Mohilev which you may make use of by filling up the blank with the person and number of horses required, but if you come yourself probably Pust: may assist you even as a Courier or rather de Bark as the Courier and you as the anybody with him.

615

Diary of Bentham's Journey from Krichëv to Warsaw[1]

19/30 November–15 December 1787 (Aet 39)

1787 Nov. 19/30 Friday

Set out from Notmans a little after day-break Stopt at the village /Usti/ 8 versts short of Cherikoff. /staid there from 10½ to 1½ or 2/ Passed Cherikoff and at the first village between Cherikoff and Riminki got Moorish horses at post price to the next village. There Notman took leave buying for 50 copecks a sledge to take his 3 horses home a bundle.

At Riminki took the post to Chaour.

A little after day-break passed through Mohileff

[7] For Du Bark and these comments, see journal 615, n. 4.

[8] The Kamenka is a small tributary flowing into the Dnieper from the north, about sixty miles upstream from Kherson. At the point of confluence there was a fortress and a major arsenal, including a dump of big guns suitable for use on ships. It does not appear that Samuel Bentham was ever there on a permanent basis.

[9] *Pravitel'*, director—i.e., the steward in charge of Potëmkin's estate at Krichëv, which would soon be passing into the purchaser's hands.

[10] *Podorozhnaya*, a warrant for horses. To the last minute Samuel Bentham hoped that his brother would come to the south to be with him for a while, instead of returning as soon as possible to England.

615. [1] B.M. XVI: 74–97 (part of a small notebook). Autograph.

Sat. 20/Dec. 1

Arrived at Tolochia[2] at 7: Found I had lost my Turkish boots out of the bags at the side of the Kabitka. Supped and slept at the Post-house tolerably decent appartment of 2 Rooms—Goose half in Soup, then other ½ roasted.

Sunday Dec. 2

Breakfast good Coffee. The three men I saw asleep on the floor in a room I passed through to come to my apartment, proved the servants of Prince Trubitski going to Moscow from Warsaw. I was surprised at hearing French and Italian mixed with Russ. My door being open one of them /in good French/ claimed a wax candle I had burning. This introduced conversation. For 8 horses to Moscow they were to pay 140 Roubles. According to him but 98 rubles from Tolochia to Warsaw—He recommended the Poste aux Juifs to Grodus and thence the regular post in preference to Carriers—saying that the post was 2 florins Polish a Mile per horse—that carriers ought not to ask more than 1½—that there would be no difficulty in meeting with horses by the Poste aux Juifs at a price less rather than greater than the regular post. The need I had of an additional person to take charge of my numerous little packages, the uncertainty of the Poste aux Juifs and the inconvenience of sparing my single attendant to look after them determined me to accept of the Carriers recommended by the Postmaster, though I took for granted he had a fellow-feeling with them I drew a contract in Latin which the Post-master a Pole translated into Russ. They proposed Polish: but I preferred a language of which I understood a few words to one of which I understood none. Agreed for 75 Roubles 2 in ducats at 280 copecks the Ducat making 27 ducats odd copecks—paid 10 at signing in advance, and afterwards on request, 3. Immediately on receipt of the money the Carriers bought a very good Horse for the Journey for which according to du Bark they paid 45 Roobles.

Prince Troubitski[3] himself had passed through a day before. He had been making the Tour of Europe in 7 years—last from Vienna through Warsaw—In the 7 years he had drawn from Russia 400,000 ducats. So he told the Postmaster who told Du Bark.[4]

[2] Now Tolochin, west of Orsha, on the main route from Moscow to Warsaw by way of Minsk.

[3] Not identified.

[4] The account Bowring obtained from Bentham about Du Bark was that he was 'a Swede, who represented himself to be of noble blood. He wrote an admirable hand, and spoke seven or eight languages: having been two years in the English service, he

The Carriers insisted upon its being 120 Miles to Warsaw, appealing to the Post-Master, who said I might ask the Director of the Custom-house. If this be true my bargain with the Carriers was rather under the mark mentioned by Troubitski's Frenchman as the reasonable one: otherwise considerably over—Situnski[?] had mentioned 20 ducats as the price from Mohileff to Warsaw. They bated from 80 to 75—Great joy testified by them on completion of the Contract. I wished to have detained the Frenchman and examined him more particularly: but my situation was too dangerous to have my thoughts at liberty, and a moments unnecessary delay might have been fatal.

Went to the Major and the Director in a sledge furnished by the Post-Master—found the Major at the Directors—They were taking their Brandy and herring before dinner of which they invited me to partake. Noble house of the Directors—extremely well fitted-up for a Russian—London Clock—In the Hall instruments for a compleat band—horns, trumpets etc.—Pots like Wedgewood's yellow ware with Mignionette and Carnations—Major much of a Gentleman spoke a little French and German—Director no French —Director a portly man, stiled by the other M. le Conseiller—civil, but condescending—a number of well powdered /and well dressed/ servants with the appearance of French or English ones in the best stile. In the hall a Piano forte made at Francfort. In one of the rooms flowered Cotton bed looked like English a Number of Prints, but coloured in the manner of the inferior English ones. Room stuccoed—good moulding, and the stucco tolerably good. The outside seemed to be stone, in a stile that might have passed for good in England or at least in France.

At Mohileff, the Archbishop's Palace a magnificent structure—The Archbishop takes in the Hamburgh Newspaper, and sends it to Gen. Bandre. The Jesuits Church magnificent on the outside and not in a bad stile. The same may be said of several other buildings I got a glance of, and which by the well-powder'd servants that were seen about them, seemed to be the dwelling-houses of the Governor or Governor General and other principal Magistrates

was perfectly master of English. He had presented himself to me in my brother's absence, soliciting employment. He had married a Polish lady of rank; but how they lived I know not.' At this time Du Bark was anxious to leave Russia and by his mastery of languages he could provide Bentham with an indispensable interpreter for his journey. Since he had been enrolled a serjeant in the Russian army, in Samuel's battalion, an exit permit was out of the question, and he had to travel as an anonymous servant of Bentham (Bowring, x, 179). Bentham was concerned about this breach of the law. Samuel considered his fears exaggerated (B.M. IV: 389–90, 429).

Decr. 3

Breakfasted at Laznihta[5]—Pretty Jewess Hogs in the stable—Turkeys and Fowls free of the house. Lucky enough to find a Coffee pot without a handle and a pipkin to boil milk

Arrived at Beresna[6] at ½ after 5. A Polish Nobleman and his Lady drunk on the only bedstead, besides a number of Moojicks, who assisted in removing his Ldship. and her Ladyship to another part of the room, as I chose their station though I preferred fresh straw to their bedstead. The lady very conversable and her conversation afforded much diversion to Du Bark as well as the rest of the company.

I had been taught /at Crechoff/ to expect a severe search at both the Custom-houses at Tolochia, on the Russian side to prevent the exportation of Russian coin: on the Polish side to enforce the payment of importation duties. At Tolochia the Postmaster upon enquiry mentioned a Rouble a piece as a proper compliment to the 2 searchers on the Russian side: as to the Polish side he afforded me no light. On the other side of Poland /at Chekanofka/ the head officer of the Custom-house had made the search in person:[7] here at Tolochia the Russian Director was by much too great a person to trouble himself about such business. According according to instructions from the Postmaster I offerd nothing either to him or to the Major for their signatures to my passport. The two searchers to whom I gave the Rooble a piece were mere underlings. As before apprised, upon receiving their fee they did not so much as pretend to search, only asked repeatedly whether I had not Russian money. I replied in the negative which was strictly true for being /pre-/ apprised of this question, I had taken care to rid my hands of every Copeck, /except the 2 Roobles reserved for feeing./

On the Polish side the first persons who presented themselves at the end of the bridge which joins the two territories were two soldiers. They stopped me with a demand of something to drink. I had still by me for such contingencies two Russian pieces of 10 Copecks each. I immediately gave them one, and upon their grumbling and saying it was too little, the other. The grumbling still continued, and they said they must search me and insisted on my getting out of the Kibitki. I asked what right *they* had to search, desiring to be conducted to the Custom-house which I conceived to

[5] Lozhnitsa, some miles east of Beresna.

[6] Now Borisov, where the road to Minsk crosses the Beresina, later to be made famous by Napoleon's retreat.

[7] I.e., on Bentham's entry into Russia at the beginning of 1786.

be the only proper place for such a business: before I had received the answer, I had got down and enter'd a small dirty hovel, like a hog-stie: and great was my surprise to be told, and as it proved truly, that that was the only Custom-house and they the only searchers. I then expressed my perfect willingness to make them a compliment suitable to their dignity, but that I must entreat their patience till I could get wherewithal having already given them all I had of less value than a ducat. Understanding that I designed them a Rooble apiece they received the news with great joy and gratitude and all idea of search was thenceforward at an end. What was my surprize, when upon enquiring for change for a Ducat at this place where no Russian money was to enter, I found it impossible to get any other money but Russian? The same impossibility was renewd at Bober[8] the first stage 30 versts from Tolochia. After that I found Polish money was to be had indeed but in very small quantities and at a considerable loss: the only money commonly current was Russian, and this I was informed would continue till I got to Minsk where Russian money ceased to be commonly current.

Dec. 4th Tuesday:

Breakfasted at Smolevitch.[9] No Coffee-pot, a dirty pipkin supplied the place. The Coffee-pot I had got made at Crechoff proved leaky: the saucepan I had got at the same place had in like manner failed upon the first trial on Sunday-night. An English Tea-kettle I was fortunately master of, and which as a teakettle would have been without employ, was now my last resource for boiling my daily repast of Sausages and Parsley-roots. Minsk being a considerable town for a Polish town may possibly supply me with a Coffee pot that will stand fire.

Set out from Smolevitch at ½ after 3. In about a minutes time an irregularity in the ground threw Du Bark of[f] his seat. He seemed to be dragged a considerable way and I expected to find him much hurt. I wonderd at the Driver's suffering the horses to go in full gallop after such an accident; I looked on that side and found the Driver had also disappeared. The ground was at the same time winding, /narrow,/ uneven, with steep descents and interspersed with stumps of trees. The horses continued at full gallop. I could see no reins. Presently I found my Turkish portmanteau, which was uppermost upon my back, and soon after the other pressing on me. I apprehended the being crushed by them: the least danger seemed

[8] Bobr, a few miles east of Krupki, on the road to Minsk.

[9] Smolevichi, some twenty miles east of Minsk.

that of their being thrown out of the Kibitki. I turned my back to the horses, and taking advantage of the retardation occasioned by an ascent found means to unbuckle the straps by which the Portmanteaus had been ill fastened and to restore them to their place. I then had leisure to face my danger, and to observe what narrow escapes I had at every turning and every stump I passed. I met a man with a sledge and horse, I waved my handkerchief to him, and cried out as well as I could to stop the horses: but he gave no signs of any disposition to assist me. I thought I saw the road divide in more places than one. I did not know what hurt /might have befallen/ my attendants: and supposing nothing the matter with them, it was a matter of chance whether they took the same road that I had done. I had before my eyes the prospect of passing the night alone in the Kibitki: and when chance should have brought a passenger that way, how could I make him understand my distress, not knowing a syllable of the language? I was entertaining myself with these thoughts when the horses came to an ascent so steep as to oblige them to slacken their pace to a slow trot. I then for the first time got a sight of the reins, and had the pleasure of finding them within my reach. I seized them and by the advantage of the ground stopped the horses without difficulty. After some time I thought I heard a noise which I ~~imagined~~ hoped might proceed from my attendants. I hallooed as loud as I could and ~~at last~~ was answer'd; and presently they came up. They had met with a man with a horse and sledge whom they engaged to take them up and follow me. Neither of them had received any hurt: but both had formed dismal apprehensions on my account, and honest Nicholas the driver, had crossed himself and ejaculated many Jesu-Marias for my benefit. The danger had not lasted above ¼ of an hour: but my anxiety had at least quadrupled the time.

In about an hour we came to a Village with a Jew Inn: and here by the Driver's recommendation we stopped, the road from thence being according to his account very bad.

Our afternoon journey did not last above a mile: we stopt as usual at a Jew Inn, the Carrier agreeing with the Jew that the Roads from thence began to be so bad as to render it totally inadvisable to proceed by night.

Decr.

arrived at Minsk about 1. Houses number'd—said to be about 2,000. Soil a rock-ground excessively rough and irregular. A large place quite shapeless where stand the Jesuits and several other churches—Fine Apothecary's shop painted in fresco in front with emblematical devices—in back front with trophees festoons etc. The house belongs to a Merchant. It makes a greater show than any of the Noblemen's houses.

Comedy in a Chapel belonging to the Jesuits' Church began about ½ after 6, was over at 8. 2 Acts—Scene a wood never shifted. Plot simple—Only one female character—5 Male, besides 2 or 3 attendants, Huntsmen. Performance better than could have been expected. The woman the lover and the womans father rather above mediocrity. None very bad, like those at Bucharest. Church impenetrable to the Sun—stone floors very cold—A stove at the entrance but no fire in it. Audience /below/ 5 or 6 Ladies and 60 or 70 Gentlemen. Ticket 45 Copecs = 3 Florins. In a Gallery above, tickets 15 copecs—a better place because boarded. At the entrance a box where refreshments were sold consisting of Wine and hot Punch, apples and confectionary—had but few customers besides myself—I was glad of some Punch to warm me. The profits of the Play go to the Jesuits. The Members of this order lost nothing individually by the Dissolution: only the benefices of those that die are not filled up.

Decr. | | morning.

Went into 3 or 4 of the Churches. The Jesuits, which is the largest and said to be the richest, not open. In one of the Churches which is not yet quite finished in the inside the Altar-piece [...?] in an elegant stile—Order Corinthian or Composite richly ornamented—Colours white and a pale green. Plaster figures of Saints /Evangelists/ white, except the eyes which are black which gives them a ghastly resemblance to life, as likewise the place for ink in their pens St. Michael and the Devil a favorite subject for the side Altars. The Archangel's armour generally of silver and in some places different members of his body. None of all this finery falls to poor Satan's share. The taste for this kind of patchwork very prevalent here. No organs in any of the Churches that I saw. Paintings upon the whole were very indifferent; though here and there a face which seemed well done. In one church two figures, wooden, as large as life, the faces pretty well done, the rest clumsy. One kneeling in a kind of theatric attitude: another—I forget in what—I believe standing. Near, though not contiguous they seemed to bear some relation to each other, but what the relation was by no means apparent to the superficial glance which was all I thought worth bestowing on them.

Decr. 8 Saty.

Arrived at Mira[10] at daybreak. Mira a little town belonging to Prince Radzivil, with a Castle, at present not occupied by the Prince but by another Polish Nobleman. This castle was occupied by the Russians at the time of the Confederacies, and bears the marks of the alterations made in it for the purposes of military defences. The Windows stopt up in several places put one in mind of the English Window Tax: but no Brickwork is to be seen any where so bad in England. On the other side of the road a garden seemingly neglected, the fences out of repair: the stile Dutch in every thing except neatness. Once a moat, but pretty well filled up. In a church in the town service performing on a small organ with ½ a dozen boys chanting. Here the snow failing, obliged to remount the Kibitki on its wheels

Slept at Stolovitch[11] at a vile Jew hovel so small and the family so numerous as hardly to have room to stir. A separate room which I should have had otherwise, render'd unoccupiable as I was told by the Stove's letting the smoke come through, a common defect incident to their wretched brickwork. In this dog-hole I observed a large quantity of home-made Macaroni, which would have looked tempting had the hands that made it been unknown.

Dec. 9.

Left Stolovitch before day break: stopt to break fast at /a Jew Inn at/ Polonka:[12] a place more pleasantly situated than any I had yet observed. Cottages in the environs had groups of trees reserved seemingly for ornament: and a few trees left here and there in the streets. The country-folks came in their Sunday Dresses: girls otherwise poorly dressed with clean handerchiefs of fine white linnen on their heads. A number of women with strings of brankas a kind of light bread in the form of a horse-collar. The sort of bread would have been good if made by cleaner hands. 2 for a Copeck, containing not so much bread as an English half-penny roll. Bread in this form I have observed in all the little towns.

Arrived at Slonim[13] before dusk—had the mortification to find

[10] Mir, some seventy miles south-west from Minsk. From Minsk to Warsaw, via Brest Litovsk, Bentham's route ran in general a few miles to the north of the line of the present railway linking these places.

[11] Stolovichi, a few miles north of what is now the important rail centre of Baranovichi.

[12] Polonka, about fifteen miles due west of Baranovichi.

[13] Slonim, on the river Shchara, about forty miles west and a little south from Stolovichi.

the New Inn kept by a German full—as likewise the only remaining Christian Inn. Obliged to take up with a room at a Jews, not an Inn but a private house—already warmed and decently fitted up. He asked 2 Roubles, but took one. Tables 3 one of them a very large oval with flaps neatly enough made and painted in compartments red and green 7 or 8 neat chairs matching it. 2 Glazed bookcases; one red and green: the other clumsy carved deal, with a clumsy oak bureau under it. Books in the 2 not fewer than 250 or 300 Vols. mostly thin folios—all Hebrew. The owner a Rabbi keeps a hardware shop with the articles painted on his window shutter. One of the books he showd me was Euclid's Elements: another on Astronomy contained a MS diagram which he said was of his own drawing. ~~The whole contents~~ A clumsy clock likewise painted green: paper hangings of the same ground. Ceiling as in Russia not plaistered but wood whitened; the boards of it not flush but alternate. A round bowl and a brush hanging up rare implements of cleanliness. Floor filthy as elsewhere.

All the contents of his shop he assured me were either English or Austrian (from Stiria) None made in Poland. No manufactory of any kind at Slonim though a pretty considerable town.

Bedsteads brought in for me and Du Bark: the bottoms of twisted straw.

The stove of embossed tiles: a kind of coarse resemblance of Dresden china.

Staid at Slonim till 12½ in expectation of a cause which was to have come on in a Court of Justice at 8. They were waiting for the President, and as the time of his arrival was represented to me as very uncertain, I would not wait longer. For the Judges a long table cover'd with green cloth—a portable crucifix on it, and an English inkstand with sliding cover—/Also a set of the Statutes at large/ A smaller table coverd also with green cloth for the Advocates, who I was told have nothing to distinguish them in their dress. While the Advocates plead, the doors are open: but when the Judges deliberate the Advocates as well as everybody else are excluded. So said a man who appeared to be an Officer of the Court. My[14] respect for Justice determined me to call in the assistance of a hairdresser. The first that presented himself disappeared upon being informed that I depended upon him for powder. He was after /a considerable length of time/ succeeded by an old German, who being apprised of my

[14] The remainder of this paragraph, and also the next, was added on one of the verso pages of the diary (most of which are blank). This seems the appropriate point at which to insert it.

wants, I expected to find prepared to supply them: but he was possessed of none of the implements of hair dressing, but an almost toothless comb and a pair of dirty hands. Powder however and Pomatum he informed me were to be bought. I commissioned him accordingly, and in about an hour he returned with a pound of powder and a tallow candle. This was the pomatum he said commonly employ'd by the officers of the regiment there in quarters: but to apply the powder he had no instrument other than the hands above-mentioned.

This regiment when compleat should consist of no more than 300: at present it has not 150 effective, 40 officers included or not included. This deficiency affords a presumption that the notion I had found entertained in Crechoff of the Poles joining the Russians against the Turks was ill-grounded.

From Slonim to Warsaw 3 roads through Briesh, through Szerchov and through Bransk and Bielsk. The former represented by the Jew Landlord as preferable, and chosen by the Carrier Nicolai.[15] Distance 50 post-miles 46 computed

---

Dec. 7 [*an addition to the journal out of date order*]

Slept at Keydanoff at a Polish nobleman's with whom the Carrier happened to have interest enough to get us quarters instead of going to the Jew Inn. This is a great luxury: enjoying a large room without any other disturbance than the intrusion of a noisy drunken Horse-doctor of his Lordship's acquaintance. He was a man of letters: and produced an Almanac in Polish for the ensuing year with the old prediction of octogesimus octavus mirabilis annus preceded by a Polish version. On this prediction he held forth with considerable energy—Seemed a great politician: perfectly acquainted with the revenue of Prince Radzwil which he maintained to be twice as great as the Kgs.

Dec. 10th Monday

Left Slonim at 12½ at about 7 arrived at Rojanka[16] distance called 7 Miles. Found 2 rooms ready warmed at the Jew Inn,

[15] From this point the renderings of place-names in Bentham's journal become increasingly uncertain and difficult to identify. The 'former' route, chosen by the carrier, was by way of Brest Litovsk. 'Szerchav' appears to be Szereszów, or Shereschev, north-east of Brest at 24° 10′ E., 52° 30′ N. Bilsk and Bryansk, on the most northerly of the three routes mentioned, lie nearly due west of Slonim, some miles to the south of Byalostok.

[16] Probably Ruzhany, west-south-west of Slonim.

happily separated by a passage from the apartments of the family. Obliged for this warm reception to a Princess one of 5 daughters of Prince Sapicha who had occupied this apartment in her way from Warsaw to Wilna. The town belongs to the Prince her father who has a palace close by. The Princess lie[s] in this dog-hole her father's house within a stone's throw? Such if I may believe my Jew Land-lord is the custom of the country: Even children who are forisfamiliated do not sleep at their Parents' houses (not to burthen them) but only eat there, having their headquarters at such Jew dog-holes as the country affords. Twas of this P. Sapicha that Potemkin bought Dubrovna. The Princess was called by the Jew *Sapijonka*.

Decr. 11. Tuesday

Left Rojanka at 8. On the left the P.'s palace a striking object. The front that first presents itself has nothing remarkable: the colour, faded I suppose, a brownish yellow. But the road turning presents a new front, not yet finished. A central building joining two wings by a curved Colonade. Materials brick, incrusted with plaister. It is only in the center and farther wing that the incrustation is finished. Colour a beautiful pale green or rather greenish white: but the moulding about the windows etc. seemed ~~to be~~ of a deeper shade. The building ornamented not over-charged with vases. A very elegant structure: the colour remarkably pleasing, though it can hardly be durable. The windows however not sashed but on hinges, and the glass seemed to be nothing better than muddy stuff which one sees in the other houses. Similar vases /and those not inelegant/ I observed on another house in the town which in other respects was as mean as its neighbours. No appearance of gardens.

Between Rojanka and | | crossed in swampy forest the road through which is made by parallel logs laid across. So intolerable a jolting I never before experienced.

Arrived at Venitz[17] distance called 5 miles between 1 and 2. Here I found a miracle—a Jew Inn tolerably clean; even the floor not much dirtier than the dirtiest one could find in England. Presently ½ a dozen Jews sat down to a good dinner with a clean tablecloth which however did not long continue so, one of the company discovering it to answer equally well the purpose of a pocket handkerchief. This preference of a clean table-cloth to the skirt of a filthy gown was the more striking to me as being the first example of personal cleanliness I had ever observed in this part of the race.

[17] Not identified.

In dividing the bouilli fingers served instead of forks, and it was thus the pieces were handed about by each man to his fellow. The plates were Queens-ware apparently English. In this extraordinary Inn the Beams as well as boards of the Ceiling were neatly plained with a bead-edge. The side boards hewn smooth and the panes regular, and the spying-hole glazed.

Left Venitz about | |: at about 6 or 7 arrived at Soritz.[18] There I had the mortification of finding the same company of Jew Travellers: who had come thus far from Selov. Here I met with some small fish which would I believe have been good, had not they been boiled to mummy in a Jew Pipkin. No separate room, nor any place to lodge my bed at a distance from other people's straw, I chose cold as a less evil than filth, and slept in my Kibitki.

At Venitz in a mean little country Church found two or three dozen fellows each with an incense wax taper burning broad-day-light at an enormous expence.

Decr. 12. Wedy.

Left Soritz about day break: at a little after 2 arrived at Kevarktch,[19] 7 miles. House tolerably clean: all the utensils remarkably so. The mistress of the house a very good looking woman's 2 sisters pretty girls, the eldest beautiful: and what is much more extraordinary clean: her hands as delicate as if she had not been used to work. A brother a comely lad: in another dress I should hardly have suspected him of Judaism certainly not the girls: the whole family fine flesh and blood not inferior to English. The mistress objected to my defiling her pipkin with my profane silver spoon: she offerd a wooden one of her own so white and clean, that I had not the least objection to the change. She entertained my men in a very elegant manner with the history of a Russian Prince who in his way to Moscow last year had made it his amusement to beat every body that came within his reach, particularly Jews, the female sex not excluded: the fair Oratrix herself had found her charms no protection against the savage Muscovite. About 7 miles short of Moscow the country rose upon him: peasants and Jews joined in the retaliations. The affair however, upon his turning complaisant in his turn, cost the Lord of the Village several thousand ducats, through the intervention of the Russians at Warsaw.

Left Kevarktch about ½ after 3. Arrived at Bratilova[20] at 10 at

[18] Not identified. [19] Not identified.

[20] Bratylowo, E. N. E. of Brest Litovsk.

night: distance called 10 miles. The driver not knowing the road, we were glad to accept of the company of a Soldier of horse who had had his quarters at the Inn at Kevarktch, and a Polish Nobleman. No separate room—Soldier, Nobleman, I and mine, joined in a snoring concert with a numerous Jew-family.

Dec. 13. Thursday

Left Bratilova a little before day-break: at about 10 arrived at the town of Briesch[21]: distance called 2 miles. Enquired in vain after a Christian Inn. (Tractec?) The Jew Inn we happened to pitch upon afforded a good dish of coffee. Here I made prize of a goose ready dressed: that is deprived by scorching of every juice except a little grease. This was laid up in the wallet as a great treasure: provisions being grown either stale or scanty. Happily this nights meal is, I hope, the last but one I shall have to make short of Warsaw, distant now only 24 or 26 miles. At this town we lost sight of the Nobleman: but the Soldier a most acceptable comrade, sticks by us. I have been sharing with him part of my provisions which he has received with thankfulness. I understand him to be bound for Warsaw. Provision of Wax-Candle presented by Gen. Bandre not to be revealed[?] in this large town; I am beholden to the Jew Religion for some yellow wax in a thick roll. The number of pieces of this wax serves with them to mark the number of the holydays.

One of the numerous churches, dated 1766, already in ruins. walls crackt, and plaister peeled all over. Of the many plaistered churches the towns in this country swarm with, I have scarce observed one that has not been in the same predicament.

Left Briesch between 12 and 1: between 6 and 7 reached Janova[22] a little town, distance 5 miles. No separate rooms pigged, as usual, Jews and Gentiles all together. Nothing more remarkable than that this place afforded the luxury of a piece of horse-radish to eat with the cold goose.

A little beyond Briesch, paid at a toll of 2 gros per horse: the first payment of this kind that had occurred during the journey. A causeway not far distant was the apparent ground. The profit goes we were told, to the King, that is I suppose to the public: it is let out to farm.

[21] Brest Litovsk.

[22] Janow, west-north-west from Brest Litovsk. Bentham's route curved to the northward nearer to the Bug than the modern highway from Brest to Siedlce.

Dec. 14 Friday

Left Janova a little after day-break: viz about 8. A little before 12 reached Loritza[23]; distance 4 miles. At this place a pair of delicate hands perfectly clean, and of a beautiful red and white /manufacturing | | a kind of Macaroni/ afforded me the first occasion I had yet met with of viewing Jewish provisions without disgust.

At my entrance a lad decently dressed presented himself with a book. I took it imagining it a book of my own dropped out of my pocket. I found it a Polish primer for teaching Latin. I returned it, but he follow'd me into the room, and not content with touching the hem of my garment, the Polish stile of supplication, prostrated himself on the ground and kissed one of my feet. His meaning was now sufficiently perceptible: he even used the first-mentioned mode of supplication to my servant to induce him to intercede. Upon inquiry, I was told he was a poor scholar and upon looking at one of his hands, found him a cripple. On this occasion I yielded for the first time to the importunities of beggars. I had been in few inns without finding one or more; taking their station by the stove with little ceremony. Most of them accompanied their petitions with a kind of muttering, which seemed to be a prayer.

Left Loritza between 2 and 3, at about 7 reached Selitz[24] distance 4 miles. This the first Jew Inn I had seen with plaistered walls plaistered in the inside. The room large /and lofty/ clumsy tin plates and dishes to the number of at least 3 dozen of various sizes a spectacle hitherto unparalleled bespoke the opulence of the owner. It was unfortunately *Sabbath* a season the effect of which is however rather the granting unwillingly than the refusing absolutely. Asking for milk, we were told there was none: desiring that some might be sent for, difficulties were made: after all they had milk themselves which at length they produced. The Sabbath it seems commands sulkiness, without forbidding lies. A Christian maid sat at a table well furnished with glasses, ready to supply beer, malt spirits, and even mead, a liquor I now heard of for the first time. The house of our Rabbi landlord at Slonim could not afford a single drinking-glass, notwithstanding the elegance of the furniture, tho' a glass of that kind cost me there not so much as two pence. The only utensil /vessel/ for liquors one can be sure of meeting with at a Polish Jew Inn is a tin can, made disproportionately tall, for the convenience of its being thrown down upon the least touch, and to render the introduction of a cleansing hand impossible. The scruples

[23] Probably Losice.

[24] Siedlce.

about the introduction of my Christian spoon into the Jew Pipkin to stir the milk were here renewed and maintained with obstinacy: a dirty wooden one being offerd instead I cut the matter short, by flinging it away and plunging my own spoon in, and all was silent. Sabbath forbidding money to be touched, the way the Devil is cheated is by making use of the intervention of some other substance than the fingers, I believe any substance whatsoever. I have just been observing the method of giving change: some money was brought in a dish: and the requisite pieces pushed out by a small loaf which happen'd to be lying on the table.

Sat. Dec.

Left Selitz a little after 7: reached Volo-calitsk[25] ½ after 12: distance 5 miles: road very bad, tho as it seems at Selitz, we had fallen onto the post-road from Warsaw to Grodno. A great part through wood ground very rugged and in some places a mixture of mud and deep water occasioned by a rapid thaw.

Left Volo-calitsk between 2 and 3. Road so bad that we could seldom keep to tolerable footplaces: between 8 and 9 were glad to stop at a place called Kooberna[26] The inn consisting of nothing but one little dirty room, kept by a Christian, a Carpenter by trade, and a fiddler for Amusement. The Virgin and our Saviour in all attitudes and colours dispelled at the first entrance the disquieting idea of Judaism: The house afforded a tolerable kind of white bread in the shape of crowdies and a tolerable kind of ale. Another evidence of christianity but two or at most 3 children, instead of 5 6 or 7. The weather being warm, the heat of the little room was such as almost stifled me, and I was forced to throw off everything but shirt and then could hardly breath. A Jew who dropt in a little before bed-time maintained all night the station he had taken on the bench close to the stove.

Left Kooberna about day-break ½ after 7. At a little before 11 stopt to breakfast at Gottslovski[?][27] 3½ miles distant but one[?] short of Warsaw. A comfortable coffee-room kept by 2 decent rosy-cheeked young German women. They say Warsaw is half full of Germans. Stove of large tiles made of a figured kind of red ware unglazed of a neat pattern. Room clean and sanded. On the lower end and side walls half a dozen pretty good heads large as life in

[25] Probably Wola Kaluska, west of Siedlce and a few miles south of Kaluszyn.

[26] Not identified; possibly near Minsk Mazowieckic, about twenty-five miles east of Warsaw.

[27] Not identified.

crayons. On the upper site 8 daubings of Mary's and Jesus's linen Window Curtains tied back with blue ribbon. Half a dozen plates of so many different sorts on the chimney piece to brown-ware Coffee pots and pewter spoons etc. cups and saucers with brass spoons. These numerous luxuries sufficiently bespoke the vicinity of the capital—tolerably neat wooden stools and a clean deal table.

The state of the road was not at all answerable and it had every ingredient to make it a bad one: deep sand to make it heavy large loose stones to make it jolting: water to make it splash and ice to make it slippery.[28]

616

Memorandum[1]

17 December 1787 (Aet 39)

Libri visendi at Berlin

Purgold de imperii Rossici ordinibus—Hale apud Gebauer 1786[2]
Vie du Baron de Trink Berlin?[3]
Harpsichord Musick
Map of Turkey in 6 sheets in German—Vienna?[4]
B. de Dahlberg Rapport de la Morale et la Politique. Berlin chez
[...?]. Trad. du Cte du Goertz.[5]
Remler Chemische Untersuchung der Tumarinden[6]
—Saure gr. 4to. 3 Gr.
Guibert Eloge du Roi de Prusse.[7]

[28] A note to Samuel Bentham from Warsaw on 17 December 1787, the day after Bentham's arrival, now missing, is acknowledged by Samuel on a scrap dated 2 March 1788 (B.M. IV: 429).

616. [1] B.M. XVI: 73. Autograph. On a blank page of the preceding diary.

[2] Joannes Purgold, *De diversis Imperii Rossici ordinibus eorumque iuribus atque obligationibus nec non de diversis foris competentibus*, Halle, 1786.

[3] *La vie de Frédéric baron de Trenck écrite par lui-même et traduite en français par M. le baron de B**** [Bock], Metz, 1787.

[4] This seems to have been obtained and presented to the Marquis of Lansdowne (see letter 622).

[5] Not traced.

[6] Johann Christian Wilhelm Remler (1759–?) was the author of various publications on chemistry about the years 1787–92. This work was published at Erfurt in 1787.

[7] Count Jacques Antoine Hyppolyte de Guibert, *Éloge du Roi de Prusse*, 1787. There was also a German edition published the same year at Leipzig.

Lettres d'un Observateur impartial sur les affaires du Pays-Bas?
Berlin?
Hertzberg sur population. Acad. Sci. 1785[8]

At Warsaw Hares down Gloves chez Richard Marchand Francois for 3 Roobles a pair. Ludwig

---

~~1. Duties~~
~~2. Best map of Poland~~
3. Polish Grammar Dicty.?
4. French books printed at Warsaw.
5. Polish Constitution new
~~6. Polish Monnaie~~
~~7. Court Calendar~~
8. Book Catalogue.

Schon
André Broadsteder
my German Valet de
Place
at Warsaw Dec. 17
1787

617

From Charles Whitworth[1]

17 December 1787

Warsaw Decr. 17th 1787[2]

Mr. Whitworth presents his Compts. to Mr. Bentham, he has but this instant heard of his being here or he would have thank'd him sooner for the offer he is so good as to make of carrying any thing to England. He has at present nothing with which he will trouble him, but to wish him a good journey, and to regret that he has not had an opportunity of making his acquaintance.
Monday Night Ten o'clock

[8] Count Ewald Friedrich von Hertzberg, *Sur la population des États en général et sur celle des États Prussiens en particulier. Dissertation…lue dans l'assemblée publique de l'Académie des Sciences et des Belles-Lettres à Berlin, le 27 Janvier*, Berlin, 1785.

617. [1] B.M. IV: 430. Addressed: 'A Monsieur / Monsieur Bentham.'

Charles Whitworth (1752–1825), a professional diplomat whose services later won him steps in the peerage, was envoy extraordinary and minister plenipotentiary to Poland, 1785–9. In 1789 he was transferred to St Petersburg, where he served in the same capacities until 1800.

[2] The dating was inserted by Bentham.

618

To Charles Whitworth[1]

17 December 1787 (Aet 39)

Warsaw
Schultz Hotel Monday night Decr. 18 1787.

Sir

On my way to England through Berlin there is a circumstance in which your assistance /or at least advice/ if it be in your power to afford me any would relieve me from a considerable embarassment. I am informed that in the Prussian Custom-houses they are so strict as even to search pockets and to make a point of opening all sealed letters. On my departure from England /in August 1785/ I took ~~various letters~~ /several/ some of which not having an opportunity of presenting them remain still with me. Concerning some of them, knowing them to be merely letters of introduction, such as official letters from Ld. Carmarthen, I should be under no difficulty. But there are others which being likely enough to contain particulars which the writers would not have wished to be known to third persons, I should be glad to return to them unopen'd. To these, would not an enveloppe from you addressed to our Minister at Berlin be a protection? In case of the affirmative, not conceiving myself to have the honour to be known to you I should beg permission to wait on you in order to ~~lay before your~~ /submit to your/ inspection such documents as between strangers might be necessary to inspire the requisite degree of confidence: in the other case, I

618. [1] B.M. IV: 432. Autograph. Draft with some corrections. Docketed by Bentham: 'Brouillion not sent / J.B. to Mr. Whitworth.' Incorrectly dated.

Bentham's reference near the end of this draft to his having already troubled Whitworth indicates that earlier in the day he had either written or left a message at the legation. Presumably this had occasioned Whitworth's note (letter 617), which seems to precede this one.

According to Bowring (x, 180), 'Bentham stopped at Warsaw, intending to pay his respects to King Stanislaus, whose correspondent he had been, through Lind, the king's agent in England. But bashfulness and gloominess interfered.' As Bentham's papers published in volume ii give no hint of such a correspondence, Bowring's remark is suspect. Moreover, apart from its being out of character for Bentham to seek such an audience, this evidently was not his intention for he gave himself no time; for Bowring's statement that he stayed a week in Warsaw is certainly wrong. The conclusion of this letter states his intention to leave on the morning of Tuesday, 18 December, within forty-eight hours of his arrival; and had he stayed much longer he would have been hard put to it to reach Berlin by 27 December (letter 620). Bowring's statement, that 'he called on the British minister, and not finding him at home, did not repeat his visit', seems to be strictly correct, but also misleading.

would not wish to add to the trouble I have already taken the liberty of giving you. In hopes of the favour of an answer, I shall not take my departure tomorrow morning before ten o'clock. I have the honour to be, with all respect

Sir,
Your most obedient humble Servant
Jeremy Bentham

619

To Jeremiah Bentham[1]

9 January 1788 (Aet 39)

Berlin Jany. 9 1788

My dear Father

I know not what fatality has hung over our correspondence. Two or three days ago Dr. Brown[2] communicated to me the letter he received from you through the messenger, Mr. Major, ~~through~~ /by/ whom I now write. Ld. Lansdown then received a letter from me dated in Septr. last,[3] and you have received neither of the duplicates which I dispatched from Crechoff about the same time.[4] One of them went in the very same enclosure with that to Ld. Lansdown. They were sent to Messrs. Comyn and Fenton Merchants ~~of~~ /at/ Riga, old acquaintances of Aiton's, my brothers Gardener, and accompanied by a letter from Aiton to them, desiring them for greater security to enclose both letters to their London correspondent. They went to Riga by the opportunity of two of my Brother's workmen, who upon the breaking up of affairs at Crechoff /were to/ returned to England. The other duplicate was enclosed in a letter to Mr. FitzHerbert and accompanied by two others, one to my Mother, and the other to Far, on the occasion of his marriage.[5] Of these, as they were short I happen to have made a Brouillon, from which I have /been/ making out duplicates or something like duplicates, which I here beg leave to enclose. That to you was too long to be made the subject of such an operation: /especially by one

619. [1] B.M. IV: 450–2. Autograph. Docketed by Jeremiah Bentham: 'Fils Jeremy / Lr. dated Janry. 9th 1788.'

Addressed: 'To / Jeremiah Bentham Esqr. / Queen's Square Place / Westminster.'

[2] Dr Charles Brown (see letter 524), instead of going to Krichëv, as had been suggested at one time, had obtained a post as physician at the Prussian court.

[3] Letter 605. [4] Letter 603. [5] Letter 602.

oppressed as I was with the whole load of my Brother's affairs:/ sending duplicates, one through the channel above-mentioned, which Aiton undertook to answer for, and the other through Mr. FitzHerbert, whose departure for England was then unknown to me, seemed to promise all the security I could wish. That enclosed to Mr. FitzHerbert went by the first post after my receipt of your two letters together[6] (the one of them a copy of /the lost one/ dated in March) and the most material part of it, was the giving the answer you desired, by a draught of /that/ £50 odd on Mr. King: it went on or about the 12/23 of Septr.[7] the day of its date. The other duplicate did not go till a week or ten days later, the men who were to take it not setting off so soon by some days as was at first expected. They gave you, amongst other things my brother's account of the commencement of the Turkish war: and an intimation of the many letters of mine which I found reason to apprehend had never reached you. Such multiplied disasters are hardly to be paralleled. To endeavour to recollect the particulars would be a very troublesome, and as I intend to tread close upon the heels of the Messenger who brings you this, an useless task.

It was no small satisfaction to me to receive so unexpectedly a printed copy of my Defence of Usury, and for that satisfaction I am much obliged to you. But I have been just tearing off a half-sheet in which[8] I had begged you in stronger terms than you would like to see, not to send any more copies in my name, much less accompanied with letters.[9] Upon turning over the copy, I was pleased to see it had suffer'd so little in point of correctness, by my distance from the press. I have however found a few errata, the list of which I inclose, that you may send it to the Printer, if you think it worth the while. Adieu, my dear Father, I hope to embrace you in a few days after your receipt of this.

Berlin Jan. 9. 1787.[10]

[6] Missing.

[7] An error for '14/25 Sept.'

[8] 'in which in which' in Ms.

[9] Jeremiah Bentham had sent complimentary copies with covering letters at least to Alleyne Fitzherbert (now back in London) and Sir James Harris at the Hague. Copies of his letters to them and of their acknowledgements are preserved, among other places, in longhand notes at the end of a copy of the *Defence of Usury* in the British Museum (press mark 8227 aa 33).

[10] Misdated '1787' by Bentham.

620

To Samuel Bentham[1]

2 May 1788 (Aet 40)

How to begin a letter, even to you, after so long an interruption of intercourse? Well, the pen, by a prodigious effort, has been set a-going, and now let it run on.

At Berlin, I arrived 16–27th December, lounged there rather more than a fortnight, waiting, the greatest part of the time, for the cursed Opera, put off from day to day by the indisposition of a cursed actress, the woman (Foote, I think her name is)[2] you have heard at Petersburg. Dr. Brown is doing there very well.[3] A great part of my time was, of course, passed with him. I saw Mrs. Brown a few days ago here on her way to Berlin, with their five children, by Hamburg; for which place, I imagine, they are already sailed. He had written to Benson a letter, full of indignation, for his rascality to you; and I found Mrs. B. in the same sentiments.[4] I was about a fortnight crawling post from Berlin to Holland through vile roads. I passed through Potsdam, Magdeburg, Brunswick, and Osnaburg. The finest situation by far, in so much of Germany as I travelled through, is Bentheim. I don't know whether I ever showed you an old MS. I have, which pretends we are descended from the Counts of that country.[5] I did not expect to have found the pretension confirmed by the identity of the arms. Of three or four coats which I observed in stone, on one side of the romantic castle, which is the family residence pertaining to the several counties which, it seems, centre in that family, one is composed of the thingumbobs called Cinq-foils, which you will find in your seal. The county is likely to be extinct, it seems, for want of heirs, and the Elector of Hanover has a large mortgage upon it. When the count dies, you may give my compliments to the empress, and desire she would lend us a body of troops to assert our claim. I lounged about ten days in Holland, seeing Sir James,[6] and as much as could well be

620. [1] Bowring, x, 181–3.

[2] Not identified. Possibly the wife of Samuel T. Foote, sometime manager of the Plymouth theatre, and mother of the actress Maria Foote, who became Countess of Harrington.

[3] See letter 619, n. 2.

[4] For Benson's 'rascality' see letters 578, 588.

[5] Now B.M. Add. Mss. 36524, fos. 13–16. The reference to Bentheim is at fo. 13v.

[6] Sir James Harris was now ambassador at the Hague, where his attempts to thwart French diplomatic influence had ended in triumph (Alfred Cobban, *Ambassa-*

seen of the Dutch towns in that time. I reached London a few days before my birth-day; that is to say, (for you remember neither day, month, nor time of the year,) February 4–15. Q.S.P., of course, in great joy, of which he has given you, no doubt, abundant particulars. His memory and bodily strength begin to fail him; but, in other respects, he is in mighty good health, humour, and spirits. His circumstances are, upon the whole, rather improved, I think, than impaired, since I left England, and his disposition towards us is certainly rather grown better, if there were room for it, than worse. Farr and I are upon as sociable terms as it is in his nature to be with anybody, besides his mother and brother.[7] He has just migrated for the summer to his country-house. During the winter, I received frequent particular invitations, though no general one. The principal cement is his wife, who plays prettily on the harpsichord, and is a mighty good creature, but timid to an excess. His behaviour is as respectful as ever. Charles I see but little of; his business increases considerably, and he is said to deserve it. Lord Lansdowne vastly civil. Upon occasion of Hastings' trial, has put himself to school to me about evidence.[8] He has accused himself repeatedly, and *sans ménagement*, for not offering me a place when he was in; and commissioned me to consider what would suit me in case of his coming in again. He supposes I should prefer a place at one of the Boards, to engaging in what is called politics, viz., coming into parliament with a precarious place. Whether he meant all this, or whether the use of it was to make me contribute to make people think he was to come in, I cannot take upon me to say. Perhaps partly one and partly t'other; but my notion is, he never will come in, in any efficient place. As for me, my real thoughts being upon that, as upon all other occasions, as you know, the easiest for me to give, I gave them him, viz., that I was not fit for a place, and that if I were, I should not wish to have one—that I hoped always to be happy enough to preserve his good opinion, and so forth, and that was enough for me. P.C.[9] is as zealous a friend of yours as ever. He

dors and Secret Agents. The Diplomacy of the First Earl of Malmesbury at the Hague, London, 1954).

[7] Bowring reads 'brothers'; but Bentham's point is that Farr Abbot's intimacy was reserved for his mother and his only full brother, Charles.

[8] Long afterwards Bentham told Bowring that his reputation as a legal theorist, left flat in the Bowood circle as a result of the critical attitude of Camden and Dunning to his *Introduction to the Principles of Morals and Legislation*, was restored in 1788 by some notes on evidence which he provided in connection with the trial of Warren Hastings. Although Bentham's opinion ran counter to Lansdowne's own views, the lawyer Sir Eardley Wilmot, whose judgment Lansdowne valued, praised Bentham's sagacity (Bowring, x, 185–6).

[9] Reginald Pole Carew. Bowring's identification as Colquhoun is incorrect. The

has been showing Vermicular to George Melville,[10] who is a very busy amateur in everything that is in any way connected with mechanics; and to Davis's friend, Lord H.[11] Melville, he says, is much pleased with it. On the cover, as returned by P.C., I see 'Lord H. to return particular thanks for the inspection of the enclosed papers.' Whether that betokens approbation, I cannot pretend to say, P.C. not having seen his lordship when I saw him last. He is certainly of my way of thinking about usury. He brought Owen Cambridge to me t'other day to acknowledge himself a proselyte; but you don't know who Owen Cambridge[12] is, and it would take up too much room to tell you. I shall endeavour to send you a copy of the Defence with this, as likewise another to Pleschejeff.[13] I choose rather to take for granted he has sent you a letter I wrote him about a month ago,[14] in which I said something of the success of the book, than to be at the pains to write it over again. Since then, it has had some little sale in Ireland, and I hope may do something towards preventing the success of the measure of reducing the rate of interest there—a measure which, after having been thrown out of the House of Lords there this winter, is to be brought on by administration the next it is said.[15]

Since my arrival in England, I have, of course, been very idle, doing very little to Code, and of course feeling like a fish out of water the whole time; but by God's assistance, I have found out a country-lodging which promises to suit me very well, and I shall migrate to it before the week is out. It is at a farm-house at Hendon, eight miles only from town—the man rents £150 a-year, and £50 of

initiative in writing to Carew seems to have been taken by Jeremiah Bentham. Copies of their exchange of letters are at B.M. XXII: 426–7, together with a memorandum to the effect that Carew was sent not only Bentham's letters describing the vermiculars (see letters 586, 591), but also his extracts of Samuel Bentham's letter describing the beginning of naval warfare between Russia and Turkey in the Liman of Ochakov (letter 603).

[10] Possibly George Melville (d. 1812), 5th son of David, 6th Earl Leven, who later entered the Indian civil service.

[11] Lord Howe, the First Lord of the Admiralty. Bowring placed a full stop after 'Davis's friend' and continued 'Lord H. Melville'. There was no such person, and the correspondence referred to in n. 9 above makes it clear that Howe is meant. Bentham no longer had as intimate a contact as formerly with Joseph Davies and his family, but evidently the friendship was not neglected after his return from Russia.

[12] Richard Owen Cambridge (1717–1802), a dilettante and mechanical inventor.

[13] Bowring mistakenly reads 'Pleschegoff'.

[14] Missing.

[15] The legal maximum rate of interest in Ireland was six per cent, one per cent higher than in England. In 1788 the movement to assimilate it to the English rate was successful (W. E. H. Lecky, *A History of Ireland in the eighteenth century*, 5 vols., London, 1913, ii, 492).

it of Mr. Brown; and his wife has the reputation of a good cook, having lived in that capacity with a good family. It is decently furnished with tapestry hangings, large carpets, and immense tables. The great inconvenience is, terrible low ceilings. I shall live on the Zadobras plan, saving and excepting fleas, gnats, mice, dirt, and interruptions. It is a very pleasant country, and being all in grass, the delights of hay-making will continue five or six weeks. The Q.S.P.'s took me down, when I saw and agreed for it, and they spontaneously promised that I should not meet with any disturbance from them so long as I staid there. I have now upon trial at my lodgings (for my chambers were let during my absence, and I am in no great hurry to get back to them) a superb harpsichord of Merlin's, which I think to buy and send into the country. It has four strings to every note, viz., besides two unisons and the octave above and octave below, and a set of hammers to produce the effect of a pianoforte. The tone is a very sweet one, but the inconvenience is, that the complexity renders it proportionably liable to be out of order, and diminishes the loudness. It is an elegant piece of furniture, very beautifully inlaid. I can have it for sixty guineas. I shall buy it, and then immediately I shall regret that I did not buy instead of it, a simple grand pianoforte; the tone of which would be louder, and is to be had for the same money. The harpsichord was made in 1781, and cost then a hundred or a hundred and ten guineas. I have got a present from Anderson of a good stock of orange marmalade, with a receipt for making it. I shall set up a marmalade *fabrique* when needful, and shall then be very happy to have the honour of your company at Hendon, at the old hour, after you have dined at Crichoff.

As soon as I have finished such parts of Code as cannot be published one without the other, I go to Paris to get it corrected, and advise about the printing of it.

I met Randal[16] t'other day in the street, who stopt me to inquire after you. Charles[17] was telling me of his having met Shairp.[18] I forget where,—S. made very particular inquiries after me, desired his compliments to me, and added, that if he had known before of my arrival, he would have waited on me.

[16] See letter 131, n. 4. Randal was senior partner in a private shipyard. In 1779 there had been suggestions that Samuel Bentham might be taken into business with him (letters 304, n. 2 and 320, n. 1).

[17] Charles Abbot.

[18] Presumably this was Mr Shairp of Shairp, Maude, and Co., Russia merchants, with whom Bentham had had previous dealings (letter 475, n. 5).

621

From George Wilson[1]

5 June 1788

5 June afternoon

Dear Bentham,

I enclose part of the Monthly Review[2] which will probably give you some pleasure notwithstanding the impertinent remarks on the Style at the end. I think upon the Whole it is better done than most articles in reviews and we have been tempted to think it written by some friend but we cannot guess who.[3]

We hope to see you soon
Yours sincerely,
G. Wilson

I have a letter from my sister with [*some words scrawled over*] Bannerman[4] goes tomorrow.[5]

621. [1] B.M. IV: 469 Autograph. Copy by Jeremiah Bentham at B.M. XXII: 425. The sheet on which this letter is written does not bear any address to Bentham, and this portion may have been detached by Bentham before he added a postscript (see n. 5) and directed it to his father. Addressed: 'To Jeremiah Bentham Esq.' Docketed by Jeremiah Bentham: 'Mr Jeremy Bentham / Lr dated June 5th 1788 / wherein is mentioned that / The Defense of Usury had / been reprinted at Dublin. / Together with a Paper / The World / dated Fryday Feb 22 1788 / containing an Account of / the Debates in the Irish / Parliament upon a Proposal / for reducing Public Interest': and also: 'Reced June 11 1788 at P. Heath Jh. B.'

[2] *Monthly Review*, lxxviii (1788), pp. 361–70. The review described the *Defence of Usury* as a 'political gem of the finest water.'

[3] At the end of this line Bentham inserted: 'Nor I neither J.B.' The reviewer has been identified as James Anderson (B.C. Nangle, *The Monthly Review, First Series, 1749–1789*, Oxford, 1934, pp. 1, 62).

[4] Charles Bannerman (d. 1813), Wilson's brother-in-law.

[5] Bentham added a note at the foot of Wilson's letter: 'P.S. On coming to town I learn that the Defense of Usury has been reprinted in Dublin. When you have done with the inclosed, return it if you please (not to Mr Wilson to whom I have given another) but to me. I may perhaps send it to Sam. June 10th.'

622

From the Marquis of Lansdowne[1]

16 June 1788

Dear Mr. Bentham,

I solemnly assure you, that it has been not only on my mind, but upon my heart, to find out this parson's house at Hendon, and to pay my court to you, not to thank you for your magnificent present of not only a most magnificent, but very useful map in the present situation,[2] because I know your nature makes you above accepting acknowledgments; but to tell you how much we wish to see you at Bowood. I am so tired of the whole human race, that we propose to bury ourselves for some time; but as happily all desires return after a certain abstinence, you will find me very happy to make peace with my fellow-creatures through you, and to begin my return to society in London, by profiting of yours for some time in the country. I need not say anything for the ladys. Though I am just now tired to death, and quite asleep, I must tell you the news of the day— which is, that Prussia, Sweden, and Denmark, have made an alliance against Russia[3]; and are, at least Sweden, immediately proceeding to action. You know the consequences of all this better than I do. The accounts from France are wonderfully serious. Sanguine people imagine a civil war must ensue. I cannot myself imagine that any other consequence can be expected, than a more speedy assemblage of the States, and a better constitution of the Cour pleniere, with a Habeas Corpus, restricted to particular descriptions and bodys.[4] Lord Wycombe sets out to-morrow, and

622. [1] Lansdowne Mss., printed Bowring, x, 183.

[2] It seems probable that this was the map Bentham put down on his shopping list when he arrived at Warsaw (see memorandum 616 at n. 4).

[3] These rumours were only partly correct. The Swedish forces attacked Russia a few days later, but the Danes stood by their alliance with Catherine II and briefly entered the war on her side in September. Prussia's first overt sign of hostility to Russia was to bring pressure upon the Danes to sign an armistice the following month. Other diplomatic moves followed but no military action.

[4] Lansdowne referred to the disorders which followed the edicts of 8 May 1788: these, among other things, suspended the *parlements* and established the *Cour plénière*, to which many of the most important functions of the *parlements* were transferred. A fragmentary note by Bentham on the *Cour plénière* is at U.C. CLXX. 36. As Lansdowne expected, the French ministers soon bowed to the storm of protest: an ordinance announcing the forthcoming summons of the States General was promulgated on 5 July, and on 8 August the *Cour plénière* was suspended and the States General definitively summoned for 1 May 1789.

goes with me as far as Bowood. He sleeps only one night at Bowood, and sails in the packet on Sunday for Lisbon. This affects me, as you know, but things must go their natural course.
Lansdowne House,
Tuesday night, 12 o'Clock.
P.S. You must not be surpriz'd if my news turns out to have no foundation, for I have it from no authority. I will take care of your letter,[5] and instructions about it, for Lord W.[6]

623

To Jeremiah Bentham[1]

28 July 1788 (Aet 40)

Hond. Sir

A pretty sort of a 'compleat victory' your's was: a victory with nothing to show for it but the destruction of 3 vessels out of 57, gained by small craft over small craft.[2] I send you something like a victory[3]: a victory, and that really a compleat one, gained over the

[5] Missing.
[6] Lansdowne's eldest son. See letter 401, n. 5.

623. [1] B.M. IV: 473–6. Autograph. Docketed by Jeremiah Bentham: 'Fils Jeremy B. / Letter datd. Hendon July 28 / 1788.'

Addressed: 'Jeremiah Bentham Esqr. / at J. Far Abbot's Esqr. / Putney Heath.'

[2] This would appear to be a reference to a letter from Bentham senior referring to the first of the series of Russo-Turkish naval engagements which took place during this summer in the Liman of Ochakov. Samuel Bentham thus described it: 'On the 7th of June [*the 18th N.S.*], when we had our first action, our flotilla consisted of about 35 vessels, counting 15 or 16 longboats carrying only one gun each: of these 22 only were in the action, when we were attacked by 57 Turkish vessels much superiour in the number of guns, but in general of less caliber than ours. They had besides a large fleet 5 or 6 times superiour to ours, who were waiting at the distance of a few versts; under the cover of which we obliged their small fleet to return, after having lost 2 or 3 we dont know which. On our part we suffered but very little; all the enemies shot went over us; we had not in all 50 men killed.' Samuel himself was fortunate not to be injured when a gun he was sighting burst, killing two and wounding another seven men of his crew (to Bentham, 12/23 October 1788, B.M. IV: 487–9). For a general account of the naval campaign of 1788 discussed in this and subsequent letters, see R. C. Anderson, *Naval Wars in the Levant, 1559–1853*, Liverpool, 1952, pp. 321–32.

[3] Bentham forwarded newspaper accounts of the second engagement, which took place during the 17/28 and 18/29 June, in which a major part was played by the light vessels with which Samuel Bentham was serving. According to Samuel's account, in the first day's fighting the Turks withdrew in face of the attack by the Russian light craft, leaving two ships of the line aground, which were destroyed by fire. Next morning it became apparent that another seven of the Turkish warships had stuck on the treacherous sandbanks of the Liman and the Russian light flotilla went in

Grand fleet of ships of the line: and what is better, by the same small craft, it should seem, that gained the former one. For you will observe that though two ships are taken with 3 or 4,000 prisoners, yet six, including the Admirals and the Vice Admirals, were burnt: so that the main of the business was done by burning: now burning is done by fireships. But the fireships /compose/ with the Bomb-vessels what Sam calls *his* division: therefore this capital and decisive victory is principally Sam's work. Q.E.D. It is the fate of the Turks to build fleets for the Russians to make bonfires of. You remember in their last war that was the way the whole fleet was destroy'd in the harbour of Chesmé or Tchesmi which I had a distant view of when I landed at the Island of Scio.

These fire-ships and bomb-vessels he made up out of the Empress's pleasure boats and other such riff-raff of which you may form a general idea from the extracts you have of old letters of his to me.[4]

Not only the business was done by fireships and gun-boats; but if it had not been done by such kind of irregular vessels, it never could have been done at all. In the open sea it was impossible the whole naval force of the Russians could have faced the half of the Turkish fleet, making every allowance for the difference betwixt the awkwardness of the Russians and the still greater awkwardness of the Turks. In the packet I returned you from Pole Carew was a state of the Russian force brought down to last Autumn[5]: ~~from~~ since then it is impossible the number of their ships of the line can have received any considerable additions, if any: and it has been diminished by one /of 74/ that was driven on shore some months ago in a storm not far from Constantinople, and there taken. The force the Captain-Bashaw took with him from Constantinople you may find, /I believe,/ by turning to the newspaper accounts about a month or six weeks back: to which is to be added the force the Turks had at Ochakoff before he came, which you will find in that letter of Sam's which gives an account of the commencement of hostilities. The expressions in Sam's letter to you are remarkable in this view. It is not merely for the Turkish Flotilla that he hopes his '*Flotilla*' 'will

once more to the attack. In the day's action the Turks lost one ship sunk, seven destroyed by fire started by shells, and one captured and subsequently refitted for Russian service. Over 3,000 Turkish prisoners were taken, and Samuel thought their dead probably exceeded this figure (B.M. IV: 487–9).

[4] See letter 603.

[5] I.e., the letters and documents about the vermicular and about the outbreak of hostilities in the Liman, which Jeremiah Bentham had sent to Pole Carew for onward transmission to Lord Howe (see letter 620, n. 9).

be a match', but for the *'Turkish Fleet'*.[6] Accordingly the terms employ'd, on the account I send you, are, on the one hand, *la Flotte Ottomane*: on the other hand (not la *Flotte* de l'Imperatrice, but /in general)/ *'Les forces Navales* de l'Imperatrice'. The Russians, as you may see from Sam's former letter above-mentioned, have, from the first commencement of hostilities, been wishing and hoping to see the Turks hamper themselves in some odd corner where they could not get away from fireships, but would be obliged to stand still to be burnt. It was on the strength of that idea that Sam wrote so sanguinely in his first letter above mentioned, upon finding the Turkish fleet venturing itself up the Dnieper, though the Russian force in ships of the line and frigates was next to nothing. It was in /pursuit of/ this idea that /in the autumn/ they formed the plan of that attack which appears to have been prevented by the hot-headedness of the Frenchman who took it into his head to break orders and plunge into the thick of the Turkish force with his own vessel alone, unsupported by the rest. Perhaps it was more fortunate upon the whole, that that project failed: had it succeded, the loss of the Turks if they had lost their all then would not have amounted to what they appear to have lost now; and the great fish, the Captain Pasha, would not have swum into the net. After all the Turks have lost more in reputation than in ships and men: the reputation of the Captain-Bashaw was the strength of their cause. Taking for granted the 8 ships captured or destroy'd were all of the line, I am very curious to know what became of the other 32: if they got out of the river safe and sound, the Russians had they twice or thrice the force they have could still never face them in the open sea. The Turkish Flotilla too? What is become of that?[7] The Russians destroy'd 3 out of the 57 in the engagement of the 19th last: but in doing so, they left just double their own number. Possibly they have got altogether into some corner, where they will abide the fate of Ochakoff.

As to Sam, whatever publick rewards other people may get, I have no expectation that any of them will fall to his share.[8] As /the

[6] On 22 May/2 June 1788 Samuel Bentham wrote a short note to his father, dated from 'Gluboka, 30 Versts below Cherson': 'I have told you that my Division consists of the Bomb and Fire Vessels. The Turkish Fleet at Ochakoff is augmenting every day; but our Flotilla, we trust, will be a match for them; I am afraid however it will be some time before any thing decisive be done' (B.M. IV: 466; endorsed by Jeremiah Bentham: 'reced. at Putney Heath / July 22 1788 / Entered in the Book of Commercial Letters, p. 67'. Copy by Jeremiah Bentham, ibid., 468. The letter-book copy, in the hand of Jeremiah Bentham, is B.M. XXII: 428).

[7] See letter 625, n. 2.

[8] This was an error of judgment. Samuel Bentham was rewarded with the Russian

fitting out for/ that kind of irregular service stands /more/ particularly in need of inventive abilities, to which I think it probable enough that nobody there has any pretensions to but himself, he was perhaps as great a contributor to the victory as the Prince of Nassau: but I believe it is not usual for the planners and fitters out to be much consider'd unless they have had a proportionable part in the execution. It may therefore be doubted, whether even Admiral Mordvinoff, though at the head of the naval department there, will have any notice taken of him: and still more, whether Sam will, who, though Mordvinoff's principal Counsellor, or rather instructor, acted in that line in no settled character, but rather as a volunteer. The Marines indeed of which Sam has the command must have been employ'd, I think in the business. But as he has had no military education nor experience, I think it not likely they should have sent him on the business, if there remained any thing for him to do at Cherson.

It should seem, though it is not expressly said so, that in this last engagement the Russians were the assailants, as the Turks had been in the first. For the business was done (says the Vienna account) as the Turkish fleet was occupied in taking post before the town of Ochakoff in order to protect it. This then was what they were employing themselves about, and not the making an attack. The experience the Russians had had of the unskilfulness of the Turks in the engagement between the flotillas, emboldened them to plan an attack upon the fleet itself.

How I do long to see particulars! but our curiosity, I doubt, will in this respect meet with but very imperfect satisfaction. The Russian accounts I think have always been very meagre.

I hope you have or will have got your book of Russian Maps at the Heath that we may talk over them when I come.

Intelligence concerning the Captain Bashaw's Fleet—extracted from the Newspapers.

Apr. the beginning	He sailed for Bujukden (the mouth of the canal where beginningitopensintotheBlackSea)withafairwind.(Extract of a letter from Constantinople Apr. 8.). Ledger June 14th.

military order of St George, advance to the rank of full colonel, and a gold-hilted sword of honour (M.S. Bentham, *Life of... Sir Samuel Bentham*, p. 88).

English paper	Intelligence where and when received	Date of the event	
Ledger July 2 Lond. Gaz. July 1	Constantinople May 22	May 20	He sailed from Bujukden for Sinope in the Black Sea. (On the Asiatic side.)
Ledger July 11	Frontiers of Poland June 16th	No day nor month	He made his appearance off Koslov in the Crimea with an evident intention of making a descent there.
Ledger July 23. Lond. Gaz. July 22.	Vienna July 9.	June 19 or 21* *See Gaz. du Leyde July 22d. This date is the most authentick	Being at anchor with his fleet near Oczakoff, he sent his small craft (57 sail) to attack the Russian small craft (27 sail) and was repulsed with the loss of 3 vessels. (The action continued 5 hours. Leyd. Gaz. July [ ])
Gaz. de Leyde July 22.	Vienna July 9. Express from arrived July 7—sent from Cherson July 2. Letter from Warsaw July 9, received at the Hague, July 21?	June 29	Being in the road of Ochakoff otherwise called the Liman, occupied in posting himself to cover that fortress from the expected attack, his *fleet* was *attacked*, it should seem, by the Russian "*naval force*" and defeated with the loss 6 ships *burned* (among which were his own and his Vice-Admiral's) and 2 taken together with between 3 and 4,000 prisoners. ——— The 32nd day after his sailing his small craft was beat: and the 40th day his Grand Fleet.

Monday 28th July 1788.

I have just received your favour, and Farr's.[9] I shall transmitt you this probably by Mr. Browne. Thanks to Far for his invitation but beg him not to look for mé any day in particular. I have depending a flying engagement of business depending upon other people; and till that is over, as I hope it will be in the course of a few days, I can not call any day my own. When I called at Lincoln's Inn Fields this last time as well as the time before, it was only to

[9] Both missing.

enquire after the family, and without any expectation of seeing any part of it.

Advise Charles, if you seem [*sic*] when he is in Italy to lay in a stock of gloves made of Rabbits' wool. I bought a pair when at Leghorn that cost but 4 *paolis* about 2s. They were much warmer and better ⟨in⟩ every respect than the Beaver or Vigogna-wooll gloves I sent to ⟨you⟩ from Paris. There is none of us all I think but would find them vastly comfortable. But he can not stuff up his portmanteau with such articles. If however he should be at Leghorn, and find any means there of sending things by sea, by means of a Merchant here, I should be obliged to him for any number of pairs not exceeding a dozen: supposing them not to be contraband, and I do not think they are. It would not be worth while to send such small articles any otherwise than through a Merchant, that is in a package separately addressed to any of us, on account of the enormous charges at the Custom-House. It might answer indeed if Far chose to get his cheese and Macaroni that way, in which case I should be glad to join with him for ¼ of a 100 lb. or so. Parmesan I gave but 8d. a lb. for in Leghorn: Macaroni but 2d. at Genoa: but the Naples sort is rather the best. Here both articles are 2s. a lb.—What a difference!

No—upon second thoughts, it is not worth while. I have seen somewhat like those gloves, as I now recollect in a shop in Cheapside—and though they may be 3 times as dear, one shall have no more than one wants at a time and be sure of fitting—But, for comparison sake, if Charles can find room for a single pair in his Portmanteau, I shall be obliged to him.

624

To Jeremiah Bentham[1]

31 July 1788 (Aet 40)

Hendon July 31st 1788.

Hond. Sir

The inclosed contains some farther particulars of the Russian naval—and some interesting accounts relative to French affairs.

624. [1] B.M. IV: 477. Autograph. Docketed by Jeremiah Bentham: 'Fils Jeremy B. / Letter datd. Hendon / July 31st 1788 / answered by Letter / datd. P. Heath Augt. 4th / with the Leyden Gazette etc. enclosed.'

Addressed: 'To / Jeremiah Bentham Esqr. / at J. Farr Abbot's Esqr. / Putney Heath,' Post mark illegible.

I promise myself the pleasure of calling on you the latter end of next week. If your bed should be occupied it will make no difference to me, so long as the couch is not. But my plan is to return in the evening, if I do not find the walk more tedious than I expect.

You will of course return these Newspapers—I need not repeat that request in future—

Your's ever
J.B.

625

To Jeremiah Bentham and The Farr Abbots[1]

14 August 1788 (Aet 40)

Mr. J. Bentham presents his respects to the family at Putney Heath, and proposes himself the pleasure of waiting on them to dinner on Saturday, if convenient to them. Monday Aug. 14 1788.

P.S. Wedn. I send a 3d victory; and still, as well as the 2d, gained by *our* Flotilla.[2]

625. [1] B.M. IV: 478. Autograph. Docketed by Jeremiah Bentham: 'Mr. Jerey. Bentham / Lr. datd. Hendon Augt. 11 1788.'

Addressed: 'To / Jeremiah Bentham Esqr. / at John Far Abbot Esqrs. / Putney Heath.' Postmark illegible.

The first part of this note relates to the invitation referred to in letter 623 at n. 9.

[2] After their defeat on 18/29 June, the main Turkish fleet took flight to the open sea and remained west of Ochakov. For fear of the fire from the batteries at Kinburn point on the south side of the entrance to the Liman the Captain Pasha dared not try again to force his way into the bay to cover Ochakov, and on 9 July he sailed south to meet the main Russian fleet, which had put out from Sebastopol a few days before. It was three days later, 12 July, that this 'third' engagement took place, an attack by the Russian flotilla upon the Turkish flotilla under the guns of Ochakov, which succeeded in causing the destruction by fire of nine of the Turkish craft and the capture of one galley and two gunboats. Samuel Bentham was then busy at Kherson and not present at this engagement (R. C. Anderson, op. cit., p. 328; B.M. IV: 487–9).

626

To Jeremiah Bentham[1]

6 October 1788 (Aet 40)

Hendon Middlesex Oct.—1788.

Hond. Sir

Double thanks to you for ~~your~~ the intelligence communicated by your two letters the one from Cheltenham, the other from Bath.[2] I have been writing to Mr. Barker[3] to thank him and accept his offer. I had before taken measures to the same end, which however were at a stand owing to the absence of the persons of whose assistance I was assured.

I have just received the means of paying you with intelligence of a more interesting nature. It is contained in a letter from Sam's friend Hynam[4] which I do not send because the principal part, relating to some concerns of Hynam's own must be kept to refer to, and it wou'd not be interesting enough to you to pay me for the trouble of transcribing.[5]

Petersburgh July 30 O.S. (Aug. 10.) 1788

'I am extremely happy to inform you, Sir, that your Brother is promoted to the rank of Colonel for his valour and prudence in two successful attacks against the Turks upon the Nieper. He is in good health. The publick papers here have announced his praise.'

I am, Dear and Hond. Sir
Ever Your's
J.B.

626. [1] B.M. IV: 486. Autograph. Docketed by Jeremiah Bentham: 'Fils Jeremy B. / Lr. datd. Hendon Middlx. / 6th Octr. 1788 / Reced. at Bath the 8th Octr. / containing an Account / of his Brother's Promotion / to the Rank of Colonel.'

Addressed: 'To / Jeremiah Bentham Esqr. / Bath.' Postmark: 'OC 7.88'.

[2] Both missing.

[3] Not identified.

[4] Robert Hynam, the empress's watchmaker.

[5] Jeremiah Bentham entered in his letter-book a copy of the extract which follows (B.M. XXII: 436).

INDEX

Note. This is an index of names of persons occurring in the text and notes. References throughout are to page-numbers, except in the case of Bentham's correspondents, where the figures in italic type after the subheadings 'Letters to' and 'Letters from' refer to the serial number of the letters. The abbreviation 'biog.' indicates a biographical note on the persons indexed.

In the case of Bentham himself (J. B.), only references to his works are indexed. His father and brother, to whom constant references are made throughout the letters, are indexed only as correspondents.

An analytical index to the correspondence as a whole will be provided in the final volume of this part of the edition.

www.ingramcontent.com/pod-product-compliance
Lightning Source LLC
LaVergne TN
LVHW082005200926
848481LV00010B/2808

* 9 7 8 1 0 1 3 2 8 7 5 6 5 *